ADELAIDE MALTING COMPANY P/L

The
BREWERIES
of AUSTRALIA

The Breweries of Australia
A HISTORY

KEITH M. DEUTSHER

Lothian
BOOKS

Disclaimer

The information in this book has been obtained from the sources referred to in the Bibliography. Every effort has been made to ensure that the information provided is as accurate as possible, and to trace and acknowledge all original source material.

A work of this nature, spanning a period of just over 200 years, can never be quite complete. As a consequence, there are instances throughout the text where details of addresses, names of breweries, and even owners were unavailable.

The author and publisher would be pleased to rectify any errors or omissions.

Hop flower

Barley head

Thomas C. Lothian Pty Ltd
11 Munro Street, Port Melbourne, Victoria 3207

Copyright © Keith M. Deutsher 1999

First published 1999
All rights reserved. No part of this publication may be reproduced, stored in a retrieval system or transmitted in any form by any means without the prior permission of the copyright owner. Enquiries should be made to the publisher.

National Library of Australia
Cataloguing-in-Publication data:

Deutsher, Keith M.
    The breweries of Australia.

    Bibliography.
    Includes index.
    ISBN 0 85091 986 X.

    1. Breweries – Australia – History. 2. Beer industry –
    Australia – History. 3. Beer – Australia – History. I.
    Title.
    338.4766330994

Design by Rob Cowpe Design
Cartoons by Jeff Hook
Printed in Singapore by Craft Print Pte Ltd

Front cover collage: John Campbell, *The Swan Brewery*, c. 1902; courtesy Lion Nathan Australia Pty Ltd; illustration from 'Ye Olde Brew Carlton Ale' label, courtesy Foster's Brewing Group Ltd; Imperial Pilsner Lager from Keith Deutsher collection.

Author photograph: Frank Park

Back cover: beer labels, from Keith Deutsher collection.

Title page: Haughton Forrest, *Cascade Brewery and Mt Wellington*, c. 1890, courtesy Allport Library and Museum of Fine Arts, Hobart.

Foreword

The Breweries of Australia is a meticulously documented insight into one of Australia's oldest industries. When Europeans first set foot on Australian soil, they had to have their liquor: the brewing of beer was a necessary part of daily life in the fledgling Australian colonies. Any town of any size had a brewery, and breweries were scattered everywhere across Australia.

This book gives, in minute detail, the history of every single brewery that has operated in Australia since colonisation.

Keith Deutsher affectionately tells the story of the gradual development of our homegrown breweries, through stifling heat, trial and error, and the growth of the temperance movement, to the consolidation of our large multinational breweries.

For anyone who has ever wondered what the X in XXXX beer means; for all those who have downed a cold one after a hot day in the backyard pushing the Victa around the Hills Hoist, *The Breweries of Australia* is an informative and fascinating guide.

Steve Vizard

Contents

Foreword by Steve Vizard	v
Acknowledgements	ix
Anecdotes	x
Introduction	1
At a Glance — Milestones in Australia's Brewing History	10

The Breweries

New South Wales	16
Victoria	86
Queensland	178
South Australia	206
Western Australia	240
Tasmania	274
Northern Territory	306
Norfolk Island	313
The Boutique Breweries of Australia	316
Lager Beer	336
How Many Xs?	341
The Temperance Movement	344
The Number of Breweries	350
Glossary	352
Conversion Table	354
Bibliography	355
Historical Societies	360
Index	362

Acknowledgements

I am indebted to many people for their contribution to the preparation of this book, far too many to name individually, but to each I offer my grateful thanks.

Andrew Bailey provided well-researched information on the breweries of early Melbourne; Rosalind Kennedy on north-eastern Victoria; Brett Stubbs on the New South Wales breweries of the twentieth century, and Geoff Spiller an appraisal of the breweries of Western Australia. Thanks also to Jeff Hook, for his contribution of cartoon humour.

Special thanks are due to Russell French for his exhaustive research on Tasmania's early breweries. Up-to-date reports on Australia's 'boutique' breweries were gathered by Alan Richards, and George Crompton gave valuable assistance in providing the production dates of the breweries' products.

I have been greatly assisted by Kerry Walton, who provided some general brewery information. In particular, he has made available for reproduction many of the photographs and labels of early breweries.

This book also owes much to the men and women of the Historical Societies listed at the end of the book. Their careful research and friendly assistance in providing valuable information is greatly appreciated.

I am thankful also for the assistance given by the La Trobe Library, State Library of Victoria, and for permission granted by breweries to reproduce their beer labels, especially Foster's Brewing Group Ltd and Lion Nathan Australia Pty Ltd.

ANECDOTES

The anecdotes in this book are selected from articles in various issues of the *Australian Brewers' Journal*, a monthly national publication that had its beginning in 1882, and continued in publication into the first half of the twentieth century.

Most of the articles are from the late nineteenth century. Today some of these sayings may be considered very odd indeed, perhaps incorrect, even humorous, but when published they were serious and factual statements and opinions of the time.

They provide a glimpse of society attitudes of a hundred years ago, and the difficulties and prejudice suffered by the brewing industry as it struggled to establish itself. It was a courageous industry, faced with factors it was often unable to cope with, and at a time when innovation and change were for the future.

Many of the articles are made all the more interesting by the wit and dry humour of the authors of those earlier times.

Introduction

> Good beer, brewed from malt, hops and sugar, has always been regarded as being among the necessities, rather than the luxuries of everyday life
> — *Anonymous*

Government Support

In the early years of Australia's colonial history the governors of the day — Phillip, Hunter, King and others — all supported the development of a local brewing industry, and for several very good reasons.

They realised the importance of having a regular supply of locally produced beer, which, with a lower alcohol content compared to rum and other spirits, would combat the effects of excessive spirit drinking and the drunkenness rampant in the community. Moreover, they believed that beer could be produced in the colony and sold at prices considerably lower than imported ales.

A most compelling reason was the prospect of the establishment and growth of both primary and secondary industries, the cultivation of barley and hops and the setting up of factories to process the products and brew the beer. Long-term potential for employment was another consideration, with attendant industries such as the manufacture of vats and barrels, as well as transport and the hotel trade.

Some governments even assisted deserving citizens to set up as brewers. They were offered grants of land on which to erect their premises, and for the first fifteen years or so of the nation's history government encouragement attracted many would-be brewers. They were among the pioneers who began their trade under the most difficult conditions, with shortages of raw materials, using substitutes, without scientific knowledge and having to cope with the vagaries of the weather. When they failed in their endeavour, as many invariably they did, others were quick to take over and try their luck.

A Difficult Beginning

Despite the commendable government encouragement, the first 100 years of Australia's history showed brewing to be a very precarious occupation. The

Hop pickers at work.
La Trobe Collection, State Library of Victoria

bewildering record of changes in ownership, partnership dissolutions, insolvencies and bankruptcies certainly suggests that brewing was a more hazardous business than most.

Brewers seemed to have a propensity for failure. When making beer, all sorts of things could go wrong, and they did. Poor quality and waste predominated. Patrick McGuire's tin-shed brewery (see the Prologue) was a typical example where things could go terribly wrong, with the causes beyond anyone's understanding.

There were much easier trades — brickmaking, carpentry, candlemaking, and many others, all predictable as to the outcome of the finished product. But not brewing. Similar to those of his cousin the goldseeker, the outcome of the brewer's efforts could never be predetermined. It was very much a matter of chance.

A Bad Reputation

For generations colonial beer had a bad reputation. Back in 1834 a Sydney book, *The Mirror of Literature, Amusement and Instruction,* said that the brewers' use of substitutes for hops 'produces the heaviest sleep, excessive pain in the head and irregularity of the bowels'. The upper-class gentry scoffed at the very thought of drinking local beer, and refused to give it a fair go. They preferred imported ale.

One early brewer, however, was given a good report in the Melbourne *Argus* of 12 January 1849:

> Mr Condell's ale is devoid of tobacco, cocculus indicus, grains of Paradise and other poisonous ingredients, which, by admixture with much of the ale brewed in the province, is the cause of the greater portion of the lunacy which prevails.

The editorial continued, at a loss to understand how anyone could be guilty of such prevalent practices as

> the atrocious villainy of administering a deadly narcotic [to the beer], gradually sipping the intellect of his fellow colonists and consigning men either to the grave, the lunatic asylum or to a state of demi-madness.

The Melbourne *Age* of 26 February 1875 claimed that Melbourne brewers used green tea leaves, tobacco, acid, quassia, green vitriol and cocculus to adulterate their product, adding that

> all over the country, suicides, murders and deeds of violence and brutality are daily occurring under the influence of mania and potu. The working man, who is the largest consumer of beer, as a consequence figures most conspicuously in the gloomy list of tragedies.

This viewpoint was supported later that year by Dr Youll, the Melbourne coroner, who blamed a number of deaths on colonial beer.

As late as 1888 it was reported by the *Australian Brewers' Journal* that

> Australian beer is not a very high-class article. The greater proportion of the beer sold and consumed is really mere swipes, soft, tasteless, insipid, sugar-and-water sort of stuff which the Australian working man drinks because he cannot get anything better at a reasonable price.

During the debate on the *Beer Duty Act* in 1894 one speaker said of colonial beer, 'some of it was bad enough that there should be legislation to prevent brewers from distributing poison'.

An Easy Occupation!

With all this bad publicity and the difficulties in making good saleable beer, why would anyone want to become a brewer? The young would-be brewer of the time had plenty of compelling and valid reasons. To begin with, he knew it was easy to start up. Very little capital was needed for a tank, a vat or two, and a few barrels and bottles. He could rent a small shed and buy small quantities of ingredients on credit. There was plenty of water in the nearby creek, and timber for fuel could be cut from forests close by. Next, there was a large ready market — practically the whole population drank beer, all his friends did, so he already had many potential customers.

He also knew that it was easy to make beer, provided he kept an eye on things. Start with malt and water, heat it up, add some hops, a bit of yeast, and that was it — let nature take its course. A few days of fermentation, and then syphon the beer into bottles and barrels. and sell to the pubs and to his mates. It was as simple as that. His beer, which he would sell for cash, would be the best in the country, there was no doubt about that.

The overpowering reason, of course, was the profit motif. He had a clear vision of the future and could imagine his own huge brewery at the end of the main street. He had done some costing, and the profit margin was incredible. His head spun at the thought of how much money he would make. What the young would-be brewer did not realise was the enormity of the problems he would face in his attempts to make good beer, and the prejudice that would follow if he sold even one poor batch. Generally, there was no such thing as a second chance. Too many brewers of the nineteenth century had a loose grip on reality, which led to disappointment through wishful thinking and shallow optimism.

Prejudice

When a beer-drinker tested the quality of his beer, and was pleased, he would come back again. But, if dissatisfied, he would never again order that beer, and would loudly proclaim, for all to hear, that the beer was bad. The word would spread, and other drinkers were easily influenced by their companions in forming a prejudice. A glass or two of a bad brew sold over the counter, and the brewer's reputation and business could be ruined. The money loss might be recovered or remedied in a short time, but it could take years to regain a reputation. Even if the brewer's next batch was perfect, the customers would not give it another go because of their stubborn prejudice.

The Problems

Occasionally, a brewer had little chance of success even if his ale was of a good standard. One problem over which the brewer had no control was the

> ## AUSTRALIAN ALE — A BAD REPORT
>
> We cannot conceal from ourselves the fact that visitors to Australia, whether they come from England, America, the continent of Europe, or elsewhere, have very little that is good to say concerning the quality of our ales, and we have all heard over and over again from such persons the remark, 'I can't drink colonial ale.'
>
> It was not to be expected that in the early days of Australian brewing, the locally produced ale would be of good quality, for appliances were then of the most primitive description, good materials difficult to be obtained, and high-class brewing skill not readily obtainable, but it seems to us regrettable that nowadays — when the possession of wealth enables us to acquire many things — effort is not made to raise the character of our ales as a whole.
>
> *Australian Brewers' Journal*, April 1889

deterioration of his beer after delivering it to the hotel. If a keg of beer was kept too long or stored in a hot environment by the hotelkeeper, it could turn sour. It was also not an uncommon practice for the beer to be watered down, giving a flat, unpalatable taste, and customers would refuse to buy any more. Even if the beer was in good condition in the hotel cellar, if drawn through a publican's pipes that had not been properly cleaned the beer could become contaminated and undrinkable. It was bad enough for the brewer having to pour his own bad beer down the drain, but a heartrending experience when barrels of beer were returned to the brewer as unsatisfactory, when he knew full well that the beer had been perfect when it left his brewery.

Why did brewers have so much trouble making good beer? The difficulties persisted for over a hundred years. Surely after a decade or two, all the problems should have been solved? But they weren't. Far from it. So, what exactly were the problems the industry struggled to overcome? Most brewers were unable to define the problems. The symptoms were there, but there was no understanding of the causes why beer would vary so much from batch to batch, and with so much waste. There were no scientific guidelines to follow, and no clear technical understanding of yeast and fermentation, and bacterial infections. Breweries had no electricity, and candles and lanterns were used in the cellars and workplaces. The brewer was frequently a one-man operation, a Jack-of-all-trades, and he had nobody to turn to for advice when things went wrong.

The brewer was at the wrong end of the social scale to start with. His brewery, large or small, always had a terrible smell about it, stale beer mostly, but also the smell of hops and yeast. The aroma was unbearable in the hotter months as it wafted in the breeze across into shops and houses. There was no way of getting rid of it, and the poor brewer had to put up with the constant complaints from irate neighbours and the local council. Temperance advocates were loud and clear in their condemnation of the horrid offensive smells that were 'the product of the devil's kitchen'.

The general public, particularly the upper class, considered a brewer as scarcely respectable. He was the unkempt person responsible for making that terrible, smelly, undrinkable, colonial beer. One brewer said that he was 'completely shut off from society in the country town where he brewed', and added that he was unable to make friends with the local butcher and baker and others in the town. Bankers and doctors ignored him altogether.

It was bad enough being ostracised by society, but worse still trying to make good beer. One of the main problems was the water. Since it represents about 85 per cent of the beer, clean pure water is absolutely essential. But frequently the brewer had no control over his water supply, and took whatever was available. All too often it was contaminated. Open drains carried refuse and pollution into rivers that were used as convenient rubbish dumps. Even after the water was filtered, the brewer had no idea of the mineral and bacterial content, or whether it was good or bad water.

Wide, open vats of fermenting beer were easy prey to bacterial infection. Pollens and dust and other undesirable substances in the air would settle in the brew. Wild yeasts and bacteria soon ruined the fermentation process, but since there was nothing visible other than the froth on the top, the brewer battled on, nervously hoping that when he tested the brew later it would taste all right.

Many brewers made their own malt, and purchased the barley from the local farmer. The barley was germinated on floors of questionable cleanliness and, since the barley chipped and cracked easily, it turned mouldy. The problem was how to prevent or destroy this troublesome fungal growth. But why bother, the grain would later be heated and ground, and then boiled.

Climate

The British system of brewing was not suitable for most Australian conditions. The majority of colonists were of British stock and, together with their material belongings, they also brought their traditions and tastes, and their methods of brewing. They used the top fermentation process, which suited the cooler English climate where beer was ideally fermented at 45°F. In Australia during the first century of white settlement, most brewing was undertaken at temperatures between 50 and 110°F, leading to the almost inevitable production of fusel oil and bad beer. Fusel oil was described in the *Australian Brewers' Journal* of June 1883 as

> a low type alcohol which exists in beer produced from inferior malt, and especially when fermentation is violent or at high temperatures and can cause giddiness, vomiting, delirium and most of the affects [sic] of a powerful narcotic poison.

When brewing in the more variable and hotter Australian climate, ventilation, dryness and low humidity were more essential conditions than coldness, but not many brewers knew that or, if they did, there was not much they could do about it. Hit-and-miss methods prevailed, and any successful brewing was the result of circumstance and the element of chance.

Other Problems

In the early days beer was sent long distances in horsedrawn wagons in sweltering heat, exposed to the sun, and over rough bumpy roads and dirt tracks. Casks and bottles were often damaged or broken, adding to the brewer's loss, but worst of all was the deterioration of the beer after lengthy periods of travel — and casks of ruined beer subsequently being returned.

La Trobe Collection, State Library of Victoria

Hotelkeepers rarely paid for their beer under three months, and expected considerable discounts for cash.

Competition was a constant problem: from nearby brewers, the large city breweries, and the superior, although more expensive, imported ales. Selling prices had to be adjusted according to the quality and popularity of the product. Poor-quality colonial beer, generally in abundance, was offered to hotels at a mere fraction of the price in an endeavour to avoid total loss. A sudden lack of sales when the beer had a bad taste or unpleasant appearance, added to the burden of the small brewer attempting to make a profit and stay in business. But these were the enthusiastic and optimistic years of the industry — tomorrow the brew would be better.

Solutions

For the struggling brewer, waste was much more than a disappointment, it could quickly lead to financial ruin. Since there were always batches of bad beer, surely something could be done to make the beer drinkable and saleable rather than tipping it down the drain. Unscrupulous brewers would 'doctor' their inferior beer with all manner of additives. Almost anything would be used in the hope that unsavoury flavour, smell or colour could be improved upon. Brewers tried alum and green vitriol to give the beer a good head, and also resorted to adding a dash of sulphuric acid, lime, potash, tobacco — and even strychnine! Other additives were honey, liquorice, treacle, ginger, capsicum, chillies, gentian and burnt sugar. It was very much trial and error — add a bit of one substance, then taste the result, and keep going until the beer seemed reasonable. The perpetrators rarely considered the consequences, and illness, even death, could result.

Advertisements

Understandably, many customers considered colonial beer to be anything but desirable, but the local brewers held a different opinion, and told the drinking public just how good their beer was in their advertising: 'We, the undersigned, have on sale superior ale and porter, brewed from the best malt and hops'. Terms such as 'good and wholesome' and 'superior to anything else' were favourite expressions. More adventurous statements included 'guarantees', 'first-class', 'genuine' and 'the best in the colony, better by far than any imports'. Many of these outrageous claims could be easily challenged today for false advertising.

An even better method of advertising was the use of credits given by well-respected authorities and members of the community. Statements made by the medical profession, attesting to the fine wholesome

---

WORLD BREWERIES

A Frenchman states that there are 51,000 breweries in the world. Germany easily leads with 26,240. Next comes England with 12,874, followed by the United States with 2,300 breweries. Austria has 1942; Belgium, 1270 and France, 1044.

Australian Brewers' Journal, July 1893

[In 1893 there were 284 breweries operating in Australia.]

qualities of a particular beer, were often repeated in newspaper and journal advertising by the brewer of the beer. As an example, an advertisement in the 1871 *Melbourne Directory* took the form of reproducing a letter sent by the Carlton Brewery to the Government Analytical Chemist, asking him to take a sample of their ale from any one of a number of their hotel outlets (list submitted), and to provide an analysis of the sample. Below the letter was the lengthy reply from William Johnson, Government Analytical Chemist, stating, 'I purchased such samples from five of the hotels mentioned … all were light coloured and clear, possessing a very pleasant aromatic odour of the hop, combined with the agreeable bitterness characteristic of good ales'. The analyst added, perhaps immodestly, that he could not detect any difference between the samples he had tested and the ales from his own cellar, 'having long been supplied with your ales for my own family use'.

Buying and selling breweries

There were almost as many advertisements for breweries for sale or to let or for auction as there were for advertisements offering 'splendid and finest' ales and porter for sale. Selling or renting out a brewery was another solution for the brewer in difficulty. Get out of the business and let someone else have the problems. The *Australian Brewers' Journal* was frequently used for advertising a brewery. One issue, for June 1886, listed several country breweries for sale in New South Wales; another in one of the largest railway towns in Victoria (£2000); one in Melbourne (£40,000); others in Gippsland, Victoria (£1200), Lithgow, NSW (£4000), Richmond, Melbourne (£4500), and several more scattered across the colonies. In the same issue of the journal there was an advertisement for 'Wanted to buy — a profitable brewery in or about Melbourne, capital say £50,000'. There were always plenty of breweries on the market and in almost any location for a buyer to choose from.

Hazardous solutions

Some desperate brewers, unable to sell and in extreme financial difficulty, went as far as scheming to collect insurance, illegally. A convenient fire at 3 o'clock in the morning, with nobody around, could solve a lot of problems. There was nothing unusual about a fire. There were fires everywhere, all the time. With open wood fires inside the brewery, dry straw used for packing lying around, and a timber and bark building, it was easy to understand why a brewery could be destroyed by fire. And just as difficult to prove that the fire was not deliberately lit. The contrived theft of barrels and bottles of beer, preferably bad beer, was another option for the unscrupulous brewer.

Growth and Decline

Toward the end of the nineteenth century there was considerable conservatism of many of the older class of brewers, and unwillingness to adopt changes or improvements. This was expressed in their determination to 'leave well alone'. They did not want the interference of science or rational theory, and many of

Number of Australian breweries, 1800–1990	
1800	1
1810	9
1820	14
1830	30
1840	48
1850	70
1860	178
1870	230
1880	241
1890	294
1900	255
1910	157
1920	77
1930	47
1940	29
1950	26
1960	22
1970	23
1980	20
1990	11

the mysteries of brewing remained as intractable as ever. Although there were some brewers in the cities and country towns who managed to brew good beer with reasonable consistency, the emergence of the brewing industry as a healthy, well-managed and profitable part of Australia's economy was painfully slow.

By the time the Australian colonies became a federation in 1901, 950 breweries had come and gone from 340 country towns and the capital cities. The maximum number operating at any one time in all the colonies was the year 1889, when 307 breweries were in business. From that time the number steadily declined, with only ten of the old breweries left by 1993.

The decline was caused in part by the severe economic depression of the 1890s, which had a profound impact on the eastern colonies, particularly Victoria and New South Wales. With much of the workforce out of work and out of pocket, beer production fell rapidly. With fearsome price wars, small breweries went out of business, and even larger ones were severely affected. In 1893 the prominent Victoria Brewery in Melbourne collapsed in bankruptcy after shares that had been valued at 22s 6d were quoted at just one penny.

Before this, however, a steady rationalisation of the industry had been taking place. Many regional and suburban breweries had been closing due to competition from the large city breweries, which had introduced a tied-house system, buying up hotels to secure outlets for their beer. By the early twentieth century about 80 per cent of Sydney hotels were tied to particular breweries, and the trend was similar in other states. In some country areas mining had ceased, and the population had drifted away. Although pastoral industries had gradually become established, state railways had been pushing further into country areas, providing the dominant breweries in the capital cities with a cheap and reliable source of transport for the sale of their products in distant towns.

One of the first Acts passed by the Commonwealth Parliament upon federation had the effect of sweeping large numbers of breweries out of existence. The *Commonwealth Beer Excise Act of 1901*, which became operative the following year, imposed stringent conditions on the industry, and heavy penalties were applied for any default. The passing of the Act seriously affected the smaller breweries and, for many, the position became so difficult that they were forced to either sell to larger and wealthier concerns, if they could, or simply go out of business.

A New Era

The beginning of the twentieth century heralded a significant and lasting change in the brewing industry of Australia. New scientific discoveries helped the brewer to understand and control the brewing processes in any climate, and the introduction of the lighter lager beer was a more appropriate and preferred beer for Australia. It was clear that the future security and prosperity of the industry lay in economy of scale, with fewer, larger, professionally managed companies. The days of the small-town brewer were disappearing along with the horse and cart.

Closures, takeovers and amalgamations became progressively evident, and the industry rapidly became more capital intensive. The few remaining breweries grew in strength, and in time consolidated further — they were the breweries that would serve the country so well in the years ahead.

Today nobody remembers the plight and struggle of the early brewers. Their successes and their failures are barely recorded in history, but through their toil and determination and spirit to achieve the foundations were laid for what is today one of Australia's most important industries.

AT A GLANCE
Milestones in Australia's Brewing History

1770 James Cook takes official possession of the east coast of Australia.

1786 Lord Sydney announces Britain's plan to settle Australia.

1788 First Fleet arrives at Sydney Cove, and the colony of New South Wales is proclaimed.

1791 Twenty convicts escape from Sydney, and attempt to reach China by land.

1793 James Squire, Australia's first brewer, commences brewing in Sydney.

1795 John Boston and his partner, James Ellis, become Australia's second brewers.

1797 Coal is discovered at Newcastle.

1803 The first Australian newspaper, the *Sydney Gazette*, is published.
The Australian Brewery, Australia's third, starts in George Street, Sydney.

1804 Australia's first and only government brewery commences at Parramatta.

1806 First country brewery is started by Andrew Thompson at Windsor, NSW.

1809 Average price of a glass of beer in Sydney is 1s 6d per gallon.

1815 Sydney has seven breweries.

1817 The Bank of New South Wales, Australia's first bank, is established.

1818 Tasmania's first brewery is started by Richard Clark at Launceston.

1820 First commercial brewery in Tasmania is established by James Whyte in Hobart.
First regional brewery in Tasmania is opened by James Austin at Austin's Ferry.

1822 10 breweries operating in Sydney.

1823 First authenticated discovery of gold in Australia, by J. McBrien, at Fish River, near Bathurst, NSW.

1826 Australia's first recorded use of gaslight, in a Sydney shop.

1827 Albion Brewery is started by Sam Terry in Elizabeth Street, Sydney; it later became Toohey's Standard Brewery.

1830 Western Australia's first brewer, Lt R. N. Bull, starts brewing at Canning Ford, near Perth.

1832 First temperance society is established in Hobart.
Australia's first Foster's Brewery is started by Thomas Foster at Hobart.
Cascade Brewery, Hobart, is opened by Peter Degraves.

1833 Tasmania has 21 breweries, New South Wales 15.

1835 William Devenish begins brewing at his East Guildford Hotel in Perth, WA.
Tooth's Kent Brewery is founded by John Tooth and Charles Newnham.

1837 James Stokes opens the Albion Brewery, Perth, the first commercial brewery in Western Australia.
South Australia's first brewery, the Torrens, is started by John Warren.
Victoria's first brewery, the Melbourne Brewery, is established by John Mills.

1838 *Port Phillip Gazette* first published in Melbourne.
South Australia's second brewery, the West Adelaide, is started by Mr Lillyman.

1841 Victoria's first country brewery, the Barwon, commences at Geelong.

1843 South Australia's first regional brewery is established at Oakbank.

1846 Melbourne *Argus* first published on 2 June.

1851 Port Phillip District of New South Wales becomes the colony of Victoria.
Payable gold is discovered in New South Wales near Bathurst, and also at Clunes and Ballarat in Victoria.
Victoria and South Australia both have 15 breweries; New South Wales 12; Tasmania 27; and Western Australia 3.

1853 Queensland's first brewery, the Brisbane Brewery, is started by John Beach.

1854 Victoria Parade Brewery (later the Victoria Brewery) is established by Thomas Aitken in East Melbourne.
The first Australian steam railway is opened: Melbourne to Port Melbourne.

1855 Van Diemen's Land is officially named Tasmania.
Opening of railway from Sydney to Parramatta.

1856 Victoria is the first Australian colony to adopt a flag.
50 breweries now operating in Victoria, and 50 in Tasmania.

1857 Swan Brewery, Perth, WA, is founded by Frank Sherwood.

1858 North Melbourne Brewery (the forerunner of Carlton & United Breweries Ltd) is started by Theodore Rosenberg in Bouverie Street, Carlton.
Castlemaine Brewery in Castlemaine, Victoria, is founded by Nicholas Fitzgerald.
Population of Australia reaches 1,000,000.

1859 Queensland is granted separation from New South Wales.

1860 Explorers Bourke and Wills commence their ill-fated journey across Australia from Melbourne, aiming to reach the Gulf of Carpentaria.
First Queensland country brewery is opened at Rockhampton by William Boldeman.

1861 Electric telegraph links Brisbane with New South Wales, Victoria and South Australia.
The first Melbourne Cup is won by Archer.

1862 Cooper's Brewery, Adelaide, is founded by Thomas Cooper.

1864 Stanbridge and Harrison begin brewing in Mary Street, Brisbane (later to become Perkins & Co. City Brewery).

1869 Patrick Perkins opens the Downs Brewery in Toowoomba, Queensland.
The largest gold nugget ever found, the 'Welcome Stranger', is discovered at Dunolly, Victoria.
John and James Toohey purchase the Darling Brewery, Sydney, laying the foundation of Toohey's Brewery.

1872 Discovery of the largest known mass of gold (235,143 g) at Hill End, NSW.

1874 Largest number of breweries to operate in Victoria — 142.

1875 Construction is completed of Toohey's Standard Brewery, Sydney.

1877 First cricket test match, England vs Australia, is played in Melbourne.
28 breweries operating in Melbourne.

1878 Fitzgerald, Quinlan & Co. is formed (the forerunner of the Castlemaine Brewery, Brisbane, later Castlemaine Perkins Ltd).

1879 Esk Brewery is started at Launceston, becoming Boag's Esk Brewery in 1882.

1881 Population of Australia is 2,250,000; there are 246 breweries.

1882 Bulimba Brewery (later the Queensland Brewery Co. Ltd) begins brewing.
Lager beer first produced commercially in Australia by the Cohn Brothers' Victoria Brewery in Bendigo, Victoria.

1883 Lager beer first produced in New South Wales by Sam Marks, in George Street, Sydney.
Charles Rasp discovers lead–zinc mineral wealth at Broken Hill, NSW.
Rail link from Sydney to Melbourne is completed.

1885 Broken Hill Proprietary Company (BHP) is floated.

1888 South Australian Brewing Co. Ltd is formed.
Tamworth, NSW, is the first country town in Australia to be lit with electricity.

1889 The greatest number of breweries operating in Australia in any one year — 307.
Foster's Brewery, Melbourne, releases its first Foster's Lager.
Lager beer first produced in Queensland by Castlemaine Brewery — selling for 6d a bottle.

1890 Regulations are introduced prohibiting the sale of intoxicating liquors at Melbourne railway stations; Melbourne then had 21 breweries.

1892	Gold is discovered at Coolgardie, WA. Three breweries are established there within four years.
1893	Paddy Hannan discovers gold at Kalgoorlie, WA.
1895	French statistician calculates 51,000 breweries in the world; Australia has 277. Coghlan & Tulloch's Ballarat Brewing Co. Pty Ltd is formed.
1897	Northern Territory's first brewery is started at Alice Springs.
1898	Western Australia has 41 breweries.
1899	Average wage paid by Victorian breweries is £2 18s 6d per week.
1900	Evocative new folksong, 'Waltzing Matilda', is written by Banjo Paterson. The population of Sydney is 475,000; Melbourne 490,000.
1901	The Commonwealth of Australia is proclaimed on 1 January. Number of breweries operating at that time: NSW 61; Vic. 71; Qld 31; SA 30; WA 41; Tas. 6 — a total of 240. Australia's total beer production (for that year) is 50,500,000 gallons (230,000,000 litres). The *Commonwealth Beer Excise Act of 1901* is introduced. Resch's Waverley Brewery is founded in Waverley, Sydney.
1902	Bottled beer costs 7d per bottle. George Adams (of Tattersalls' fame) starts his brewery in Hobart. Excise duty on Australian beer is 3d per gallon. Swan Brewery, Perth, WA, instals a new machine for wiring corks into bottles; its capacity is 70 dozen bottles per hour, a saving in wages of £4 per week.
1904	Melbourne Co-operative Brewery Co. Ltd is formed (later to become the brewing headquarters in Melbourne of Carlton & United Breweries Ltd).
1907	Carlton & United Breweries Pty Ltd (CUB) is formed.
1913	Crown seals are introduced, gradually replacing corks. CUB becomes a public company, Carlton & United Breweries Ltd. Canberra is named the capital city of Australia.
1914	Castlemaine Brewery, Brisbane, advertises for a head brewer at a salary of £500 per year.
1915	Victorian hotels close at 9.30 p.m.
1917	Prohibited imports into Australia: 'any preparation purporting to be a remedy for Drunkenness, Alcoholic Habit, Opium Habit, Tobacco Habit or Cocaine Habit'.
1918	Excise duty on Australian beer is 1s per gallon.
1919	Six o'clock closing is made permanent for hotels.
1920	The retail price of beer in Perth is increased to 4d per glass; 5d per pot and 1s per bottle.
1924	First release of Castlemaine XXXX Bitter Ale.
1925	64 breweries operating in Australia.
1927	Ballarat Bertie first appears on the labels and advertising of the Ballarat Brewing Co. Pty Ltd. Transfer of the seat of government from Melbourne to Canberra.
1928	Grant Hay opens his Richmond Brewery, Melbourne. Castlemaine Perkins Ltd is formed by the amalgamation of Perkins City Brewery and the Castlemaine Brewery, Brisbane.
1929	Resch's Waverley Brewery is taken over by Tooth's Brewery, Sydney.
1932	Stainless steel kegs progressively replace wooden barrels. Sydney Harbour Bridge is opened.
1941	Excise duty on Australian beer is 3s per gallon.
1949	The average price of a small glass of beer is 7d.
1950	26 breweries operating in Australia.
1952	Grafton Brewery, NSW, commences production.
1953	First discovery of oil in Australia, at Exmouth, WA.
1956	Introduction of steel cans.
1957	CUB commences brewing in Darwin.
1958	CUB establishes brewery in Fiji; acquires Ballarat Brewery, Ballarat, and Volum Brewery, Geelong (closed).
1961	Huge iron-ore discoveries in Pilbara region of Western Australia. Queensland Brewery in Brisbane, Toowoomba Brewery, and Fitzroy Brewery in Rockhampton, acquired by CUB.
1965	Excise duty on Australian beer is 11s 4d per gallon.
1966	Decimal currency is introduced.

1967	Stubby beer bottle is released.
1968	Courage Brewery commences brewing at Melbourne.
1969	Swan Brewery, Perth, WA, releases ring-pull cans.
1970	Boags Brewery, Tasmania, is the first to use aluminium cans. Regulations are introduced requiring licensed hotelkeepers to provide a fresh glass with every drink served.
1972	Packaging capacities of beer changed from fluid ounces to metric (ml).
1973	Courage Brewery introduces Melbourne's first litre beer bottle.
1975	South Australian Brewery trial release of 'pop-top' cans.
1978	Excise duty on Australian beer is now 52c per litre.
1979	Castlemaine Perkins, Brisbane, and Toohey's Brewery, Sydney, merge to form Castlemaine Tooheys Ltd.
1980	Tooheys Brewery, Sydney, and Castlemaine Perkins Brewery, Brisbane, merge to form Castlemaine Tooheys Ltd. 20 breweries still operating in Australia.
1982	Courage Brewery, Melbourne, is purchased by CUB, and closed.
1983	Takeover of Tooth's Brewery, Sydney by CUB. CUB closes its Victoria Brewery, East Melbourne. Resch's Waverley Brewery, Sydney, is closed. Australia wins America's Cup yachting contest.
1984	First of the boutique breweries, the Sail & Anchor Pub Brewery, begins brewing at Fremantle, WA.
1985	Castlemaine Tooheys Ltd is taken over by Bond Corporation.
1987	CUB closes its brewery in Bouverie Street, Carlton; most of the buildings are later demolished.
1988	Powers Brewery commences production at Yatala, Queensland (later to become the brewing base for CUB in Queensland).
1989	Darwin and Ballarat breweries are closed by CUB.
1990	New Zealand-based Lion Nathan group acquire the Swan Brewery, Perth, and the Castlemaine Tooheys breweries in Brisbane and Sydney.
1990	Foster's Brewing Group Ltd is formed.
1991	Old Goulburn Brewery, NSW (founded 1838) is reopened as a boutique brewery.
1993	Hahn Brewing Co. is taken over by Tooheys Brewery, Sydney. Power Brewing Co. Ltd at Yatala, Qld, now wholly owned by CUB. New Zealand-based Lion Nathan Group acquires South Australian Brewing Co. Ltd. Cascade Group Ltd forms a joint venture with CUB.
1995	Sanctuary Cove Brewery in Queensland is taken over by CUB.
1996	Buffalo Brewery in Boorhaman, Vic., commences brewing, and claims to be the smallest commercial brewery in Australia. CUB commences brewing again in Darwin.
1998	28 boutique breweries operating in Australia.

The lone figure sat on a wooden stool, hunched forward. He stared blankly at the bubbling brown froth as it oozed over the top of the vat and down the sides, spilling out across the dirt floor. Outside, the searing heat swept in from the north, its relentless force swirling the red dust, penetrating every crack in the small building.

Elbows on his knees, head cupped in the palms of his hands, the young man sat motionless, watching with sightless eyes as the foul-smelling sludge kept spreading out across the floor. This was Patrick McGuire's beer, his fifth attempt in as many weeks to make something he could sell.

Desperate now for funds to buy more barley and hops, and to provide for his family, he sat in numb hopelessness and despair. He recalled the long sea voyage with his wife and two young children, and the excitement of a new life in Australia, the land of hope and opportunity. Patrick had worked at a brewery at his home town of Shannon, Ireland. Since there was a ready market of thirsty miners in the small community where he had settled, he decided to start his own brewery. But the vision had soon turned sour. Earlier, his hard work and eager anticipation of a quick fortune at the goldfields had met with no success.

The past month had been a nightmare for Patrick McGuire, with brew after brew a failure. The first two barrels had turned out reasonably well, so he thought, and he had taken them to the hotel down the road. After one drink the fussy patrons had complained bitterly, and refused to have any more. Now the two returned barrels of beer sat on the dirt floor in a corner of the tin shed brewery, a stark reminder of his failure and his predicament.

Week after week, batch after batch, he had watched the excessive fermentation of the beer, helpless to stop the process in spite of his urgent treatments. In his attempts to salvage the brew, he had tried adding salt, then more salt, even some crushed-up tobacco and all sorts of other ingredients but nothing worked. If only the wretched heat and the wind and the dust would go away.

His tiny tin-roofed shed was his office, storeroom and his brewery. It was his castle. He was painfully aware that it was too small and far too hot, but the shed had to be kept closed to keep out the hot dusty wind.

The brown froth was now creeping across Patrick's boots, soaking into his socks. His face drawn, he stared blankly down without reaction, then, with a shake of his foot, he jolted back to reality. He raised himself slowly from his seat, the exhaustion of inadequacy and the stress of being constantly aware of it now affecting his physical wellbeing. Whatever resolve he had when he had started the brewery had now evaporated, and his decision born of despair then came easily. No more brewing, no more futile attempts, no more anxiety and frustration. He would sell the business. But he had no business, no customers and no beer that was any good.

Patrick McGuire's dilemma cannot be truly appreciated today, 150 years later. The hardships of those times were handicaps beyond the imagination of our present generation.

Months passed, and the brewery was now in the hands of another eager enthusiast who had taken over Patrick's modest equipment of two tanks, a vat and some barrels. Once again, there would be the delusion of easy profit, the anticipation of a long and successful career and a brewery that would one day become the grandest in the land.

New South Wales

Colonisation of Australia began on 26 January 1788. On that day Governor Arthur Phillip arrived at Sydney Cove with the First Fleet of eleven ships, carrying fewer than 1500 people, the majority of them convicts.

Because of its isolation from other countries, it was essential for the new settlement to be made self-sufficient as quickly as possible. Provisions aboard the fleet were limited, and England was an eight-month sea voyage away.

As the settlement slowly developed, coinage was in such short supply that rum and other spirits became a popular means of bartering. Trading and wages were settled by payment in rum, but its excessive consumption had disastrous effects throughout the small community. Convicts became unfit for work and unable to improve their way of life. Free settlers and emancipists (convicts who had served their sentences or had been pardoned) struggled to exist on their farms, and many set up stills to illegally brew liquor, both for their own consumption as well as a source of ready currency.

The Beginning of an Industry

The government, anxious to see improvement in the drinking behaviour of the small population, welcomed the efforts of James Squire who started brewing the less-volatile beer during the second half of 1793. He was Australia's first brewer, and the business that he started continued, off and on, for thirty-seven years.

Australia's second brewer was John Boston, a free settler who began brewing beer in September 1795. After a year or so he stopped brewing to take up farming, and later he began trading in the South Pacific, sailing his own ship.

Other brewers soon followed: Daniel Cooper ran his Australian Brewery in George Street in 1803, and Larkin's Brewery was operating in Castlereagh Street the following year. By 1810 there were five more breweries in Sydney.

Government Brewery

Australia's first and only government brewery started in business in 1804 at Parramatta, now an outer Sydney suburb. The authorities hoped that the availability of cheaper beer with a much lower alcohol content would improve the drinking habits of the people and reduce the effects of overindulgence of rum. There would be the added benefit of new primary industries — the growing of hops and barley. This was a commendable project, but after twelve months the government venture ended in financial disaster, and the brewery closed.

Growth of the new colony was slow, and by 1828, forty years after the arrival of the First Fleet, the population was only 11,000. Surprisingly for such a small community, there were ten breweries operating in Sydney at that time, and six others had started and closed.

The year 1835 saw the beginning of a great depression in the colony, and within ten years the number of breweries in Sydney had dropped from thirteen to six. There was little change for the next forty years.

Country Breweries

Most of the area near the main Sydney settlement was infertile, prompting exploration to find land suitable for pastures and crops. An early rural settlement at Windsor, located on the Hawkesbury River, 55 km west of Sydney. Australia's first country brewery was established at Windsor in 1806 by Andrew Thompson, another ex-convict who brewed there for four years.

The exploration of New South Wales and the development of country towns was slow, and as a consequence there were very few country breweries until the 1840s. But for the next fifty years there was steady growth, and any town of modest size had a brewery. Over time, some townships supported more than one brewery. Seven breweries have operated at Goulburn, the first of which was the Riversdale Brewery, where, in 1832, Matt Healy brewed beer at the back of his hotel. The town of Bathurst, Australia's oldest inland settlement, has had four breweries; the first two both started in 1835, and one of these, the Great Western, continued under various names for almost 100 years.

Six breweries have operated at the border town of Albury, five at Wagga Wagga, and five at Newcastle. Dubbo and Orange each had four; and at Broken Hill, in the far west, eight breweries plied their trade. The size of a town was sometimes judged by the number of its breweries.

The big inland rivers of New South Wales played an important role in provincial development. The Lachlan, Murrumbidgee, Darling and Murray Rivers began to carry paddle steamers on regular runs, and 'port' towns were established on these and other rivers. They acted as bases for the transport of wool, wheat and other produce, and were ideal locations for breweries. In addition to servicing the transient

---

FEDERATION?

Federation of the Australian colonies is, for the time being, dead and nearly buried. The colony that professed to have the greatest interest in it, Victoria, undeniably did so from a selfish motive.

New South Wales was never greatly in its favour, although the Parkes Ministry gave it a limited measure of support, but the new Protectionist Ministry — the Dibbs Government — were exceedingly cold towards it when they sat on the Opposition Benches and now they wield the sceptre of power, they have other matters needing their attention. Consequently federation, so far as New South Wales, the premier colony, is concerned, is a thing of the past and we venture to assert that it is buried for the next fifty years.

Australian Brewers' Journal,
February 1892

New South Wales

1 Adelong	F7	26 Cootamundra	F6	51 Junee	E6	76 Silverton	A4
2 Albury	E7	27 Corowa	E7	52 Kempsey	J3	77 Singleton	H4
3 Araluen	G7	28 Cowra	F5	53 Kiama	H6	78 Stroud	I4
4 Armidale	I2	29 Currawang	G6	54 Lismore	J1	79 Sydney	H5
5 Balranald	C6	30 Deniliquin	D7	55 Lithgow	G5	80 Tamworth	H3
6 Barringun	D1	31 Drake	J1	56 Maclean	J2	81 Temora	E6
7 Bathurst	G5	32 Dubbo	F4	57 Maitland	H4	82 Tibooburra	A1
8 Bega	G8	33 Eden	G8	58 Menindee	A4	83 Tuena	G6
9 Berrima	H6	34 Forbes	F5	59 Molong	F5	84 Tumbarumba	F7
10 Blackheath	H5	35 Garryowen	F7	60 Moree	G1	85 Tumut	F7
11 Blayney	G5	36 Girilambone	E3	61 Morpeth	I4	86 Ulladulla	H7
12 Boorowa	F6	37 Glanmire	G5	62 Mt Hope	D5	87 Urana	E7
13 Bourke	D2	38 Glen Innes	I2	63 Mudgee	G4	88 Wagga Wagga	E6
14 Braidwood	G7	39 Goulburn	G6	64 Muswellbrook	H4	89 Walgett	F2
15 Branxton	H4	40 Grafton	J2	65 Narrabri	G2	90 Wallacia	H5
16 Broken Hill	A4	41 Grenfell	F5	66 Narrandera	E6	91 Wellington	G4
17 Bukkulla	H2	42 Gulgong	G4	67 Nerrigundah	G7	92 Wentworth	A6
18 Burrundulla	G4	43 Gundagai	F6	68 Newcastle	I5	93 Wilcannia	B3
19 Captains Flat	G7	44 Gunnedah	H3	69 Nymagee	E4	94 Windsor	H5
20 Carcoar	G5	45 Hay	D6	70 Nyngan	E3	95 Wollongong	H6
21 Cobar	D3	46 Hill End	G5	71 Orange	G5	96 Woodburn	J1
22 Condobolin	E5	47 Hillston	D5	72 Parkes	F5	97 Wyalong	E5
23 Coolah	G3	48 Howlong	E7	73 Purnamoota	A3	98 Yass	G6
24 Cooma	G7	49 Inverell	H2	74 Queanbeyan	G7	99 Young	F6
25 Coonamble	F3	50 Jerilderie	D7	75 Raymond Terrace	I4		

New South Wales — 19

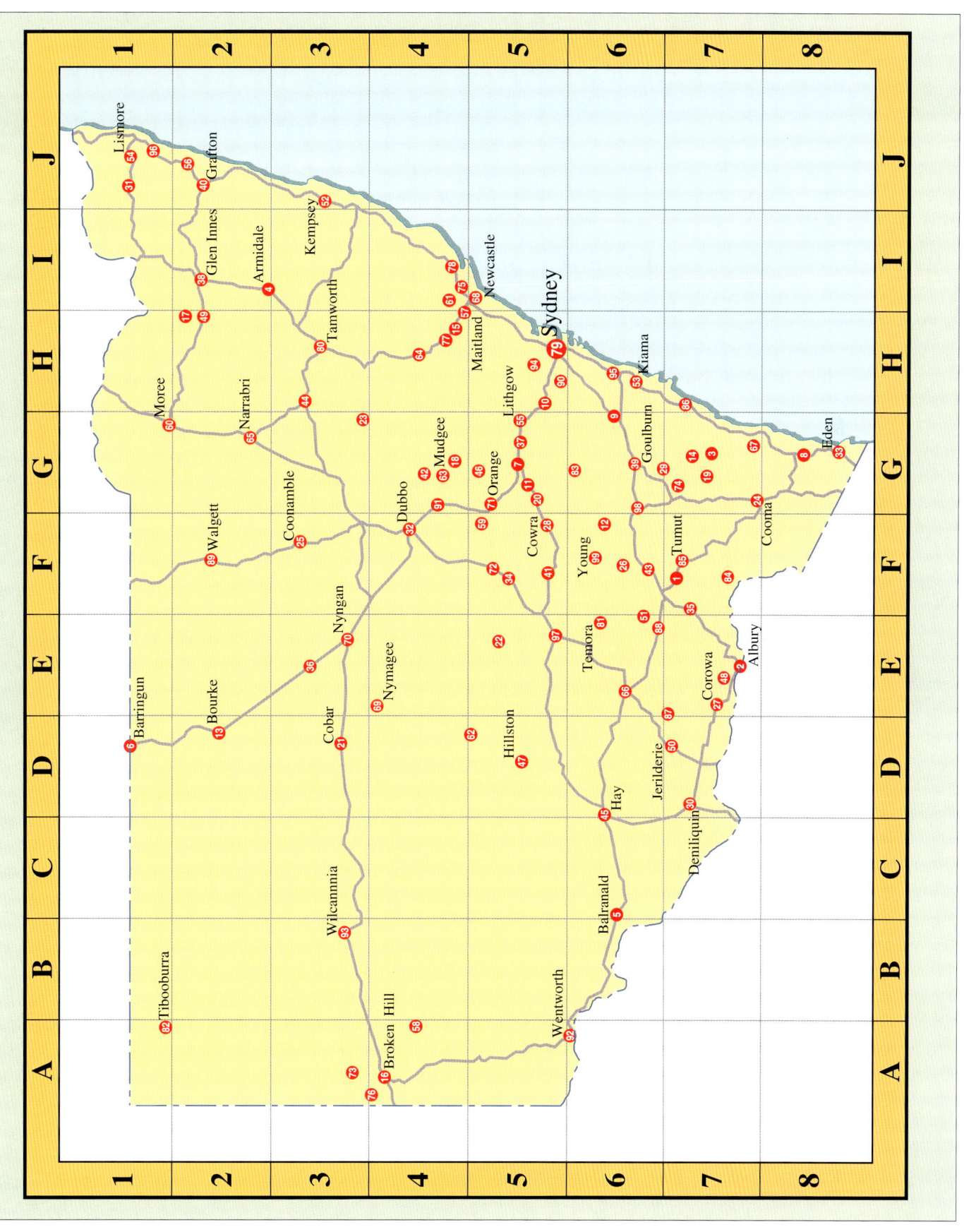

trade and the permanent population, the breweries used the river systems to transport their beer to smaller towns, a much quicker method than the long overland travel by bullock drays.

Change

Brewing reached its peak during the 1880s in country New South Wales, with 100 breweries operating in almost as many townships and villages. But the decline was rapid, and by the turn of the century the number had dwindled to less than fifty. By the early 1930s only two country breweries remained, one at Lithgow and the other at Mudgee. Both have since closed.

The trend in Sydney toward fewer breweries was much the same as in the country towns. During the 1880s at least twenty-three breweries were in business in Sydney and its suburbs, but by 1917 only three remained. The number fluctuated between three and five for the next sixty-six years, and finally there were only two.

What was the cause of this decline? There was almost no competition from overseas imports, and little, if any, competition from other Australian states. Of the many reasons for brewery failures around the turn of the century, the most compelling factor was competition from a few powerful Sydney-based breweries. The industry was becoming more capital intensive, and the big breweries had the economy of large-scale production. They owned hotels that sold only the products of the parent brewery. Sound financial management, scientific methods of production and quality control, coupled with attractively packaged popular beers, made it virtually impossible for smaller operators to compete. They were gradually squeezed out of business or taken over.

Tradition

Since colonisation in 1788 at least 170 breweries have operated in close to 100 New South Wales country towns. A further eighty have brewed in Sydney. Today only two major breweries operate in the state. Of these, the Sydney-based Tooth Brewery is the second-oldest operating brewery in Australia; it opened as the Kent Brewery in 1835. The other Sydney brewery, Toohey's, can trace its history back to 1869, when it was first known as the Darling Brewery.

The early New South Wales brewers laboured under the most difficult of conditions, using primitive equipment and whatever raw materials were available. Lacking scientific knowledge, they carried on their businesses with a great deal of trial and error, and failure. Through generations of time, their determination and perseverance gradually brought the industry forward to higher levels of achievement.

A SUM OF BEER

According to the 'New South Wales Teacher and Tutorial Guide', the following letter was sent to a country teacher:

Sir — Will you in future give my boy easier soms to do at nite? This is what he's brought hoam two or three nites back: If 4 gallons of bere will fill 32 pint bottles, how many pints and half-bottles would 9 gallons of bere fill? Well, we tried, and could make nothing out of it at all, and my boy cried and laughed, and sed he didn't dare go back in the morning without doing it.

So I had to go and buy a 9 gallon keg of bere, which I could ill afford to do, and then he went and borrowed a lot of brandy bottles. We filled them, and my boy put the number down as an answer. I don't know whether it is right or not, as we spilt some while doing it.

P.S. — Please let the next som be in water, as I am not able to buy more bere.

Australian Brewers' Journal,
May 1908

Adelong

Eaton, William 1897–1901

William Seymour Eaton had been involved in breweries at Albury, Tumbarumba and Wagga Wagga from the early 1880s, and his son, William, also operated a brewery at Temora.

The Adelong venture was shortlived. There was strong competition close by from Dennis Kenny's brewery at Gundagai, 50 km to the north, and Johnnie Beale's brewery, 22 km east at Tumut. Both of these breweries had been in business for a long time, and their beers were popular throughout the pastoral districts of south-eastern New South Wales. Faced with this competition and the small local population of Adelong, William Eaton Snr decided to close his brewery in 1901.

Albury

Settlement of the Albury region began as the result of the important overland journey from Sydney to Melbourne by the explorers Hume and Hovell in 1824. Named after a village in Surrey, England, Albury was gazetted in 1839, became a municipality in 1859, and a city in 1946.

A road from Sydney to Melbourne, which passed through Albury, was marked out in 1838, and the first punt service to operate across the Murray River was established in 1849. In 1855 the steamer *Albury* reached the town, marking the beginning of the significant river transport that followed.

The district now supports agricultural, pastoral and dairying industries, as well as an expanding secondary industry.

Albury Brewery
See Albury Brewing & Malting Co. Ltd; Hume Brewery, Wodonga Place.

Albury Brewing & Malting Co. Ltd 1857–1915
Wodonga Place, adjoining the Union Bridge

The *Albury Post* of 31 January 1857 reported that Davison & Co. had completed the construction of the first brewery in the town, the Albury Brewery, on the south-east corner of Dean and Townsend Streets. The population at the time was 600.

Robert Davison and his partner, John Kaleski, were not destined to become famous brewers. Davison left after one year, and six months later Kaleski became insolvent. This was a dismal start to the brewery that was to become the largest in the district, but many more failures and changes were to occur during the fifty-eight years of the brewery's existence.

The next owner was John Dickson. He took over in August 1860, but died early in the following year; the brewery was put up for auction on 16 March 1861. Four days later the *Border Post* recorded that the brewery was purchased by E. Clarke for £620.

During the nineteenth century there were frequent changes in the name and ownership of many of the breweries throughout all of the Australian colonies. New owners were often undercapitalised, lacked brewing experience, but mostly they were unable to produce beer of a consistent and acceptable standard. Bad batches were common, and the public soon refused to drink the beer. Bankruptcy followed, and then a new owner or lessee would try his luck.

The new owner of the Albury Brewery, E. Clarke, was a speculator, and he resold the brewery to Thomas Bullock in 1862. Bullock advertised, inviting readers to 'Encourage Native Industry', and added that he 'continues to brew the best ale in Australia'. As a sideline he sold wine casks, vinegar, hay, corn and chaff.

Bullock brewed his 'best ale in Australia' for four years, and then leased the brewery to James Liddle from 1866 to 1870. The *Albury Border Post* of 16 November 1870 gave a poor account of Liddle's beer, stating that it was only fit for consumption when nothing better was available. James Liddle left in 1870 to start up another brewery, still in the township of Albury.

In 1871 the partnership of Richard O'Keeffe and John Lister took over the lease of the Albury Brewery. The owner, Thomas Bullock, died that year, and the investor, Kenneth McLennon, purchased the property in 1872. During March of that year the O'Keeffe & Lister partnership was dissolved. Two months later O'Keeffe left the Albury Brewery and took over the lease of the brewery and cordial factory that had been started by James Liddle two years earlier. The Albury Brewery, Dean Street, had probably closed at this time.

Richard O'Keeffe did not stay long at Liddle's Brewery, which was auctioned and then closed after six months. In March 1874 O'Keeffe purchased the Hume Brewery in Wilson Street, closed it, and used the equipment for the new brewery he was constructing in Wodonga Place, adjoining the Union Bridge.

O'Keeffe again traded as the Albury Brewery, enjoying some initial success, but after five years he was almost bankrupt. In May 1879 he sold the brewery to George H. Billson.

COMPULSORY BEER DRINKING

At the district race meeting on Boxing Day, at Albury, New South Wales, all the water and soft drink gave out and the whole assemblage were obliged to drink beer. This is not surprising considering that the temperature was over 107 in the shade.

Australian Brewers' Journal, January 1897

George Billson had left his father's brewery at Beechworth, and had decided to start his own brewery in Albury. In April 1879 he purchased land in Hovell Street, intending to build on the site, but two months later he purchased the readymade Albury Brewery from Richard O'Keeffe.

During the next few years Billson built a new four-storey brewery complete with a 50-foot-high chimney stack. A bottle department was added, and a malthouse was built in Olive Street. On 20 July 1888 the Albury Brewing & Malting Co. Ltd was floated, taking over the assets of Billson's Albury Brewery, and also the Hume Brewery, Wodonga Place, which was owned by Headley & Langhammer. The Hume Brewery was closed, and Headley became the manager of the new company, with Langhammer in charge of brewing. George Billson remained a director of the company.

On 2 January 1907 the company advertised:

No Christmas Dinner complete without a bottle of Albury Brewing Co.'s Light Pale Ale or Table Beer which contains absolutely nothing but malt, hops, sugar, yeast and water. If you don't believe it, have them analysed.

This was a safe challenge, since facilities for any sort of analysis would have been almost impossible to find; more likely, they did not exist. Moreover, advertising on 2 January was decidedly late for the previous Christmas dinner!

Another advertisement said that their Light Pale Ale 'is equal to any imported beer but is a long way inferior in price. No chemicals, added gas or concoctions, but a slight sediment'.

The Albury Brewing & Malting Co. Ltd amalgamated with the Anglo-Australian Brewery Co. Ltd of Beechworth, and the name of the new company, Border United Co-operative Breweries Ltd was registered in Melbourne on 30 June 1911. Both breweries continued to operate. The brewery at Beechworth was sold in 1914 to Murray Breweries Pty Ltd, and by 1915 the grand old Albury Brewery had closed.

Albury Brewery (cnr Dean & Townsend Streets)

Robert Davison & John Kaleski	1857
John Kaleski	1858, closed
John Dickson	1860–61
E. Clarke	1861
Thomas Bullock	1862–66
James Liddle (lessee)	1866–70
Richard O'Keeffe & John Lister (lessees)	1871–72
Kenneth McLennon	1872, closed

Albury Brewery (Wodonga Place)

Richard O'Keeffe	1874–79
George H. Billson	1879–88
Albury Brewing & Malting Co. Ltd	1888–1911
Border United Co-operative Breweries Ltd	1911–15

Billson's Brewery   1894–1903
Dean Street

George Billson had been the owner of the Albury Brewery, and in 1888 he sold his interests when the Albury Brewing & Malting Co. Ltd was formed. Within a year he moved to Melbourne to join his brother in running an aerated-water business.

In 1894 George Billson returned to Albury, and started a new brewery in Dean Street.

Wearing his top hat for the occasion, George Billson, the owner of the Albury Brewery, poses proudly with his workers, c. 1880.

State Library of NSW

After George's death, his son, Walter Joseph Billson, continued to run the brewery, and stayed on as the brewer when the partnership of John Edwards and Henry Mitchell took over in 1900. The following year the new partners were prosecuted and fined for attaching fraudulent excise stamps on beer casks. Following a brief closure, the brewery was reopened by Alex McGee in 1903.

Border United Co-operative Breweries Ltd
See Albury Brewing & Malting Co. Ltd.

Colonial Porter Brewery
See Hume Brewery, Wodonga Place.

German Brewery
See Hume Brewery, Wilson Street.

Hume Brewery (Wilson Street)   1871–74
Wilson Street

The Hume Brewery was started late in 1871 by the partnership of Frederick Gleich and A. Frew. They traded as Gleich & Co., and claimed to be the only Australian brewers of pure German ale. The *Albury Border Post* of the time referred to the company as the German Brewery.

Brewing entrepreneur Richard O'Keeffe purchased the brewery in March 1874, then closed it and used the equipment for his newly-built Albury Brewery in Wodonga Place, adjoining the Union Bridge.

Hume Brewery (Wodonga Place) 1872–88
Wodonga Place

The *Albury Border Post* of 19 October 1872 carried an advertisement:

> Colonial Porter Brewery, Wodonga Place, Albury, R. Manning begs to inform the public that he is now making and ready to supply orders for bottled Colonial Porter — a really first class article. The public are invited to try it.

The name of the brewery varied. In his first advertisement Robert Manning chose the name Colonial Porter Brewery, although several correspondents made reference to the Wodonga Place Brewery. During 1877 Manning advertised his business as the Albury Brewery and, to add further confusion, it was listed as 'Robert Manning, Hume Brewery', in *Government Gazettes* from 1878. There is even further confusion in the fact that another Hume Brewery operated, in Wilson Street, during the early 1870s.

The Hume Brewery was named after the explorer of that name, and also because of its location on the site of the Old Hume Inn, which had burnt down in suspicious circumstances in 1868.

In December 1882 William S. Eaton purchased the Hume Brewery from the trustees of the estate of Robert Manning. Eaton had been the owner of the Wagga Wagga Brewery, and by 1883 he had passed the control of the Hume to his son-in law, H. S. Headley, and his partner, Mr Langhammer. The partnership proved to be highly successful, and five consecutive first prizes were secured at the Albury Annual Shows. Their ale also won second prize at the Sydney Show of 1884.

The Hume Brewery, Wodonga Place, amalgamated with George Billson's Albury Brewery in June 1888 to form the Albury Brewing & Malting Co. Ltd. Headley was appointed manager of the new company, and Langhammer the brewer. Billson stayed on as a director. The business then continued to operate from the Albury Brewery premises adjoining the Union Bridge, and the Hume Brewery was closed.

Liddle's Brewery 1871–72

James Liddle leased the Albury Brewery in 1866, but had difficulty in brewing good-quality beer. He laboured on for four years, then left to start his own brewery, which was to become known as 'Liddle's Folly'.

Liddle advertised in 1871 as 'Liddle's Original Albury Brewery' — hardly 'original' since the first Albury Brewery began in 1857. He put out what he called his Celebrated Pale Ale, apparently not worth celebrating since he stopped brewing after a few months, and leased the brewery and cordial factory to Robert Thompson in October 1871.

On 1 May 1872 Richard O'Keeffe advertised in the *Albury Border Post* that he had succeeded Thompson & Co. He was a lessee, since James Liddle still owned the property. O'Keeffe's brief involvement with Liddle's Brewery ended when the land and brewery were auctioned in November 1872. Five years later the property was acquired by Watson & Young, manufacturers of aerated waters and cordials.

Manning, Robert   1883–84
Cnr Townsend & Hume Streets

Robert Manning had been the proprietor of the Hume Brewery, Wodonga Place, Albury. When he ran into financial difficulties in 1882, the trustees of his estate sold the brewery to William Eaton.

Still the eager brewer, Manning managed to start up again in January 1883, this time at the corner of Hume and Townsend Streets. He was bold enough to advertise that he could supply his old customers — but not for long, since there is no record of Manning and his second brewery after 1884.

Wodonga Place Brewery
See Hume Brewery, Wodonga Place.

Araluen

The small town of Araluen is situated in high mountainous country to the west of the coastal town of Bateman's Bay in New South Wales.

During 1866 miners rushed to the area following the discovery of gold. The huge new finds were soon worked out, and with no better work opportunities elsewhere many of the settlers stayed on and turned to fruitgrowing and dairyfarming. The fact that a brewery operated at Araluen was probably due to its isolation and difficult access, making it relatively free from competition. At one time the home to thousands of miners, today the town is little more than a place of tourist interest.

Araluen Brewery 1868–72

In 1868 when Richard Chynoweth started the brewery, Georgina Auld was also registered as a brewer and was possibly the silent financial partner. Her husband, Thomas Auld, operated the brewery until it closed in 1872.

Armidale

In 1839 G. J. MacDonald, Commissioner of Crown Lands, established his headquarters in the district that he named Armidale, after his father's estate in Scotland. The town was gazetted in 1849, and proclaimed a city in 1885. Today Armidale is well known as an educational centre. Among the many facilities in the city are the University of New England (founded in 1938), the Armidale College of Advanced Education, and the Armidale College of Technical and Further Education.

Armidale Brewery 1850–1917

John Tuck advertised in the *Maitland Mercury* of 13 March 1850 that his Armidale Brewery was operating, and that he could supply 'good ale, equal to any ale in the colony and at a reasonable price'. As with many brewers of the time, John Tuck's attempt at brewing was a failure, and the brewery was put up for auction in February 1852.

The auction advertisement was lengthy, and advised would-be purchasers that

the brewery, in the hands of a resident proprietor, will, of necessity, lead to the realization of a rapid fortune at this eventful period of the colony's history, when, from the discovery of our splendid goldfields, Australia's population will speedily become tenfold.

The brewery closed after it failed to sell at auction, and in the late 1850s Richard Jenkins and his brother, Charles, purchased the property; they worked the brewery until 1865. The population of the township was then 950. The new owners, Butler & Baker, lasted a year, and by 1867 the brewery had closed again.

Two of the early owners, John Tuck and Charles Jenkins, joined Benjamin Blencowe, and the three partners ran the brewery from 1871 to 1873. When Tuck left, the others continued for another year. The brewery then closed for the third time.

The next owner was J. F. McKinley, who sold to Peter Simpson in 1882.

Following a meeting of creditors in 1887 the Armidale Brewery became the property of Walter Billson, the son of George Billson of Albury brewing fame. Walter Billson changed the name to the City Brewery, and worked it for about a year. In 1888 he sold to the partnership of A. M. Solomon & S. Hillier.

Nobody seemed to last long at the brewery. James Rampling took over in 1890 and traded as Rampling & Scholes, but by October that year J. F. McKinley was once again the proprietor.

Left: *The City Brewery, Armidale, NSW, during its period of ownership by Hillier & Solomon, 1888–90.*

Right: *Although the name of the brewery was changed to the City Brewery in 1887, Steven Hillier's advertisement used the original name, Armidale Brewery.*

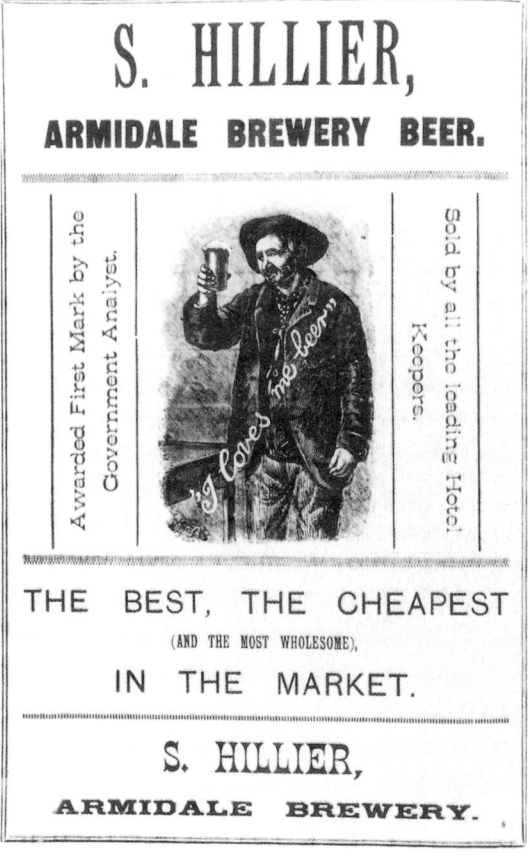

Steven Hillier came back into the business in 1893, but by 1896 there was another owner, William Allen. He had previously owned breweries at Blackheath and Goulburn, and became the most successful of all the brewers at Armidale, running the brewery for twenty-one years.

Armidale Brewery

John Tuck	1850–82, closed
Richard & Charles Jenkins	1858–65
Butler & Baker	1866–67, closed
Tuck, Jenkins & Blencowe	1871–73
Jenkins & Blencowe	1873–74, closed
J. F. McKinley	1880–82
Peter Simpson	1882–87

City Brewery

Walter Billson	1887–88
A. M. Solomon & S. Hillier	1888–90
Rampling & Scholes	1890–90
J. F. McKinley	1890–93
Steven Hillier	1893–96
William Allen	1896–1917

Balranald

Balranald Brewery   1883–88
Turandury Street

The brewery commenced in 1883, and three years later the owner Henry Simmons tried unsuccessfully to auction the business. Thomas Boynton purchased the brewery in 1888, but it closed soon after.

Barringun

The small township of Barringun, located on the Queensland border in western New South Wales, was once a Customs Post for the trade between New South Wales and Queensland.

Barringun Brewery   1883–94
Cnr Anderson & Scott Streets

The brewery, conveniently situated on the corner of Anderson and Scott Streets, was started by the partnership of Lee & Hine in 1883. Lee left three years later, and the new partnership of Gustavus Klaeby and Henry Hine continued to run a moderately successful business. By 1890 Henry Hine was the sole proprietor.

Bathurst

Australia's oldest inland settlement, Bathurst, was named by Governor Macquarie in May 1815. It was an important pastoral district, and in the 1850s the discovery of payable gold changed Bathurst into a boom town. The bushrangers, Ben Hall, John Gilbert and others, rode through the main streets in 1863, captured the Gold Commissioner and held him to ransom. The previous year, the overland transport business of Cobb & Co. moved from Victoria to set up their national headquarters at Bathurst.

Today, the city has many beautiful historic buildings, and the Mt Panorama racing circuit, a major tourist attraction where car and motorcycle racing events are held.

Albion Brewery   c. 1835
John Neal was the proprietor.

Bathurst Co-operative Brewing Society Ltd
See Crown Brewery.

Burton Brewery
See Great Western Brewery Co. Ltd.

Crown Brewery   1883–1920
Cnr Durham & Rankin Streets

James Stewart built the Crown Brewery in 1883, and a year or so later he sold the business and property to the partnership of F. McKenny and Eugene Parker. Daniel Fitzpatrick took over Parker's share about 1885, and the business then traded as McKenny & Fitzpatrick.

The Crown Brewery enjoyed a good reputation, and, as well as selling to local residents and hotels, delivered beer as far north as the Queensland border. At the Adelaide International Exhibition of 1887 Crown beer attracted second prize against 250 competitors. By 1888 Daniel Fitzpatrick had become sole owner, and during the early 1890s J. H. Gracie was involved in the business.

In August 1892 one of the employees who had been dismissed for drunkenness broke into the brewery and, in an act of vengeance, turned on the taps of the beer and porter vats, allowing the vats to drain out until

---

A REMARKABLE PATENT

The object of my invention is to manufacture an improved description of ale and stout which will be a valuable medium for supplying nourishment to persons who are in ill-health and unable to take food in its solid form.

I introduce during the process of brewing, for every barrel of beer, 15 pounds of calves' head or calves' feet, 10 pounds of bullocks' heads and shins of beef, 2 bushels of malt, 12 pounds of hops and 4 grains of quinine. And in my treatment of the liquor, I produce an entirely new beverage.

Australian Brewers' Journal,
March 1895

In 1908 James Walker formed Walker & Co. Ltd, which acquired the assets of the Great Western Brewery in Bathurst and the Standard Brewery, Orange. He used the unimaginative trademark, OB, for his advertising, the letters referring to the towns of Orange and Bathurst.

Defiance Brewery
See Great Western Brewery Co. Ltd.

Federal Brewery c. 1899
Howick Street

For a short period in 1895 Patrick J. McGrath had been a partner in the Great Western Brewery, Bathurst, but later that year he shifted to Melbourne. After a few years he returned to Bathurst, and in February 1899 he gave notice in the *National Advocate* that he intended to open 'The Federal Brewery (late the Acme Flour Mills) centrally situated, a First Class Brewery, everything up-to-date to turn out a First Class Article'.

The advertisement was repeated during the next two months, and on 18 April 1899 he advised that the brewery was 'now in full swing and turning out a splendid quality of beer. Everything tip-top, modern and up-to-date'. In earlier years Patrick McGrath had gained his brewing experience when he worked for P. J. Martin at the Australian Brewery in Melbourne.

Great Western Brewery Co. Ltd c. 1835–1927
Cnr Morrisett & Peel Streets

The first brewery in the district was established by George Rankin at One Tree Hill (or Eglington as it is now known), 5 km north-west of Bathurst. Known then as the Kelloshiel Brewery, it operated in conjunction with a mill. Brewing started about 1835, and after a few years the partnership of Heathorn & Price took over. Price dropped out soon after, leaving Heathorn to continue on his own. Both the brewery and the mill were destroyed by fire, as reported in the *Free Press and Mining Journal* of 24 March 1852. Heathorn then started brewing again at Morrisett Street in the town centre.

A number of lessees followed from 1864. At that time the township had fifty hotels and a population of 5000. Robert Springett ran the brewery from 1864 to 1866. It was known then as the Burton Brewery, and was advertised to let in the *Bathurst Times* of 27 November 1867.

John Beatty held the brewer's licence from 1869 to 1871, and the brewery may have closed then. Coyle, Holman & Inch were the lessees by 1875, and on 2 October of that year an advertisement in the *Bathurst Times* announced that 'The partnership of W. Holman and J. Kerry, Defiance Brewery, is dissolved'. The name had been changed to the Defiance Brewery, but the new owners, J. Kerry and C. Mullins, changed the name again, this time to the Great Western Brewery.

Charles Mullins became the sole proprietor in 1883. He was a popular personality in the district, and was involved in many community activities, including the Bathurst Turf Club, the Building Society and the local council.

Edward Mullins ran the business in 1891, and with a syndicate he formed the Great Western Brewery Co. Ltd. Several years later the brewery closed. It was reopened in 1895 by James Walker and Patrick McGrath.

empty. Reporting on the incident the *Bathurst Daily Times* commented on the smell and the flooding of the cellar that was 'knee deep in beer'.

The brewery was put up for auction as a going concern in 1912. Daniel Fitzpatrick had retired, and, when the brewery was passed in at the auction, the business was continued by his son, Vincent Fitzpatrick, with the assistance of William Strickland. By 1917 Strickland had become the owner, but the business was struggling.

Two years later Albert Dalton tried unsuccessfully to run the brewery, and the assets were acquired by a group of hotelkeepers who formed the Bathurst Co-operative Brewing Society Ltd. The brewery closed the following year.

James Stewart	1883–84
F. McKenny & E. Parker	1884–85
F. McKenny & D. Fitzpatrick	1885–88
Daniel Fitzpatrick	1888–1912
V. Fitzpatrick & W. Strickland	1912–17
William Strickland	1917–19
Albert Dalton	1919
Bathurst Co-operative Brewing Society Ltd	1919–20

McGrath, previously the manager of the Crown Brewery, Bathurst, left within a year, leaving James Walker to continue as sole proprietor. In 1908 he formed Walker & Co. Ltd, which acquired the assets of the Great Western Brewery, Bathurst, and the Standard Brewery, Orange, which he also owned.

Walker's Pale Ale was popular in the district, and was distributed under the unimaginative trade mark of 'OB', the letters representing the townships of Orange and Bathurst where the breweries were located. During his period of residence at Bathurst, Walker was prominent in public affairs, and was mayor on several occasions.

Kelloshiel Brewery
George Rankin	c. 1835–c. 1838
Heathorn & Price	c. 1838–c. 1840
Henry Heathorn	1840–52

Burton Brewery
Henry Heathorn	1852–64
Robert Springett	1864–66, closed
John Beatty	1869–71, closed

Defiance Brewery
Coyle, Holman & Inch	c. 1875
W. Holman & J. Kerry	1875

Great Western Brewery
J. Kerry & C. Mullins	1875–83
Charles Mullins	1883–1891

Great Western Brewery Co. Ltd
Edward Mullins	1891–c. 1893, closed
James Walker & Patrick McGrath	1895
James Walker	1895–1908
Walker & Co. Ltd	1908–27

Kelloshiel Brewery
See Great Western Brewery Co. Ltd.

Bega

The name Bega comes from an Aboriginal word meaning either 'a large camping ground' or 'a beautiful place'.

Bega Brewing Co. Ltd   1872–1900
Auckland Street

When Richard Rogers started the Bega Brewing Co. in 1872, and during the life of the brewery there was no other brewery for 100 km in any direction.

Three years was enough for Richard Rogers; he went out of business and the brewery closed.

Peter Sharp reopened the brewery in 1882, and was joined in 1891 by Robert Sharp. The brewery was sold to Augustus Arnold in 1897, and the vendor, Peter Sharp, stayed on as the brewer and manager until 1900, the year the brewery was destroyed by fire.

Berrima

Berrima has been declared a historic village by the National Heritage Council. Situated 140 km south of Sydney, this picturesque town is a favourite tourist attraction. Australia's oldest jail, and the oldest licensed inn in New South Wales, are two of the many historic buildings in the town.

Kentish Arms Inn & Brewery   c. 1860
James Atkinson was a pioneer farmer and distiller of the Berrima district. In 1829 he wrote a treatise on the need to establish a distilling and brewing industry in New South Wales, but he himself never brewed or distilled. He set up a large cattle station and pastoral business, and after his death in 1834 his wife and his younger brother, John, continued to manage the family interests.

John Atkinson held the licence for the family-owned Kentish Arms Inn (later known as the Three Legs of Man), which was located a short distance south of Berrima. A brewer's licence was taken out in 1860, and Atkinson was content to brew sufficient beer to satisfy the customers of his inn.

Blackheath

Mountain Brewery Co. Ltd   1884–92
Because of its wild and black appearance the town was named Blackheath by Governor Macquarie in 1815. The brewery, located in the beautiful Blue Mountains district, was built alongside Centennial Creek. According to the Sydney *Illustrated News*, it was almost hidden in a gully, not for secrecy reasons, since its licence had been gazetted, but for easy access to the clear mountain-stream water.

William Allen founded the Mountain Brewery in 1884, and sold out to James Daley in 1888. The business was incorporated the following year, but less than a year later the brewery closed. Daley, still in the liquor business, built and operated the Ivanhoe Hotel in Govett Street.

The brewery was leased to Frederick Wilkins in 1890, was passed in at auction in August 1891, and a month or so later Henry Hargen took over the lease. Hargen was less successful than his predecessors, and the premises and equipment were taken over in 1892 by William Young for the production of cordials and aerated waters.

Blayney

Blayney Brewing & Cordial Mfg Co. Ltd   1882–95
During 1882 C. & C. H. Inch began brewing at the small township of Blayney, 40 km south-west of

Bathurst. Uriah Wright held the brewer's licence from 1883 to 1885, followed by John Renateau in 1886. Three years later Renateau formed the Blayney Brewing & Cordial Mfg. Co. Ltd.

The brewery was purchased in 1891 by D. J. Inch, who changed the name to the Carlisle Brewery. The last brewer was William Wittaker who operated from 1893 to 1895.

Carlisle Brewery
See Blayney Brewing & Cordial Mfg. Co. Ltd.

Boorowa

Milne, G. D. 1881–82

Old Mill House Brewery 1891–94
Patrick Murphy was granted a brewer's licence in 1891, and started brewing in the premises of the old Shamrock Hotel. Under Murphy's ownership it was quaintly named the Old Mill House Brewery, and for a few years he supplied the small community with his local brew, before leaving the district.

Bourke

For more than 100 years Bourke has been the centre of a large pastoral district. The town, in the far north-west of New South Wales, was established in 1862 as a distribution centre for supplies to surrounding properties and also for the export of wool.

Early means of transport was by horse, camel, bullock teams and mail coach (Cobb & Co.). Paddle steamers also moved supplies along the Darling and Murray Rivers, and to and from the coast of South Australia. The same methods of transport were used by the only brewery in the town, the Red Lion.

Red Lion Brewery 1879–1901
Henry L. Lindsay operated breweries at Bourke, Cobar, Hay, Hillston and Orange — all in New South Wales. For much of the time during the 1880s he lived in Sydney and appointed managers to run the breweries, each manager applying for and receiving the brewer's licence. Using the name Red Lion Brewery for each operation, Lindsay began business at Bourke in 1879, and on 31 May 1883 Lindsay's Brewery Co. Ltd was floated to take over the Red Lion breweries at Hay and Bourke.

Thomas Hardwick became the manager in 1889, followed by Philip Hardwick in 1891. The business went into liquidation in 1893, and, following reconstruction, other managers continued to run the business: Digby Trew in 1894, James Liddington from 1895 to 1896, and Herbert Coomber late in 1896. For the last two years Charles Long worked the brewery.

Braidwood

Britannia Brewery 1859–60
Monkittee Street

Gold was discovered in the area in 1852, and Braidwood quickly developed as the principal town of the southern goldfields. While the rush was still on, Edward Smith advertised in the *Braidwood Dispatch* in 1859:

> to Innkeepers, heads of families and the public generally ... Edward Smith having completed his brewery and commenced operations on an extensive scale, is now in a position to supply all orders he may be favoured with.

Smith's advertisement continued, describing how farmers, diggers and men in business could now get his local brew, 'resembling as close as possible the ales of Great Britain ... the whole surrounding district will see the benefits ... at a considerably lower price than imported ales'.

The brewery had a short life, probably less than a year. It was situated in an area that was liable to flooding, and there was a massive flood in February 1860. The old town has now been classified as a historic village by the National Trust.

Branxton

Hunter Valley Brewing Co. Pty Ltd   1951–53
Russell & Short Streets

The company was granted a brewer's licence on 18 December 1951, and operated from premises that had previously been a dairy. The first brew was tapped five days before Christmas 1951, and production reportedly reached 4000 gallons of beer per week in the new year.

There were grand plans for a bottling department and large-scale production, but the venture turned out to be decidedly unsuccessful, and the brewery closed either late in 1953 or early in 1954. The Hunter Valley brewery was one of only a few breweries to start in the mid-1900s. Strong competition and a host of other reasons forced its closure after two years.

Broken Hill

In the early days of the township of Broken Hill severe droughts and the high cost of water were constant problems. The occasional rainwater, collected from roofs, was heavily contaminated with lead from the dust falling from the smelter chimneys. Sanitation barely existed, and there was widespread disease, yet people came and stayed, determined to exploit the huge mineral deposits that were the sole reason for the town's existence.

Berliner Brewery
See South Broken Hill Brewery.

Broken Hill Brewing Co.   1888–89
Beryl Lane (now Silica Street), North Broken Hill

During a visit to Broken Hill Theodore Bruce from Adelaide purchased an acre of land where excellent well-water was available on the site. Subsequently, he built a brewery on the land, and was ready for business on 24 July 1888.

The local newspaper, the *Silver Age*, gave a lengthy description of the brewery and its facilities on 25 July 1888. The tower was four storeys high, and under the high-pitched roof there were water-storage tanks with a capacity for 1600 gallons, filled by means of a pump from the well. On the top of the tower there was a turret for ventilation, complete with an ornamental weather vane.

The brewery went into liquidation in 1889, and in July of that year, the South Australian Brewing Co. Ltd of Adelaide, purchased the property and equipment. This enabled the company to become quickly established in the rapidly expanding mining town.

See also South Australian Brewing Co. Ltd (Broken Hill).

Burton Brewery & Aerated Water Co. Ltd   1891–1900
Cnr Bromide & Blende Streets

Peter McIndoe had been a wine-and-spirit merchant, and also a manufacturer of aerated water and cordial. His partner in the brewing side of the business was James Sloan, owner of the local Globe Hotel. They set up a small 12-hogshead capacity plant at the back of the hotel, and began producing beer in 1891. After four years the partnership was dissolved, and Sloan joined the opposition, Shamrock Brewery.

Peter McIndoe continued on his own, and restructured the business as the Burton Brewery & Aerated Water Co. Ltd. The brewery sold Sparkling Pale Ale for 2s per gallon, stout for 7s 6d a dozen bottles, and Champagne Ale for 4s 6d a dozen bottles.

The *Barrier Miner* of 3 April 1895 recorded that the Licensing Court had granted a transfer of the brewer's licence from P. McIndoe to W. H. Alton. Alton continued to run the Burton Brewery at Broken Hill for a further four years, and McIndoe left the district to take over the Burton Brewery in West Melbourne.

Simpson, Beaglehole & Co. of the Waverley Brewery, Broken Hill, bought the Burton Brewery on 1 March 1900, and closed it. The manager of the defunct brewery, F. W. Smalpage, purchased most of the equipment and took it to Echuca, Victoria, where he opened the Clarion Brewery.

The old Burton Brewery premises were acquired by the Shell Co. in 1932. Later, the tower was demolished, the well was filled in, and the site became the Broken Hill Tourist Centre.

Clayton's Barrier Brewery
See Silver City Mineral Water Co.

Lee's Barrier Brewery
See Silver City Mineral Water Co.

Shamrock Brewery
See West End Brewery.

Shelley & Co.   c. 1900
Cnr Morgan & O'Farrell Streets

John Shelley's factory, which was set up in 1893, was primarily a producer of soft drinks and cordials. The company also produced a light non-alcoholic hop beer. For a brief few years, when a brewer's licence was granted, some alcoholic beverages were produced, including a XXX Ale.

Silver City Mineral Water Co.   c. 1890–c. 1910
Argent Street

In addition to cordials and aerated waters, the company produced a lager beer under the name of Lee's Barrier Brewery. Soft drinks comprised the company's main output, and a non-intoxicating Golden Ale was marketed under the name of Clayton's Barrier Brewery.

Label for the Hunter Valley Brewing Co. Pty Ltd.

The South Australian Brewing Co. Ltd, Broken Hill, supplied bulk beer for bottling by hotels in Broken Hill and outback townships such as Port Pirie. Labels had similar themes, depicting industry in the background and the worker enjoying his glass of beer.

South Australian Brewing Co. Ltd (Broken Hill)   1889–1925
Cnr Beryl & Buck Streets

In 1883 Charles Rasp, a German migrant from Hamburg, Germany, collected specimens of dark heavy rock from an outcrop on one of the low hills of the Barrier Range, about 25 km from Silverton; where the jagged crest had given it the name of Broken Hill. Eighteen months later a syndicate formed a public company to develop the rich and extensive silver and lead ore deposits. The name chosen for the company was Broken Hill Proprietary Co. Ltd (known today as BHP, one of Australia's largest companies).

The Broken Hill Brewing Co. went into liquidation in 1889, only a year after it was formed, and the South Australian Brewing Co. of Adelaide purchased the substantial brewery property for £6000. This gave them a readymade base to enter the market of the rapidly growing mining township. There were already sixty-seven hotels in the town.

For a short period the brewery continued to be referred to as the Broken Hill Brewery, and the name was used on the bottle labels of the company's XXX Dinner Ale. The South Australian Brewery's Broken Hill venture was highly successful, in spite of the strong competition from the nearby Waverley Brewery. To eliminate this opposition the Waverley Brewery was taken over and closed in 1906. It was demolished the following year. In 1918 the local West End Brewery was also purchased and closed.

The South Australian Brewery was the last company to brew beer at Broken Hill. Production ceased in 1925, and supplies were shipped up from the parent company in Adelaide to the Broken Hill Brewery, which was then used as a distribution depot.

South Broken Hill Brewery   1891–c. 1900
274 Knox Street

This small brewery was operated by Louis Berliner and his son, Morris. The *Barrier Miner* of 30 December 1897 advertised the brewery for sale as a going concern, explaining that Louis Berliner was retiring due to old age; eight months earlier Louis had advertised and thanked his customers for their patronage over the previous six years.

Time went by, and the brewery didn't sell. During the latter part of 1898 the brewery was put up for auction, complete with the land, premises, appliances, horses, wagons and furniture. There were still no buyers. By 1904 Louis Berliner had shifted to Melbourne, and, despite his presumed old age, he started brewing again at North Fitzroy.

Waverley Brewery   1887–1906
Beryl Lane (now Silica Street), off Buck Street

The following article appeared in the May 1888 issue of the *Australian Brewers' Journal*:

> At Broken Hill there is already a 14 hogshead brewery in full working order, the income of which, from the sale of water alone, is stated to be £20 per week.

The article referred to the Waverley Brewery, and said that, at that time, there were over fifty hotels in the town. The editor added that

> the population, although rapidly increasing on the field, numbers are said to be dying from typhoid fever, due to the exceedingly bad sanitary condition of the place and the difficulty of obtaining good water.

Typical transport of the nineteenth century. Wagons loaded with casks of beer leave the South Australian Brewing Co. Ltd, Broken Hill, c. 1890.

A novel method of transporting beer. Teams of camels take a consignment en route from the Waverley Brewery, Broken Hill, to districts in the far west of New South Wales. The beer frequently suffered in quality when exposed to the scorching heat during long days of travel.
La Trobe Library, State Library of Victoria

The article gave some indication of the appalling state of the township shortly after it was settled, and at the time when the town's first brewery, the Waverley, began to brew beer. The proprietors were George Simpson and Thomas D'Arcy Burke. Burke left the business in 1889 to take over the management of the Union Barrier Brewery at Silverton, and the Waverley Brewery was then operated by Simpson, Johnston & Co.

By 1896 business had increased to such an extent that an extra tower had to be added and more cellars provided. George Simpson was the brewer and managing partner. William Beaglehole joined the company, and the business was then conducted as Simpson, Johnston & Beaglehole & Co. Ltd. Both Beaglehole and Johnston had interests in the Lion Brewing & Malting Co., Adelaide; Beaglehole was also a director of several mining companies in Broken Hill, and Johnston was the owner of the Oakbank Brewery, South Australia.

The Waverley Brewery produced excellent-quality beer. It was the most popular of all the beers put out by the five breweries operating in Broken Hill toward the end of the nineteenth century. Kegs of beer were transported as far as the Queensland border, and most hotels in 'the back country' were staunch customers.

The *Barrier Miner* of 8 September 1906 reported that

> Mr George Simpson, proprietor of the well-known Waverley Brewery at Broken Hill, which for many years has traded under the name of Messrs Simpson, Beaglehole & Co., has sold the brewery and its business connection to the South Australian Brewing Co. at, it is understood, a high figure.

The Waverley Brewery was then closed. In spite of the never-ending heat and dust and disease, the Waverley Brewery at Broken Hill was indeed a remarkable success during its nineteen years of operation.

West End Brewery   c. 1895–1918
Cnr Kaolin & Morgan Streets

The brewery was originally called the Shamrock Brewery by the proprietor, J. F. Molony, but when he took on James Sloan as a partner the name was changed to West End Brewery.

John Molony moved to Mt Gambier in 1911 and purchased the Standard Brewery there, but he still retained a 50 per cent interest in the West End Brewery at Broken Hill.

James Sloan then ran the West End Brewery at Broken Hill until 1918, when it was bought by the South Australian Brewery Co. and closed. The old brewery buildings were pulled down in 1930, and the site was cleared before the subdivision of the area for housing.

Bukkulla

Wyndham, Wadham   1882

Wadham Wyndham chose the tiny township of Bukkulla to brew and sell beer. The size of the village, located in the far-north east of New South Wales, and the limited market were probably the reasons for the brewery's failure.

George W. Simpson was the founder of the Waverley Brewery, Broken Hill, one of the largest and most profitable in the district during its operation from 1887 to 1906. He was said to be 'an exceedingly popular business man, just and generous, prompt and decisive in his actions, and with ever a kindly shake of the hand'.

During their tour of England in 1901, this photograph of Mr and Mrs G. W. Simpson was taken by Lafayette, the well-known and famous London court photographer of the time.
La Trobe Library, State Library of Victoria

Burrundulla

Burrundulla Brewery
See Sydney Brewery.

Sydney Brewery   1861–90
The old flourmill at Burrundulla, 10 km south of Mudgee, was converted to a brewery by Andrew Caxton in 1861. He used the name Burrundulla Brewery, and continued to run the business until 1876.

The new owner was G. J. Southward. Within a few years he had twenty men working for him. He brewed every day, and grew his own barley, which he converted to malt at his brewery.

During the 1880s E. W. Daley took control of the business, which then became known as the Sydney Brewery. He advertised in the *Mudgee Guardian* of 26 May 1890:

> Drink Pure Californian Golden Drop Ale — the Best and Purest Summer Beverage in the Market; Invigorating, Light and Appetising. This Acknowledged Superior Ale is recommended by the Medical Faculty and may be obtained from E. W. Daley, Sydney Brewery, Burrundulla.

Directly above this advertisement was another, put in by the Royal Oak Hotel, telling readers that it stocked beer from Marshall's Brewery, Sydney.

During the latter part of 1889 Daley purchased the Mudgee Co-operative Brewery, and closed his Sydney Brewery at Burrundulla, probably through lack of business in that small town.

Captains Flat

Leon, Henry W.   1892–97

A QUESTIONABLE PRACTICE

The means by which some brewers gain their trade cannot but be considered as highly discreditable to themselves. We have heard of instances where there were two or more breweries in one city, where one of them to gain trade is in the habit of giving to working men a few shillings to go and ask for their beer at a house [hotel] where they know the opposition brewery company's ale is alone drawn, with instructions that they are to turn up their noses at it, and reject it as vile and undrinkable. Trade gained by such means, although for a while enriching the profits of the unscrupulous brewer, is sure to have its just reward, and to use a very trite but true saying, 'such birds come home to roost'.

Australian Brewers' Journal,
February 1892

Carcoar

The mid-west township of Carcoar nestles like a charming English village in a picturesque valley alongside the Belubula River. It is the third-oldest town west of the Blue Mountains, and is classified in its entirety by the National Trust. It was at Carcoar that the infamous bushranger, Ben Hall, was sentenced to death.

Australian Brewing Co.
See Carcoar Brewery.

Carcoar Brewery   1889–1913
Belubula Street
When William Derwin began brewing at Carcoar in 1889, there were sixteen hotels in the township. Derwin's drive and energy enabled the family brewing business to continue profitably for twenty years. There was a steady supply of clear, fresh spring-water, and with astute attention to the brewing process William Derwin and his sons produced beer of consistently high quality. As well as supplying the hotels in town, beer was sent by bullock wagon to Orange, Cowra and other western townships.

In 1896 the control of the business was taken over by William's sons, Charles and William Jnr. Charles became mayor of the town on several occasions.

Joseph Derwin held the licence from 1904 until 1910, when the brewery was sold to Robert S. Raymond. He changed the name to the Australian Brewing Co., but the brewery closed in 1913. It was later used as a cordial factory.

Cobar

Following the discovery of copper in the district in 1869, Cobar became one of the largest copper-mining operations in Australia. Today it remains a quiet township of historical interest.

Australian Brewery   c. 1880–86
Saul's Tank, on the road from Cobar to Louth
The *Forbes and Parkes Gazette* of 31 December 1880 announced that John Parker Snr had recently purchased the Fair Hill Brewery and renamed it Australian Brewery. The previous owner of the Fair Hill Brewery is unknown, but John Parker brewed until 1885, and James H. Parker continued for another year.

Fair Hill Brewery
See Australian Brewery.

Red Lion Brewery   1884–90
Henry L. Lindsay owned a number of breweries in country New South Wales. He either leased or operated these through the appointment of a manager.

Wood, Samuel R. 1888–c. 1893
It was reported in the *Australian Brewers' Journal* of October 1888 that 'S. R. Wood is adding a brewery to his cordial manufacturing business'.

A number of Cobar brewers were listed in trade directories and *Government Gazettes*. Some of these may have been involved with the Fair Hill, Australian or Red Lion breweries.

Baxter, Robert 1893–95
Robert Baxter held a brewer's licence from 1893 to 1895, and possibly continued on at the Red Lion Brewery.

O'Brien, Thomas 1879
Thomas O'Brien started brewing in 1879 at East Cobar, fronting Cobar and Nyngan Roads. It appears that the brewery was idle for some time until 1884, when O'Brien began brewing again. He sold out in 1885 to the partnership of Hopkin Lewis and Edward Freeman, and they continued until 1895.

Williams, G. 1880
Marshall Street
Another brewer was G. Williams who started up a business in 1880. Samuel Williams followed in 1881, and Capel H. Lewis (probably the Hopkin Lewis above) was listed as a brewer, at the same address, in 1884. Hugh Sutherland followed in 1885.

Condobolin

Condobolin Brewery 1892–1900
William Street
At the Condobolin Brewery there were frequent changes in management, with people joining and leaving. Each new brewer would eagerly settle into his business with impetuous disregard of the past failures, and carry on regardless. Conventional wisdom was certainly not at work, and with predictable results!

Graf & Adams	1892–93
Daniel Comans	1894–95
Thomas Dowling	1896–97
Daniel Comans	1898
Stephen Byrnes	1899
Sam Plunkett	1900

The brewery burnt to the ground in November 1903, although the adjoining house and stables were saved. The local press said 'the fire brigade did a good job'.

Coolah

Mead, Richard 1886–93

KEEP THE FLOORS CLEAN

Nothing militates more against the production of really sound beer than a dirty or 'slimy' cellar, and yet in a vast number of breweries the cellars are by no means what they should be. A recent investigator has found that in many cases the 'slime' which accumulates on cellar floors and elsewhere in breweries consists almost entirely of 'wild yeast' cells, which, of course, work an immense amount of mischief in brewing.

We once were in a brewery where for six months the beer had been very inferior indeed, and where we were convinced that the one and only cause of the trouble was the slimy and 'greasy' state of the floors, due to the neglect of the cellar-man, an 'old hand,' who 'got to know too much,' as the saying is, and neglected his every-day duties.

Australian Brewers' Journal, February 1889

Cooma

Cooma, situated in high mountainous country, was a long way from the nearest brewery, and access was treacherous and slow at those times. Local brewing provided a simple solution.

Cooma Brewery 1886–92
On the Murrumbidgee River, near Cooma
The partnership of Sir James Ashton and Hugh Stewart lasted barely a year before Sir James decided to pull out of the brewing business, leaving Stewart to continue on his own. Stewart owned the Pine Valley Inn, about 6 km from Cooma on the Adaminaby road, and it was thought that the brewery may have been started to supply the inn's customers.

Coonamble

Coonamble takes its name from an Aboriginal word meaning 'plenty of dirt' or 'bullock dung'. The town has a reticulated supply of bore water, and the principal produce of the district are wool, wheat, fat lambs and beef cattle.

Coonamble Brewing & Cordial Mfg Co. Ltd
See Red Lion Brewery.

Red Lion Brewery 1887–1904
When the partnership of R. E. Rule and E. R. Shone started the brewery, they traded as R. Rule & Co., and employed John Atkinson as the brewer and manager. Atkinson had previously managed a brewery at

Walgett, and had worked at the Black Horse Breweries, both at Wilcannia and Hay. At Coonamble, in 1888, Atkinson secured first prizes for his ales and cordials against strong competition.

The brewery was purchased by Samuel Carmichael and R. J. Boyle in 1889. Two years later they formed the Coonamble Brewing & Cordial Mfg. Co. Ltd. Carmichael was a member of the local municipal council at the time.

When Henry Parsons acquired the brewery in 1893, he changed the name to the Red Lion Brewery. For the next seven years ownership changed almost yearly.

The brewery closed in 1900, and became the venue for more sinister activities. In 1903 the police raided an opium den in the old brewery. They confiscated five tins of opium, various items of smoking equipment, and arrested seventeen Chinese men and two white women.

The brewery enjoyed a new lease of life in 1904 when it was reopened by John and Ernest Fletcher. They traded as Fletcher & Sons, and were also involved in a brewery at Walgett. However, their effort at Coonamble lasted less than a year.

R. E. Rule & E. R. Shone	1887–89
S. Carmichael & R. J. Boyle	1889–91

Coonamble Brewing & Cordial Mfg Co. Ltd
S. Carmichael & R. J. Boyle	1891–93

Red Lion Brewery
Henry Parsons	1893–96
George Adams	1896–97
David Edwards	1897–98
Charles Vaughan	1898–99
Stratton, Lang & Co.	1899–1900, closed
John & Ernest Fletcher	1904

Reminiscent of an English castle, the brewery (below) was originally known as the Burton Brewery. The name was changed to Lion Brewery by Edmund and Richard Resch when they took over in 1883. Brewing continued for twenty years.

Cootamundra

The Cootamundra district was settled by pastoralists in the 1830s, and a village was officially established in 1861. It became a municipality in 1884.

The town of Cootamundra is the home of the Cootamundra wattle (*Acacia baileyana*), and the birthplace of Sir Donald Bradman, Australia's most famous cricketer.

Burton Brewery
See Lion Brewery.

Cootamundra Brewery
See Excelsior Brewery.

Excelsior Brewery　　　　1879–1913
Olney Street

In 1879 a brewer's licence was issued to J. & E. Barnes, and the following year separate licences were granted to Michael McTherney and Patrick McCormack.

During 1888 Thomas Rankin became the owner of the Cootamundra Brewery, as it was then known, but changes in ownership continued. Rankin sold the brewery the following year to the partnership of W. Jones & T. F. Lincoln, who controlled several breweries in other country towns. William Jones sold his share in the business in 1894, and the company then traded as McIntyre, Lincoln & Co.

Within a year the Cootamundra Brewery was resold to Benjamin Bartley, who changed the name to the Excelsior Brewery. Benjamin Bartley also owned breweries at Chiltern and Maryborough in Victoria, and with shrewd business sense he had McIntyre, Lincoln & Co. execute a bond whereby they agreed not to carry on trade as brewers, cordial or aerated water manufacturers within 30 miles of Cootamundra (except at Junee Junction) for a period of five years. Later Benjamin Bartley's sons, Edmund and Alfred, ran the brewery until it closed in 1913.

Cootamundra Brewery
J. & E. Barnes	1879–80
M. McTherney & P. McCormack	1880–88
Thomas Rankin	1888–89
W. Jones & T. F. Lincoln	1889–94
McIntyre, Lincoln & Co.	1894–95

Excelsior Brewery
Benjamin Bartley	1895–
Edmund & Alfred Bartley	–1913

Lion Brewery　　　　1882–1903
Murray Street

When the brewery was started in 1882 by the partnership of Rochester, Morton & Jackson, it was known as the Burton Brewery, but late the following year it was taken over by Edmund and Richard Resch. They renamed the brewery the Lion, and Richard Resch shifted from

Wilcannia to Cootamundra to manage their new brewery. By coincidence, James Howison had operated a Lion Brewery near Temora, on the Cootamundra–Temora Road during 1881 and 1882. This had no connection with the Lion Brewery at Cootamundra.

The Resch family were involved in other breweries at Wilcannia and Silverton, and Edmund Resch Snr later became the founder of the famous Waverley Brewery, Sydney. At Cootamundra the business traded as E. & R. Resch & Co.; the brewery was on a 5-acre site, now bounded by Lawrence, Richards and Cowcumbla Streets and Centenary Avenue. At the time of acquisition it was decided to advertise the fact in the *Cootamundra Herald* of 3 December 1883 that E. & R. Resch had recently purchased the Burton Brewery and 'for clearness, condition, fullness of the palate, great keeping qualities and a mellow vinous character, our ales cannot be surpassed'.

Edmund Resch had remained at Wilcannia, and Richard Resch continued to manage the Lion Brewery at Cootamundra.

During 1888 the brewery was offered for sale, but there were no buyers. Richard stayed on until 1903, then left the district to take up the position of brewer at the Clarence River Brewery in Maclean.

Corowa

Tom Roberts, the famous Australian artist of the Heidelberg School, visited the Brocklesby Station shearing shed (16 km from Corowa) over a period of two years, making sketches and finally putting onto canvas that typically Australian rural scene, *Shearing the Rams* (now held in the National Gallery of Victoria in Melbourne).

When the Colony of Victoria was proclaimed in 1851, customs duties were imposed on goods moving between the states of Victoria and New South Wales. The duties caused much hostility, which led to the 1893 Federation Conference, held in Corowa, and ultimately to the federation of Australia on 1 January 1901.

Corowa & Wahgunyah Brewing & Malting Co. Ltd   1871–1917
Albury Road, near Corowa

There was only one brewery at Corowa, but there were many owners who followed one after the other. The first to try his luck was Thomas William Brady. He built the brewery in 1871, on the bank of the Murray River about 2 km upstream from the bridge linking Victoria with New South Wales.

Brady built up a good business, and after two years he sold to Edward Clayton. Clayton was less successful, and the following year Dennis Hallahan became the new owner. He also happened to be the owner of the brewery at Wahgunyah, Victoria. At Corowa he brewed with reasonable success before selling to Henry Moras. This was a disaster for Moras, and within a year he went into liquidation. This happened in 1889, and during August of that year Thomas Ogilvie bought the breweries at Corowa and Wahgunyah, and formed the Corowa & Wahgunyah Brewing & Malting Co. Ltd. He rebuilt the Corowa Brewery on the same site, but the change in name and the new building did nothing to improve his business. The heat and the brewing problems still remained, and the brewery closed in 1891.

George Abbot reopened the brewery, but lasted less than a year. The next brewer, in 1892, was Frederick Hose, but he fared no better and the brewery closed again.

There must have been some attraction about a vacant brewery, surely an easy challenge for someone to take over and make a fortune. In January 1893 along came Harry Ogilvie, a relative of Thomas's, and where so many before him had failed Harry kept on brewing for twenty-four years.

Corowa Brewery

Thomas Brady	1871–73
Edward Clayton	1873–74
Dennis Hallahan	1874–88
Henry Moras	1888–89

Corowa & Wahgunyah Brewing & Malting Co. Ltd

Thomas Ogilvie	1889–91, closed
George Abbot	1891–92
Frederick Hose	1892, closed
Harry Ogilvie	1893–1917

Corowa Brewery
See Corowa & Wahgunyah Brewing & Malting Co. Ltd.

Cowra

During World War II a Japanese prisoner-of-war camp was located at Cowra. In August 1944 the prisoners staged a suicidal break for freedom, in which four Australian soldiers and 247 Japanese died, many of the Japanese committing suicide.

Clifton's Brewery   1882–98
Redfern Street

Although Cowra was first settled early in the nineteenth century, the population was sparse and a brewery was not a proposition until the 1880s. The first brewery was at the back of a house in Redfern Street, opposite the Canowindra railway line, and brewing began on 8 September 1882. The partners were William Larkin and David Clifton.

William Larkin left in 1884 to set up a brewery at Forbes, and for the next five years Dave Clifton ran the brewery as sole proprietor.

From 1889 the partnership of Clifton & Howey operated the brewery for a further nine years.

Connolly's Brewery
See Phoenix Brewery.

Phoenix Brewery 1889–1904
Darling Street

John Connolly started the brewery in 1889 and, although the business traded as Boxall & Connolly in 1892 Connolly was the major shareholder. Connolly's Brewery, as it was known, closed in 1895, and remained idle for the next seven years.

Tom Comerford reopened the brewery in 1902, and named it the Phoenix. Two years later he had to close the brewery since only three hotels could buy his beer; the others were 'tied houses' owned by the large city breweries.

Currawang

Currawang Brewery 1876–78

The tiny town of Currawang, 35 km south of Goulburn, near Lake George, was where Samuel Williams decided to seek his fortune as a brewer. After two years Sam moved on to pursue other endeavours.

Deniliquin

Deniliquin was named after Denilakoon, the elder of the local Aboriginal tribe. The town is famous for its sheep and wool industry, particularly the Peppin Merino bred by George Peppin and his sons when they settled outside Deniliquin in 1858.

Ernstsen's Brewery 1878–1902
Crispe Street

Ernst Ernstsen, a Dane, came to Australia in 1853. He was a publican at Dunolly, Victoria, for twenty-five years before building his brewery at Deniliquin in 1878. At that time he would have experienced strong competition from Elliott's Riverine Brewery, which had been in business in nearby George Street for twelve years.

Six years after starting his brewery Ernstsen attempted to raise capital for expansion. A meeting was held in January 1884 to consider converting his business into a proprietary company to be called Ernstsen's Brewing Co. After three months the proposal was dropped, and money was returned to the prospective shareholders. The brewery may have closed in 1900.

In 1902 George Guinn leased the brewery for one year.

Ernst Ernstsen died on 13 June 1908 at the age of eighty-five, and was buried at Dunolly. He had been a resident of Deniliquin for thirty-two years. After his death, the business having failed, his assets, which included the local Bridge Hotel, were sold at auction.

Riverine Brewery, Aerated Waters & Milling Co. Ltd 1866–1924
Beside the Edward River, north side of George Street

The brewery, built by George Elliott of Sandhurst, Victoria, was set on 5 acres of land that had been bought for £225 in February 1866. The brewery was the first of Deniliquin's ventures into secondary industry. It followed the settlement of the area by sheep breeders in 1858, and was to become an important part of the town's economy for fifty-seven years.

The first brew was drawn by George Elliott in October 1866, and, proud of his effort, he advertised in the *Deniliquin Pastoral Times* of January 1867:

> Riverine Brewery — George Elliott advises that he has, at an expense of 1000s of pounds, erected a large brewery on the banks [sic] of the Edward River and begs to inform all classes in the southern Riverina that they now can have first rate beer and porter, fresh [sic] brewed at Deniliquin at a price defying competition and delivered by his own teams immediately orders are received. Also bottled ales and porter.

George Elliott built up a fine business, and took on Phillip Holler as a partner in 1880. Early in 1884 the Riverine Brewery, Aerated Waters & Milling Co. Ltd was floated with a capital of £25,000 and a promise to pay 12.5 per cent on the investment.

In January 1891 a hurricane severely damaged the brewery, blowing away the whole roof structure.

Various managers ran the business: William Tindale from 1885 to 1894; Henry Tippins in 1895; James Skinner from 1896 to 1911; then John Atkinson, followed by W. T. McGee. During World War I the company's fortunes began to decline. The plant was later modernised, but at a meeting of shareholders held on 28 June 1924 it was resolved to discontinue brewing and to concentrate on the mill, wines, spirits and

The motto on the Riverine Brewery's bottle label, 'Dum Vivo Cano', literally translated means 'While I Live I Crow'.

cordial departments, and to act as distributors for Carlton & United Breweries Ltd of Melbourne.

Drake

Drake Brewery   1888–89
The small township of Drake is situated in the north-east of New South Wales, 130 km west of the coastal town of Ballina. The owners of the brewery there were Joseph and James Thomas and George Beet. For their short period of brewing they traded as Thomas Bros. & Co.

Dubbo

The City of Dubbo was founded as a town in 1849 and rapidly developed as a rich rural district. Today, the city's famous tourist attraction is the Western Plains 'open-range' zoo.

Dubbo Brewery   1880–1914
West side of Macquarie Street, at the junction of Boundary Road (now Kelvin Grove)

James Stevens's substantial brewery had a five-storey tower, and a capacity to brew 100 hogsheads of beer per week, with only a few hands needed to do all the work. The Dubbo Brewery was highly profitable, and survived the depression years of the 1890s. The partnership of Treacey & Stevens worked the brewery until 1910, and then Martin Treacey and John Seage continued until the brewery closed.

Dubbo Co-operative Brewery
Early in 1919 there was a proposal to establish a co-operative brewery in Dubbo. A prospectus was issued by the enthusiastic proposer of the venture, Fred Lanfear (formerly of the Stanley Co-operative Brewery in Perth, Hannan's Co-operative Brewery in Kalgoorlie, WA, and the Burton Brewery in Lithgow, NSW). With such credentials the project had to succeed. The capital of the concern was to be £20,000, and Fred took out an option over the old Dubbo Brewery, which had closed in 1914.

It was reported in February 1919 that 'the project is bounding along successfully on the interest and enthusiasm of the local and district people … it only needs 'good goods' to make an immense success'. Unfortunately for Fred Lanfear and the local and district people there were no 'good goods', and nothing came of the proposal.

Macquarie Brewery   1875–1900
Brisbane Street, North Dubbo

Two Scots, Archibald and John McCullam, founded the Macquarie Brewery, which stood on 2 acres of land a short distance from the Macquarie River. The building was constructed of freestone 2 feet thick; it had two large cellars and the 60-foot-deep well provided an ample supply of clear water. Beer was cooled in large vats by a steam-powered fan.

The brewery was gradually extended to cope with demand, and production reached 100 hogsheads per week in 1886. John McCullam sold his interest in the business to his brother Archibald in 1892, but Arch died the following year and the business was taken over again by brother John.

Brewer's licences were granted to James Cudden in 1894, John McCullam in 1895, and Narcisse Muller from 1896.

Well Park Brewery   1875–78
James Osborne and his partner, Narcisse Muller, started Dubbo's first brewery, the Well Park Brewery, in 1875. Three years later the plant and equipment were purchased by Archibald and John McCullam, who transferred it to their brewery in Brisbane Street a short distance away. Muller then worked for the McCullams at their Macquarie Brewery, and James Osborne converted the Well Park Brewery into a cordial factory.

'DOCTORING' BEER

In the course of a tolerably varied experience, we have frequently been asked many questions what — for want of a better term — we are obliged to call 'doctoring' of beer. By this term we mean to describe all dodges or expedients resorted to to give beer a fictitious 'body,' artificial 'condition,' particular flavour, &c., or to restore old or sour beer, stout, &c., to their original soundness.

Some of the questions asked were as follows:-

'Would you advise me to use mustard, potash, and grains of Paradise when bottling stout?' Answer: 'Yes; if you want to get twenty years for manslaughter.' Again: 'Can you tell me any chemic [sic] that will make old beer [meaning stale, flat and undrinkable beer] sound? I hear there is such a thing; if so, and you know it, I can make your fortune and my own.' Answer: 'If I knew of such a chemic I would be worth a million in five years; but I don't know it, or anybody else either, for there is no such thing on earth. You might as well try to bring a dead man to life as to restore to its original soundness a fluid like old beer, every constituent of which, roughly speaking, has been altered by the life action of complex organisms, about which the most advanced chemists living know scarcely anything.'

Again: 'What is a good thing for 'putting life' into beer?' Answer: 'I don't know, but fancy that anything you might use to 'put life' into beer would be very likely to 'put death' into those who drank the stuff.'

Still another: 'What can I 'put into' beer to prevent sediment?' Answer: 'Nothing that you could 'put into' beer would prevent sediment; careful brewing will alone do this.

Australian Brewers' Journal, January 1888

Eden

The township of Eden, on the southern coast of New South Wales, was planned in 1842. It is the centre for the district's pastoral and fishing industries, and also a popular tourist resort.

Eden Brewery 1861

Thomas Auld apparently brewed at Eden for a very brief period during 1861. Several years later he and his wife, Georgina, were involved in a brewery at Araluen.

Forbes

Following the discovery of gold in the Forbes area in 1861, bushranger gangs roamed the district, relieving the unwary of their gold and other possessions. In 1865 the notorious bushranger, Ben Hall, was shot dead by police in bushland near Forbes; his grave is in the town's cemetery.

The town is named after Sir Francis Forbes, the first Chief Justice of New South Wales and not the Dr Forbes who owned the Kent Brewery.

Kent Brewery 1885–98
Camp Street

The Kent Brewery was started by William Bray in 1885. It was almost destroyed by fire in 1892, and two years later Bray was declared bankrupt.

Frank Calder ran the brewery for a year or so, and in 1895 Dr Forbes became the owner. He employed William Bray, the original owner, as the brewer and manager, but the business failed a few years later.

Lachlan Brewery Co. 1879–1928

James Howison was the first brewer in Forbes. He advertised in the 28 March 1879 edition of the *Forbes and Parkes Gazette* with the simple message: 'Lachlan Brewery, Howison & Co. Ales, Porter, Yeast and Grains'.

Howison left the district in 1880 to start another brewery at Temora, and the Lachlan Brewery was taken over by the Baker brothers. The brewery was frequently referred to as the Park Brewery.

When William Larkin acquired the brewery in 1884, the address was 'near Ferry Street, South Forbes, on the north bank of the Lachlan River'. Brandon Street was the address from 1885. After working the brewery for six years, Larkin sold to Thomas Sprunt.

Dr Forbes bought the brewery in August 1895, and

apparently leased it to George Simpson. At that time Dr Forbes also owned the Kent Brewery, which was managed by William Bray. Other lessees followed at the Lachlan Brewery: Arthur Marrin, and finally Patrick McGrath. In December 1898 the brewery burnt down 'under suspicious circumstances'. The firm of Marrin, Vincent & Co. purchased the property, and rebuilt the brewery.

The Lachlan Brewery closed in 1906, but was reopened the following year by Frank Broughton & Co. The Lachlan Brewery Co. was registered on 22 January 1910. The partners were Roy Strickland, Michael Newell, and the executors of the estate of Frank Broughton. Newell continued to run the brewery from 1912 to 1928.

James Howison	1879–80
Baker brothers	1881–84
William Larkin	1884–90
Thomas Sprunt	1891–93
John Sprunt	1894
Sprunt & Stirling	1894–95
Stirling	1895
Dr Forbes	1895
George Simpson	1895–96
Arthur Marrin	1896–97
Patrick McGrath	1898
Marrin, Vincent & Co.	1898–1906, closed
Frank Broughton & Co.	1907–9
Lachlan Brewery Co.	1910–28

Park Brewery
See Lachlan Brewery.

Garryowen

Gregson, W. 1878–79
The Gregson brothers started their brewery on the bank of Billabong Creek in 1878, but all the equipment was sold at auction on 23 August of the following year.

Girilambone

Mullard, Isaac 1882

Glanmire

Glanmire Brewery 1870–75
The small township of Glanmire is located 10 km east of Bathurst, and the owner of the Glanmire Brewery was E. Combes. He advertised 'Combes' XXX Ale, Entire Brown Stout and Porter' in the *Bathurst Times* during 1873 and 1874.

Late in 1874 the residence of Mr E. Combes, MP, was advertised for sale, in consequence of his intended visit to Europe. The list of articles for sale included household furniture, oil paintings, rare wines and a fine collection of books, but no mention was made of the brewing equipment.

Glen Innes

Glen Innes Brewery 1883–94
56 East Street (now Church Street)

Although W. Twedall received a licence to brew in Glen Innes in 1881, he may not have brewed, since his licence was not renewed. More purposeful plans for a brewery were reported in the *Glen Innes Examiner* of 27 September 1881:

> we learn that J. A. Spier has purchased two acres of land in East Street whereon he intends erecting the necessary buildings ... has arranged for the transportation of his extensive plant from Wagga Wagga.

The partnership of J. A. Spier and Thomas C. Gillies began brewing in 1883, but within a year or so they sold their brewery to Peter Simpson. Simpson was also the owner of the Armidale Brewery, but he went out of business, both at Armidale and Glen Innes, during 1886, and the Glen Innes brewery closed.

Thomas Gillies, one of the original owners, was still living in the district, and he reopened the brewery in 1887.

By 1889 the brewery was owned by Francis Dixon Kite & Co. Kite had arrived at Glen Innes during the 1870s, and achieved some recognition when he was awarded the Victorian Humane Society Medal for saving two men from drowning. Kite ran into financial difficulties and was declared bankrupt in 1893, forcing the closure of the brewery once again. Later, he became a shearing contractor at Narrabri.

Henry Floyd had worked at the brewery as a cooper for six years, and he reopened the brewery in 1893, but it closed permanently the following year.

The brewery was subsequently converted to a cordial factory, demolished some time later, and a service station erected on the site.

Goulburn

From the 1830s Goulburn was a centre for police operations in the southern regions of New South Wales, searching out bushrangers, and keeping law and order over a wide area.

Goulburn was proclaimed a city in March 1864, the first inland city in Australia, and the last in the British Empire. It was so proclaimed by virtue of being created a bishopric by Royal Letters Patent. Goulburn was officially declared a city in 1885. Many of the city's civic buildings date from the latter part of the nineteenth century, and are registered with the National Trust.

Argyle Brewery 1883–94
Cnr Clifford & Faithful Streets

The Argyle Brewery was built in 1882 by Edward and Joseph Kennedy, and was officially opened the following year. The brewer was John Lang, a Victorian with thirty-three years' brewing experience, but his problem was the lack of a ready supply of fresh water. For cleaning, and for the production of ale and porter, water had to be carted by dray from the Wollondilly River.

Henry Chard purchased the brewery in 1887, and sold three years later to William Allen, who had been the owner of the Mountain Brewery in Blackheath. Allen stayed at Goulburn for four years, then left the district and settled in Armidale, where he purchased the Armidale Brewery.

Bartlett's Brewery
See Goulburn Brewery.

Bradley's Brewery
See Goulburn Brewery.

Capel's Brewery 1849–c. 1851

Thomas Capel was one of Melbourne's early brewers, having started the Britannia Brewery there in 1838. He moved to Sydney, and his pregnant wife followed later in the brig *Britannia*. The ship was wrecked on its journey, and the sole survivor, Mrs Capel, was captured by Aboriginals. She and the child were discovered many years later, but Mrs Capel was by then incurably insane.

Thomas Capel, in his grief, worked as a brewer in Sydney for a short period before moving south to Goulburn, where he took up farming. Later, he worked at Bradley's Goulburn Brewery as a miller, subsequently becoming a malster.

In 1849 he started his own brewery. John Blackshaw, Capel's brewer, left within a year, and Capel then worked the brewery on his own, producing 'a light and exceeding [sic] pleasant summer drink' until the early 1850s.

Foston Brewery 1853–73

Goulburn resident, John Blackshaw, called his home 'Foston' after his home town in England. He had worked as a brewer for Thomas Capel before becoming the brewer and manager at the Bradley family's Goulburn Brewery. In 1853 he set up his own Foston Brewery.

In June 1864 the Blackshaw family had to be rescued from the roof of their house during a particularly heavy flood, but apparently the brewery was not affected.

John Blackshaw died in 1873, but during the twenty years that the Foston Brewery was in existence Blackshaw was renowned for the purity of his well-water, which he sold in Goulburn for 'nine pence a gallon, delivered'.

Goulburn Brewery 1838–1929
Bungonia Road

The Goulburn Brewery, malthouse, mill and mews were designed as a single complex for the Bradley family — Jonas, Catherine, Thomas and William. Jonas Bradley, the father of William, was the founder of the Australian tobacco industry. Construction of the complex was under way in 1834, and the mill bears the date 1836.

Thomas Bradley died in 1835, and in 1838 William Bradley began brewing, in partnership with his uncle, William Shelley. Bradley worked the brewery on his own after the death of Shelley in 1844. Throughout Australia it was a common practice for a brewery to be referred to by the owner's name, and 'Bradley's Brewery' was used by locals, the media and in advertisements.

The *Goulburn Herald* of 25 August 1849 gave some qualified approval of the brewery's product:

> Great praise is due to Mr. Bradley for the excellent ale they produce ... we do really think that it is being daily improved upon and that the late brews have approximated, if possible, closer to the quality of the first class English ales'.

The article went on to praise the Lansdowne Ale, which was half the price of imports, and said that 'very soon every publican would stock Bradley's Entire'.

William Bartlett's Goulburn Brewery, c. 1900. The Goulburn Brewery is the oldest intact brewery and flour-mill remaining in New South Wales. The mill bears the date 1836, and brewing commenced in 1838. Restoration began in 1982, and the grand old buildings are now licensed premises, open to the public as a tourist attraction. A boutique brewery now operates in the premises.

This label for Fine Sparkling Ale was produced during the 1920s after the Goulburn Brewery had been taken over by Tooth & Co. Ltd.

William Bradley died in 1865, and the following year a consortium of Walford, Sparkes and Emanuel took over Bradley's assets. They continued to operate the flour mill, but closed the brewery.

In 1870 the brewery was leased to Melville & Milne, then to George Milne in 1873, and then again in 1874 to William Bartlett and Joseph Oddy.

Flourmilling had ceased in 1869, and in 1877 Bartlett & Oddy purchased the entire complex for £3000. After the retirement of Joseph Oddy in 1879 William Bartlett became sole proprietor, and built up a fine reputation for his ales and Bartlett's Goulburn Stout. He was involved in many civic activities, and made a presentation of the Rocky Hill Memorial site to the City of Goulburn.

The brewery was let to the Raymond brothers, James and Robert, in 1887. They ran the Goulburn Brewery until 1896, when the owner, William Bartlett, took over once again. The brewery was now known mostly as 'Bartlett's Brewery'. In 1920 it was purchased by Tooth's Brewery, Sydney, for £14,000. Brewing continued until August 1929, and the premises were then used by the company as a warehouse and depot until 1956.

William Bradley & William Shelley	1838–44
William Bradley	1844–68
Walford, Sparkes & Emanuel	1868, closed
Melville & Milne (lessees)	1870–73
George Milne (lessee)	1873–74
W. Bartlett & J. Oddy (lessees)	1874–77
W. Bartlett & J. Oddy	1877–79
William Bartlett	1879–87
James & Robert Raymond (lessees)	1887–96
William Bartlett	1896–1920
Tooth & Co. Ltd	1920–29

Riversdale Brewery   c. 1832–c. 1840

Matt Healy's hotel licence was first issued in 1832. His hotel was near the Riversdale property, and he 'brewed his own' before the Bradley family started their Goulburn Brewery in 1838. John Richards purchased the Riversdale property in 1837, and continued to brew beer there until his death in 1838. His widow ran the brewery for another year or two, and employed John Walton as the brewer.

Thorne Brothers Brewery   1847–49

Another early Goulburn brewery was conducted by George and Daniel Thorne at Mulwaree Ponds. Daniel was active in community affairs and became a member of the first municipal council in 1859.

Wollondale Brewery   1884–1900
Tuena Road, on the Wollondilly River near Marsden Bridge

In 1884 John Farrell and Tom Gulson advertised that they had completed the erection of a new brewery on the eastern flat of the Wollondilly River. Five years later Farrell retired, and Tom Gulson, a member of the family that manufactured bricks and tiles at Albury, continued to run the Wollondale Brewery on his own.

By 1894 the company was trading as R. A. & T. Gulson, and they claimed to produce 4000 gallons of ale and porter per week. They sold the ale for 1s 2d per gallon wholesale, and 2s retail. Bottled ale was 6s per dozen, and porter 7s per dozen.

When a sustained drought caused the Wollondilly River (the source of the brewery's water supply) to dry up, Tom Gulson managed to keep the business going by buying beer from Tooth's Brewery in Sydney. It was incomprehensible that, when the river ran again, he was unable to brew beer of a satisfactory quality. Some chemical change in the riverbed was the verdict of the experts who had attempted to solve the problem. By that time Tom Gulson was nearly bankrupt, and the brewery property was sold.

Grafton

Grafton Brewing Co. Ltd   1952–98
170 North Street

The Grafton brewery was incorporated in March 1949 as a private company, and construction of the brewery commenced in September 1950. It was completed in 1952, and sales of the first beer, Grafton Lager, took place during December of that year. The business was registered as a public company in February 1953.

The Sydney brewer, Toohey's Ltd, acquired the brewery in April 1961, and continued to operate it as a wholly owned subsidiary. Brewing ceased in May 1998. The equipment was sold at auction, and the premises were also sold. A section of the property was leased by Toohey's Ltd as a sales office and warehouse.

SELLING WITHOUT A LICENCE

A party of Grafton [NSW] citizens decided upon a picnic. One of their number purchased the beer that was part of the dinner dainties, and paid for it. After the picnic, all the men settled up, repaying the money paid for the beer, to the picnic member who purchased it on their behalf.

This unfortunate individual was subsequently hied before the magistrate and fined £30 with costs. An appeal to Mr. Justice Ferguson to restrain the magistrate from proceeding further in the matter was upheld. On an application for costs by the appellant, Mr. Justice Ferguson said the magistrate made a mistake.

Australian Brewers' Journal, April 1920

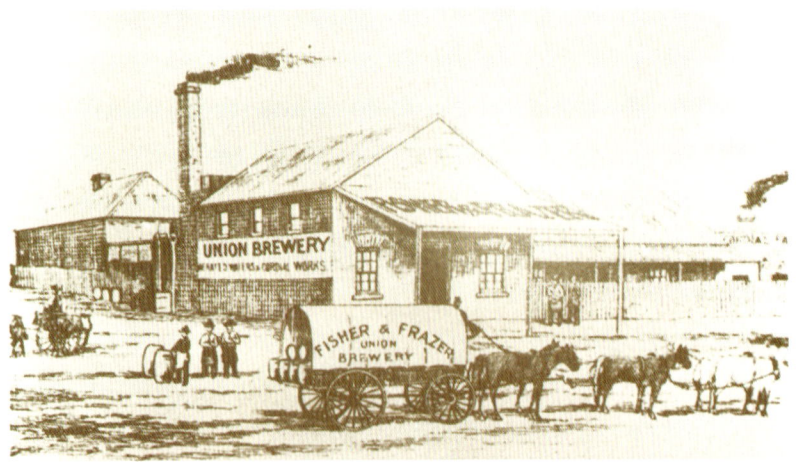

The Union Brewery, Aerated Waters & Cordial Works, Grenfell, c. 1890. It was one of the successful NSW country breweries and continued in business for twenty-eight years.

Looking very much like the barrel of a cannon, the chimney for Kenny's Brewery, Gundagai, is hauled across the river, to be taken up the hill and fitted to the brewery building in the background, c. 1879.

Grenfell

The rush to the Grenfell goldfields began during October 1866, and within three months there was a rambling tent village. The following year the township was marked out and named after J. G. Grenfell, a gold commissioner in the area who had been shot by bushrangers in December the previous year.

Australia's famous short-story writer and poet, Henry Lawson, was born at 'One Mile' near Grenfell, and a monument marks his birthplace.

Union Brewery   1886–1914
Wood Street

In 1857 Thomas Nelson began making cordials, and nine years later he sold his business to Fisher & Frazer. They added a brewery, called it the Union, and to their credit brewed excellent beer for the next twenty-eight years — all the more remarkable considering that neither partner had any brewing experience.

Thomas Fisher was a well-educated man and a fine musician. Born in France, he came to Grenfell in 1866 and took on work as a signwriter, painter and decorator. His partner, James Frazer, was born at Bathurst, and came to Grenfell with his parents. He worked in the Consols goldmine at the age of thirteen.

The two men began brewing Colonial Ale in 1886, and won prizes at the Chicago Exhibition in the USA that year, and at the Sydney Show in 1902. Thomas Fisher retired from the business in November 1912, and two years later the Union Brewery discontinued beer production. Cordial manufacture was carried on by the Frazer family until the 1930s.

Gulgong

Gulgong Brewery   1872

The three partners in the brewery — Eli Allan, James Jackson and Thomas Largey — were each registered as a brewer for the year 1872. It is not known who did the brewing, if, in fact, any brewing took place.

Gundagai

The early settlement of Gundagai suffered Australia's worst flood disaster in 1852 when a flood drowned 89 people (30 per cent of the population). The river bank, where most people lived, was almost swept away. Following the flood, the town moved up the slopes of Mt Parnassus to its present location.

Much has been written, music composed and many stories have been told about the origin of the famous pioneers' monument, the Dog on the Tucker Box, situated '5 miles from Gundagai'. The monument gives expression to that sentimental piece of Australian folklore — mateship between man and dog.

Kenny's Brewery   1879–1910
South Gundagai

It is not commonly known that a brewery operated at Gundagai, and about the same time, as the Dog on the Tucker Box legend had its beginning over 100 years ago. A Frenchman, Frederick Gasse, owned a hotel and store at South Gundagai, and the store was later used as a brewery by Dennis Kenny. The red-bearded Kenny had been a farmer, but in 1879 he put a few brewing utensils into the store and began brewing. He worked his brewery for thirty-one years, a remarkable achievement for that period when the lifespan of most breweries was exceedingly brief. In Kenny's favour, the brewery was on a hill on the Hume Highway, then little more than a dirt track, halfway between Melbourne and Sydney, a prime location to service customers travelling north and south. Gundagai was also central to large crop-farming and sheep and cattle properties.

Gunnedah

Perseverance Brewery   1880–88

Throughout the nineteenth century a prevailing characteristic of the Australian brewing industry was the short tenure of the operators, be they owners, partners, lessees or managers. For some, it didn't seem to matter that they would be following on from a succession of failures, that none previously had been able to make good beer, that the water supply might be bad, or whatever. To them, these were matters of little consequence.

Contrary to its name, the Perseverance Brewery was a typical example where perseverance alone was no measure of success. During its eight years of beer production, there were six operators. The brewery property was finally put up for sale in October 1888.

C. E. Beauvais	1880
J. W. Conlon	1880
Conlon & Goddard	1881
Charles Goddard	1882–83
Frederick Wilkins & O. N. Funnell	1884–86
William Tyrell	1887–88

Hay

Hay, situated on the Murrumbidgee River, was at one time the centre for an extensive wool-producing region; it was a busy river port where paddle-steamers called to collect bales of wool and other produce.

The town was gazetted in October 1859, and named after John Hay, the local parliamentary member at that time.

Black Horse Brewery   1879–99
Leonard Street, South Hay

John Simpson started the Black Horse Brewery in 1879, worked it for a year or two without much success, and then closed the brewery. Allan Lakeman took over in 1883, but two years later he was out of business and the brewery closed again.

The brewery remained idle until 1891, when it was reopened by Jones, Lincoln & Co., who already owned a number of breweries in country New South Wales. Actually, the company took over two breweries in Hay in 1891; the other was Patrick McGrath's Brewery that was also idle, having closed in 1887. The Black Horse Brewery was closed, and McGrath's brewery was used by the company

In 1897 Jones, Lincoln & Co. changed their brewing location back to the old Black Horse Brewery premises. The brewery finally closed in 1899 after it had been taken over by John McIntyre and Thomas Lincoln. At that time they also purchased and operated the Red Lion Brewery in Hay.

John Simpson	1879–80, closed
Allan Lakeman	1883–85 closed
Jones, Lincoln & Co.	1891, closed
Jones, Lincoln & Co. (McGrath's Brewery)	1891–97
Jones, Lincoln & Co. (original location)	1897–99
McIntyre & Lincoln	1899

Excelsior Brewery
See Red Lion Brewery.

Lincoln Brewery
See Red Lion Brewery.

Lindsay's Brewery Co. Ltd
See Red Lion Brewery.

McGrath's Brewery   1885–87

Patrick McGrath started his brewery at a time when there was another well-established brewery in town, the Red Lion. Either McGrath's beer was not up to standard or the competition was too strong, or both, since after two years he closed the brewery. It remained closed until 1891 when Jones, Lincoln & Co. acquired the premises, and brewed under the name of the Black Horse Brewery.

Red Lion Brewery   1868–1912
West Hay

In 1868, nine years after the founding of the township of Hay, the partnership of Albert Elliott and John Mennon began in business as the Excelsior Brewery. Mennon sold his share in the brewery to Thomas Simpson in 1870, and about three years later the partnership of Albert Elliott and Henry L. Lindsay became the proprietors. Elliott was the youngest of a family of nineteen children, and the cousin of George Elliott who had previously owned the London Brewery in Bendigo, Victoria.

The name was changed to the Red Lion Brewery, and by 1875 Lindsay was running the business with notable success. Lindsay's Brewery Co. Ltd was formed on 31 May 1883, with the new company acquiring the assets of the Red Lion breweries at Hay and Bourke.

Other breweries were established, as advertised in the *Bathurst and District Directory* of 1886/87:

> Lindsay's Brewery Co. Ltd, Red Lion Brewery;
> Hay, Hillston, Cobar, Bourke and Orange:
> Agencies at Balranald and Mosgiel.
> Bottled ale and porter in splendid condition.
> H. L. Lindsay, Managing Director.

Lindsay either leased out the breweries or appointed managers.

On 18 May 1891 fire destroyed the brewhouse and plant at the Red Lion in Hay, and the brewery was closed during a period of reconstruction. James

Label used by John Simpson when the Black Horse Brewery, Hay, was first opened in 1879. Simpson brewed for less than a year.

Whitson was the manager at the time, followed by James Liddington in 1893. Two years later Charles Long was the manager until 1899.

River boats frequently pulled in at the Red Lion wharf on the Murrumbidgee River to collect beer for distribution to other settlements along the Murrumbidgee, Murray and Darling River systems.

The brewery was taken over in 1899 by McIntyre, Lincoln & Co., and Tom Lincoln became sole owner in 1907.

After the brewing side of the business was closed in May 1912, and the premises were used as a depot and for the production of cordial. Beer supplies were then obtained from the company's brewery at Narrandera.

Excelsior Brewery
Albert Elliott & John Mennon	1868–70
Albert Elliott & Thomas Simpson	1870–73

Red Lion Brewery
Albert Elliott & Henry Lindsay	1873–75
Henry Lindsay	1875–83
Lindsay's Brewery Co. Ltd	1883–99
McIntyre, Lincoln & Co.	1899–1907
Lincoln & Co. Ltd	1907–12

Hill End

About 1860 the village was known as Bald Hill, but in August that year it was gazetted as Forbes. The error was not corrected until 1862, and the name was then shown as Hillend, finally becoming Hill End in 1870.

During the brief goldmining boom at Hill End between 1871 and 1874 the population of the town rose from a mere handful to 8000. The business area consisted of nearly 2 km of shops, including twenty-eight hotels, five banks, two newspapers, and a brewery. Hill End became one of the largest inland towns of New South Wales, but after 1874 the gold yield swiftly declined, mines closed, prospectors moved on, stores ceased trading, blackberry weeds invaded the buildings, and entire streets disappeared. Today, the small quiet township retains some unique buildings and mining memorabilia from its golden past.

Barley Sheaf Brewery   1873–c. 1883
Southern side of Bald Hill in Spring Creek

The brewery was started in 1873, at the height of the gold boom, by Edward Inch and Albert Jeffree. Edward Inch was a member of the Inch family who had involvements in breweries in several other New South Wales country towns. The brewer's licence was issued to Inch & Jeffree in March 1873, and to Coyle, Holman & Inch in January 1875. In August of that year Richard Inch advertised in the *Hill End and Tambaroora Times*:

> Inch's Barley Sheaf brewery, Hill End — try Inch's Celebrated XXX Ale, which for quality and flavour, cannot be excelled.
> R. Inch Sole Proprietor.

Richard Inch worked the brewery for a few years, and then moved to Lithgow where he set up the Eskbank Brewery. At Hill End Charles Inch continued to run the Barley Sheaf Brewery until it was no longer a viable business.

Hillston

The town of Hillston, located on the Lachlan River, was first known as Redbank, and later named after William Hill who built and owned a hotel there. Roads radiated out from the town like the spokes of a wheel, leading to other pastoral towns and districts.

Star Brewery   c. 1878–c. 1907
High Street

The town's centralised location may have influenced Henry Lindsay to build a brewery in the town, and some time before 1878 his Star Brewery was open for business. He appointed A. W. Todd as manager. Lindsay already controlled breweries in several other country towns of western New South Wales.

In 1888 the Star Brewery was purchased by Jones, Lincoln & Co. Thomas Byrnes was the manager, followed by Peter Simpson from 1890 to 1895, at which time the brewery closed. When McIntyre, Lincoln & Co. reopened the brewery in 1896, they retained the name Star Brewery, and J. Flynn was appointed manager.

During the 1880s and 1890s the firm of Jones, Lincoln & Co. built one of the largest brewing empires in country New South Wales. At one time or another they owned breweries at Cootamundra, Hay, Hillston, Jerilderie, Narrandera, Temora and Urana. The partners were William Jones and Thomas Lincoln, and they specialised in taking over breweries that had closed or were run down and in financial difficulty.

Ownership of most of the Jones, Lincoln & Co.

CANCER CURE

CANCER CURED WITHIN A WEEK
BY DR ETTINGE'S INFALLIBLE REMEDY
NO OCCASION TO LEAVE HOME
NO CHARGE IF NOT CURED WITHIN ONE MONTH
FOR FURTHER PARTICULARS APPLY THE OFFICE OF THE
HILLSTON NEWS

[The above advertisement appeared in the *Hillston News*, Saturday, 25 November 1882]
Australian Brewers' Journal, December 1882

breweries later changed to McIntyre, Lincoln & Co., but by the end of the nineteenth century almost all of their breweries had closed. Early in 1900 Tom Lincoln became sole proprietor, and traded as Lincoln & Co. Ltd until at least 1907. Tom Lincoln ran one or two of the breweries for a few more years on his own.

Howlong

Howlong Brewery　　　　　　　　1874–77

It is difficult to understand why Henry Edwards started a brewery at Howlong in the 1870s. At that time there were no fewer than six breweries operating within a 30 km radius of the town: one each at Corowa, Chiltern and Wodonga, and three at Albury. There was also very little local trade in the small township, but Edwards managed to carry on for about three years.

Inverell

The town of Inverell had its beginnings in 1833 when the Ross family started a store for the settlers who had moved into the district. The name Inverell combines the meanings of a meeting place ('inv') and swans ('ell'); so named because there were many swans in the area.

Within the district there are many fossicking areas where sapphires, quartz, and even diamonds, may be found. It is claimed that the Inverell district produces almost 75 per cent of the world's sapphires.

Inverell Brewery　　　　　　　　1885–1914
Glen Innes Road, near the MacIntyre River

Early in 1885 the Thomas brothers, natives of Cornwall, England, shifted from St Arnaud in Victoria, where the elder brother John had worked at the local brewery. John and his family and younger brother settled in Inverell, and started a brewery near the MacIntyre River, east of town.

The brewery's New England Pale Ale attracted considerable patronage, but when the railway arrived at Inverell, the publicans began to bring in beer from Sydney. The Thomas brothers attempted to meet the competition and updated their equipment, but the brewery closed in 1914 after it failed to sell as a going concern.

For some unknown reason the brewery always had trouble making its beer keep. Each New Year's Eve the Brewery Handicap was held, and a keg of beer was rolled out, with free beer for everyone. The first keg was reputedly good, but, after that, flat and sour beer, plus that left unsold from the Christmas rush, would be gladly drunk by those with alcohol-diminished judgement.

Victoria Flour Mill & Brewery　　　　　　1884–86
Cnr Greaves & Lawrence Streets

Inverell was renowned for its wheat production, and the 120,000 bushels produced yearly by farmers during the 1880s supported three local flour mills. One of these mills was the Victoria, built around 1875, and purchased by Henry Edmeades in 1884. He set up a brewery at the mill, but brewing ceased when the flour mill was resold in 1886.

Jerilderie

Jerilderie, one of the Riverina's prettiest towns, is famous for its woolgrowing, rice and wheat production. In February 1879 there was some excitement and alarm in the town when the local Telegraph Office was raided by the bushranger, Ned Kelly, and his gang.

Jerilderie Brewery　　　　　　1879–97
North side of Billabong Creek

Production of beer commenced in Jerilderie in 1879. The first few years of the brewery's operation saw rapid changes in ownership: D. Campbell, then J. D. Rankin, then F. A. Hoverden — each lasted for one year.

The business stabilised under the direction of Jones, Lincoln & Co. after they purchased the brewery in 1883.

The partners were Thomas and William Jones and Susannah Lincoln, and they ran the brewery successfully until 1897.

The firm of McIntyre, Lincoln & Co. took over during that year, and used the brewery building as a depot for supplies of casks of beer that were sent by rail to Jerilderie from the company's Narrandera Brewery.

During 1924 Sydney brewer Tooth & Co. purchased both the property of the Narrandera Brewery, which had closed, and the premises of the old Jerilderie Brewery. Both were used as distribution depots.

Junee

The town of Junee is set in gently rolling hill country in the south-west of New South Wales. The name, originally Jewnee, is derived from an Aboriginal word meaning 'speak to me'. The town, officially gazetted in 1863, experienced a goldmining boom from the late 1860s to about 1880.

Junee Brewery　　　　　　　　1894–95
Lorne Street

Although Thomas Edmunds was granted a brewer's licence on 5 February 1894, it is possible that he never brewed at Junee.

Kempsey

Emms, Jonathan　　　　　　　　1872

Label from the Inverell Brewery c. 1895. The trademark, TB, was used by the Thomas brothers, owners of the brewery.

Kiama

Kiama is located on the south coast of New South Wales, and was originally a port for the export of cedar taken from nearby forests. A well-known tourist attraction is the Blowhole on a rocky headland close to the town, where surging tides force sprays of seawater out from the crevice high into the air, creating an awe-inspiring roar and spectacle.

Fitzroy Brewery 1854–57
Collins Street

William Gard had been a cooper at the Woodstock Mill & Brewery, located inland, about 10 km west of Kiama. He was there when the brewery started in 1844, but moved to Kiama after a year or so.

In 1848 Gard built his own Fitzroy Brewery on the north bank of the Terralong Street water reserve, the town's only water supply. He also owned two hotels in the town. It was reported that Gard's Brewery was renamed the Fitzroy (along with one of his hotels) after the then Govenor Fitzroy had stayed at the hotel. Unfortunately, William Gard was only able to run his brewery for five years, since on 8 April 1853 he 'died by drowning while intoxicated'.

Samual Bonham and George Hunt were granted a brewer's licence in 1854, and they leased the Fitzroy Brewery from William Gard's widow. She had re-married and was now Mrs Elizabeth Chester. The Bonham–Hunt partnership operated the brewery until the end of 1856, and Hunt subsequently took over the local Illawarra Brewery.

On 20 January 1857 Mrs Chester leased the brewery to David Smith for a period of seven years. Smith had been the publican of Kiama's first hotel, the Gum Tree Inn, from 1837. David Smith may not have operated the Fitzroy Brewery for very long, since there is no further information of his brewing activity.

Illawarra Brewery 1855–95
Manning Street

John and Francis Seager started the Illawarra Brewery in 1855, and were listed as brewers until 1856. The brewery possibly closed at that time. Meanwhile, George Hunt had left the nearby Fitzroy Brewery and purchased the Illawarra Brewery in 1858. Having learnt the brewing trade in England, Hunt was confident of success, and quickly settled into his newly acquired stone-constructed brewery, house and shop alongside a crystal-clear stream.

'Among commercial buildings in 1870,' it was reported, 'Kiama boasts the only brewery that has stood the ordeal of public opinion and private taste in the district.'

George Hunt was doing very well, and decided in 1887 to let his sons, James and John, take over the running of the business. They traded as Hunt Brothers, ran the brewery for three years, and then sold out to the partnership of C. F. Hustwick and A. C. Westley. Arthur Westley carried on by himself during the closing stages of the business, and following a meeting of creditors in 1892 it was decided to close the brewery.

James Hunt reopened the brewery in 1893, and his father, George Hunt, came back into the business in 1895, the year the brewery closed for the last time.

Woodstock Mill & Brewery 1844–c. 1850
Jamberoo (approx. 10 km west of Kiama)

When Captain John Collins built his flour and timber mill at nearby Jamberoo in 1838, he called it the Woodstock Mill, and the surrounding area became known as the village of Woodstock.

In 1844 Henry Heathorne took over the management of the mill, and added a brewery, complete with a cooperage for the manufacture of barrels. He left to start the Defiance Brewery at Bathurst, and Charles Newnham, recently retired from the Kent Brewery in Sydney, was appointed manager of the brewery at Kiama.

When the son of the original investor came from England to retrieve the capital, the property was sold.

Lismore

Northern Brewery 1979–86

The Sydney-based brewer, Tooth & Co. Ltd, built their Northern Brewery at Tuncester, 6 km west of Lismore, at a cost of $15 million. It was designed to produce Tooth's products for distribution to the north coast and northern tablelands of New South Wales, and was opened in September 1979. When Carlton & United Breweries Ltd of Melbourne acquired the Tooth Co. in 1983, the Northern Brewery continued for a few more years.

There had been much celebration when the brewery opened, but it was a sad day for the townspeople and the employees when the brewery finally closed in March 1986.

Richmond River Brewery 1886–88

The Richmond River Brewery was started by Chynoweth & Co., in a new building on the side of Gerrard's Hill. In October 1886 the local newspaper, the *Northern Star*, gave a lengthy description of the brewery and its unique method of refrigeration: 'the cooler is 30 foot long by 6½ foot wide and is supplied with a circular fan that performs 700 revolution per minute to assist in cooling'.

Lithgow

Situated in the north-western sector of the Blue Mountains, the city of Lithgow is an important manufacturing centre. In the early 1980s coal production was at its peak; however, most of the coal mines in the Lithgow Valley are now worked out.

The area is noted for its beautiful mountain scenery. Tourists are attracted to the reopened Zig Zag railway, whose steam engine chugs its way through tunnels and across viaducts as it winds its way through the mountains. The rail line was completed in 1869, and enabled trains to descend the steep west face of the Blue Mountains by three viaducts and two tunnels cut through the sandstone. The Zig Zag was replaced in 1910, and the old railway has now been opened as a tourist attraction.

Blue Mountains Brewery (Lithgow) Ltd
See Terry's Brewery Ltd.

Burton Brewery
See Lithgow Burton Brewing Co. Ltd.

Eskbank Brewery
See Lithgow Burton Brewing Co. Ltd.

Eskbank Brewery, Wine & Spirit Co. Ltd
See Lithgow Burton Brewing Co. Ltd.

Lithgow Brewery Ltd
See Terry's Brewery Ltd.

Lithgow Burton Brewing Co. Ltd   1878–1917
Near Burton Street, off Brewery Road (now Inch Street), Eskbank

Richard Inch had owned a small brewery at Hill End, and established another brewery at Lithgow in 1878, possibly earlier. He traded as R. J. Inch & Sons, and a Mr Passmore was a partner for a brief period during 1883. The company was first known as the Eskbank Brewery, and in 1887 the Eskbank Brewery, Wine & Spirit Co. Ltd was formed.

Inch's estate was sequestrated in 1889, and the business and brewery property was purchased by R. Blackford, who floated the Lithgow Burton Brewing Co. Ltd. Most references record the company simply as the Burton Brewery.

Richard Inch came back into the business, and was granted a brewer's licence for the years 1902 to 1904. He may have leased the brewery during that period, but in November 1905 the company went into liquidation. After reconstruction, the brewery continued to operate until 1917.

Stahl, Louis   c. 1860
Victoria Avenue

Louis Stahl was Lithgow's first brewer, but for reasons unknown he brewed for only one year.

Terry's Brewery Ltd   1884–1958
Brewery Gully, Oakey Park

The site for the brewery was selected because of the purity of the water of the stream that ran through the property, and at an altitude of 3000 feet above sea level the cold climate was ideal for brewing.

For the first forty-four years of the brewery's existence it was known as the Zig Zag Brewery, so named after the famous Zig Zag steam railway in the Blue Mountains. Henry P. Corbett built the Zig Zag Brewery in 1884, and when Alfred Goodeare became a partner four years later they traded as Corbett & Goodeare. From 1891 Corbett was again the sole proprietor. One of the brewery's products was Wombat Stout, the name having been chosen after a mob of marauding wombats had caused considerable damage by burrowing under the foundations.

By 1896 the brewery had been taken over by Corbett's stepson, John Alexander Stammers Jones, who expanded the business into a highly profitable enterprise. He became one of the most successful men in the district, owning the brewery, ten hotels, a mansion at Lithgow and another at Darling Point, Sydney. He was a keen horseman and billiards player, and was the first person in Lithgow to own a motorcycle.

John Stammers Jones sold the brewery in 1928, and retired. The newly-formed company, the Lithgow Brewery Ltd, secured a twenty-year lease on the brewery property and took control of the ten 'tied' hotels, but for the next seven years or more the fortunes of the brewery gradually declined, with a succession of owners, failures and closures.

The brewery, running at a loss, was leased to Mr Dodimeade, who was forced to close after eighteen months. The brewery was reopened by the partnership of Gale & Henry, who were later joined by Messrs Cornell and Bond. They had no success, and after six months the brewery closed again and remained shut for eighteen months.

Mr Mallen was next, but he failed to pay his excise duty, and the Bathurst Bankruptcy Court took over. They found another brewer, Mr Wolfensohn, who subsequently ran into heavy debt and left the country for England. The brewery closed for the fifth time in 1934.

In 1935, with dauntless courage, C. N. Wingate Terry reopened the brewery as Terry's Brewery, and appointed Frederick Lanfear as the brewer. Terry was unable to do much better than all the others in running the business, but Lanfear carried on. He was originally from Queensland, and a member of the well-known Lanfear family of brewers who had established breweries in at least three Australian states.

When Frederick Lanfear died in 1939, the brewery interests passed to the Official Receiver in Bankruptcy. Later that year the brewery was leased by Alfred Norman Wyld. P. Newdick was a partner for about two years, but from 1942 Wyld was the sole proprietor. Norman Wyld died in 1951, only two months after the company had been floated as Terry's Brewery Ltd.

From 1955 the brewery traded as the Blue

This colourful label shows the Great Western Zig Zag Railway, c. 1930. At that time the brewery was known as the Lithgow Brewery Ltd.

Terry's Brewery Ltd, c. 1936.

Lithgow Burton Brewing Co. Ltd, c. 1890.

Mountains Brewery (Lithgow) Ltd, but brewing ceased in 1958. Years later the premises were used as a soft drink and cordial factory.

Zig Zag Brewery

Henry Corbett	1884–88
Corbett & Goodeare	1888–91
Henry Corbett	1891–96
John Stammers Jones	1896–1928

Lithgow Brewery Ltd

Dodimeade	1928, closed
Gale & Henry	1929, closed
Gale, Henry, Cornall & Bond	1930, closed
Mallen	1932, closed
Wolfensohn	1934, closed

Terry's Brewery

C. N. Wingate Terry	1935–36
Frederick Lanfear	1936–39
Alfred N. Wyld	1939–40
Wyld & Newdick	1940–42
Alfred N. Wyld	1942–51

Terry's Brewery Ltd   1951–55

Blue Mountains Brewery (Lithgow) Ltd
                                         1955–58

Zig Zag Brewery
See Terry's Brewery Ltd.

Maclean

Clarence River Brewery Co. 1881–1914
Stanley Street

The first record of the Rocky Mouth Brewery, as it was first known, was in 1881 when it was reported as being near completion. Neil McAuley was the owner, followed by J. & D. McAuley in 1882, and H. Morton in 1883.

Morton sold in 1884 to Flowers, Bond & Co., who used the name Clarence River Brewery. Although John Flowers was an experienced brewer, he left within a year, and Bond carried on alone.

Robert Bond had come to Australia from Liverpool, England, as a boy of seven, and lived in Tasmania where he was trained as a cooper. He moved to Maclean, previously known as Rocky Mouth, and by 1886 he was trading as Bond, Berry & Underwood. Berry left the company in 1889, as did Bond the following, year leaving Frank Underwood to continue alone. John Hickson was involved during 1892, but the business was now in financial difficulty.

It was unbelievable when in 1893 the brewery was offered as first prize in an Art Union raffle. The value was said to be £4000, but the raffle venture fell through. Two years later Thomas D'Arcy Burke bought the brewery, stayed on for five years, then closed up in 1901.

J. G. Kempnich tried to revive the business in 1903, and upgraded the brewery on a grand scale. A splendid opening was held on 9 March 1904, with free beer for the public. Cordial and aerated waters were also produced, but the main products were Bulldog beer and Crab stout. The stout labels showed a large red crab, and the words 'Have a Nip with Me'.

Brewing ceased some time before the sale of the buildings in 1915. The purchaser was Charles Goddard, a builder by trade. He removed the tower section, and converted the rest of the building into two residences that were separated by the old brewery archway through which the beer wagons had passed many years earlier.

Rocky Mouth Brewery Co.

Neil McAuley	1881–82
J. & D. McAuley	1882–83
H. Morton	1883–84

Clarence River Brewery

Flowers, Bond & Co.	1884–84
Robert Bond	1884–86
Bond, Berry & Underwood	1886–89
Bond & Underwood	1889–90
Frank Underwood	1890–92
Underwood & Hickson	1892–95
Thomas D'Arcy Burke	1895–1901, closed
J. G. Kempnich	1903–14

Rocky Mouth Brewery Co.
See Clarence River Brewery Co.

Maitland

A number of time-expired convicts were allowed to occupy land in the Maitland district as early as 1813. A

Clarence River Brewery, Maclean, c. 1890.

village came into existence during 1825, and the government township that became East Maitland was surveyed in 1829. West Maitland came into existence five years later. Ultimately, in 1944, the two municipalities, and also the municipality of Morpeth, merged to form the City of Maitland.

Burton Brewery 1844–c. 1848

William Tinson had left the Hunter River Brewery in Maitland, and began brewing again at his home in 1844. After four years he was joined by John Edwards, who had been associated with the Maitland Brewery in the early years when it was known as the Millstream Brewery.

William Tinson was more of a cooper than a brewer, and advertised widely of his experience and ability to produce casks and vats of all sizes. He told the public of his 'fine full flavour ale, second to none in the colony for its brilliancy and keeping qualities, brewed on an entirely new principle'. The fact that he had only recently received the recipe for the process, and instructions from a friend, did little to enthuse the locals. Tinson brewed for a few years, and then concentrated on coopering — making barrels and vats for the trade.

Hunter River Brewery c. 1840–c. 1846
West Maitland

In the early 1840s Alexander Berrie began brewing, and in 1842 he took on the experienced cooper, William Tinson, as a partner.

At least one journalist of the time thought their beer was good:

> The Hunter Brewery — we are ever averse to give publicity to anything that may be construed into what is vulgarly called 'puffing' and from the operation of this conscientious feeling, we have frequently refrained from mentioning circumstances when our object in doing so, to the public, appear at all questionable. We do not suppose however that we shall lay ourselves open to this charge when we recommend to the taste of the inhabitants, the beverage concocted at the above establishment by Messrs Berrie and Tinson. We have received a sample of the Pale Light Ale, which they have succeeded in bringing to a state of great perfection and can pronounce it a mild and invigorating summer drink. When it can be done without a sacrifice, as in this case, the community ought to encourage as much as possible, colonial industry and skill.

No doubt the journalist had another Pale Light Ale after writing all that.

By June 1844 the Berrie–Tinson partnership had ended, and the business continued as Berrie & Underwood. Sales were slow, and the new partners advertised in the 11 January 1845 issue of the *Maitland Mercury* that they had reduced the price of their ale to 1s per gallon for quantities not less than 10 gallons. Five months earlier Henry Gooch, the Maitland agent for R. & E. Tooth & Co., Sydney, had put an advertisement in the same newspaper, dropping the price of Tooth's Best XXX Ale from 2s to 1s 6d per gallon.

Alexander Berrie left the business in February 1845; Thomas Underwood then became the sole owner.

Maitland Brewing Co. Ltd 1845–1915
High Street, West Maitland

During the latter part of 1845 John Edwards and James Stuart agreed to start a brewery as a joint venture. After three months there were losses, and since Stuart argued that Edwards had made insufficient contribution to the loss Edwards was ' kicked out', and Stuart continued on his own for the next thirty years. After this long period of successful brewing by one owner, there were seven ownership changes over the next thirty-seven years and a change in location.

January 1876 saw Williams & Cohen in charge; two years later, George Milne; and four years further on three partners, George Milne, H. J. Adams and T. Morrow. They purchased the old Northumberland Flour Mill in 1887, and relocated the brewery to that site. The brewery had been known as the Millstream Brewery, and its Crystal bottled beer and Millstream draught beer were popular in many districts of New South Wales and Queensland.

The name was changed to the Maitland Brewing Co. Ltd, and in 1891 the new owners, Henry Adams and Arthur Wall, began a major rebuilding and expansion programme. A new four-storey brewery was built and installed with the most modern equipment available. The construction was based on the gravitation system of brewing. Malt, hops and liquor were hoisted to the top of the tower, and the result of their admixture then flowed from vessel to vessel by gravitation until the brew reached the cellars. The method dispensed with the need to raise the wort by pumping, and eliminated pipe exposure and contamination.

The new brewery complex consisted of the brewery and tower, brewery yard, cask sheds, coopers' shop, stables, coach-house and buggy sheds, all arranged so that the manager could supervise the whole at a glance. Part of the old dismantled brewery was used as a wine-and-spirit and bond store.

The buildings stood in the middle of 15 acres of land, 10 acres of which were under lucerne cultivation, all presenting quite an attractive sight to folk passing along the road.

The Maitland Brewery had an office at 34 O'Connell Street, Sydney, and later a bottling depot and head office was established at the corner of Bayview and Mills Streets, Pyrmont. This was shifted to the corner of King and Day Streets in 1912.

Henry Everett became the owner in 1908, and in

1913 the Sydney brewer, Tooth & Co. Ltd, acquired the brewery, which continued to operate as Tooth & Co. Ltd, Successors to the Maitland Brewing Co. Ltd. Brewing was discontinued in 1915, and the buildings were later remodelled and converted into the Hampton Court Flats.

Millstream Brewery

John Edwards & James Stuart	1845
James Stuart	1845–76
Williams & Cohen	1876–78
George Milne	1878–82
G. Milne, H. J. Adams & T. Morrow	1882–87

Maitland Brewing Co. Ltd (new location)

G. Milne, H. J. Adams & T. Morrow	1887–91
Henry Adams & Arthur Wall	1891–1908
Henry Everett	1908–13
Tooth & Co. Ltd	1913–15

Millstream Brewery
See Maitland Brewing Co. Ltd.

Menindee

The small township of Menindee is located in the arid inland plains area of New South Wales, 120 km east of Broken Hill. The name Menindee is derived from an Aboriginal word meaning 'egg yolk'.

During the heyday of river transport, Menindee served as a port for paddle-wheel steamers hauling barges of produce along the Darling River.

Menindee Brewery 1870–74
For Charles Medlicott the town held great prospects for the sale of beer, and in 1870 he set up the Menindee Brewery. Four years later the brewery closed through lack of trade.

Molong

Swan Brewery 1892–98
Betts Street, East Molong

Although the government had established a stockyard in the Molong area in 1828, the township itself only began to take shape in the late 1840s when the first copper mine was opened. Almost fifty years later the partnership of Hirons, Clifton & Hughes set up their Swan Brewery, located to the east of the small township. Robert Clifton was the brewer and manager, and beer was sold to hotels and individuals in the surrounding districts.

The brewery was sold to Henry Martin & Co. in 1897, but the following year the only sale for Swan Brewery beer was to Mrs Flynn of the Post Office Hotel.

Moree

Gwydir Brewery 1889–1907
Culloden, near Moree

'If you want to keep warm during the cold weather, drink good sound Moree Beer' —that was part of the advertisement in 1901 for the Gwydir Brewery. It continued: 'Magnificent A1 Moree Extra Double Stout available, brewed with a splendid water'.

The brewery was 5 km west of Moree, near what is still known as Brewery Flat. At least one Moree resident recalls the time when Brewery Flat was known as Tickle Belly Flat, where the boys and girls would go for a little wooing.

The owner of the Gwydir Brewery was Charles Collins, who also operated breweries at Narrabri and

The label of the Gwydir Brewery, Moree, featured the waratah, the floral emblem of the state of New South Wales.

HOW TO CURE DRUNKARDS

Amongst other things discussed at the Medical Congress, assembled here . . . during this present month, was 'Dipsomania; and How to Cure Drunkards of their Propensities.' Dr. P. Smith, of Queensland, read a paper on the subject, in which he laid down this dictum:- 'The man who gave way to drink was afflicted with some lesion or flaw of the brain, whereby the organ was placed in a state of unstable equilibrium.'

I don't know about that; but I do know that when a man has had too much, there is decidedly an 'unstable equilibrium' about the feet and legs. Dr. Smith recommends that all persons habitually given to excessive drinking should be shut up in asylums for periods ranging from one year to five years. I would recommend the longer period, so that whether they get cured or not they may at least be kept away from respectable hotel-keepers.

Australian Brewers' Journal, January 1889

Walgett. When the brewery was started at Moree, C. Lindsay was the manager. He was followed by Benjamin Joseph, then a Mr Thomas, and in 1898 by Henry Joseph, a former partner with Charles Collins at the Narrabri Brewery. More managers came and went; George Lindsay, George Dewar and Albert Collins all took their turn during 1900, and Septimus Faulkner ran the business for a few months during 1901.

Albert Collins (brother of Charles) and T. A. Stirton worked the brewery from 1901 until it closed in 1907.

Moree Brewery
See Gwydir Brewery.

Morpeth

Morpeth Brewery　　　　　　　1863
At one time Morpeth was a small town east of Maitland; today it is a suburb of Maitland. When Johnson & McClelland were brewing there in 1863 they would have experienced strong competition from the well-established Maitland Brewery.

Mt Hope

Mount Hope Brewery　　　　　1883–86
The brewery was established by Edward Evans, who sold out to William Small the following year. When the brewery closed in 1886, Isaac Mullard was the proprietor.

Mudgee

The original inhabitants of the district were the Wiradhuri Aboriginals; the Aboriginal word 'mudgee' means either 'nest in the hills' or 'contented'. The area was surveyed for a village in 1823, and Mudgee was proclaimed a municipality in 1860. The district is noted for its fine wool and other primary production, including many wineries.

Broombee Brewery　　　　　　c. 1883
The *Mudgee Guardian* of August 1883 reported that the Broombee Brewery shareholders had held their first meeting. It was explained at the meeting that 'there were more swallowers in summer than winter', and that 'business will improve'. Regrettably, business didn't improve.

Crossing's Brewery　　　　　　c. 1858
The address for the brewery was 'next to Crossing's Mill and Settlers Stores, Mortimer Street'. There was at least one advertisement for Richard Crossing's Brewery and its products in the *Mudgee Newspaper and Mining Advocate* during 1858.

Dressler's Brewery (Australia) Pty Ltd
See Federal Brewery Ltd.

Federal Brewery Ltd　　　　　1883–1956
Cnr Mortimer & Lawson Streets

The Mudgee Co-operative Brewing Co. was formed in 1883. Six years later the owners, J. H. McCarthy & Sons, sold the business to E. W. Daly, who happened to be the proprietor of the Sydney Brewery at the township of Burrundulla. He lasted for two years at Mudgee.

When the partnership of George Young and John Ferrier took over in 1891, two changes took place: the brewery was shifted to the corner of Mortimer and Lawson Streets, and the name was changed to the Federal Brewery. The partners leased the brewery to D. Edwards & Co. in 1892, but took over again the following year.

The Young & Ferrier partnership had lasted for eight years when they advertised that their final day of business would be 1 March 1901; G. H. O'Connor had purchased the brewery.

Nine years passed, and in January 1910 an advertisement appeared in the *Western Post*:

> Federal Brewery, George Young, Proprietor — patronize local industry, support the district instead of helping to swell the already overpowering influence and importance of Sydney.

The lengthy and challenging notice told the reader that he, George Young, had repurchased his old business, the Mudgee Brewery, that the plant would be upgraded, the very best materials would be used, and he guaranteed that his beer and stout would be 'pure, wholesome, sound and saleable'. Living up to his promise, George Young won first prize for his bottled stout at the 1918 Royal Agricultural Show in Sydney.

With the business in good shape, he decided to sell out in 1921, and the Federal Brewery was bought by the three-way partnership of Alfred C. Wade, Henry Smith and Jack Birtles. With well-deserved pride, they claimed their beer to be 'good beer because it is skilfully brewed in the pure country air', an original approach to advertising. In fact, their beer was regarded as 'one of the best drops in the country'.

During World War II the brewery operated three shifts, and beer was shipped to Darwin and several Pacific Islands.

When Wade, Smith and Birtles ran the business, they had an arrangement with Bruce Merrin, who had a well on his farm near the river. The water seeped through gravelly soil and came out clean and crystal clear. The partners purchased a large tankful of the water twice a week, but this was tedious and costly. The arrangement ended when the town water supply was connected to the brewery, but the water evidently contained some impurities. The partners tried to correct the problem, but their ale was just not as good as it

During the 1920s the Federal Brewery, Mudgee, had its watercart filled twice a week with clean, clear well-water from a nearby property.

had been. Drinkers referred to the brew as 'Mudgee Mud', with grimaces and a jerk of the head thrown in for good effect after a drink or two.

The Federal Brewery Pty Ltd was formed in 1946 when beer production was 1000 gallons per week. After extending the buildings and putting in new plant, output gradually increased. The quality of the beer improved remarkably, and at the end of 1951 eighty men were employed, working two shifts, and beer was sent to Sydney and Melbourne. Also during that year the company was floated as the Federal Brewery Ltd.

In 1953 the Dressler family purchased the business, and formed Dressler's Brewery (Australia) Pty Ltd — although locals still called the brewery 'the Federal'. Lack of outlets for the company's beer was the major cause of the brewery's closure in 1956, and the many devotees sadly missed their 'Mudgee Mud'.

Mudgee Co-operative Brewing Co. Ltd

J. H. McCarthy & Sons	1883–89
E. W. Daly	1889–91

Federal Brewery (new location)

Young & Ferrier	1891–92
D. Edwards & Co.	1892–93
Young & Ferrier	1893–1901
G. O'Connor	1901–9
George Young	1910–21
Wade, Smith and Birtles	1921—46

Federal Brewery Pty Ltd	1946—51
Federal Brewery Ltd	1951—53
Dressler's Brewery (Australia) Pty Ltd	1953–56

Mudgee Co-operative Brewing Co. Ltd

See Federal Brewery Ltd.

Muswellbrook

Muswellbrook Brewery   1868–70

There were several owners during the short life of the Muswellbrook Brewery. The first, in 1868, was Eli Allen. The following year Edward Heley took over, then George Cadell, followed by William Tinson, who had been involved in breweries at Maitland. Tinson & Wharton were the owners when the brewery closed.

Narrabri

The town of Narrabri, located at the junction of Narrabri Creek and the Namoi River, is the centre of a rich cottongrowing industry.

Narrabri Brewery   1881–96
Cnr Maitland & Fitzroy Streets (opposite what is now the RSL Club)

Toward the end of 1881 Thomas Usher was granted a brewer's licence, and he started brewing ale and porter in premises at the southern end of the town. Six years later he sold the brewery to Peter Simpson, who had owned breweries at Glen Innes and Armidale, both of which had been in the hands of trustees in January 1887.

In 1888 Simpson invited the *Narrabri Herald* reporter to visit the brewery and sample the beer. The reporter wrote:

Mr. Simpson has now turned out the first batch of the present season's brew and must be congratulated on having succeeded in producing a light, wholesome, thoroughly drinkable beverage.

High praise, but the reporter continued, 'It is not quite as good now as it will be when a few days older'.

Another report in an earlier 1888 edition of the *Narrabri Herald* quoted, with dry humour:

Among our Saxon forefathers, there was a law under which any person brewing bad beer was pinioned to a chair and ducked 'till he was half drowned in a vat of his own brew. There is not much probability that Mr. Simpson will render himself liable to such a penalty as he has acquired a reputation for brewing a wholesome and drinkable article.

In spite of the friendly editorials, Peter Simpson gave up brewing at Narrabri in 1889. He had been there less than two years.

Next to take over were Charles Collins and Henry Joseph. They owned breweries at Moree and Walgett, and did quite well at Narrabri until 1896. Collins was much respected in the district. He was the first mayor of Narrabri, and owned a large general store there.

The railway reached Narrabri West in 1882, and the town proper in 1889. Gradually the large Sydney brewers began to offer strong competition by rail-freighting their beer to country towns, including Narrabri. That was the finish of the local brewery.

Narrandera

Crystal Fountain Brewery
See Oakbank Brewery.

Narrandera Brewery   c. 1879–1925
On the bank of the Murrumbidgee River

Some time before 1880 George Wildman established his Narrandera Brewery, which he sold in 1880 to William Jones and Susannah Lincoln. Although water had been drawn from the river and used after proper filtration, it was decided to sink a well, and at a depth of 120 feet a flow of excellent water was tapped. This was then used as the primary source of water for cleaning and brewing.

By 1888 the partnership had changed to William Jones and Thomas Lincoln. During the 1880s and 1890s the firm of Jones, Lincoln & Co. owned a considerable brewing empire, with breweries at Cootamundra, Hay, Hillston, Jerilderie, Narrandera, Temora and Urana.

In 1888 the company purchased and closed the local Oakbank Brewery. It was then decided to change the name of their existing operation from the Narrandera Brewery to the Oakbank Brewery. The Narrandera Brewery name, as such, no longer existed.

Disastrous floods swept through the district in 1891, and the brewery was flooded four times in five weeks, washing away part of the brewery. Three years later the firm of McIntyre, Lincoln & Co. became the owners, but later that year the brewery was totally destroyed by fire.

In time the brewery was rebuilt; and in 1900 Thomas Lincoln became sole proprietor. After 1907 he traded as Lincoln & Co. Ltd. Tom Lincoln died in 1920, and his brother, Harry, carried on at the brewery. In October 1924 Tooth & Co. Ltd took over, and closed the brewery. Years later the property was sold, and converted to a soft drink factory. In spite of the fact that the name had changed to Oakbank many years before, because of its location in Narrandera and earlier history most people still referred to it as the Narrandera brewery.

The Oakbank Brewery, 1911. It was originally called the Narrandera Brewery, with the name changing to the Oakbank in 1888 when it was taken over by Jones, Lincoln & Co. Three years later the brewery was flooded four times, and was partly washed away. In 1894 it was completely destroyed by fire, was rebuilt, and continued operating until 1925.

Oakbank Brewery   1882–88
Richard Heath was the owner of the Newtown brewery at Wagga Wagga, and in 1882 he built another brewery at Narrandera. He sold the brewery three years later to George Rogers, who gave it the fairylike name of the Crystal Fountain Brewery.

George Young and John Ferrier were the owners from 1886 to 1888, followed by Jones, Lincoln & Co., who immediately closed the brewery. Jones, Lincoln & Co. happened to own the Narrandera Brewery only a few streets away, and for reasons unknown they changed the name of their Narrandera Brewery to the Oakbank Brewery.

See also Narrandera Brewery.

Nerrigundah

Nerrigundah Brewery   1863
Thomas Auld, T. H. Saunders and George Hopkins were issued with brewers' licences in 1863, and were no doubt partners in the Nerrigundah Brewery. Auld had operated a brewery at Eden, and after leaving Nerrigundah he and his wife settled in Araluen, and became involved in a brewery there.

The Castlemaine Brewery, Newcastle, 1878.

Newcastle

Newcastle was founded in 1804 as a penal settlement. Although coal had been discovered in 1814, free settlers did not enter the area until 1824, after the prison had closed.

Today Newcastle is the second-largest city in New Sosuth Wales, and the sixth city of Australia. It is one of the largest ports in Australia, particularly for the export of coal. Its major industry is the Broken Hill Proprietary Co. Ltd's steelworks.

Castlemaine Brewery & Wood Brothers & Co., Newcastle, New South Wales Ltd   1876–1931
Charlton Street (now Hunter Street)

During 1874 Robert Prendergast and Nicholas Fitzgerald of the Castlemaine Brewery, Sydney, prepared plans to start a brewery in the New South Wales coastal town of Newcastle. The plans were made in association with Wood Brothers & Co., a long-established wine, spirit and import company that had held an agency for the sale of Castlemaine ale since 1868.

The brewery began production in 1876 under the name of Prendergast, Wood & Co. This was changed in 1887 to the Castlemaine Brewery & Wood Brothers & Co., Newcastle, NSW, Ltd — generally called the Castlemaine Brewery for simplicity.

The nearby Great Northern Brewery had run into difficulties, and was taken over by the Castlemaine Brewery during 1890, and closed. Tooth & Co. Ltd of Sydney had been operating a small depot in Telford Street, Newcastle, and as part of their expansion programme they acquired all the assets of the Castlemaine Brewery & Wood Brothers in 1921. Tooth then had a well-established brewing base in the fast-growing city of Newcastle. However, at the end of June 1931 brewing ceased, and the brewery buildings were used as a Tooth & Co. depot.

Ferndale Brewery, Wine & Spirit Co. Ltd
See Park Brewery.

Great Northern Brewery & Malting & Wine & Spirit & Aerated Waters Co. Ltd   1888–89
The partnership of Cowlishaw & John Armstrong started the brewery, and with much enthusiasm for a bright future they appointed J. B. Magney as managing director. One year later the business was in liquidation.

The other brewery in town, the Castlemaine, took over the Great Northern in March 1890, and closed it to prevent competition. The premises were subsequently leased to an icemaking company.

Hunter Brewery   1970–87
Cardiff

Sydney brewer, Toohey's Ltd, commenced brewing at Cardiff, near Newcastle, in August 1970, although the official opening was not until 3 February 1971. The modern brewing plant and the brewery's location, gave Toohey's a strategic production base to service the immediate district and the widespread areas of northern New South Wales. It so happened that the rival Sydney brewer, Tooth & Co., opened a depot next door to the brewery in 1974.

Toohey's Ltd, Sydney, and Castlemaine Perkins Ltd, Brisbane, merged in 1980 to form Castlemaine

Toohey's Ltd. The new company was taken over by Bond Corporation in August 1985, and the Hunter Brewery in Newcastle was closed in August 1987.

Park Brewery 1887–88
Albert Street, Wickham

The Park Brewery was opened for business by Clarence Linden in 1888, and the following year it was proposed to form a new company to further develop the brewery. The new company was to be known as the Ferndale Brewery, Wine & Spirit Co. Ltd. It anticipated a bright future in supplying beer to the large population of the rich coalmining city, but the project failed to proceed.

Scarr's Brewery c. 1825

The *Sydney Gazette* of 3 February 1825 announced that

> Thomas Scarr intends to proceed to Newcastle immediately for the purpose of commencing the brewing business, he having obtained from His Excellency the Governor, permission to establish a concern there.

Nymagee

Nymagee Brewery 1881–89

Within a year of starting the brewery Samuel Williams sold to David Thomas. Thomas lasted two years, and was followed in 1884 by Isaac Mullan, whose address was Milford Street. Herbert Harris then took over the brewery in 1887, and his address was 'Sawmill tank, near Nymagee'; by 1889 he was bankrupt. At that time the dry arid area in western New South Wales was sparsely populated. Lack of water, extreme heat and few customers would seem to be the obvious reasons for the brewery's failure.

Nyngan

Nyngan Brewery 1892–97
Bogan Road

The brewery lasted for about five years, during which time there were three owners. The first was Peter Crane, who employed James Howison as the brewer. In 1893 the partners, Donald Sanderson and W. M. Connell, owned the brewery; and they sold to J. Sloane around 1895.

Orange

In 1846 the Surveyor-General of New South Wales, Major Thomas Mitchell, named Orange after Prince William of Orange, later the King of Holland. The first goldrush in New South Wales occurred at nearby Ophir in 1851, and the quiet grazing district changed to a scene of furious activity as thousands of hopefuls from all over the world, flocked into the area. Orange became an ideal place for a brewery. Paradoxically, the area around the town of Orange produces about 10 per cent of Australia's apples; peaches and cherries are also grown, but no oranges.

One of Australia's best-known poets, 'Banjo' Paterson, was born at Narrambla, near Orange. He is well remembered for his ballads, 'The Man from Snowy River', 'Waltzing Matilda' and 'Clancy of the Overflow'.

Boxall, Henry W. c. 1852

Henry Boxall emigrated from England, and in 1852 he was granted a brewer's licence for premises described as a slab building at Narrambla, near Orange.

Burton Brewery
See Red Lion Brewery.

Chynoweth, John 1875–82

The brewery once stood on the triangle of land on Bathurst Road, now known as Colvin Park.

Lindsay's Brewery
See Red Lion Brewery.

Lord's Place Brewery
See Red Lion Brewery.

Orange Brewery
See Red Lion Brewery.

Red Lion Brewery 1879–1903
Lord's Place

During the course of the brewery's history it was known by a number of different names. The original proprietor, Charles Graham, called it the Burton Brewery. When the Lindsay Brewery Co. took over in 1884, it became the Red Lion Brewery, the name used by Lindsay for his other country town breweries. The name Lindsay's Brewery was commonly used, also Lord's Place Brewery and the Orange Brewery.

Henry Lindsay, the owner, lived in Sydney for much of the time, and the Orange Brewery was maaged by an Englishman, Thomas Hardwick. The product range was incredibly large. The company advertised their bottled ale and porter, ginger ale, peppermint, cloves, lemon syrup, lime juice, gingerette, quinine, ginger wine, ginger brandy, bitters, lemonade, soda water, raspberryade, nectar, champagne, cider, ginger beer, seltzer and tonic water.

John Martin ran the brewery from 1891, but two years later the company went into liquidation. Charles Bromilow, who had recently left the Standard Brewery, Orange, believed the brewery could be run at a profit, so he took over in 1894. He lasted a year, and was then followed by Henry Laurance from 1895 to 1896.

Left: *The Standard Brewery, Orange, c. 1880. The proprietor at that time was Edward Heap.*

Right: *The brewery was substantially upgraded and extended in 1881 by William Elwin.*

James Walker, owner of the Great Western Brewery in Bathurst, purchased the brewery in 1897. Six years later he bought the other brewery in Orange, the Standard, and closed the Red Lion.

Standard Brewery 1861–1926
Intersection of Hill & Moulder Streets

Thomas Lane, the founder of the Standard Brewery, advertised his best ales for sale at 2s 6d per gallon. He brewed until 1864. Apparently the brewery then closed for a few years.

The next owner was Henry O'Neill, whose name appears, off and on, in New South Wales *Government Gazettes* from 1869 to 1874.

Heap & Bothwell were at the brewery from 1870 to 1874, and then Edward Heap became sole proprietor. A few years later he was joined by William Elwin, and they traded as Heap, Elwin & Co. until 1881. The business then continued as William H. Elwin & Co.; C. W. Bromilow became a partner and, later, A. J. Maude.

William Elwin's business prospered, and to keep up with the demand new equipment was installed and the buildings extended. The brewery became a huge complex of buildings, sheds, stables and cellars. The outstanding feature was the lofty five-storey tower. They carried out their own malting, cooperage and bottling, and had an abundant supply of water noted for its purity.

William Elwin was described as a 'likable gentleman'. He was a Justice of the Peace, and, as a member of the Hospital Committee, he raised funds by keeping a money box at his brewery where those who had a 'long beer' had to contribute a silver coin. A keg was always on tap for visitors and for entertainment purposes. For those with a thirst on Sunday mornings, they could call on their friend at the brewery, who would take them to the cellar and pull a beer for them.

James Walker was born in Scotland, and came to Australia in the 1870s. He took any job he could get, and went on to become a bridge builder, sugar miller, gold digger and brewer. He did well at the Coolgardie goldfields in Western Australia, and settled in Bathurst with sufficient funds to enter the brewing business.

He negotiated the purchase of the Standard Brewery in 1903, and closed the Orange Brewery, which he had acquired six years earlier. Walker also owned the Great Western Brewery at Bathurst, and in 1908 Walker & Co. Ltd was formed to take over the assets of both breweries.

The Standard Brewery was purchased in 1926 by Toohey's Brewery, Sydney, who closed the Standard and used the premises as a depot; the buildings were subsequently demolished.

Thomas Lane	1861–64, closed
Henry O'Neill	1869–70
Heap & Bothwell	1870–74
Edward Heap	1874–79
Heap, Elwin & Co.	1879–81
William H. Elwin & Co.	1881–1903
James Walker	1903–8
Walker & Co. Ltd	1908–26
Toohey & Co. Ltd	1926

Parkes

The district of Parkes remained relatively unsettled until 1862, when the discovery of gold led to a hastily erected 'canvas town' known as Currajong. By 1867 the gold rush was almost over, but in 1871 a further discovery was made at the nearby Bushman's Gold Mine. The district went on to become one of the richest gold-producing areas in the colony of New South Wales. On 1 December 1873 the settlement was renamed Parkes in honour of the then Prime Minister of New South Wales, Henry Parkes.

Parkes Brewery c. 1875–79

The first and only brewery was established in the town about 1875. Although the brewery operated for a mere four years, quite a few people were involved: Isabella Rippendale, c. 1875; Surrey & Myers, 1876; James Bothwell, 1876; Bothwell & Prior, 1877; James Bothwell, 1878–79; Mark Coleman, 1877–79.

James Howison, formerly the brewer at the Union Brewery in Grenfell, was 'about to start a brewery at Parkes' in June 1891, but the proposal did not proceed.

Purnamoota

The tiny town of Purnamoota is located in a hot and arid area, 20 km north-east of Silverton in far-west New South Wales.

Falcon Brewery 1884–86
Gum Well

Three partners began making beer at the outset: John Cocks, Alfred Martin and Charles Kite. They traded as Cocks, Martin & Co., but the partnership was dissolved in 1885, not long after the Falcon Brewery started.

John Cocks and Charlie Kite continued to run the brewery in the sweltering heat where temperatures could rise to 46°C. Somehow they managed to brew an acceptable beer that drew the comment, 'a sample of their beer was classed as a nice light and very palatable drink'.

Queanbeyan

Bradbury's Brewery 1845–60; 1884–85
Trinculo Place

Alfred Bradbury's brewery was a strange, rambling brick building dominated by a three-storey tower. For fifteen years Bradbury turned out very good beer, which was said to be due to the excellent waters of the Queanbeyan River, fed from the surrounding high mountains. Before his death in 1866 Bradbury's business had collapsed, and he ended his days, poor and lonely, at the inn next door.

The brewery remained closed for twenty-four years, until in 1884 George Billson and John Farrell refurbished the equipment, tidied up the place, and reopened the brewery. Billson owned the Albury Brewery, and Farrell was a partner in the Wollondale Brewery in Goulburn. Both men were entrepreneurs, and their decision to set up another brewery in a likely township was typical of many experienced brewers of the time. Few of these ventures proved successful for any length of time, and Billson and Farrell's attempt was no exception.

Raymond Terrace

Haviland, Francis 1860–62

Raymond Terrace, located at the junction of the Hunter and Williams Rivers just north of Newcastle, was a thriving river port in the 1840s. Twenty years after the town was established Francis Haviland set up a brewery in the town, and worked it for two years.

Silverton

Silverton owes its origin to the discovery of useful grades of silver and lead ore found in the district in the late 1870s. Situated 25 km west of Broken Hill in the far south-west of New South Wales, it was a hot, dry and dusty town when the prospectors started to arrive. Although transport to and from the remote area was difficult and relied on bullock wagons, camel teams and horsedrawn carts, the population quickly increased from 250 in 1883 to over 3000 in 1885, the year when Silverton was proclaimed a township.

The supply of drinkable water was a constant problem. In 1883 a bucket of water of doubtful quality cost 6d; better-quality cost 1s. The summer heat was dreadful, and it is difficult to imagine how the settlers were able to cope with the primitive and harsh conditions. It is also difficult to imagine how anyone could brew beer in such an environment — but they did.

Lion Brewery 1885–1901

The Resch brothers, Edmund and Emil, joined John Penrose in opening the Lion Brewery at Silverton in 1885. The Resch brothers were already operating breweries at Cootamundra and Wilcannia, and later they set up a soft drink factory at nearby Broken Hill.

Penrose was the owner of the Queen's Head Hotel in Wilcannia, and had been successful in mining speculation in the early boom days. At the peak of his career

E. Resch & Co., Lion Brewery, Silverton, before the flood in 1898.

he was reputed to be worth £100,000, and had been mayor of the town. The local recreational centre carries his name. Sadly, he died penniless in Melbourne in 1908.

The Lion Brewery was built on the south bank of the Umberumberka Creek, and it was a familiar sight to see women and children lined up with billycans to buy a pennyworth of yeast from the brewery for making bread. In 1888 the yearly output of the brewery was an incredible 600,000 bottles each of cordial and aerated waters, and 90,000 gallons of beer.

Following the dissolution of the partnership in 1893, John Penrose and Emil Resch continued at the Lion Brewery, and traded as E. Resch & Co. Early in 1898 the building was flooded, but eager workers soon had the brewery running again, at least for a further three years.

Nectar Brewery
See Unicorn Brewery.

Topman's Brewery 1891
Burke Street
T. Bock.

Unicorn Brewery 1886–c. 1900
North bank of the Umberumberka Creek

John Crossing started his brewery, the Nectar Brewery, in 1886. It was described as

> prettily situated, surrounded by waving gum trees and other green foliage, a pleasant change from the everlasting salt bush and sand so prevalent on the Barrier … The men employed at the brewery live and board on the premises. A neat little garden is fenced in and all the useful table vegetables are to be seen growing which gives the place quite a homely appearance.

John Crossing, possibly a descendant of Richard Crossing who had owned a brewery at Mudgee in the late 1850s, sold the Nectar Brewery to a syndicate, who formed the Union Barrier Brewing Co. Ltd in 1888. Thomas D'Arcy Burke was the manager; he had previously been in charge of brewing at Thomas Aitken's Victoria Parade Brewery in Melbourne, and also at John Primrose's Union Brewery in Adelaide. He had a record of thirty-two prizes for draught and bottled ale and stout, but in spite of these impressive credentials the company went into liquidation in 1890. It was subsequently reformed by the partnership of A. Gillett & E. Phillips as the Unicorn Brewery.

Union Barrier Brewing Co. Ltd
See Unicorn Brewery.

Singleton

Singleton Brewery 1867–68
William Tinson had been involved in both the Hunter Brewery and Burton Brewery in Maitland during the 1840s. At Singleton his beer may have been passable for some, but certainly not the majority, and that was the problem. Instead of his business growing, it declined rapidly. He was more experienced as a cooper than as a brewer, and this third attempt at making beer was a failure.

Stroud

Australia Inn & Brewery c. 1879
In the early years at Stroud the Australia Inn was an important meeting place for locals and visitors passing through. The inn had quarters for coachmen and travellers, a smokehouse, several other buildings at the rear, and a number of wells where fresh water was drawn.

The first owner, Charles Dee, sold the Australia Inn to John Williams in 1854. The inn was a considerable distance from the nearest town with a brewery, and Williams probably engaged in some brewing at the inn. This was not an uncommon practice in remote areas, and the brewer rarely bothered to register as a brewer. However, Samuel Williams, the son, did receive registration as a brewer in 1879.

Sydney

Adelaide Brewery
See Waverley Brewery (Waverley).

Albion Brewery 1827–52
Elizabeth Street

For an ex-convict, Samuel Terry did very well for himself. He was a stonemason by trade, and before his sentence expired he had been the superintendent for the building of the Parramatta gaol. Sam became a

The brewery, in Singleton, was originally called the Nectar Brewery. When it was taken over in 1888 by Thomas D'Arcy Burke, the name was changed to the Union Barrier Brewing Co. Ltd, and changed again to the Unicorn Brewery in 1890 by A. Gillett and E. Phillips.

storekeeper, publican, and a substantial land and property owner. At one time he owned close to 20,000 acres of agricultural and pastoral land in the settled districts. In conjunction with a butcher named Smith, he had interests in Emu Station in the Liverpool district; they ran 150,000 head of sheep, 400 horses and 200 head of cattle.

In earlier years Sam Terry had been a partner with Daniel Cooper in the Australian Brewery, George Street, and in 1827 he started his own brewery, the Albion, in Elizabeth Street. The location was chosen because of the proximity of a spring of fresh water that flowed down to Cockle Bay (Darling Harbour). The site was later to become the premises of one of Australia's most famous breweries, Toohey's Standard Brewery.

After the death of Sam Terry in 1838 his son-in-law, John Terry Hughes, carried on the business for four years; he then sold the brewery to Gavin Ralston & Co. in 1842. Brewing ceased about nine years later, and the premises were converted to a soap and candle factory. The buildings burnt down in the 1860s, and the site remained vacant. John and James Toohey had been working the Darling Brewery in Sydney for some time, and in 1873 they purchased the old Albion Brewery property, built their Standard Brewery on the site, and closed the Darling.

The Albion Brewery has long since disappeared, but it can be remembered by the names of Albion Street and Terry Street, which, with Elizabeth Street, formed the boundaries of the old brewery.

Allt's Brewery & Wine & Spirit Co. Ltd

See Surrey Brewery; Waverley Brewery (Waverley).

American & German Lager Beer Brewing Co. Ltd

A prospectus was issued in 1891 for the formation of the company intending to take over the Carrington Brewery in Marrickville. Perhaps they intended forming a Carrington Brewery, since there was no brewery of that name in Sydney at that time. The directors were to be mainly hotel owners, and the brewing expertise was to be provided by Ralph Foster, the co-founder of the Foster Brewing Co. in Melbourne. The proposal did not proceed in spite of the promise to pay 50 per cent return on capital.

The Carrington Brewery referred to may have been the Eagle Brewery, Marrickville, which had many changes of ownership during the late 1880s, or it may have been a non-operating company that had been formed at that time.

Anchor Brewery 1865–76
Johnstone Street, Woollahra

The various owners/managers of the brewery were Samuel Studd, 1865–71; David Price, 1871–72; John Heinz & Co., 1872–75; Tighe & Co., 1876.

Anglo Australian Brewery 1882–90
555 Harris Street, Ultimo

During the eight years that the brewery operated it was known by three different names, had five different owners and two locations. In the early years the brewery earned the distinction of being the first to commercially produce lager beer in New South Wales, and second only in Australia to Cohn Brothers of the Victoria Brewery in Bendigo, Victoria, who had brewed and sold lager beer earlier, in 1882.

The partnership of Marks & Murphy began brewing at 709 George Street South in 1882. The *Australian Brewers' Journal* of August 1883 reported that during a visit to New South Wales by their representative he was surprised to find that lager beer was being successfully manufactured by Marks & Murphy. The beer was excellent, no doubt due to the fact that Sam Marks had had fifteen years' experience in brewing lager beer in the USA, where lager beer had been popular since 1860.

By 1885 Sam Marks was sole proprietor, and about that time he shifted the brewery operations to 555 Harris Street, Ultimo, and used the name Sydney Brewery. William Jones & Co., late of Narrandera, purchased the brewery in 1886, and Marks moved on to start the New York Brewery in Newtown.

The next owner was John Derwin, who changed the name to the Red Heart Brewery. George Miller and Samuel Mason had been brewers in Hamilton, Victoria; and when they took over the Red Heart in 1888 they immediately renamed it the Anglo Australian Brewery. Brewing stopped in 1890, and Miller & Mason sold the equipment and moved out of the premises.

Marks & Murphy (George Street)	1882–85
Sydney Brewery (Harris Street)	
Sam Marks	1885–86
W. Jones & Co.	1886–87
Red Heart Brewery	
John Derwin	1887–88
Anglo Australian Brewery	
Miller & Mason	1888–90

An Albion Brewery letterhead, c. 1845. The brewery had been taken over by Gavin Ralston & Co. in 1842. Nine years later the brewery closed, and was used as a soap and candle factory before being destroyed by fire in the 1860s. In the years that followed, John and James Toohey built a new brewery on the site, and named it the Standard.

The Red Heart Brewery was operated by John Derwin during 1887 and 1888. Previously called the Sydney Brewery, it later became the Anglo Australian Brewery.

> ## 'IT'S TRUE, YOUR HONOUR'
>
> *Thirty-nine Pints of Beer Have No Apparent Effect*
> That her husband, James McDonald, could drink 39 pints of beer without its having any effect on him, was a statement made by Lily McDonald in the Newtown [Sydney] Police Court on 14th February, 1917.
> *Australian Brewers' Journal*, February 1917

Annandale Brewery 1884–89
16 Collins Street, Annandale (between Nelson & Trafalgar Streets)

Shortly after starting the brewery William Bogie formed a partnership with a Mr Liardet. The union was brief, and Bogie was on his own again for several years. Later he took on the position of brewer at Marshall's Paddington Brewery.

Australasian Breweries Ltd 1933–34
66 Castlereagh Street, Redfern

Australian Brewery (Bourke Street)
See Australian Brewery & Wine & Spirit Co. Ltd.

Australian Brewery (George Street) 1803–c. 1856
George Street

When Daniel Cooper began his Australian Brewery in 1803, he did not know that his was the third brewery to commence in Australia. Brewers before him were James Squire in 1793, and John Boston in 1795.

William Hutchinson and Samuel Terry joined Daniel Cooper as partners for a while, but left in the early 1820s. In the early days of the colony money in the form of coinage was in short supply, and the barter system of trading was common practice. Cooper advertised in the 25 August 1824 edition of the *Australian*:

> payment will be taken in colonial property or produce, at the market price of the day including land, houses, grain, cattle, sheep, horses, pigs, pork, poultry, eggs, cheese, butter, lard, tallow, wool, hides, leather, shoes, soap, candles, tobacco, hemp, flour, wattlebark, salt, kangaroo skins, seal skins, fish oil, sawn timber, cedar logs, shingles, laths, wood, fuel or coal.

Cooper's brewery must have looked like a general store. Whether or not his finances benefited from all this bartering, his career as a brewer finished in January 1825.

When James Wright took over the Australian Brewery in 1826, he extended the buildings to include stores for barley, sugar and hops, a fermenting room, cooling store and a 50-foot-high kiln stack. The brewery complex was situated between Bathurst and Liverpool Streets, and took up a large frontage in George Street. Horsedrawn drays would plod through the settled districts around Sydney supplying ale and porter, and the brewery even delivered as far as Windsor and Pitt Town, and the lower parts of the Hawkesbury.

The Australian Brewery was closed after it was purchased by Tooth & Co. about 1856.

Australian Brewery & Wine & Spirit Co. Ltd 1883–1906
4 Bourke Street, Waterloo

Both John and Samuel Cornwell had worked for the large Sydney brewery, Tooth & Co., and, having decided to start out on their own, they imported a complete brewing plant from England and traded as the Australian Brewery. Sam was the brewer and managing director.

The Castlemaine Brewing Co. had closed its brewery in Hay Street, Sydney, in 1890, but maintained a brewing interest in Sydney by amalgamating with the Australian Brewery in May 1890. The new company, the Australian Brewery & Wine & Spirit Co. Ltd, was declared bankrupt eight years later. After reconstruction, and improvements to the equipment, the business stabilised, and good sales were obtained along the Northern Rivers districts.

Misdemeanours were treated harshly by the law in those days. Two of the brewery workmen were arrested in April 1900, and charged with stealing a keg of beer. The magistrate fined each of the accused £10 (a considerable sum at that time) or two months' hard labour.

The business went into liquidation for the second time in 1906, and the premises were subsequently sold to the Sydney Municipal Council and used as a fruit and vegetable market.

Bathurst Street Brewery 1858–61
107 Bathurst Street

The owner and operator of the brewery was Patrick McGuigan.

Bennett's Brewery c. 1830–c. 1835
Goulburn Street

Another early Sydney brewer was Francis Bennett, who, as did so many others, brewed for only a few years.

Boston, John 1795–96
O'Connell Street

John Boston and his partner, James Ellis, were Australia's second brewers. They were free settlers, and were brewing and selling beer as early as September 1795 (James Squire had started brewing two years earlier). Boston's background was ideally suited to successful settlement in the new colony of New South Wales. In his letter of application to migrate to Australia, dated 5 December 1793, Boston wrote:

I was brought up as a surgeon and apothecary, but have never since followed that profession ... have a knowledge of brewing, distilling, sugar making, vinegar making, soap making etc., ... I likewise have a theoretical and some practical knowledge of agriculture.

John Boston arrived in Sydney with his wife and two children on 25 October 1794. He and his partners, James Ellis and Thomas Fyshe Palmer (a well-connected, well-off clergyman), in the following year erected a small brewery in the vicinity of the present Government House. The partners were men of considerable enterprise and, in addition to brewing beer, they made and sold vinegar, salt and soap, and were involved in farming, sealing and shipbuilding.

Boston's beer was made from Indian corn, properly malted and bittered with the leaves and stalks of the love apple (the tomato) or the cape gooseberry — there were no hops available at that time. The beer sold for 1s 6d a bottle, undercutting the price of a bottle of London porter by sixpence.

The brewing venture was shortlived, most probably due to the restrictive and oppressive monopoly of the military officers who had control of the purchase of all liquor from all ships that came to the harbour. Local brewing would have an adverse effect on the huge profits made by the military, and Boston and Ellis were refused a grant and permission to employ servants. This abuse of power by the military and their grip on the liquor trade was soon to change, but at the time, for Boston and Ellis, there were other more attractive business opportunities for them to follow without such restrictions.

In order to establish a time when Boston first started brewing, credence can be given to a letter from the Reverend T. F. Palmer to the Reverend T. Lindsey of Essex Street Chapel. The letter, dated 15 September 1795, deals at length with the treatment meted out to Palmer by Captain Campbell of the *Surprize*. Palmer talks about how Boston and Ellis insisted on the right of British subjects to carry on any trade, and the oppression they suffered:

had it not been for the courageous and active friendship of James Ellis and Mr. Boston, the young man I wrote to you about, and his wife. They were threatened with irons ... They [Boston and Ellis] manufacture beer, salt, soap etc. for sale ...

John Boston took up pigfarming for a while, and then began trading in the South Pacific, sailing his own ship. His last voyage was to Tonga, in 1804, where he was killed and apparently eaten by cannibals, a terrible and tragic end to one of the very few men who pioneered the Australian brewing industry in the late eighteenth century.

Brickfield Hill Brewery
See Rushton's Brewery.

British Breweries Pty Ltd 1935–c. 1951
610 Parramatta Road, Petersham

When the brewery officially opened in September 1935, it traded as British Breweries Ltd. In December 1937 the brewery licence was transferred to Robert William Miller, chairman of directors of the company, and the business then traded as British Breweries Pty Ltd. During the early 1950s the name was changed to Miller's Brewery Pty Ltd.

See also Miller's Brewery Pty Ltd.

Brookvale Brewing Co. Pty Ltd 1952–56
Mitchell Road, Brookvale

The company started brewing in January 1952, and entered into an arrangement with the Union of Registered Workers' Clubs to supply beer to member clubs. In addition, the brewery supplied licensed golf and social clubs, and sold direct to consumers in the Brookvale area. It was the brewery's policy not to cater to the hotel trade.

According to a contemporary *Sydney Morning Herald* report, the Brookvale Brewery produced beer 'of a type new to Sydney, brewed on [sic] a continental recipe, using glucose instead of sugar'.

Later, the brewery (which was often called the Union Brewery) changed over to the production of normal beer, but this didn't help the company's fortunes, and the last brew was on 10 July 1956.

British Breweries Pty Ltd started in 1935. The company changed its name to Miller's Brewery about 1951, and was subsequently taken over by Toohey's.

During its short life the Brookvale Brewing Co. was frequently called the Union Brewery; it marketed pilsener, ale and beer under the Union brand.

During Australia's Bicentennial year, 1988, the Castlemaine Brewery in Brisbane released this John Boston Special Lager, suggesting on the label that Boston was the first man to brew beer in Australia in 1796. John Boston and his partner, James Ellis, were actually brewing and selling beer as early as September 1795. Boston, however, was Australia's second commercial brewer — the first was James Squire, who began brewing in 1793.

Burton Brewery 1822–c. 1835
George Street, Parramatta

Enterprising shipowner and merchant J. H. Grose started brewing at Parramatta in 1822, a time when Parramatta was considered a country township. The Burton Brewery put out a powerful brew, as described in the *Sydney Gazette*:

> This beverage possessed such strength that many who drank of it, upon the cask being tapped at both ends, soon betrayed that reason was dethroned and madness and folly reigned instead.

J. H. Grose ran the business until 1833, when the brewery was taken over by James and William Burns. As well as running the brewery, the Burns brothers had a wine-and-spirit business, a general store and a soap and candle factory. Before the brewery closed, ownership had been transferred to Francis Lowe.

Byrne's Brewery c. 1815–23
Near cnr Pitt & King Streets

Michael Byrne started brewing some time between 1815 and 1820. His brewery was at the back of a large block of land that he owned. Byrne later built an inn on the land, and christened it the Three Legs O' Man.

Caledonian Brewery 1832–34
Market Street, near the corner of George Street

The premises of the Caledonian Brewery had been Natty's Brewery until January 1826, when Nathaniel Lawrence, the owner, 'died by the visitation of God'.

William Watt refitted the place in 1832, and started it up as the Caledonian Brewery. At the same time he ran a ginger-beer factory in Clarence Street. John Tooth, later of Tooth Brewery fame, held a bill of sale over the Caledonian Brewery property. William Watt died in 1834, and the premises ceased to be used as a brewery.

Carrington Brewery
See American & German Lager Beer Brewing Co. Ltd.

A STIFF PENALTY

On 24th ult., Edward Chapman, 54, was charged at the Central Police Court, Sydney, with selling liquor without having a licence to do so. The evidence was that a probationary constable called at Chapman's residence at 28 Charles Street, city, at midnight on the previous day. The accused sold the constable four bottles of ale and a flask of whisky for which three shillings was charged. Chapman had been convicted on similar charges on two previous occasions. The magistrate inflicted a fine of £100 or nine months' imprisonment with hard labour.

Australian Brewers' Journal, September 1914

Castlemaine Brewing Co., Sydney 1869–90
69 Hay Street

The Castlemaine brewing empire had its beginning in 1858 in the Victorian country town of Castlemaine, with Nicholas Fitzgerald as the founder. Progressively, other Castlemaine breweries were established in Sydney, Melbourne, Newcastle, Brisbane and Perth.

Robert Prendergast was a close associate of the Fitzgerald brothers, having managed their Castlemaine Brewery in Victoria. He had also been a partner with Nicholas Fitzgerald in a brewery at Newbridge, also in Victoria.

In 1869, in partnership with Nicholas Fitzgerald, Robert Prendergast set up the first branch brewery outside Castlemaine. Originally called the Castlemaine Brewing & Malting Co. in 1881, it became the Castlemaine Brewing, Malting & Wines & Spirits Co. Ltd in 1884. The brewery closed in 1890, but the company continued to maintain a brewing interest in Sydney by amalgamating with the Australian Brewery, Bourke Street, Waterloo, in 1890 to form the Australian Brewery & Wine & Spirit Co. Ltd.

Centennial Brewery 1888–1911
1 Short Street, Leichhardt

The owners of the business chose the appropriate name, Centennial Brewery, since the opening of the brewery was 100 years after the founding of Australia in 1788. There were too many changes in the running of the business for the brewery to achieve any degree of success, as the following summary indicates.

Centennial Brewery

George Rodwell	1888–89
Samuel Turrell	1889–90
Turrell & King	1890–91
Louis King & Co.	1891–c. 1895
William Harrison	c. 1895–1904

Sydney Co-operative Brewing Co. Ltd

	1904–8, closed
John Woods & Richard Gant	1909, closed

Leichhardt Brewery

James Walker & Co.	1910, closed
Marshall's Co-operative Breweries Ltd	1910–11

When the Sydney Co-operative was formed in 1904, arrangements were made for the shareholders to obtain beer at reduced prices. The company, desperate to increase business, dropped the price of barrelled beer by 15 per cent. This gave a short-term surge in sales, but fierce competition forced the company into liquidation. John Woods and Richard Gant reopened the brewery late in 1909, but soon had it on the market again as a going concern, complete with a bottling plant and refrigerator. James Walker took over the following year, changed the name to the Leichhardt Brewery and became bankrupt later that year.

Marshall's Co-operative Breweries Ltd relocated their brewery to the Leichhardt Brewery site in 1910, and their first brew was tapped in June of that year. Brewing ceased a year later, and Tooth & Co. Ltd took over the premises.

City Brewery c. 1900
Turner & Co.

Clarence Street Brewery 1809–c. 1847
55 Upper Pitt's Row (now Pitt Street south of King Street)/
8 Clarence Street

The desire to foster the brewing industry in the rapidly growing community of Sydney, led Governor Macquarie to grant a number of brewing licences during his term of office. One of the fortunate to receive a licence was Enoch Kinsela, previously the manager of the government saltworks at Rose Bay. By December 1808 he was ready to start brewing.

He advertised in the *Sydney Gazette* of 29 January 1809:

> Strong Beer Brewery — E. Kinsela.
> The public can be supplied at his brewery with Strong Beer at two shillings per gallon, Table do., one shilling and sixpence, do. for ready money only.

After eighteen months Kinsela shifted to larger premises in Castlereagh Street. With continuing success, he then built a new brewery in Clarence Street, which was completed in March 1813. The public was informed that good beer could be supplied regularly, 'warranted to keep sound for six months, perfectly clear, fine and free from any nauseous flavour'. True to his word, Kinsela's beer was good. It attracted a large country following, and on market days country carts would pull into the brewery yard to load up supplies of bottled or keg beer.

The brewery was bought in 1831 by William Evisson, a bottler of 'superior ale', which he had been buying in bulk from the Australian Brewery in George Street. At the Clarence Street Brewery Evisson sold his own beer at extremely low prices to anyone who paid cash. He worked the brewery himself until his death in 1830, and the business was continued for a few more years on behalf of his heirs.

E. J. & A. Blaxland bought the brewery, and continued until its closure, about 1847.

Strong Beer Brewery
Enoch Kinsela (Pitt Street)	1809–11
Enoch Kinsela (Castlereagh Street)	1811–13

Clarence Street Brewery
Enoch Kinsela	1813–31
William Evisson	1831–c. 1838
E. J. & A. Blaxland	c. 1838–c. 1847

Clarkson's Brewery 1810–32
Cnr Hunter & Elizabeth Streets

Directly opposite Thomas Rushton's Brewery in Hunter Street, Thomas Clarkson, 'a brewer of the old school', ran a substantial hostelry.

Clarkson began making his own beer in 1810, and as a retailer of his own product he did his best to encourage the drinking of colonial beer in preference to imported beer. His brewery was housed in a group of buildings standing some distance back from the roadway so that carts would have room to move about. There was a granary, malt store and cooperage, and the brewhouse was fitted out with coppers and coolers. A large sign, 'Clarkson's Brewery', was proudly displayed over the gateway so that people knew what went on inside the premises.

Governor Macquarie, and later Governor Brisbane, encouraged Clarkson in his brewing endeavour, and both gave him their patronage. Clarkson died at the Sydney General Hospital on 26 May 1832, and his widow, Catherine, assisted by Thomas Rowley, carried on the business for several more months. The following year Clarkson's Brewery became known as the Imperial Brewery when the firm of J. B. Smithers & Co. bought the property.

See also Imperial Brewery.

Colonial Brewery
See Larkin's Brewery.

Constitution Brewery 1812–34
Thomas Collicott chose 'The Rocks' area of Sydney for the location of his brewery, and after setting up in 1812 he supplied nearby publicans with beer at moderate prices. He also owned a hotel, which he sold in order to open a larger brewery in Pitt Street.

In 1828 Collicott shifted again to Castlereagh Street, where he set up his new Constitution Brewery. He believed that the government should encourage the brewing of beer from barley and hops, to the exclusion of sugar, in order to benefit the farming industry. His efforts, and interest in the brewing trade generally, contributed much to the improvement and growth of a very young Australian brewing industry.

Continental Brewery
See Eagle Brewery.

Darling Brewery
See Steam Engine Brewery; Toohey's Ltd.

Darlinghurst Brewery c. 1845
R. Thompson & Co.

Eagle Brewery 1887–98
Shepherd Street, Marrickville

During the 1880s more and more breweries started up all over Australia, particularly in the eastern states. The economy was booming and anyone with an ounce of

> ### TRANSPORT OF THE FUTURE
>
> We hear that Tooth's Brewery, Sydney, have placed an order with the Sydney agents of Fiat's for £10,000 worth of Fiat motor lorries. The head of the Sydney firm of representatives of these great cars will leave for Turin and London at an early date to see the order properly executed.
>
> *Australian Brewers' Journal*, May 1912

brewing experience was eager to start his own brewery and make a fortune. Of those who did start their own brewery, very few stayed in the business for more than a few years, mainly because of the difficulty in brewing top-quality beer consistently, and the increasing competition from the large city breweries. The brief history of the Eagle Brewery is a typical example.

John Stevenson established the Eagle in 1887, and the following year, took on two partners — Tyler and Lewis — trading as James E. Tyler & Co. Thompson & Bishop took over the business in 1889, then Welwood Thompson continued on his own later that year.

Alfred Pond (who previously had set up Ponds Brewery in Newtown) bought the brewery in 1890, and, compared to the previous owners, he did quite well. He changed the name to the Continental Brewery, and kept brewing for eight years.

Edinburgh Brewery 1884–93
Cnr Emma & Bungay Streets, Leichhardt

After brewing for seven years, George Vincent, the senior partner of Vincent, McDonald & Co., advertised that he wished to retire and offered to sell his interest in the Edinburgh Brewery. Thomas Vincent, presumably a relative of George, joined McDonald, and they kept the brewery going for two more years.

Emu Brewery
See Parramatta Brewery, Macquarie Street, Parramatta.

English Ale Brewery 1855–66
157 Bourke Street/6 Bank Street

The name, English Ale Brewery, was rather odd for an Australian brewery, but Colman R. Springett was quite satisfied with the name, since many Sydney residents of the time preferred English ale to the questionable local brews. Even though his was a local brew, the name of his brewery obviously contented those who bought his beer. The business later shifted from Bourke Street to Bank Street.

Evestaff, William 1809–11
Pitt Street

William Evestaff's property, 'in a most desirable part of Pitt Street', consisted of a two-storey brick dwelling and outbuildings including a capital malt-kiln, malt-house, brewery, with a spacious copper fixed, and all utensils complete, together with a granary capable of containing 1000 bushels of grain, [and] a capital covered well.

By 1811 Evestaff had left the colony.

Federal Brewery 1900–1
Mansfield Street, Balmain

Henry Arnold & Co.

John C. Fletcher & Co. 1881–89
Cnr Bailey Street & Enmore Road, Newtown

Gas Light Brewery c. 1826–29
Pitt Street

The brewery advertised in the *Sydney Gazette* of 29 July 1826: 'Gas Light Brewery, T. Wilson, Best Colonial Ale at Three Pounds Five Shillings per Hogshead'.

Goerin's Brewery c. 1830–c. 1835
Kent Street

Harry Goerin was the proprietor.

Government Brewery
See Parramatta Brewery (George & O'Connell Streets).

Imperial Brewery 1833–c. 1841
Cnr Hunter & Elizabeth Streets

Toward the end of 1833 John Smithers took over the premises formerly known as Clarkson's Brewery. The old brewery signboard over the gateway was taken down and another one was put up, proudly displaying the new name, Imperial Brewery.

Although Smithers & Co. were warehousemen, they were determined to produce and market good beer. Of course, everyone who started a brewery had the same idea, but John Smithers engaged a competent brewer of many years' experience, both in England and the colonies.

Circulars were sent out on 30 November 1833 informing the public of their intentions: 'Having engaged a thoroughly efficient brewer, we flatter ourselves that we will be enabled to offer to the public of Australia a refreshing and wholesome drink'. The circular message offered advice barely understandable to the average reader of the day:

> Under the impression that an improvement in the manufacture of beer in the colony will doubtless tend to check the immoderate use of ardent spirits which is said to be the result of the uninviting quality of the more simple beverages it will be our study as it will be our interest to endeavour to effect that important object.

During the next twelve months, Smithers's travellers brought in many orders from the town and country — business was good. Smithers sold the brewery in November 1834 to John Matthewman, an

English and colonial brewer of good repute. A further sale took place in 1840, the new owner being Richard Crampton.

Johnson & Sands Brewery   1870–c. 1872
4 Hancock Lane, off George Street

Jon's Breweries Ltd
See Kops Brewery Ltd.

Kent Brewery
See Tooth & Co. Ltd.

Kissing Point Brewery
See James Squire.

Kops Brewery (Australia) Ltd   1910–16
Roberts Street, Rozelle

The company formed as Kops (Australia) Ltd was for the purpose of acquiring the businesses of Jons Breweries Ltd in Balmain, and C. F. Johnson, ginger-beer manufacturer of Erskinville.

The new company obtained the sole rights for Australia for brewing and bottling the famous English beverage, Kops Ale. It is doubtful if any alcoholic beers were produced by the company, which was wound up in 1916.

Larkin's Colonial Brewery   1804
45 Chapel Row (now Castlereagh Street)

The *Sydney Gazette* of 23 December 1804, carried an advertisement advising the small Sydney community that Larkin's Colonial Brewery could supply 'Ales — Pale, Brown and Amber; Twopenny and London Porter prepared after the system of the British Breweries'.

Patrick Larkin opened his brewery at a time when hops and barley were scarce in the colony, and it is difficult to imagine how Larkin could have made any sort of beer as being 'prepared after the system of the British breweries'. There is no further evidence of his brewing activity subsequent to his first hopeful invitation in the *Sydney Gazette*.

Leichhardt Brewery
See Centennial Brewery.

Lion Brewery   1889–90
553 King Street, Newtown

Christopher Bellett was the proprietor.

Marshall's Co-operative Brewery Ltd
See Marshall's Paddington Brewery Ltd.

Marshall's Paddington Brewery Ltd   c. 1857–1911
Cnr Oxford Street & Dowling Street, Paddington/ Short Street, Leichhardt

The Yorkshireman Joseph Marshall landed in South Australia in 1840. He became involved in the distilling business for a few years, then moved to Sydney and set up in business as a chemist. He experimented in making his own beer, a hobby that ultimately led to him becoming one of the foremost brewers in New South Wales.

At the outset Marshall made only sufficient beer for his private use, but his home brew soon became well known and sought after. He purchased land in Paddington, and built a house for himself and his family. He added a small brewery, and supplied beer to his friends and a few families.

Joseph Marshall's beermaking hobby was so successful that he was soon selling his beer to hotels and taverns.

For more than fifty years Marshall's Brewery was one the best-known breweries in Sydney. Founded in 1857, it was a vast complex of buildings, including the brewery, granary, cellars, malthouse and stables. The company became Marshall's Co-operative Breweries Ltd in 1904.

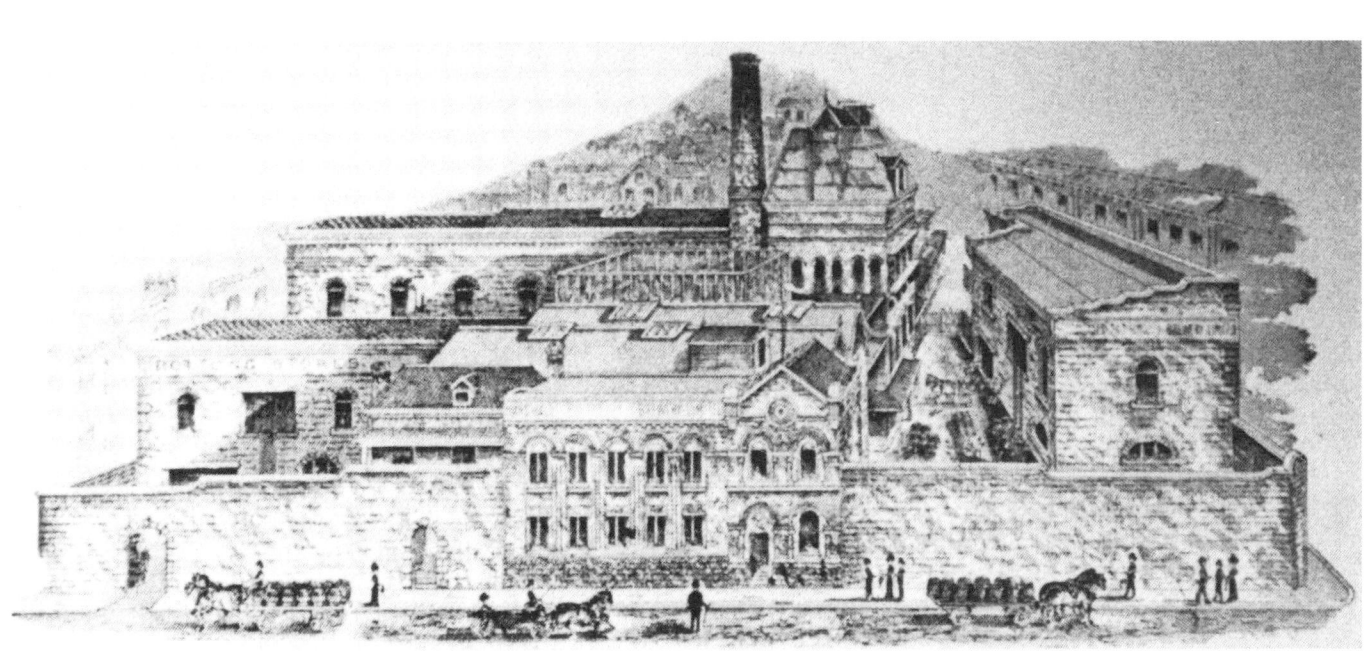

His business rapidly expanded mainly because of the excellent quality of his beer, and a number of prizes were awarded at various agricultural shows for Marshall's draught and bottled ales and porter, including first prize at the Intercolonial Exhibition of 1876.

When Joseph Marshall Snr died in 1880, his brewery was one of the largest in Sydney. The sons, Joseph and James, kept the business going as a private concern until July 1888 when Marshall's Paddington Brewery Ltd was floated.

Three years later James Marshall retired, and on 9 February 1904 the business was restructured as Marshall's Co-operative Brewery Ltd. In 1909 an offer was accepted to buy the property on which the brewery was situated, and the brewery's operations were transferred in 1910 to premises in Short Street, Leichhardt (previously those of the Sydney Co-operative Brewing Co. Ltd and, before that, of the Centennial Brewery). Brewing commenced at the new location in June 1910, but the brewery was purchased by Tooth & Co. Ltd and closed the following year, ending a long history of fifty-four years when it had been one of the best-known breweries in New South Wales.

Metropolitan Brewery   c. 1850–98
119 Castlereagh Street (between Moore & Hunter Streets)/35 Castlereagh Street

Although there were several changes in ownership and two locations, the name Metropolitan Brewery did not change during its life of forty-eight years. The business was established about 1850 by William Henfrey. Much later, in 1869, John T. Toohey became a partner for three years or so.

Henfrey shifted to premises in Castlereagh Street about 1880, and Edmund O'Farrell joined the firm. Henfrey had been in the business for thirty-five years when he finally sold out to O'Farrell and A. T. Herald in 1885. Three years later O'Farrell and H. F. Marr were recorded as running the Metropolitan Brewery, but they still traded as Henfrey & Co. Edmund O'Farrell was the sole proprietor when the brewery closed in 1898.

The 1899 issue of the *Australian Cordial Maker and Brewer* revealed some interesting history of the earlier brewery premises:

> the whole of the walls were of extraordinary thickness; three feet being the thickness of those in the basement. The old walls are composed of solid blocks of stone and were built by convict labour at a very early date. The front portion of the basement is divided into compartments, each one being slightly oblong and comparatively small; these, I have been informed, were used as prison cells for convicts in early days.

Miller's Brewery Pty Ltd   c. 1951–75
610 Parramatta Road, Petersham

Formerly British Breweries Ltd, the company assumed the name of the founding chairman of directors, Robert W. Miller, to become Miller's Brewery Pty Ltd, probably in 1951. The new company rapidly expanded as a highly successful business, in spite of the dominance of the two large Sydney breweries, Tooths and Tooheys. Miller's Brewery owned or had interests in many hotels, which assisted their marketing; and patrons, finding the beer amply satisfying, continued their patronage.

Toohey's Ltd acquired Miller's Brewery in April 1967, and continued to run the brewery until 1975.

Today the old brewery building still stands, tall and stately, high on a hill in Parramatta Road, a reminder to many who pass by of the period when an independent brewery sought to challenge the might of Sydney's two powerful breweries.

Mountain Brewing Co. Ltd   1884–c. 1890
The brewery was established in 1884, and became the Mountain Brewing Co. Ltd in 1890.

Natty's Brewery   1810–26
34 Pitt Street/Market Street

The public house called the 'Pine Apple' was owned by Nathaniel Lawrence, who had arrived in New South Wales in 1806. Nat also ran a bakery. Not content with merely selling beer across the counter of his pub, he decided to make his own beer and started brewing in 1810.

The brewery, which became known as Natty's, was a weatherboard, brick-nogged building, which housed a copper boiler with a capacity of 70 gallons. Attached to the brewery was the bakehouse, a granary, stables, and a deep well, conveniently located alongside. Nat Lawrence's main contribution to the wellbeing of his fellow-citizens, apart from his bread, was the excellent quality of his ale, which he sold more cheaply than any other brewery.

During the 1820s Nat shifted his brewing operation to Market Street, but unfortunately he lived only a short time after the move. On 4 January 1826 he attended a convivial gathering, returned home and went to bed, only to be found dead the next morning. The Coroner's jury gave a verdict of 'died by the visitation of God'. A large crowd of friends followed him to his grave in the Strawberry Hills cemetery, near the present site of the Central Railway Station.

Nelson Brewery   1820–29
29 Pitt Street, between Spring & Hunter Streets

The founder of the Nelson Brewery, T. W. Middleton, issued circular letters to his customers, thanking them for their business, and pointing out with a touch of pride that thanks were due to him anyway because of the wholesome quality of his beer.

During 1822 and 1823 Middleton issued more circulars, again thanking his customers, and conveying the glad tidings that he had received a large consignment of fine Kentish hops and could continue to sell his beer at the usual price of 1s 6d per gallon. This sending out of letters grew to be a habit. He did it again in 1824, 1825 and

1826, combining his thanks with an appeal to those of his customers who may have been short of currency that 'Salt, pork or beef, wheat and maize etc., will be received at marketable rates in payment for the same [beer]'.

The Nelson Brewery went out of business in 1829, the closing brought about by the demolition of buildings and property improvements in the vicinity.

New South Wales Lager Bier Brewing Co. Ltd 1896–98
South Dowling Street, Redfern

The company was registered in September 1896 with a capital of £100,000. In December that year 2 acres of land were purchased at Redfern. According to one journalist, the brewery, when completed, 'started with a flourish and was one of the finest, if not the finest in the colony'. It was fitted out specially for the production of lager beer, but brewing lasted for less than two years. During that time a reasonable South Pacific Island trade had been established in New Guinea, New Caledonia and Fiji.

The magnificent brewery, with its new equipment, closed in 1898 and remained idle for two years. It was reported that the problem was excessive capital expenditure and insufficient working capital. Moreover, the drinking population still preferred the traditional ale compared to the new lager beer.

In June 1900 Edmund Resch purchased the property and all the equipment for £16,000. This was about a quarter of the cost, and well below the amount of the mortgage. Resch centralised his brewing business at this new location after closing his Waverley Brewery, which he had bought only three years earlier. He renamed the New South Wales Lager Bier Co., the Waverley Brewery.

See also Waverley Brewery, South Dowling Street, Redfern.

New York Brewery 1887–1905
22 King Street (cnr Fitzroy Street), Newtown

After selling his Sydney Brewery in Harris Street, Samuel Marks started business again as the New York Brewery in the inner Sydney suburb of Newtown. Marks had been in the brewing business in New York, for fifteen years, and his choice of name was a reminder of his time in that city.

The main products of the New York Brewery were, in contradiction to the brewery's name, English-style ales, porter and stout that were sold in quart bottles for 6s per dozen. Kegs containing 3 gallons and 5 gallons were sold for 1s 6d a gallon, and 1s 4d if a 10-gallon keg was ordered. Brewing ceased in 1905, and the business was wound up the following year.

Nicholls Tasmanian Dandelion Ale Co. 1889–1915
8 George Street, West Camperdown/Trafalgar Street, Annandale

Arthur Howe was the owner of the brewery when it opened for business in 1889. The brewery closed the following year; five years later it was reopened by George Nicholls.

When Nicholls shifted the brewery to Annandale in 1907, he leased it to A. Cross & Co. The business continued to operate as Nicholls & Co., and in 1913 this was changed to Nicholls Tasmanian Dandelion Ale Co.

Orient Brewery
See Surrey Brewery.

Paddington Brewery
See Marshall's Paddington Brewery Ltd.

Parramatta Brewery (George & O'Connell Streets) 1804–10
Cnr George & O'Connell Streets, Parramatta

The arrival, in 1800, of Governor King in New South Wales marked the beginning of positive action to stop the monopoly of the liquor trade. By 1801 King had taken steps to stop all future imports of spirits into Australia, anticipating that the production of beer in the colony would reduce the craving and excessive use of spirits among all classes in the community. He had requested the English authorities to send out some hop plants, arguing that the establishment of colonial brewing would not only stop the terrible effects of overindulgence of spirits, but would also establish and encourage three new industries, the growing of hops and barley, and brewing of beer.

On 29 August 1802 Lord Hobart sent a despatch to Governor King, agreeing with King's actions to outlaw spirits and commence local brewing, at the same time advising that he was sending out 10 tons of porter, six bags of hops, and two complete sets of brewing utensils. The shipment included 1818 lbs of the best-quality hops. By the first quarter of 1804 a brewery had been constructed, the first and only government brewery to be established in Australia. It stood on the north-east corner of George and O'Connell Streets, Parramatta, a site later occupied by the maternity wing of the Parramatta District Hospital.

At the time the brewery was built the district was known as Rose Hill, and Governor Phillip had supervised the laying out of the town as early as 1790. The area had good soil, far better for crop cultivation than the region around Sydney Cove.

Experienced brewer Thomas Rushton was brought from Van Diemen's Land to run the brewery, and on 15 September 1804 the beer began to flow. The price was 1s 4d per gallon to licensed persons, on the condition that the resale price would be no more than 6d per full quart, payment to be made in wheat, barley, hops, casks or iron hoops. At the end of three months 4247 gallons of beer had been produced.

For all of Governor King's enthusiasm and high hopes, the enterprise from which he had expected so much and laboured so diligently to establish was destined to early failure. The first twelve months ended in financial disaster for a number of reasons: the govern-

The New South Lager Bier Brewing Co. Ltd operated from 1896 to 1898, and was the forerunner of Resch's Waverley Brewery.

ment employees were each allowed 5 gallons of beer a week; there were far too many employees, many of them unreliable and prone to stealing; barley was scarce; and supervision and management were inadequate.

Governor King decided at the end of 1805 that the Government Brewery had to close.

For several months the brewery lay idle, a great misfortune, not only for the government but also for the general public, many of whom had developed a preference for the beer. On 17 February 1806 the brewery was leased to brewer Thomas Rushton to brew on his own account, but there were qualifications. He had to supply 'table beer' for 6d per gallon, and 'strong beer' for 1s. The method of rental payment was unique — it was paid for in beer. Each month Rushton supplied 200 gallons of beer to the government for the use of prisoners of the Crown employed on public works.

Thomas Rushton decided not to renew the lease, and left Parramatta to start his own brewery at Brickfield Hill in Sydney. The premises at Parramatta remained idle, and were offered at auction, for rent, in June 1809, and again on 30 June 1810, but the brewery never reopened.

Parramatta Brewery
(Macquarie Street) 1830–1910
Macquarie Street, Parramatta

The brewery was owned by Thomas Bedding, and adjoined the Rose Hill Cottage. The spacious and beautiful verandah-style cottage was almost hemmed in by cellars, storehouses, ovens and fermenting rooms. There was also a granary, huge water tanks, and the brewery building had three tall chimneys. There was still room, however, for a fine garden of fruit and other trees.

When Thomas Bedding died in 1839, Pat Hayes took over the property, called it the Emu Brewery, and employed an English brewer, James Vallack. In June 1845 Hayes was caught, redhanded, producing illicit spirit. Penalties were harsh, and Hayes was fined £110, and his brewing equipment was confiscated. That was the finish of the Emu Brewery, leaving James Vallack without a job.

Fortune favoured Vallack when his well-to-do father-in-law set him up in business back at the old Emu Brewery. Now the proud owner, Vallack changed the name to the Parramatta Brewery, although there were frequent references to the Rose Hill Brewery. James Vallack died in 1883, having been at the brewery for most of forty-four years. His daughter, Emily, was the sole beneficiary, and she sold the property to the partnership of A. H. Emanuel & S. R. Walford. They built a new brewery on the site, which occupied a block in Macquarie Street (twenty years earlier the partners had been the owners of the Goulburn Brewery).

A new partnership of Oscar Burrows and Alfred Emanuel took over the brewery from 1887 to 1902, but the business still traded as Vallack & Co. Beer sales began to dwindle, and on 21 July 1902 the Parramatta Brewery was advertised for sale. Brewing ended about 1910, and the premises were used as a linseed oil factory. All traces of the brewery disappeared when the buildings were totally destroyed by fire in 1914.

Rose Hill Brewery
Thomas Bedding   1830–39

Emu Brewery
Pat Hayes   1839–45

Parramatta Brewery
James Vallack   1845–83
Emanuel & Walford   1883–87
Burrows & Emanuel   1887–1910

Ponds Brewery 1888–90
Cnr King & Maria Streets, Newtown

Alfred Pond ran a modest brewery at Newtown for a year or two, and then closed it when he took over the Eagle Brewery at Marrickville.

Pyrmont Brewery Co. Ltd 1880–87
Cnr Union & Murray Streets, Pyrmont

During the seven years of the company's existence the brewery operators were:

W. H. Felmingham	1880
J. G. H. Swan & Co.	1881–84
Edwards & Co.	1884
Henry Edmeades	1884–85
Edward Wehlow	1886–87

The Pyrmont Brewery Co. Ltd was formed in 1886, six years after the brewery started. It was put up for sale, in full working order, on 1 August 1887, but there were no buyers.

Red Heart Brewery
See Anglo Australian Brewery.

Resch's Brewery
See Waverley Brewery (Redfern).

Rose Hill Brewery
See Parramatta Brewery (Macquarie Street).

Rushton's Brewery 1808–26
Brickfield Hill (near Bathurst Street)/cnr Bell Row (now Hunter Street) & Elizabeth Street

When the government of New South Wales started a brewery at Parramatta in 1804, Thomas Rushton was brought from Tasmania to take charge of the brewing. The government venture failed, and in 1806 Rushton leased the brewery for a period of two years. He then left to start his own brewery.

In 1808 Rushton began brewing at Brickfield Hill. James Wilshire had financed the building of the brewery and the purchase of the equipment, all of which he leased to Rushton.

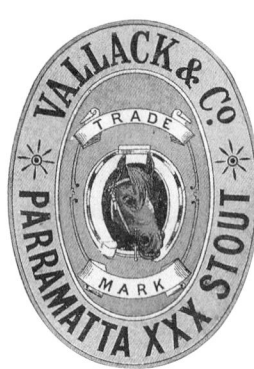

Originally the Rose Hill Brewery when it commenced in 1830, it later became the Emu Brewery, and finally the Parramatta Brewery. Most breweries of the nineteenth century were shortlived, but the Parramatta operated for an amazing eighty years. For more than half a century it traded as Vallack & Co.

The *Sydney Gazette and New South Wales Advertiser* of 16 April 1809 carried an advertisement:

> To be let, situated near the Brickfields, Sydney, a brew-house, malt-house and malt-kiln and other brewing utensils belonging to James Wilshire but now in the occupation of Thomas Rushton. N.B. Any person wishing to take the same who may not be conversant in malting and brewing, the proprietor has no objection to give such needful instructions as if pursued, cannot fail of making good beer.

Rushton left the brewery, and took up farming and pastoral interests. About 1810 he built a larger brewery in a more central location at the corner of Bell Row and Elizabeth Street; most of the equipment was from his earlier brewery. Rushton amassed a fortune, but frittered it away; he died in 1822 at the age of seventy-eight.

For some years the business was carried on by Mrs Elizabeth Smith and Charles Rushton (one of his sons). During November 1826 there was a sale of brewing equipment on account of Charles Rushton, 12 Hunter Street, so ending Rushton's Brickfield Hill Brewery.

Squire, James   1793–c. 1830

James Squire arrived at Sydney in 1788 with the First Fleet, his journey being decided upon by those who did not consider his personal wishes in the matter.

Dr David Hughes, in 'Australia's First Brewer' (*Journal of the Royal Historical Society*, December 1996, vol. 82), states that on 29 December 1820 James Squire gave oral evidence to the Bigge Inquiry into New South Wales and Van Diemen's Land that he had made some beer 'from some hops that I got from the *Daedalus*. I also brewed for General Grose & Col. Paterson for their own consumption, from English malt'. The *Daedalus* first arrived in Sydney on 20 April 1793, carrying, among other things, sixteen casks of essence of malt, seven casks of malt and four casks of hops. The hops and English malt used by Squire could have come from no other source than from the *Daedalus*, and both Grose and Paterson were in Sydney at that time. Although there is no corroborating information of Squire brewing at this time, the evidence is sufficient to accept that, by late 1793, James Squire was brewing beer, but how much we do not know.

By 1795 Squire had been conditionally pardoned after serving his sentence of seven years' transportation, and on 22 July 1795 was granted 30 acres of land at Kissing Point (now the outer Sydney suburb of Ryde). However, the land was a kilometre from the Parramatta River, and since Squire's brewery was erected on property having a river frontage with wharf and jetty, the brewery could not have been built on his original land grant. In fact, Squire's Kissing Point Brewery was built on a grant of land made by Governor Hunter to John Pollard on 15 September 1796; Squire had bought the 25-acre farm, known as Kissing Point Farm, for £5 late in 1796, and he resold his original 30 acres for £50 in 1799.

By 1797 (some writers suggest 1791 or 1795, others say between 1797 and 1800) Squire had established himself at Kissing Point as a commercial brewer, operating in a legitimate and open manner. The brewery consisted of a brewhouse with two sets of coppers, and a cellar. Various theories have been advanced as to what Squire used as a bittering agent when hops were not available. The most logical would seem to be horehound, which was available from government stores.

Although early Sydney Town news sheets said the beer was of excellent quality, not everyone had held the same opinion. On an epitaph in a Parramatta churchyard the following words are inscribed: 'Ye who wish to lie here, drink Squire's beer'. Inscribed on Squire's headstone is a different story, and worthy of the man who pioneered Australia's brewing industry: 'Under his care, the hop plant was first cultivated in this settlement and the first brewery was erected which progressively matured to perfection'.

James Squire came from Kingston, a hopgrowing district in Surrey, England, and he knew a great deal about hops and brewing. From experiments as early as 1802 he ultimately established a highly successful hop plantation, Australia's first. The hops were used for his beer production, and he also prepared yeast for breadmaking. On 23 December 1804 Squire advertised, asking for barrels and kegs to be returned, and stating that the brewery would be shut on Christmas Day. His table beer sold for 6d a gallon, and strong ale for 1s a gallon.

The *Government Gazette* of 16 March 1806 reported:

> On Friday, Mr. James Squire, settler and brewer at Kissing Point, waited upon His Excellency the Governor, at Government House, with two vines of hops taken from his own grounds. On a vine from last year's cuttings were numbers of very fine bunches and upon the two-year-old cutting, the clusters, mostly ripe, were innumerable … and of a most exquisite flavour. As a public recompense for the unremitting attention shown in bringing this valuable plant to such a high degree of perfection, His Excellency has directed a cow to be given to Mr. Squire from the Government herd.

After the death of James Squire in May 1822, at the age of sixty-seven, the brewery business was carried on by his eldest son, James, until he, in turn, died in 1826. The brewery closed down for a time, and was reopened

---

BEER AT £25 PER BOTTLE

For having sold two bottles of beer to a constable at a house in Meagher Street, Sydney, recently, without a licence, an unfortunate named Edward Bloomfield was, the other day, fined £50, in default six months' imprisonment. In such cases as this, the interesting question always arises, 'What becomes of the beer?'

Australian Brewers' Journal, May 1914

in 1828 by one of Squire's sons-in-law, Thomas Charles Farnell, one of whose children, James Squire Farnell, became Premier of New South Wales.

The brewery probably closed about 1830, and at a later date a boatbuilding firm took over 5 acres of the property, including the portion that included the old wharf and brewery.

Stabler, William 1803

An advertisement appeared in the *Sydney Gazette* on Christmas Day 1803 for William Stabler's beer, guaranteed 'of superior strength and quality'. This would give Stabler the credit of being Australia's fourth brewer. Before him were James Squire in 1793, followed by John Boston in 1795, and Daniel Cooper, earlier in 1803.

Apart from William Stabler's advertisement, there is no further record of his brewing endeavours.

Standard Brewery
See Toohey's Ltd.

Steam Engine Brewery 1827–c. 1833
Goulburn Street

The first steam-engine brewery to operate in Australia was built at the west end of Goulburn Street, facing Dickson's Mill Dam, at the head of Cockle Bay (Darling Harbour). The area was called the Brickfield Hill district in the early days.

John Dickson arrived at Port Jackson in 1813, bringing with him a steam engine that he had operated in Southwark, England. Soon after his arrival he built a flourmill, which was opened in 1815 with Governor Macquarie officially setting the steam engine in motion. Ten years later Dickson turned his attention to brewing. He extended the buildings, and built another steam engine to power the machines in the brewery. In partnership with John Mackie, the Steam Engine Brewery was officially opened on 8 December 1827.

Dickson advertised at some length in the *Sydney Monitor* during 1828:

> The undersigned respectfully announces that at the Steam Engine Brewery, malt liquor brewed from malt and hops only, is now in ripe state for delivery on the following terms: Fine, bright and fragrant beer, one shilling and sixpence per gallon, or £4 per hogshead; Potent, lively brisk pale ale of very superior quality, £6 per hogshead. John Dickson & Co.
> N.B. Purchasers of smaller quantities than a hogshead will be pleased to send their own casks.

Dickson put similar advertisements in the *Sydney Gazette*.

John Dickson was his own malster, looking after the steeping, flooring and kiln-drying of the grain, which was mostly barley. With regulated kiln temperature, the malt acquired distinguishing colours — pale brown, amber or black. His light beers were made from the pale and amber varieties, the sweet from the brown, and porter from the black. Dickson retired in 1833, and sold his brewery interests to his partner, John Mackie.

There is no evidence to suggest that brewing continued much beyond 1833, although the site, bounded by Harbour, Dixon and Goulburn Streets later became the Darling Brewery of John and James Toohey.

Strong Beer Brewery
See Clarence Street Brewery.

Surrey Brewery 1879–88
Bourke Street, Waterloo

When Cobb & Co. started the brewery in 1879 it was called the Orient Brewery, and it continued to trade under that name for the next eight years. The partnership of H. Burrows & F. B. Kyngdon purchased the Orient Brewery in 1886, but within a year N. Bladen and Oscar Burrows took over the business, renaming it the Surrey Brewery.

In 1888 the Surrey Brewery amalgamated with the wine-and-spirit firm of Allt & Co., and the Waverley Brewery of Burrows & Gleeson, to form Allt's Brewery & Wine & Spirit Co. Ltd. Each of the sellers entered into an undertaking not to be connected with any other brewery or wine-and-spirit business in Sydney, or within 50 miles, for a period of ten years. The Surrey Brewery was closed, and the new company continued to operate at the Waverley Brewery premises.

See also Waverley Brewery (Redfern).

Sydney Brewery (Harris Street)
See Anglo Australian Brewery.

Sydney Brewery (Parramatta Road) 1834–37
Parramatta Road, Ultimo

The following advertisement appeared in the *Australian* of December 1834:

> Sydney Brewery, Parramatta Road, opposite Ultimo House. Colonial Beer of the best quality delivered from the above brewery, in Sydney,

---

SYDNEY BREWERIES IDLE

Starting at 10 o'clock on the night of 3rd December [1919], a strike of employees threw the Sydney breweries into idleness. The breweries of Tooth & Co., Tooheys Ltd. and Reschs Ltd. are involved, and about 1,500 employees of those three establishments are 'doing nothing'.

A meeting of the Federated Liquor Trade and Allied Trades' Employees' Union was advised that the Brewery Association would not concede the demand for a minimum adult wage of four pounds seven shillings per week.

Australian Brewers' Journal, December 1919

[The strike lasted for three weeks.]

Liverpool, and Parramatta on reasonable terms. William Blackwell & Co.

That same year Newnham & Tooth laid the foundations of the Kent Brewery on property originally purchased by John Tooth. William Blackwell died in 1837, just three years after he had opened his brewery. Blackwell's land later became incorporated in the property of Tooth & Co. Ltd. The Sydney Brewery was therefore selling beer while the Kent Brewery, later to become the largest in Sydney, was in the course of construction.

Sydney Co-operative Brewery Co. Ltd
See Centennial Brewery.

Toohey's Ltd 1869–
Auburn

The Toohey family, Matthew, his wife Honora and son John, emigrated from Ireland and settled in Victoria, where they raised beef cattle during the goldrush boom. Beef was in constant demand at the diggings and Matthew prospered, supplying the miners with their daily needs. About 1865 the family moved north to New South Wales, where the elder son, John Thomas Toohey, purchased a cattle station near Lismore. The younger son, James Matthew Toohey, then about sixteen, 'squatted' on a large station near Coonamble.

During a visit to Sydney in 1869 John was informed that the Darling Brewery was for sale at a very reasonable price, and a year or so later he bought the brewery that stood at the corner of Dixon and Harbour Streets, at the western end of Goulburn Street. He persuaded brother James to join him as a junior partner in the brewery. They traded as J. T. & J. Toohey, and continued to use the name Darling Brewery.

In 1874 the Toohey brothers purchased the site of the old Albion Brewery. It had been started in 1827 by the ex-convict Samuel Terry, but the brewery had been gutted by fire in the 1860s. The brothers set about building a new brewery on the site, and when it was completed in 1875 it was an impressive series of stone buildings covering 2 acres. The main building was six storeys high, complete with an 80-foot tower. There were cellars below and a well, 200 feet deep, was sunk through solid rock. The brothers named their new complex the Standard Brewery, and used the old Darling Brewery as a store. The Standard Brewery was a success from the start, and depots were progressively opened at Newcastle, West Maitland, Goulburn, Orange, Narrandera and Wagga Wagga.

On the death of James Toohey in 1895 his son, John Thomas Jnr, joined the firm in partnership with his uncle, John. A share in the business was also held by Thomas Hughes, a descendant of Sam Terry, as equity represented by the transfer of the freehold of the old Albion Brewery site.

In 1902 the business was floated as Toohey's Ltd, with members of the Toohey family engaged in various

capacities until shortly after the end of World War I. By 1910 the brewery was capable of producing 2500 casks of beer per week. There were 400 employees, and 150 horses in the stables. The chief brewer frequently had to 'camp' on the premises, which had a neat, well-appointed office and bedroom on the third floor.

In the early 1930s the company was divided into two separate entities, both reporting to the chairman. There was a manager responsible for administration, but without any control over the head brewer, who also reported directly to the chairman. In those days the actual brewing section was off limits to everyone — even the manager could not enter without permission from the head brewer. When the position of general manager was created, practically everybody reported to him; very little authority was delegated, management was autocratic, and communications within the company were minimal. By the late 1950s profit was in

Above: *The Darling Brewery, c. 1870. It was taken over by John and James Toohey in 1869, and closed in 1875.*

Below: *Toohey's Standard Brewery, shortly after completion in 1875.*

John Thomas Toohey was the founder of one of Australia's most well-known breweries. Originally called the Standard Brewery, it was built at Darling Harbour in 1875. Although now at another location, the brewery continues to be referred to as Toohey's, a lasting monument to the memory of the founder.

Born in Limerick, Ireland, in 1837, John T. Toohey was brought to Australia by his parents when he was twelve months old. He received a sound education, and held a keen affection for the lands of his birth and of his adoption.

In 1892 the Hon. J. T. Toohey, MLC, MP, was appointed to the Legislative Council, and later he was created a Knight of the Order of St Gregory. It was a sad loss for the many deserving institutions that he had so generously supported, when on 5 May 1903 he died during a visit to the USA.

La Trobe Library, State Library of Victoria

serious decline, and there was growing concern for the company's survival. Drastic changes were made, and the brewery slowly emerged from its periods of difficulty.

The Standard Brewery in Orange was purchased from Walker & Co. Ltd in 1926 and closed, and the premises were used as a depot. In April 1961 the company succeeded in a takeover bid for the Grafton Brewery, and in 1967 acquired Miller's Brewery in Sydney, together with trading arrangements related to Miller's hotels.

Toohey's built a new brewery at Cardiff, Newcastle. It was called the Hunter Brewery, and was officially opened in February 1971. During that decade the company purchased both Seaview Wines and Wynn's Wines, with further diversification into the tea and coffee industry with the purchase of Robert Timms.

The year 1978 saw the transfer of all brewing operations to the company's brewery at Auburn in the western suburbs. It had been officially opened in May 1957, and was first used for the bottling of beer, which was sent across by tanker from their Standard Brewery.

Miller's Brewery was closed in 1975, and on 23 March 1978 the Standard Brewery closed its doors for the last time. The buildings were subsequently demolished with the exception of some facades under heritage classification. The names of Albion Street and Terry Street are reminders of the precincts of the old Albion Brewery that Sam Terry had started all those years ago.

In March 1980 Toohey's Ltd merged with the Castlemaine Perkins Brewery of Brisbane to become Castlemaine Toohey's Ltd, and in August 1985 ownership changed to Bond Corporation Holdings Ltd.

Toohey's elaborate float in an Eight Hours' procession in Sydney, 1910. It was drawn by a splendid team of grey horses.

La Trobe Library, State Library of Victoria

The Toohey's Brewery, together with the Swan Brewery in Perth and the Castlemaine Perkins Brewery in Brisbane, were all taken over from Bond Corporation in October 1990 by the New Zealand-based Lion Nathan Group. The three Australian breweries were then controlled by the new company, National Brewing Holdings Ltd.

Early in 1993 Toohey's bought the Hahn Brewing Co., which had been established in January 1988. The acquisition was a positive and successful move, and gave Toohey's an entry into the growing premium and specialty beer market.

In spite of the temporary destabilising effects of the changes in ownership, the Toohey's Brewery today is a progressive and innovative company producing a range of popular beers that are marketed nationally and exported to many countries. It is one of Australia's great breweries with a long and proud heritage — John Toohey and his brother, James, would be proud to know that the symbol of a stag, head held high, which they had used to promote their ale in 1869, is still used today by the company they founded.

Tooth & Co. Ltd   1835–
Broadway

The Tooth Brewery is the oldest operating brewery in New South Wales and the second oldest in Australia, topped only by the Cascade Brewery, in Hobart, which was established in 1832.

John Tooth, a native of Kent, England, arrived at Sydney in the early 1830s, and became a merchant and commission agent before entering the wine-and-spirit trade. He realised the potential for a brewery, and in partnership with his brother-in-law, Charles Newnham, built a brewery on a 5-acre block of land at what was then called Blackwattle Creek. The site was near a beautiful stream of fresh water that flowed through the government paddocks into Blackwattle Bay. Apart from the tollgate, the only other buildings in the area were Cooper's distillery, Shepherd's nursery and a few minor business establishments. The Caledonian Brewery was not far away, and John Tooth held a bill of sale over the property. Brewing had ceased at the Caledonian after the lessee, William Watt, died in 1834.

John Tooth nostalgically named the brewery the Kent, after his home county in England, and used a rampant white horse as his trademark. The brewery was officially opened on 5 October 1835.

The partners were the first in Australia to use the letter X to indicate the strength of their ales, and on 16 September 1835 they advertised:

> Newnham & Tooth intimate that on Monday October 5th, they will have ale ready for delivery at prices, viz.,
> X Ale   one shilling per gallon
> XXX Ale   one shilling and sixpence per gallon
> XXXX Ale two shillings and sixpence per gallon
> Orders left at the brewery or at the counting house of Mr. Tooth will meet every attention.

During 1843 Newnham retired from the business to pursue pastoral interests. Soon after, John Tooth relinquished active management, and the brewery was leased to his nephews, Robert and Edwin Tooth, who were later joined by their brother, Frederick. Trading as R. E. & F. Tooth, they had an agent, Henry Gooch, in Maitland as early as 1844, and Nehemiah Bartley became their Brisbane agent in 1854. Before that, on 20 June 1846, J. Harris was advertising in the *Moreton Bay Courier*, Brisbane, that he had Tooth's ale and porter for sale 'at Sydney prices'.

On 16 January 1853 the brewery was almost destroyed by fire. The *Sydney Morning Herald* reported that, in addition to the efforts of the fire brigade, soldiers of H.M. 11th Infantry had to be called in. Fire engines pumped water on the smoking ruins for five days.

Edwin Tooth died in 1859, and some time later Robert Tooth retired. They were replaced by Robert Lucas Tooth and James Mitchell. Frederick Tooth retired in 1873.

After the great fire the brewery was rebuilt, and the business flourished. On 30 June 1888 the company was incorporated as Tooth & Co. Ltd, with a share capital of £900,000. Although the depression years of the 1890s brought fierce competition from Toohey's, Resch's and Marshall's breweries, the Kent Brewery survived. Another fire, in 1903, destroyed the bottling plant, including 600,000 bottles of beer, a serious loss since it happened just before the Christmas period. The brewery also made a range of aerated waters and cordials, marketed under the Blue Bow label, and large quantities of beer were exported to India.

During the early part of the twentieth century the company expanded through the acquisition of many country breweries. Most were closed, effectively shutting out competition, but some continued brewing for a few more years. Many of the closed breweries were used as depots.

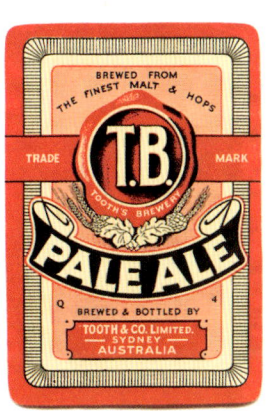

Brewery Acquisitions

		Acquired	Closed
Goulburn	Goulburn Brewery	1920	1929
Jerilderie	Jerilderie Brewery	1924	1924
Maitland	Maitland Brewing Co. Ltd	1913	1915
Melbourne	Courage Breweries Ltd	1978	1982
Narrandera	Narrandera Brewery	1924	1924
Newcastle	Castlemaine Brewery	1921	1931
Sydney	Marshall's Co-operative Brewery Ltd	1911	1911
Sydney	Waverley Brewery (Redfern)	1929	1983
Temora	Temora Brewery	1918	1918
Tumut	Tumut Brewery	1919	1919
Wagga Wagga	Federal Brewery	1924	1924

The company's most important acquisition was Resch's Waverley Brewery in 1929. This removed a

Etching of the New South Lager Bier Brewing Co. Ltd, Redfern, at the time it was taken over by Edmund Resch in 1900. He changed the name to the Waverley Brewery.

Although this label, c. 1950, is for Resch's Lager, the brewery had been taken over by Tooth & Co. Ltd.

major competitor and placed the Kent Brewery in a dominant position in New South Wales. The Waverley Brewery continued as a separate brewing unit. The lion emblem of Edmund Resch was used until 1979, when it was replaced by Tooth's white horse emblem.

A new brewery was started at Lismore in September 1979. Trading as Tooth's Northern Brewery, it produced Resch's and Tooth's beers for distribution to the northern coast and tableland districts. The Courage Brewery in Melbourne was taken over in 1978, a decision that was later regretted. Courage had been operating unprofitably, and Tooth, in an attempt to market its products in Victoria, removed the Courage name and cockerel emblem and the product names, replacing them with Tooth names and emblems. It then brewed and sold its own Sydney brands of beer in Melbourne. The exercise was a failure, and Carlton & United Breweries Ltd (CUB) in Melbourne took over the languishing brewery and closed it in April 1982.

Some Sydney drinkers may have shed a tear when CUB acquired the assets of Tooth & Co. Ltd on 9 August 1983; the acquisition included the rebuilt Kent Brewery and the Lismore plant. Indeed, there was much amazement and even indignation that their own Tooth Brewery, after 148 years, was now going to be owned and controlled by upstarts from the south. If it was any consolation, after the acquisition the Tooth Brewery still produced all the popular brands of beer that had for so long been consumed with affection by the New South Wales drinking public.

Resch's Waverley Brewery was closed in 1983, and the Northern Brewery in Lismore in 1986.

The parent company, Carlton & United Breweries Ltd, became part of the Foster's Brewing Group Ltd on 13 November 1990. The brewery in Sydney is still called Tooth's Brewery — named after the founder, John Tooth, who, in 1835, began brewing his X Ale, which he sold for a shilling a gallon.

Tooth's Brewery
See Tooth & Co. Ltd.

Union Beer Co.   1897–98
527 Kent Street

James Hamilton was the Managing Director.

Union Brewery
See Brookvale Brewing Co. Pty Ltd.

Union Brewery   c. 1830–c. 1835
35 Upper Pitt Street

Waverley Brewery
(Redfern)   1900–83
South Dowling Street, Redfern

The Resch brothers, Edmund, Richard and Emil, were German emigrants who arrived in Australia during the 1860s. They became involved in cordial manufacture at Wilcannia and later at Broken Hill, but their main endeavour was to be brewing. In time, they established Lion Breweries at the New South Wales towns of Wilcannia, Silverton and Cootamundra.

By 1895 Edmund Resch had moved from Wilcannia to Sydney to manage Allt's Brewery & Wine & Spirit Co. Ltd, then in liquidation. It was known as the Waverley Brewery, and, before that, the Adelaide Brewery. The location was the corner of Edgecliff Road and Adelaide Street, Waverley. In 1897 Edmund Resch purchased the assets of the company.

Three years later, in 1900, Resch purchased the New South Wales Lager Bier Co. Ltd in Redfern. He closed the Waverley Brewery, shifted the equipment across to Redfern, and began brewing there in 1901. He upgraded the brewery with the most modern equipment available, and the imposing group of buildings covered more than an acre. Resch continued to use the name of his previous brewery, the Waverley.

The business became Resch's Ltd in 1906, and with the energy and sound management of Edmund Resch, the Waverley Brewery was soon out-performing most of the other Sydney breweries. One of the most popular beers was Resch's Dinner Ale, which, after almost a century and now brewed at another location, is still one of Sydney's favourite beers.

Edmund Resch died in 1923, and the brewery was then managed by his sons, Edmund Jnr and Arnold. The business and property of the Waverley Brewery were taken over by Tooth & Co. Ltd in 1929 but the brewery continued to operate as a separate unit, brewing the same products and using the same name of Waverley Brewery. Edmund Resch's lion emblem continued to be used until 1979, when it was replaced by Tooth's white horse emblem.

Following the acquisition of Tooth & Co. Ltd by the Melbourne-based CUB in 1983, the grand old Waverley Brewery was closed. The majestic buildings in Dowling Street have been a striking landmark in Sydney for generations, and what now remains of the buildings is a lasting testimony to the enterprise of one of Australia's great brewers, Edmund Resch.

Waverley Brewery (Waverley)

Adelaide Brewery	1874–76
Waverley Brewery	1876–88

Surrey Brewery (Bourke Street)

Orient Brewery	1879–87
Surrey Brewery	1887–88

Amalgamation in 1888 of the Surrey Brewery, Waverley Brewery and Allt & Co. to form Allt's Brewery & Wine & Spirit Co. Ltd, but trading as the Waverley Brewery.

Waverley Brewery (Waverley)

Edmund Resch (manager, in liquidation)	1895–97
Edmund Resch (owner)	1897–1900, closed

New South Wales Lager Bier Brewing Co. Ltd
(South Dowling Street, Redfern)
                                     1896–98, closed

Taken over by Edmund Resch, and renamed the Waverley Brewery.

Waverley Brewery (Redfern)

Edmund Resch	1900–6
Resch's Ltd	1906–29
Resch's Waverley Brewery (owned by Tooth & Co.)	1929–83, closed

Label used by the Adelaide Brewery, Waverley, when it was opened in 1874 by the founders, William Simms, Edgar Chapman and Hampton Gleeson.

Waverley Brewery
(Waverley)   1874–1900
Cnr Edgecliff Road & Adelaide Street, Waverley

It seems odd that a brewery in Sydney should be named the Adelaide, after the capital city of South Australia. This was probably because two of the proprietors owned a brewery in Adelaide and felt inclined to retain a reminder of their home town. Adelaide Street, where the brewery was located, may well have been named after the brewery.

The Adelaide Brewery commenced in 1874; the partners were William Simms, Edgar Chapman and Hampton Gleeson. Simms and Chapman owned the West End Brewery in Adelaide, and had sent their head brewer, Charles Mallen, to Sydney to take control of the new venture. Mallen ran the Adelaide Brewery in Sydney for a year, and then returned to Adelaide to start his own brewery.

Burrows & Gleeson bought the Adelaide Brewery in Sydney in 1876, and changed the name to the Waverley Brewery. During that year the brewery suffered severe damage from floods, and brewing stopped

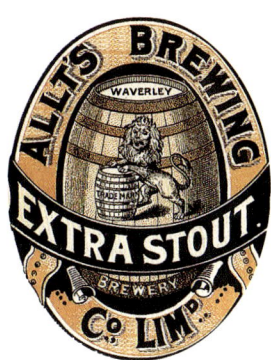

Allt's Brewery & Wine & Spirit Co. Ltd was formed in 1888 by the amalgamation of Allt & Co., the Waverley Brewery and the Adelaide Brewery. The business then continued to operate as Allt's Brewing Co. Ltd, Waverley Brewery.

Resch's Waverley Brewery, 1897. It was originally the Adelaide Brewery, located in the inner Sydney suburb of Waverley. Edmund Resch took over in 1897, closed the brewery three years later, and transferred his business to the new, larger brewery at Redfern.

The Adelaide Brewery Waverley, 1874.

Edward Fagan's Wellington Brewery advertisement, c. 1830.

for quite some time. To keep the business going, beer was obtained from Toohey's Standard Brewery.

In 1888 Allt's Brewery & Wine & Spirit Co. Ltd was formed by the amalgamation of Allt & Co., wine-and-spirit merchants (established thirty-one years), the Waverley Brewery of Burrows & Gleeson (formerly the Adelaide Brewery, established fourteen years), and the Surrey Brewery of Bladen & Borrows (formerly the Orient Brewery, established eight years). The business continued to trade as the Waverley Brewery at the same address, and W. H. Tulloch was appointed managing director; the Surrey Brewery was closed.

By 1895 Allt's Brewery & Wine & Spirit Co. Ltd, the holding company of the Waverley Brewery, was in liquidation, and Edmund Resch was brought in as manager. Resch ultimately took over the company in 1897. Three years later he bought the New South Wales Lager Bier Brewery in Redfern, which had been closed for two years. He closed the old Allt's Waverley Brewery in 1900 and transferred all his brewing business to the more spacious premises at Redfern. Edmund Resch still called his business the Waverley Brewery — it was destined to become one of the largest breweries in Sydney.

See also Waverley Brewery (Redfern).

Wellington Brewery   1820–c. 1833
George Street

The Wellington Brewery was one of the most notable brewing houses of the early 1820s. It occupied a large area of land next to the site of the present Sydney Post Office, and the Wellington Inn was alongside the brewery.

Matthew Bacon, the owner, brewed a very strong ale, using malt and hops exclusively. He had several employees, and three horse-drawn drays were used to carry the ale and porter around Sydney.

Bacon suffered from poor health, and invited an English brewer, John Payne, to join the business. In July 1823 the partners announced that they would pay 'the average market price in barter for shop goods at ready money price for locally grown barley'. Farmers were unable to supply the demand for barley at that time.

Bacon's health deteriorated, and he passed the business over to Payne, entering into an agreement whereby Payne would pay, on the due date, three promissory notes. Payne only paid one of these, and said he would contest the other two in court. In the meantime, Bacon, instead of dying, took on a new lease of life, and claimed he was still a partner, a claim that Payne denied. The battle was only terminated on Bacon's death in August 1825.

Payne carried on with the brewery, but financial problems, brought about by poor-quality beer, forced him to reduce his prices. To make ends meet he started making soap and candles at the brewery, and dealt in consignments of brandy and gin. In 1826 he sold his business to Edward Westbrook, who immediately began selling English Ale and Taylor's London Porter, as well as his Wellington Brewery beer. By 1828 Westbrook had achieved a monthly output of 465 hogsheads of beer. It was a good time to sell.

An Irishman, Edward Fagan, purchased the brewery in the early 1830s. He added more buildings, and updated the equipment in anticipation of a long and profitable brewing business, but the brewery closed after a few years.

West, Absolem   1809–c. 1811
1 and 2 Cambridge Street (close to Dawes Point)

Absolem West was a free settler, and since he was growing his own barley he decided to use it for brewing. In 1809 he requested permission to build a brewery in the populous area known even at that time, as 'The Rocks'. He undertook to brew a wholesome, nourishing and cheap beer from barley and hops — hopgrowing had started in the settlement a few years earlier.

West's petition was granted, and he built a malt-house, malt kilns, cellars and stables, and installed his brewing vats and tanks. The brewery site commanded a splendid view of Port Jackson, the Parramatta River and Cockle Bay (as Darling Harbour was then called). Brewing commenced on 25 October 1809.

Together with the few other breweries operating in Sydney at the time, Absolem West contributed quite significantly to weaning the hard-drinking population from rum and other strong spirits, and the government applauded his enterprise.

The prices charged by West were set out in a notice, which was posted outside his brewery in October 1809:

Brewery – Absolem West gives notice to his friends and the public in general that he will supply beer as follows:
Best Strong Beer   Four Shillings per Gallon
Best Table Beer   Two Shillings per Gallon

Wetherhill's Brewery   c. 1830–c. 1835
Upper Clarence Street

Robert Wetherhill.

Windsor Brewery c. 1835
Bridge Street

Thomas Cadell already had a brewery in Windsor, and decided to start another, under the same name, in Sydney.

Woolpack Brewery c. 1829
Brickfield Hill

Yorkshire Brewery 1888–90
Cnr Parramatta Road & Elswick Street, Leichhardt

Shortly after Joseph Smith started the brewery he was joined by Henry Moss, but the partnership lasted a little over a year, leaving Moss to continue for a few more months on his own.

Tamworth

Tamworth is named after a town in Staffordshire, England, and in 1888 it was the first Australian town to have electric street lighting.

Tamworth was incorporated as a borough in 1876, and during that decade three flourmills operated. The Royal Standard Brewery opened in 1879, and by 1914 became the largest in New South Wales outside Sydney.

The Australasian Country Music Festival and Awards have been held in the city in January each year since 1973, justifying Tamworth's claim to be the 'Country Music Capital of Australia'.

Royal Standard Brewery 1879–1921
Park Street

Charles Britten came directly from England to supervise operations at the Phoenix Flour Mill, Tamworth. After two years he left the mill, and in 1885 he bought the local Royal Standard Brewery, which had been founded by Joseph Oddy in 1879 (Oddy had been declared bankrupt in 1884).

Within a few years Britten had become well known in the district, and was to serve for five consecutive terms as mayor. In 1896, with business thriving, he re-equipped the plant with a giant 13-ton boiler; he added a new two-storey malthouse the following year.

By 1901 there were twenty-three hotels in the town, and Britten had reportedly gained a near monopoly of the Tamworth beer trade. Although there were varying accounts of the quality and flavour of the beer, he was selling it widely throughout the north and north-western districts of New South Wales. There were more extensions in 1903; a towering four storeys were added, an electric generator installed, and brewing capacity increased to 60 barrels a day. The brewery employed over 100 men, who attended to the malting, brewing, bottling and soft-drink manufacture. By 1914 the Royal Standard was reputedly the largest brewery in New South Wales outside Sydney.

Charles Britten grew his own barley, and was able to produce almost 3000 kg of ice daily. He was a lover of dogs and birds, and was the foundation president of the Pigeon, Caged Birds and Kennel Society, Tamworth.

Britten's fortunes began to decline through over-capitalisation on machinery, the failure of several rural schemes, and increasing competition from the large Sydney breweries. His health deteriorated, and on his death in 1919 the business passed to his son, Carl. Unfortunately Carl was unable to prevent the business from going into liquidation two years later.

Charles Britten's Royal Standard Brewery, Tamworth, c. 1896. The elaborate construction of the brewery was similar in design to a number of country railway stations of the time.

Tamworth Brewery 1877–85
Elsworth Street, South Tamworth

In May 1877 John Milne and James Graham started Tamworth's first brewery, and gave it the appropriate name of the Tamworth Brewery.

In March 1879 Graham took over Milne's share of the business, and within a few months there was a three-way partnership made up of James Graham, Cleveland Solomon and Nathan Cohen. This new arrangement contributed nothing to the welfare of the business, and after a few months the brewery closed.

The Ross brothers reopened the brewery in July 1881. At first, their beer was criticised for being too sweet, but they corrected the problem and went on to win a prize at the Liverpool Annual Show.

It was common practice throughout the nineteenth century for the purchaser of a brewery to change the name. Frequently the old name carried a poor reputation for the quality of its beer or service, or ability to pay debts, and, understandably, a proud new owner would wish to establish his own identity. For whatever reason, John Bisby chose the name Tiger Brewery when he secured the lease of the Tamworth Brewery in September 1882. Robert Campbell owned the premises at the time.

The change of name did little to advance the fortunes of the proprietors who followed. After Bisby came A. C.

Label of the Royal Standard Brewery.

Hill, and then Samuel Johnston. By 1885 the brewery had closed permanently, and it failed to sell two years later when it was advertised at one-sixth its original cost.

Tiger Brewery
See Tamworth Brewery.

Temora

The town of Temora rapidly developed in 1880 when goldseekers swarmed to the area following the discovery of the famous Mother Shipton gold nugget, which weighed 258 ounces. In time the gold ran out, and Temora became a major wheatgrowing district.

Jones, Lincoln & Co. 1892–1900
When this company began brewing at Temora, it was already operating breweries in five New South Wales country towns: Cootamundra, Hay, Hillston, Jerilderie and Narrandera. At Temora it is possible that they had taken over Robert Ecclestone's Temora Brewery.

As with most of the Jones, Lincoln & Co. breweries, their brewery at Temora was bought by McIntyre, Lincoln & Co. This occurred in 1895. Four years later the business was owned by Bartley & Co.

Lion Brewery 1881–84
Cowan's Lagoon
The town's first brewery was started in 1881 by James Howison, the former proprietor of the Lachlan Brewery, Forbes. He advertised in the *Cootamundra Herald* of 10 May 1881 that he had opened 'the Lion Brewery, situated on the Cootamundra–Temora Road, would be in a position to supply all orders after April 15, 1881'.

The brewery, which closed in 1884, had no connection with the Red Lion breweries that Henry Lindsay had established in many New South Wales country towns.

Temora Brewery (Junee Road) 1884–94
Junee Road
Robert Ecclestone started the brewery in partnership with P. Lugton. A Mr. Hughes was involved for a while, but from 1888 Ecclestone was sole owner.

Temora Brewery
(Upper Temora) 1891–1918
Upper Temora
W. S. Eaton and A. R. Tewksbury were the owners of the Wagga Wagga Brewery, and in 1891 they decided to start another brewery at Temora. When Eaton left a few years later, his share of the business was taken up by James Bellair. The partners then traded as Tewksbury & Bellair from 1894 until 1898.

Alphonso Tewksbury continued to run the brewery as sole owner until 1918, and he then sold the brewery section of the business to Tooth & Co. Beer production ceased, but Tewksbury stayed on at the premises making soft drinks and acting as the local agent for Tooth's.

Tibooburra

Wittabrinna Brewery 1889–c. 1890
The tiny settlement of Tibooburra is in harsh semi-desert country in the far north-west of New South Wales, close to the Queensland and South Australian borders.

John Guritson states in his book *Tibooburra: Corner Country*:

> The brews dispensed generally came from down south or 'inside', but for a brief period around 1890, David Scott, formerly of the Wittabrinna Run, ran the Wittabrinna Brewery, supplying the district's hostelries with that vital foaming liquid.

Michael Nolan held the brewer's licence in 1889.

Tuena

Tuena Brewery 1872–75
Tuena is a small township about 150 km west of the Blue Mountains. Samuel Williams ran the brewery there in 1872, as did George Milne in 1875.

Tumbarumba

Alpine Brewery 1883–1925
Before the arrival of rail transport, country-town brewers generally supplied their beer to customers within their immediate district. A few of the larger breweries in provincial cities shipped their beer far and wide, but for most smaller operators it was too expensive to service

---

CAT-ASTROPHIC

A remarkable invasion of cats has taken place this month in the Thargomindah district, NSW [on the border of Queensland].

'Thousands upon thousands of cats are advancing from the north', says a correspondent of one of the daily papers, 'and are infesting the bush.'

'It is supposed they are following the plague of rats which recently passed through here. The noteworthy fact is that the cats, which are of ordinary size, and of the domestic species, are all pretty nearly of the same colour, namely sandy, which proves that they have reverted to the original stock.

'They are in very poor condition, showing that their migration is due to the scarcity of their habitual food. It is hoped they will keep down the rabbits which still keep pouring into the colony through the 17 mile gap in the rabbit-proof fence'.

Australian Brewers' Journal, July 1888

other towns — unless large quantities of beer were involved, horse-and-cart transport was too costly for a mere barrel or two. Another problem was the constant shaking and jolting of the barrelled beer as it travelled over bumpy dirt tracks, frequently in sweltering heat. The result was deterioration of the beer, quite often leaving it unfit for drinking, to be returned to the brewer, at more cost, and then thrown out.

As a consequence, breweries started up in many country towns and provided the beer was good, the brewery owners were relatively safe from competition. When William Seymour Eaton started his brewery at Tumbarumba, the isolated location in high mountain country offered some degree of security from competition. The nearest brewery was a difficult day's journey away. Moreover, Eaton knew how to make good beer, and already owned breweries at Albury and Wagga Wagga.

William Eaton called his brewery the Tumbarumba, but when he sold to John Chapman in 1889 the name was changed to the Alpine Brewery. Chapman had the misfortune of having to rebuild the brewery after it was destroyed by fire in 1902. Later that year, he was fined for delivering casks of beer with insufficient duty stamps attached.

Austin Cowley took over the Alpine Brewery in 1911, and continued brewing there until 1925.

Tumbarumba Brewery
See Alpine Brewery.

Tumut

In 1824 the explorers Hume and Hovell crossed the Tumut River slightly south of Tumut. Local natives called the area Tumottt, which to them meant 'quiet resting place by the river'. The modified name of Tumut was used for both the township and the adjacent river.

In the early years the Tumut district was sparsely populated, mostly by unfriendly natives. By 1856 the town had one small school, and the few other scattered buildings were of slab and bark construction. Although a small town, there were three hotels. Ten years later, there were eleven.

Anderson's Brewery 1860–69
Eastern side of the Tumut River
The Atkinson family had a farm on the east side of the Tumut River, upstream from Anderson's Bridge, and they operated a small brewery on the property. Anne Atkinson held the brewer's licence from 1860, and later the brewery was leased or managers were put in charge.

Tumut Brewery 1873–1919
Between Russell & Fitzroy Streets (now Beale Street)
The Anderson family were early settlers at Tumut, and in 1873 Thomas Anderson began brewing at the family's farm property near the bank of McFarlane's Creek. John Beale, more affectionately known as Johnnie, became a partner in 1878, and they traded as Anderson & Beale until 1881.

Johnnie Beale had been involved in mining and the cartage business, and earlier still, back in England, he had been a brushmaker and had served with the mercantile marine. His only brewing experience was what he picked up while working with Thomas Anderson.

The Tumut Brewery turned out beer acknowledged by competent judges to be as good as any in the colony. Johnnie Beale, as the beer was called, was a favourite beverage in Tumut, and 'Beale's magnificent team of van horses delivered beer to Gundagai, Adelong, and Bartlow', servicing all the hotels along the way.

A descendant of an early resident recalled being told that his auntie, when a child, would go to the brewery and ask for 'Ginger' Whyburn, an employee, to buy threepence worth of yeast for her mother to make bread. Ginger would give the children barley sugar: 'it was like coarse salt, only yellow, and was used in the beer'. There was a little ditty sung by some locals:

> Beer, beer, beautiful beer, fill yourself right up to here.
> Drink a good deal of it, make a good meal of it.
> Nothing can come up to Johnnie Beale's beer.

The brewery was taken over by Tooth's Brewery, Sydney, in 1919, and closed. It was the finish of Johnnie Beale's beer, so fondly appreciated for forty years.

Ulladulla

Ulladulla Brewery 1877–c. 1883
Jonis Dommichetti and J. Hoe were registered as brewers for the year ending 31 March 1887. Hoe was recorded as brewing on his own in 1879.

Urana

Urana Brewery 1884–c. 1901
Brongon Street
William Jones started the brewery in 1884, and two years later Thomas Lincoln joined as a partner. They traded as Jones, Lincoln & Co., and were to build a chain of breweries across country New South Wales. Their breweries were established at Cootamundra (1889–94), Hay (1891–98), Hillston (1888–98), Jerilderie (1883–97), Narrandera (1888–94), Temora (1892–95) and Urana (1884–96).

E. Rankin took over the Urana Brewery in 1898, worked it for two years, and then sold to H. T. Holt in 1901.

Wagga Wagga

The area of Wagga Wagga was explored in 1829 by Captain Charles Sturt. The town is located on the banks of

The Albion Brewery, Wagga Wagga, was never very successful — eight people had been involved in less than ten years. Richard Mooney was the lessee during 1892 and 1893.

Below left: The Federal Brewery, Wagga Wagga, c. 1900.

Below right: Additions to the brewery included this handsome entrance, c. 1910. The brewery closed in 1924.

the Murrumbidgee River, and was once home to the largest Aboriginal tribe in New South Wales, the Wiradjuri. It is from their language that the city's name Wagga Wagga is derived. It has many meanings, the most accepted being 'many crows' (repetition of Wagga signifies the plural).

Albion Brewery 1889–1900
Baylis Street

When William Davoren and Hugh McDonnell started their Albion Brewery in 1889, they had two competitor breweries to contend with: the Murrumbidgee and the Wagga Wagga. Both were well established, and this was probably one reason why the Albion Brewery was never a success. Another factor was the death of William Davoren shortly after the brewery started.

The Albion Brewery was then leased to Richard Mooney, who lasted for only a year or two; the brewery was then controlled by the executors of Davoren's estate. Thomas Loughlin and James Bellair operated the brewery from 1895 to 1898.

The new owner in 1898 was James Beatie, an aerated-water and cordial manufacturer. However, one year was enough for Beatie.

The final owner, in 1899, was William Robertson, who was joined by Thomas D'Arcy Burke of the Clarence River Brewery, Maclean, in September that year.

Federal Brewery 1899–1924
The Esplanade

The Murrumbidgee Brewery was destroyed by fire in 1896, and three years later the site was purchased by a cordial-maker, John Hogan. In partnership with Patrick J. Mahon, they built a brewery on the bank of the Wollundry Lagoon, directly opposite the Wagga Wagga Brewery. Their Federal Brewery did quite well for some years, but there was always strong competition from the Sydney breweries.

By the turn of the century the Federal had only one local competitor, the Wagga Wagga Brewery. John Hogan had died in 1909, and in 1914 it was decided that the Wagga Wagga and Federal breweries should amalgamate. The Wagga Wagga Brewery of Henry Headley was closed, and the equipment was transferred to the Federal Brewery. The business then traded as Mahon & Headley.

With the Federal now the only brewery in town, business began to pick up. In 1921 it was sold as a going concern to John and Andrew Whelan. It was taken over by Tooth & Co. three years later, and they used it only as a depot for kegged beer, which was sent by rail from their Kent Brewery in Sydney.

Murrumbidgee Brewery 1881–96
The Esplanade (south side of the Wollundry Lagoon)

Irishman Martin Treacey was a builder by trade, and with his brother, John, they built the Murrumbidgee Brewery in 1881. Their beer was popular, and they won several medals at International Exhibitions. The brewery was destroyed by fire on 28 January 1896. As Martin Treacey had died less than two weeks before the fire, his share in the business went to his daughter, Kathleen. Unfortunately for her, because of the fire there was no business left, and it was strongly sus-

A busy day at the Wagga Wagga Brewery, c. 1910. The proprietor, Henry Headley, is in the foreground, driving his Ford car.

pected that the fire was deliberately lit to obtain the insurance.

Newtown Brewery 1866–87
Cnr Murray & Forsyth Streets

In August 1866 the *Wagga Wagga Express* announced that a man named Strickland 'has excavated a large cellar and is erecting a commodious superstructure of wood, almost ready to receive the necessary boiler and vats'. During 1868 the local Royal Hotel was advertising 'a splendid light sparkling ale from the Newtown Brewery'. It was priced at 6d a pint, and everyone was invited to 'come and try it, you will never drink the heady English ale again'.

The brewery and parlour were leased to Chris Godhead and Jonathon Riley for 40s per week during the mid-1870s, and later the partnership of Godhead & Spier ran the brewery.

By 1881 Richard Heath had become the owner. He built a cordial factory alongside the brewery, but six years later he stopped brewing and concentrated on the more profitable cordial business.

Wagga Wagga Brewery 1866–1914
Western end of Johnston Street (on the bank of the Wollundry Lagoon)

The first location of the Wagga Wagga Brewery was in Baylis Street, in premises adjoining the rear of the Royal Hotel. As reported in the *Wagga Wagga Express* of August 1866, George Ralston was the owner of the brewery.

Several changes in ownership followed, and in 1875 George Wildman, a former publican at the Royal Hotel, purchased the brewery. He also owned another brewery, which he had started two years earlier in Johnston Street. With two breweries to operate, Wildman appointed William Ovenden to manage the brewery in Baylis Street.

William Seymour Eaton, a previous partner with Wildman in a cordial business, took over Wildman's brewery in Johnston Street in 1879, and the brewery in Baylis Street was closed. Eaton brewed ale, stout and a non-intoxicating lager beer, as well as a comprehensive range of cordials, essences and liqueurs. The quality of the products was consistently good, and the company was awarded a gold medal for its Strong Bottled Ale at the Melbourne International Exhibition of 1888. A branch was established at Tumbarumba in 1883, and another at Temora in 1891.

By 1888 the Wagga Wagga Brewery was being operated by William Seymour Eaton's son, William Henry Eaton, in partnership with A. R. Tewksbury. Eaton Jnr supervised the brewing, and Tewksbury looked after the financial side of the business. They traded as Eaton & Tewksbury for four years, and then Eaton Jnr became the sole proprietor.

By 1903 the business was being conducted by Eaton Snr's son-in-law, Henry S. Headley, previously the manager of the Albury Brewing & Malting Co. Ltd. He was also a former mounted trooper, and had been involved in the capture of the bushrangers, the Captain Moonlight Gang. One policeman, two bushrangers and three horses died as a result of the battle; Headley and others were later presented with awards, Headley also receiving £60.

In 1914 the firm amalgamated with the other brewery in town, the Federal, and after brewing for forty-eight years the Wagga Wagga Brewery was finally closed.

Baylis Street

George Ralston	1866–68
O'Keefe	1868–73
Mathew Callaghan	1873–75
George Wildman	1875–79, closed

Johnson Street

George Wildman	1873–79
William Seymour Eaton	1879–88
Eaton & Tewksbury	1888–92
William Henry Eaton	1892–1903
Henry Headley	1903–14

Walgett

Castlemaine Brewery
See Waratah Brewery.

Waratah Brewery   1883–1913
Warren Street

For some unknown reason Thomas Simpson used the name Castlemaine Brewery when he began brewing at Walgett in 1883. A more appropriate brewery name could have been the town name of Walgett, which comes from the Aboriginal word meaning 'meeting of the waters'.

Thomas Simpson had come from Wilcannia, where for the previous three years he had owned a cordial factory and small brewery. At Walgett he employed John Atkinson to do the brewing and act as manager, but after a few months he had a better idea, and leased the brewery to Thomas and William Willis for a year. Atkinson had stayed on as the brewer, and when he left in 1887 Simpson decided to get out of the brewing business altogether and sold the brewery to two Narrabri storekeepers, Charles Collins and Henry Joseph. They changed the name to the Waratah Brewery.

The business must have been trading satisfactorily, for after two years Collins started the Gwydir Brewery at Moree, and also purchased the Narrabri Brewery. After the death of Charles Collins early in 1889, the Waratah Brewery was bought by Archibald Skinner, and during the next fourteen years the brewery changed hands many times.

Archibald Skinner	1889–1902
James Glass	1903–4
John Fletcher & Son	1904–6
Arthur Colless	1907–12
Robert Wilson	1912–13

Wallacia

Luddenham Brewery
See Mulgoa Brewery.

Mulgoa Brewery   1808–c. 1820
As early as 1808 Gregory and John Blaxland were brewing beer and growing hops on their Newington estate beside the Parramatta River, not far from present-day Parramatta. A few years later the brewery was shifted 40 km west to Wallacia, beside the Nepean River. The name Mulgoa Brewery was chosen, and the Blaxland's supplied the western-road traffic with Mulgoa Brewery ale and beer.

The brewery went through several changes of name and ownership, becoming, in turn, the Luddenham Brewery, the Nepean Brewery and the Regentville Brewery.

Neapean Brewery
See Mulgoa Brewery.

Regentville Brewery
See Mulgoa Brewery

Wellington

Wellington is located at the junction of the Macquarie and Bell Rivers, and was established as a convict settlement in 1823. Later it became a squatting area, and in 1846 it was gazetted as a township.

Bell Brewery   1880–1932
Brewery Lane

Fifty-two years was a long time for any brewery to stay in business in country New South Wales, particularly to survive the depression years of the 1890s, the ceaseless competition from the powerful Sydney breweries, and the effects of World War I. Although there were some minor setbacks along the way, the Bell Brewery achieved that distinction, without changing its name and with few changes in ownership

There were already nine hotels in Wellington when C. F. W. Kirchner set up the Bell Brewery in 1880, under the supervision of Peter Sharp. The buildings were of white cypress pine covered with galvanised iron, and large woodburning brick fireplaces heated the boiling vats that were one storey above ground. The location was close to the Bell River, which joins the Macquarie River a short distance north. Brewery Lane is now closed because of erosion from the river.

When brewing commenced, it was expected that seventy casks of beer could be produced each week, an optimistic target. The brewery closed early in 1882. Six months later Restall & Dymond started the brewery again, extended the premises, and soon had six employees turning out 45 hogsheads of good-quality beer each

Left: *Peter Jager, of the Bell Brewery, Wellington, and his penny farthing bike, c. 1908. Note the stacks of empty bottles in the background.*

Right: *The Bell Brewery, Wellington, 1883. The two wood-burning brick fireplaces at the top of the loft were used for heating the vats inside the building. After operating for fifty-two years, the brewery was destroyed by fire.*

week. One of the employees was nineteen-year-old Peter Jager, who became an apprentice brewer in 1883, and later head brewer and cooper, and part-owner.

John Restall had been a baker by trade, and after fossicking unsuccessfully for gold in Victoria he moved to Wellington in 1878. He went back to baking before taking on brewing as a livelihood. Difficult times forced Restall to sell the Bell Brewery in 1908 to the partnership of Peter Jager and Hugh Kelly. They renovated the brewery, increased production, and sold their beer as far west as Bourke.

Business prospered, at least until 1918 when the partners closed the brewery for a short period because of high costs and poor returns. Soon they were back in business, and continued brewing until April 1932 when the brewery was destroyed by fire. Peter Jager and his son, Harry, made Horehound and Hop Beer in part of the old cellar that had remained intact after the fire.

C. F. W. Kirchner	1880–82
Restall & Dymond	1882–1908
Jager & Kelly	1908–32

Wentworth

The town of Wentworth, in the far south-west of New South Wales, sits peacefully at the junction of two of Australia's longest rivers, the Darling and the Murray. The region was sparsely settled by sheep graziers in the 1840s, and the small town was named in 1859 after the explorer and politician William Wentworth.

Wentworth Brewery 1889–98
Darling Street

Joan Moody was brewing at Wentworth between 1867 and 1869.

Twenty years later, in the latter part of 1889, John Dunn built a small brewery in Darling Street. He called it the Wentworth Brewery, and managed to continue brewing for nine years.

Wilcannia

During the 1870s and 1880s the townships of Wilcannia and Bourke were principal ports on the Darling River. Paddle-steamers and barges plied their trade along the river, despite the vagaries of the river level as drought and flood alternated, with drought the more common condition. Supplies, including beer and soft drinks, were often slow in arriving and prices were exorbitant.

Black Horse Brewery Co. Ltd 1880–87
The first advertisement for this brewery appeared in the September 1880 edition of the *Wilcannia Times*. It gave the proprietor's name, Thomas Simpson, and assured the public that 'the finest ingredients have been purchased and courteous service is assured'. Simpson also produced cordials.

In 1883 the Black Horse Brewery Co. Ltd was formed to acquire the brewery and cordial factory of Thomas Simpson. Simpson then left the district to settle in Walgett, where he started another brewery.

John Wright was appointed manager of the Black Horse Brewery, the major shareholders being Thomas Whyte and James Counsell of Adelaide. Unfortunately, after four years, the company was wound up.

Edmund Resch, owner of the nearby Lion Brewery, apparently took over about that time, possibly to utilise some of the equipment. Two years later the brewery building was destroyed by fire.

Lion Brewery 1879–1930
Bourke Street

This was one of the few successful breweries to operate in the far west of New South Wales, surviving the effects of drought, flood, depression and war for more than fifty years.

Edmund Resch had been in the cordial and soft-drink business at Wilcannia since 1875. He had migrated from Germany in 1863, and his brothers, Emil and Richard, followed later. They worked together for a few years before pursuing independent careers.

Edmund and his younger brother, Richard, began brewing at Wilcannia in 1879. Four years later Richard left to manage their Lion Brewery at Cootamundra. In 1895 Edmund moved to Melbourne, and then to Sydney, where he later established one of the largest breweries in that city, Resch's Waverley Brewery.

Charles Norman ran the Lion Brewery at Wilcannia from 1908 to 1925; followed by Vincent Mitselberg, who continued until the brewery closed.

Part of the old brewery still stands alongside the Wilcannia Golf Club.

Wilcannia Brewery 1867–73

Although the Wilcannia Brewery was the first to operate in the town, it was the least successful. James Parker established it in 1867, but the following year the brewery closed.

The next owner, J. P. Tripp, reopened the brewery in 1871, and leased it to Robert Bruce & Co. late in 1872. The property and all the equipment were auctioned in March 1873.

Windsor

Windsor, named after an English town on the Thames River, is the second-oldest town in Australia after Sydney. (Parramatta was settled earlier, but is now a suburb of Sydney.)

Dickens, Daniel c. 1825

'July 7, 1825. To let or for sale. Dwelling with malt and brewhouses, granary, bakehouse and cellar, Apply at the premises to Daniel Dickens, Windsor.' This may have been Henry Kable's brewery being advertised for sale.

Hawkesbury Brewery 1833–c. 1870
Cornwallis Road (near Riccaby Creek)/
cnr Kable Street and the river bank

Thomas Cadell had a brewery and malthouse in Windsor. When he started brewing in 1833, samples of his beer were sent to the editors of Sydney newspapers, and excellent reports were given concerning the quality of Cadell's beer. One local connoisseur declared that the beer was

> quite equal to the best quality of beer drunk from the cask at gentlemen's tables in England and besides being more wholesome than the vile stuff produced from sugar, it was cheaper.

Another kindly editorial appeared in the September 1833 issue of the *New South Wales Magazine*:

> It has been the fashion to plead in extenuation of the prevalent use of ardent spirits in the Colonies that Colonial Beer was not fit to drink, and that British made liquor was too expensive. We have much pleasure in intimating that this excuse is now likely to be altogether set aside. An ale has been produced at Windsor by a Mr. Cadell of so excellent a quality that it falls little short of the celebrated Hudgson's Pale Ale. We strongly recommend our readers to taste and judge for themselves.

Thomas Cadell was persuaded to set up depots in Sydney, and by 1835 he had started another brewery, the Windsor, in Bridge Street, Sydney. After ten years the Hawkesbury Brewery was rebuilt at the corner of Kable Street and the river bank. It was described as being the largest in the district, with three-storey buildings of brick construction and slate roofs. After visiting the brewery in 1861, Governor Young doubted that there was any brewery as large and as ably conducted in the colony.

Kable's Brewery 1811–c. 1830

At the beginning of 1811 Henry Kable and Richard Woodbury built a large and well-equipped brewery on a 2-acre block of land, with a freshwater creek flowing alongside. The complex consisted of a brick brewery, malthouse, kiln, granary, and a comfortable house. In keeping with the custom of the period, Kable & Woodbury advised all and sundry, by card, of their superior products and terms of trading.

Richard Woodbury retired in 1816, and sold his interest to his partner. By 1820 the management had been taken over by Henry Kable's son, George, who ran the business until the late 1820s or early 1830s.

Windsor Brewery 1806–10

For years Andrew Thompson was a figure of importance in the colony — a man of substance, a public benefactor, head constable of the Hawkesbury, and a confidant and friend of governors. A native of Scotland, Thompson's transport to Australia had been at government expense, and his first work was with stone gangs at Parramatta. On the expiration of his sentence he became a watchman in Sydney, and later he set up as a storekeeper at Greenhills (as Windsor was known at that time). His progress was rapid; he became a farmer, dairyman, auctioneer, publican, land and house proprietor, general merchant, shipbuilder, saltmaker and brewer.

When Governor King acknowledged the arrival of equipment for the Government Brewery at Parramatta, he asked the Home Authority to send out more brewing equipment so that other breweries could be started at Sydney, Windsor and Norfolk Island. When the goods arrived two years later in 1806, the Government Brewery at Parramatta had, by this time, proved to be a total failure, and King had no intentions of repeating the mistake.

In April 1806 Andrew Thompson was offered the brewing equipment and an opportunity to start a brewery at Windsor. He accepted, and entered into an agreement on 11 May 1806 whereby payment for the equipment was to be made in beer to be supplied to the Crown. Sales to the public were to be 1s per gallon.

Andrew Thompson had a public house attached to the brewery. He also had an illicit distillery, and traded in spirits — which attracted a £100 fine. Thompson died in 1810 at the age of thirty-seven, and the brewery closed. The *Sydney Gazette* of 8 December 1810 advertised the brewery: 'To be let. Extensive farm and properties including a large and convenient brewery at the Green Hills on the bank of the South Creek, the property of Andrew Thompson, deceased'. By 1816 the buildings had been converted to the Windsor Public Hospital.

Woodburn

Pedley, Arthur 1887

Wollongong

Young, George 1869–11

Wyalong

Wyalong Brewery 1894–1901

When the brewery started, the proprietors Alphonso Tewksbury and James Bellair were also the owners of the Temora Brewery, 60 km to the south. By 1896 the Wyalong Brewery had been bought by McIntyre, Lincoln & Co.; William Henry Eaton was involved in the business at the turn of the century.

Yass

Europeans first entered the Yass area in 1821. Settlement started soon after, following the Hume and Hovell Expedition in 1824. Settlement was slow, and by 1848 there were only 55 houses and 274 inhabitants in the district.

Star Brewery 1882–87
Bowning Road, near Yass

After selling his share in the Standard Brewery at Orange, Edward Heap settled in Yass. He converted a disused tannery into the Star Brewery, and 'soon made a name for his liquor'. Heap supplied the principal hotels and private families in the district.

Yass Brewery 1864–65

Milne & Woodman began brewing ale for the locals in 1864. The following year Milne was brewing on his own, and later that year the brewery closed. The population of Yass was then 1200, sufficient, it would seem, to have supported a brewery.

Young

Crystal Spring Brewery 1885–1916
Clarke Street

George Cranfield was in business as a baker, confectioner and aerated-water manufacturer, and was the mayor of Young, during the 1880s. In 1885 he started the Crystal Spring Brewery, in spite of the fact that there was already a well-established brewery in town. Cranfield's brewery was at the foot of Burrowa Street, beyond the Australia Hotel and facing Clarke Street.

Cranfield managed to brew good beer, and received distinction by winning second prize for his ale at the Melbourne Exhibition in 1888. He also received an award at the Brewers' Show in London in 1891.

Young Brewery 1874–97
Garibaldi Gully

In August 1874 work commenced on the construction of an 'up-to-date' brewery at Young. It was about a mile from the centre of the town, 'on the slope of a hill by the side of Garibaldi Gully, to the left of the Burrowa Road, close to the recreation ground'.

The proprietors were Frederick Gleich and William Hills. Gleich had been the owner of the Hume Brewery in Albury in the 1870s. A reporter from the *Young Chronicle* visited the building site in October 1874 and said, 'after a short walk through light scrub ... came upon the brewery, a neat brick building situated on the edge of the creek'. There was also a brick cellar, many large sheds, and an engine room with two large boilers that used water from a nearby dam.

William Hills ran the brewery on his own in 1881, but he began to devote more of his time to grazing and breeding cattle. He owned considerable property at Young.

During the late 1880s new owners, Frederick Sibbald and Henry Simmond, ran into some trouble with the law. Both were fined £30 plus costs, in default six months' imprisonment, for allowing a cask of beer to leave their brewery fraudulently stamped. Their horse, cart and chattels were also confiscated — in all, a severe punishment for a relatively minor misdemeanour.

The partnership of Lang & Parker operated the brewery in 1893, then Lang on his own for the next two years. Harry Tovey was the owner when the brewery closed in 1897.

Victoria

The first attempted settlement of Victoria occurred in October 1803 when Lieutenant-Colonel David Collins, under the direction of Governor Philip Gidley King in Sydney, landed a party of soldiers, convicts and free settlers at Port Phillip Bay near modern-day Sorrento. Three months later Collins was compelled to abandon the scheme and transferred his party to Van Diemen's Land, as the southern island of Australia (Tasmania) was then known.

In May 1835 cattlebreeder John Batman sailed to Port Phillip Bay from Van Diemen's Land, and on 8 June that year he noted a good site for a village a short distance above the Yarra River estuary. Soon after, on 29 August, another party, organised by John Pascoe Fawkner, settled on the northern bank of the Yarra River near the present location of Spencer Street, and the site of early Melbourne was established. The group did not include Fawkner, who arrived with his wife two months later. He then started a small store and inn at the new settlement.

Both Governor Richard Bourke, who had visited the site in 1837 and Captain William Lonsdale, the resident magistrate, believed the estuary would become the site of the major settlement, and named it Williamstown after King William IV of England. The area a short distance up river was named Melbourne, after the then prime minister of England.

The Early Brewers

By 1838, less than three years after the first permanent settlement, four breweries were operating in Melbourne, all producing ale and porter of very questionable quality. The population at the time was 3511 (3080 males and 431 females).

The first brewer was John Mills, who owned and operated the Melbourne Brewery & Distillery from either July or August 1837. A former convict, Mills had trouble with the authorities and was fined for trading on Sundays. Earlier, he had been sentenced to fifty lashes for drunkenness. In 1843 Mills was forced by the Melbourne Health Department to close his brewery, as it was thought that his beer, brewed from polluted Yarra River water, had caused the death of sixteen people.

The Britannia Brewery was also in business in 1838. The owner, Thomas Capel, suffered the terrible misfortune of losing his young, pregnant wife when

John Mill's Brewery, c. 1839. John Mills was Melbourne's first brewer. He traded as the Melbourne Brewery & Distillery, but was forced to close on 12 January 1843 as it was thought that the brewery's beer had caused the death of sixteen people.

From a watercolour by W. E. Liardet, La Trobe Library, State Library of Victoria

she was shipwrecked off the eastern coast of Victoria and captured by Aboriginal people. She and her young child were rescued years later, but Mrs Capel was by then incurably insane.

The early Melbourne brewers found it almost impossible to brew anything approaching good beer. The Murphy brothers owned the Wharf Brewery in Flinders Street and, like that of their competitor, John Mills, the beer they produced was barely drinkable. When Murphy's Swipes, as their beer was called, was served at the Governor's Ball, many of the guests required medical attention after drinking the beer, and some were ill for days.

Another Melbourne brewer in 1838 was John Moss, a free settler, who brewed at the back of his modest Ships Inn. He had trouble with the law — his crimes were Sunday trading, and allowing his customers to gamble. His beer, Sheoaks Tops, sold for 2s a gallon.

By 1843 Melbourne had become a fast-growing centre for shipping, supply and banking, and the population of just over 4000 could buy beer from six breweries. Twenty years later the number had increased to twenty, and the peak was reached in 1874 when no fewer than thirty-one breweries were flourishing in Melbourne.

Country Breweries

Victoria has had far more breweries than any other Australian state. In total, no fewer than 300 breweries have existed in Victoria, including 90 in Melbourne. The first Victorian country brewery, the Barwon Brewery, started in Geelong in 1841. The owner, Oliver Adams, advertised in the *Geelong Advertiser* of 24 April 1841:

> Barwon Brewery — The friends of temperance as well as the lovers of good beer will be glad to learn that a pleasant and wholesome liquor is now brewed in Geelong … We

hope that the host of spirit drinkers, if they can't keep sober … will substitute ale and beer for rum and gin.

In November 1834 Edward and Francis Henty crossed Bass Strait from Van Diemen's Land, and landed at Portland Bay on Victoria's south-west coast. They established a whaling depot, and formed sheep and cattle stations on rich pasture lands to the north. Portland was actually Victoria's first permanent settlement, predating Melbourne by six months or more. After Geelong, Portland was Victoria's second country township to have a brewery when William Johns started making beer at the back of the London Inn in 1842.

On 1 July 1851 the Port Phillip District of NSW separated from Sydney as the Colony of Victoria. It was during that year that gold was first discovered in central Victoria; the goldrushes that followed, and the development of townships, were of unprecedented proportion in the history of Australia. Victoria's population in 1851 was 77,000. Ten years later it was 540,000 and still growing as the result of the surge of gold seekers from around the world.

During the 1860s more than 80 breweries were operating in no fewer than 34 country towns, and the spread continued. The goldmining town of Bendigo had 25 breweries, the most by far of any Australian country town. Second was Castlemaine with 16 breweries, followed by Geelong with 11, Ballarat 10 and Beechworth 8. With the exception of Geelong, all of these were rich gold-mining townships.

The pastoral towns of Hamilton and Wangaratta each had 6 breweries as did the port of Echuca on the Murray River. During the depression years of the 1890s there were still more than 100 breweries operating in Victoria, including 30 in Melbourne. But the era of the small country and city breweries was slowly to end.

Decline

Gradually, country breweries were forced to close, some because of the declining population of townships after the gold ran out, but mostly because of the competition from the large Melbourne breweries with their lower prices and incentives, better-quality beer and company-owned hotels. From the 1860s railways began to fan out across the colony, providing rapid and cheap transport for the Melbourne breweries to distribute their products. Country Victoria had 91 breweries in 1870. Twenty years later this was down to 66 and by 1910, the number was 33. Only six remained by 1930.

At the turn of the century there were far too many breweries in Melbourne — of the eighteen breweries, very few were solvent and the competition was crippling. As a

---

INTERESTING CALCULATION

The total quantity of beer ('colonial' and 'lager') that was brewed in the colony of Victoria during 1899 was 15,555,455 gallons. If this huge quantity of beer was put into hogsheads, 311,109 would be required to hold it all. If placed together end to end, they would stretch along a distance of over 181 miles, or would form a continuous line from Melbourne to Wodonga on the border of New South Wales.

Australian Brewers' Journal, April 1900

measure of necessity, six of Melbourne's largest breweries amalgamated in 1907 to form Carlton & United Breweries Pty Ltd (CUB). After taking over its competitor, the Melbourne Co-operative Brewery Co. Ltd in 1925, CUB was then the only major brewing company in Melbourne, and it held a monopoly on much of the beer trade throughout Victoria. But competition was soon to arrive.

A Challenge

During 1928 a Tasmanian hopgrower, Grant Hay, set up his Richmond Brewery. Although the new company was small in size compared to CUB, its products attracted considerable popularity. To retain its outright supremacy, CUB purchased the Richmond Brewery in 1962, and closed it.

The only other local challenge to CUB occurred in 1968 when Courage Breweries Ltd built a substantial brewery in the northern Melbourne suburb of Coolaroo. Its effect on CUB's business was minimal, although it was ultimately taken over by CUB and closed. From 1983 CUB has been the only major brewery operating in Melbourne; after 1989 it remained the only major brewery in Victoria.

Although a number of small boutique breweries have been started in Melbourne and country Victoria since the late 1980s, CUB, now restructured as the Foster's Brewing Group, maintains its pride of place as arguably the largest brewing enterprise in Australia.

Throughout the state it is unfortunate that there is very little structural evidence left standing as witness to the heritage of Victoria's brewing history. Of those that do remain, there are two in Melbourne of relative significance: the tower of the Yorkshire Brewery in Collingwood, and the grand facade of the Victoria Brewery in Victoria Parade, East Melbourne.

VICTORIA

#	Location	Grid	#	Location	Grid	#	Location	Grid
1	Alberton	G8	25	Dooen	B5	49	Lilydale	E6
2	Alexandra	F6	26	Dunolly	D5	50	Maindample	F5
3	Amherst	C6	27	Echuca	E4	51	Maldon	D5
4	Ararat	C6	28	Eddington	D5	52	Malmsbury	D6
5	Bacchus Marsh	E6	29	Eldorado	G4	53	Maryborough	C5
6	Bairnsdale	H6	30	Enoch Point	F6	54	Melbourne	E6
7	Ballarat	D6	31	Fernshaw	F6	55	Mildura	A1
8	Beaufort	C6	32	Gaffneys Creek	D7	56	Moonambel	C5
9	Beechworth	G4	33	Geelong	G5	57	Mooroopna	E5
10	Benalla	F5	34	Germantown	E6	58	Mt Beckworth	D6
11	Bendigo	D5	35	Gisborne	G5	59	Mt Macedon	E6
12	Blackwood	D6	36	Glen Creek	F5	60	Newbridge	D5
13	Bridgewater	D5	37	Gobur	B6	61	Nhill	A4
14	Bright	G5	38	Hamilton	E5	62	Port Albert	G8
15	Buninyong	D6	39	Heathcote	B5	63	Port Fairy	B7
16	Camperdown	C7	40	Horsham	D5	64	Portland	A7
17	Carapooee	C5	41	Inglewood	G6	65	Quantong	A5
18	Carisbrook	D5	42	Jamieson	E6	66	Riddell's Creek	E6
19	Castlemaine	D5	43	Kilmore	D3	67	Rochester	E4
20	Chewton	D6	44	Koondrook	E6	68	Rushworth	E5
21	Chiltern	G4	45	Kyneton	E6	69	St Arnaud	C5
22	Colac	C7	46	Lancefield	D6	70	Sale	G7
23	Creswick	D6	47	Leigh Creek	E5	71	Seymour	E5
24	Daylesford	D6	48	Lillicur	C6	72	Shepparton	E4
						73	Smythesdale	C6
						74	Stanley	G5
						75	Stawell	B5
						76	Stratford	H7
						77	Talbot	D6
						78	Tallangatta	H4
						79	Tanjil South	G7
						80	Taradale	D6
						81	Tarraville	G8
						82	Trentham	D6
						83	Vectis	B5
						84	Wahgunyah	G4
						85	Wail	B5
						86	Walhalla	G7
						87	Wangaratta	G4
						88	Warracknabeal	B4
						89	Warrnambool	B7
						90	Wodonga	G4
						91	Woodend	E6
						92	Woods Point	G6
						93	Yackandandah	G4
						94	Yarrawonga	F4

VICTORIA — 91

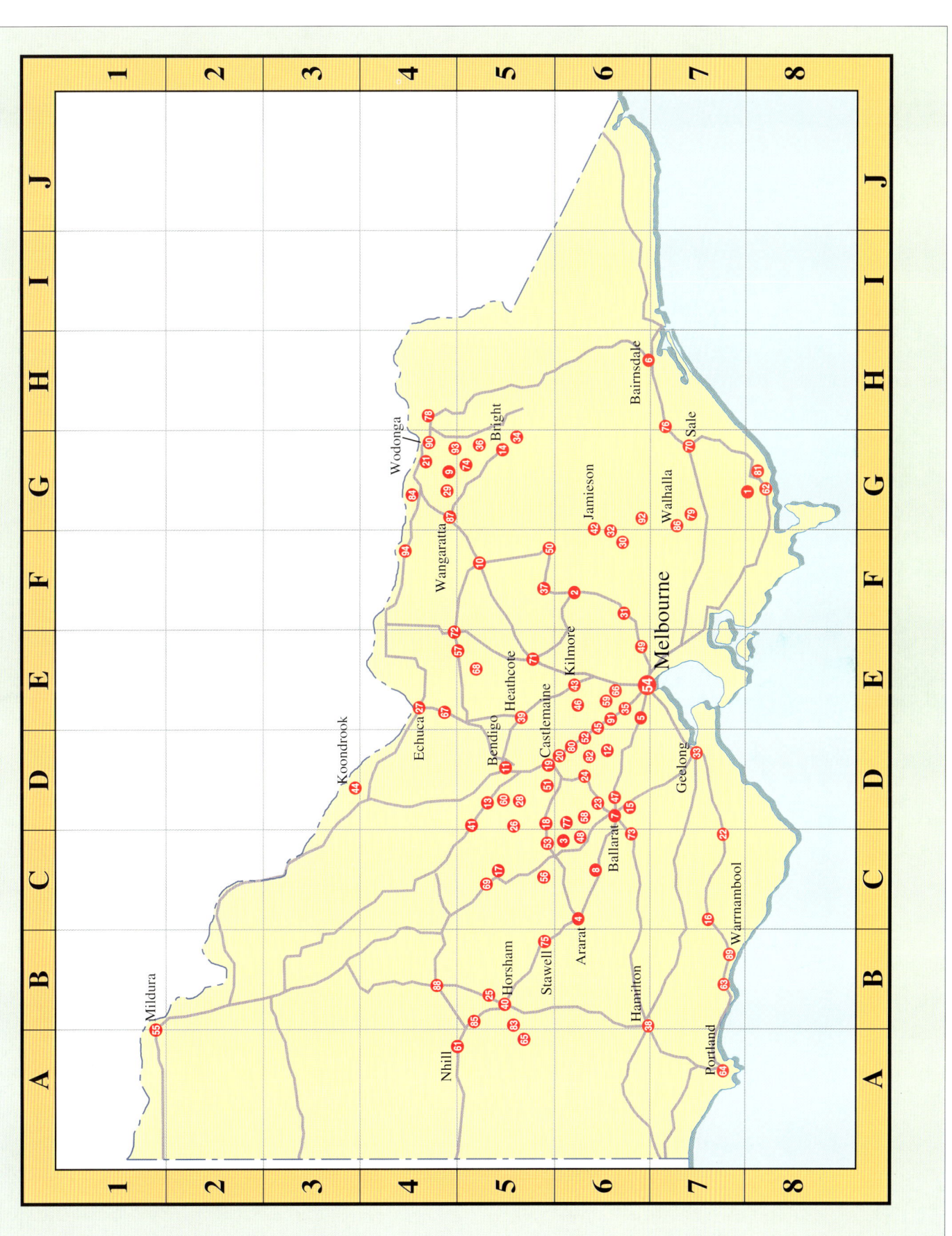

Alberton

Alberton Brewery 1851
Johnson Street

It was an adventurous undertaking when Newton & Martin started brewing at Alberton in 1851. The tiny township was located in the south-west coastal region of Gippsland. Apart from the few locals, the only other customers were the crews from passing ships as they came and went, staying briefly on each visit.

Alexandra

Goldmining, and the heavily timbered fertile soil surrounding the Upper Goulburn River, provided the initial attractions for settlers to the district. When the gold was worked out, timber-milling became the district's main economic activity, and the population was enough to warrant a brewery.

Burton Brewery
See Lion Brewery.

Lion Brewery c. 1867–85
Goulburn River

The partnership of Power & Blain started the Lion Brewery at Alexandra about 1867, but by October of that year the brewery and plant were offered for sale. James Blain continued brewing on his own, and on 21 August 1871 new owners, Eagles & Gruby, advertised under the name of the Burton Brewery. The name was changed back to the Lion Brewery before 1878. Later, Henry Knight advertised in the *Mansfield Guardian* of 2 November 1878 that 'he has just purchased the Lion Brewery and … can supply a First Class Ale at a moderate price'.

Typical label used by many country hotels that bottled bulk beer purchased from Melbourne breweries. The label was overprinted with the hotel name.

Amherst

Mayton's Brewery c. 1860
The *North Western Chronicle* of 25 October 1860 referred to Mayton's Brewery. Sam Marks was brewing at Amherst at that time, and probably started the Red Lion (Mayton's Brewery) that he sold to James Neave.

Red Lion Brewery 1860–c. 1864
McCullum's Creek

Several Red Lion breweries operating in western NSW during the latter part of the nineteenth century were owned by Henry Lindsay, and were not connected with the Red Lion Brewery at Amherst.

James R. Neave advertised in the *Maryborough and Dunolly Advertiser* of February 1860 that he could supply XXX Malt Ales and Stout. Another advertisement in the *Talbot and North Western Chronicle* of 1 January 1862 said that

> in order to meet competition, he is able to reduce prices:- XXX Ale and Porter to two shillings and sixpence per gallon and XX Ale to two shillings per gallon. Free delivery within 15 miles of the brewery.

Ararat

Mt Ararat was named in 1841 by the first squatter in the district, Horatio Wills, whose journal records: 'I name this place Mount Ararat for, like the ark, we rested there'. By 1854 gold had been discovered in the region, and the miners rushed to the area, digging out the precious metal until no more could be found. Many workers stayed on after the gold rush to become merchants and farmers.

Ararat Brewery 1859–1905
One of the local residents, John (Jens) Kofoed, a shipwright from Denmark, built his Fountain Head Brewery at Armstrong, about 6 km north-west from Ararat. It stood on the bank of a creek at a picturesque spot a short distance to the east of the main road. Kofoed put an advertisement in the *Mount Ararat Advertiser* of 17 May 1859:

> John Kofoed, Fountain Head Brewery, Armstrong, has completed his large and extensive brewery …
> has available Colonial Malt Ale, Lemonade, Ginger Beer, Cider and Cordials.

The brewery was a large building, four storeys high, and close to two streams where clean, fresh water came from a natural underground spring. Kofoed supplied the miners with his beer in the early years, and continued to do so until his death in 1887. Visiting journalists spoke highly of the brewery as 'probably the most self-contained and compact and certainly the cleanest brewery in the colony or on the continent of Australia'.

Mrs Kofoed, assisted by the manager Alex Belperoud, ran the brewery for several years, and then sold in November 1891 to Joseph Block. Block was a jeweller by trade, and after labouring on for a year or so decided to quit.

The new owners in 1893 were C. H. Chateau and James Calvert, and the first thing they did was to change the name to the Chateau Brewery. In 1896 it was changed again, to Ararat Brewery, after Chateau had left to become brewer at the South Australian Brewery in Broken Hill. (It was not uncommon for a good brewer to shift from time to time to another brewery where the pay or incentive was better. Chateau had been at the Esk Brewery, Launceston; six years at the Carlton Brewery, Melbourne; the West End Brewery, Brisbane; the Ararat Brewery, and now on to Broken Hill.)

James Calvert was left on his own to run the Ararat Brewery. His wife, Florence, was running the business in 1899, followed by H. Brinkley & Sons, who purchased the brewery and everything that went with it in 1900. One of the sons, R. B. Brinkley, had been the head brewer at McCracken's City Brewery, Melbourne. The Brinkleys applied for a trademark registration of a label, comprising the device of an ark, the word 'ARK', and a monogram consisting of the letters B and S (Brinkley & Sons), in respect of ales and beers.

Late in 1901 James Elliott (of Western Australian brewing fame) took over from Mary Jane Brinkley.

Fountain Head Brewery
John Kofoed	1859–87
Mrs Kofoed	1887–91
Joseph Block	1891–93

Chateau Brewery
Chateau & Calvert	1893–96

Ararat Brewery
James Calvert	1896–99
Florence Calvert	1899–1900
H. Brinkley & Sons	1900–1
Mary Jane Brinkley	1901
James Elliott	1901–5

Chateau Brewery
See Ararat Brewery.

Fountain Head Brewery
See Ararat Brewery.

Bacchus Marsh

Symington's Brewery   1858–86
Symington's Brewery has long since been demolished, but it was originally located about 5 km on the Melbourne side of Bacchus Marsh. A roadhouse now occupies the site.

William Symington ran the brewery until his death in March 1867, and his son, also William, continued the business, producing an average of 16 hogsheads of beer per month. The brewery was in a good position to attract the passing trade, being on the main road from Melbourne to Ballarat.

Bairnsdale

Bairnsdale Brewery   1868–72
Nicholson Street

The *Gippsland Times* of 10 October 1868 reported that

> A brewery has been established … the first brew from which was completed on the 7th inst. Some of the local publicans have taken umbrage at the fact that the proprietor has adopted the course of disposing of his article to the limited population of Bairnsdale, in small kegs.

The proprietor was Joseph Day. He brewed for only five months, and on 16 March 1869 another editorial in the *Gippsland Times* advised that Edward Thomas was now working the brewery.

By April 1872 brewing had stopped, and the property was advertised to let.

Bairnsdale Brewing & Distilling Co. Ltd   1887–90
Pope Street, Picnic Point

The brewery was built during 1886, and was formally opened on 5 January 1887. The first hogshead was tapped, the new brew declared to be of good quality, and the proprietors were congratulated on their enterprise. The owners were the Spargo brothers of Melbourne, in partnership with W. Gowers. They built a malthouse, used locally grown hops, and chose the name Picnic Point Brewery because of its location at Picnic Point, to the west of the township, near the Mitchell River.

In June 1890 the Bairnsdale Brewing & Distilling Co. Ltd was established

> for the purpose of purchasing the goodwill, freehold property, machinery, plant etc., at Bairnsdale, of the Bairnsdale Brewery and Malthouse, for the sum of £2,250 and to carry thereon the business of malting, brewing and distilling.

The vendors were W. H. Gowers and B. B. Spargo. They had every confidence in the success of the new company, and agreed to take up 2000 shares and to give a guarantee to the other shareholders that a dividend of not less than 10 per cent would be paid for three years. Their own shares would be lodged as security for the due performance of the guarantee.

In September 1890, following the first general meeting of shareholders where directors were elected, a dinner was held on the verandah of the Victoria Hotel, specially walled-in with canvas for the occasion. The chairman, in congratulating the company and directors, said:

> the brewery should be of great advantage to the district and apart from proving a payable concern to the shareholders, would be a powerful factor in the district interests of hop growing and barley growing.

The following month, October 1890, shareholders were advised that their share certificates were ready, and could be collected at the office of the company in Bailey Street. Within weeks, however, doubts and problems began to surface.

In a 'Letter to the Editor', quoted in the *Gippsland Daily News* of 31 October 1890, one shareholder asked the directors if they intended having an investigation made to disprove the many rumours concerning the unsatisfactory state of the supposed assets of the company. The situation worsened the following month when judgements were given in the Bairnsdale Police Court against the brewery company, and in favour of claimants for monies overdue.

It had been said that 'the beer from the Picnic Point Brewery tasted awful and they went broke'. However, after the assessment of assets and liabilities, the result showed a surplus of £139.

The large building forming part of the old brewery had been used as a barn, and was burnt to the ground with its contents of basketmaking material in 1903.

Goold's Brewery 1875–80
Cnr Service & Francis Streets

Although Michael Goold had started the brewery, within a year or so it had changed hands; the new owner was Charles Cima. Hops were available locally, and soon Cima had a thriving business. He advertised in the *Bairnsdale Courier* in December 1877 that he was bottling stout, ale and porter.

James Pettit of the Victoria Brewery in Sale had advertised in the *Gippsland Mercury* of June 1877 that he was the proprietor of breweries at Sale, Bairnsdale and Walhalla. He had apparently purchased the brewery at Bairnsdale from Cima in 1877. Cima continued to work there as manager until 1878, when he died as the result of an accident: while repairing a pump at the bottom of a well, part of the connecting rod fell down the shaft onto his chest, and he died several weeks later.

In 1860 the township of Bairnsdale was laid out, grid-iron fashion with wide streets, by James Pettit. He combined brewing and surveying with auctioneering and other ventures, but his brewing endeavours at Bairnsdale were the least successful, and the brewery closed in 1880.

Picnic Point Brewery
See Bairnsdale Brewing & Distilling Co. Ltd.

Ballarat

Ballarat is Victoria's largest inland city and takes its name from an Aboriginal word meaning 'resting place'. At one time the name was spelt 'Ballaarat'.

In the late afternoon of 21 August 1851 John Dunlop and James Regan found gold at Poverty Point, about 1 km from what is now the centre of Ballarat. With their picks and shovels, and tin dishes, goldseekers swarmed to the area in their thousands, and a vast settlement of tents and huts soon spread around the diggings. Within eighteen months the population had grown to 22,000, and the fortune seekers still kept coming.

One of the largest gold nuggets ever found, the Welcome Stranger, was discovered near Ballarat by two Cornish miners in 1869. About 53 cm long and 25 cm thick, the nugget weighed 73,381 grams, and was sold for £10,500.

Men who toiled under the scorching sun developed a compelling thirst, but officialdom sought to keep the district free from liquor. For the first year or two no liquor licences were granted on the diggings, and sly grog flourished — anything by the name of liquor had a ready sale at an exorbitant price. Some of the concoctions were little better than poison, with ingredients of stale wine, opium, rum, cayenne pepper and tobacco.

When liquor licences were granted in Ballarat in 1853, small breweries quickly started up in huts and wooden shacks, and the beer produced was generally not much better than the foul sly grog. However, a few brewers began to produce beer of better quality — those who didn't soon went out of business.

Ballarat was the scene of Australia's most famous civil insurrection. On 3 December 1854, at Eureka, miners clashed with Victorian military and police forces. Arising from a series of miners' grievances, it resulted in about thirty deaths.

Ballarat is famous for its parks and gardens, and the annual Begonia Festival, first held in 1953, attracts many visitors. At Sovereign Hill, close to the centre of the city, a goldmining township has been authentically reconstructed. Visitors can pan for gold, watch working exhibits and wander through the many period buildings that recapture the atmosphere of old Ballarat.

Albion Brewery c. 1860
Errard Street

In the newly-settled goldmining township of Ballarat, a gold seeker with a 'strike' would have immediate success to show for his efforts. Not so the brewer. His chances of success, to put out a saleable beer, were generally very slim because of the heat and the dust and the polluted creek water.

George Hinyard expected success when he started the Albion Brewery around 1860, but nobody liked his beer, and poor George had to close his brewery. The premises subsequently became an aerated-water factory, and later a malthouse that was operated by the partnership of the brewers, Elliot & Magill.

Ballarat Brewing Co. Ltd 1895–1989
Armstrong Street

This well-known Victorian brewing company was formed in 1895 as Coghlan & Tulloch's Ballarat Brewing Co. Pty Ltd, by the amalgamation of the Phoenix Brewery of James Coghlan (established at nearby Warrenheip in 1857) and the Royal Standard Brewery of William Tulloch (established in Armstrong Street in 1853).

At the time of amalgamation the new company also purchased the Barley Sheaf Brewery of Henry Leggo & Sons (established at Creswick Road in 1857). The Barley Sheaf Brewery was closed, but the acquisition, and the amalgamation of the Phoenix and Royal Standard breweries, included a considerable number of properties, grazing and crop land and about sixty hotels. The trademark of the new company was made up of the phoenix (a large mythical bird rising from flames) of the Phoenix Brewery, holding the royal standard of the Standard Brewery in its beak.

An advertisement of the Ballarat Brewing Co. Pty Ltd, 1930.

Strong and progressive management, and popular beers, led to the company's rapid growth. Gradually more hotels were acquired and depots were established at Melbourne, Geelong, Creswick, Scarsdale, Horsham and Hamilton. The Barley Sheaf Brewery was used as a malthouse and for storage until its destruction by fire in 1954.

Both the Phoenix and Royal Standard breweries continued to operate independently until 1911, when the Phoenix was closed. The big horse-drawn wagons laden with hogsheads of beer, ready for bottling at the depot at Doveton Street, Ballarat, no longer rumbled through the hills on their journey from Warrenheip.

The small Maryborough brewery, which the company had bought in 1897, continued to operate until 1911, and it was during that year that the company name was simplified to the Ballarat Brewing Co. Pty Ltd.

Both James Coghlan and William Tulloch, the founders of the brewery, became active in community affairs. As a justice of the peace, Coghlan attended the Bungaree Court, while Tulloch became a city councillor and a member of the Art Gallery and Mechanics' Institute.

On 1 February 1915 the company struck water at a depth of 80 feet in a shaft near the intersection of Lydiard and Dana Streets. The water was excellent, and the output of 3300 gallons per hour came at an appropriate time when the Ballarat reservoirs were almost empty.

In 1936 the business became the Ballarat Brewing Co. Ltd, and in 1953 the Volum Brewery in Geelong was taken over, together with its chain of twenty-one hotels. By 1958 the company owned 114 hotels. During that year the Ballarat Brewing Co. Ltd sold its brewing assets, and also the building in Armstrong Street (the site of the old Royal Standard Brewery), to Carlton & United Breweries Ltd, Melbourne. The Ballarat Brewing Co. Ltd, although no longer involved in brewing, retained its head office in Dana Street, its chain of hotels, and its name, and continued to manage its hotel, motel and other investment businesses.

During the 1980s production of Ballarat Bitter was transferred to CUB, Melbourne, and the Ballarat Brewery then produced only one product, Invalid Stout. Brewing at Ballarat ceased altogether in 1989, 136 years after William Tulloch had started as the Royal Standard Brewery. It had been Victoria's longest operating brewery.

Ballarat Brewing Co. Ltd

Coghlan & Tulloch's Ballarat Brewing Co. Pty Ltd	1895–1911
(amalgamation of Phoenix Brewery, at Warrenheip (founded 1857), and Royal Standard Brewery, at Ballarat (founded 1853); both breweries continued to operate)	
Barley Sheaf Brewery purchased	1895, closed 1897
Maryborough Brewery purchased	
Ballarat Brewing Co. Pty Ltd	1911–36
Phoenix and Maryborough breweries closed in 1911	
Ballarat Brewing Co. Ltd	1936–58
Volum Brewery, Geelong purchased	1953; closed 1958
Carlton & United Breweries Ltd	1958–89

The Ballarat Brewing Co.'s famous character, 'Ballarat Bertie', has been used as a symbol on bottle labels and advertising since 1927. Ballarat Bertie, the little man with a walrus moustache, clad in an apron and holding up his foaming glass of beer, became a household name throughout central Victoria.

Barley Sheaf Brewery   1857–95
15 Creswick Road

In 1857 Henry Leggo formed a partnership with his brother-in-law, J. B. Murton, and at the start they made beer in an unpretentious, small wooden shed. The business traded as H. Leggo & Co., and was called the Barley Sheaf Brewery. The partnership was successful, lasting for sixteen years, and was amicably dissolved in 1873.

By 1888 the business was trading as H. Leggo & Sons, but within a few years the company was in financial difficulty, and in 1893 the brewery and hotel properties were offered for sale. Joseph Leggo was in charge at that time.

One of the Leggo sons, Charles, met with a fatal

Henry Leggo's Barley Sheaf Brewery, Creswick Road, Ballarat, 1888.

accident in May 1891 when he stepped off a moving tramcar; he was crushed to death when he fell under the wheels of the vehicle.

In 1895 the Barley Sheaf Brewery was purchased by the Coghlan & Tulloch's Ballarat Brewing Co. Pty Ltd. Brewing ceased, and the premises were used as a malthouse and store until it was destroyed by fire in 1954.

Black Horse Brewery   1862–96
7 Ripon Street, Ballarat West

When George Lee started the Black Horse Brewery in 1862, he traded as Lee & Hull, although he was the major partner. In February 1885 Lee was fined £10 for trading without a licence. In defence, he said he had been paying his licence fees for twenty years, always during the second week in January — some bureaucrat had discovered that the Act required payment to be made by the first day of January each year.

George Lee took on Francis Drew as a partner in 1890, but on 29 May the following year Drew was found dead in his office, shot through the heart. The case was determined as suicide. It was said that the deceased had been unfortunate in investments, and that the losses had preyed on his mind. Shortly after, a meeting of creditors of the firm of Lee & Drew was held, but the Black Horse Brewery continued for a few more years.

Late in 1896 J. J. Trait leased the brewery from George Lee. At that time it was called the XXX Brewery, and there was also a branch at Geelong. In 1897 F. J. (Jessie) Evans acquired the Ballarat premises, but conducted no business there.

BOTTLED STOUT AT AUCTION

At the auction sale of railway passengers' 'lost property', Melbourne, on 12th March [1914], the clerk read out the item — 36 bottles of Ballarat Brewing Co.'s stout! The crowd bid spiritedly. The lot was 'knocked down' for twelve shillings. This worked out at fourpence a bottle.

Australian Brewers' Journal, March 1914

Coghlan & Tulloch's Ballarat Brewing Co. Pty Ltd
See Ballarat Brewing Co. Ltd.

Coghlan & Crabbe   1883–c. 1894
Doveton Street

After arriving in Melbourne in 1863 W. J. Coghlan immediately made his way to Ballarat, and started work at the Phoenix Brewery, which was owned by his uncle, James Coghlan. After fifteen years at the Phoenix, W. J. Coghlan sought the experience of station life in the Western District of Victoria. According to W. B. Kimberley, *Ballarat and Vicinity* (1894), Coghlan then went to the Gympie goldfields in Queensland, and joined a Mr Finselbach at the Brewery Tap Hotel and Brewery.

In 1883 Coghlan returned to Ballarat, and began brewing in Doveton Street. Two years later a Mr Crabbe became a partner, and they traded as Coghlan & Crabbe. Crabbe subsequently left, and in 1891 a Mr Naples joined the firm.

Eureka Aerated Waters & Brewing Co.   1897–1905
103 Creswick Road

The original proprietors were Alfred Clarke, Jessie Evans and David Jones. Clarke and Evans were also the proprietors of the Bux Brewing Co., Melbourne, and non-alcoholic Bux Ale and Progress brand soda water were produced at their breweries at both Melbourne and Ballarat. Just before Christmas 1897, during hot weather, the company sold their entire stock of 48,000 bottles of Hop Beer in three days.

Priscilla Nicholas and Alice Clarke became the owners in 1902, and the operation was shifted to 103 Creswick Road during 1905. With Nicholas sole proprietor at that time, the business was registered as the Eureka Aerated Waters & Brewing Co. It is doubtful whether any alcoholic beverages were brewed after 1905, and the company continued making cordials and soft drinks until the late 1920s.

Gilchrist's Brewery   1855–59
Warrenheip

W. J. Gilchrist built his brewery on the western side of Mt Warrenheip, about 6 km from Ballarat. He was an experienced chemist, and using the excellent springwater on his property, he made ales and porter of such high quality that he was awarded a Silver Medal at an Industrial Exhibition, Melbourne. For some unknown reason he left the district in 1859, and took on work as a brewer in Bendigo.

Napier Brewery   1856–69
Specimen Hill Road

The address of the brewery was variously referred to as Specimen Hill, Eureka Street, Main Road, or the Flat, presumably all referring to the same location of the brewery.

Scrase & Fry were brewing on the Flat early in 1856, and in January 1857 they advertised in the *Ballarat Star* as the Specimen Hill Brewery. At that time the Flat was the hub of Ballarat, the plateau on which the present city stands. The beer was quite good, and the partners were able to compete with the five other local breweries. The spacious cellars, 100 feet by 50 feet, were almost underneath the old Charlie Napier Theatre from which the brewery derived its name.

The partnership changed to Edwin Scrase and Edward Ainley in the early 1860s, and before the brewery closed Scrase was working the brewery on his own.

Phoenix Brewery   1857–1911
Warrenheip

During 1857 the Irishman Alex Magill started his Phoenix Brewery near the crystal-clear springs of Warrenheip, about 6 km east of Ballarat. Magill worked the brewery on his own for the first year, and then formed a partnership with his brother-in-law James Coghlan. Coghlan came to Victoria in 1853, tried his luck on the goldfields with little success, and then worked at Murphy's Wharf Brewery, Melbourne, in 1856.

The experience of both partners, and the excellent water, resulted in top-quality beer and a very successful business. The population of Ballarat was expanding, and by 1864 it had grown to 64,000, including 6000 Chinese.

The price of good beer, in 1870, was 6d a pint, but poorer quality could be bought for as little as 2d. These prices were quite high for the time, but earlier, in 1855, the cost was exorbitant at 2s a glass. The stomach ache that often followed was free.

The Magill & Coghlan partnership lasted a creditable thirty years, and was terminated only on the death of Alex Magill in 1887. Coghlan purchased the Magill family's interest, and continued to run the brewery and bottle department.

According to W. B. Kimberley in *Ballarat and Vicinity* (1894), the brewery was considered to be the largest industry of its kind in Victoria, outside Melbourne. It employed fifty men, and had an annual capacity of 20,000 hogsheads of beer. The three-storey main building had an ornamental tower, and a private farm kept 200 acres under grass and under cultivation. A private telephone connected the brewery with the offices in Dana Street, Ballarat, and also with Coghlan's private residence. The company had depots at Creswick and Scarsdale.

In later years James Coghlan used to recall to his children how well he remembered hearing, on Sunday morning, 3 December 1854, the gunshots of the Eureka uprising echoing across the hills from the scene of Australia's only battlefield. He also recalled how the local Aboriginals would creep up to the windows of his home to peer at the white people.

The year 1895 marked the amalgamation of the Phoenix Brewery with the Royal Standard Brewery, Ballarat, to form Coghlan & Tulloch's Ballarat Brewing Co. Pty Ltd. The breweries continued to operate as separate production units until the Phoenix was closed in 1911, ending a period of fifty-four years of continuous brewing.

The Phoenix Brewery, Warrenheip, c. 1880.
La Trobe Library, State Library of Victoria

Royal Standard Brewery   1853–95
Armstrong Street

Thomas McLaren migrated from Scotland, and in 1853 he started brewing in a small way in Armstrong Street. Ten years later a fellow-Scotsman, William Tulloch, became a partner, and they called their business the Royal Standard Brewery — Tulloch, previously a cattledealer, gold-digger and storekeeper, had obtained approval from the Duke of Wellington to use the name Royal Standard.

The company traded as Tulloch & McLaren until 1890, and the business then continued as Tulloch & Sons. William Tulloch's son, James, one of sixteen children, worked at the brewery as an executive officer and brewer. Branch depots were established at Melbourne and Geelong. Tulloch Snr became a member of the town council, the Old Colonists' Association, the Art

The Royal Standard Brewery, Ballarat, c. 1880. It merged with the Phoenix Brewery, Warrenheip in 1895 to form Coghlan & Tulloch's Ballarat Brewing Co. Pty Ltd.
La Trobe Library, State Library of Victoria

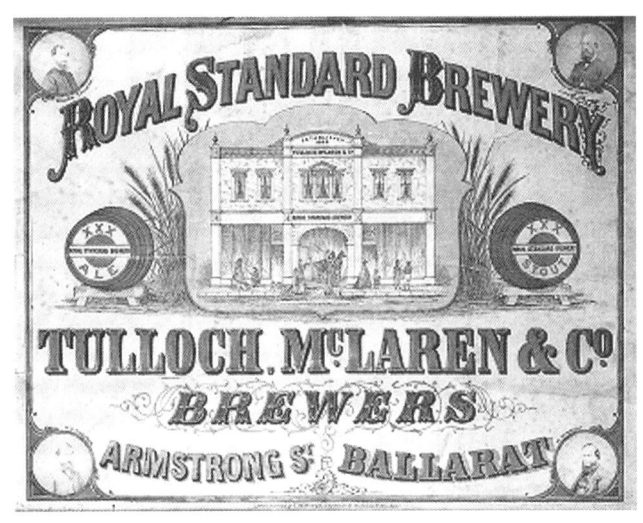

Gallery and the Mechanics' Institute. He was also an excellent brewer, and his Bitter Beer and Ale were said to be the best beers on the market.

In 1895 the Royal Standard Brewery of Tulloch & Sons amalgamated with the Phoenix Brewery of James Coghlan to form Coghlan & Tulloch's Ballarat Brewing Co. Pty Ltd. The breweries continued to operate as separate units: the Phoenix at Warrenheip, and the Royal Standard at Armstrong Street.

See also Ballarat Brewing Co. Ltd.

Specimen Hill Brewery
See Napier Brewery.

Warrenheip Brewery   1887–1914
Warrenheip

Irishman William Kenna had worked at the Phoenix Brewery, Warrenheip, for twenty years, and also at the Queen's Head Brewery, Geelong, for two years, before starting his own brewery at Warrenheip in 1887. This was a bold move for Kenna, since his neighbour, the Phoenix Brewery, was well established, and there were also many large breweries just a few kilometres away at Ballarat. William Kenna, however, was not deterred, and built quite a large brewery on the crown of a hill. He had ample fresh spring-water, and his long experience of brewing in the area ensured a quick acceptance of his beer among the locals, many of whom he had known for years.

In 1898 William Kenna was saddened by the loss of his sixteen-year-old son, Leonard, from influenza. Earlier, he had lost another son through pneumonia, and before that three other adult members of his family had died in prevailing epidemics. Five sons died within a span of eight years.

In 1891 the Breheny Brothers joined the firm, which then traded as Breheny Bros & Kenna. William Kenna died in 1910, and two years later his widow sold her interest in the brewery to the Brehenys. By 1914 brewing had ceased, and the company diversified into grain-distilling and whisky and gin production. Federal Distillers took over in 1922, and in 1932 a merger with the Distillers Company of Edinburgh saw the formation of United Distillers Limited.

XXX Brewery
See Black Horse Brewery.

Beaufort

Norfolk Brewery   c. 1866–75
Bourke Street

Henry Bourne was the owner of a hotel in Havelock Street, Beaufort; it originally had the unusual name of the Barley Mow Hotel, which was later changed to the George Hotel. In 1870 Bourne took over the Norfolk Brewery, which had been started by John Smith about 1866. A year or two later the brewery was sold to John Phillips, and Bourne went back to hotelkeeping.

Beechworth

The northern Victorian town of Beechworth came into being as the result of the rich gold discoveries in 1852. The huge demand for goods and services by the goldseekers and camp-followers attracted all types of traders, and also brewers. By 1874 there were sixty-one licensed hotels in the town, and the breweries were doing a roaring trade.

The infamous bushranger, Ned Kelly, when captured, was sent to Beechworth from Melbourne, and preliminary proceedings in connection with his trial were held in the local court.

Beechworth is a picturesque town of considerable tourist attraction. Many of the fine buildings date from the 1850s and are classified by the National Trust.

Anglo-Australian Brewery Co. Ltd 1897–1914
Last Street

The Anglo-Australian Brewery Co. Ltd owned a small brewery at Yarrawonga on the Murray River, and also another at Tallangatta. In 1897 the business and assets of Billson's Brewery in Beechworth were acquired, and the vendor, Alfred Billson, an experienced brewer and an influential personality in the district, stayed on as an active director.

The Benalla Brewing & Malting Co. was acquired in 1902, and continued brewing for a further three years. The only competition in Beechworth at that time was the Spring Creek Brewery, which was taken over in 1906, and closed. It was later converted to a jam and fruit-preserving factory.

A major change took place during 1911 when the company amalgamated with the Albury Brewing & Malting Co. (NSW) Ltd to form Border United Co-operative Breweries Ltd. Three years later the new company was sold to Murray Breweries Pty Ltd.

Beechworth Brewery Co. Ltd 1857–73
North-east corner of Camp & Last Streets

The *Ovens District Directory* of 1857 carried an advertisement of George B. Kerferd & Co. announcing that his new brewery was completed, and strong ales and beers could be delivered on the shortest notice. This was just three years after Kerferd had arrived in Australia from England. The Hon. G. B. Kerferd went on to take an interest in local and political affairs, becoming a member of the Legislative Assembly for the Ovens District, and ultimately the Premier of Victoria.

Kerferd's Brewery was soundly managed and highly profitable. It had a huge market, since the population of the Beechworth goldfields in 1863 was almost 38,000. An aggressive marketer and wide advertiser, Kerferd distributed his superior Kerferd's Entire to most of the northern Victorian towns and the Riverina district of New South Wales.

On 4 April 1868 George Kerferd structured his business as the Beechworth Brewery Co. Ltd, and employed William Dyer as manager. The new company ran into financial difficulties, and early in 1872 the shareholders agreed to the company being wound up. As a result, the land, buildings and plant were sold at auction in April 1872 to John Clark for £560. Clark leased the brewery to the brothers, Patrick and James Durham, who traded as Durham's Brewery until bankruptcy forced them to close in 1873. Six months later the brewery was passed in at auction and brewing was never resumed.

George Kerferd died on the last day of 1889. The brewery property was finally sold, and the new owner leased the premises for use as a gymnasium and later, a skating rink.

Alfred Arthur Billson was not content as a mere member of various organisations, and became the President of the Beechworth Branch of the Australian Natives' Association; President of his shire; three times President of the Ovens District Hospital; and three times President of the Liedertafel. At various times he was President of the Beechworth Gun Club, the Cricket Club, and the Beechworth Racing Club.
La Trobe Library, State Library of Victoria

Billson's Brewery 1872–97
Last Street

The best-known brewery in Beechworth was Billson's. George Henry Billson had been a publican in the Wood's Point area, and in 1872 he purchased the Ovens Brewery in Last Street, Beechworth, and traded as G. Billson & Son. Last Street was an ideal site for a brewery because of the abundance of fresh spring-water. Billson built a larger brewery and an aerated-water factory soon after buying the Ovens Brewery. The business was conducted in conjunction with his eldest son, George.

George Billson Snr died in 1886, but four years earlier the brewery had been taken over by the youngest and most versatile of his three surviving sons, Alfred Arthur Billson. The eldest son, George, had purchased the Albury Brewery (NSW) in 1879, and left the district.

Trading as A. A. Billson & Co., Alfred Billson's beer, aerated-waters and cordials sold well locally and throughout north-eastern Victoria. The brewery's specialty, Anglo-Australian Ale, was particularly popular, and markets extended into southern New South Wales. The soft-drink factory, opened at Tallangatta in 1884, also served as a depot for the company's bottled and draught beer.

Alfred Billson adapted to the pressure of the growing temperance movement by producing non-alcoholic drinks such as his Social Ginger Cup. In conjunction with his friend, Dr David Skinner, they

One of Alfred Billson's most popular beers was Anglo-Australian Ale.

> ### DON'T BLAME THE BEER
>
> Of the murders in the United States last year, 1267 were committed by drunkards and 1282 by total abstainers, which effectively disposes of the favourite teetotal theory that murder is almost invariably commited by people whilst under the influence of intoxicating liquor.
>
> *Australian Brewers' Journal*, October 1892

developed one of the doctor's prescriptions as a palatable drink. This popular drink, Ecks, was a non-alcoholic beverage that contained herbs.

In the mid 1890s Billson converted his old factory into a storage warehouse, and erected a new two-storey stone-and-brick brewery. The tower was 50 feet high, and according to one reporter who visited the brewery

> the extension of the trade in bottled ale and porter is shown by an inspection of the spacious cellars where no less than 84,000 bottles of ale and porter are stacked from floor to ceiling.

During 1897 the business was incorporated as A. A. Billson & Co. Ltd, and, when the Anglo-Australian Brewery took over later that year, Alfred Billson and Dr Skinner were two of the first four directors. Alfred Billson was elected President of the Ovens District Hospital three times, and he was also President of the Beechworth Gun Club and the Beechworth Racing Club.

Ovens Brewery	1856–72
Billson's Brewery	1872–97
Anglo-Australian Brewery Co. Ltd	1897–1911
Border United Co-operative Breweries Ltd	1911–14
Murray Breweries Pty Ltd	1914–54

Border United Co-operative Breweries Ltd
See Anglo-Australian Brewery Co. Ltd.

Durham's Brewery
See Beechworth Brewery Co. Ltd.

Kerferd's Brewery
See Beechworth Brewery Co. Ltd.

Murray Breweries Pty Ltd   1914–54
When Billson's Brewery was taken over in 1897 by the Anglo-Australian Brewery Co. Ltd, the company continued until 1911, at which time the Border United Co-operative Breweries was formed. Three years later Murray Breweries Pty Ltd became the new owners.

The directors of the company were Albert Zwar, A. W. Foster and Michael Daly. Production of beer ceased in 1920, but stout continued until 1954. The Ecks brand, and other aerated waters and cordials that had been an important part of the business, continued in production. Much of the original buildings still stand, and the name A. A. Billson & Co. is clearly visible at the top of the tower.

Ovens Brewery   1856–72
Last Street

Peter Sharp and Henry Edwards started the Ovens Brewery in November 1856, four years after gold had been discovered in the area. Within a matter of months the partnership had changed to Peter Sharp & John Ross. Another partnership, Edwards & Hatt, ran the brewery from 1859 to 1861. Henry Edwards then became the sole proprietor.

George Henry Billson purchased the brewery in 1872, and continued to brew under the name of Billson's Brewery.

See also Billson's Brewery.

Spring Creek Brewery   1870–1906
Railway Avenue, Spring Creek

George Lyon arrived in Victoria from New York, USA, in 1853. He settled in Beechworth, and started in business as a newsagent and tobacconist in Ford Street. He sold his business in 1870, purchased a cordial factory from E. H. Dunn, and transferred the equipment to the area known as Spring Creek, where he began making beer.

Lyon sold the Spring Creek Brewery to Edward Hurst in 1885, but a year later Hurst was declared bankrupt, and Frederick Allen became the new owner. Allen had been the proprietor of the local Star Hotel for the previous fourteen years. Henry Clements became his partner in the brewery for about a year.

A sample of the brewery's bottled ale was sent in July 1894 to the editor of the *Australian Brewers' Journal* in Melbourne, who predicted that 'the beer will earn credit for Australian brewed bottled ale wherever it is introduced'. During 1903 Frederick Allen started another Spring Creek Brewery at Tallangatta.

Frederick Allen died in 1906, and the brewery was taken over by the Anglo-Australian Brewery Co. Ltd, and closed. Some years later the premises were use as a jam and fruit-preserving factory.

Williams Brewery   1856–59
Lock Street

Shortly after starting the brewery, the owner Charles Williams took on Thomas Reynolds as a partner. Williams Brewery advertised in 1857 that they 'can supply prime sparkling ales in any quantity above five gallons'.

Benalla

The town of Benalla was laid out in 1848, and was proclaimed a city in 1965. The city is noted for its regional art gallery, located in gardens beside the Broken River.

The Benalla Rose Festival, with many supporting events, is held annually in November.

Benalla is recognised as Victoria's gliding centre, and in 1987 hosted the World Gliding Championships.

Benalla Brewing & Malting Co. 1858–1905
Arundel Street

In common with many other Australian breweries of the nineteenth century, the Benalla Brewery had a succession of owners.

Richard Clarke	1858–68
Jesse Watts	1871–81
Henry Bolton & William Humphrey	1882–84
John de Grout	1884–88
Robert Cock & Cecil Barney	1888–89
Cock & Featherstonhaugh	1889–92
Robert Cock	1892–1900
W. Magill & R. Foristal	1900–1
Robert Foristal & Patrick Green	1901
Patrick Green	1901
A. A. Billson & Co.	1901
Anglo-Australian Brewery Co. Ltd	1902–5

Richard Clarke had built his brewery in Shadforth Street, Benalla, in 1858, but ten years later a court case cost him his whole fortune — the Black Swan Hotel, numerous town allotments, a flourmill, two squatting stations, and the brewery. In January 1869, only a few months after the financial disaster, Clarke died, and the brewery closed.

The *Ovens and Murray Advertiser* of 27 February 1869 stated:

> A new brewery and malting company is about to be formed at Benalla. There is no brewery at Benalla at present. Mr Sharpe [Clarke], some years ago, built a very large brewery in connection with his flourmill which he proposes to lease to the new company at a very small annual rental.

Not only had the editor misspelt the name, but obviously was unaware of the death of Richard Clarke.

During 1882 the river end of Shadforth Street was closed, seemingly making the brewery part of Arundel Street. After several changes of ownership, the Cock family took over in 1888, and with various partners they ran the brewery for the next twelve years. In 1897 the brewery was passed in at auction when the reserve of £450 was not realised.

There were more changes in ownership at the turn of the century, and when Magill & Foristal took over in 1900 they changed the name to the North Eastern Brewery. The Billson family bought the brewery in 1901, and traded as A. A. Billson & Co. with Walter Billson in charge. The following year they sold out to the Anglo-Australian Brewery Co. Ltd, where Alfred Billson was the chairman of the company. Brewing ceased in 1905.

North Eastern Brewery
See Benalla Brewing & Malting Co.

Bendigo

In December 1852 the booming goldmining town of Bendigo was gazetted as Castleton. In January the following year the name was changed to Sandhurst by the British authorities, although locally the name Bendigo was mostly used. In 1891, fifty years after the town was settled by the goldseekers, the colonial government agreed to officially name the city Bendigo.

Bendigo ultimately became the greatest Victorian goldfield, reaching its record output in 1856. The Victoria mine, with its depth of 1400 metres, was for a time the world's deepest goldmine. Active mining ceased in 1954–55, although renewed interest has resulted in further exploration and mining.

Tourism is one of the city's major industries. The local Chinese community is represented by the famous Joss House and also the Dai Gum San Wax Museum. Another popular tourist attraction is the Central Deborah goldmine, now open to the public for guided tours, both on the surface and underground.

More breweries have operated in Bendigo than any other country town in Australia — no fewer than twenty-five having been in business there since 1853.

Adelaide Brewery 1855–1918
111 Lucan Street

When J. Nelson Jones arrived in Australia in the 1840s, he went straight to Adelaide and opened a chemist shop. He moved to Bendigo in 1852, one year after the start of the goldrush, and set up the first chemist shop in the sprawling tent township.

During 1855 the partnership of Jones & Farrington opened the Adelaide Brewery on Commissioners Flat, now known as Lucan Street. They advertised in the *Bendigo Advertiser* of 18 March 1858: 'Adelaide Brewery, Farrington & Co., Ale and Porter — Two Shillings and Six Pence per Gallon'. Nelson Jones bought out Farrington's share in 1860 and took on Charles Chamberlain as head brewer, and also Thomas Pritchard. The foundation was now laid for a brewing business that was to become one of the largest in the district.

From 1878 the brewery was generally referred to as Pritchard & Chamberlain, since the partners had secured a twenty-year lease on the property. Jones stayed in the area to look after his various interests, including several hotels.

Pritchard & Chamberlain modernised the brewery by adding steam lifts, a malt crusher, and a large cooperage for the manufacture of barrels. Output soon reached 75 hogsheads of beer per week, and the business was expanding and very profitable.

Section of a sketch of the old Benalla Brewery.

Courtesy Jean Dennis.

Chamberlain did the brewing, and Pritchard looked after the hotel trade, which was largely tied. At the end of the lease the partners purchased the brewery. Pritchard died in 1909, and after Chamberlain's death in 1914 his son, George, ran the business until 1918.

Albion Brewery 1853–1912
Lethaby Road, Sailor's Gully, Eaglehawk

The Albion was probably Bendigo's first successful brewery. It began in 1853 with the partnership of Irving & Bull, sometimes referred to as Irvine & Ball. Three years later Peter Pursy became the owner.

Meanwhile, James Steward had arrived in Australia in 1853. He was twenty-one, and, like so many other immigrants of the time, he went straight to the Bendigo goldfields. He prospected at Red Hill with reasonable success, and in 1857, with Joseph Cross as a partner, bought the Albion Brewery from Peter Pursy. Two years later Steward became the sole owner. He built a malthouse, and used only the best-quality materials. From 1865 to 1892 he took no less than forty-one prizes for his ales and porters at shows in the Bendigo district.

James Steward died in 1898, and the business was taken over by the three youngest sons, William, Abraham and Henry. They traded as Steward Brothers Albion Brewery, although it was frequently referred to as the Eaglehawk Brewery.

In 1912 the brewery was taken over by the newly-formed Bendigo & Northern District Co-operative Brewing Co. Ltd, and the Albion Brewery was closed.

Alpine Brewery & Cordial Co. 1905–15
Lucan Street/Eaglehawk Road

By the beginning of the twentieth century the number of breweries operating in Bendigo had dwindled from twenty-five to five. In spite of the intense competition at the time, Clarke & Evans believed they could make good beer and capture some of the market, and in 1905 they started in business as the Alpine Brewery.

Five years later C. H. Ellis purchased the business, and in 1911 he shifted the equipment to premises in Eaglehawk Road. The brewery had never done very well, and to boost trade Ellis started making cordials as well as beer. Two years later he sold the lot to Robert Harper and Daniel Climas, who fared no better.

Anchor Brewery
See City Brewery.

BB Brewery
See William Bruce & Sons.

Bendigo Brewery 1856–77
Myrtle Street

When the brewery was started by George Coates in 1856, it was known as the Burton Brewery. Four years later, on 18 May 1860, the name was changed to the Liverpool Brewery by the syndicate of Jackson, Jones & Nash. They stayed in business at the brewery for six years.

The liquor trade was becoming overcrowded in Bendigo with too many hotels and breweries. In 1866 there were 320 hotels and 12 breweries in the town, and the competition was formidable. There was a constant battle for survival, with rapid changes in brewery names as ownership passed from one to the next. It was during that year, 1866, that the ownership and name of the brewery changed for the third time in less than ten years. The optimistic new proprietors, Burrowes & Vickery, chose the name Bendigo Brewery, but they lasted for less than three years.

The brewery had never been a success right from the start. It had been put up for auction in 1863 and again in 1866, and by 1870 another group of hopefuls, Bain, Elliott & Jackson, was ready to try their luck; they lasted for three years.

Along came William Bruce, a man of considerable brewing experience on the goldfields, and for the first few years at the Bendigo Brewery he had Thomas Barrett as a partner. In 1873 William Bruce transferred the equipment from his other brewery across to the Bendigo Brewery, and he stayed there until 1877. He then shifted again, this time to the Norfolk Brewery, which he had purchased in 1874. So ended the Bendigo Brewery.

Burton Brewery	
George Coates	1856–60
Liverpool Brewery	
Jackson, Jones & Nash	1860–66
Bendigo Brewery	
Burrowes & Vickery	1866–70
Bain, Elliott & Jackson	1870–73
Bruce & Barrett	1873–75
William Bruce	1875–77

Bendigo & Northern District Co-operative Brewing Co. Ltd
See Bendigo United Breweries Pty Ltd.

Bendigo United Breweries Pty Ltd 1907–47

The Bendigo & Northern District Co-operative Brewing Co. Ltd had been formed by a group of Bendigo hoteliers for the purpose of acquiring the City Brewery owned by the Breheny brothers. The purchase took place in October 1907.

The Albion Brewery (then owned by the Steward brothers) was taken over by the group in 1912, and closed, as was the Kent Brewery (run by the Hunter brothers), in 1913. The name was changed to the Bendigo United Co-operative Breweries Ltd, but the difficulties of trading during the period of World War I forced the company into voluntary liquidation in 1917.

It was still for sale in 1919, and following a restructure in 1920 the name was changed yet again to Bendigo United Breweries Pty Ltd, which was registered in June 1920.

Carlton & United Breweries Ltd, Melbourne, purchased and closed the brewery in 1947.

Bendigo United Co-operative Breweries Ltd
See Bendigo United Breweries Pty Ltd.

William Bruce & Sons   1864–94
Bridge Street

William Bruce, a native of the Shetland Islands, landed at Port Melbourne in 1852. He immediately went to the Bendigo goldfields where he opened a store at Irishtown (Lower Bridge Street). Within a few years he was making and selling ginger beer, and in 1864 he started a career that led to his involvement in four breweries and recognition as one of the foremost brewers in the district.

In 1864, two years after the railway link with Melbourne was opened, William Bruce became involved in two breweries. He formed a partnership with James Fawns in the London Brewery by buying out the silent partner, George Elliott. At the same time he formed another partnership with Michael McNamara to produce cordials, aerated-waters, ginger beers, stout and strong ale. This second venture traded as William Bruce & Co. The partnerships of both breweries were ultimately dissolved, with McNamara leaving after a year to become an agent for Bruce. In 1872 Bruce sold his interest in the London Brewery.

Bruce's next acquisition was the Bendigo Brewery in 1873, in partnership with Thomas Barrett. All brewing operations were then centralised at the Bendigo Brewery at Myrtle Street.

The old Norfolk Brewery was auctioned on 1 June 1874, and William Bruce, the compulsive collector of breweries, was the successful bidder. He stayed on at the Bendigo Brewery until 1877, and then shifted all the equipment over to the Norfolk Brewery in Bridge Street.

William Bruce first released his popular BB beer in January 1874, and won two prizes at the 1875 International Exhibition. The BB monogram was adopted as his business trademark and the name BB Brewery was quite often used, the letters representing either Bill Bruce, Bruce's Beer or, most likely, Bruce's Brewery.

The partnership with Thomas Barrett was dissolved in 1875, and by 1883 Bruce's two sons had joined the business. William Bruce was a popular and well-known personality throughout the district; a keen cricketer, he formed the Bendigo United Cricket Club, and was president for forty-three years.

The City Brewery took over Bruce's Brewery in Bridge Street in June 1894, and closed it.

London Brewery
Elliott & Hill	1854
Elliott & Fawns	1858
Fawns & **Bruce**	1864
James Fawns	1872
Helen Fawns	1891
Taken over by the City Brewery	1894, closed

William Bruce & Co.
McNamara & **Bruce**	1864
William **Bruce**	1865
Bruce shifted to the Bendigo Brewery	1873

Bendigo Brewery
George Coates	1856

Liverpool Brewery
Jackson, Jones & Nash	1860

Bendigo Brewery
Burrowes & Vickery	1866
Bain, Elliott & Jackson	1870
Barrett & **Bruce**	1873
William **Bruce**	1875
Bruce shifted to the Norfolk Brewery	1877

Norfolk Brewery
Charles & James Sayer	1856
William **Bruce**	1874
William **Bruce** & Sons	1883
Taken over by the City Brewery	1894

Burton Brewery
See Bendigo Brewery.

City Brewery Co.   c. 1860–1909
High Street, Golden Square

The London Brewery had been operating in High Street, Golden Square, since 1854, and it is surprising that another brewery, the Anchor Brewery, started up next door. In 1866 it was purchased by John Holmes.

In November of that year he sold the brewery to James Liddle and George Hunter, owners of the Edinburgh Brewery in Bridge Street. They immediately shifted all of the equipment out of the Edinburgh and across to the larger premises of the Anchor Brewery in High Street.

New owners came and went. The name was

BB Brewery, Bendigo, c. 1883.

changed to the City Brewery when William Johnston took over in 1871, and he continued to use the old Anchor trademark. By 1888 the brewery was owned by John Illingworth, Duncan Graham and William Johnston. Both Johnston and Illingworth had gained brewing experience at the Norfolk Brewery, and Illingworth had also worked at the Albion and Sandhurst breweries.

The City Brewery Company was registered on 2 February 1893; the partners at that time were William Johnston and John Illingworth. They boiled their beer in an open iron vessel over an open fire, and their end product sold for 6s per dozen bottles. The London Brewery next door was merged with the City Brewery in 1894, and William Bruce's Brewery (the old Norfolk Brewery) was taken over and closed the same year.

After 1900 the business continued as Illingworth's City Brewery until March 1904, when the Breheny brothers took control. Three years later they sold the brewery to the Bendigo & Northern District Co-operative Brewing Co. Ltd.

Unknown	c. 1860–66
Anchor Brewery	
John Holmes	1866
James Liddle & George Hunter	1866–68
George Elliott & James Armstrong	1868–71
City Brewery	
William Johnston	1871–88
Graham, Johnston & Illingworth	1888–93
City Brewery Co.	
Johnston & Illingworth	1893–1900
Took over the London Brewery	1894, merged
Took over William Bruce's Brewery	1894, closed
John Illingworth	1900–4
Breheny brothers	1904–7
Bendigo & Northern District Co-operative Brewing Co. Ltd	1907

Kent Brewery, Bendigo, c. 1900.

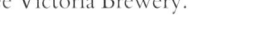

Cohn Brothers Brewery
See Victoria Brewery.

Dublin Brewery   c. 1860
High Street

The Dublin Brewery was owned and operated by Burke & O'Neill.

Eaglehawk Brewery
See Albion Brewery.

Edinburgh Brewery   1853–66
Bridge Street

The partnership of Liddle & Cooper had started brewing in High Street late in 1853. After four years Liddle left and formed a partnership with George Hunter, and they started the Edinburgh Brewery in Bridge Street. Their business was small and they advertised in the *Weekly Mercury and Bendigo Mining Journal* of 20 January 1860: 'Liddle and Hunter, Edinburgh Brewery, Lower Bridge Street'.

During November 1866 they bought the Anchor Brewery in High Street, and closed the Edinburgh.

High Street Brewery   1860–67
High Street

The Strickland brothers, Robert and William, ran their small brewery for five years. William then continued on his own. He advertised in the *Bendigo Advertiser* of 21 September 1865: 'William Strickland (late Strickland Bros.) High Street Brewery. First class ales and porter'. Strickland claimed that his brewery was the only one in the district supplying private families 'in quantities of not less than 3 gallons or one dozen bottles. Pale Ale and Stout, 8 shillings per dozen'.

Hindmarsh Brewery   c. 1862
High Street

The following advertisement appeared in the *Bendigo Independent* newspaper of 13 May 1862: 'Hindmarsh Brewery — Top of High Street. S. M. Crawford Prop'.

Kent Brewery   1870–1913
Cnr McCrae & Chapel Streets

The Hunter brothers were well-known personalities in the Bendigo district, and from father to sons their brewing and soft-drink businesses spanned a period of almost seventy years. George Frederick Hunter had started the Kent Brewery in partnership with James Liddle. The two of them had been together at the Edinburgh Brewery, but Liddle stayed for only a few months at the Kent.

The Kent Brewery was actually the premises of Slattery's Brewery, which had closed in the late 1860s. As the years passed, the Kent Brewery prospered and expanded, selling a large range of pale ales and stout. Some of the bottle labels depicted a greyhound, which formed part of the Hunter crest.

George Hunter's wife, Elizabeth, became the proprietor in 1886, and in 1895 she formed a partnership with her sons, Frederick and Thomas. The business traded as Hunter Brothers Kent Brewery until 1913, when it was taken over by the Bendigo & Northern District Cooperative Brewing Co. Ltd.

No longer brewers, the Hunter brothers continued in business as manufacturers of aerated waters, and in 1914 they joined the Steward brothers to form Steward & Hunter Pty Ltd. Unfortunately, the business was placed in liquidation in 1917, but the following year the Hunter brothers were trading again. Thomas O. Hunter was in charge from 1923 to 1939.

Liverpool Brewery (Myrtle Street)
See Bendigo Brewery.

Liverpool Brewery (White Hills)
See White Hills Brewery.

The London Brewery, Bendigo, c. 1880. The gentleman in the top hat is probably the owner, James Fawns.

London Brewery 1854–94
Kangaroo Flat/High Street, Golden Square

The first reference to the London Brewery is an advertisement in the *Bendigo Advertiser* of 13 October 1854: 'Messrs Elliott & Hill, London Brewery, Kangaroo Flat, have commenced brewing from malt'. The goldrush was well under way at the time, and breweries operated under appalling conditions with the heat and dust, lack of hygiene and the scarcity of clean water. It was almost impossible to make a pleasant-tasting, wholesome beer.

The London Brewery managed to survive better than most, and after a year or two George Elliott relocated to larger premises at Golders Flat, Golden Square. In May 1858 James Fawns joined the company, and four years later, in July 1862, Elliott retired from the daily routine of the brewery, leaving Fawns in charge.

William Bruce acquired George Elliott's interest in 1864 and the London Brewery was then conducted by Bruce & Fawns, a partnership that lasted until 1872. Fawns then continued on his own until his death in 1891. His wife, Helen, kept the business going for three years, and then accepted a takeover offer from the City Brewery. The London and City breweries were next to each other in High Street, Golden Square and the merger meant the closure of the London Brewery.

Lucan Street Brewery 1856–79
Lucan Street

When T. Delaney started the brewery in 1856, he called it the Sandhurst Brewery — the town at that time was known as Sandhurst.

Delaney sold out to Glasgow & Thunder the following year, and then a massive flood caused considerable loss and damage. Two years later, to avoid a recurrence, another larger brewery was built in Lucan Street immediately opposite the site of their old brewery and above the level of any possible flood.

As an aid to their beer production, a Harrison ice-making machine was installed in 1861, one of the earliest to be used in Australia, but at that time such innovations were looked upon with ignorant suspicion.

The Sandhurst Brewery was offered for sale in the *Bendigo Advertiser* of 9 October 1862, 'together with the

The Lucan Street Brewery, Bendigo, c. 1870. It was called the Sandhurst Brewery when it started in 1856 (Bendigo was then known as Sandhurst).

The brothers Charles and James Sayer opened their Norfolk Brewery in Bridge Street, Bendigo, in 1856. The large sign above the entrance, with barrels at the top, left little doubt as to the nature of the business.

trade, stock, plant, casks, horses, drays, cart etc.' Apparently there was no sale, and by 1863 Alfred Thunder was the sole proprietor.

The brewery was generally called the Lucan Street Brewery, at least until 1879 when it was purchased by George Elliott, and closed. Alfred Thunder moved to Melbourne and became the manager of the Metropolitan Brewery before starting his own brewery in Port Melbourne.

Manchester Brewery   c. 1862
The Manchester Brewery was offered at auction in 1862.

Murphy's Brewery   1859–62
The brewery, which was located at Kangaroo Flat, began trading as James Murphy & Co. in 1859. Two years later Mrs Murphy was running the brewery, with the assistance of J. McClelland.

Norfolk Brewery   1856–74
Bridge Street

The Norfolk Brewery was of brick and weatherboard construction, and was opened for business by Charles and James Sayer in 1856. James left in 1867, and Charles subsequently auctioned the brewery on 1 June 1874. The successful bidder was William Bruce, who traded under his own name for the next three years. He then shifted his Bendigo Brewery operations, which were at Myrtle Street, across to the Norfolk Brewery site at Bridge Street. The name Norfolk Brewery was discontinued.

Phoenix Brewery   1855–72
High Street

Edward Emmett was a well-known auctioneer in the Bendigo district, and he advertised in the *Bendigo Advertiser* of 17 January 1855: 'Vine Street Malt Brewery, Sandhurst, Emmett & Co. ... in full operation and respectfully solicit patronage'.

When Emmett shifted the business to High Street in 1858, he changed the name to the Phoenix Brewery and advertised the fact in the *Bendigo Advertiser*.

James Armstrong bought the brewery in 1859; three years later Thomas Brown was the proprietor.

Pritchard & Chamberlain
See Adelaide Brewery.

Refreshment Tent & Brewery   c. 1854
Long Gully

The only reference to the brewery is an advertisement in the *Bendigo Advertiser* of 22 August 1854:

> To a small capitalist — For Sale — The Stand, Tent and Fixture of that well known Refreshment Tent and Brewery, now in the occupation of Mr Meaton, situated at the Crossing Place of the Long Gully.

Sandhurst Brewery
See Lucan Street Brewery.

Sandhurst Brewing & Malting Co. Ltd
The prospectus for the Sandhurst Brewing & Malting Co. Ltd, issued in July 1888, proposed to amalgamate and carry on the businesses of William Bruce & Sons, brewers and aerated-water manufacturer; Graham, Johnston & Illingworth's City Brewery; Pritchard & Chamberlain's Adelaide Brewery; Hedley Bros' Bridgewater Brewery; J. Wharton & Co., aerated-water manufacturers; and C. Hoffmeyer, wine-and-spirit merchant. The grand scheme anticipated profits at the rate of 17 per cent on the proposed capital, and dividends of 10 per cent were guaranteed for three years. The brokers, Chapman & Wakeley Ltd of Queen Street, Melbourne, would have been disappointed when the venture did not proceed.

Again, in 1890, another prospectus was issued, this time for the Sandhurst Brewing Co. Ltd, which proposed to amalgamate James Fawns's London Brewery and Johnston & Illingworth's City Brewery. This proposal also failed to proceed.

Slattery's Brewery   1856–69
McCrae Street

Known as Slattery's Brewery, its partners were John Slattery and Michael McNamara. By 1862 Slattery was working the brewery on his own, and he continued for the next five years until it closed in 1869.

The premises were later sold to James Liddle and George Hunter, who started up as the Kent Brewery in 1870.

Union Brewery   1854–58
High Street

The Union Brewery began early in 1854 and was advertised for sale in the *Bendigo Advertiser* of 26 September 1854:

> For Sale, the well known Union Stores and Brewery, Golden Square, belonging to Messrs Howe, Rogers & Co. The brewery with plant and utensils is the most complete in Bendigo ... apply on the premises.

The partnership had been dissolved, but the brewery kept operating for a few more years.

Victoria Brewery Co. Ltd   1858–1925
Bridge Street

The three Danish-born Cohn brothers, Moritz, Julius Isaac and Jacob, arrived at Port Phillip during August

Cohn Brothers label, celebrating fifty years of continuous brewing, 1907.

1853 at a time when Melbourne was almost deserted because of the Bendigo goldrush. Even members of the police force had left their jobs to hurry to the goldfields.

The brothers decided to try their luck, and set out on foot for Bendigo. Moritz, the eldest brother, had the family fortune of 60 sovereigns sewn into the lining of his vest, but while they were passing through the Black Forest all the coins were lost through a hole worn in the lining. Fortunately, by backtracking the next day, they recovered most of the sovereigns.

When they reached Bendigo, the brothers found the area to be a sprawling canvas town, and work difficult to find. They were able to open a general store in Camp Street, and during 1854 they built the Criterion Hotel, a 'marvel of elegance', and acknowledged as the premier hotel of the district.

After twelve months, the Criterion Hotel, was sold and the brothers began making cider, raspberry vinegar and other beverages, all of which found a ready market with the miners and traders. They constructed a 'substantial brewery' and the *Bendigo Advertiser* of 11 October 1858 reported the opening of the new 'Victoria Brewery of the enterprising Cohn Brothers'. As well as brewing their own beer, they transported barrelled beer from Melbourne and bottled it at their brewery, to be resold to hotels and through their own wine-and-spirit store.

During 1861 Moritz Cohn started a brewery in the nearby township of Talbot, the Talbot Brewery, and maintained his involvement with that brewery until it was sold in 1872. In the meantime, Julius and Jacob Cohn had been running the Victoria Brewery in Bendigo. After selling the brewery at Talbot, Moritz acquired Julius's shareholding in the Victoria Brewery, and Julius moved to Melbourne and started his own brewery there.

It was during 1882 that Cohn Bros' Victoria Brewery produced the first lager beer in Australia under the brand name Excelsior. To maintain a chilled temperature, the company installed the first refrigeration and icemaking plant outside Melbourne. Other brands of ales were introduced, including Old Style Colonial Beer, Australian Pale Ale and Lion Stout. In addition to the production of ale, lager and beer, they also made and sold ice, soft drinks and cordials, and a new non-intoxicating lager called Tonic Ale. This was later called 9.30 Lager, then 6 O'Clock Lager during World War I. The name continued until 1966 when the closing time of hotels was extended to 10 p.m.

The business became a public company on 17 November 1887, and the following year the aerated-water factory of John Wharton was purchased. The company took over the Bridgewater Brewery in 1893, and continued to expand through acquisitions of aerated-water and cordial factories, hotels, and wine-and-spirit outlets.

The brewing interests of the Cohn Bros, together with forty freehold hotels, and the mortgages, bills of sale and bank guarantees on an additional forty hotels, were sold to Carlton & United Breweries Ltd on 30 April 1925, and beer production ceased at Bendigo. Cohn Bros continued to produce aerated waters, ginger beers and cordials, and were involved in many investment ventures. A branch factory was established at Swan Hill in 1923, and the business then traded as Cohn Bros Bendigo and Swan Hill.

Cohn Brothers' Victoria Brewery, Bridge Street, Bendigo, c. 1885.
From a sketch printed on silk; courtesy Jack M. Cohn

Vine Street Brewery
See Phoenix Brewery.

White Hills Brewery   1853–58
New Street, White Hills

The following advertisement appeared in the *Bendigo Advertiser* on 21 July 1854:

> To be sold by private contract, the Liverpool Brewery, situate opposite the First and Second White Hills, the largest and oldest place on [*sic*] Bendigo. The property of Lawrence & McGrath. Premises consist of a shop, kitchen, bedroom, brewery, stabling, out-houses and all the brewing utensils.

The brewery had actually started the year before, and when there were no buyers as a result of the advertisement the owners tried again, in the same newspaper, on 18 March 1858, this time using a name for the brewery more descriptive of its location: 'For sale, White Hills Brewery, New Street, White Hills. Tenders invited'. White Hills, now part of Bendigo City, is about 4 km east of the city centre. A series of hills in the area were covered with a hard white clay and gravel, hence the name given to those early landmarks.

Blackwood

Blackwood Brewery   1854
George Knight, a brewer from London, England, arrived in Australia in 1852. Two years later George

The Bridgewater Brewery, Bridgewater, was owned and operated by James and William Hedley.

Sketch of the Bright Brewery, Bright, c. 1880. It had a 44-year history of producing ales and stout considered to be 'unsurpassed in the country'. Brewing was discontinued in 1916; later, motel units were built on the site.

arranged for his son to join him. Together they started a brewery at the small country town of Blackwood, between the two main roads leading out from Melbourne, one to Ballarat and the other to Bendigo. As a consequence, there was very little passing traffic, and after a year both father and son left the district. They settled in Maryborough, about 80 km to the north-east, and opened the Two Brewers Hotel and Brewery, an appropriate name for father and son to use.

Bridgewater

Bridgewater Brewery 1874–93

James Hedley landed at Melbourne in 1856 at the age of eighteen. He took up gold-digging at Ballarat, and became an engine driver and bookkeeper before returning to the goldfields, where he earned good money.

After working as a traveller at James Steward's Albion Brewery in Ballarat, James Hedley and his brother, William, began brewing in 1874 at the northern Victorian township of Bridgewater, on the Loddon River. They stayed in business for sixteen years, and prizes were taken all over the country, as well as in London, England.

The Hedley brothers retired in 1890, and the Bridgewater Brewery was sold to the partnership of George Elliott and Phillip Holler. They lasted three years. The brewery premises were then purchased by the Cohn Brothers of Bendigo.

Loddon Brewery c. 1875

Cornelius Hegarty.

Bright

The old goldmining township of Bright, situated on the Ovens River, is in the heart of north-eastern Victoria's spectacular alpine region.

Hopgrowing is an important local industry, and the quiet picturesque village is a popular tourist resort and the gateway to Mt Buffalo and the snowfields.

Bright Brewery & Alpine Aerated Water Works & Cordial Co. 1872–1916

William Hooper was the owner of a hotel at nearby Porepunkah, and in 1872 he started the Bright Brewery with William McLean as a partner. Hooper's son-in-law, J. B. Berry, worked at the brewery, and became a partner in 1884 following the death of McLean. William McLean's nephew, another William, was involved in the brewery until 1889.

Advertisements quoted the lengthy title of 'The Bright Brewery and Alpine Aerated Water Works and Cordial Company' and also the lengthy list of products: 'Bottled Ale and Porter, Bitters, Lemon Syrup, Raspberry, Cloves, Peppermint, Ginger Wine, Limejuice, Ginger Ale, Pineapple, Lithia and Soda Water, Sarsaparilla, Lemonade, etc., etc.'

Brewed in the cool mountain country, the products were of consistently high quality, and became very popular over a wide region. They were considered to be 'unsurpassed in Australia', and the Bright Brewery was awarded first prize for its bottled ale and stout at the 1891 Wangaratta Show.

Thomas Cock was the brewer and manager in 1889, followed by Alex Belperound in 1900.

By 1905 Mrs Ellen Hooper was in charge, and she managed the business for six or seven years.

The last proprietor of the brewery was George Abrahams, and when beer production was discontinued in 1916, the company continued to make soft drinks. Years later, motel units were erected on the site.

Kelly's Brewery c. 1870–98

The Railway Hotel was opposite the council chambers in Ireland Street, on the east bank of Bakers Gully Creek. It was managed by Mrs Kelly who was 'separated' from her husband, James Kelly. In conjunction with William Cardwell, he ran a brewery, which was a short distance upstream from the hotel. The beer from Kelly's Brewery

would be brought down to the Railway Hotel. Each delivery would be attended by loud haggling on either side, with Ma Kelly complaining about the poor quality of the beer and the high price.

Some years later William Cardwell worked the brewery on his own. After his death there were three quick changes in occupancy: Robert Moyes; then three months later, in March 1898, James Locke; and shortly after that, W. Magill & Co.

Buninyong

Buninyong claims to be Victoria's first inland settlement when, in 1837, early colonists explored inland from Geelong in search of grazing land for their sheep. By the early 1840s the first hotel was established to serve the travellers as land was settled further out. The discovery of gold at Buninyong in 1851 was just four weeks after the discovery at nearby Clunes, and predates the initial Ballarat discovery by several weeks.

Buninyong Crystal Temperance Malt Ale Co. 1855–1900

The brewery was started by a Mr Allen in 1855. He sold to Thomas Sheppard shortly after, and by 1857 Sheppard's Crystal Malt Brewery, as it was then called, had an output of 50 hogsheads of beer per week. Sheppard leased the brewery to Ryan & Iveson for a few years from about 1860, and following Sheppard's death in 1873 the brewery closed.

Other brewers either leased or owned the brewery over the next several years: William Saunders, Augustus Peyroux and Charles Topp. The business was renamed the Buninyong Crystal Temperance Malt Ale Co. in 1880, and alcoholic beverage production ceased in 1900.

It was a peculiar circumstance when public demand forced the factory to close, or so it was reported — some of the local lads had become intoxicated from drinking so-called 'lemonade' that was produced at the factory.

Crystal Malt Brewery
See Buninyong Crystal Temperance Malt Ale Co.

Camperdown

Leura Brewery 1875–98
Tait Street

William Strickland was having difficulty in building up sufficient business at his Colac Brewery, and took the decision to start another brewery at Camperdown, 50 km west, to see if he could do better there. Later, in 1875, he was involved in a law suit that resulted in the closure of his breweries in both Colac and Camperdown.

The Leura Brewery at Camperdown, together with an eight-roomed dwelling and a stable, was sold at auction to William Ower on 5 March 1875. Ower was an investor, and immediately rented the brewery to James Jackson.

As the new proprietor, James Jackson advertised in the *Hampden Guardian* of 8 June 1875: 'Leura Brewery, Camperdown, J. & W. Jackson, Ale and Porter Brewers, Bulk and Bottled; all cordials, aerated waters, ginger beers, etc., kept in stock and the trade supplied'. The advertisement was placed intermittently in both the *Hampden Guardian* and the *Camperdown Chronicle*.

Glen Archibald owned the property in 1884, and James Jackson continued to rent the brewery and dwellings.

The Buninyong Brewery, Buninyong, Victoria, c. 1870. Much of the old bluestone brewery still stands.

Carapooee

Western Creek Brewery 1860–85

Archie Faulkner started the Western Creek Brewery in 1860. It was located in the quiet little town of Carapooee in central Victoria, and William Wheeler was the brewer. Wheeler subsequently started his own brewery at St Arnaud, 10 km south.

Faulkner managed to survive the bushfires that raged through the district on 12 January 1869, and kept on brewing until 1875.

Sam Fletcher took over at that time, and Daniel Cunningham ran the brewery from 1880 to 1885.

Carisbrook

Carisbrook Brewery 1856–68

James Flett, in his book *Old Pubs*, states there were two breweries at Carisbrook in 1856, Arnold's and Chaplin's, but Arnold's brewery was apparently at the township of Moonambel, about 60 km west of Carisbrook.

In the 1850s there were five hotels in Carisbrook, plus the one brewery that had been started in 1856 by Mitchell & Hall.

In July 1860 the Melbourne *Argus* advertised a mortgagee's auction, and the brewery was bought by Thomas Laski. By December 1862 the brewery was up for sale again, and was advertised in the Melbourne *Herald*: 'To distillers, brewers, millers and others; For Sale, the extensive premises known as Laskie's [Laski's] Brewery, situated at Carisbrook'.

March 1866 saw a similar advertisement: 'Carisbrook Brewery, with plant, easily converted into a flourmill or factory'. According to the *Maryborough and Dunolly Advertiser* of October 1868, the Standard Brewery of Castlemaine purchased the brewery, and used it as a depot.

Castlemaine

The central Victorian town of Castlemaine developed as the result of the rush for gold that started toward the end of 1851. The deposits proved to be the richest alluvial goldfield the world had ever seen, and the town quickly attracted a population of 30,000. The young township was named after a small village in Ireland where a castle stood on the bank of the Maine River, hence the name Castlemaine.

Advance Brewery 1855–59
Forest Creek

Following the discovery of gold and the later development of pastoral industries, the township of Castlemaine became second only to Bendigo for the number of breweries to operate in any country town in Australia.

When Amour & Hatton opened the Advance Brewery in 1855, there were already three breweries in the district. Not long after the brewery had started, Armour decided to leave, and Hatton took on a new partner, James Oddy. Hatton later left, and Oddy continued on his own. About twenty-six years later James Oddy was recorded as brewing at Cooktown in northern Queensland.

Anderson's Brewery
See Imperial Brewery.

Andrews Brewery 1860–67
Fryers Creek

William Andrews commenced brewing in 1860, and it is possible that he took over the Advance Brewery, which had closed the previous year.

Barker's Creek Brewery
See Castlemaine Brewery (Kennedy Street).

Bellvue Brewery 1861–76
Kennedy's Flat, Fryers Creek

Partners Bell & Holmes ran the Bellvue Brewery from 1861 to 1868. John Benallack bought the brewery at that time, and changed the name to Benallack's Brewery.

Benallack's Brewery
See Bellvue Brewery.

Boyle, Henry 1861–62
Fryers Creek

It was reported that Henry Boyle's production of beer was only 10 gallons per month, and his brewing business was probably little more than that of a home brewer.

Castlemaine Brewery (Kennedy Street) 1854–58
Kennedy Street

During October 1854 Walter Smith advertised that he had commenced brewing ale and porter at his Castlemaine Brewery. This was Castlemaine's second brewery, and was located in Kennedy Street near the railway goods sheds. It was also known as the Barker's Creek Brewery.

The business was a small concern, but it was of interest to Edward Fitzgerald who bought the brewery on 8 December 1858. Fitzgerald closed the brewery and probably used what equipment there was for his own brewery (Fitzgerald's Brewing & Malting Co., Castlemaine, Ltd) that he had recently built at Winters Flat. 'Watty' Smith was given the job as brewer.

Castlemaine Brewery (Winters Flat)
See Fitzgerald's Brewing & Malting Co. Castlemaine, Ltd.

Crown Brewery Co. Ltd 1857–79
Elizabeth Street, Winters Flat

The brewery, which was started by Elias Siddall in 1857, was originally located at Churches Flat, Fryers

Creek. Two years later brother Paul was running the business with William Ryan and John Anderson as partners, and in 1864 they shifted to Winters Flat.

By 1866 Paul Siddall was on his own but not doing very well, and the brewery was put up for sale in 1869. There were no buyers until 1874, and James Dickinson then became the new owner. He had previously been the manager of the Standard Brewery in Castlemaine, and in February 1875 he structured his business as the Crown Brewery Co. Ltd. A depot was opened at the Western Market in Melbourne in 1872, but on 26 May 1879 the Crown Brewery was declared insolvent.

Fitzgerald's Brewing & Malting Co., Castlemaine, Ltd 1858–1925

Elizabeth Street, near cnr Mt Tarrengower & Campbell's Creek Roads, Winters Flat

A native of northern Ireland, Edward Fitzgerald, arrived at Forest Creek, Castlemaine, during 1857, and proceeded to build a brewery. Edward's father, Francis, applied for the brewer's licence in December 1858, and possibly helped in the financing of the venture.

Throughout the history of the company it was simply called the Castlemaine Brewery, even though it became Fitzgerald's Brewing & Malting Co., Castlemaine, Ltd, twenty-nine years after it had opened. It was the founding company of a number of Castlemaine Breweries that were to operate in four Australian states. One of these breweries, in Brisbane, was to produce the now-famous Castlemaine XXXX Bitter Ale. The Perkins brothers, Paddy and Thomas, of later Queensland brewing fame, were small shareholders in the Castlemaine Brewery, Victoria, but sold their interest in 1867, and left for Queensland.

The company's early brews, Pale Ale, XX Ale and XX Porter, sold for 3d a pint in the seventy or so pubs in the town. This was a high price for the time but the people liked the beer. Edward's brother, Nicholas, arrived from Ireland in 1859, and helped in running the business. He was later to become the Hon. Nicholas Fitzgerald, and a prominent figure in political life and in the brewing industry in Victoria and other colonies. He married the daughter of the Premier of Victoria (Sir John O'Shanessy), and had seven sons.

The Fitzgerald brothers appointed Robert Prendergast as manager of their Castlemaine Brewery, and James Perrin as their traveller. Prendergast, in conjunction with Nicholas Fitzgerald, set up the Newbridge Brewery Co. at Newbridge, on the Loddon River, in 1860. This was sold nine years later and Prendergast went to Sydney to start the Castlemaine Brewing Co. Ltd, Sydney. Meanwhile, in 1863 James Perrin joined the Fitzgerald brothers in purchasing the Daylesford Brewery. Six years later Perrin moved to Melbourne, and started another Castlemaine Brewery at Moray Street, South Melbourne. He stayed there as the manager.

At Castlemaine James Newman became a partner on 1 January 1876, and was active in the supervision of the brewery and the substantial wine-and-spirit business; the

Fitzgerald's Brewing & Malting Co. Ltd, Castlemaine, c. 1880. It was generally referred to as the Castlemaine Brewery. Although other Castlemaine breweries were opened in Sydney, Melbourne, Newcastle, Brisbane and Fremantle, the famous Castlemaine XXXX Bitter Ale has only been brewed in Brisbane.

company traded as Fitzgerald & Newman. The Fitzgerald's Brewing & Malting Co., Castlemaine, Ltd, was floated on 12 February 1887, and the vendors, James Newman and the Fitzgerald brothers, guaranteed dividends of 10 per cent — the shares were oversubscribed within an hour! The business flourished and expanded and the dividends declared were actually 12.5 per cent.

Under the initiative of the Hon. Nicholas Fitzgerald, other Castlemaine breweries were established, leading to the largest brewing enterprise in Australia in the late nineteenth century.

	Established
Castlemaine Brewery, Castlemaine	1858
Castlemaine Brewing Co., Sydney	1869
Castlemaine Brewing Co. Ltd, Melbourne	1871
Castlemaine Brewery, Newcastle	1876
Castlemaine Brewery, Brisbane	1885
Castlemaine Brewing Co., Fremantle	1898

By 1891 James Perrin owned the brewery at Castlemaine, and he upgraded the brewery and equipment. Output had quadrupled by the time he retired in 1905. He died five years later at his East Melbourne home.

Late in 1911 Fitzgerald's Brewing & Malting Co. Ltd took over the Standard Brewery in Castlemaine and closed it, marking the end of one of the oldest operating breweries in country Victoria.

The Castlemaine Brewery was purchased by Carlton & United Breweries, Melbourne, in 1925 and closed, ending a memorable life of sixty-seven years. But the dynasty was to continue, with the Castlemaine Brewery, Brisbane, merging its operations with the Perkins City Brewery to form Castlemaine Perkins Ltd in August 1928.

Although other takeovers have occurred since that time, Castlemaine XXXX Bitter Ale is still one of Australia's popular beers, carrying the name of the Victorian town where the Castlemaine Brewery was born in 1858.

This picture of the Standard Brewery, Castlemaine, c. 1870, provides an interesting view of the early gold-mining township at that time.

Castlemaine Brewery	1858–87
Fitzgerald's Brewing & Malting Co., Castlemaine, Ltd	1887–1925
Newbridge Brewery purchased	1860–68, closed
Daylesford Brewery purchased	1863–73, sold
Standard Brewery (Castlemaine) purchased	1911, closed
Carlton & United Breweries Ltd (Melbourne)	1925

Imperial Brewery 1870–71
Near Cemetery Road, Campbell's Creek

John Anderson, being the proprietor, thought it appropriate to call his brewery Anderson's Brewery, but James Kinkead soon changed that to the Imperial Brewery when he became the owner. It was of little consequence since the brewery lasted only a year.

Loddon Brewery 1855–76
Junction of the Loddon River & Fryers Creek

Label for the Standard Brewery.

One of the pioneers of the Castlemaine district was Benjamin Edhouse. He had a large general store, and made 'sugar beer' that he sold to other storekeepers. His friend, William Thorne, persuaded Edhouse to extend his premises and make ordinary beer, and eventually the store was closed and made into a brewery. Thorne was the brewer. When brewing started in 1855, there were already two other breweries in town.

During 1856 Ben Edhouse advertised his ale and porter for sale at £7 per hogshead. This was expensive beer at the time, particularly in bulk, but the beer was popular and sold well. The factory (the old store) had to be extended several times. 'Old' Edhouse built a malthouse, and since no barley was grown in the district he used wheat for malting.

Willy Thorne left in 1856 to start up his own brewery at Maldon. Fortunately, Edhouse found another brewer, Charles Bryant, who was taken on as the brewer and manager. Bryant married Ben Edhouse's daughter, but, even so, he left in 1863 and also moved to Maldon to start brewing for himself.

After that, Edhouse's fortunes began to wane. The old boiler, which had been replaced, was sold to Fitzgerald's Castlemaine Brewery in South Melbourne in the early 1870s. At one time Edhouse had twenty-five horses carting beer to the hotels and various mine locations, but gradually the quality of his beer began to deteriorate, and too many batches of bad beer led to insolvency.

McBride's Brewery 1861–c. 1867
Foot of Redfearn's Hill, Campbell's Creek

The brewery was started by John McBride in 1861. Although Walter Smith and Allan Chambers were partners, the business traded as McBride & Co. Earlier, 'Watty' Smith had his own Castlemaine Brewery in Kennedy Street, and later he became the head brewer at Fitzgerald's Castlemaine Brewery. Allan Chambers retired in 1863, and McBride's Brewery kept going for a few more years after that.

Phoenix Brewery 1853–62
Main Road, Campbells Creek

The Phoenix was Castlemaine's first brewery, and was the forerunner of the Standard Brewery, which continued in business until 1911. The proprietors of the Phoenix Brewery were James A. Wheeler and his brother, Edmund. Trading as Wheeler Brothers, they began brewing the usual ale and porter only a year or so after gold was discovered in the area. McCracken's City Brewery in Melbourne held an interest in the Phoenix Brewery until 1858.

The brewery was purchased in 1862 by a syndicate, and the Wheelers stayed on to manage the business.

James Wheeler was killed in an accident. When Edmund left the district to settle in Warrnambool, the company appointed James Robertson as manager. At the time of acquisition in 1862 the business was reformed as the Standard Brewery Co. Ltd.

Standard Brewery Co. Ltd 1862–1911
Main Road, Campbell's Creek

Castlemaine's first brewery, the Phoenix, had been started by the Wheeler brothers, James and Edmund, in 1853, and they stayed on to manage the brewery when it became the Standard Brewery Co. Ltd in 1862. Later, James Robertson became head brewer and George Millar was the major shareholder. Millar got into such financial difficulty that he decided to leave the country, 'with stealth and speed'. He was eventually apprehended in London.

The brewery was auctioned in 1864; the successful bidders were four Castlemaine businessmen, Joseph Myring, William Halford, David Murray and Dr David Mackay. They thoroughly overhauled the brewery, put in a new cleansing process, and their first beer was pronounced to be 'a fine pale ale which would turn out well'.

J. H. Dickinson was the manager. He increased the output but not the profits, and was replaced by John McBride, who had owned a brewery at Castlemaine in the early 1860s.

The company was restructured in October 1869 with Myring and Halford as the joint owners. Halford left in 1871 to return to the grocery and wine-and-spirit business, leaving Joseph Myring the sole proprietor. He died in 1886, and his wife Annie tried to run the brewery but sold soon after.

More owners were to follow; the first was Henry Lindsay who sold the same year to George Elliott and Phillip Holler. They were also lessees of the Hedley brothers' Bridgewater Brewery.

George Elliott retired from the partnership around 1890 because of ill health, and the Standard Brewery, which was then in some difficulty, was put up for auction. Only the horses and wagons and some of the plant managed to sell, and the brewery closed.

Two years later the brewery was reopened by a syndicate that traded as Joseph Young & Co. The members were Joseph Young, Horace Collett and J. C. Greaves.

The Castlemaine Brewery (Fitzgerald's Brewing & Malting Co. Ltd) took over, and closed the Standard Brewery late in 1911. Throughout the brewing history of Castlemaine, no fewer than sixteen breweries had been licensed, with many more operating illegally, particularly during the goldrush period. The closure of the Standard Brewery marked the end of fifty-eight years of brewing by one of the district's most famous breweries.

Phoenix Brewery	
James & Edmund Wheeler	1853–62

Standard Brewery Co. Ltd	1862–1911
Myring, Halford, Murray & Mackay	1864–69
Myring & Halford	1869–71
Joseph Myring	1871–86
Annie Myring	1886
Henry Lindsay	1886
Elliott & Holler	1886–90, closed
Joseph Young & Co.	1892–1911

Star Brewery 1869–76
Gingell Street, south (now Gaulton Street)

William Ryan's first attempt at brewing had been at the Albion Brewery in Inglewood in 1859. A year later he was a partner in the Crown Brewery, Castlemaine.

By 1869 he had long since disposed of his interests in both breweries, and during that year he started the Star Brewery in Gingell Street, Castlemaine. Unfortunately for Ryan, it was destroyed by fire in 1876.

Strathloddon Brewery 1869–71

This was not a very successful brewery. After two years of hard work, John Ludlow sold his Strathloddon Brewery to Luke Thompson. Luke gave up after a few months.

Victoria Brewery 1859–78
Kennedy's Flat, Fryers Creek

In 1859 Henry Sheppard started brewing in a two-storey stone building and was soon ready to supply his 'best ale and porter'. Four years later he became insolvent, but managed to start up again the next year under the name of the Victoria Brewery.

Walder's Brewery 1868–75
Chapel Hill, Fryerstown

Thomas Walder brewed a small amount of beer in conjunction with his general store and hotel, sufficient only for his hotel trade.

Chewton

Mount Alexander Brewery 1873–84
Main Street

The Mount Alexander Brewery operated in conjunction with a hotel of the same name, and both were owned by Joseph Barnes. He tried to sell the brewery in 1876 but there were no buyers, and so he continued to brew until 1884. There was too much competition from the Castlemaine and Standard breweries at the neighbouring township of Castlemaine, so Barnes left the district and started another brewery at Trentham.

Chiltern

The Chiltern district was originally known as Black Dog Creek, and with the discovery of gold in the area in 1859 there was a steady influx of miners. By 1865 the population of Chiltern reached 2200, and there were twelve hotels in the town.

Bartley's Brewery 1861–1913
Indigo Road

Benjamin Bartley had been a cordial manufacturer and hotel owner before starting his brewery 'on the Indigo, about two miles from Chiltern on the Howlong Road'. Business was good, despite there being many breweries already in business in at least six nearby towns.

Bartley became president of the Agricultural and Horticultural Society, the Chiltern Racing Club, a justice of the peace and, for a long time, coroner for the district. He was considered 'one of nature's gentlemen and a model of integrity'.

In 1884 Bartley, with his sons, opened the Maryborough Brewery in Maryborough, Victoria, and both breweries ran successfully under the Bartley name.

Early in 1897 tenders were invited for the purchase or rental of Bartley's Chiltern brewery, the reason being the failing health of Benjamin Bartley; he died two years later. His son, Theodore, carried on as A. E. T. Bartley until 1913 when the brewery closed. The site of the brewery was sold by the Bartley family in 1989, and is now included in the Chiltern Regional Park.

Colac

Colac Brewery 1867–98
Murray Street

The Colac Brewery was typical of many country breweries that struggled on, with owners coming and going, all trying to produce a good beer and build a good business. Very few succeeded.

William Strickland bought land in Murray Street, and built a brewery using bricks and stone. He had excellent water from a nearby spring, and started brewing in March 1867, but unfortunately he couldn't build up enough business — the large Melbourne breweries were cutting prices, and he began losing much of the hotel trade.

In 1875 he became involved in a law suit and the Colac Brewery closed. On 1 January 1875, just before the brewery closure, an advertisement appeared in the *Hampden Guardian*: 'Strickland's Brewery and Cordial Manufacturer, Colac and Camperdown'. Strickland had started another brewery (the Leura Brewery) at Camperdown, 50 km to the west, but this had to be auctioned off in March 1875.

Thomas Harris, Strickland's brewer, reopened the Colac Brewery but fared no better than his former employer, and the brewery was up for sale in 1884.

James Jackson, owner of the Leura Brewery, Camperdown, tried to run the Colac Brewery but had to give up. Several others followed, and the brewery was finally closed in 1898. When the property was auctioned, only two of the six lots of land were sold.

William Strickland	1867–75, closed
Thomas Harris	1884
James Jackson	1884
Albert Elliott	1884–88
William Ritchie	1888–89, closed
Richard Escott	1892–98

Creswick

Creswick Brewery Co. Ltd c. 1866–75
Cabbage Tree Flat

When Thomas Quinn started brewing about 1866, he also had a malthouse and store. In September 1873 the Creswick Brewery Co. Ltd was incorporated, but the business was wound up two years later.

Daylesford

The huge hills of grey shale that surround Daylesford are a vivid reminder of the town's early goldmining history. Daylesford is also well renowned for its

James Dolphin's Daylesford Brewery, c. 1880.

natural, crystal-clear mineral water. Of Victoria's 110 documented mineral springs, 72 are at Daylesford. Brewing has long since ceased in the peaceful historic town, but the mineral water still flows.

Daylesford Brewery 1861–1916
Bridport Street

Gold had been discovered at Daylesford, originally called Wombat Hill, in 1851, and the one and only brewery in the town followed ten years later. Known simply as the Daylesford Brewery, it was started by the Borsa brothers, Antonio and Battista. Later, Antonio ran the brewery on his own.

After two years the brewery was taken over by Nicholas Fitzgerald, in partnership with James Perrin. The Fitzgerald brothers owned the Castlemaine Brewery, the Newbridge Brewery and wine, spirit and produce stores at Creswick and Daylesford.

The Daylesford Brewery was of weatherboard construction, and the water for brewing came through fine rocks into a crystal-clear well. Perrins managed the brewery until 1871.

Two years later James Dolphin became the owner, brewing consistently good-quality beer for almost forty years: 'Mr Dolphin does his own brewing, considers that boiling by steam is the best method, less expensive and much less labour than boiling by direct fire'.

By 1895 the town had grown to a population of 4500, and Dolphin was selling 'bottled ale, 6 shillings per dozen large bottles, and 4 shillings, small'. Late in 1908 he installed a new boiling copper, and at that time it was said that 'the capacity is about 30 hogsheads … the old boiler certainly had its day having been in use for over 30 years'.

Frank Sheppard took over the brewery in 1910, and 'spent money freely in making the place up to date'. Six years later the brewery closed.

Antonio & Battista Borsa	1861–62
Antonio Borsa	1862–63
Nicholas Fitzgerald & James Perrin	1863–73
James Dolphin	1873–1910
Frank Sheppard	1910–16

Dooen

Dooen Brewery 1884
When John Lawther began brewing in the small township of Dooen in 1884, he would have had competition from the two large and well-established breweries (the Victoria Brewery and the Wimmera Brewery) at Horsham, just 10 km to the south.

Dunolly

The discovery of gold in the area in 1853 determined the site of the original township of Dunolly. As more gold was found downstream, the town followed, culminating in the fifth and present siting of Dunolly during the big rush of 1856 when the population had grown to 35,000. The Welcome Stranger gold nugget, claimed to be the largest ever discovered, was found at Moliagul, nine miles from Dunolly.

Burnt Creek Brewery 1854–62
Burnt Creek

The town's first brewery commenced soon after the gold-rush started, and the owners, Collier & Gunn, decided to trade as the Burnt Creek Brewery. It was situated close to Wigham's Junction Hotel, on the Burnt Creek.

John and Sibley Collier had taken over by 1860. In December the following year there were two serious accidents in one week: on both occasions, loads of barrels fell on the driver (there was no mention if it was the same driver).

Frayne, Peter 1860
Peter Frayne's Brewery was near Dunolly's soap factory.

Noblett, George 1859–62
Many owners of small breweries did not bother to choose a fancy name for their brewery, and George Noblett was one such. He was a brewer of old Dunolly (site of the first Dunolly), and his brewery was located a few miles north-west of Dunolly at Goldsborough, on the creek.

Windsor Brewery 1856–63
The owner of the Windsor Brewery and the adjoining Windsor Castle Hotel was Frederick Finch. The buildings, which were constructed in 1856, were of wood and canvas, but were rebuilt three years later as a two-storey brick building.

Fred Finch delivered ale for £5 per hogshead, also lemonade and cordials.

Before production of beer was discontinued, John Shelley was leasing the brewery.

Echuca

The Murray River is Australia's largest and longest river. For 100 years and more, from the 1850s it has provided a major source of transport. Echuca was the epicentre, being the closest river town to Melbourne; at its peak it was the largest inland port in the southern hemisphere, working 100 vessels a week.

An ex-convict, Henry Hopwood, founded Echuca in 1853, and took over a river-punt service. He built the Bridge Hotel beside the punt landing, and shrewdly staggered the punt schedules to keep customers drinking at his bar. If trade in the pub was slow, the punt was delayed.

The city is situated at the junction of the Murray, Campaspe and Goulburn Rivers, and is the centre of a pastoral and agricultural district. With the substantial river trade, Echuca was an ideal place for a brewery — in fact, no fewer than six breweries have operated there.

Today, tourism is a major industry. Attractions include the re-created Port of Echuca, which incorporates the wharf, wharf station and rolling stock, and restored paddle-steamers and barges.

Australian Brewery & Aerated Water Co.
See Echuca Brewing & Malting Co. Ltd.

Black Horse Brewery 1877–80
George Elliott started the brewery in partnership with a Mr Clegg, but after three years Elliott left the district and the brewery closed.

> ## CLEANING BOTTLES
>
> It is surprising, says Dr. F. Sawyer, how many persons persist in cleaning bottles with [lead] shot after the frequent cautions which have been given from time to time.
>
> Nothing cleans bottles so easily as a handful of lead shot, which can be shaken into every corner until the glass fairly shines with cleanliness. But the danger of lead poisoning is great, even when the bottle is rinsed out with clean water. It is doubly dangerous when there is no rinsing out at all, as is frequently the case.
>
> *Australian Brewers' Journal*, July 1893

Clarion Brewery 1900–1
Hopwood Street

Frederick Smalpage had been the manager and ultimately the proprietor of the Burton Brewery in Broken Hill, and when it closed early in 1900 he thought Echuca would be a good place to settle and to start another brewery. There were no breweries at Echuca at that time.

The Echuca Brewing & Malting Co. Ltd had been destroyed by fire the previous year, and Smalpage purchased the derelict property and converted the undamaged two-storey malthouse into a brewery. He used some of the equipment from the old Burton Brewery that he had brought with him from Broken Hill.

Energetic and resourceful, Smalpage soon had his Clarion Brewery working at a capacity of 20 hogsheads of beer daily. The *Riverine Herald* of 15 August 1900 said that the beer produced at the Clarion Brewery was 'brewed from malt, hops and sugar only, no acids or poisons whatever being allowed to be used'. In the past, locally made beer had been noted for its non-keeping qualities, and the general excuse for this failure was that the local water was not suitable. Fred Smalpage said he had the same trouble at Broken Hill, but had found a method of treating the Murray River water that enabled him to 'turn out a splendid article'. But not for long.

After one year, Smalpage 'was compelled to give it up as a bad spec [sic]'. Some months later he was drowned at Manly beach, Sydney, while attempting to rescue a girl who had been swept out to sea.

Echuca Brewing & Malting Co. Ltd 1884–99
Hopwood Street

Echuca supported a number of breweries, the largest of which was the Echuca Brewery, started by the Guinn brothers, Harry and George, in 1884. The name New Brewery was frequently used. A malthouse was added, and the Guinn brothers were the first brewers in Echuca to make their own barley malt.

The *Riverine Herald* of 11 May 1889 reported on the first half-yearly meeting of the company, listed on the Melbourne Stock Exchange as the Echuca Brewing & Malting Co. Ltd. Many local hotelkeepers and traders were shareholders, and the brewery was managed by Harry Guinn and cordial-manufacturer John Patterson. During 1890 the company completed the installation of two artesian wells, 200 feet deep. The water from one well was used for cooling purposes and the other for brewing. It was claimed that the artesian water was better than that drawn from the Murray River.

Harry Guinn retired in 1890, and the following year George Mapleback became the new manager. Beers produced included Echuca Liquid Gem and Superior Pale Ale.

For a brief period A. Elliott and S. G. Elliott controlled the brewery, but the company went into liquidation in 1893. It was taken over by the partnership of P. J. Martin and A. McMillan the following year, but they decided to sell; the brewery was purchased by A. Siddall in 1894. He changed the name to the Australian Brewery & Aerated Water Co. and employed his father, Paul Siddall, as the brewer.

During 1899 the brewery was destroyed in one of the largest and most destructive fires seen in Echuca. Frederick Smalpage bought the ruined property the next year, and repaired and converted the malthouse into a brewery. He changed the name to the Clarion Brewery, but it closed the following year.

New Brewery
See Echuca Brewing & Malting Co. Ltd.

Riverine Brewery c. 1860–71
The brewery was started by a Mr Jones around 1860. It is uncertain how long Jones brewed for, since by 1869 a tannery business occupied the premises and the brewery equipment had been shifted to Conolly Street.

In May 1869 an advertisement was placed in the *Riverine Herald*: 'having completed their new brewery, Messrs Lowden & Nash are ready to supply the public with ales and porter of the best quality'.

In October 1869, only five months later, Nash was insolvent, and the brewery was sold to John McDowell who chose the name Riverine Brewery.

Springvale Brewery 1858–66
The owner of the Springvale Brewery was T. H. Freeman.

Standard Brewery 1861–75
Hare Street

William James Disher arrived in Echuca in 1861 to manage the new Standard Brewery for one of the Elliott brothers. In January 1865 Disher placed an advertisement in the *Riverine Herald* announcing that he had purchased the brewery from Elliott. The next month he appeared in court, charged by Elliott with trespass and embezzlement. Although Disher had negotiated the purchase, he had difficulty in raising the cash, and, in fact, he was still paying off outstanding debts incurred in Melbourne.

On 5 April 1865 William Disher finally became the legal owner of the Standard Brewery and started advertising. One advertisement appeared in the *Pastoral Times & Echuca & Moama Chronicle* of 20 January 1866 with the simple message: 'Standard Brewery, Echuca, W. J. Disher. Disher's Celebrated X, XX and XXX Ales and Porter'.

The brewery was purchased by a member of the McCracken family of Melbourne in 1867, and it was either leased or sold shortly after.

Late in 1869 Neil McArthur was the owner and he advertised in both the *Riverine Herald* and the *Echuca & Moama Advertiser* on 8 January 1869 that 'having completed his arrangements … is now in a position to supply beer'. Fifteen months later he advertised again, advising the readers that he had 'perfected his plant'. Apparently McArthur took a long time to put out a satisfactory beer, but he stayed in business for another two years or so.

From 1873 to 1875 the brewery was either owned or leased by James Liddle.

Eddington

Eddington Brewery 1880–96

It is surprising that the Eddington Brewery lasted for sixteen years. The goldrush had finished, and there were many well-known, long-standing breweries in nearby townships such as Bendigo, Castlemaine, Maryborough and Maldon. Undeterred, John Sheridan started brewing at the much smaller town of Eddington, and after five years he took on a partner, Frederick Appleton.

During 1894 the company sued the Water Supply Department, claiming damages of £8000 because of the contamination of their water supply caused by the construction of a weir at Laanecoorie to the north. The brewery had to stop operating for an extended period.

Two years after the brewery started operating again, it was closed.

Eldorado

Eldorado Brewery c. 1870

The partners, Russell & Taylor, had been wine-and-spirit merchants in nearby Beechworth during the 1860s. About 1870 they set up a small brewery at Eldorado (Spanish for 'The Golden One'), and advertised 'The primest ales always on sale'.

Enoch Point

Macintosh, David c. 1870–75
Sullivan Street

David McIntosh was brewing at Enoch Point in the high mountainous country of Victoria about 1870. At the time the brewery closed five years later, F. C. Stander was the owner.

Fernshaw

Toogood, William 1866–72

Bailliere's Official Post Office Directory of Victoria lists William Toogood, brewer, Fernshaw, for the years 1868 to 1872. Toogood is also listed as a brewer in *Butler's Woods Point and Gippsland General Directory* in the 1866 and 1866–67 editions. Toogood's property happened to be between two hotels. Whether he brewed at that location or whether he actually had a brewery at Fernshaw is unknown.

Gaffneys Creek

The small township of Gaffneys Creek was originally called Lauraville, and was the site of the first gold discovery on the Jamieson–Walhalla goldfields in 1859.

Lauraville Brewery
See Mountain Brewery.

Mountain Brewery 1860–1900
View Street

The brewery, which was opened in 1860 by William Mountford, was first known as the Lauraville Brewery. In 1864 Mountford advertised: 'Hogsheads of ale, 10 guineas, or 4 shillings & 8 pence in small casks'.

The name had changed to the Mountain Brewery by 1875. During that year Charles Mountford, presumably a son or brother of William, had sold his Mountain Brewery at Woods Point about 20 km south, so that he could concentrate on running the brewery at Gaffney's Creek.

The brewery was offered for sale in 1883, but there is no record of any new owner after that date.

Geelong

In 1824 explorers Hume and Hovell travelled overland to the western shore of Corio Bay. They heard the natives call the bay 'Jillong', and hence named the place Geelong. White settlers arrived at the Geelong area late in 1835, and in November 1837 it was declared a town. Three years later the *Geelong Advertiser* was in production, and flourmills, tanneries, soap and candle works, and breweries soon followed.

Barwon Brewery c. 1841

The Barwon Brewery was Geelong's first brewery. It was owned by Oliver Adams who advertised in the 24 April 1841 issue of the *Geelong Advertiser*:

Barwon Brewery — the friends of Temperance, as well as the lovers of good cheer, will be glad to learn that a pleasant and wholesome liquor is now brewed in Geelong ... We hope ... that the host of spirit drinkers, if they can't keep sober, ... will substitute ale and beer for rum and gin.

It is not known how long the brewery lasted, although in April 1846 Adams was described as a hotelkeeper. A. McGill and P. O'Hara had been partners in a brewery in Geelong, and had announced the dissolution of their partnership in the *Geelong Advertiser* of 14 June 1845; O'Hara was to carry on alone. Their brewing activity may have been a continuation of the Barwon Brewery.

Bollington Hop Beer Co. 1903–8
Little Malop Street

Although the company was licensed to brew alcoholic beverages, beer, ale and porter were probably never produced.

Corio Brewery 1851–94
Little Malop Street

Scottish-born Thomas Aitken arrived in Victoria in 1842, moved to Geelong, and started the Corio Brewery either late 1850 or early 1851. He sold the brewery almost immediately to Thomas Powell, and moved back to Melbourne, where he started up again as the Union Brewery. Later, he achieved fame and fortune when he established the Victoria Parade Brewery, which was to become one of the largest in Melbourne.

Thomas Powell had been a wheelwright and blacksmith, and later he built and occupied the Union Hotel in Malop Street.

After working the Corio Brewery for seven years, Powell retired, and for a while the brewery was in the hands of James Brown, who described himself as an ale-and-porter brewer.

In 1858 the brewery property was purchased by Henry Elmes, who had owned a brewery in Melbourne in the 1840s. He rented the Corio Brewery to the original owner, Thomas Powell, in July 1862, and Powell's Brewery was frequently referred to in journals and directories.

It was the practice of some of the more enterprising breweries throughout Australia to establish agents in other towns. The agents would promote the brewery's products, book orders, and attend to the return of empty casks. Provided the beer was satisfactory, this was worthwhile business for the brewery and the agent. Thomas Powell was doing business, through an agent, as far away as Port Fairy on Victoria's south-west coast, and he advertised in the *Banner of Belfast* (Port Fairy) on 29 August 1866: 'Corio Brewery. Powell's XXX, in bulk and bottle'. The agent's name and address were included.

Thomas Powell died in March 1877 during a visit to his Excelsior Brewery at Stawell. His daughter, Miss M. J. Powell, continued to run the Corio Brewery, Geelong, for a very brief period, and the brewery closed. Michael Clanchy, licensee of the Queen's Head Hotel, purchased the Corio Brewery in 1886. He employed William Kenna as the brewer, a wise choice since Kenna had a reputation as being one of the best brewers in the state, having brewed at the Phoenix Brewery in Ballarat for twenty years.

Unfortunately for Clanchy, Kenna left the following year to start his own brewery in Warrenheip, near Ballarat, and by 1894 Clanchy was bankrupt. That was the finish of the Corio Brewery.

Three years later Coghlan & Tulloch's Ballarat Brewery bought the premises, which were then used as a depot.

Thomas Aitken	c. 1851
Thomas Powell	1851–58
James Brown	1858
Henry Elmes	1858–62
Thomas Powell	1862–77
Miss M. J. Powell	1877
Michael Clanchy	1886–94

Geelong Brewery 1845–57
Between Corio Street & Corio Terrace, east of Yarra Street

From the time of settlement Geelong rapidly developed as an important port facility and main outlet for the rural produce of Victoria's Western District. One of the early industries was brewing, and the Geelong Brewery was one of the first. It was started by John Cumming in 1845. He had come from Aberdeen, Scotland, to Van Diemen's Land in 1833, subsequently moving to Melbourne, and then to Geelong in the 1840s.

The Geelong Brewery, which traded as Cumming & Son from 1853, became one of Geelong's best-known landmarks. It was built on high ground overlooking the eastern foreshore, and the 80-foot high chimney-stack, built in 1876, was a conspicuous feature of the town.

The name was changed to the Volum Brewery following the purchase of the property and goodwill by Captain James Volum, who took possession in January 1857.

See also Volum Brewing Co. Ltd.

Hodges Brothers Brewery
See West End Brewery.

Kildare Brewery c. 1860
The premises were adjoining the Sportsman's Arms Hotel.

Newtown Brewery 1858
Western end of Skene Street

The partners were Shaw & Pagden.

Pivot Brewery 1865
Cnr Little Malop & Bellarine Streets

The Pivot Brewery was in a new building adjoining the Clare Hotel, but after a few months of operation both the brewery and hotel were auctioned — £700 bought the lot.

Powell's Brewery
See Corio Brewery.

Retreat Inn & Brewery   c. 1843–50
Fyans Street, South Geelong

During the 1840s there were several breweries in Geelong, most of them in south Geelong, which was almost a separate township at the time. One of these small brewing concerns was associated with the Retreat Inn, which opened in December 1840. Joseph Griffin was the proprietor. On 7 January 1846 he advertised his hotel and brewery for sale.

The brewery was rented in 1847, and on 11 February 1848 the *Geelong Advertiser* reported that J. Skerret was in charge. The stock was up for sale late in 1850, and at that time brewing would have ceased.

Royal Brewery   1868–82
Malop Street

The old Theatre Royal in Malop Street had closed in 1867, and the fittings and properties were auctioned. Henry Elmes purchased the building, converted it to a brewery and when this was completed, he sold it to Isaac Hodges, late of the local Prince of Wales Hotel. Elmes was also the owner of the Corio Brewery, which he was leasing to Thomas Powell at that time.

Isaac Hodges took control in July 1868, and used the name of the old theatre by trading as the Royal Brewery. After the death of Isaac Hodges in 1875, his sons carried on the business, which expanded rapidly.

More space was required, and in 1881 they purchased the West End Brewery in La Trobe Terrace, and the equipment from their Royal Brewery at Malop Street was transferred there.

The Royal Brewery was taken over by James Miller in 1881, but his tenure was brief. The property was bought by the Salvation Army in 1883.

Volum Brewing Co. Ltd   1857–1958
Corio Street

The Volum Brewery was second only to the Ballarat Brewery as the longest-running brewery to operate in country Victoria. Brewing continued for 113 years, starting in 1845 as the Geelong Brewery, and changing to the Volum Brewery when Captain James Volum purchased the property in January 1857.

Volum, an enterprising businessman, opened a paper mill on the bank of the Barwon River near Buckleys Falls. He lived in a house attached to the brewery, and died there in 1884 at the age of eighty.

The son, Andrew Volum, ran the business from 1875, and formed the Volum Brewing Co. Ltd, which was registered in October 1887. Directors included John Sommers, Charles Cole and Samuel Young. By 1891 output of the brewery had increased to 350 hogsheads of beer per month, plus 2500 dozen bottles of ale and stout, much of which went to Melbourne and nearby provincial towns.

Samuel Young's son, John James Young, was managing director from 1923 to 1953, when the business was acquired by the Ballarat Brewing Co. Ltd.

In 1958 Carlton & United Breweries (CUB), Melbourne, took over all the brewing operations of the Ballarat Brewery, including the Volum Brewery. Brewing was discontinued at Geelong and beer was transported by tanker from CUB, Melbourne, put into kegs at Geelong, and marketed in Geelong and surrounding areas.

Sectional view of the Volum Brewery, Geelong, showing the manager's residence in the foreground.

Geelong Brewery	1845–57
Volum Brewery	1857–87
Volum Brewing Co. Ltd	1887–1953
Ballarat Brewing Co. Ltd	1953–58
Carlton & United Breweries Ltd	1958

West End Brewery   1865–1924
La Trobe Terrace

Martin Augustus Treacey was the owner of a brewery at Wagga Wagga, NSW, and also a hotel in Geelong. He leased a three-storey building in La Trobe Terrace, near Spring Street, and converted it into the West End Brewery. The opening was celebrated on 22 May 1865; friends were invited to a champagne luncheon and a tour of the plant.

Treacey returned to Wagga Wagga in 1881, and the West End Brewery was offered for sale by auction. The Hodges brothers, who were brewing at their Royal Brewery in Malop Street, needed more space, so they bought the West End Brewery for £925. Brewing operations were then centralised at La Trobe Terrace, and the business continued as Hodges Brothers Brewery until 1924.

Carlton & United Breweries Ltd, Melbourne, purchased the brewery at that time, and used the premises as a depot.

Germantown

Germantown Brewery   1895

Germantown is located in rugged mountain country in north-eastern Victoria, and was never an ideal location for a brewery. The population was sparse, and very few travellers passed that way. In spite of these disadvantages, Albert Elliott set about brewing there in 1895, but moved out very soon after.

Gisborne

During the 1850s Gisborne had thirteen hotels and one brewery. The township was a stopping-off place for people travelling between Melbourne and the goldfields of Bendigo and Castlemaine, and the hotels and brewery enjoyed good business for a while. Travellers invariably stayed overnight, since the road conditions were difficult for travel, even in the daytime. The main problem, however, was the danger of travelling through the Black Forest at night, where highwaymen lurked ready to relieve unfortunate prospectors of their winnings.

Gisborne Brewery 1854–61
Calthorpe Street

Alfred Terry had started brewing at Gisborne in 1854, and supplied the transient population, lumber-yard workers and the hotels with his traditional ales and porter.

W. Lane & Son ran the brewery for the last two years. The brewery closed in 1861 — during that year the rail line went through to Bendigo, and people then travelled mostly by rail, leaving the brewery with insufficient custom.

Glen Creek

Eagle Brewery 1870–80

The brewery was built in 1870, and the proprietor, John Lawther, advertised that, 'regardless of expense', he had completed the Eagle Brewery at Glen Creek, and could 'supply the district with genuine, pure and unadulterated Ale and Porter and trusts, by unremitting attention to business and producing a first class article, to merit the approbation of publicans and others'.

A fire destroyed the buildings in 1885, although the brewery had closed several years earlier.

Gobur

Gobur Brewery c. 1880

Gobur is quite a small township about 30 km east of Seymour in central Victoria. There were no major towns in the surrounding district, and the trade of the Gobur Brewery would have been limited.

Edhouse & Whittington owned the Gobur Brewery: both partners had left the Castlemaine district, where Benjamin Edhouse had previously been the proprietor of the Loddon Brewery. Gobur was not their best move.

Hamilton

Settlement of the Hamilton district dates back to 1837, following exploration of the area by Major Thomas Mitchell. Hamilton was known as The Grange until 1851, and was first occupied by Scottish settlers.

Collins Street Brewery
See Sheldrick & Co.

Grange Brewery 1861–82
Gray Street, through to Lonsdale Street

Hamilton's first brewery was opened for business in 1851 by Thomas Smith, with Francis Rentier in charge of the brewing. The following year the brewery closed. It remained idle for the next ten years. It was purchased in 1861 by Charles Haferkorn, who brewed ale and porter in addition to the ginger-beer and cordial that he had been making for the previous three years. For part of the time Haferkorn was assisted by Francis Rentier.

Preoccupied with his hotels at Balmoral and Coleraine, Haferkorn leased the Grange Brewery to Robert Younger in 1873, and then to Thomas Sloan from 1877 to 1882, at which time the brewery closed. Charles Haferkorn built his Grange Family Hotel on the brewery site, and Thomas Sloan, the previous lessee of the brewery, started his own North Hamilton Brewery at the corner of Collins and Pope Streets.

Hamilton Brewery
See Sheldrick & Co.

Herman, Frank 1911
Cnr French & Brown Streets

Within a year of starting his brewery, Frank Herman sold out to the Ballarat Brewing Co. Pty Ltd, who used the ideal corner position as a depot.

North Hamilton Brewery 1883–c. 1930
Cnr Collins & Pope Streets

Thomas Sloan had been the owner of the White Horse Brewery at Portland during the 1860s, and then moved to Hamilton where he worked at the Grange Brewery for several years. He decided to start his own brewery in 1883, and built a brewery and family home on two blocks of land at the corner of Collins and Pope Streets. Sloan produced aerated waters, as well as the usual ale and porter.

The brewery had closed, but was reopened and leased by John Currie early in 1885.

Robert and James Sloan became involved in the business, and after the death in 1910 of Thomas Sloan his widow, Susan, assumed control. By 1919 Millie and Anne Sloan had joined the firm, frequently called Sloan's Brewery.

Sheldrick & Co. 1868–1920
Collins Street, through to McPherson Street

During the life of the brewery it was known by four different names, was closed three times, and close to twenty different brewers were involved.

Ferdinand Heinze was a cooper by trade, and he built his house and brewery on a large block of land with a frontage to both Collins and McPherson Streets. He ran the brewery in partnership with Johann Rottger for the first few years, and traded as the Hamilton Brewery. It was a small business and the proprietors just managed to scrape together a living. Lack of good water was one of the problems.

The brewery was then leased to John Smith, and when Heinze took over again he built a new brick brewery.

A number of lessees followed, and finally Heinze sold the brewery to George Miller and Sam Mason in 1888. They changed the name to the Western City Brewing Co., but left after two years, and more owners followed. Their failure was put down to the 'scarcity of water' and 'having to pay seven shillings for 100 gallons of water'.

The Warrnambool-based brewery, Sheldrick & Co., purchased the Western City Brewery in 1900, and it continued to be called Sheldrick & Co. until the brewery closed in 1920.

Hamilton Brewery

Heinze & Rottger	1868–71
John Smith (lessee)	1871–74, closed
Ferdinand Heinze	1877–81

Collins Street Brewery

William Hill (lessee)	1881–83
John Thomas (lessee)	1883–84
George Dilnot (lessee)	1884–85
George Scrase (lessee)	1885–88

Western City Brewing Co.

Miller & Mason	1888–90

Western City Brewing Co. Ltd

Williams & Phillips	1890–96
Haley & Taylor	1896–97
Wilkins & Grogan	1897–99, closed

Sheldrick & Co.

Sheldrick & Co.	1900–11
Silberberg & Sidney	1911–19
Francis McGee	1919–20

Sloan's Brewery
See North Hamilton Brewery.

Smith's Brewery 1851–52
See Grange Brewery.

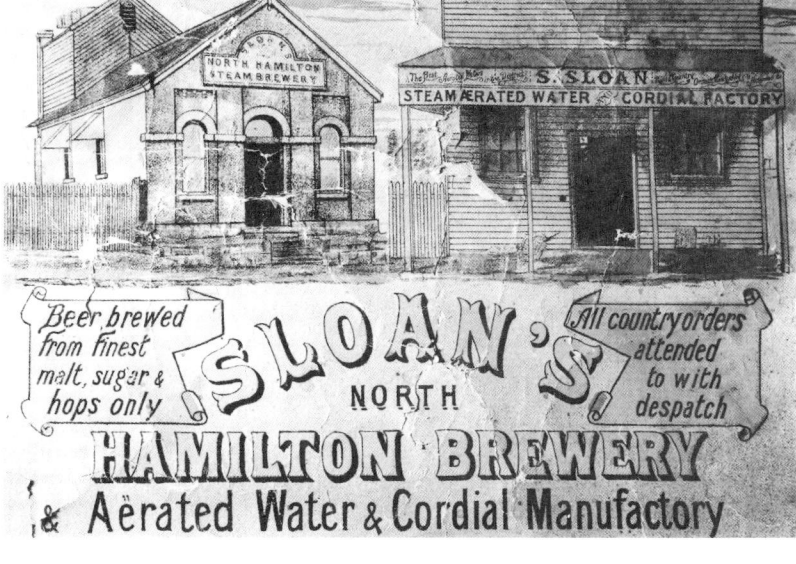

Waterfield, William 1866–69
Cnr Kenny Lane, North Hamilton

William Waterfield's brewery was a short distance from his hotel, and he brewed only sufficient for sale at the hotel.

Western City Brewing Co. Ltd
See Sheldrick & Co.

Heathcote

Heathcote Brewery 1855–81
High Street

Not long after starting the brewery in 1855, John Fynn sold the business to his brother-in-law, James Tierney. Fynn went back to his home country (Ireland), but returned to Heathcote in 1862 and renewed his interest in the brewery by becoming a partner, and later a substantial landowner.

Henry Bolton, Fynn's nephew, ran the brewery from about 1865 to 1869, and at that time Bolton, Fynn and Tierney set up a brewery (the Seymour Brewery) at Seymour in central Victoria. Earlier, in 1864, Fynn and Tierney had purchased the Kilmore Brewery. On 14 January 1869 Bolton advertised in the *Waranga Echo* with the brief message: 'Henry Bolton, Brewer, Heathcote'. Later that year M. J. Jefferson was in charge of the brewery and Patrick O'Meara held the brewer's licence after 1870.

Brain & Humphreys were the proprietors in 1875 and they employed Albert Elliott as their brewer. Elliott had won numerous awards for his ale, beer and porter when he was the brewer at various breweries at Bendigo, Echuca and Geelong.

This photo, from a very poor original, was taken about 1915. The name on the building to the right is S. Sloan. The founder of the North Hamilton Brewery, Thomas Sloan, died in 1910, and his widow, Susan, then took control of the business.

Horsham

Federal Brewery
See Victoria Brewery.

Horsham Brewing, Ice & Cordial Co. 1904–11
McPherson Street

Having completed their brewery in 1904, Heinrich Haustorfer and Gustave Kanter launched their beer with a tasting at the local Royal Hotel. There was a choice of dark and light beer, and the invitees were told that no chemicals or preservatives were used. They were also told that the beer was excellent — at least Kanter, one of the proprietors, said so.

Gustave Kanter left after two years, and in July 1910 the brewery was for sale as a going concern. It closed the following year.

Meadowbank Brewery
See Wimmera Brewery.

Victoria Brewery c. 1874–1907
McPherson Street

Peter Stevens, the proprietor of the Victoria Brewery, had trouble with the local council for many years. During 1890 there were complaints about the run-off liquids from his brewery, but he argued that the health officers were satisfied with the way he washed his casks. The brewery was on the bank of the river, and 'in no way did he want to run his wash water to the river because he would spoil his own water supply for the brewery'.

At the council's insistence, Stevens built a brick tank, but the problem persisted because he wouldn't clean it. By 1892 there had been five visits to the brewery by various council officials, and the problems were apparently rectified, although the waterhole at the back of the brewery still gave off offensive odours.

Problems of a different nature surfaced in August 1904 when the Collector of Customs presented evidence that the brewery was supplying beer without recording the details. The inspector said that 'he had been examining Stevens' books for 14 years and always had difficulty in understanding the irregular way in which they were kept'.

During the last few years the business was known as the Federal Brewery and traded as P. R. Stevens & Sons, with Augustus Stevens as the manager from 1899.

Wimmera Brewery 1874–98
Beside the Wimmera River

An advertisement in the *Horsham Times* of April 1874 stated:

> WIMMERA BREWERY.
> R. Bauer has much pleasure in announcing that he has opened the above-named brewery and is prepared to supply Ale and Porter of the best quality on the shortest notice.

By about 1880 the partnership of Treacy & Smith had taken over, and the name Meadowbank Brewery was sometimes used. Ernst Seeliger bought the brewery in 1883, and continued brewing good beer for the next fifteen years. He had previously been a brewer at the South Australian towns of Penola, Lobethal and Mt Gambier.

Inglewood

Albion Brewery 1859–c. 1867
Tarnagulla Road

Although gold had been discovered at Inglewood in 1859, the find was not extensive and William Ryan, who had only just started brewing at Inglewood, moved to Castlemaine where he believed the prospects would be better.

Robert Day and George Elliott owned the Albion Brewery at Newbridge, and decided to start another Albion Brewery at Inglewood, 20 km to the north. They began brewing there in 1860, and possibly took over William Ryan's brewery.

Jamieson

Alpine Brewery 1862–c. 1876
Northern end of Bridge Street

In its heyday the mining township of Jamieson, situated on the Goulburn and Jamieson Rivers, had two breweries and ten hotels. Dances were held at the hotels, admission free, and most hotels had their own two-piece band of piano and violin.

The first brewery was the Hibernian, built by Daniel Finn on the western bank of the Jamieson River. The

Situated in the high country beside a mountain stream, the Alpine Brewery, Jamieson, was in an ideal location. Unfortunately for the brewery, when the gold ran out, most of the population left the district.

name was later changed to the Alpine Brewery. Finn's beer was said to be excellent; it sold well in the nearby townships of Mansfield and Woods Point.

Goulburn Brewery
See Rock Brewery.

Hibernian Brewery
See Alpine Brewery.

Rock Brewery 1864–1901
End of Perkins Street

The Goulburn Brewery, as it was first known, was built on the eastern bank of the Jamieson River by William Power. He was a well-educated Irishman, and his interests extended to mining administration and local government.

When William Power moved to Queensland in 1873, the Goulburn Brewery was acquired by T. Holdsworth and Alfred Ingham. Two years later Richard Dale purchased the brewery, which included 'the substantial brewery, a five room cottage, horse works [sic], a pump, two malt mills, cold and hot water tanks … and 200 casks'.

Before the end of the nineteenth century there were several changes in ownership. In 1897 Mrs M. A. Dale, presumably Richard's wife, sold the brewery to George Lindsay and his brother. They extended the buildings, put in some new plant and set about competing for the trade of the district. They also changed the name to the Rock Brewery.

In 1899 Henry Edhouse of the Stawell Brewery purchased the Rock Brewery, and installed his stepson, Richard Cowman, as the brewer and manager. Progressively, cordial and aerated-water production became a more important part of the business, and by 1901 beer production had ceased.

Kilmore

Kilmore Brewery
See Victoria Brewery.

Victoria Brewery 1850–1902
Mitchell Street, near cnr Sydney Street

The founder of the Kilmore Brewery, as it was first known, was Stephen Nelson who advertised in the Melbourne *Argus* of 24 December 1850 that he had just completed his brewery. The area's rich volcanic soil had attracted squatters from NSW as early as 1837 when Melbourne, only 60 km south, was just two years old. The township was named Kilmore in 1841, and the subsequent settlement experienced a boom period in the 1850s with coaches arriving daily from Melbourne.

In spite of the growing population and business prospects, Stephen Nelson sold the Kilmore Brewery in 1855 to Howard Allt, who kept brewing until his death in 1862.

By 1864 John Fynn and his brother-in-law, James Tierney, had taken over the brewery. Fynn had started the Heathcote Brewery in 1855, and in Kilmore he became a large landowner, and was the mayor in 1865.

The following year John Fynn leased the brewery to Thomas Roberts, the owner of the town's general store. Roberts chose the name Victoria Brewery. Some years later John Brady was managing the brewery, and after the death of Fynn Brady managed to buy the brewery in 1881 for £390. In 1888 Brady sold out to the partners, Thomas Hunt and Thomas Ryan. After the sale, for reasons unknown, Brady committed suicide by cutting his throat with a table knife.

Thomas Hunt was the local newspaper proprietor, and in 1890 he became the sole owner of the brewery.

The *Kilmore Advertiser* of 25 June 1890 reported that a brewery worker, John Robinson, had been charged with burglary and larceny of a bucket. Police found him drinking in his room, with a bucket of beer locked in a box under his bed.

During March 1902 the brewery was completely wrecked by a severe storm. Only the chimney was left standing.

Koondrook

Victoria Brewery 1890–94
Michael Kean owned a flourmill in the small township of Koondrook, on the Murray River. He added a brewery and, with state pride, named it the Victoria.

A year later Kean sold to Robert Moyes, but brewing ceased in 1894, and the brewery and flourmill were offered for sale by tender. Early in 1897 the brewing equipment was bought by Gracie & Sleigh, who freighted it over to their new brewery at Fremantle, WA.

The Victoria Brewery, Kilmore, during the time it was leased by Thomas Roberts, 1866 and 1867. During its fifty-two years it was generally known as the Kilmore Brewery.

Right: *Although the Kyneton Brewery had started in 1857, the Nation brothers were only involved from 1904 until the brewery closed in 1916.*

Kyneton

Similar to many central Victorian towns of the time, the growth of Kyneton was due firstly to the hectic goldrush days of the 1850s, followed by sustained growth of commercial and pastoral activity.

Jowett & McKenna 1859–87
Ebden Street/Beauchamp Street

William Jowett and Martin McKenna set up their brewery in Ebden Street, and enjoyed a good business partnership for the next twenty-two years.

McKenna became sole owner in 1881, and then moved the brewery to Beauchamp Street. In 1887 the breweries of Martin McKenna and Robert Cock amalgamated to form the Kyneton Brewing & Malting Co. Ltd.

Kyneton Brewing & Malting Co. Ltd 1857–1916
Beauchamp Street

Matthew Johnson and Robert Cock began brewing in 1857, in modest premises in Mitchell Street, Kyneton. They continued for twenty-four years at that address, and in 1881 they shifted to a better location in Beauchamp Street, adjoining the Campaspe River.

On 23 October 1887 the Kyneton Brewing & Malting Co. Ltd was formed by the amalgamation of the breweries of Robert Cock and Martin McKenna. The new company was soon sending beer to Echuca and Tatura to the north, and as far as Sunbury to the south. Malting also became an important part of the company's business, with sales extending throughout the eastern states.

Robert Cock left the company in 1892, and moved to Cairns in Queensland, where he started the Burton Brewery Co. Ltd. This left Martin McKenna in charge of the Kyneton brewery until his retirement in 1904.

The company experienced financial difficulty, and was placed in liquidation in June 1906. Tenders were invited for the purchase of the brick brewery and malthouse in Beauchamp Street, together with all equipment and stock; also a group of malthouses at the corner of Ebden and Jennings Streets, and the lease and goodwill of a wine-and-spirit store at the corner of Piper and Wedge Streets.

The brewery was leased to George Mapleback, who tried to run the brewery in 1907. The next year the Nation brothers took over and changed the name to the Trent Brewery. Early in 1914 Kyneton & Trentham Breweries Ltd was formed to acquire the freehold property, plant and machinery of the Trent Brewery in Kyneton, and the Trentham Brewery in Trentham, 20 km to the south. The Nation brothers owned both breweries, and with the formation of the new company they intended to reopen the breweries that had recently closed.

Two years later, in May 1916, another company was registered as the Trent Brewery Pty Ltd, again, with the Nation brothers as the owners of both breweries. The brewery at Kyneton was closed, with brewing to continue at Trentham. On 7 February 1917 the freehold, plant and equipment were sold at auction.

Kyneton Brewing & Malting Co. Ltd, c. 1890.

Johnson & Cock (Mitchell Street)	1857–81
Johnson & Cock (Beauchamp Street)	1881–87
Kyneton Brewing & Malting Co. Ltd	1887–1906, liquidated
George Mapleback (lessee)	1907
Trent Brewery	
Nation Brothers	1908–14
Kyneton & Trentham Breweries Ltd	
Nation Brothers	1914–16
Trent Brewery Pty Ltd	
Nation Brothers	1916

Kyneton & Trentham Breweries Ltd
See Kyneton Brewing & Malting Co. Ltd.

Trent Brewery Pty Ltd
See Kyneton Brewing & Malting Co. Ltd.

Lancefield

Lancefield Brewery
See Trent Brewery Co.

Trent Brewery Co. 1880–97
The Lancefield Brewery was started by George Abbott, but after two years he was trying to lease or sell the brewery. In the meantime, Henry Lindsay had converted a local flourmill into a brewery. He bought all of Abbott's brewing equipment, fitted it into position

and began brewing, but within a year the brewery was idle and for sale.

The partnership of Henry Rickettson and Edmund Young reopened the brewery, and traded as the Trent Brewery Co. Young retired in 1891, and Rickettson, a well-known squatter from Barratta, NSW, employed E. W. Cockrane as the brewer and manager. He was replaced by J. T. Enright in 1895.

By this time a good share of the company's beer was sold in Melbourne and suburbs through their Melbourne agent, H. W. Perry.

The bore water used by the brewery had been too soft, and the condition was remedied by the addition of gypsum.

P. S. Tucket leased the brewery in 1895, but his efforts failed and the brewery was put up for auction twice in 1897. The brewery was still owned by Henry Rickettson, and he tried to auction the property once more on 10 March 1898. There were no bidders, and perhaps it was a mere coincidence that the brewery was destroyed by fire that very night.

Leigh Creek

Well Park Brewery   c. 1875–85

The proprietor of the Well Park Brewery, James McGrath, had found a permanent supply of spring water at Leigh Creek, and started brewing there some time before 1875.

Leigh Creek is only 6 km east of Ballarat, and it is difficult to understand why McGrath chose the location for his brewery, since there were at least four well-established breweries operating at Ballarat at that time. The ample supply of clear spring water may have influenced his decision, and, surprisingly, the Well Park Brewery stayed in business for ten years.

Lillicur

Bet Bet Brewery
See Black Horse Brewery.

Black Horse Brewery   1860–92
Bet Bet Creek

Scrase's Brewery was built on the bank of the Bet Bet Creek by the Scrase brothers, Edwin and Samuel, and it was described as a fine large building with a tall chimney. They advertised in the *Maryborough and Dunolly Advertiser* of 29 June 1860: 'to bakers and cow keepers; yeast and grains always on hand at Scrase's Brewery, Bet Bet Creek, three miles from Lamplough'.

The brewery was actually in Lillicur, almost centrally situated between Lamplough and Amherst. Many incorrect references show the brewery to be in either Lamplough or Amherst; even nearby Talbot has been stated as the location.

Another advertisement, this time in the *North Western Chronicle* of 12 December 1860 reads: 'Bet Bet Brewery, Scrase Bros. XXX Ale'. A further advertisement appeared in the same newspaper, on 19 October 1861: 'Black Horse Brewery, Bet Bet Creek, Scrase Bros., proprietors of the old firm of Scrase & Co. Ballarat'. The 'old firm' referred to was the Napier Brewery, Ballarat.

What began with the name Scrase's Brewery, quickly became the Bet Bet Brewery, and less than a year later, the Black Horse Brewery. With the changes in brewery name and the conflicting references to the address, the activities of the Scrase brothers have been difficult to follow. However, it was apparently an easy task for the brewery's traveller, Mr Eastwood, to slip away with £350 of the company's money in January 1869.

Edwin Scrase died in 1883 and his brother, Sam, in 1893, one year after the brewery closed.

Scrase's Brewery
See Black Horse Brewery.

The Maldon Brewery, Maldon, was started by Charles Bryant in 1863. The adjacent Springs Brewery, founded in 1856, had been idle for several years and the property was acquired by the Maldon Brewery for additional work space. There are some ruins of the old brewery at the rear of a private home.

Lilydale

Kobbell's Brewery 1870–84
Main Street

The township of Lilydale was founded and named in 1860, and ten years later locally-produced beer was available. The brewery formed part of the residence and shop of John Kobbell, who was listed as a cooper in council rate books.

Kobbell's wife, Louisa, was in charge of the brewery in 1881, but brewing ceased soon after. She was then occupying lodgings described as a boarding house.

Maindample

Lawther's Brewery 1880–84

The town of Maindample is on the Maroondah Highway, west of Mansfield and close to Lake Eildon. John Lawther was the town brewer for four years, and supplied the locals with the usual ale and porter. In 1884 he left the district to start another brewery at Dooen.

Maldon

The Maldon area was settled by Lachlan MacKinnon who took up holdings as early as 1839. He named his run 'Tarrangower'. The pastoral nature of the district changed with the discovery of gold, and the influx of 20,000 goldseekers led to the surveying of the township site of Maldon in 1854. Today Maldon is arguably Victoria's best example of a remarkably intact nineteenth-century mining town, and is a popular tourist attraction.

Laski, Thomas 1854

The Springs area, where Thomas Laski's brewery was located, was commercially important according to William Howitt in his writings of May 1854:

> water dealers had sunk wells with great success. They are called the Springs and here, during the summer, all the people would congregate and pitch their tents for the sale of water.

Howitt also reported on the first brewer in the area:

> In the pleasant valley of Tarrangower, we met with an old Bendigo acquaintance, Mr. Thomas Laski, from London … who has established a brewery there and is supplying almost the whole of the Tarrangower diggings with a wholesome beer instead of deleterious grog.

Nothing more seems to be recorded about Laski's brewery at Maldon, which may have been the forerunner of the Springs Brewery. Laski had started brewing at Talbot in 1855, and by 1858 he was brewing at Maryborough, Victoria.

Maldon Brewery Co. Pty Ltd 1863–1916

Charles Bryant, an immigrant from Portsmouth, England, was twenty-three years of age when he arrived in Melbourne in 1853. He began prospecting at Castlemaine, with only modest success, and then joined the Loddon Brewery, which he successfully managed for several years. Later, he married the daughter of Benjamin Edhouse, the owner of the brewery.

In 1863 Charles Bryant moved to Maldon and started his own brewery; three years later, it was sold at auction to the Warnock brothers. They also owned the Springs Brewery, which happened to be adjacent, and had been closed for a year. Bryant continued to lease the brewery from the Warnock brothers, and later the buildings were extended to take over the derelict premises of the old Springs Brewery.

Richard Marks joined the company, and by 1879 the Maldon Brewery traded as R. Marks, with Bryant retaining a half-share in the business. Bryant was also a partner with his nephew, Henry Edhouse, in the Stawell Brewery in Stawell, and also with William Sheil Snr, in the Shepparton Brewery in Shepparton.

R. Marks & Co. was registered on 21 January 1893, and the certificate of registration shows the partners as Charles Bryant, manager; Richard Marks, gentleman; and William Johns, traveller for the firm. The company produced bulk beer, which sold for £4 per hogshead. Their stable of twenty horses carted beer as far as 30 miles from the brewery.

Charles Bryant became President of the Maldon Shire Council on two occasions, and was a praiseworthy supporter of charity. Following his death in 1898, his son, Charles William Bryant, assumed control of the business, with William Sheil Jnr as a partner.

By 1901 William John Bryant had become the sole proprietor, although the company continued to trade as R. Marks & Co. until the beginning of World War I.

The *Australian Brewers' Journal* of May 1916 reported that

> the Maldon Brewery was sold by auction in one lot, last month, for £1,050 to a small syndicate from Brunswick [Melbourne] who dismantled the plant and buildings and resold them in several lots at, it is reported, a good profit.

Spring Creek Brewery
See Springs Brewery.

Springs Brewery 1856–66
During the latter part of 1856 William Thorne and Edward Scott began brewing at Maldon. They may have taken over Thomas Laski's brewery, which was in the Springs Creek area, hence the name Springs Brewery. Thorne had been the brewer at the Loddon Brewery in Castlemaine, and by 1857 he was the sole lessee of the Springs Brewery, sometimes referred to as the Spring Creek Brewery. In May 1861 the brewery was advertised to be auctioned, and the following month Thorne became insolvent.

The property passed to the mortgagees, the Warnock brothers, and, after trying unsuccessfully to sell the brewery, they leased it in November 1864 to A. A. Fielder.

Within months the lease was taken over by Chambers & Stowe. Chambers left after a year and the brewery closed again in 1866. (The owners of the brewery, James and Samuel Warnock, also owned the Beehive Stores, which comprised four shops: grocery, ironmongery, drapery and footwear shops.)

The Warnocks tried to lease the brewery again, and advertised in January 1867: 'To let, with plant, in complete working order'. A year passed, and by June 1868 the property was described as a wreck and unlettable. James Warnock offered the property to anyone, free of rent, if they would repair the buildings.

Malmsbury

Malmsbury Brewery 1855–59
John Clarke, the owner of the Malmsbury Brewery, leased out the property, but none of the lessees was able run the brewery with any success. There was too much competition from a number of breweries at Castlemaine to the north and from the Kyneton Brewery a short distance south.

John Lester & Albert Terry	1856
John Lester & Co.	1857
Robert Cock & Co.	1857
George Whightman & Co.	1858
William Lyon & Co.	1858

The 13 August 1860 edition of the Melbourne *Argus* advertised:

> To Brewers and Capitalists — Malmesbury [sic] Brewery and Malt House — for Sale or to Let. This brewery is well known and centrally situated. The business has heretofore been large and there is every prospect of a rapid increase from the extensive works now being carried on in the vicinity.

In August 1897 'the Malmsbury United Brewing Co. Ltd was struck off the register since the company had long ceased operating'. The company was probably never utilised.

Maryborough

The town of Maryborough, in central Victoria, was founded in 1854. In June of that year gold was discovered, and within three months there were 30,000 gold-seekers on the field. There was no brewery in the town, although at that time there were no fewer than ten at Castlemaine, six at Ballarat, and at least fifteen at Bendigo.

Maryborough Brewery 1884–1911
Derby Road

Benjamin Bartley had been running a profitable brewery at Chiltern since 1861. Twenty-three years later, with the help of his sons, he decided to start another brewery at the central Victorian town of Maryborough. During November 1884 'a good brew of Bartley's ale' was on sale, and he named the brewery the Maryborough (Victoria) District Brewery.

The company traded as Bartley Bros. in 1893, and as William Bartley in 1896, but at that time the economic depression was severe and resulted in Benjamin Bartley being declared insolvent in 1897. There was a deficiency of almost £2000, and the main creditor, the City of Melbourne Bank, was also in liquidation.

In April 1897 the brewery was purchased as a going concern by Coghlan & Tulloch's Ballarat Brewing Co. Ltd for £1700, and brewing continued until 1911.

O'Connor's Brewery 1869–89
Napier Street

The original partners were Nicholas O'Connor and Nicholas Prendergast. In the late 1870s, when O'Connor was sole proprietor, he had such grand ideas of extending his trade to Melbourne that 'very soon a glass of Maryborough Ale will be procurable at any of the principal hotels in Melbourne'.

The brewery cellar was extended to a length of 112 feet, and was said to be the finest cellar in any Victorian country town. Many men were employed, and about twenty horses were stabled for the transport of the company's ale and porter.

Smith & Laski's Brewery 1858
Thomas Laski had been brewing at Maldon in 1854 and Talbot in 1855. Neither venture was successful, and he tried again at Maryborough under the name of Smith & Laski.

Two Brewers Hotel & Brewery 1862–c. 1880
Cnr Nolan & Napier Streets

In June 1862 the Two Brewers Hotel & Brewery was opened by George Knight, who 'gave an excellent supper to his numerous guests on that occasion'. Knight and his son had previously operated a brewery at Blackwood.

The brewery at Maryborough operated in conjunction with the hotel. The owner, George Knight, was mayor at the time of his death in 1882.

Sayers & Co. of the Norfolk Brewery in Bendigo, purchased the Two Brewers Hotel & Brewery about 1865. George Elliott followed in the 1870s, and in 1880 the brewery was bought by James Steward of the Albion Brewery, Bendigo, and brewing at Maryborough was apparently discontinued.

Melbourne

Abbotsford Brewery
See Melbourne Co-operative Brewery Co. Ltd.

ANA Brewery
See Australian Natives Association Brewing Co.

Anglo-Bavarian Brewery Co.   1890–93
131 William Street

F. Tizard Welch was the manager.

Armstrong, Alfred   1858–c. 1862
Eltham

Artillery Brewery   1864–89
Nelson Place, near Cole Street, Williamstown

The woolstore, close to the old Bayview Hotel in Nelson Place, Williamstown, had been used as a marine stockade for prisoners who were set to work on the construction of roads and piers. In 1856 the Defence Ministry took over the building and it became a drill hall for the Volunteer Rifles.

When John Breheny leased the property in 1864, he converted it to the Marine Stockade Brewery, and soon carts laden with barrels of beer were lumbering down the little laneway next to the Bayview Hotel. Some of the barrels were sent by train to Melbourne. As early as 1867 the brewery was advertised as the Williamstown Brewery, and was still advertised as the Williamstown Brewery in the *Williamstown Chronicle* of October 1882.

William Hornby had become a partner, and was in charge of the business in 1868. The following year William Disher also became a partner, and the business, now known as the Artillery Brewery, traded as W. Hornby & Co.

William Disher, a big burly man, had gained his brewing experience in England. At the Artillery Brewery he put out Disher's 10-Guinea Ale, which was much advertised in Melbourne. Although a jovial, good-natured gentleman, he was better at talking about brewing than making good beer, according to an observer.

Albert Terry of the West End Brewery, Melbourne, purchased the Artillery Brewery in 1883. Six years later, in 1889, he amalgamated his Artillery and West End breweries with the Melbourne Brewing & Malting Co. to form Carlton & West End Breweries Ltd. This new company became the Carlton Brewery Ltd in 1896.

The old Artillery Brewery at Williamstown was used as a storage depot, and the historic buildings were unfortunately demolished to make way for the construction of the Aitken Street Housing Commission flats.

Marine Stockade Brewery (Williamstown Brewery)
John Breheny	1864–68
Breheny & Hornby	1868–69

Artillery Brewery
W. Hornby & Co.	1869–83
Albert Terry	1883–89

Austral Brewing Co.   1900–6
33 Stanley Street, West Melbourne

The company used the trademark Boz Ale, presumably a contraction of the Australian colloquialism 'Bonza', meaning excellent. The ale was non-intoxicating, and apparently no alcoholic beverages were produced.

Australian Brewery   1853–86
175 Flinders Lane, east

The following simple advertisement appeared in the *Melbourne Directory* of 1853: 'J. Henderson, Brewer of Family Ales, Flinders Lane, Eastern Hill, House 179'. John Henderson worked the Australian Brewery with his sons, and in 1862 he sold the business to P. J. Martin.

The new owner employed a brewer manager, Martin Hood, a lifelong teetotaller who never tasted a drop of his own product. Martin, the owner, moved with his sons to Townsville in Queensland in 1885, and started brewing there as the City Brewery.

Australian Brewery & Malthouse   1843–44
Flinders Lane, east

Captain James Dunbar opened the Australian Brewery & Malthouse in October 1843, offering 'ale and porter of pure, pleasant and healthful quality'. In April the following year Dunbar filed for insolvency, and allegations of fraud occupied the court for years with no clear result.

Australian Natives Association Brewing Co.   1893–1906
180 Nelson Road, South Melbourne

The Hannay brothers began brewing in 1893, and when they sold in 1900 the new proprietors, J. L.

A COMPLIMENT

Our contemporary thinks it not at all improbable that ale from Melbourne-on-Yarra may become as famous as beers from Burton-on-Trent and complacently reflects that 'if Australia can meet England on the vatted field, and beat her on her beer barrels, there is undoubtedly a great future awaiting this Austral continent.'

Australian Brewers' Journal, December 1891

Horne and W. T. Burbury, chose the name Australian Natives Association Brewing Co. — ANA Brewery for short. Later, one of the brothers joined the Federation Brewery in La Trobe Street as head brewer.

The Horne and Burbury partnership was dissolved in August 1903, and Burbury carried on alone for the next three years.

Ballenger Brewery Co. Pty Ltd   1908–9
82 Wellington Street, Collingwood

When the brewery was founded by John Wood in 1858, it was known as the Yorkshire Brewery Co. Ltd. During its life it had closed on several occasions. In 1893, after it had closed again, three Melbourne breweries, the Carlton, McCrackens and the Castlemaine, rented the brewery to prevent another company starting up again in opposition.

Years passed, and in 1908 Colonel John Ballenger leased the brewery and gave it a new name, the Ballenger Brewery Co. Pty Ltd. Ballenger had been at the Carlton Brewery for forty years, the last twenty years of which he had been head brewer. It was reported that Col. Ballenger was 'a firm believer in the value of printer's ink' and the magic words, 'Drink Ballenger's Beer', could be found in almost every newspaper and journal. The centre of the main curtain of the King's Theatre in Russell Street displayed a classical female figure holding two shields: one set out the merits of Ballenger's brew, and the other the superior quality of Hutton's bacon.

In November 1908 Ballenger's advertisements stated that the demand was so great that 'the company at present cannot book country orders'. Indeed, the beer was said to be 'an excellent drop'. There was a choice of XXXX Lager, XXX Stout and Pale Ale. While the Colonel was a first-class brewer, he was apparently not such a good businessman. On 23 November 1909 he went into liquidation, and the brewing equipment and unexpired lease were taken over by Carlton & United Breweries Pty Ltd (CUB). The name was changed back to the Yorkshire Brewery, which was then kept as a standby plant by CUB. The telephone number at the time was 56 City.

Berliner Brewing Co.   1903–4
216 Nicholson Street, North Fitzroy

It is surprising that Louis Berliner took up brewing again in Melbourne in 1903. Six years earlier he had tried to sell his South Broken Hill Brewery because he said he was retiring due to old age. When the brewery didn't sell, he stayed on at Broken Hill until 1903.

In Melbourne Louis Berliner intended supplying ale to private houses in 'handy size vessels'. The proprietor of the business was his son, Maurice Berliner, and Louis was merely an employee working for wages.

Maurice was successfully sued in January 1904 for non-payment of goods received on credit, and the brewery closed later that year.

Billson, George H.   1888–c. 1905
Brighton Road, Elsternwick

Although George Billson's factory at Elsternwick produced only soft drinks, this listing is included as an example of how some aerated-water manufacturers were producing so-called soft drinks and hop beer with more than just a touch of alcohol.

George Billson had been brought up in the brewing business. As a lad, he worked at his father's brewery at Beechworth and later, he had his own brewery at Albury. In the late 1880s he moved to Melbourne and began brewing hop beer and other aerated non-alcoholic beverages.

The *Australian Brewers' Journal* of March 1898 reported:

> At the St. Kilda Court on the 15th inst., G. H. Billson, aerated water manufacturer, was fined £10 with costs of one guinea, for selling hop beer with 4.5 per cent of proof spirit.

The judge commented:

> The fact of the matter is that some temperance people have been getting the worse for liquor on your beer and we are compelled to fine.

Similar situations were not uncommon throughout the colonies. Again, in the *Australian Brewers' Journal* of January 1898 mention was made of a ginger beer with an alcoholic content of 13.5 per cent. Victorian excise officers at the turn of the century began to clamp down on manufacturers of beverages containing 3–11 per cent of alcohol, which were sent out under such names as Hop Beer, Dandelion Ale and Temperance Beer. In most cases where charges were laid it was shown that the defendants had no intention of evading the duty, and that the offences were committed in ignorance.

Bollington Brewery   1888–1904
171 Stawell Street, Richmond

George Bollington migrated from England in 1886, worked at Townsville and Brisbane, and then came to Melbourne in 1888. He established a factory at Richmond in partnership with John and Richard Lee, trading as the Victorian Hop Beer Co., to produce Lager Bier, Dandelion Ale, Hot Tom, Kola, Cordial and A1 Hop Beer.

When the Lee brothers took over in 1893, Bollington formed the Bollington Hop Beer Co., and set up his factory at the corner of Somerset and Burnley Streets in Richmond. E. L. Deumer was a partner for a few months.

Ballinger Brewery label, 1908.

Later, Bollington shifted his business to 171–179 Stawell Street, Richmond, and used the name Bollington's Temperance Brewery. The use of the word 'Temperance' may have been inappropriate, since in May 1898 the company was charged with brewing without a licence. Their hop beer contained 6 per cent alcohol, and the defendants were fined £10.

Although George Bollington was primarily a manufacturer of cordials, aerated waters and hop beer, some alcoholic beverages were produced during his early partnership with the Lee brothers.

In later years William Roberts became the owner of the Bollington Brewery, and in 1904 it continued to trade as the Bollington Hop Beer Co. under the ownership of Walter Hacker.

Brighton Brewery 1859–83
Cockrane Street, Brighton

Melbourne's southern suburb of Brighton was first settled by Henry Dendy in 1841, just six years after the founding of Melbourne. Named after the town in England, Brighton was created a borough in 1859, and it was during that year that the small population of the district was able to buy locally-made ale and porter.

When John Penny started brewing at Brighton, he had no competition, and for twelve years he supplied the local farmers and travellers with his beer.

John Dodds took over the brewery in 1871, and John Simpson was involved for a year or two in 1875.

Britannia Brewery (Melbourne) 1838–39
Near Queen Street Wharf

Thomas Capel claimed to be Melbourne's first brewer, and advertised in his circulars dated December 1838: 'Capel's beer entire; beer equal to any brewed in Melbourne is to be had at the Britannia Brewery near the wharf, at 2s per gallon'. Capel also sold hogsheads of beer for £5, both prices being the same as that of his competitor, John Mills of the Melbourne Brewery.

The fact that Capel stated in his advertisement 'equal to any brewed in Melbourne' clearly suggests that other brewers were in business at that time. In fact, there were three others: Moss's Brewery in Little Flinders Street; the Wharf Brewery owned by the Murphy brothers, in Flinders Lane west, and John Mills, the ex-convict, who worked his Melbourne Brewery in Flinders Street east.

In February 1839 Capel's beer was on sale at Fawkner's Hotel for the exorbitant price of 1s per quart at the bar, for cash.

Thomas Capel married early in 1839, and he disposed of his business after receiving an offer to manage one of Sydney's larger breweries. He departed for Sydney, leaving his young bride to follow later in the brig *Britannia*. The ship was wrecked during its voyage, and portions of the wreck were subsequently found along that stretch of Victorian coastline now known as the Ninety Mile Beach. The only survivor was Mrs Capel, who was captured by Aboriginal people. She was seven months' pregnant at the time, and this was probably the reason her life was spared.

'Garryowen', in *The Chronicles of Early Melbourne, 1835–52* (1894), gives a lengthy account of the various sightings of a white woman and a white child living with Aboriginals. After several unsuccessful rescue attempts Mrs Capel and her young child were finally rescued and reunited with Thomas, but the long trauma left Mrs Capel permanently insane.

After brewing for several years in Sydney, Thomas Capel moved to Goulburn, NSW, and took up farming before starting his own brewery there in 1849.

Britannia Brewery (Prahran) 1857–73
Raleigh Street, Prahran

The partnership of Phimister & Thompson started the brewery. When Thompson left the following year, William Phimister continued by himself for a year or two. By 1860 the business was conducted by Phimister & Webster.

Henry Shakespeare took over the premises nine years later, and named his brewery the Britannia, an appropriate British title considering the location in Raleigh Street, and his surname.

Brunswick Brewery Ltd 1876–98
Cnr Glenlyon Road & Evelyn Street, Brunswick

The Brunswick Brewery Ltd was incorporated on 29 March 1876, and the partners were George Barker and William Brett. For most of the time Brett worked the brewery on his own.

Burnley Brewery 1892–99
Gibdon Street, Burnley

The owner of the Burnley Brewery was Edward Terry, son of Albert Terry, the former owner of the West End Brewery, Melbourne. Brewing commenced in November 1892, and was discontinued in 1899 when supplies of beer and stout were obtained from the Carlton Brewery. The beer was then redelivered to the Burnley Brewery's regular customers.

Edward Terry moved to Sydney, and became the brewer for Marshall's Paddington Brewery.

In April 1898, before brewing had stopped, a hotel proprietor was charged with unlawfully returning to the Burnley Brewery 7 gallons of what was purported to be sour beer. A customs officer found that the returned beer was nearly all water. The watering down of beer by hotelkeepers, both for public consumption and for return to a brewery for credit, was not an uncommon practice, particularly during the depression years of the 1890s.

Burnley Brewery Co. 1913–22
492 Swan Street, Richmond

This Burnley Brewery, as it was first known, produced no alcoholic beverages, and brewed 'Absolutely Non-Intoxicating' Burnley Ale and Stout.

The company became the Silverstream Mfg Co. Pty Ltd, and was operated by James Evans until 1922.

Burton Brewing Co. Ltd   c. 1867–99
33 Stanley Street, West Melbourne

The first brewer at Stanley Street was A. Levi. This was about 1867, and after a year or so the brewery was bought by Joseph McBride and Peter J. Martin. They chose the name Melbourne Brewery, since there were no other breweries by that name at that time.

The Melbourne Brewery was purchased by James Hennelly in 1881. He was the owner of the Metropolitan Brewery in La Trobe Street, and, for reasons unknown, he closed the Melbourne Brewery.

Walter James, a brewer from Hobart, Tasmania, reopened the brewery in 1885, and called it the Tasmanian Brewery. It was reported in June 1886 by the *Australian Brewers' Journal* that 'Mr Green, manager of the Tasmanian Brewery, West Melbourne, has broken his arm in a fall at the brewery'.

By 1887 the brewery had closed again, and Walter James tried unsuccessfully to auction the business. The following year he managed to negotiate a sale to Malcolm Macpherson and W. F. Smee. They used the name Burton Brewery Co.

Smee retired in 1889, and in 1894 the business was registered as the Burton Brewery Co. Ltd. The new company secured the trade of about sixty-five hotels formerly served by the Yorkshire Brewery, which had closed. G. H. Jamieson, the former manager of the Yorkshire Brewery, rebuilt the Burton in 1894. The last owner, two years later, was Peter McIndoe.

A. Levi	1867–68
Melbourne Brewery Co.	
J. McBride & P. J. Martin	1868–81
James Hennelly	1881, closed
Tasmanian Brewery	
Walter James	1885–87, closed
Burton Brewery Co.	
Macpherson & Smee	1888–89
M. Macpherson	1889–94
Burton Brewery Co. Ltd	
G. H. Jamieson	1894–96
P. McIndoe	1896–99

Bux Brewing Co.   1898–1929
120–126 (later 466) Nicholson Street/677 Nicholson Street, North Fitzroy

Although licensed as a brewery, the Bux Brewery probably had only a minimal production of alcoholic beverages. The owners, Alfred Clarke and Jessie Evans, started brewing in North Fitzroy in 1898. The previous year they started the Eureka Aerated Waters & Brewing Co. at Ballarat. Both breweries produced a non-intoxicating Bux Ale and Progress Brand soda water. Their rather unoriginal motto was 'You can never get too much of a good thing'.

Clarke ran the business from 1910 until his retirement in 1920, when the premises were purchased by the Defence Department and used as an ordnance store.

By 1922 the Bux Brewery was in business at 677 Nicholson Street, North Fitzroy, the site of the defunct Stacey Brewing Co.

James Byrne & Co.   1874–76
Stokes Street, Port Melbourne

James Byrne, a Melbourne publican, was a good-natured, rough-tempered Irishman of varied experiences. He had been a cabinet-maker, then a caretaker of the Melbourne Public Baths, afterwards the proprietor and licensee of the Argus Hotel in Collins Street, and a brewer for two years at Sandridge (now known as Port Melbourne). When he stopped brewing, he became the landlord of the Duke of Wellington Hotel.

Cambridge Brewery   1858–82
48 Cambridge Street, Collingwood

The partners, William Allen & John Sneath, started the brewery in 1858. A year or two later Allen was the sole owner.

During 1861 Edward Crispe was the proprietor, and he shifted the business in 1869 to the Collingwood Brewery, which he had purchased from Charles Vaughan and Edward Wild; the Cambridge Brewery was closed. It was reopened in 1872 by Oscar Gruenert, who was joined by George Ball in 1876.

Carlton & United Breweries Pty Ltd
See Carlton & United Breweries Ltd.

Carlton & United Breweries Ltd   1907–
16 Bouverie Street, Carlton

Carlton & United Breweries Ltd is arguably Australia's best-known brewery. Generally referred to as CUB, it has extensive national product distribution and acceptance. It also has by far the broadest international reputation of any Australian brewery because of its large-scale export marketing and ownership and equity in overseas breweries. The company has granted licensing

---

TOP JOB

Mr. R. J. Dooley has been appointed representative of the Ballarat Brewing Co., in succession to the late Mr. Harry Thompson whose dead body was found in the bay at Mordialloc. There were no fewer than 150 applicants for the position which carries a salary of £5 per week, all expenses paid and a free pass over the Victorian Railways.

Australian Brewers' Journal,
December 1907

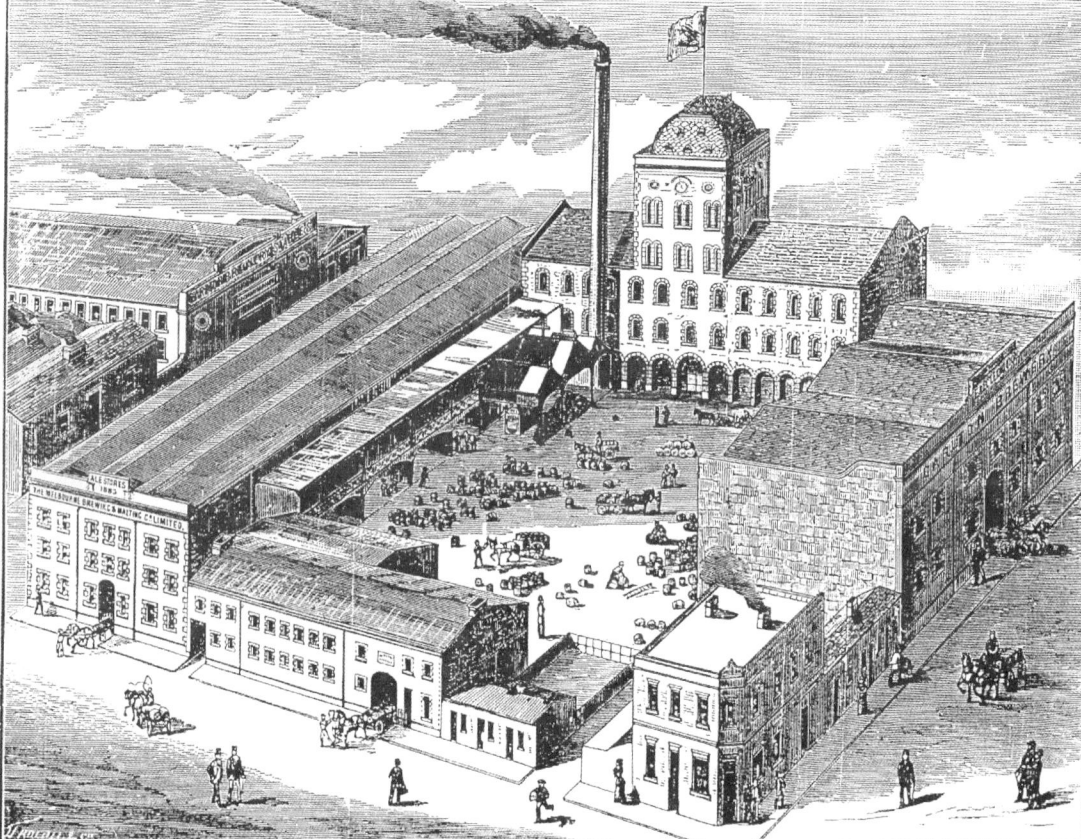

The Carlton Brewery, Bouverie Street, Melbourne, 1883. The old bluestone building at the corner of Bouverie and Victoria Streets, Carlton, is the only building remaining.
La Trobe Library, State Library of Victoria

This early label was used by Carlton & United Breweries when the company was formed as a Proprietary Limited company in 1907. It became a Limited company in 1913.

agreements to a number of overseas breweries, particularly for the production and sale of its most famous product, Foster's Lager.

CUB can trace its history back to August 1858 when Theodore Rosenberg set up a modest brewery in Bouverie Street, Carlton. It was known then as the North Melbourne Brewery, and although the name changed many times the brewing location at Bouverie Street remained from 1858 until 1987.

The depression of the 1890s had a severe effect on the eastern states of Australia, and particularly Victoria where it reached catastrophic proportions. Breweries were closing or otherwise struggling to exist, and the introduction of the beer duty in 1892 added to the burden. By the turn of the century most of the breweries in Melbourne had closed. In an attempt to stay in business, those remaining engaged in fierce price competition which had the inevitable effect of even greater losses.

In November 1905 members from several breweries held a meeting to consider the consolidation of six of Melbourne's largest breweries. Negotiations for this huge business undertaking took almost two years, culminating in the formation of Carlton & United Breweries Pty Ltd, which was registered on 8 May 1907.

The amalgamation was literally the salvation for some of the six breweries in the group. A receiver and manager had been appointed at the Victoria Brewery in East Melbourne in 1905, and the following year it was taken over by the Carlton Brewery. In 1903 McCracken's City Brewery earnings were not sufficient to meet interest payments, and it was still losing money before the amalgamation. The Castlemaine Brewery at South Melbourne lost heavily when its beer was affected by bacteria, and no dividend was declared for several years. The Shamrock and Foster breweries, both small operations compared to the others, had managed to survive; and the Carlton, after many years of heavy losses, managed to become profitable by 1907.

The six breweries that formed Carlton & United Breweries Pty Ltd are listed in order of their foundation.

McCracken's City Brewery Co. Ltd

McCracken & Robertson	1851–61
R. McCracken & Co.	1861–88
McCracken's City Brewery Co. Ltd	1888–1907

Victoria Brewery Pty Ltd

Victoria Parade Brewery:	
Thomas Aitken	1854–84
Archibald Aitken	1884–87
James & Alfred Nation	1887–88
Victoria Brewing, Malting & Distilling	
Co. Ltd	1888–92
Liquidated, and taken over by Nation	
Brothers	1892–94
Melbourne Brewery & Distillery Co.	1894–1904
Receiver and manager appointed	1904–5
Victoria Brewery Pty Ltd, owned by	
Carlton Brewery Ltd	1905–7

Carlton Brewery Ltd

North Melbourne Brewery:	
Rosenberg & Co.	1858–64
Phoenix Brewery	1864
Carlton Brewery:	
John Bellman	1864–65
Edward Latham	1865–81
Melbourne Brewing & Malting Co. Ltd	1881–89
Carlton & West End Breweries Ltd	1889–95
Carlton Brewery Ltd	1896–1907

Shamrock Brewing & Malting Co. Ltd

Graham's Brewery	1865
Murcutt's Brewery	1865–66
Simpson's Road Brewery:	
Graham	1866–71
Shamrock Brewery:	
Boyd & Head	1874–87
Shamrock Brewing & Malting Co. Ltd	1887–1907

Castlemaine Brewery Co., Melbourne, Ltd

Castlemaine Brewery, Melbourne	1871–85
Castlemaine Brewery Co.,	
Melbourne, Ltd	1885–1907

Foster Brewing Co. Pty Ltd

Foster's Brewery	1888–89
Foster Brewing Co. Ltd	1889–97
Foster Brewing Co. Pty Ltd	1897–1907

STEALING BEER FROM A BREWERY

A curious case of larceny was brought under notice on the 28th ult., when four young men were charged at the South Melbourne Court with stealing beer from the premises of the Castlemaine Brewery Company, Moray Street, South Melbourne, on the previous evening.

Constables were sent on 'special duty' in plain clothes and saw the accused outside the brewery. They had a piece of gas-pipe about twelve feet long and bent in the form of a syphon, which was stuck through one of the windows of the cellars, into a large vat of newly-brewed beer. They were drawing beer off into three billycans. The offenders were each sentenced to seven days' imprisonment.

Australian Brewers' Journal, April 1898

Of the six breweries that amalgamated, only two continued to operate. The Carlton Brewery in Bouverie Street became the company's headquarters and major production centre, supported by the output from the Victoria Brewery, which continued to brew until 1983. Brewing ceased at the Castlemaine, Shamrock and City breweries, and the Foster Brewery was retained as a standby plant until December 1910 when the property was sold.

The success of the new company was largely due to the wise and dynamic management of Emil Resch. Appointed general manager, he was one of Australia's most outstanding brewers of the time. He directed the installation of a laboratory, and the old 'rule of thumb' practices gave way to scientific methods of controlling the quality of beer production.

In January 1913 CUB became a public company, Carlton & United Breweries Ltd. The post-World War I period saw considerable expansion in production facilities and export growth, and the installation of plumbing and beer-drawing equipment to almost 1000 hotels and clubs in Melbourne and country Victoria.

The acquisition of other breweries began in 1924 with the takeover of Hodges Brothers Brewery, Geelong. The following year Fitzgerald's Brewery, Castlemaine, and the Victoria Brewery of Cohn Brothers, Bendigo, were also taken over. All three were closed, but the acquisitions included no fewer than eighty-four hotels spread throughout northern and central Victoria.

A merger with CUB's main competitor, the Melbourne Co-operative Brewery Co. Ltd, took place in 1925 to make CUB the largest brewing enterprise in Australia.

Other acquisitions followed, particularly in Queensland, and branch breweries were started in Darwin and in Fiji.

Acquisitions and expansions, in chronological sequence:

Yorkshire Brewery Co. Ltd, Melbourne
Yorkshire Brewery:
John Wood	1858–65
John Wood & Sons	1865–80, closed
James, Charles & John Wood	1883–87
Yorkshire Brewery Co. Ltd	1887–93, closed
Ballenger Brewery Co. Pty Ltd	1907–9, closed
Yorkshire Brewery, owned by CUB for a brief period	1909

Hodges Brothers Brewery, Geelong, Vic.
Royal Brewery, Malop Street	1868–81
Hodges Brothers Brewery, La Trobe Terrace	1881–1924
Taken over by CUB	1924, closed

Fitzgerald's Brewing & Malting Co. Castlemaine, Ltd, Castlemaine, Vic.
Castlemaine Brewery:
Fitzgerald Brothers	1858–76
Fitzgerald & Newman	1876–87
Fitzgerald's Brewing & Malting Co., Castlemaine Ltd	1887–1925
Taken over by CUB	1925, closed

Victoria Brewery Co. Ltd, Bendigo, Vic.
Victoria Brewery, Cohn Brothers	1858–87
Victoria Brewery Co. Ltd	1887–1925
Taken over by CUB	1925, closed

Melbourne Co-operative Brewery Co. Ltd, Melbourne
	1904–25
Taken over by CUB	1925–

Northern Australian Breweries Ltd, Cairns, Qld
Cairns Brewing Co. Ltd	1925–27
Northern Australian Breweries Ltd	1927–31
Taken over by CUB	1931–72
Carlton & United Breweries (N.Q.) Ltd	1972–86
Carlton & United Breweries (Queensland) Ltd	1986–92, closed

Bendigo United Breweries Pty Ltd, Bendigo, Vic.
Bendigo & Northern District Co-operative Brewing Co. Ltd	1907–14
Bendigo & United Co-operative Breweries Ltd	1914–20
Bendigo United Breweries Pty Ltd	1920–47
Taken over by CUB	1947, closed

Carlton & United Breweries Ltd, Darwin Brewery, Darwin
Carlton & United Breweries Ltd, Darwin Brewery	1957–73
N.T. Brewery Pty Ltd	1973–89, closed

Carlton Brewery (Fiji) Ltd, Fiji 1958

Ballarat Brewing Co. Ltd, Ballarat, Vic.
Phoenix Brewery	1857–95
Royal Standard Brewery	1853–95
Coghlan & Tulloch's Ballarat Brewing Co. Pty Ltd	1895–1911
Ballarat Brewing Co. Pty Ltd	1911–36
Ballarat Brewing Co. Ltd	1936–58
Taken over by CUB	1958–89, closed

Volum Brewing Co. Ltd, Geelong, Vic.
Geelong Brewery	1845–57
Volum Brewery	1857–87
Volum Brewing Co. Ltd	1887–1953
Taken over by Ballarat Brewing Co. Ltd	1953–58
Taken over by CUB	1958, closed

Queensland Brewing Co. Ltd, Brisbane
Bulimba Brewery	1882–83
Queensland Brewery Co.	1883–85
Queensland Brewery Co. Ltd	1885–1961
Taken over by CUB	1961–71
Carlton & United Breweries (Queensland) Ltd	1971–84
Carlton & United Breweries	1984–93, closed

Queensland Brewery Ltd, Toowoomba, Qld
Silverstream Brewery	1881–1923
Queensland Brewery Ltd	1923–61
Taken over by CUB	1961–71
Carlton & United Breweries (Queensland) Ltd	1971–76, closed

Thomas McLaughlin & Co., Rockhampton, Qld
Fitzroy Brewery	1880–93
Thomas McLaughlin & Co.	1893–1961
Taken over by CUB	1961–70
Carlton & United Breweries (Rockhampton) Pty Ltd	1970–76, closed

Richmond N.S. Brewing Co. Pty Ltd, Melbourne
	1928–62
Taken over by CUB	1962, closed

Courage Breweries Ltd, Melbourne
Courage Breweries Ltd	1968–78
Taken over by Tooth & Co. Ltd	1978–82
Taken over by CUB	1982, closed

Tooth & Co. Ltd, Sydney
Kent Brewery:
Newnham & Tooth	1835–43
John Tooth, and later descendants	1843–88
Tooth & Co. Ltd	1888–1983
Taken over by CUB	1983–

Northern Brewery, Lismore, NSW
Tooth & Co. Ltd	1979–83
Taken over by CUB	1983–86, closed

Matilda Bay Brewing Co. Ltd, Fremantle, WA
Anchor Brewing Co. Pty Ltd   1984–88
Matilda Bay Brewing Co. Ltd   1988–90
Taken over by CUB   1990–

Power Brewing Co. Ltd, Yatala, Qld
Power Brewing Co. Ltd   1988–93
Taken over by CUB, and used for all
    Qld beer production   1993–

Sanctuary Cove Brewing Co., Hope Island, Qld
Sanctuary Cove Brewing Co., then
    Luka Brewery   1988–95
Taken over by CUB, trading as the
    Gold Coast Brewery Pty Ltd   1995–

Cascade Brewery Co. Pty Ltd   1993–97
(wholly-owned CUB subsidiary; joint venture with
    Cascade Group Ltd, whereby J. Boag & Son Ltd
    retained Tasmanian distribution rights of Cascade-
    branded beer products)
Agreement terminated   1997
(CUB then had total control of Cascade Brewery
    Co. Pty Ltd)

Carlton & United Breweries Ltd, Darwin Brewery, Darwin
Carlton & United Breweries Ltd,
    Darwin Brewery   1996–

After World War II the company continued with its policy of hotel acquisitions and the use of the best brewing equipment available. The bottling of beer was transferred to both the Victoria and Abbotsford breweries, and ultimately only the Abbotsford Brewery, where a large new bottling plant was installed. The Carlton Brewery at Bouverie Street concentrated on the production of bulk beer.

The company has been a consistent leader in innovation. During the early 1910s crown seals were introduced, and gradually replaced corks. Soon after, motor vehicles took the place of horsedrawn lorries — at one time there had been as many as a hundred horses in the Bouverie Street stables. Stainless-steel containers were first used experimentally by CUB about 1932, and, in time, they replaced all of the company's wooden casks. Canned beer came on the market in 1958, and later the plastic six-pack beer can carrier was adopted as a convenient and economic method of packaging.

The remarkable progress of CUB continued with the acquisition of the large Sydney brewer, Tooth & Co. Ltd, in August 1983. The takeover, which included the newly-rebuilt Kent Brewery, Sydney, and the Northern Brewery, Lismore (NSW), made CUB the largest brewing company in Australia, with breweries located in Victoria, New South Wales, Queensland, the Northern Territory, and Fiji.

By the middle of 1984 the Melbourne-based company, Elders IXL, had taken control of CUB, and the spread of Foster's Lager as an international beer gained momentum. Under new direction the company embarked on grand schemes of expansion through the purchase in September 1986 of the Courage Breweries in the United Kingdom (subsequently resold), and the Canadian brewer, Carling O'Keefe Ltd of Toronto, early in 1987.

In Australia the company had been gradually rationalising brewing operations, beginning with the closure of the Victoria Brewery, East Melbourne, in 1983. This marked the end of 129 years of continuous brewing from the time Thomas Aitken had started the brewery in 1854. The Lismore Brewery, NSW, was closed in 1986, and the Darwin and Ballarat breweries closed three years later. The Cairns Brewery followed in 1992.

There was much nostalgia and reminiscence of earlier times, and no doubt more than a touch of sorrow when brewing finally ceased at the Carlton Brewery in 1987. During that year a new keg-filling plant opened at the Abbotsford Brewery where all beer production and packaging was carried out.

Carlton & United Breweries Ltd and the Cascade Group Ltd of Tasmania formed a joint venture company in January 1993 to acquire the Cascade Brewery in Hobart. This joint venture, called the Cascade Brewery Co. Pty Ltd, was then a wholly-owned subsidiary of Carlton & United Breweries Ltd. However, at that time J. Boag & Son Ltd retained the distribution rights in Tasmania of Cascade-branded beer products. The distribution agreement was terminated on 3 October 1997.

Today Australia's best-known brewery operates as the Foster's Brewing Group Ltd, the change taking place on 13 November 1990.

By 1998 the company had established brewing operations in China, Vietnam and India.

Close to their production headquarters at Abbotsford, the company has built a modern Brewery Museum and Visitor Centre, where visitors now, and for generations to come, may appreciate the history of Australia's brewing industry.

Carlton & West End Breweries Ltd
See Artillery Brewery; Carlton Brewery Ltd; West End Breweries Ltd.

Carlton Brewery Ltd   1864–1907
Bouverie Street, Carlton

When John Bellman took over the North Melbourne Brewery in 1864, he changed the name to the Carlton

---

AT IT AGAIN

A number of roughs assembled on the night of the 8th inst. outside the Carlton Brewery, Melbourne and, by putting a syphon through an open window into a cask, they succeeded in filling a bucket with beer. However, they got drunk and five of them were arrested and punished.
Australian Brewers' Journal, February 1884

The Carlton Brewery, Edward Latham, proprietor, c. 1875.

Brewery. Five years later, on 9 August 1869, the Sheriff's Office auctioned the brewery, horses and equipment, 90 casks of ale and 150 empties. The brewery was purchased by Edward Latham and his partner, George Milne, and the business then began operating on a sound and progressive basis. Milne retired in 1871.

Edward Latham was born in England and came to Victoria in 1862. He crossed to Tasmania, married a year later, and returned to Melbourne with his young bride. When he bought the Carlton Brewery, he was fortunate in securing the services of Alfred Terry, an experienced brewer whose integrity and ability was widely known in the colony. Alfred Terry died in 1881, and Colonel John Ballenger then became the head brewer, continuing the Carlton Brewery tradition of brewing first-class ales and stout of consistently high quality.

After running a highly successful business for seventeen years, Edward Latham sold the brewery, which was reformed in January 1881 as the Melbourne Brewing & Malting Co. Ltd. Latham retained a large interest in the new company, and stayed on as managing director until his retirement in 1884. Not content in retirement, he reopened the Southern Brewery in Richmond in 1892. The 1890s, however, were disastrous times for Latham, and he lost his considerable fortune during the depression years through unsuccessful land speculation.

After its formation in 1881 the Melbourne Brewing & Malting Co. Ltd prospered. At the second annual meeting, held at Scott's Hotel, Collins Street, on 23 May 1883, a dividend of 10 per cent was declared for the previous six months, making a total of 20 per cent for the year. The company owned a wine-and-spirit store, and a bore 1000 feet deep was completed to supply the brewery with water for cooling.

In 1889 the Melbourne Brewing & Malting Co. Ltd amalgamated with the West End Breweries Ltd to form Carlton & West End Breweries Ltd. The West End Breweries were owned by Albert Terry, the brother of Alfred Terry, Carlton's first brewer.

The Carlton Brewery in Bouverie Street continued at full production, and the West End's Artillery Brewery in Williamstown continued for a few more years. The West End Brewery in Flinders Street was closed in 1889, and the wine-and-spirit department closed in 1893.

During September 1892 the head brewer, Colonel R. J. Ballenger, created a record when he brewed eight times in twenty-four hours, producing 700 hogsheads of beer. This was in anticipation of the proposed beer duty, and the task was completed the day before the passing of the Bill by the Legislative Assembly.

Carlton & West End Breweries Ltd was affected by the financial crisis of the 1890s, and went into liquidation in 1896. The subsequent reconstruction of the company resulted in the formation of the Carlton Brewery Ltd, which was registered on 5 March 1896. And so, for the second time, the Carlton Brewery was born, this

Edward Latham is considered by many historians to be the founder of what is now Carlton & United Breweries Ltd. For seventeen years he was identified with one of the most successful concerns in the colony.

Latham was said to be 'a man of unswerving integrity and an ornament to the brewing profession'. Among other deeds of benevolence, Latham founded and financed the Clergymen's Retreat at Queenscliff.

The depression years of the 1890s had a disastrous effect on Latham's fortunes, and in 1892 he found himself compelled to return to business. He started another brewery in Richmond, and ran this for ten years before retiring permanently from the brewing industry.

La Trobe Library, State Library of Victoria

The Carlton Brewery was reformed in 1881 as the Melbourne Brewing & Malting Co. Ltd, and continued to trade under that name until 1889.

Originally the Carlton Brewery, then the Melbourne Brewing & Malting Co. Ltd in 1881, the business changed again in 1889 to the Carlton & West End Breweries Ltd. This label was issued in 1889, one year after the Centennial Exhibition, held in the Exhibition Buildings, Melbourne.

Carlton Ale was one of Melbourne's most popular beers, and was widely distributed in bulk to country hotels. The hotels bottled the ale for resale, using their own labels.

Labels used by the Carlton Brewery Ltd, c. 1900. The company was registered on 5 March 1896, and was one of the six Melbourne breweries that amalgamated in 1907 to form Carlton & United Breweries Pty Ltd.

time as a 'Limited' company. Unfortunately, the formation of the new company did not increase trade or improve profitability. Reporting to the meeting of shareholders in February 1897, the chairman attributed the company's troubles to the beer duty, the economic crisis and the heavy burden of old debts. The beer duty of 2d per gallon on malt ales, and 3d per gallon on beer made with sugar, had been introduced in 1892, and was a contributing factor to the financial collapse of many breweries.

By 1897 the Carlton Brewery Ltd was 'on the wrong side of the ledger', despite the fact that sales were the second-highest of all the Melbourne breweries. The company also had the largest interest in freehold and leasehold properties, but rents were often unpaid.

By the turn of the century Carlton Ale was a much favoured beverage, and the brewery began to see steady recovery. In 1899 the Carlton Brewery secured the trade of the Burnley Brewery and the Burton Brewery, both of which had ceased brewing. Output had increased to such an extent that, during April 1901, each workman received an extra day's pay when the week's production exceeded 2000 hogsheads for the first time. During that year the company also purchased Edward Latham's Ye Olde Tymes Brewerie and closed it.

The Carlton Brewery grew to be one of the largest and most profitable in Melbourne, supplying more country town hotels than any other brewery. In 1907 the Carlton Brewery Ltd joined with five other Melbourne breweries to form Carlton & United Breweries Pty Ltd.

Cascade Brewery
See Clifton Hill Brewery.

Castlemaine Brewery Co., Melbourne, Ltd   1871–1907
Moray Street, South Melbourne

The Castlemaine Brewery, established by Edward Fitzgerald in 1858 in Castlemaine, was the foundation of the largest brewing empire in Australia during the latter half of the nineteenth century. Over time, substantial breweries were established at Sydney, Melbourne, Newcastle, Brisbane and Perth, and the name

View of the offices and main buildings of the Castlemaine Brewery, South Melbourne, c. 1890.
La Trobe Library, State Library of Victoria

Clifton Hill Brewery, c. 1890.

'Castlemaine' is perpetuated in the brand name of the famous beverage, Castlemaine XXXX Bitter Ale.

The popularity of Castlemaine beers influenced the rapid expansion of the company, and their second brewery was established at Sydney in 1869.

There was much opportunity for business in Melbourne, and Edward and Nicholas Fitzgerald, in partnership with James Perrins, opened a brewery in South Melbourne in 1871. They traded as Fitzgerald & Perrins, and after the first few weeks of operation weekly beer production was 30–40 hogsheads, increasing to 100 hogsheads by the end of the first year.

The Castlemaine Brewery Co., Melbourne, Ltd was floated on 1 March 1885, with the shares selling quickly at a premium of 20 per cent. James Perrins was the first managing director, and the company prospered. A 20 per cent dividend was declared in 1888, and during that year another brewery was built immediately opposite the existing brewery. By January 1890 weekly output had reached 1400 hogsheads of beer, plus 6000 dozen bottles of ale and porter.

In an obituary on the death of James Perrins, the *Australian Brewers' Journal* of April 1892 described the Castlemaine Brewery, Melbourne, as

the best paying joint-stock brewery in the world for we know of no other on the surface of the earth which pays 25% per annum and possesses a reserve fund nearly equal to its share capital.

The comments were premature, since by 1896 the company's shares had dropped from a high of 58s in 1891 to a mere 8s 6d, and no dividends were paid for the next three years.

By 1900 there had been some recovery, and a new Hercules icemaking machine was installed. A vat was specially made, the largest wooden receptacle in Australia at that time, having a capacity of 16,000 gallons.

More trouble surfaced in 1902, when microbes and unfriendly bacteria seriously affected the beer. The chairman reported that 'it was no one's fault but a great misfortune as demand for our beer has fallen away'. Sales had slumped badly and no dividends were paid until 1905, and then only a modest 4 per cent was declared.

In 1907 the Castlemaine Brewery amalgamated with five others to form Carlton & United Breweries Pty Ltd. Brewing was discontinued, and the premises were later used as ordnance stores.

City Brewery
See McCracken's City Brewery Co. Ltd.

Clayton's Brewery Pty Ltd 1914–20
William Street, Balaclava

Although the operating company was Clayton's Brewery Pty Ltd, the owners had also registered another company, Golden Ale Pty Ltd.

Clifton Hill Brewery 1881–1905
Hoddle Street, Clifton Hill

The owners of the brewery were James Daly and his son, Dominic. A few years later they were joined by Edward Daly, but after ten years the Daly family wanted to sell. In 1891 they advertised the Clifton Hill Brewery for sale, 'including land, goodwill, stock-in-trade and plant in full working order'. The buildings included a two-storey stone-and-brick brewery and a double-fronted villa of six rooms.

It was 1895 before the Daly family sold their brewery, the buyer being George Wilcox. He had been at the Union Brewery, Richmond, for the previous two years, and before that, he had been a partner in the Warrnambool Brewing & Malting Co. Wilcox changed the name of the Clifton Hill Brewery to the London Brewery, but the name was changed again to the Cascade Brewery by Thomas Stacey when he took over in 1899. In choosing the name, Stacey may have been inspired by the nearby Dights Falls on the Yarra River.

Thomas Stacey upgraded the brewery, installed new pumps, casks and a refrigeration unit, and supplied a private trade with small 3-gallon kegs of XXX Sparkling Ale. The brewery was described as 'a picturesque little place nestling in the midst of tall willow trees and with ivy trailing around the walls of the buildings'.

Charles Barrett ran the brewery for a brief period during 1902, then William Williams continued until 1905. During this time the business was known as the Crystal Malt Ale Brewery, and, in addition to beer, it made a non-intoxicating Temperance Ale.

Clifton Hill Brewery	1881–95
London Brewery	1895–99
Cascade Brewery	1899–1901
Crystal Malt Ale Brewery	1901–5

Cohn, Julius Isaac   1872–74
140 La Trobe Street, west

In 1872 Julius Cohn sold his shares in the Victoria Brewery, Bendigo to his brother Moritz, and moved to Melbourne, where he opened his own brewery in La Trobe Street opposite the Flagstaff Gardens.

Financial difficulties forced Julius to sell the brewery. The buyer was James Hennelly, owner of the Richmond Brewery, who closed the Richmond, shifted the equipment across to La Trobe Street, and then traded as the Metropolitan Brewing Co.

Julius Cohn returned to Bendigo, leased a building in Bridge Street, and started in business by bottling and selling beer that he obtained in bulk from his brother's Victoria Brewery.

Collingwood Brewery   1840–74
Junction of Smith, Bedford & Otter Streets, Collingwood

Melbourne's first suburban brewery was in Smith Street, Collingwood. It was started by Charles Vaughan and Edward Wild in 1840, just five years after the first settlers had arrived in Melbourne and in the year when Queen Victoria of England married her first cousin, Prince Albert. At that time the area where the brewery was located was called Newtown, but two years later it became Collingwood, named after Admiral Lord Collingwood.

When the Collingwood Brewery opened for business, the competition consisted of the Wharf Brewery, the Melbourne Brewery & Distillery and Condell's Brewery in Little Bourke Street, a total of four breweries to service Melbourne's population of just over 3000.

In their circular soliciting business for their No 3 Pale Ale Vaughan & Wild described it as

> a light, wholesome and eminently palatable beer, a pure and honest beer suitable for general consumption and for the hotel and family alike. We ask your patronage solely on the ground of the thorough excellence of the article we propose to supply.

Progressively, Vaughan & Wild extended their brewery and facilities as the population expanded, particularly during the goldrush era that began in the 1850s.

An editorial in the *Argus* of 4 December 1867 stated:

> One of the many charges made against colonial ale is that it will not keep. This charge however is baseless, as many others which have been disproved. We yesterday tasted some of Mr Wild's No 3 Pale Ale, eighteen months old, and have no hesitation in saying that there is very little imported ale which comes into the colony that can at all be compared with it. It is clear, bright sparkling and of admirable flavour ... it is difficult to see why we should import any from other countries.

In later years Charles Vaughan became mayor of Fitzroy. His partner, Edward Wild, 'a genial gentleman', possessed two ambitions: one in connection with freemasonry, and the other to perfect a system of book-keeping related to brewing.

By 1869 the firm of Crispe & Co. had taken over the Collingwood Brewery. Crispe closed his Cambridge Brewery, which was close by, and shifted everything over to the Collingwood Brewery. Five years later the Collingwood Brewery, now a substantial business, was sold to C. Forbes and B. Elam, and they changed the name to the Star Brewery.

See also Star Brewery.

Condell's Brewery   1839–45
Little Bourke Street, through to Lonsdale Street

One of Melbourne's early brewers was Henry Condell. He was born in Madeira in 1799, and at an early age was sent to Scotland to his grandfather, a distiller and brewer, to gain experience in the brewing industry. In 1822 he sailed from England to Van Diemen's Land, and started the Bevley Bank Brewery in Hobart Town in 1830.

In 1839 Condell sailed with his family to the infant settlement of Port Phillip (Melbourne). He purchased some land a short distance east of the north-east corner of Swanston Street and Little Bourke Street, and erected a brewery there. Although the population of Melbourne was only about 3000 at that time, there were already three breweries in the town.

THE FIRST PUBLICAN'S LICENCE IN VICTORIA

It is only 53 years ago [1837] since the first publican's license was granted in Melbourne, then the centre of what was then known as the 'Port Phillip District.' The 'district' had reached a population of about 2,500, and in September 1837, there was a general desire that a licensed public house should be established.

Mr. J. P. Fawkner started a tavern at the rear of the present Custom-house building but there was some difficulty about obtaining a licence. Eventually, Captain Lonsdale, P.M., the then 'Governor' of the province, declined to grant Fawkner's application, for one without reference to the Treasury in Sydney, namely, a 'certificate.' Shortly after, the Sydney Legislature passed an Act, empowering Captain Lonsdale to grant licenses at his own discretion.

In 1838, there were, according to the Evening Standard, eight licensed houses in Victoria, seven of which were in Melbourne. There is now no trace of Fawkner's first tavern, or of his second inn which was situated in Collins Street, near Market Street, in 1838.

Australian Brewers' Journal, November 1890

Courage Breweries Ltd 1968–82
Maffra Street, Coolaroo

The company, formed in Melbourne in 1964 as Kejam Pty Ltd, was named after former Melbourne stockbroker, Keith Jamieson. Initially, the capital was held by the British Tobacco Co. (Australia) Ltd and the British brewer, Courage, Barclay & Simonds Ltd.

The name was changed to Courage Breweries Ltd in November 1966. During that year, after extensive market surveys, a decision was made to establish a new brewery in Victoria. Construction commenced during August 1967 at Coolaroo, 20 km north of Melbourne. Courage floated publicly in October 1968 with 3.4 million ordinary shares offered at par. The issue was oversubscribed nearly fifteen times.

Following a ten-month advertising campaign, Courage Bitter was launched in Melbourne on 10 October 1968. The cockerel symbol, historically an international symbol of bravery and courage, was introduced three weeks later. Public response to Courage beer was overwhelming, and new products were released, including Courage Draft, Crest, Premium and Export Lager, and Tankard Bitter.

During 1971, by arrangement with Cooper's Brewery of Adelaide, Cooper's transported their stout by wine tanker to the Courage plant at Broadmeadows for bottling and marketing in Victoria. In reverse, Courage trucked its packaged beer to the Cooper plant in Adelaide in an attempt to benefit both breweries.

Courage Brewery introduced a litre beer bottle in February 1973, the first in Australia. The bottles were returnable, but few found their way back to the brewery since home brewers found the larger bottle an ideal size.

The rush to sample the new Courage beers began to slow down, and the company started to sustain substantial losses. More new beers were put on the market, but in spite of considerable advertising programmes Courage was unable to overcome the deeprooted preference of Victorian drinkers for their favourite Carlton brands.

Courage Breweries Ltd was taken over by the Sydney brewer, Tooth & Co. Ltd, in 1978, and several of Tooth's popular Sydney beers were brewed for the Victorian market. The endeavour was unsuccessful.

In 1982 the plant was advertised for sale world wide, and Carlton & United Breweries quickly purchased it to avoid facing another competitor. The brewery was closed in April 1982, and the premises were used as a warehouse.

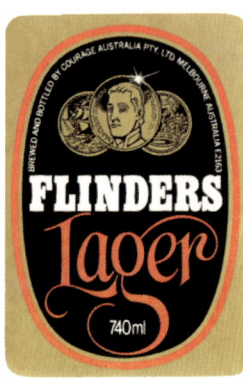

Henry Condell's first beer was called Condell's Entire, a blend of ale and stout, which was not the best on the market. It improved in time, and achieved such popularity that Condell became one of the richest men in Melbourne. When Melbourne became a town, he was the first mayor, and, through his well-established brewing business he commanded respect and held considerable influence in the community. His private house fronted Little Bourke Street and was at the rear of the brewery facing Lonsdale Street. He owned the Royal Hotel (which began as the Lamb Inn and was later renamed the Clarendon), and it was used as the venue for council meetings. At one time, there had been three William Streets in the Collingwood area. One was changed to Condell Street in recognition of his services as Melbourne's first mayor.

On 15 July 1845 fire almost destroyed the malthouse and brewery, causing damage amounting to £700. He had no insurance cover, and Condell decided to retire from brewing.

Coppin's Brewery c. 1855–65
Simpsons Road (now Victoria Street), East Collingwood

George Coppin's brewery was in Simpson's Road and the property ran down to the Yarra River. It happened to be near Graham's Brewery, which became the Shamrock some years later. By the mid-1860s George Coppin had closed his brewery. He was well known at the time as an actor and comedian, and later as a politician.

Cremorne Brewery 1852–83
Cremorne Street, Richmond

The founder of the Cremorne Brewery, James Crawford, had several partners until his death in 1862. James Wood was one of the partners who left after a brief period, probably because of his preoccupation with his Admiral Hotel in Richmond and the Prince George Hotel in Swanston Street, both of which he owned.

The longest period of operation by one ownership was from 1863 to 1877, when the four Mitchell brothers ran the business. During that period they traded as William Mitchell & Co. The name Mitchell's Brewery was often used. One observer declared that 'John Mitchell was one of the best fellows and most highly respected travellers who ever booked an order'.

The last proprietor was John C. Winn. The premises later became a malthouse operated by Smith & Winn.

James Crawford	1852–53
Crawford & Wood	1853
James Crawford	1853–60
Crawford & Cox	1860–62
William Mitchell & Co.	1863–77
John Winn	1877–83

Crown Brewery
(Collingwood) 1859–75
Clarke Street (near cnr Johnston Street), Collingwood

The location of the Crown Brewery was described as 'at the bottom of Johnston Street, Abbotsford, near the Yarra River'. There was certainly ample water close by, but the brewery had to remove the debris and thoroughly clean and filter the water before use. At that time the Yarra River was a convenient place to dump rubbish, and for the disposal of industrial and human waste.

Although there were many partnerships, lessees and proprietors during the life of the brewery, the founder, Charles Lister, had the most involvement. At one time Robert Montgomerie was employed as the brewer and 'made some of the best beer ever brewed in Victoria'. He left the Crown in 1873 to become head brewer at McCracken's City Brewery, and later started his own brewery at West Melbourne.

After Montgomerie's departure, business at the Crown Brewery quickly declined. When the brewery closed, the owner, Mathew McNamara, left the brewing industry, and became the first secretary of the Brewer's Club established in Melbourne in 1875.

Charles Lister	1859–66
George Elmes & Co.	1866–67
Charles Lister & Co.	1867–68
T. B. Alexander	1868–69
Maunsell & Co.	1870–71
Lister & McCarthy	1872–73
Mathew McNamara	1873–75

Crown Brewery (Fitzroy) 1871–79
61–69 Webb Street, Fitzroy

The premises had been a vinegar factory, and the partners, Henry Boyd and Francis Head, cleaned up the place and had it ready for brewing in 1871. When established, the Crown Brewery was described as a small, compact, well-managed concern, and the only reason the partners sold in 1874 was to shift to a larger factory.

After Boyd & Head shifted out of the Crown Brewery, Edmund Baron took over.

Baron was followed in 1878 by Paul Siddall, probably a partner, who apparently had an obsession with the name Crown. He had been involved in two breweries in Victoria; the Crown in Castlemaine; and, with his partner Baron, they built and operated the Crown & Junction Brewery in Seymour. Neither of these ventures was very successful, and their Crown Brewery in Fitzroy also failed after five years.

Crystal Malt Ale Brewery
See Clifton Hill Brewery.

Dandelion Ale Brewery (Brunswick)
See Temperance Brewery.

Dandelion Ale Brewery
(Richmond) 1886–c. 1892
Lennox Street, Richmond

The owner, Walter James, also owned the Tasmanian Brewery in West Melbourne, which he had been desperately trying to sell for some time. At Richmond he used the name Dandelion Ale Brewery, but sold after a few years to George Pearson, whose specialty was bottled stout.

Dandelion Ale & Weiss Brewery 1891–97
Clowes Street, South Yarra

The firm of F. W. Reichelt and H. W. Corbett produced a non-alcoholic dandelion beer, and also a Weiss beer. When the Victorian customs analysed the Weiss beer, they found that it contained more than the maximum percentage of alcohol allowed for non-alcoholic beers. Since there was a good demand for Weiss Lager Beer, Frederick Reichelt took out a brewer's licence, which allowed him to brew and sell alcoholic beverages.

When the Reichelt–Corbett partnership was dissolved in 1895, Reichelt kept the business going for two more years. Later, he started up again at Brunswick as the Temperance Brewery.

Dublin Brewery 1852–1902
Church Street, Richmond

William Dart was the owner of the brewery, although for the first few years a Mr Machin was a partner. The business traded as the Richmond Brewery at that time.

In 1864 a tailor by the name of Joseph Jeffries became the proprietor. He sold to Ernest and Louis Millcr in 1869, and they changed the name to the Dublin Brewery. There were more changes in ownership, and cordials and sauces were added to the product range.

Edward White began working at the Dublin Brewery in 1878 and became a partner with Samuel Stokes four years later. Stokes retired the following year, leaving

The Cremorne Brewery, Richmond commenced in 1852, with John Winn as the proprietor from 1877 until the brewery closed in 1883.

The Dublin Brewery, Richmond, was operated by Edward White from 1882 to 1902.

1021 HOTELS CLOSED

Ten Years' Work of Licences Reduction Board

Under the licensing law, as it at present stands, the Licences Reduction Board of Victoria will cease to operate at the close of the present year. As a result of ten years' operations, the Board, although excluded from dealing with hotels in a large proportion of the licensing districts of the State, has closed over a thousand hotels — a number between one-third and one-fourth of the total number of hotels in the State at the time it was appointed.

The question whether this system of closing hotels where, on enquiry it is held that they are not necessary, and paying compensation from a fund provided by the trade itself, is to be continued, will be a matter for early consideration by the Cabinet.

When the Board began its work in the latter half of 1907, there were 3448 hotels in the State, apart from 74 roadside licences. Since then, eight licences had been added, as a result of local option polls, and 39 had lapsed. Except for further surrenders, the total open next year would be 2396 or 1052 fewer than when the Board began its work.

Australian Brewers' Journal, August 1916

Edward White as sole proprietor. His brother, Elliott, joined the firm in 1886, and together they ran a highly successful business for the next fifteen years. During the 1890s they marketed Dingo Brand Bitter Ale, Lion Brand India Pale Ale and Nursing Stout. These were sold to hotels, grocers and other storekeepers.

Edward White became mayor of Richmond in 1898. Three years later his brother, Elliott, left the business; the brewery closed the following year.

The premises were acquired by R. Bell & Co. and used as a match factory. The firm eventually became Bryant & May. Although match production has ceased, the large and impressive buildings in Church Street, Richmond, still stand on the site of the former Dublin Brewery.

Richmond Brewery

Dart & Machin	1852–55
William Dart	1855–64
Joseph Jeffries	1864–69

Dublin Brewery

Ernest & Louis Miller	1869–71
Miller & Brownscombe	1871–72
Stokes & Brownscombe	1872–77
Sam Stokes	1877–82
Stokes & White	1882–83
Edward White	1883–86
Edward & Elliott White	1886–1901
Edward White	1901–2

Eagle Brewery   1876–78
Spencer Street

A gentleman named Thomas Hearty, who kept the Eagle Tavern in West Melbourne, became obsessed with the idea that brewing his own beer would lead to a fortune, and so he erected 'a snug little establishment' at the rear of his hotel in Spencer Street.

A small plant was installed, and Thomas Thurston (previously from the Yorkshire Brewery, Collingwood) was employed as the brewer. Old Tom happened to be the licensee of the Royal Sovereign Hotel in Smith Street, Fitzroy, at the time, and acquaintances commented that he was a better host than a brewer.

East End Brewery
See Star Brewery.

Elmes Brewery   1843–47
Flinders Lane

When Melbourne had developed beyond a small village, it became notorious as a town of many stenches. Pigs wallowed in backyard manure heaps, decaying rubbish overflowed into open gutters, and animal refuse poisoned the Yarra River. Most large houses, even in the middle of the town, had their own cowsheds, stockyards, piggeries and fowlhouses. These all added to the smells since there was no effective reticulation for waste products to flow into drains or sewers.

Typical of the problem was a complaint in 1843 by a neighbour that drainage from Henry Elmes's brewery was flowing underneath his house. The Town Surveyor gave Elmes a chance to construct a proper drain to the street before taking him to court.

The *Port Phillip Gazette* of December 1846 noted that the brewery had been let to a Mr Norman.

Some years later Elmes became the owner of the Corio Brewery in Geelong.

Excelsior Brewery   1876–83
Clarke Street, Collingwood/236 Church Street, Richmond

The proprietor, Timothy Lane, had acquired the Collingwood premises of the closed Crown Brewery, and he set about specialising in brewing porter, using the name Excelsior Brewery. Later, the brewery was shifted to Church Street, Richmond.

In 1882 George H. Bennett (later the MLA for Richmond) joined the firm, which continued as Lane & Bennett — Bennett had previously been a bottler of ale and porter. However, after a year, brewing was discontinued, but the substantial aerated-water and cordial manufacturing section of the business continued under the name of G. H. Bennett for many years.

Federal Dandelion Ale Brewery   1885–90
424 Bridge Road, Richmond/8 Duke Street, Abbotsford

Henry Rowland started in business in Richmond in 1885, and after shifting to Duke Street, Abbotsford, in

1888, he traded under the name Federal Dandelion Ale Brewery.

The owners of the brewery, H. Rowland & Son, offered the brewery for sale at auction as a going concern, but bidding fell short of the reserve price, and the brewery closed.

Federation Brewery Co. 1864–1907
Lincoln Street, Richmond/140 (later 523) La Trobe Street

Thirty-four years were to pass before this business became the Federation Brewery Co., and during that time there were numerous changes in name and location and ownership.

Originally started by Paul Siddall in 1864 in Lincoln Street, Richmond, it was called the Lincoln Brewery at that time. Five years later it was owned by James Massey, followed by J. G. Farmer & Sons, and then James Hennelly from 1871, who used the name Richmond Brewery. After two years he moved his business to La Trobe Street in Melbourne, using the more appropriate name of the Metropolitan Brewery Co.

In 1882 the Metropolitan Brewery Co. was sold to John McGee, and it was during his ownership that a tragic death occurred. In November 1895 the brewer, Henry Lindsay, was drowned in a vat of beer, apparently falling in as he leaned over to examine the beer. There was nobody about at the time, and the sides of the vat were too high for Lindsay to escape. The beer, obviously polluted, was poured down the drain under Custom's supervision, and the vat was destroyed.

Lindsay had been the founder of many Lindsay Breweries, which he had established in a number of New South Wales country towns; he had also started the Trent Brewery in Lancefield.

The business became a 'Limited' company in 1893, and five years later John McGee decided to change the name to the Federation Brewery Co. A. W. Hannay (formerly of the ANA Brewery in South Melbourne) was the brewer, and Herbert Coomber (formerly of the Fremantle Brewing & Ice Co. in Western Australia) was the manager.

John McGee became insolvent in the summer of 1904, and the equipment was put up for auction. Later that year the brewery was re-opened by McGee's son, Francis, and in partnership with A. W. Hannay, he formed a new company. Early in 1907 the company was wound up.

Flagstaff Brewery 1872–79
131 La Trobe Street

The owners of the brewery were Edward White (1872–74) and Thomas D'Arcy Burke (1874–79).

Foster Brewing Co. Pty Ltd 1888–1907
15 Rokeby Street, Collingwood

There have been two Foster brewing companies in Australia: the first was started by Thomas Foster at Glenorchy, Hobart, in 1832, and lasted for only a few years; the other, which commenced over fifty years later in 1888 in the inner Melbourne suburb of Collingwood, was destined to have its name perpetuated by that world-famous beverage, Foster's Lager.

William M. Foster and his brother, Ralph R. Foster, built their ultra-modern lager-beer brewery in Rokeby Street, Collingwood, a few doors north of Victoria Parade where the Victoria Brewery was located. The brothers had arrived from New York in 1887, bringing with them a Mr Sieber, a German-American who had studied brewing in Cologne, Germany. Most of the equipment, which was designed specially for the production of lager beer, and also the icemaking plant, had been imported from the USA.

All ale and porter produced in the Australian colonies had been brewed by the top-fermentation process, resulting in brews that were relatively strong, slightly thick and malty, and consumed at room temperature. This was the English tradition, a brew that the Australian population had been accustomed to, and preferred. Today, virtually all beer produced in Australia is of the lager type, brewed by the bottom-fermentation process — a lighter type of beer, clearer and thinner, served chilled at a temperature of around 4°C.

The change to lager-beer production in Australia was gradual, and began in the 1880s. Although the Foster Brewery is generally credited with being the first brewery in Australia to make lager beer, there were several others that had started earlier, the most notable being that of the Cohn brothers, who were brewing Excelsior brand lager beer at their Victoria Brewery in Bendigo in 1882.

Lincoln Street, Richmond:

Lincoln Brewery
Paul Siddall	1864–69
James Massey	1869–70
J. G. Farmer & Sons	1870–71

Richmond Brewery
James Hennelly 1871–73

140 La Trobe Street, Melbourne:

Metropolitan Brewery Co.
James Hennelly	1873–82
(same location, but the street number had changed to 523 La Trobe Street)	
John McGee	1882–1893

Metropolitan Brewery Co. Ltd
John McGee 1893–98

Federation Brewery Co.
John McGee	1898–1904
F. McGee & A. Hannay	1904–7

The Metropolitan Brewery Co. commenced in 1873 and became a Limited company in 1893. Five years later the name was changed to the Federation Brewery Co.

The Foster Brewery, Collingwood, 1888.

Right: *During 1903 the word 'Wattle' was registered and used by the Foster Brewery for their newly-released Wattle Ale.*

The Foster brothers started brewing in November 1888, and the public received their first taste of Foster's Lager on 1 February 1889. At the start, only bottled beer was available; it was supplied in heavy champagne-type bottles with the corks wired in.

The brothers were undercapitalised, and when they sold their interests to a syndicate on 13 November 1889 the business became a public company, and the Foster brothers no longer held any interest in the brewery.

In 1891 Ralph Foster was involved in a proposal to form the American & German Lager Beer Brewing Co. Ltd, by taking over the Carrington Brewery in Marrickville, Sydney. Foster was to provide the technical and brewing expertise, but the proposal did not proceed.

By the early 1890s the Foster Brewing Co. Ltd was in difficulty. Output was small, the debt large, and there were many staff changes. However, the company was fortunate in having the services of the experienced chemist, August de Bavay, and the quality and production output saw a remarkable improvement. The company's lager beer became so popular by the mid-1890s that the monopoly it exerted on the bottled-beer market in Melbourne was the subject of questions in the colonial parliament.

From the outset, every hotel taking the new lager received a free supply of ice to keep the beer cool. When draught lager was put on the market, chilled casks were delivered during the summer months. In 1895 small 5-gallon kegs of lager beer were delivered to leading cafes and hotels, an innovation new to the trade. Production of stout had commenced in October 1892, and a Light Running Ale was marketed in 1899 under the name of Foster XXX Ale. Other brands were Empire Pale Ale and India Pale Ale. All were lager beers.

The letter 'F' has continued in use as a symbol for Foster's Lager since the time it was introduced in 1889.

During 1894 serious consideration was given to starting a lager beer brewery in Sydney, but the proposal was ultimately abandoned. Instead, a branch store was opened at 11 Castlereagh Street, Sydney, under the management of T. Oxley, and operated from 1896 to 1898. On 10 February 1897 the company structure was changed to that of the Foster Brewing Co. Pty Ltd.

Foster's lager beers sold well in other states, and in 1901 thirty cases of Topaz Lager were shipped to South Africa. At that time Foster's appeared to be the only Victorian brewery making any attempt to develop export markets.

In 1907 the Foster Brewing Co. Pty Ltd amalgamated with five other Melbourne breweries to form Carlton & United Breweries Pty Ltd. The Foster brewery was kept as a standby plant until 13 December 1910, when the property was auctioned and subdivided into four lots. Foster's lager continued to be brewed at the Victoria Brewery, and later at CUB's plant at Abbotsford.

The last section of wall of the old brewery was demolished in 1997, but at least one interested historian was able to salvage a few of the original Northcote bricks as souvenirs from the brewery that made the first Foster's Lager.

Foster's Brewing Group Ltd
See Carlton & United Breweries Ltd.

Gambrinus Lager Beer Brewery Co. Ltd 1885–87
Duke Street, Collingwood

When Leopold Renne, Rudolph Friederich and Joseph Warburton started the Gambrinus Brewery, they traded as Renne, Friederich & Co., and production was devoted solely to the brewing of lager beer. All the employees were German, and the brewer, Leopold Renne, brewed on the true German system, using only malt and hops.

The Gambrinus Lager Beer Brewing Co. Ltd was registered on 25 September 1885, but shortly afterwards the company was wound up.

William Curry purchased the brewery in 1886, but it closed the following year.

Although the Gambrinus Brewery produced lager beer well before the more famous Foster's Brewery, other Australian breweries were brewing lager earlier still. The Cohn brothers of the Victoria Brewery in Bendigo had been supplying the public with their Excelsior brand lager beer since 1882, and Sam Marks of the Anglo-Australian Brewery in Sydney was making lager beer in 1883.

The German brewer, Leopold Renne, had chosen an appropriate name for his ill-fated brewery. Johann Gambrinus was born in the year 1251, the son of Henry III of Germany. Brewers' societies then in existence chose him as their 'guardian angel', as he gave them full freedom throughout the land and fostered the industry in many ways. His picture, or statue, may be seen at some European breweries, and he is recognised as the 'God of Lager.'

Graham's Brewery
See Shamrock Brewing & Malting Co. Ltd.

Henden's Brewery 1850–61
Richmond/Heidelberg

Henry Henden started brewing at Richmond in 1850. Eight years later he was trading as Henden & Edney, and had apparently shifted his business to the outer Melbourne suburb of Heidelberg. During the final year, the partners were Henden & Green.

Hennelly's Brewery
See Federation Brewery Co.

Hobson's Bay Brewery 1872–82
8 Osborne Street, Williamstown

German tinsmith, Frederick Taegtow, had been a long-time resident of Williamstown when he started his modest brewery in 1872. Bottles were a scarce commodity at the time, and Taegtow frequently advertised for empty bottles for his Hobson's Bay Brewery.

After the death of his wife, he sold the brewery to Frederick Jones, and returned to Germany. A few months later the brewery was destroyed by fire.

Horonda Brewery Ltd c. 1900–c. 1920
130 Miller Street, North Fitzroy

The Horonda Brewery appears to have been part of the Moonee Valley Aerated Water & Cordial Co., and it is doubtful if any alcoholic beverages were produced.

The Moonee Valley's factory was described as a little community, with everything, as far as possible, being done on the premises. There were blacksmiths, painters, coachbuilders and harnessmakers. About sixty horses were stabled, and the company grew its own horse feed, with the hay converted to chaff on the premises. A glassworks produced all the bottles required for their cordials and aerated waters. The company was the sole manufacturer of the soft drink Horonda, brewed from horehound and other herbs.

Imperial Inn & Brewery c. 1841
Collins Street

During the early years of the settlement of Melbourne, licences were not required for the brewing of beer, and it was not uncommon for inns and taverns to brew small quantities of ale for sale to their customers. Brewing tended to be intermittent, the quality frequently questionable, and the small output only a secondary activity.

As soon as Henry Baker took over the Imperial Inn in Collins Street in 1841, he began making his own beer. He advertised meals for a shilling, and added,

> N.B. 50% increase on the charges for those individuals who practise teetotalism. Henry Baker, having completed his brewing arrangements, is prepared to offer an article that is unparalleled in Melbourne. Customers bringing their own jugs are supplied with wholesome Table Ale at four pence a quart.

Another hotel brewer was Tom Halfpenny, who moved his hotel licence to the corner of Elizabeth Street and Little Collins Street in 1841, and began making his own beer. Hotel brewing was a widespread practice throughout all the Australian colonies, and these activities were not always recorded or reported. During the earlier years of the Australian colonies considerably more brewing would have taken place than has been included in this book.

Johnston Street Brewery 1858–70
33 Johnston Street, East Collingwood

Gideon & Wheeler	1858–59
Gideon & McKaige	1859–61
Jonathon Rudkin	1861–63
J. McLaughlin	1864–65, vacant
Smith & Horwood	1870
Henry Austin	1870

Kent Brewery
See Kew Brewery.

Kent Brewery Co. 1870–71
54 Chancery Lane, Melbourne

The owner of the Kent Brewery Co., James Churchman, decided to end his career as a brewer in less than two years, not an uncommon decision for many brewers of the day. It was difficult to make good beer consistently week after week; there was always too much competition, publicans were slow payers, it was a seven-day-a-week job with long hours of strenuous work, and in social circles the occupation of a brewer was one held in very low esteem.

Kew Brewery 1873–80
Bulleen Road, Kew, near the Clifton Hotel

Alfred Fuller started brewing as the Kent Brewery, and after four years decided on the name Kew Brewery, the name of the suburb where the brewery was located.

Kooyong Brewery 1902
St John's Avenue, Camberwell

Licensed Victuallers Brewery Co. Ltd 1877–83
Smith Street, Collingwood

Lincoln Brewery
See Federation Brewery Co.

Lincolnshire Brewery 1868–89
180 Chapel Street, Prahran

Although Thomas Hotchin started brewing in 1868, eight years went by before he decided on the name Lincolnshire Brewery. It is possible that Hotchin had taken over Orme's Brewery.

London Brewery (A'Beckett Street, Melbourne)
See Phoenix Brewery.

London Brewery (Clifton Hill)
See Clifton Hill Brewery.

Lonsdale Street Brewery 1849–52
Lonsdale Street

T. G. W. J. Robinson arrived in Melbourne in 1840, and began working at the Melbourne Brewery owned by John Mills. When Mills died, Robinson took over the management of the brewery, and later he married Mills's widow. According to Thomas Strode who founded the *Port Phillip Gazette* on 27 October 1838, 'it was not until the arrival of Robinson that the Melbourneites [*sic*] had the opportunity of enjoying a fair imitation of the good old English glass of ale'.

Thomas Robinson advertised in the Melbourne *Argus* of 23 November 1849 with the simple message: 'Thomas Robinson, formerly of the Melbourne Brewery, has taken over Henry Condell's Brewery'. Four years earlier a fire had all but destroyed Condell's Brewery. After rebuilding and fitting out with new equipment, Robinson started again as the Lonsdale Street Brewery, but he closed after four years and became a consultant to the brewing industry.

It was said that Tom Robinson led a flamboyant life, and wore loads of jewellery that included an Albert chain made entirely of sovereigns. As a 'beer doctor', he would move from brewery to brewery, giving advice when things went wrong. For most of the breweries of the time, things were always going wrong and there was a fortune to be made for anyone who had simple effective solutions. Robinson was a likeable fellow, but his ability to fix the things that went wrong was limited. He had a vivid imagination, and his services took the form of trial and error — any cure or improvement was sheer luck!

McCracken's City Brewery Co. Ltd 1851–1907
110 Little Collins Street, west

It was a remarkable achievement that what began as a three-man brewery ultimately became one of the largest and best known in Melbourne. Brothers Robert and Peter McCracken arrived in Melbourne from Scotland in 1841, and ten years later they formed a partnership with their brother-in-law, James Robertson. With Melbourne only sixteen years old, the partners built a brewery at the west end of Little Collins Street, and in their small way they laid the foundation of a brewing business that was destined to flourish as one of the most prominent in Melbourne.

At first the partners traded as McCracken & Robertson. With a staff of only two, very soon the out-

McCracken's City Brewery was located almost opposite the Rialto building in Collins Street, Melbourne. It was second only to the Carlton Brewery at the turn of the century, and formed an impressive group of buildings that reflected the architectural splendour of the 1880s. Note the catwalk on top of the roof.
La Trobe Library, State Library of Victoria

put reached 4 hogsheads of ale per day. When Robertson left in 1861, he sold his shares to the McCrackens, and the firm then traded as R. McCracken & Co., City Brewery.

Business expanded rapidly following the appointment of Robert Montgomerie as head brewer, and during his eleven years with the company beer production quadrupled. At his farewell in 1884 he was presented with a valuable gold watch and chain in recognition of his excellent service. Ironically, he started up in opposition, building his own substantial brewery only a few blocks away in Jeffcott Street, West Melbourne.

At the City Brewery there was more family involvement in 1884, with two of the sons becoming partners; Collier McCracken, son of Peter, and Alexander McCracken, son of Robert. Robert, however, continued to run the business until his death in 1885, and then his son Alexander took over.

Benjamin Fink, a well-known land speculator, floated McCracken's as a public company in April 1888. He subsequently became bankrupt, owing Peter McCracken £113,000. The 1880s had been a period of frantic growth and speculation, and at the time of flotation £2 million was raised, with a guaranteed dividend of 8 per cent for at least three years. Then the great depression of the 1890s began to take its toll. There was no dividend in 1892, and a year later £1 shares were worth 1s 6d. Somehow, the business managed to survive, and by the end of the century it held the largest trade of all the Melbourne breweries.

McCracken's City Brewery was one of the six Melbourne breweries that amalgamated in 1907 to form Carlton & United Breweries Pty Ltd. The final brews were taken in April 1908, and by June the magnificent City Brewery had closed. The front section of the brewery, facing Collins Street, was rebuilt by Alex Cowan & Sons, wholesale stationers and paper merchants, and the rear section was converted into offices and factories that were occupied by printing and hardware firms.

CUB continued to use the McCracken name on products such as AK Light, McCracken's Australian Bitter Ale, Invalid Stout and Khaki brand Extra Stout, which were still produced as late as the 1940s.

McCracken's Lane, which runs south from Little Collins Street between King and William Streets, is lasting evidence of where one of Melbourne's grand breweries once stood.

Marine Stockade Brewery
See Artillery Brewery.

Melbourne Brewery & Distillery   1837–52
71 Flinders Street, east

According to 'Garryowen' in *The Chronicles of Early Melbourne, 1835–52* (1894),

> When Mr La Trobe [later Governor of Victoria] arrived as superintendent in 1839, there were in Melbourne two fellmongeries, one tan yard, some 70 shops, 500 houses and three breweries. The population was about 3,000 and police protection consisted of four constables.

One of the breweries referred to was the Melbourne Brewery & Distillery owned by John Mills, a former convict, who on 6 March 1837 had been sentenced to fifty lashes for drunkenness; he had been a bricklayer, hotelkeeper and a former brewer in Van Diemen's Land. Mills purchased a half-acre block of land in Flinders Street, between Elizabeth and Queen Streets, for £35 at the first government land sale held in June 1837. He built a complex of brick and stone buildings that included a brewery and a house, both of which were two storey. When his daughter was born on 10 January 1838, his occupation was listed as brewer.

In December 1837 Mills was in trouble for trading on Sundays, and was fortunate in receiving only a warning. According to the *Historical Records of Victoria*, Foundation Series, volume 4, 'In March or April 1838, John Mills applied for permission to begin distilling spirits at his brewery premises in Flinders Street'. Mills had actually started brewing about August 1837, which would credit him with being Victoria's first brewer. He was lucky to get his distiller's licence, since he was not in Captain Lonsdale's good books. In November 1839 he was found guilty of selling inferior barley to John Cumming of the Geelong Brewery, and was fined £50.

John Mills turned out 'a palatable ale', which he sold for 2s a gallon and £5 a hogshead. As reported in the *Port Phillip Gazette*, 'the beer is a fair imitation of English ale and has diminished the demand for "Sheoak Tops" put out by his rival John Moss'. John Moss had a small brewery in Flinders Lane about two blocks west from the Melbourne Brewery, and his Sheoak Tops, as his beer was called, was considered a very heady brew.

The site of the Melbourne Brewery was close to the Yarra River, and in January 1840 Mills requested permission to lay a conduit, six feet deep, across Flinders Street (then a dirt track) down to the river, to bring up water direct from the river to his brewery. The request was declined. According to the minutes of early

---

BOTTLE COLLECTORS

There are no fewer than 4,000 licensed bottle collectors in Melbourne and suburbs. There are considerably more than 900,000 dozen of beer bottles gathered in Melbourne in twelve months. As probably more than 100,000 dozen are broken, cast away, or used privately, it may be presumed that at least 1,000,000 dozen of bottles are emptied of 'colonial' beer in one year in this city and its suburbs.

The gatherers also bring to the depots, lager beer, English beer, stout, spirit, sauce, pickle, and other bottles, but the reason for the trade is the thirst for bottled beer.

Australian Brewers' Journal, February 1910

Melbourne Council Health Department meetings, the Melbourne Brewery was made to close on 12 January 1843 for health reasons. It was thought that the brewery's beer had caused the death of sixteen people because it was brewed from polluted water from the Yarra River.

John Mills had died in 1841, and his foreman, Tom Robinson, continued to run the brewery; he subsequently married Mills's widow. After eight years he left to start his own brewery in Lonsdale Street.

Melbourne Brewery & Distillery Co. Ltd
See Victoria Brewery Pty Ltd.

Melbourne Brewery Co.
See Burton Brewery Co. Ltd.

Melbourne Brewing & Malting Co.
See Carlton Brewery Ltd.

Melbourne Co-operative Brewery Co. Ltd   1904–25
Bent Street, Abbotsford

In 1903 a meeting of free hotelkeepers (not brewery tied or owned) decided to start a new co-operative brewery, and in February 1904 the Melbourne Co-operative Brewery Co. Ltd came into existence. The brewery was situated close to the bank of the Yarra River in Abbotsford, and was frequently called the Abbotsford Brewery.

The new brewery was an instant success, and as much as 110 per cent dividend was paid to shareholders. Hotelkeepers who purchased the company's beer received a 2½ per cent discount, and the impact on other brewers was considerable. There was already too much competition, with at least sixty breweries operating in Victoria, including eighteen in Melbourne, and a hotel for every 350 persons in the state.

The first brewer for the new company was James Breheny; followed by Thomas Breheny, who left in 1916 to become head brewer at the Tooth's brewery in Sydney. The third brewer was Peter Breheny, brother of James and Thomas.

In 1920 the Melbourne Co-operative Brewery was restructured, and shareholders received a £1 share for every 5s share held (4 to 1). The business kept expanding, and prospered, paying high dividends. The company was more than just a minor nuisance to Carlton & United Breweries, and after much negotiation a new company was formed in 1925 with the Melbourne Co-op. amalgamating with CUB. In the new company structure of Carlton & United Breweries Ltd the allocation of 650,000 CUB shares to the Melbourne Co-operative Brewery shareholders made that group of shareholders the largest stockholders in the business at that time.

By 1987 the Abbotsford Brewery was the only CUB beer-production centre in Melbourne. Many of the original Melbourne Co-operative Brewery brand names such as Abbots Lager and Melbourne Bitter have continued in production to this day.

An early picture of the Melbourne Co-operative Brewery Co. Ltd. It commenced in 1904 and was often referred to as the Abbotsford Brewery. In 1925 it amalgamated with Carlton & United Breweries Ltd. Today the CUB brewery at Abbotsford is the largest in Victoria.

Metropolitan Brewery Co. Ltd
See Federation Brewery Co.

Miller Lager Beer Brewing Co.
See Royal Artillery Brewery.

Mitchell's Brewery
See Cremorne Brewery.

Montgomerie's Brewery   1884–1910
41 Jeffcott Street, West Melbourne

Robert Montgomerie had gained his brewing and malting experience in Tasmania. After arriving in Melbourne, he became head brewer at McCracken's City Brewery, achieving considerable success with that company for eleven years, and in 1884 he branched out on his own. He designed and built his own brewery in six months: it was a three-storey building with lofty towers, fitted out with the best equipment available, and stood at the corner of King and Jeffcott Streets, West Melbourne. Although the business was floated as the New Brewery Ltd in 1888, it was still called Montgomerie's Brewery.

The first partners were R. Montgomerie, J. W. Moreland and W. Henderson; Moreland withdrew in 1886.

Montgomerie, the senior partner, was, by the standards of the time, an excellent brewer, and the high quality of his beer was widely acclaimed. He received an award at the Colonial and Indian Exhibition, London, in 1886 for his Ordinary Ale. He also made Pale Ale, Lager Beer, Malt Ale, Golden Ale and Stout. He was the first brewer in Australia to introduce the eight-hour system of shift work, and he had men working 'around the clock' on three shifts. Many other breweries adopted the practice.

The *Australian Brewers' Journal* reported:

> Montgomerie's Brewery. The official opening of the new Princes Bridge (the main bridge crossing the Yarra River) took place on September 7, 1886 … After the ceremony, food was offered to the politicians and notables and consisted of the cold meat left over from the Mayor's Ball held the night before in the Melbourne Town Hall. The band was kindly lent for the occasion by R. K. Montgomerie of the New Brewery, West Melbourne.

The business was sold to David Munro in 1888, but sales and profit declined during the 1890s, severely affecting the value of the shares. As an indication of the impact of the depression years, at an auction sale in 1894 of an insolvent estate, 300 shares in Montgomerie's Brewery sold for 10s the lot.

David Munro and the New Brewery went into liquidation in 1899. The following year, the brewery, plus twelve hotels, were purchased by a syndicate for £26,500. Two years later the properties were valued at £158,000. Although the company continued in business, brewing had ceased, and beer was obtained from the Shamrock Brewery.

By 1904 the New Brewery was again in liquidation, and the brewery finally closed in 1910. Later, the premises were used as a cordial factory and oil store.

Moss's Brewery   1838–39
Cnr Flinders Lane & William Street

At the first land sale held in Melbourne in 1837, John Moss purchased an allotment of land that ran from Flinders Street to Flinders Lane near King Street; the price was £35.

In 1838, one year after Melbourne received its official name and only three years after the founding of the colony, John Moss set up his tiny brewery at the back of his tavern, which he had called the Ship Inn. The location was the south-west corner of Flinders Lane and William Street, and not on the land he had purchased. The population of Melbourne in March 1838 was about 600.

John Moss began brewing beer that became known as Sheaoks Tops, so named after the sheoak trees that grew nearby on the crest of Batman's Hill. This was sold for 2s a gallon or £5 a hogshead.

Moss was a free settler, and he was frequently in trouble with the authorities. On 19 September 1837 he was fined £5 for allowing gambling to take place at his Ship Inn, and the following month he was fined £4 for trading on a Sunday. A year later, on 29 October 1838, he was fined 5s for drunkenness (free men were usually fined for this offence, but for convicts the sentence was generally twenty-five or fifty lashes).

By 1840 John Moss had stopped brewing, and was listed only as a publican.

Murcutt's Brewery
See Shamrock Brewing & Malting Co.

Murphy's Brewery
See Wharf Brewery.

New Brewery Ltd
See Montgomerie's Brewery.

North Carlton Brewery   c. 1880
Drummond Street, North Carlton

J. W. Beard & Co.

North Melbourne Brewery   1858–65
Bouverie Street, Carlton

The brewery was the forerunner of Carlton & United Breweries Ltd. It was started in August 1858 by Theodore Rosenberg, who sold to the partnership of Savage & Clifford the following year. By 1860 the brewery had closed, and apparently remained vacant for a few years.

The date when the brewery reopened is uncertain, but, at least by November 1864, it was known as the Phoenix Brewery. A bill of sale of the Phoenix Brewery, Bouverie Street, Carlton, dated 26 November 1864, shows the purchaser to be a Mr James, Earl of Zetland.

The goods were listed as:

Oct 19	to 1 Hogshead Ale	4–0–0	
Nov 8	2 Do.	8–0–0	
			12–0–0
Discount	1–4–0		
5 empty h/hs	2–5–0	3–9–0	
			8–11–0

The docket was signed, on behalf of the Phoenix Brewery, by what appears to be Thos Wm Dougall.

The brewery was taken over in 1865 by John Bellman who changed the name to the Carlton Brewery. The name, North Melbourne Brewery, was most likely decided upon by a journalist or reporter of the time.

See also Carlton Brewery.

Orme's Brewery   1861–68
Chapel Street, Prahran

The partnership of Orme & Ryall ran the brewery for a year, and then Frederick Orme continued on his own.

Parker Brothers Brewery   1861–73
312 Brunswick Street, Fitzroy

The Parker Brothers Brewery was at the corner of Cecil Street and Brunswick Street, Fitzroy. Although there were many breweries operating within a short distance, the Parker boys did quite well for twelve years, even though the brewery had been offered to let in 1862.

Phoenix Brewery
See North Melbourne Brewery.

Phoenix Brewery Co.   1871–76
A'Beckett Street, west

When Allen & McKay began brewing in 1871, they traded as McKay & Co., using the name Phoenix Brewery Co. Allen had worked at breweries in Castlemaine, whereas McKay, a coppersmith, had no brewing experience at all but, 'imagined there was money to be made in beer'.

In 1874 the brewery was owned by Wolf Isaacs, well known for his geniality and popularity with customers.

CLOSING OF MELBOURNE HOTELS

A proclamation ordering all hotel and registered club bars within a radius of 15 miles of the Elizabeth Street Post-office to close, in consequence of the influenza epidemic, was issued by the Minister for Health, Mr. Bowser, on 12th February [1919] and as a result, no hotel, club or wine bar was permitted to open on the following morning.

Australian Brewers' Journal, February 1919

He changed the name to the London Brewery but closed up after two years.

Queen's Brewery   1887–88
Brooke Street, Collingwood

Richmond Brewery (Church Street)
See Dublin Brewery; Richmond N. S. Brewing Co. Pty Ltd.

Richmond Brewery (Lincoln Street)
See Federation Brewery Co.

Richmond N.S. Brewing Co. Pty Ltd   1928–62
654 Church Street, Richmond

The Kentdale Hop Estate was one of the finest properties in Tasmania. It was located 50 km from Hobart, and the owners, Coulson, Hay & Co., harvested about 30 hectares of finest-quality hops. During 1927 there was a business disagreement with their largest customer, a Melbourne brewery, which cancelled their business and purchased their substantial requirements of hops elsewhere. This was a disastrous loss of business. Resentful of the attitude of the executive authority of big business, Peter Grant Hay announced his intention of starting his own brewery. It was no idle threat. Hay managed to offload his surplus stock of hops to breweries in other states, and with much courage and purpose went about the task of starting a brewery.

To embark on such a programme would surely have been courting disaster, as he had to compete with the powerful Carlton & United Breweries, with its vast resources, popular beers, price-fixing policy and huge chain of tied hotels. Many said that Grant Hay was foolhardy, that he didn't recognise the risks, and they predicted his financial ruin. Hay brushed aside the warnings and went ahead regardless. He contacted Dr Leopold Nathan in Europe, and purchased the right to use, in Victoria, Nathan's world-famous brewing system. Then followed the building and equipping of the Richmond Brewery, a strenuous and nerve-wracking effort that took almost two years, extending from 1927 to 1928.

Land had been acquired in East Richmond, having a frontage to Church Street and adjacent to the Yarra River. Hay was ready to begin construction when the problems started. Neighbourhood residents objected to the development — they didn't want a smelly brewery nearby. That difficulty took time to settle, and at length a contract was let for the excavation of foundations and cellars. After two weeks the contractor complained that the rock was entirely honeycomb, and refused to continue without a price increase. He was promptly released from his contract, and Hay arranged and supervised the excavation himself. More problems followed when Hay started blasting. The properties of surrounding residents were bombarded with rock shrapnel, and the local council threatened to close the works.

The Richmond Brewery's first label showed the Church Street Bridge, which crossed the Yarra River a short distance from the brewery.

With dogged determination and a lot of capital, Grant Hay finally began brewing Richmond Lager and Bitter Beer in 1928. In its infancy, beer output was a meagre 88 dozen bottles per week. But the quality of the beer, and the fact that it had been produced free of any combine, commended the beverage to public taste. Within three years output of beer had grown to 1000 hogsheads per week, and Richmond beer couldn't be produced fast enough.

The Melbourne *Sporting Globe* of 4 March 1931, had favourable comments:

> Wherever it goes, Richmond beer receives an enthusiastic welcome and in no instance has the demand been known to abate. Absolute purity, wholesomeness and delicious flavour commend the beverage to a discerning public who 'know a good thing when they taste it'.

The brewery's hops were still grown in Tasmania, with a yield of 875 bales in 1930. Kentish hops, with the characteristic Kent (England) flavour, were in constant demand by the breweries.

The Richmond Brewery was a remarkable success. By 1930 shipments of Richmond Lager were eagerly consumed in Sydney and Brisbane. Exports to India followed, with the bottle labels of Richmond Pilsner, Lager Bitter and Stout showing an elephant's head. Most of the product labels for the domestic market were illustrated with a tiger's head.

The company established sales offices at 86 King Street, Perth (Shaws Ltd, 1931–34); 5 Cliff Street, Fremantle (1935–60); 26 Hunter Street, Sydney (1933–35); and at Sussex Street, Sydney (1935–60).

At the time of Grant Hay's death in 1961 the Richmond Brewery held about 6 per cent of the Victorian market, and sales were on the increase.

After negotiation with the heirs to his estate, Carlton & United Breweries purchased the brewery, and closed it on 13 April 1962. Saddened ex-brewery workers received half an hour's free beer at the brewery-owned Prince Alfred Hotel, opposite.

The brewery has since been demolished, but for many long years there were legions of drinkers who would chat with fond memories about the flavour of Richmond beer.

Roxburgh Brewery 1861–c. 1870
Arthur Street, Prahran

The brewery, which was next to the Roxburgh Castle Hotel, was operated by Henry Wilcox.

Royal Artillery Brewery c. 1875–89
New Street, Elsternwick

Ernest Miller started brewing at Wattle Grove in Richmond in 1869, and later that year he and his brother Louis took over the Dublin Brewery in Church Street, Richmond. They sold the Dublin in 1872. A few years later Ernest opened the Royal Artillery Brewery in Elsternwick. In 1888 the name was changed to the Miller Lager Beer Brewing Co., and the sons were then employed in the business.

Lager beer was very much experimental in Australia at that time. The technique was new, the public was sceptical, and the Miller family's attempt to produce and sell lager beer met with failure. The brewery closed in 1889.

During November 1897 the unoccupied premises were destroyed by gale-force winds.

Royal Mint Brewery 1876–84
Cnr William & Lonsdale Streets

Patrick Coyle was said to be a thoroughly genial, kindhearted host when he ran the Grace Darling Hotel in Collingwood. He also built the Albion Hotel, but he was apparently too kindhearted and liberal to become a successful brewer. His brewery name was appropriate, since it was located opposite the Royal Mint, which had been established in June 1872 for the minting of gold sovereigns.

Henry Edhouse was connected with the brewery until 1879, but five years later the Royal Mint Brewery was put under the auctioneer's hammer. Patrick Coyle and his brewer, E. T. Moulden, moved on to the northern Victorian township of Mooroopna and purchased the Goulburn Valley Brewery — that was to prove to be another unsuccessful venture.

Scrase Brothers Brewery 1854–61
Rouse Street, Port Melbourne

About the time the Scrase brothers started brewing at Port Melbourne in 1854, Australia's first railway was built, linking Melbourne to Sandridge (as Port

Ernest Miller of the Royal Artillery Brewery, Elsternwick, was one of Australia's early brewers of lager beer. He was producing his Lager Bier in the late 1880s, and recommended that if the bottles were stored on their side, the beer would keep for several years.

Melbourne was then known). This was the Scrase brothers' first attempt at brewing, not a successful venture, and after a year or so they moved to Ballarat and tried again, this time under the name of the Napier Brewery.

At Sandridge the brewery remained idle until 1861, when Henry Vezey tried unsuccessfully to get the brewery going again.

Shamrock Brewing & Malting Co. Ltd   1865–1907
Victoria Street, East Collingwood

In the early years the Melbourne suburbs of Richmond and Collingwood played a significant role in the development of Australian industry. Mostly the industries were of a noxious nature and concerned with animal products: slaughter yards, tanneries, soap and candle works, and factories for cleaning sheepskins and wool. There were also brickworks and breweries. All these contributed to the pollution of the environment, and, as an economic necessity, the Yarra River was used as a sewer. Water used for washing beer barrels either flowed into the river or onto the flat lands where it stagnated.

Brewing was one of Collingwood's first and fastest-growing industries, and by 1865 there were at least six breweries operating in the district. One of these belonged to Thomas Graham, who began brewing in new premises at the corner of Simpson's Road (now Victoria Street) and Walmer Street, East Collingwood (now Abbotsford). Within a few months Thomas Graham leased his brewery to Robert Murcutt, who traded as Murcutt's Brewery. This was in 1866, and by April that year the entire plant and equipment, together with the unexpired term of the lease, were put up for auction. Since there were no buyers, Thomas Graham, the owner, resumed control, and continued running the business as Simpson's Road Brewery until his death in 1871.

Meanwhile, Henry Boyd and Francis Head had sold their Crown Brewery in Fitzroy, and in 1874 they took over Graham's Brewery and changed the name to the Shamrock Brewery. For thirteen years Boyd & Head ran a very successful business, and when Francis Head retired in 1887 the business was floated as the Shamrock Brewing & Malting Co. Ltd with a capital of £10,000.

The bottling department of the Shamrock Brewery was described as being one of the largest and best equipped in Melbourne, and the company's Strong Ale was awarded Second Order of Merit at the 1888 Melbourne Centennial Exhibition.

After four years, extensive alterations were made to the buildings, but lean times followed and no dividends were paid for some years.

Business then gradually improved, and by the turn of the century the Shamrock Brewery had become one of the most solvent and progressive breweries in Melbourne.

Henry Boyd was the man who guided the business through the difficult years, and it was a shock to the company and a loss to the brewing industry when he died suddenly in 1904. His son, Lt C. J. K. (Charles) Boyd, a Boer War veteran, then became the head brewer. He put out two very popular beers, Pilot Ale and Anchor Stout.

In 1907 the Shamrock Brewery, together with five other Melbourne breweries, amalgamated to form Carlton & United Breweries Pty Ltd. The Shamrock ceased to operate, and in December 1907 the plant and equipment were auctioned. Within a few years the premises were being used as a factory for the manufacture of compressed yeast. As a reminder of the brewery's former glory, Shamrock Street remains near the site of the old brewery.

For a summary, see Carlton & United Breweries Ltd.

Silverstream Mfg Co. Pty Ltd
See Burnley Brewery Co.

Simpson's Road Brewery
See Shamrock Brewing & Malting Co. Ltd.

Southern Brewery   1874–91
Cnr Lyndurst & Abinger Streets, Richmond

When William Findlay and his brother, Thomas, commenced brewing, their only product was a bottled ale of intense bitterness; it was said to be recommended by the medical profession.

Thomas Findlay died in 1886 at the age of thirty-eight, and the business was acquired by George Anthoness, previously a traveller for the Carlton Brewery, Melbourne. He died in 1891, and the Southern Brewery closed.

It was subsequently reopened by Edward Latham (former owner of the Carlton Brewery Ltd) as Ye Olde Tymes Brewerie.

Stacey Brewing Co.   1899–1910
677 Nicholson Street, North Fitzroy

Thomas Stacey, the former owner of the Cascade Brewery in Clifton Hill, started brewing at North Fitzroy in May 1899, and his output appears to have been limited to non-alcoholic beverages, including Stacey's Ale.

He closed his brewery at North Fitzroy around 1910, and in 1922 the premises were taken over by the Bux Brewing Co.

Star Brewery   1874–83
258 Smith Street (cnr Bedford Street), Collingwood

The history of the Star Brewery began in 1840 when the inner Melbourne suburb of Collingwood was known as Newtown. The brewery had been started by Charles Vaughan and Edward Wild, and when the district was named after Admiral Lord Collingwood in 1842 they decided on the name Collingwood Brewery,

Southern Brewery, Richmond, c. 1890.

and it continued under that name for the next thirty-four years.

During 1874 two aspiring young men, Charles Forbes and Benjamin Elam, purchased the Collingwood Brewery from Edward Crispe, the owner at that time. Forbes had been the manager of Graham's Brewery (later the Shamrock). They set about cleaning and renovating, used the name Star Brewery, and were soon turning out an incredible 400 hogsheads of beer a week.

Forbes and Elam saw themselves on the road to wealth and prosperity, and for twelve months or more the quality of the beer and the profits were excellent. Then the trouble started. The beer would not mature and something seemed to be wrong with the finings and the yeast. Nobody knew the cause, least of all the brewer, who was a 'rule of thumb' operator who made good beer on chance and was completely in the dark when there were problems with the brew.

The troubles persisted and the situation deteriorated. Finally, the financier, a local Collingwood personality, took over, and eventually disposed of the business to a syndicate that formed a co-operative company. After several unprofitable years the company failed, and in 1882 the brewery was leased to John Anderson, who wisely traded under a new name, the East End Brewery.

Anderson and his partner R. Hay fared no better than any of the others, and the following year they decided to sell. They advertised in the *Australian Brewers' Journal*:

> On Wednesday, August 22nd, 1883, at Eleven O'clock, to be auctioned on the premises, the East End Brewery ... the whole of the fixed and unfixed brewing plant, rolling stock, engine and boiler, horses, lorries, drays, water meters, office furniture, brewery utensils etc., without the slightest reserve. Terms Cash.

The lease had expired, and at the auction Albert Terry of the West End Brewery, Melbourne, was able to buy some cheap brewing equipment for use at his recently acquired Artillery Brewery at Williamstown. After forty-three years the old Collingwood Brewery had reached the end of its life.

Collingwood Brewery
Vaughan & Wild	1840–69
Crispe & Co.	1869–74

Star Brewery
Forbes & Elam	1874–78
Co-operative Co.	1878–82

East End Brewery
J. Anderson	1882–83
Anderson & Hay	1883, closed

Tasmanian Brewery
See Burton Brewing Co. Ltd.

Temperance Brewery 1899–1908
27 Overend Street, Brunswick

As the brewery name would indicate, no alcoholic beverages were produced, although the owner Frederick Reichelt had brewed and sold an alcoholic Weiss beer some years earlier when he owned the Dandelion Ale & Weiss Brewery in South Yarra.

During the later years the Temperance Brewery, sometimes called the Dandelion Ale Brewery, was operated by A. Mueller.

Terry's West End Breweries Ltd
See Carlton Brewery Ltd; West End Breweries Ltd.

Thunder & Co. 1884–86
Beach Street, Port Melbourne

> Yet another brewery in Melbourne. A company has rented the buildings known as the 'Sugar Works', Port Melbourne and are [sic] fitting them up as a porter brewery, the first purely porter brewery, we think, started in Australia.

This was part of the editorial in the *Australian Brewers' Journal* of July 1884. The proprietor of the brewery was Alfred Thunder, previously the owner of the Lucan Street Brewery in Bendigo, and later the manager of the Metropolitan Brewery in La Trobe Street.

Trades Union Co-operative Brewery Co. Ltd
A proposal to start a Trade Union Brewery was first discussed by Union Committee members in 1906. Three years later, in August 1909, a prospectus was issued for the Trades Union Co-operative Brewery Co. Ltd, showing a nominal capital of £25,000. The provisional directors were officers of various Victorian Trade Unions.

At a meeting of directors held at the Trades Hall, Melbourne, it was reported that the company had on offer the premises of Latham's old brewery, Richmond, previously known as Ye Olde Tymes Brewerie, and before that as the Southern Brewery. The Trades Union venture was ultimately abandoned.

Union Brewery (Little Lonsdale Street) 1852–54
Manton's Lane, off Little Lonsdale Street

Born in Scotland, Thomas Aitken arrived in Victoria in 1842, founded the Corio Brewery in Geelong in about 1851, sold out soon after, and moved to Melbourne, where he started his Union Brewery in Little Lonsdale Street. Two years later, he shifted his brewing operations to East Melbourne to start the Victoria Parade Brewery, which was to become one of the largest in Melbourne.

Union Brewery (Richmond) 1857–95
Cnr Stephenson & Lesney Streets, Richmond

Melbourne's first Union Brewery was located in Lonsdale Street, and it operated from 1852 to 1854.

The second Union Brewery was situated in the inner Melbourne suburb of Richmond, and was started by William Stephenson in 1857. Most of the owners had limited success in running the brewery, which closed on three occasions.

William Stephenson	1857–58
Stephenson & Priestly	1858
Stephenson, Cooper & Co.	1859
Pearson & Gray	1861–63
Daniel Clancy	1868–80
George Wilcox	1893–95

The last owner of the Union Brewery was George Wilcox who brewed on a small scale for family trade.

After two years he purchased the Clifton Hill Brewery, and the Union, at Richmond, closed for the last time.

Victoria Brewery   1857–75
Chapel Street, Prahran

The brewery was started by the partnership of Terry & Lister, but this changed to Terry & Thomas a year later. By 1861 the partners were Albert Terry, Robert Murcutt and Robert Cunningham. They bought Murphy's Wharf Brewery in Flinders Lane, closed it, and transferred the equipment to their brewery at Prahran.

The Victoria Brewery, traded as A. Terry & Co. until March 1872, and later that year the partnership of Strachan & Minter became the owners.

The company was incorporated as the Victoria Brewery & Malting Co. Ltd on 23 March 1874, but was wound up in January the following year.

Victoria Brewery Pty Ltd   1854–1907
Victoria Parade, East Melbourne

Thomas Aitken came to Victoria from Scotland in 1842 at the age of nineteen. In 1851 he founded the Corio Brewery in Geelong, and later started the Union Brewery in Melbourne.

By 1854 he was in business at Victoria Parade, East Melbourne, where he had built a new brewery, distillery and malthouse. The large complex was called the Victoria Parade Brewery and a substantial business developed.

In 1862 the brewery kept sixteen horses for the transport of beer, and the malthouse was guarded from rats by an army of cats, estimated by one reporter to be about a thousand!

Following the death of Thomas Aitken in 1884 the business passed to his son, Archibald. At that time the brewery was described as being 'one of the largest and

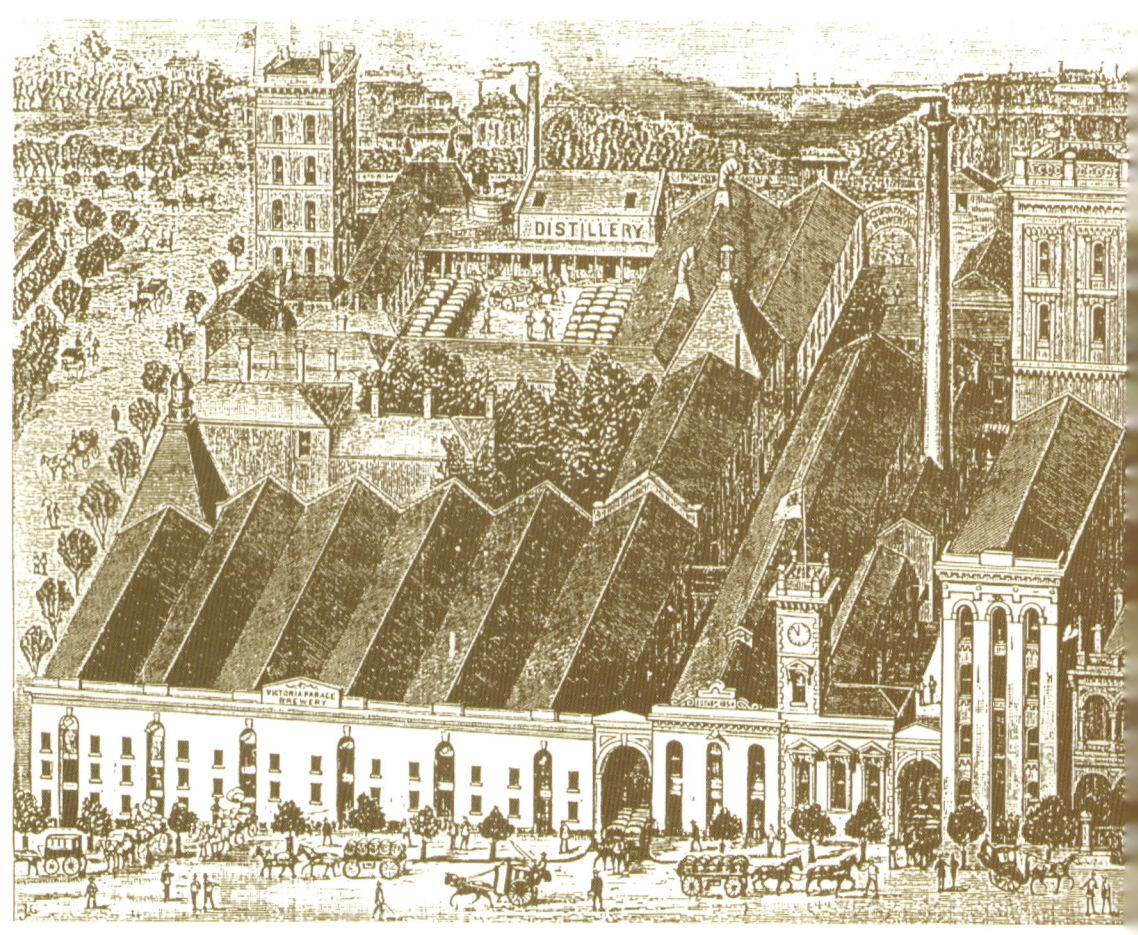

Thomas Aitken's Victoria Parade Brewery, c. 1880. The premises in Victoria Parade, East Melbourne, covered an area of 1½ acres. At the top of the tower a lead-lined reservoir contained 10,000 gallons of filtered water in case of emergency. The complex consisted of a malting house, a storage building for barley, a granary, a distillery, and the four-storey brewery.

La Trobe Library, State Library of Victoria

handsomest in Victoria'. Telephone communication had been linked between the exchange in the city and the company's distillery in Collingwood, and further innovations included gas for heating, and electric bells to assist communication between and within the buildings.

Archibald Aitken retired in 1887, and James and Alfred Nation purchased the total business for £80,000. On 13 March 1888 the business was floated as the Victoria Brewing, Malting & Distilling Co. Ltd, with Alfred Nation continuing as managing director. At the Centennial Exhibition at Melbourne in 1888, the Victoria Brewery was awarded First Order of Merit for its entry of bottled beer in the Light Sparkling Ale section.

The company was in financial difficulty by 1892. The Foster Brewery was taking a substantial slice of their business, competition was rampant, and the company was running at a loss. The share value had dropped to 3d, and late in 1892 the company went into liquidation when the shares were quoted as low as one penny. The former proprietors, the Nation Brothers, took over until August 1894, at which time the business and assets of the company were bought by a group of London investors. They changed the name to the Melbourne Brewery & Distillery Co. Ltd. A new lager beer plant was installed, and the first lager beer came off the line in February 1896. Business slowly started to pick up.

Breweries, in general, had always been a ready target for theft, and the courts of the day dealt harshly with anyone caught pilfering beer. At the Victoria Brewery (now the Melbourne Brewery & Distillery Co. Ltd) one unfortunate by the name of William Thompson was caught trespassing on the premises on the night of 14 May 1900. No theft charges were laid, only a charge for unlawful intrusion, but that was enough to earn him a sentence of one month's imprisonment. Another less fortunate employee was sentenced in December 1899 to nine months' imprisonment for stealing fourteen dozen bottles of beer.

In 1904 the Court appointed Emil Resch as receiver and manager, a position he held until 11 May 1905, when the brewery and several of its hotels were purchased by the Carlton Brewery Ltd.

Emil Resch and his brother, Edmund, retained a shareholding in the new company, which was formed in October 1905 as the Victoria Brewery Pty Ltd. T. L. Parker was appointed manager, and the brewery operated as a separate business from its owner, the Carlton Brewery.

The Victoria Brewery Pty Ltd was one of the six breweries that amalgamated in 1907 to form Carlton & United Breweries Pty Ltd (CUB). Beer continued to be produced at Victoria Parade, with bottle labels and promotional material retaining the name Victoria Brewery until the 1960s.

In June 1983, after 129 years of continuous operation, brewing ceased at Victoria Parade, and the facility was converted to a warehouse. Production of Foster's Lager, Carlton Draught and Victoria Bitter was transferred to the CUB Abbotsford plant.

CUB finally sold the Victoria Brewery site in 1984, and the magnificent facade still stands, an imposing reminder of Melbourne's early brewing history. During 1993 the property was converted to a residential development in a manner that complied with the heritage controls imposed by the Historic Buildings Council.

View of the north-west corner of the Victoria Brewery, c. 1896. Long since closed as a brewery, the magnificent facade remains under heritage control.

La Trobe Library, State Library of Victoria

Originally named the Victoria Parade Brewery, early labels proudly featured Queen Victoria of England.

Labels of the Victoria Brewery, East Melbourne, c. 1900.

In 1904 the Court appointed Emil Resch as receiver and manager of the Victoria Brewery, a position he held until May 1905. The brewery was then purchased by the Carlton Brewery Ltd. Resch retained a shareholding in the new company formed later that year as the Victoria Brewery Pty Ltd.

Emil Resch was one of the most successful of the Australian brewers, and through his experience and wise council the Victoria Brewery held its place among the finest and most successful in Melbourne.

La Trobe Library, State Library of Victoria

Victoria Brewery & Malting Co. Ltd
See Victoria Brewery.

Victoria Brewing, Malting & Distilling Co. Ltd
See Victoria Brewery Pty Ltd.

Victoria Parade Brewery
See Victoria Brewery Pty Ltd.

Victoria Temperance Brewery   1861–62
100 Bourke Street, east

The brewery name, using the words 'Temperance' and 'Brewery', would appear to be a contradiction as to the products made by the company, and probably only non-alcoholic beverages were brewed. August Puctalko was the proprietor in 1861, and William Crellin in 1862.

Victorian Hop Beer Co.
See Bollington's Brewery.

Vienna Lager Beer Brewery   1889
28 Studley Street, Abbotsford

The beer of the future was certainly lager beer, according to the experts of the day. Foster's Lager had reached the market early in 1889, and had taken an incredible hold on public taste. Quick to respond to this new market potential, William Eaton, a country brewer of considerable experience, started to brew lager at Abbotsford under the name of the Vienna Lager Beer Brewery. Unfortunately for Eaton, his long experience in brewing ale was of little use in his attempts to produce lager, which required radically different brewing techniques.

West End Breweries Ltd   1872–89

The original West End Brewery, started by Glynn & Co. at 135 Flinders Street West, was taken over by Albert Terry in 1875. While still operating this brewery, he purchased the Artillery Brewery at Williamstown, and in 1883 he formed West End Breweries Ltd, which acquired the assets of both breweries. They continued to operate independently, and T. L. Parker was appointed manager.

West End Brewery (Flinders Street)
Glynn & Co.   1872–75
Albert Terry   1875–83

West End Breweries Ltd   1883–89
(amalgamation of West End Brewery (Flinders Street) and Artillery Brewery (Williamstown))

Carlton & West End Breweries Ltd   1889–96
(amalgamation of West End Breweries Ltd and Melbourne Brewing & Malting Co. Ltd)

During 1889 Terry's West End Breweries Ltd amalgamated with the Melbourne Brewing & Malting Co. Ltd to form Carlton & West End Breweries Ltd. The Artillery Brewery at Williamstown continued for a short period, but the West End in Flinders Street was closed and the premises sold.

Wharf Brewery 1838–61
86 Flinders Lane, west

One of Melbourne's very early breweries was the Wharf Brewery, which started in the latter part of 1838. Brothers John Robert Murphy and James Murphy started brewing in a small wooden building, and for much of the time the locals used the name Murphy's Brewery. Later, a more substantial stone building was constructed.

John Murphy achieved the distinction of becoming a member of the first Board of the Victoria Fire and Marine Insurance Company in 1848.

On the night of 26 November 1849 a violent storm swept across the township of Melbourne causing enormous flooding and damage. Murphy's Wharf Brewery was completely swamped, ruining the stocks of all the raw materials. However, the brothers managed to survive the loss.

Murphy's beer was poor quality, to say the least. At the Governor's Ball in 1855 Murphy's Swipes, as the beer was referred to, was served as refreshment. Many of the guests were subsequently ill for days. As reported in the Melbourne *Herald*:

> Poor Mrs P and her daughter have been obliged to take a glass of flour and water twice a day … the doctor says it will be weeks before they are right again.

James Coghlan (later of Ballarat Brewery fame) worked at the Wharf Brewery during 1856.

Murphy's Brewery was sold in 1861 to the partnership of Albert Terry, Robert Murcutt and Robert Cunningham. They shifted the equipment to their Victoria Brewery in Prahran, and that was the end of the Wharf Brewery.

Wheeler's Brewery c. 1860–69
19 La Trobe Street

Jabez Wheeler first began brewing at 226 Wellington Street, Collingwood, and shifted to La Trobe Street several years later. Before branching out on his own he had been a partner in a brewery in Johnston Street, Collingwood.

Williamstown Brewery
See Artillery Brewery.

Ye Olde Tymes Brewerie 1892–1901
Cnr Lyndhurst & Abinger Streets, Richmond

The brewery was first known as the Southern Brewery and the owners, the Findlay brothers, brewed excellent beer for seventeen years. The brewery had closed in 1891, but the following year it was reopened by Edward Latham, considered by some to be the founder of the Carlton Brewery. He had retired from the Carlton Brewery in 1884, and when he started brewing again in the old Southern Brewery premises he chose a quaint name reminiscent of old England — Ye Olde Tymes Brewerie — and traded as E. Latham & Sons Pty Ltd.

The brewery was refitted with new equipment including an enormous 7500-gallon capacity vat. The Latham family concentrated on the production of ale that was sold in bulk and in jars for family use, through stores and grocery shops.

During 1894 'Edward Latham was fined a nominal

West End Brewery label.

Murphy's Wharf Brewery was one of Melbourne's earliest breweries, located at the west end of Flinders Lane, where the brothers, John and James Murphy, commenced brewing late in 1838.

La Trobe Library, State Library of Victoria

The Yorkshire Brewery, Collingwood. The majestic tower and parts of the old buildings still stand, and are now classified by the National Trust.

La Trobe Library, State Library of Victoria

The business traded as Wood & Ware until 1865, and then changed to J. Wood & Sons, Yorkshire Brewery. To cater for the growing trade, a new building was erected in 1876. The foundation stone weighed 5 tons, and the six-storey brewing tower, complete with hydraulic lift, was topped with a spire and flagpole. There were stables for twenty-six horses. With its 205-foot chimney-stack, the brewery was a most impressive feature in the district.

The brewery closed in 1880, but was reopened three years later by James, Charles and John Wood, all sons of the late John Wood, the founder of the business. In 1887 the brothers formed the Yorkshire Brewery Co. Ltd and appointed G. H. Jamieson as manager. Although the company was awarded first, second, third and fourth prizes for its ale and porter at the Centennial Exhibition in Melbourne in 1888, the brewery closed again in 1893. At the auction sale of the goods and chattels, casks, lorries and wagons were purchased by eager bidders for very low prices.

Three years after the sale the Carlton Brewery, McCracken's City Brewery and the Castlemaine Brewery in South Melbourne arranged to rent the Yorkshire Brewery premises in order to prevent another company starting up again in opposition. It was reported that in January 1896 Charles Wood was busy getting the brewery ready for the new occupants.

Years went by with the brewery unoccupied, and in 1907 it was leased to Colonel John Ballenger, who traded as the Ballenger Brewery Co. Pty Ltd. By the end of 1909 Ballenger had been placed in liquidation. The newly-formed Carlton & United Breweries Pty Ltd purchased some of the casks and other assets, plus the unexpired term of the lease, and changed the name back to the Yorkshire Brewery. The premises were kept as a standby plant, and later they were used as a cooperage.

penalty of 5 shillings with one guinea costs for allowing smoke from the chimney of his brewery to cause a nuisance'.

After ten years the business was no longer viable, and the brewery was taken over in 1901 by the Carlton Brewery Ltd, and closed. Years later the premises were used as a jam factory.

Yorkshire Brewery Co. Ltd   1858–93
82 Wellington Street, Collingwood

The brewery was originally a small wooden building that John Wood had erected on a 2-acre block of land on the east side of Wellington Street, Collingwood. Wood also owned a wine-and-spirit store and the Yorkshire Arms Hotel, and was to become one of the largest property owners in East Collingwood.

Mildura

Mildura Brewery Ltd
See Northern Brewing Co. Pty Ltd.

Northern Brewing Co. Pty Ltd   1966–89
217 Wade Street

The Heley family were soft-drink manufacturers in the small township of Ouyen, and as a result of a fire in the town the family decided to relocate to the larger northern Victorian town of Mildura on the Murray River. By 1922 the Heley family was back in business producing soft drinks and cordials for the Sunraysia and Riverina districts.

In 1965 the Northern Brewing Co. Pty Ltd was formed, and the following year Frank Heley, son of the founder, Walter Heley, began brewing low-alcohol beer. An early order from Sydney was for 320 dozen

Showing typical Australian fauna motifs, these labels were used for exports to the USA by the Northern Brewing Co. Ltd, Mildura.

large bottles of a non-excisable low-alcohol beer called 2 ON Lager.

The company began brewing standard-strength beers in 1970, marketed under such labels as Mildura Lager, Mildura Draught and Mildura Bitter. By 1980 yearly output had reached 80,000 dozen bottles of the various beers.

New owners took over in 1985, and they introduced Premium Lager. Other products followed, including Koala Bear Lager and Kangaroo Beer, both attractively packaged for the US market. Another export product was Down Under Lager Beer, put out by Mildura Brewery Ltd (as the company was then called), but by the end of 1989 beer production had ceased.

Moonambel

Moonambel Brewery 1862
Cherry Creek

The tiny township of Moonambel is located in the south-east corner of Victoria's Wimmera district, and there must have been some attraction for F. P. Arnold to brew there in 1862.

Mooroopna

Goulburn Valley Brewery Co. Ltd
See Mooroopna Brewery Co.

Mooroopna Brewery Co. 1882–85
Two years after the Goulburn Valley Brewery Co. Ltd was formed, it was purchased by Patrick Coyle and his partner, E. T. Moulden. Coyle had been the proprietor of the Royal Mint Brewery in Melbourne, and Moulden had been his brewer.

The partners changed the name to the Mooroopna Brewery Co., which did little to assist them in their short-lived country brewing venture. It was rumoured that there were suspicious circumstances concerning the fire that completely destroyed the brewery in 1885.

Mt Beckworth

Beckworth Brewery 1872–77
The owner of the Beckworth Brewery, Charles Holmes, advertised from time to time in the *Clunes Guardian and Gazette*. The first advertisement was in 1873, and another, on 9 July 1874, advised readers, 'Prize Mild Ale and Double Strong Do. This celebrated ale has taken the only three prizes awarded within a circuit of twenty miles for the last two years'.

The brewery was near McCallums Creek, about midway between the two goldmining towns of Clunes and Talbot. During the time the brewery was operating there were about fifty hotels within a 10-mile radius of the brewery. As noted by one historian,

> most if not all of the hotels would have been struggling to reach the one star bench mark, but a glass of double strength Beckworth beer would have been a great start to any festive occasion.

Mt Macedon

Mount Macedon Brewery
Early in 1884 there was a proposal to start a brewery at the small township of Mt Macedon, 70 km north-west of Melbourne. The *Australian Brewers' Journal* of April 1884 reported that William J. Disher, a consulting brewer from Melbourne, was the proposer.

William Disher's brewing experience was minimal. Back in 1875 he had tried unsuccessfully to run the Imperial Brewery in Adelaide. Before that, in 1865, he had lasted less than two years as the proprietor of the Standard Brewery in Echuca. Perhaps it was good fortune that the Mt Macedon proposal did not proceed.

> ### TOO MUCH
>
> A death from over-indulgence in beer occurred towards the end of last month at the Commercial Hotel, Nhill, Victoria. A party of five navvies came into town on Saturday evening. On the road, they had one or two drinks. Upon their arrival, they bought a supply of goods for the week and then proceeded to the hotel to have drinks.
>
> One of the party was a man commonly known as Scottie Allan whose real name is supposed to be Aleck Roy. After having had a drink, he stated that he had won a large wager by backing himself to drink nine pints of beer in seven-and-a-half minutes, and he offered to repeat the feat.
>
> The wager was not taken up and he then undertook to drink six pints in seven minutes, for fun. He accomplished the task in five-and-a-half minutes, stood up alongside the counter for about five minutes, after which he fell down.
>
> He never recovered and died shortly afterwards. An inquest was held, when it transpired that the deceased had drunk seven pints of beer in ten minutes, prior to which he had had three pints in less than half an hour, making a total of ten pints within the hour.
>
> *Australian Brewers' Journal,* June 1886

Newbridge

Albion Brewery   1860–c. 1878

George Elliott and Robert Day set up their brewery on the high bank of the Loddon River, about 2 miles from Newbridge on the Bridgewater Road, and began brewing in February 1860. Later that year Robert Day also ran the Albion Brewery at Inglewood, a short distance north.

During January 1870 Day advertised for a partner, apparently without success. His wife, Eliza, had died the previous year, and when Day died in September 1873 he was only forty-five years of age.

On 12 February 1874 John Carden, Thomas Smith and Lawrence Roberts took over the brewery, which was described at that time as being of brick construction, with a weatherboard superstructure. Little more is known of the brewery, although a tender to grub 40 acres of land opposite the brewery was called by John McGuiness of the Albion Brewery on 23 April 1878. The brewery building was destroyed by fire in July 1900.

Newbridge Brewery Co.   1860–76

After arriving in Australia from Ireland in 1859, Nicholas Fitzgerald joined his brother, Edward, in the running of the Castlemaine Brewery in Castlemaine. Early the following year Nicholas set up a brewery at Newbridge, in partnership with Robert Prendergast.

The business traded as Fitzgerald & Co. until 1868 when the firm of Balsillie & Crawford purchased the brewery. Both partners had worked at the brewery from the time it started, and they advertised in the *Maryborough Advertiser* of October 1868 that they were the new proprietors, 'Successors to Fitzgerald & Co.'

The brewery won first prizes at the Newbridge, Sandhurst and Ballarat shows in 1870, but in spite of the high quality of the company's beers the brewery was put up for auction on 28 February 1872. Andrew Balsillie left the district later that year.

On 1 January 1876 Joseph Webster, J. P. Gaulston and Thomas Crawford registered the Newbridge Brewery Co. Later that year Crawford assigned his equity in the brewery to James Service, but by then the brewery was almost ready to close. It was advertised for sale or lease on 5 September 1876, and even a follow-up advertisement two months later failed to attract a buyer.

During earlier years the company had set up an ale-and-porter depot at Maryborough.

Nhill

The small township of Nhill, in the Wimmera district of western Victoria, is exactly halfway between Melbourne and Adelaide. It became an important service centre for the rich farming and grazing region, which produced wool, dairy products, wheat and other grain crops. During the time the brewery operated there were seven hotels in Nhill.

Nhill Brewery   1889–1902

Nicholas Rauert had a cordial factory at Nhill and decided to try his hand at brewing. He traded as N. Rauert & Son, and his first batch of ale was ready for sale in January 1889. Alex Belperoud was employed as the brewer in 1895, and when Rauert died in 1898 the business was conducted by Belperoud & Lambert.

Alex Belperoud left in 1900 to become the brewer at the Bright Brewery, and by 1902 the Nhill Brewery had closed through lack of local support.

Port Albert

Port Albert Brewery   1859

In its early years Port Albert was a port of entry for thousands of migrants, many of whom were destined for the Omeo and Walhalla goldfields. It was the discovery of gold that led to the settlement of the entire Gippsland region.

At the time Richard Williams began brewing at Port Albert, his choice of location appeared to be ideal. The seaport was isolated and there was no competition. Unfortunately, the seafarers and whalers were away most of the time, and there were not enough customers left to keep Richard Williams in business.

Port Fairy

In the early nineteenth century Port Fairy was an operating base for sealing and whaling ships, and the tiny settlement took its name from one of these ships, the *Fairy*, which sheltered there in the 1820s. In 1843 the area was renamed Belfast, although the harbour continued to be called Port Fairy. In 1887 the name of the town was changed back to Port Fairy as a result of a petition from local residents. During that decade the port was second only to Sydney in volume of trade.

Belfast Brewery
See Victoria Brewery.

Victoria Brewery 1844–1911
Gipps Street

In 1844, when the town was known as Belfast, John Finn set up his Belfast Brewery. Only two other Victorian country towns had a brewery at an earlier date: Geelong in 1839, and Portland in 1842. The *Portland Gazette and Belfast Advertiser* of 3 November 1844 ran the following editorial:

> A brewery has been erected a few months since by Mr Finn and his knowledge of the business is sufficiently attested by the superiority of the article he produces and the great demand it has already secured.

Alex Magill of Cox Street, Belfast, received a brewer's licence for the year 1851, and either leased the brewery or worked there as the brewer.

Henry Hobbs ran the brewery for a brief period, and advertised in the *Belfast Gazette* of 17 November 1855:

> Genuine, brilliant, home brewed ale of superior quality in two gallons and upwards. Henry Hobbs can confidently recommend the above to the attention of families. Grain and yeast on sale at the brewery. Belfast brewery, Gipps Street, near the bridge. November 3, 1855.

Shortly after this advertisement, Hobbs left the brewery, and the following year John Finn was back again, running the business as the proprietor.

During the early 1860s the name was changed to the Victoria Brewery, and the business traded as Finn & Meagher. Others became involved, and the brewery apparently closed around 1866.

Alfred Guinn was the owner in 1868, and was assisted by his son, Frederick. Both father and son ran hotels as well as the brewery, and after about nine years the son became the sole proprietor. The Victoria Brewery continued for a further twenty-four years, making a total of forty-three years of successful brewing by Alfred and Frederick Guinn, and sixty-seven years in all since the brewery stared.

Belfast Brewery
John Finn	1844–55
Alex Magill	1851
Henry Hobbs	1855–56
John Finn	1856–60

Victoria Brewery
Finn & Meagher	1860
R. Spry	1860
Charles Brooker	1860–64
William Flattelly	1864–66, closed
Alfred & Frederick Guinn	1868–87
Frederick Guinn	1887–1911

Portland

Edward Henty is considered to have been the first permanent European settler in Victoria, having arrived at Portland Bay in 1834 to establish an agricultural settlement. Portland is therefore Victoria's oldest town. In those early years the only means of transport to other settlements was by sea, and the small community became self-sufficient for much of its daily needs.

Clark's Brewery 1845–75
Cnr Richmond & Henty Streets

Alexander MacKinlay used the name Portland Brewery when he started brewing in 1845. Good beer was very difficult to make in those early years, and by 1846 MacKinlay had stopped brewing and had left the district. The brewery was reopened in November 1849 by James Smith, who was ready to settle into a steady career as a brewer. However, he lasted less than a year.

The next owner was William Robinson. The *Portland Guardian* of June 1851 referred to 'William Robinson, Henty Street, Portland Brewery', but by December that year, although the same name and address were used, it was called the Victoria Brewery. The name change made little difference, however, since the brewery closed again the following year.

Portland Brewery
Alexander MacKinlay	1845–46, closed
James Smith	1849–50
William Robinson	1851

Victoria Brewery
William Robinson	1851–52

Clark's Brewery
Thomas Clark	1853–56
Maria Clark	1856–60
William Marshall (lessee)	1860–66
John Gibbs (lessee)	1867–68
Patrick Brown (lessee)	1869–73
William Kirby (lessee)	1874–75

Thomas and Maria Clark had arrived at Portland in 1852, and Thomas reopened the brewery in 1853. He used his own name for the brewery — simply Clark's Brewery. Thomas died in 1856; his widow Maria continued to manage the brewery until 1860. She then leased the brewery, firstly to William Marshall, then John Gibbs, followed by Patrick Brown, and finally to William Kirby, owner of the nearby Foresters Brewery.

Foresters Brewery 1856–79

William Kirby operated the brewery at Walook, or Double Bay, at the upper end of Hurd Street, a few doors from the Wheatsheaf Hotel. Obviously a successful brewer, he worked the Foresters Brewery for twenty-three years. Perhaps to stop competition, he took over the lease of Clark's Brewery in Henty Street in 1874, and brewed there for the next year or so, while still continuing to run his Foresters Brewery.

Johns, William, & Gibbons, Henry 1842–43
Gawler Street

The first recorded brewers at Portland were William Johns and Henry Gibbons. They began brewing in 1842 at the rear of the London Inn, Gawler Street. Later that year, the partnership was dissolved, leaving William Johns to continue on his own.

Marshall's Brewery
See White Horse Brewery.

Portland Brewery
See Clark's Brewery; White Horse Brewery.

Victoria Brewery
See Clark's Brewery.

White Horse Brewery 1859–82
Glenelg Street/20 Gawler Street

The first location of the White Horse Brewery was in Glenelg Street, opposite the Botanical Gardens. The Portland rate book of 1857/58 lists the Glenelg Street land as an industrial site, with a tannery, woolwash, brick kiln, and Thomas Must's iron shed, which housed the brewery.

According to the *Portland Guardian* (first published in 1842), Thomas Sloane was the owner of the brewery in 1865. Before that had been William Marshall, who started the brewery in 1859, but his tenure was only a year and the brewery closed in 1860; Marshall then took over the lease of Clark's Brewery, which was close by.

After running the White Horse Brewery for two years, Sloane shifted his brewing operations in 1867 to 20 Gawler Street, renting the premises for two years, before purchasing the property in 1869. Four years later he leased the brewery to David Mackie. The final lessee was the original owner, William Marshall, who brewed until 1882. During his period of operation the names Portland Brewery and Marshall's Brewery were used.

Glenelg Street
William Marshall	1859–60, closed
Thomas Sloane	1865–67

Gawler Street
Thomas Sloane	1867–74
David Mackie (lessee)	1874–76
William Marshall (lessee)	1876–82

Quantong

Quantong Brewery 1893–96

The little township of Quantong is on the Wimmera River, 15 km west of Horsham. When the brewery commenced in 1893, there were three partners: George Thistlewaite, William Waygood and Hector Wilson. Wilson retired after a few months.

During 1875, possibly earlier, William Sloane had been brewing in Jacob Street.

Riddell's Creek

Macedon River Brewery Co. Ltd 1888

Rochester

William Laitz 1895
Gillies Street

Rushworth

Phoenix Brewery 1856–85
High Street

Wolton H. Wigg started the Phoenix Brewery a few years after gold was discovered in the area. As goldmining declined, the extensive ironbark forests gave rise to a considerable timber industry, which attracted sufficient population to support the brewery.

Henry Groom, a brewer from Bendigo, was involved in the Phoenix Brewery from 1858 to 1860. Later came Alexander Hall, and then Robert Francis from 1880 until the brewery closed.

Rushworth Brewery Co. Ltd 1888–1910
High Street

The brewery was built on the site of Wolton Wigg's old Phoenix Brewery and, when completed, it was said to be one of the finest in the colony. The four-storey building was 50 feet high and had a flagpole on top of

Label used by William Marshall, Portland Brewery, c. 1880.

the tower. A steam-operated lift worked from the underground cellars, between each floor, to the top of the tower.

In spite of the considerable investment, the business began to fail soon after the opening. The owners were unable to find a good brewer, and Wolton Wigg Jnr, son of the founder of the old Phoenix Brewery, travelled to Melbourne to search for someone suitable. Finally, in 1889, Edward Hughes was given the job.

Over time there were several changes in the management of the brewery. William Magill was there in 1897, then A. W. Hannay, followed by E. H. Humphreys, but by 1898 the brewery had closed.

There seemed to be no explanation as to why Wolton Wigg's old Phoenix Brewery equipment and old-fashioned methods and recipes had produced better beer and ale for thirty years, far better than the new equipment and supposedly more knowledgeable brewers could produce at the new brewery.

The shareholders of the Rushworth Brewery Co. Ltd offered the plant and buildings for sale by auction in June 1898, but the highest bid of £950 failed to reach the reserve. After the auction some of the equipment, including barrels and a bottling machine, sold cheaply.

George Mapleback and Patrick Hallahan reopened the brewery, put it back in working order, and began brewing in October 1899. Both partners were experienced brewers, Mapleback having worked at the Corowa Brewery in New South Wales and Hallahan at the Federal Brewery at Wahgunyah. After two years George Mapleback was the sole owner, and he produced Diamond Brand ale, which he sold in bulk and in bottles.

In 1903 Mapleback was charged at the police court with having defrauded the federal customs by sticking cancelled duty stamps on his casks of beer. The fine was £20, with £6 6s in costs. Brushing this aside, Mapleback managed to run a reasonable business until 1910.

Phoenix Brewery

Wolton H. Wigg	1856–58
Wigg & Groom	1858–60
Wigg & Hall	1860–80
Wigg & Francis	1880–85, closed

Rushworth Brewery Co. Ltd

Wolton Wigg Jnr (manager)	1888
Edward Hughes (brewer)	1889
William Magill (manager)	1897
A. W. Hannay (manager)	1898
E. H. Humphreys (manager)	1898, closed
George Mapleback & Patrick Hallahan	1899–1901
George Mapleback	1901–10

St Arnaud

St Arnaud, first known as New Bendigo, became notable as a goldfield during the mid-1850s. The Borough of St Arnaud was proclaimed in 1863, and the town in 1950.

The town is noted for the cast-iron 'lace' to be found on many of the buildings, a number of which are classified by the National Trust.

Albion Brewery 1864–1911
Inglewood Road

Gavinus McRoberts opened his St Arnaud Brewery on 4 October 1864, and at the banquet there were no complaints about the quality of the first samples of beer.

The Albion Brewery, St Arnaud, Victoria, c. 1900, previously known as the St Arnaud Brewery. James Steward changed the name to the Albion when he took over in 1896 — the previous owner had died after being bitten by a redback spider.

He had sold his hotel, but one year of brewing was enough for him, and he went back to hotelkeeping.

In 1865 the St Arnaud Brewery, together with a substantial house, was leased to William E. Wheeler. He had previously worked at Archie Faulkner's Western Creek Brewery at the nearby township of Carapooee. After two years Wheeler bought the brewery, the house and all the outbuildings, and constructed a 15-foot dam for his supply of water. The water from the St Arnaud Creek, which ran past the brewery, was brackish.

It was not long before William Wheeler had to double his brewing capacity to keep up with the demand for his very popular Pale Ale, but tragically he died in 1894 as the result of a bite from a redback spider. His wife, Ann, kept the business going with the aid of her sons, Jack and Frank, but finally she sold the brewery and property to James Steward on 6 June 1896.

When Steward took over, he changed the name to the Albion Brewery, set about extending and upgrading the buildings and equipment, and appointed his eldest son, James George Steward, to take charge of the brewing and management of the business. James, the father, died in 1898, and the Albion Brewery, together with the residence and other buildings, plus the sum of £3000, were bequeathed to his son, who then ran the business on his own.

Brewing was suspended for about eight months during 1903 because of severe drought, and beer supplies were sent from Steward's brother's Albion Brewery at Eaglehawk (Bendigo).

The last decade of the brewery's history was plagued with difficulty and change. During 1905 a partnership was formed with Thomas Bilton, and before the closure of the brewery Charles McLean was the owner.

St Arnaud Brewery
See Albion Brewery.

Sale

The name Sale came into official use around 1850, and gradually the small township became a busy stopover for travellers, and an important supplier of goods to the prospectors moving to and from the Gippsland goldfields. During the 1870s there were thirteen hotels in Sale, and although the population was only 3000, there were three breweries: McIver's, the Sale and the Victoria. Between them, they were producing 100,000 gallons of beer annually.

Gippsland Brewery Pty Ltd 1897–1936
Dawson Street/York Street

Richard Jamieson started brewing in Dawson Street in 1864, shifted to York Street soon after, and sold out to James Pettit in 1871. He named the brewery the Victoria, and after twenty-six years, he sold his well-established business to the Breheny brothers, who changed the name to the Gippsland Brewery Pty Ltd.

The new company formed in 1897 continued to prosper. Edward Breheny was the brewer-manager, and Gippsland Brewery beers and stout were distributed widely throughout Victoria's East Gippsland district. Later, Edward's brother, Michael B. Breheny, took over the management of the business. Of Irish descent, the Breheny family, fathers and sons, brothers and cousins, all at some period from the 1850s, and for the next 130 years, had been involved in the brewing industry in Australia.

Breheny Brothers' Gippsland Brewery, Sale, showing the three-storey addition that was completed in 1911.

The Breheny brothers sank a well, which provided ample pure water for brewing and cooling. Previously, they had been dependent on the town supply, where the water was not quite as suitable for brewing. They installed a whistle, and its shrill sound, announcing the starting and finishing of shifts, was part of daily life at Sale. Part of daily life was also the consumption of the company's very popular Lager, Stout and Gippsland Bitter.

The company advertised in *Every Week* newspaper on 22 August 1933:

> The Gippsland Brewery notifies that four non-intoxicating Stout, Vitex, Maltx and Hop Beer, all at 6 shillings per dozen for quarts and 4 shillings per dozen for pints.

'Fern Tubs for Sale' concluded the advertisement.

The brewery finally closed in 1936, and by 1953 the buildings had become so dilapidated that the council ordered their demolition.

McIver's Brewery   1866–82
Reeve Street

The brewery was located in Reeve Street, behind the present-day St Patrick's College. When brewing started in August 1866, the owner of the brewery, John McIver, advertised that he was ready to supply his 'Superior Ale'.

McIver died in 1874 and his widow, Mary, continued to run the business until 1879; she then leased the brewery to Maurice Coleman.

During December 1882 the brewery was offered to let, and brewing had probably ceased. Two years later Arthur Ralston of the Sale Brewery purchased McIver's old brewery, probably to acquire some of the equipment.

Roxburgh Brewery   c. 1866

On 27 March 1866 George Wilcox advertised in the *Gippsland Times* that he was 'now producing ale and porter free from all adulteration, the same as that celebrated Roxburgh Ale brewed by his father in Prahran [Melbourne]'.

Sale Brewery   1861–88
Cnr Barkly & Foster Streets

The following advertisement appeared in the 21 August 1861 edition of the *Gippsland Times*:

> Good samples of English barley will be purchased at the Sale Brewery at six shillings and six pence per bushell.
> G. Ralston.

Three months later another advertisement informed the public that ale, porter, grains and yeast were available at the Sale Brewery. Ralston also said that he would, 'soon be able to supply soda water, lemonade, ginger beer, raspberry vinegar and all kinds of cordials'.

Gavin Ralston had been the owner of the Albion Brewery in Sydney in 1842, and was now a well-established and successful brewer in Sale. He died in 1874, and the Sale Brewery was leased in 1878 to Michael Coffey.

Two years later the business was conducted by the partnership of Ralston & Wishart. Gavin Ralston's son, Arthur Ralston, had become the proprietor by 1884, and during that year he purchased McIver's Brewery in Reeve Street, which had been closed for two years. The acquisition was evidently to obtain the equipment, since the Reeve Street brewery was never reopened.

A similar circumstance occurred in 1888 when James Pettit of the Victoria Brewery, only a few streets away, purchased Ralston's Sale Brewery and closed it.

Victoria Brewery   1864–97
York Street

In 1864 Richard Jamieson started brewing in Dawson Street. He placed small advertisements in the *Gippsland Times*, offering yeast for sale at his brewery. The brewery may have closed for a period, since he advertised again in September 1867: 'the Sale Brewery has now reverted into my hands' — he had possibly leased the business and had then taken it back; the 'Sale' brewery refers to the town name, as distinct from a brewery name.

Richard Jamieson shifted his brewery to York Street, between Macalister and Foster Streets, and continued producing 'Celebrated Light Bitter and other Ales and Porter'.

James Pettit bought the brewery in 1871. He was one of the earliest residents of Sale, having arrived there when there were only three houses. Since there was already a 'Sale' Brewery in town, Pettit chose the name Victoria Brewery, and began brewing his 'Fine Sparkling Ales'. He advertised extensively, and advised readers in the *Gippsland Mercury* of 9 June 1877:

> **Victoria Brewery, J. G. Pettit, Prop., Sale, Bairnsdale and Walhalla.**
> Mr Pettit assures customers in the Bairnsdale and Walhalla districts that the production from his establishments in those towns are equally on a par with his Sale ales.

Pettit had taken over the Alpine Brewery at Walhalla and Goold's Brewery at Bairnsdale earlier in 1877.

James Pettit was awarded first prize for his ale at the North Gippsland Agricultural Show in April 1876, and he continued to win prizes over successive years, proudly advertising the fact almost three times a week in the *Gippsland Mercury*.

The Sale Brewery was purchased from Arthur Ralston in 1888, and closed, leaving the Victoria the only brewery operating in Sale.

During 1897 the Breheny brothers bought the Victoria Brewery from the executors of the estate of James Pettit, and the name was changed to the Gippsland Brewery Pty Ltd.

See also Gippsland Brewery Pty Ltd.

Gippsland Brewery Pty Ltd label, c. 1915.

Seymour

Crown & Junction Brewery 1869–c. 1871
On the Goulburn River

Paul Siddall had been the owner of the Crown Brewery in Castlemaine, but, with increasing competition, he decided to move to Seymour. With Edmond Baron as a partner, they advertised in the *Waranga Chronicle & Goulburn Advertiser* of 18 November 1869:

> Crown & Junction Brewery – Goulburn River. Messrs Siddall & Baron beg to inform … that at a great outlay, have established a brewery on the Goulburn River and are now in a position to defy competition in the production of First Class Ales.

Siddall and Baron would surely have known that another brewery had started at Seymour the same year, further along the Goulburn River, and that three very experienced brewers (Henry Bolton, James Tierney and John Fynn) were the owners. Siddall obviously ignored this competition, but not for long. After a year or two he and his partner, Baron, left for Melbourne, where they took over the Crown Brewery in Fitzroy.

Goulburn River Brewery Co. 1869–98
Hanna Street, on the bank of the Goulburn River

Henry Bolton, together with his uncle John Fynn, and James Tierney, started the brewery, which at that time was generally referred to as the Seymour Brewery. At one time or another all three partners had been involved in the Heathcote Brewery, about 40 km to the west. Bolton, sometime Postmaster-General of Victoria, had brewing interests in Benalla and elsewhere.

The partners advertised in the 18 November 1869 issue of the *Waranga Chronicle & Goulburn Advertiser* simply as 'Bolton, Tierney & Co. Brewers, Seymour'.

The Goulburn River Brewery Co. was formed in 1874. Five years later Bolton became the sole owner. Percival Renou bought the business in 1880, and did reasonably well until he became insolvent in 1892. The brewery was offered for sale by the mortgagee, and a year later it was purchased by Henry Bones & Sons for £2000. Bones was the owner of the local Prince of Wales Hotel, and he found that selling beer was easier than making it, and he closed the brewery after a few months.

The Carlton Brewery, Melbourne, supplied bulk beer to many Victorian hotels, including some at Seymour. To demonstrate its public spirit, and no doubt to gain publicity, the Carlton Brewery rallied to the request of the newly-formed Seymour Volunteer Fire Brigade in 1891 and made a donation of a hose and reel.

The Goulburn River Brewery had been closed for four years until in 1896 when along came Paul Siddall with his two sons, eager to try their luck. Paul had owned the Crown & Junction Brewery at Seymour twenty-five years earlier. Although that venture had lasted for only two years, he had learnt a lot since then; besides, he said, he knew the district very well. The Siddall family's attempt to get the brewery going again lasted for two years, and the buildings were later converted to a butter factory.

Seymour Brewery
See Goulburn River Brewery Co.

Shepparton

Irrigation came to the Shepparton district in 1912, followed by stock fattening and dairying, and the start of the fruit industry. The well-known Shepparton Fruit Preserving Co. (SPC), a growers' co-operative venture, was formed, and commenced operating in 1917; it continues as one of the town's major industries.

Shepparton Brewery 1885–1929
Welsford Street

One of the largest industries in Shepparton at the turn of the century was Bryant & Sheil's Shepparton Brewery. It was built on the bank of the Goulburn River in 1885 at a cost of £5500, including the plant and equipment. The original partners were Charles Bryant Snr and William Sheil Snr. Bryant already had interests in the Stawell and Maldon Breweries.

The Shepparton Brewery built up a fine reputation throughout the colony. The quality of the beer was consistently good, due in part to the excellent springwater drawn from a well alongside the river. After the death of Charles Bryant in 1898, the brewery was conducted by William Bryant and William Sheil, sons of the original partners. The sons also set up the Buffalo Brewery at Wangaratta in 1902.

The Shepparton Brewery and hotel properties were sold to the Goulburn Valley Investment Co., although the brewery was repurchased by William Sheil Jnr just before his death. Brewing had ceased by 1929, and the buildings were demolished in 1938.

Smythesdale

Smythesdale Brewery 1872–75
Gregory Street

Charles Tait obtained a licence at the Police Court, Smythesdale, as licensee of his hotel at Staffordshire Reef. Tait also owned many allotments of land in the town, including an area that is still called Brewery Dam (recently restored by the Smythesdale Progress Association for swimming and picnicking). Tait's occupation in the 1872 rate book is shown as 'brewer', and in 1876 as 'publican' and also 'hotelkeeper'.

The Brewery Dam site was where Charles Tait had his brewery. The large section that had been excavated was where the beer barrels were stored — the machinery and other equipment were further south.

William Park was granted a brewer's licence for one year in 1861, but it is doubtful if he started a brewery.

Stanley

When the Stanley area was settled in 1852, it was known as both Nine Mile and Snake Gully — it was Nine Mile if you approached it from Myrtleford, and Snake Gully if you approached it from Beechworth! In 1858 the name was changed to Stanley (from whichever direction it was approached).

Aitken & Fraser c. 1866–77
Little Scotland Road

Some time after 1866 Anthony Aitken and David Fraser ran a brewery on Crown land. They lasted three years, and the *Ovens and Murray Advertiser* of March 1870 carried an advertisement that gave details of the forthcoming auction of 'the well known brewery lately occupied by Messrs Aitken & Fraser'. The same paper listed, under insolvencies, both Anthony Aitken and David Fraser.

The brewery was purchased by Alexander Dunn, who immediately let it to Cornelius Collins and William Morton. By January 1873 both were insolvent, and the brewery was in the hands of the owner, Alexander Dunn. One year later, Dunn also was insolvent.

There must have been something wrong with the brewery — to a cynic, three insolvencies in less than eight years would be ludicrous, but, for those directly involved at the time, the events were quite tragic. Alexander Dunn's son, John, had worked at the brewery. He went on a drunken spree — and they dragged his body out of Lake Kerferd. Three days later, after returning from his son's funeral, the father attempted to drown his sorrows — his son's death and his own insolvency. 'Drown' was the operative word. The next morning he was also fished out of Lake Kerferd, making it a busy time for the undertaker with two funerals from the same family in one week.

From 1874 the brewery was known as Little's Brewery, and was worked by Joseph Edwards.

Crawford's Brewery
See Star Brewery.

Little's Brewery
See Aitken & Fraser.

Nine Mile Brewery
See Star Brewery.

Star Brewery 1856–1906

John Alston Wallace started the brewery in the main street of Stanley, next to his general store and Star Hotel. He became a member of the Legislative Council, representing the North-Eastern Province, and in later years was involved in his various mining ventures. He was born at Rutherglen, Scotland, and the town of Rutherglen was named after his birthplace as a compliment to him by the townsfolk.

John Wallace sold his Star Brewery to Francis Mitchell in 1863, and when Charles Dyring took over two years later it was called the Nine Mile Brewery. According to the *Ovens and Murray Advertiser*, Stanley had 380 residents in 1868, certainly insufficient to support two breweries, and in 1869 the Nine Mile Brewery was offered for sale, and finally leased to the local baker, James Muter.

The brewery owner, Charles Dyring, appeared in the Beechworth Insolvency Court in 1870, and the brewery was subsequently taken over by James Crawford. Finally, here was someone able to run a successful brewing business, and Crawford continued to brew for the next thirty years. He died in 1900, and his widow, Jane, continued to work the brewery for a few more years with the assistance of James Clingin. In June 1906 there was a 'clearing sale at Crawford's Stanley Brewery', and, with no other brewery in town, the townsfolk were no longer able to buy locally made beer.

Stawell

Gold was discovered in the Stawell district, first known as Pleasant Creek, in the 1850s, and by 1857 the population had grown to 30,000. The following year the

---

A DREADFUL OCCURRENCE

An accident, attended with the most distressing consequences, happened in a large brewery where the brother of an old friend of mine was brewer. This young man was of very fine physique and, unlike many men so gifted, was also very bright and clever. One evening, when he was going home, he walked across a sort of gangway which led over the hop-back, at that time filled with scalding hot wort. He had changed his soft brewery hat for a 'bell-topper,' and unfortunately had the latter knocked off when passing under a beam. The hat fell into the wort and he leant over the hand-rail of the gangway and was trying to lift it up with his umbrella, when the frail hand-rail gave way and precipitated him head first into the scalding wort. Blinded and agonized, he half-swam, half-waded and half-crawled through the torturing fluid to the side of the vessel, over which he managed to scramble and then fell exhausted. His parents were sent for but he died in his mother's arms in the course of an hour.

Australian Brewers' Journal, April 1890

A cooper at work at the Stawell Brewery. The manufacture and maintenance of wooden beer barrels was a highly skilled and substantial industry until they were gradually replaced by stainless-steel kegs in the 1930s.

settlement was proclaimed, and named after the then Attorney-General, William Stawell.

Today, Stawell is the home of the Stawell Gift, Australia's most famous professional foot race.

Excelsior Brewery
See Stawell Brewery.

Marshall's Brewery
See Stawell New Brewery.

Nicholls, James   1859–61

James Nicholls and Archie Faulkner had been in partnership as ginger-beer and soda-water manufacturers. When they separated, Faulkner went to Carapooee and started the Western Creek Brewery there. Nicholls stayed on at Stawell, and decided to expand his product range to include beer. He advertised in the *Mount Ararat Advertiser* of 18 January 1859 that he was 'carrying on business at the Pleasant Creek gold-diggings as general brewer and cordial manufacturer'.

James Nicholls died in 1861 at the age of thirty-five. During that year the Stawell District Rates Board rate book showed William Frayne rated for a brewery at Commercial Creek, the location of the brewery in the Pleasant Creek area. Frayne apparently continued to make only cordials, but later erected a flourmill in the town.

Stawell Brewery   1869–1918
Seaby Street, Pleasant Creek

Spirits of one form or another had always been a popular and convenient drink on the goldfields — for storage and transport there was more alcohol in less volume compared to beer. The beer, with a lower alcohol content, was generally an unstable drink, difficult to keep cool, or to keep at all for very long after it was brewed.

The miners were not known for their moderate spirit drinking, and drunkenness and outrageous behaviour were commonplace. The problem was eased to some extent when Thomas Powell opened his brewery in 1869. He called it the Excelsior at the time, and the timber building was located outside the racecourse gate and near the botanical reserve. Powell, who also owned the Corio Brewery in Geelong, advertised in the *Pleasant Creek News* of 31 July 1869, 'Excelsior Brewery; Strict attention paid to country orders; Encourage local industry'.

There were about sixty-two licensed hotels in the town, an enormous market for anyone who could make good beer, and Powell made the best of it until his death in March 1877. His daughter tried to run the business, but knew nothing about brewing; the brewery was then put up for auction 'By order of the Mortgagees, on March 24, 1879'. The brewery failed to sell, and two years went by before Charles Bryant purchased the property and business. Bryant was part-owner of the Maldon Brewery.

After extending the premises, now known as the Stawell Brewery, Bryant began advertising that his

'Bright Sparkling Ales were brewed only from the renowned Grampian Water'. Bryant's nephew, Henry Edhouse, managed the brewery, and in 1893 he became the proprietor. He also owned several hotels in the town, and became involved in many community affairs.

Richard Cowman, Henry Edhouse's stepson, was registered as a brewer in 1916, and managed the business, but by 1918 the brewery had closed. Four years later Henry Edhouse died.

The shutting down of the Stawell Brewery was symptomatic of the fate of other country breweries. They were unable to compete with the consistent beer quality, pricing and efficient distribution of the larger city breweries with their network of tied houses and hotel ownership. There were also fewer hotels. Temperance campaigners in Victoria had welcomed the setting up of a Licences Reduction Board in 1906, which resulted in the gradual reduction in the number of hotels in the state. By 1917 only nine of Stawell's hotels retained their licences. Ballarat had lost thirty-seven hotels, and others chose not to renew their licences over the same period.

By 31 October 1929 only 818 of the 2002 Victorian country hotels licensed in 1906 remained open for business. Some, especially on the outskirts of towns, were left abandoned. These delicensed hotels soon became derelict, a nostalgic reminder of the past, a source of adventure for children, and a welcome campsite for swagmen.

Stawell New Brewery 1881–89
Patrick Street

William Marshall advertised in November 1881: 'Stawell New Brewery; splendid Ale in bulk and in bottles at six shillings per dozen. Fresh yeast always on hand. W. Marshall'. By coincidence, the advertisement was directly below a similar advertisement for Henry Edhouse's Stawell Brewery.

This 'new' brewery was generally called Marshall's Brewery by locals and others, probably for convenience, as a means of distinguishing between the two 'Stawell' breweries. Marshall was renting the premises, but after eight years the brewery closed.

Stratford

Alpine Brewery 1866–69

The brewery stood prominently in the main road of Stratford, a small picturesque township on the Avon River, north of Sale in Victoria's East Gippsland district. Although the town has no historical link with the birthplace of that famous English author, William Shakespeare, a Shakespeare Festival had been part of its annual calendar. The River Avon was actually named by the explorer Angus McMillan after a stream in his native Scotland, and the name Stratford is derived from the river's 'Straight' Ford.

The proprietor of the Alpine Brewery was Edward Thomas, owner of the local Brewery Arms Hotel. After three years he left the district and settled in Bairnsdale, where he bought another brewery. The Avon had been one of the most flood-prone rivers in Victoria, possibly the reason for Thomas's departure.

Talbot

Hope & Anchor Brewery c. 1860
Back Creek

The brewery, which was opened by S. Marks about 1860, may have been the forerunner of the Talbot Brewery.

Laski's Brewery 1855
Scandinavian Crescent

In 1855 Thomas Laski introduced a sugar beer that critics said was palatable and wholesome. A year earlier Laski had been brewing at Maldon; after one year at Talbot he moved on to Maryborough and started another brewery.

Talbot Brewery 1862–c. 1881

Gold had been found at Talbot during the late 1850s, and the town was reported to have had a floating population of 50,000. Prospects were good for a brewery, and Moritz Cohn of the Victoria Brewery at Bendigo opened a branch brewery at Talbot in 1861 — Talbot lies some 70 km south-west of Bendigo.

The *Maryborough and Dunolly Advertiser* of January 1862 carried an advertisement for the Talbot Brewery, Back Creek, advising that the brewery had been completed and that ales and porter were available.

Moritz Cohn took a leading part in the civic affairs of the district and became the mayor.

The mining of gold began to decline, and in 1866 the population had dropped to 8000. With the continuing decline, Moritz Cohn sold the Talbot Brewery to George Jacobson in 1872 and returned to Bendigo. Jacobson shifted the brewery from Elgin Street to Talbot Street in 1881.

Tallangatta

Spring Creek Brewery 1903–6
Main Street

Frederick Allen was the owner of the Spring Creek Brewery at Beechworth, and in 1903 he started another Spring Creek Brewery at Tallangatta. When Allen died in 1906, both breweries were acquired by the Anglo-Australian Brewery Co. Ltd, and both were closed.

Tanjil South

Tanjil Brewery 1870

The brewery was set up by J. Robinson on behalf of Albert Harris & Co. of Walhalla. During 1870 Harris & Co. advertised their 'pure and sparkling XXX ales and porter, Tanjil Brewery, Tanjil River'. The small town of Tanjil South is about 10 km north of Moe in Victoria's West Gippsland district.

Taradale

Clarke, John 1860

Tarraville

Brown's Brewery c. 1850–c. 1862

The address of Brown's Brewery was listed in the *Victorian Government Gazette* as the 'north bank of the Tarra Rivulet, adjoining a place known as Turnbull's Bridge'. The location, on the south Gippsland coast, is 10 km south of Yarram, and was a rather remote area for a brewery.

Gilbert Brown may have started brewing before 1850, but he was still brewing in the early 1860s.

Trentham

Trentham Brewery 1884–1913
Blackwood Road

The sparkle of gold brought the first settlers to the Trentham area in 1854 when two men, searching for lost bullocks, returned home with pockets full of gold nuggets that they had found lying in the river bed just below the mineral springs. However, the gold had long since run out when Joseph Barnes moved into the area to set up his Trentham Brewery. He spent most of his time at his hotel, and employed a brewer to look after the daily operation of the brewery. In case of emergency, electric bells were connected from the brewery to Barnes's bedroom so that he could be called at night if necessary.

Joseph Barnes's wife, Annie, looked after the Criterion Hotel at Castlemaine, about 30 km north, and served beer that came from her husband's brewery at Trentham. Three months after Barnes died the son, also Joseph, ran the brewery with all its complexities, and had Edgar Flanagan helping with the more difficult tasks.

A year went by and Annie Barnes decided to lease the business. In 1899 the Nation brothers (James, Thomas, Alfred and Walter) were working the brewery, which they purchased in 1908.

Early in 1914 the Kyneton & Trentham Breweries Ltd was formed to take over the freehold property and brewing equipment of the Trent Brewery at Kyneton and the Trentham Brewery. The Nation brothers owned both breweries, which had recently closed, but the brewery at Trentham was never reopened.

Vectis

Vectis Brewery 1893–96

Vectis today is little more than a railway siding, about 10 km from Horsham in Victoria's central Wimmera District. The brewery was opened by the Sudholz brothers in 1893, and at that time Edward Walsh, George Ward and James Williams were either partners or employees at the brewery.

Wahgunyah

Belltopper Brewery
See Wahgunyah Brewery.

Federal Brewery
See Wahgunyah Brewery.

J. Knight & Son 1860–c. 1862

J. Knight & Son had their first brew ready for delivery in October 1860.

McSweeney's Brewery 1884–89

During the first year of the brewery's operation, the owner, Eugene McSweeney, sold the property to R. McKenna. Three years later John McKenna & Son were running the brewery.

Wahgunyah Brewery 1866–1900

When Dennis Hallahan started the brewery in 1866, he called it the Belltopper Brewery. He changed the name four years later, as noted in his advertisement in the *Ovens and Murray Advertiser* of May 1870 that his 'Wahgunyah Brewery has First Class Winter Ales for sale'.

John Crisp, previously a storekeeper, bridgebuilder and flourmiller, leased the brewery in the late 1870s with his father-in-law, William Thorne, as a partner.

Ownership of the brewery changed from Dennis Hallahan to Hallahan & Tyrell in 1886, and they continued to lease out the brewery to Crisp and Thorne.

Thomas Ogilvie leased the brewery in 1887; he purchased it two years later, together with the Corowa & Wahgunyah Brewing & Malting Co. Ltd in Corowa, NSW. Ogilvie became bankrupt in 1891, and Patrick Hallahan, probably Dennis's son, then continued to run the business at Wahgunyah as the Federal Brewery. John Hallahan became involved in the business in 1894, and R. Savage & Co. in 1897.

Brewing has long since ceased, but grapegrowing and wine production, which also started in the 1860s, has developed as a major industry in the district.

Wail

Ward, Charles 1893

Walhalla

Toward the end of 1862 payable gold had been discovered at Springers Creek (later named Walhalla). A goldrush started, and breweries were quick to follow.

Similar to other goldmining towns throughout Australia, the gold at Walhalla was ultimately worked out, and most of the population moved on.

Today the township is a tourist attraction of historical significance, and is classified by the National Trust.

Alpine Brewery 1865–c. 1890

Within a few years of the discovery of gold at Walhalla the Alpine Brewery was flourishing. Thomas Perkins Jnr had started the brewery in 1865, at much the same time that his brother Paddy had opened an Alpine Brewery at Woods Point, 50 km north. Both Thomas and Paddy eventually settled in Queensland.

After Thomas Perkins left Walhalla, Arthur Ralston, the well-known brewer from Sale, bought the Alpine Brewery and worked it for the next six years. Arthur was the son of Gavin Ralston, who had been the owner of the Albion Brewery in Sydney, later the site of Toohey's Brewery.

James Rice operated the Alpine Brewery in 1875, and then another brewing identity from Sale, James Pettit, bought out the previous owner, and ran the brewery until it closed about 1890. The buildings were later converted to a hotel.

Anchor Brewery 1866
Main Street
William E. Ball.

Junction Brewery
See Star Brewery.

Star Brewery 1878–98

James Austin built a hotel at Walhalla in 1873 and called it the Star. Five years later he opened the Junction Brewery. A year or so later Lewis Loan purchased the property, and in harmony with the name of the hotel he renamed the brewery the Star.

The clear stream-water and cool mountain climate favoured the brewing of first-class beer, and Loan had the distinction of winning an award at the 1880 Melbourne Exhibition. Other prizes were taken at Paris and Calcutta.

Lewis Loan died in 1898, and the houses and brewery were sold at auction by his widow, Elizabeth, in February 1889.

Wangaratta

The name Wangaratta is an Aboriginal word meaning 'resting place of the cormorant', and although the region was opened up by the explorers Hume and Hovell in 1824 settlement did not start until twenty or more years later.

Buffalo Brewery 1902–50
Boundary Road (now Phillipson Street)

Mt Buffalo, 70 km south-east of Wangaratta, was named by the explorers Hume and Hovell during their expedition from Sydney to Port Phillip Bay in 1824. From one vantage point the mountain resembles a buffalo, and it was this mountain view that inspired Bryant & Sheil Brothers to name their new brewery the Buffalo Brewery.

Construction was under way early in 1901, and brewing was started in 1902 by the partnership of Garnet Bryant and William Sheil. This was the fourth brewery to be built by the company. Charles Bryant, Garnet's father, had started brewing at Maldon in 1856; he had operated other breweries in Stawell in 1884, and in Shepparton in 1888.

The Buffalo Brewery was built on farmland away from rivers, and at times it was completely surrounded by crops. Wells and a spring provided an unlimited supply of pure, crystal-clear water. It was the only brewery on the main road (now the Hume Highway) between Melbourne and Albury, and the excellent-quality beer was immediately popular. The company brewed Prize Ale, Bohemian Lager, Victorian Bitter Ale, and Buffalo Ale and Stout.

Walter Bryant became involved in the business in the early 1900s. During 1914 he commenced production of aerated water and cordials in a new factory. On 4 August 1920 the business was registered as the Wangaratta Brewery Pty Ltd, but continued to trade as the Buffalo Brewery. Brewing ceased about 1950, and the five-storey tower and the chimney were demolished in 1957.

Cohn Brothers of Bendigo purchased the premises in 1961, and continued to make soft drinks.

Dodsworth's Brewery 1880–87
Templeton Street

John Dodsworth was involved with several breweries in Wangaratta. He had been a brewer at the Wangaratta Brewing & Malting Co. Ltd in 1868, and ultimately became the manager. After leaving there in 1872 he started out on his own, and set up the Victoria Brewery, which he worked until 1877. Michael Moloney was a partner during the final year.

John Dodsworth was a popular personality in Wangaratta, but he was plagued with financial difficulties, and in 1877 he sold his Victoria Brewery. His old workplace, the Wangaratta Brewing & Malting Co.

Ltd, had failed, and later that year he took over that brewery and lived in a house on the premises. He apparently did not operate the brewery, which he sold a year or two later.

Victoria Brewery

John Dodsworth	1872–76
Dodsworth & Moloney	1876–77
Baynes & Hearn	1877–86
Edward Hurst & Co.	1886–87
Stewart & Dodsworth	1887–88
A. E. Clarke & Co.	1888
J. M. Walters	1888–93

Victoria Brewery Co. Ltd 1893

William Halligan	1899
Halligan & Dale	1900
R. E. Dockendorff & Dale	1901
McLean & Hannay	1902
Moloney & Dale	1903

Wangaratta Brewing & Malting Co. Ltd

H. Kett (manager)	1868–77
J. Dodsworth	1877
Dale, Rundle & O'Neill	c. 1880–87, closed

Perseverance Brewery

Henry Simmons	1869–75, closed

Dodsworth's Brewery
(reopened the Perseverance Brewery)

Dodsworth & Son	1880–84
Stewart, Dodsworth & Son	1884–87

(Dodsworth then returned to the Victoria Brewery in 1887 in partnership with Stewart)

Meanwhile, the Perseverance Brewery in Templeton Street had been idle for several years, and in 1880 John Dodsworth acquired the property. The small dilapidated brewery of timber construction and bark roof then became known as Dodsworth's Brewery. It traded as Dodsworth & Son, and after 1884 as Stewart, Dodsworth & Son.

During 1887 Stewart and Dodsworth purchased the Victoria Brewery from Edward Hurst & Co. The premises were larger, so Dodsworth's old brewery in Templeton Street was closed and the surplus equipment sold. Dodsworth was then back again at the Victoria Brewery (which he had started 1872), and he stayed there until his death in 1893. Although he was frequently in debt, he was well liked in the community; he had been a Wangaratta councillor and a captain of the Volunteer Fire Brigade.

Meldrum's Brewery
See Wangaratta Brewery.

Perseverance Brewery   c. 1869–75
Templeton Street

Henry Simmons's brewery was small and crude, and did not live up to its name 'Perseverance', since it closed about six years after it started.

John Dodsworth and his son reopened the brewery in 1880, and traded as Dodsworth's Brewery.

Victoria Brewery
See Victoria Brewing Co. Ltd.

Victoria Brewery Co. Ltd   1872–1904
Grey Street, on the bank of the Ovens River

John Dodsworth was a pioneer of the brewing industry in Wangaratta, and at various times he was involved in three breweries in the town. In 1872 he started the

John Dodsworth had been involved in several breweries in Wangaratta. This dilapidated building of timber construction and bark roof was his brewery during the 1880s.

The partnership of Arthur Baynes and William Hearn ran the Victoria Brewery in Wangaratta from 1877 to 1886.

Victoria Brewery, and after a few years he took on Michael Moloney as a partner.

Dodsworth always seemed to be in financial difficulty, and in 1877 he sold the Victoria Brewery to the partnership of Arthur Baynes and William Hearn. Baynes ran a successful business and won a number of prizes for his beer, including First in the Colony, at the International Exhibition in Melbourne.

Baynes sold the brewery to Edward Hurst & Co. in 1886, and shifted to Benalla. Hurst had been the owner of the Spring Creek Brewery in Beechworth, and had been declared bankrupt earlier that year.

In the meantime, the partnership of Stewart & Dodsworth had been brewing at Dodsworth's Brewery in Templeton Street. They closed that brewery, and purchased the Victoria Brewery only a few months after it had been acquired by Edward Hurst. Dodsworth was now back at the brewery he had started in 1872, but he brewed there again for only one year.

In 1888 it was purchased by A. E. Clark & Co., who built a new brewery adjoining the existing brewery.

When the brewery was let to J. M. Walters later in the same year, John Dodsworth accepted the position as manager, and stayed on in that capacity until his death in 1893 at the age of fifty-five.

The Victoria Brewery Co. Ltd was formed in 1893 to acquire the business and property owned by A. E. Clark, Francis Clark and Robert Wallen. Various managers then operated the brewery: William Halligan; Halligan & Dale; Dockendorf & Dale; McLean & Hannay, followed by Moloney & Dale in December 1903.

Wangaratta Brewery 1853–69
Cnr Mackay & Templeton Streets

The first brewer's licence issued in Wangaratta was granted to James Meldrum in 1853. Seven years later Meldrum was insolvent, and the brewery was closed. The *Ovens and Murray Advertiser* of 22 January 1863 advised that

> Meldrum's Pale Ale was joyously quaffed throughout the length and breadth of the Murray Valley … but Kerferd's Entire has actually flooded the original article [Meldrum's Pale Ale] out of Wangaratta. It is hoped that the brewery, now in new hands, will resume its pristine prosperity.

Kerferd's Entire was brewed at Kerferd's Brewery at the nearby township of Beechworth.

Meldrum's Brewery, was bought by Louis McDermott Ward in 1863, and it was then called the Wangaratta Brewery.

Ward also owned the hotel across the road. He and his barman had a fight with Richard Atlas, nicknamed 'Ham & Eggs'. 'Ham & Eggs' was killed, and Ward and his barman were arrested and taken to Beechworth. Ward died there, awaiting trial — he was only thirty-four years of age. In that year, 1869, the brewery closed again.

Wangaratta Brewery Pty Ltd
See Buffalo Brewery.

Wangaratta Brewing & Malting Co. Ltd 1868–87
Chisholm Street (near Ely Street corner)

The Wangaratta Brewing & Malting Co. Ltd was formed on 2 June 1868, with Henry Kett the chairman and manager, and John Dodsworth the brewer. Four years later Dodsworth left and started his own brewery the Victoria Brewery, which he worked for five years. Then, in 1877, he took over his old workplace, the Wangaratta Brewing & Malting Co., which had failed and had closed. Apparently, Dodsworth didn't operate the brewery, and used a house on the property as his home.

The Wangaratta Brewing & Malting Co. was purchased by Dale, Rundle & O'Neill some time before 1880, and for some years after 1887 the buildings were used only for the storage of chaff and produce by a local grocer. The brewery was destroyed by fire in 1908, and under the foundation stone was found a bottle containing a scroll, still in a well-preserved condition, with the words:

> This scroll was placed under the foundation stone of the Wangaratta Brewing and Malting Company Limited on Saturday, 19th day of September 1868.

Warracknabeal

The town of Warracknabeal derives its name from an Aboriginal word meaning 'large gum trees'. It was relatively late in its settlement, 1885 being the year when the Scott brothers started the Warracknabeal Station. Five years later there was sufficient population in the town and district to justify a brewery.

Federal Brewery 1890–1917
Cnr Phillips & Jamouneau Streets

Shortly after starting the Federal Brewery Peter Stevens transferred the ownership to his son, Ernest. The original building was a flourmill, and two storeys were added to meet the requirements of the gravity system of brewing.

A 17 March 1893 advertisement of P. R. Stevens & Sons offered 'Superior Pure Ale', but mineral waters, and lemonade, soda water, ginger ale and ginger beer were also made on the premises. Beer and soft drinks were delivered by horse and cart to local hotels, and by rail to customers in Beulah, Hopetoun, Roseberry, Sheep Hills, Minyip, and many other townships in north-western Victoria. Additional business was picked up at race meetings, picnics and clearing sales.

Peter Stevens had also owned another Federal Brewery, which operated at Horsham from 1874 to 1907.

Warrnambool

The area between Warrnambool and Port Fairy, on the south-west coast of Victoria, has been considered to be one of the richest belts of farming land in Australia. Through the latter half of the nineteenth century, there was also considerable industrial development in Warrnambool. There were tanneries, flourmills, soap works, bacon factories, boot factories, a meat cannery and four breweries, all of which have long since gone.

Corio Brewery 1865–88
Cnr Raglan Parade & Liebeg Street

The Corio Brewery was opened for business in May 1865 by John Smith, licensee of the Flying Buck Hotel. Two years later the new owner of the brewery, John Rowley, advertised in the *Warrnambool Examiner* of 8 October 1867: 'XXX Ale and Stout in bulk and bottled in splendid condition, pronounced the best and purest. Colonial Ale on tap at every respectable hotel within 50 miles of Warrnambool'. Rowley was a member of the local council for twenty-four years.

After ten years or so John Rowley decided to stop making beer, and specialised in the production of hop beer, aerated waters and cordials.

Cutts' Brewery 1851–52
Timor Street

James Cutts's attempt at brewing lasted a year, then the brewery closed. Three years later an editorial in the *Warrnambool Examiner* of 27 November 1855 reported that

> a brewery is about to be established in this town on the premises known as Cutts' old brewery in Timor Street … About five years ago there used to be a brewery in the town.

The report was premature, since no new brewery was started that year or the next.

New Brewery
See Sheldrick's Brewery.

Sheldrick's Brewery 1869–1922
North-east corner of Timor & Fairy Streets

During May 1868 a syndicate of hotel owners formed the Warrnambool New Brewery Co. Ltd. They planned to set up the brewery in Burt's Bacon Curing Works at the corner of Timor and Fairy Streets, but by September the following year the company was in liquidation. This was a most unfavourable beginning for a brewery that was to continue in business for the next fifty-three years.

Two members of the original syndicate, Walter Sheldrick and Thomas Price, converted the substantial stone buildings of the old bacon-curing works into a brewery, and they traded as Sheldrick's Brewery, although the name New Brewery was often used.

The business was highly successful. When Walter Sheldrick died in 1876, Thomas Price continued in control of the brewery until his death in 1891.

The new owners were E. Hutton, R. Sheldrick and W. Twigg; the managers of various departments were: R. Sheldrick, brewing; E. Price, bottling, and also accountant; Heydeck and Heard, cooperage; Richter, traveller; Mitchell, engineer; Kelton, cellarman; and Robinson, groom.

During 1892 many additions and alterations were carried out to cater for the increasing demand. Later that year R. Sheldrick decided to leave the company. He sold his interest in the brewery to Edward (Ted) Price, the son of the founding partner, Thomas Price. At that time twelve men were employed, and the annual wages bill was £2000.

By the turn of the century James McGee was connected with the company, and about 1911 the partners were known to be Ted Price and Mrs F. M. McGee. Her sons, William and Alex McGee, were wine-and-spirit merchants, and were also active at the brewery.

The year 1916 saw the McGee brothers running the brewery, but by 1922 Sheldrick's Pale Ale was only a memory.

Warrnambool Brewing & Malting Co. 1866–1911
Timor Street, east

The old store of Stevens & Denny was bought by W. Martin & Sons in 1866, and with much pride and care it was converted to the Western Brewery. The following year the Martins sold to Edmund Wheeler, who put an advertisement in the *Warrnambool Examiner* of 8 October 1867: 'Imperial Pale Ale and Extra Stout, orders by post promptly attended to. Edmund Wheeler, Western Brewery'.

Advertisements were also placed in the *Banner of Belfast* (Port Fairy): 'Western Brewery, Timor Street, Warrnambool, Edmund Wheeler. Western Pale Ale for private families and Prime Stout as recommended by the Faculty for Invalids'.

After Wheeler left in 1875, various owners came and went, very few lasting for more than a few years. One of them, Arthur Baynes, left in 1877 to take over the Victoria Brewery in Wangaratta.

The name Western Brewery was changed to the Warrnambool Brewery when the Crawford brothers took over in 1885.

Dennis O'Driscoll sold the Warrnambool Brewery

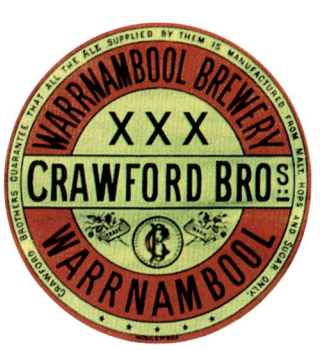

Warrnambool Brewery, Crawford Brothers, 1885–86.

in 1890 to George Wilcox and Daniel Hodgens, who formed the Warrnambool Brewing & Malting Co.

Wilcox left during 1891, and the following year D. Hodgens, son of Daniel, became the proprietor.

Western Brewery

W. Martin & Sons	1866–67
Edmund Wheeler	1867–75
W. Hill	1875
Arthur Baynes	1875–77
August Landmann	1880
Landmann & Mitchell	1880–85

Warrnambool Brewery

J. & E. Crawford	1885–86, insolvent
Dennis O'Driscoll	1886–90

Warrnambool Brewing & Malting Co.

Wilcox & Hodgens	1890–91
D. Hodgens	1891–1911

Warrnambool New Brewery Co. Ltd
See Sheldrick's Brewery.

Western Brewery
See Warrnambool Brewing & Malting Co.

Wodonga

Wodonga was first settled in the 1830s, but the population remained small and was spread over a wide area of sheep-grazing country. In 1973 Wodonga was proclaimed the Rural City of Wodonga.

Wildman, W.   1870–75
Sydney Road

Wodonga Brewery   1889–98
Hume Street (now Church Street)

After selling his breweries in Corowa, NSW, and Wahgunya, Victoria, Dennis Hallahan moved to Wodonga, and began brewing there in 1889. Later that year he sold the brewery to W. D. Bush, and stayed on as the brewer for a number of years, working for new owners as they took over.

Dennis Hallahan	1889
W. D. Bush	1889–90
L. D. Winkelman	1890–91
Patrick Flanagan	1891–95
J. R. Martin & A. Wilcox (lessee)	1895–96
Patrick Flanagan	1896–98

Woodend

Evans, John   c. 1862

Woods Point

Alpine Brewery   1861–69

Patrick (Paddy) Perkins had arrived in Australia with his father, Thomas, and his brothers, James and Thomas Jnr, in 1855. They had some success on the Ballarat and Bendigo goldfields, and later as storekeepers and brewers in Castlemaine. In years to come Paddy was to achieve fame and fortune as a brewer in Queensland.

Paddy and James moved to Jamieson, Victoria, and became hotelkeepers there, but they shifted to Wood's Point soon after, where business opportunities were much better. It was here in the high rugged mountainous country that Paddy started his Alpine Brewery, trading as Perkins & Co.

Paddy, later the Hon. Patrick Perkins, became the mayor of the newly-formed Borough of Wood's Point, but after eight years he moved to settle permanently in Queensland. Before shifting, he had purchased and closed the Wood's Point Brewery Co. Ltd.

Mountain Brewery   1863–92
Scott Street

A notice appeared in the *Wood's Point Times* of 1 March 1865:

> Mountain Brewery – Wood's Point and Gaffney's Creek. Messrs. Mountford & Co., Ale and Porter Brewers, beg to announce ... extensive alterations in their premises ... prepared to furnish their customers with an article superior to any yet produced in the colony.

The owner of the Mountain Brewery was Charles Mountford, who had started brewing at Woods Point in October 1863. He was also the owner of the local Bridge Inn and Store, as well as the Mountain Brewery at Gaffney's Creek, 20 km to the north. Mountford advertised again in the *Wood's Point Times* in April 1866: 'excellent ale and stout in bottles, always on hand, at 20 shillings per dozen'.

Later that year the brewery was offered for sale, but there were no ready buyers until about 1875, when Peter Simpson took over. He left a year later, after selling to the cordial-maker H. Palling.

Mrs Mary Palling owned the brewery from 1888 to 1892.

Wood's Point Brewery Co. Ltd 1865–66

The first report, by the local *Wood's Point Times*, of the Wood's Point Brewery Company's new beer, although favourable, did not give the reader any assurance as to the quality of the beer: The report said:

> making an allowance for the newness of the casks, etc., we must say that the sample of beer which we tasted was very excellent and we doubt not but that it will be improved upon.

Two weeks later, in the same newspaper:

> its products do not seem to have supplanted in public esteem that of its older brother, the hotel-keepers and the public, appearing to recognise the principle, and reduce it to practice, of no one like an old friend.

Still not a very good report. The older brother referred to was the nearby Alpine Brewery. A week later, however, the beer was apparently much better: 'We believe a much better sample of ale has been produced this week than previously disposed of'.

The Wood's Point Brewery Co. Ltd was registered on 13 April 1865, but by October that year the brewery was in difficulty, and it was decided to wind up the company.

A local mining syndicate tried unsuccessfully to run the brewery, and in June 1866 Perkins & Co. of the local Alpine Brewery took over and closed the brewery.

Yackandandah

This attractive old goldmining town, with its avenue of English trees and verandahed buildings, is classified by the National Trust.

Crystal Springs Brewery 1857–82

The brewery was first known as the Yackandandah Brewery, and there were three owners in as many years: Samuel Berwick in 1857, and then Edward Lancaster later that year tried to sell the brewery by advertising in the *Ovens and Murray Advertiser* in September 1857; by 1859 Alfred Lawton was the owner.

The address of the brewery was simply 'On the township flat'.

When Flynn & Unmack took over in 1860, they changed the name to the Crystal Springs Brewery. The premises had been unoccupied, since most of the building had burnt down a year earlier. Lawrence Unmack had the brewery rebuilt, and brewing continued for the next twenty-two years.

CURIOSITIES OF ANCIENT BREWING

The following collection of quaint recipes and advice to brewers of 300 years ago is exceedingly curious and in this scientific age, can only be read with amusement.

The brewers, as a class, were superstitious, which the following, found in a work written by Johann Colery in 1593, will readily prove:-

> To prevent beer from turning sour, open the bung of the barrel, take a fresh laid egg, put it in a small linen bag together with a few hops and a few grains of barley, tie the bag up and hang it in the bung-hole. Then drive the bung in tightly and the beer will never sour as long as there is a drop left.
>
> To prevent beer from getting flat, put a little salt in a linen cloth and wrap the bung in it before driving it in.
>
> The putting of a few peach leaves in the barrel will make the beverage most beneficial to the kidneys and will also remove worms.
>
> A good thing for all breweries to do is to write a verse from the Bible and have it blessed by the priest during mass, then nail it on the outside of the barrel, or in any secret place in the brewery. It will prevent witchcraft from having any power over the brewery.
>
> A brewer who desires to sell a large quantity of beer, must get the thumb of a man that has been hung, tie it to a string and hang it in his brewing kettle.
>
> Thistles laid on a beer barrel prevent refermentation during a thunder storm.
>
> The drinking of beer with oak leaves in it will prevent poisoning from snake bites.
>
> Those who drink beer in Lent will not be troubled by mosquitoes.
>
> Water must never be drunk during Lent, for anyone who does not drink beer, but does drink water during that time will surely die before the year ends.

Australian Brewers' Journal, November 1891

Sheffield's Brewery 1870–c. 1871
In March 1870 J. Sheffield brewed in a small wooden building on the town site of Commissioner's Creek, and 'made casks from timber from Hillsborough'.

John Hattersley, the local soda-water manufacturer, took over the brewery in 1871, but made very little beer.

Wardley & Potts c. 1855
In January 1855 the brewery, owned by Wardley & Potts, was advertised for sale. Its location was given as 'up the Creek', which would be Upper Yackandandah, or 'Yack' as it was referred to by the locals.

Yackandandah Brewery
See Crystal Springs Brewery.

Yarrawonga

Anglo-Australian Brewery Co. Pty Ltd 1886–1912
Hunt Street

The Anglo-Australian Brewery Co. Pty Ltd took over the brewery that had been started by James Gibson in 1886. The company also acquired other breweries at Tallangatta and Beechworth, and a branch depot operated at Rutherglen in the early 1900s.

Yarrawonga Brewery 1885–1907
John Crisp had been in the Royal Navy before coming to Melbourne in 1854. He spent twenty years in Maldon as a butcher, and then became involved in mining speculation. He won numerous prizes as a marksman when he was a member of the 2nd Castlemaine Rifle Corps. In 1877 he went to Wahgunyah, and entered into a partnership with his father-in-law, William Thorne, before settling in Yarrawonga in 1885.

John Crisp built his Yarrawonga Brewery near the bank of the Murray River, on the western side of the town, and used the river-water for his beer. Meticulous in his habits, he watched over the production of every batch of beer, which he sold for 6d a bottle. Stout was 7d, and both were of excellent quality.

After John Crisp died in December 1894 his widow, Eliza, carried on the business with the assistance of her sons, Walter, Charles and Fred. The *Australian Brewers' Journal* of September 1896 included an editorial:

> Mr Walter Crisp of the Yarrawonga Brewery is proud of the beer he produces from the River Murray water and sent us some for our opinion. The member of our staff who is paid to drink beer was highly pleased with Mr Crisp's production and, like Oliver Twist, had the impudence to ask for more.

In the late 1890s Fred Crisp was lucky to survive a near-fatal accident at the brewery. He was washing out a cask using steam with a pressure of 50 pounds when the cask exploded, causing severe and critical scalding.

Business for the Crisp family prospered until the Victorian government introduced restricted hotel trading in the early 1900s. Within a few years half the hotels in the district, and the brewery, had closed.

Queensland

Unlike most of the other Australian colonies where breweries quickly followed the first settlements, many years went by before Queensland had its first brewery. In fact, the capital city, Brisbane, had only three breweries in its first fifty years, with only one remaining at the end of that period.

The surveyor, John Oxley, was sent by the Governor of New South Wales, Sir Thomas Brisbane, to explore the area around Moreton Bay to find a suitable site for a penal colony. In 1824 the first batch of convicts was sent to what is now the north Brisbane suburb of Redcliffe. Early the following year, lack of water and the hostility of the Aboriginal people forced the colony to move about 30 km upstream to the present site of Brisbane.

Between 1826 and 1830 the garrison commander, Patrick Logan, drew up a plan for the budding town, but by 1839 the colony was abandoned, and squatters were then legally free to move into the area. The first land sales were held in 1842, but growth was very slow. The early 1840s were plagued with drought and disease, but the Moreton Bay pioneers survived. In 1846, when the population was only 346, their own newspaper, the *Moreton Bay Courier*, came into being.

The First Brewery

Queensland's first brewery was known simply as the Brisbane Brewery. It was started by John Beach in 1853, and was located in Queen Street, then called North Brisbane. Beach had been in the drapery business, and in 1855 he was advertising soap, beer and yeast for sale. He brewed for three years, and was then declared insolvent. Only two other breweries started in Brisbane before 1880. The City Brewery was operating in Mary Street in 1864, and the Castlemaine Brewery began brewing at the inner Brisbane suburb of Milton in 1878.

Gold

Queensland had been part of New South Wales until 1859 when Sir George Bowen arrived as the first governor of the newly-proclaimed colony of Queensland, named in honour of Queen Victoria. In 1853 traces of gold were found in the Port Curtis region, which covered a wide area from present-day Gladstone up to Rockhampton. Some years later modest discoveries occurred in other areas, but the big rush to Queensland started in October 1867. A prospector in the Wide Bay district had come across some 'colour' — a small indication of the presence of gold, and within a few hours he had found so much gold that he decided to inform the commissioner at Maryborough. Soon, half the population of the town had staked their claims. Struggling settlers left their farms, diggers swarmed in from the south, and a mass of shanties appeared at the newly-founded township of Gympie. Within a year two breweries were busily brewing in the shanty town, unable to cope with the demand.

The pastoral industry became firmly established in the colony, and agriculture, particularly the cultivation of sugarcane, flourished along the coastal areas, where towns such as Cairns, Townsville and Rockhampton quickly developed into important regional centres. As these and other towns were settled, most supported one or more breweries at one time or another.

Country Breweries

The first Queensland country brewery began in 1860 at the coastal town of Rockhampton; and four more were to follow in later years. Toowoomba had its first brewery in 1869, and many more followed in other townships during the 1880s. The population of the colony in 1860 was 23,500, and by 1880 the number had grown to 211,000. The most populated areas in the 1880s were Brisbane where nine breweries were in business, Townsville had four, and Bundaberg, Cooktown, Gympie, Mackay, Maryborough, Rockhampton and Toowoomba each had two breweries during that decade. The peak was reached during the 1890s when thirty-two breweries were operating in twenty-seven Queensland country towns. By 1910 there were only nine.

Brisbane

The capital city, Brisbane, had fewer breweries by far than any other Australian capital city except Darwin. In total, only twelve breweries have existed in Brisbane, of which nine were operating in the 1880s, and only five by the turn of the century. This pattern of gradual decline was consistent with the trend throughout Australia, and only two major breweries now operate in Queensland. One of these is Carlton & United Breweries Ltd, which acquired the Queensland Brewing Co. Ltd in 1961. The brewery was subsequently closed

THE POPULATION OF AUSTRALIA

The Victorian Premier lately called upon Mr. Hayter, the Government Statist, to furnish an approximate return, showing what will be the probable population of the Australian colonies in 100 years from date (*i.e.*, the year 1985).

Mr. Hayter based his calculations on the same rate of increase in population as actually occurred between 1871 and 1881.

At the end of 1884, the population of the colonies stood at 3,247,365. It is estimated, that by the year 1984, the population will reach 108,246,657.

Australian Brewers' Journal, February 1885

following the takeover of the Power Brewing Co. Ltd in 1993. Brewing continues at this modern plant, located at Yatala, 70 km south of Brisbane.

The City Brewery, which began in Mary Street, Brisbane in 1864, was taken over by Paddy Perkins in 1872. It was later floated as Perkins & Co. Ltd, and the brewery became one of the largest and most profitable in Queensland. On 1 August 1928 Perkins City Brewery amalgamated with the Castlemaine Brewery, Brisbane, to form Castlemaine Perkins Ltd. The Castlemaine Brewery, located in the inner Brisbane suburb of Milton, had started in 1878, and was one of a chain of Castlemaine breweries established across Australia. The first was at Castlemaine, Victoria.

Tradition

In February 1928 the now-famous Castlemaine XXXX Bitter Ale was introduced, and the characteristic yellow label with a picture of the brewery in the background has remained virtually unchanged since that time. Castlemaine XXXX Bitter Ale, or simply 4X, has become very much a part of Queensland's heritage and one of Australia's most popular beers.

Barcaldine

The central Queensland town of Barcaldine, which was established in 1886 with the arrival of the central railway line, is historically significant as being the centre of the shearers' strike of 1891. About 400 men, striking against the use of non-union labour in the sheds, formed camps on the outskirts of the town. The dispute resulted in the formation of an organisation that ultimately developed into the Australian Labor Party.

At the same time, the Graziers' Association of Central and Northern Queensland was formed — this later became the modern-day National Party.

Barcaldine Brewing Co. Ltd 1892–1906
Cnr Oak & Myall Streets

A group of local business people planned to start a brewery, and in 1892 the Barcaldine Brewing Co. Ltd was formed, financed by local subscription. The brewery, when completed, was a four storey-building facing the railway line east of town. On 1 August 1892 the manager, Henry Hargan, turned out a sample of the brewery's first beer.

During November 1892 the Governor of Queensland, Sir Henry Norman, visited the brewery, where he was given a tour of inspection. Returning to the first floor, he found a banquet table had been laid out with champagne, but no beer. With some embarrassment, it was explained that the first brew was not quite ready to be tapped. At the opening ceremony, His Excellency expressed regret, stating that he 'much preferred a glass of good beer to the best of wines'.

By January the following year production had reached 19 hogsheads of beer weekly, and supplies were being sent to nearby townships. Unfortunately, although described as having a 'clear, pleasant, slightly bitter taste' by the *Western Champion* newspaper, the beer didn't appeal to the public. Drought and poor-quality bore water were said to be the problems.

Barcaldine became the first town in western Queensland to have reticulated water, but pressure from the bore could not keep up with the demand. During summer the mains had to be turned off at night to allow the bore water to flow into Lagoon Creek for stock watering, and it was not until 1899 that an ample supply of quality water became available. All this had a serious effect on the quality of the beer, and less than two years after production had commenced the brewery closed in June 1894.

The brewery remained closed until November 1897 when W. J. Humphreys and his son took out a five-year lease. Their first beer was ready for sale on 11 December 1897. Humphreys' beer was little better than the earlier production, and competition from the Fitzroy Brewery in Rockhampton forced the brewery to close again. The son, E. H. Humphreys, was the last person to brew at Barcaldine.

Beenleigh

Two Englishmen established the first permanent settlement at Beenleigh about 1865. They began to grow sugarcane on their plantation, which was named Beenleigh in memory of a family estate in Devonshire, England. Today, the district is still noted for its sugarcane and also the production of rum.

Beenleigh Brewery 1886–87

Swedish-born August Thorsborne had a varied career after arriving at Melbourne in 1861. He tried gold-mining in central Victoria, then went to New Zealand, returning soon after to Queensland where he tried gold-mining again, and then took up hotelkeeping at Gympie.

After an unsuccessful attempt at storekeeping, he settled at Beenleigh, and took on contract work in the town. In 1873 he started a cordial factory, which proved to be reasonably successful, and late in 1884 he purchased the Victoria Brewery in Brisbane. When that venture failed, he decided to add a small brewery to his cordial factory at Beenleigh. Due mainly to inexperience, Thorsborne and his sons closed the brewery section of the business with the intention of reopening it at a later date. That never eventuated.

During the limited period of the brewery's operation only 2544 gallons of beer were produced for the period 1 April 1886 to 3 March 1887, as recorded in the Return of Registered Breweries.

Brisbane

Bond Brewing Queensland Ltd
See Castlemaine Perkins Ltd.

Brisbane Brewery 1853–56
Queen Street

Brisbane was named in 1834, although ten years earlier an attempt had been made to establish a penal colony north of Brisbane. Open settlement was declared in 1842, but growth was slow, and by 1846 the population numbered less than 400.

Queensland's first brewery was known simply as the Brisbane Brewery. It was owned and operated by John Stewart Beach, and was located in Queen Street, then called North Brisbane. In September 1849 he started a drapery shop in Queen Street, but sold the business in 1854 in order to devote more time to his Brisbane Brewery. An editorial in the *Moreton Bay Courier* of 6 August 1853 provided some qualified comments:

> Brewing — Mr. J. S. Beach of Brisbane has lately commenced brewing an article very much in request in this climate and one which would no doubt realise handsome profits to the successful producer here — namely beer. The article is very palatable and we trust that Mr Beach's experiments may result in improvement and ultimate success.

Queensland

#	Location	Grid	#	Location	Grid
1	Barcaldine	D8	20	Macrossan	E6
2	Beenleigh	H10	21	Mareeba	D4
3	Brisbane	H10	22	Maryborough	H9
4	Bundaberg	H9	23	Mungindi	F10
5	Cairns	D4	24	Millbong	H10
6	Cawarral	G8	25	Miriwinni	E4
7	Charleville	E9	26	Nerang	H10
8	Charters Towers	E6	27	Owanville	H9
9	Cooktown	D4	28	Reid River	E6
10	Croydon	C5	29	Rockhampton	G8
11	Cunnamulla	E10	30	Roma	F9
12	Eidsvold	G9	31	St George	F10
13	Gympie	H9	32	Stanthorpe	G10
14	Harrisville	H10	33	Thargomindah	D10
15	Herberton	D5	34	Tiaro	H9
16	Hughenden	D6	35	Toowoomba	H10
17	Ipswich	H10	36	Townsville	E6
18	Longreach	D8	37	Warwick	H10
19	Mackay	F7	38	Yatala	H10

There was a similar editorial in the *Sydney Morning Herald* of 29 September 1853.

John Beach placed an advertisement in the *Moreton Bay Courier* of 24 December 1853, which stated: 'Brisbane Brewery, J. S. Beach has now on sale at the brewery a large supply of excellent beer'. He began to extend his business, and in February 1855 he was advertising soap, beer and yeast for sale; later that year he opened a general store. By September he had been declared insolvent, and his assets, which were minimal, were put up for auction.

Somehow, Beach managed to survive and advertised again in the *Moreton Bay Courier,* on 5 January 1856, that he had resumed business and 'hopes, through care and attention, to secure the patronage of those who can appreciate a good glass of beer'. Two months later Beach and his family departed for Sydney.

Bulimba Brewery 1882–83
Oxford Street, Bulimba

R. Tooth was the head of a syndicate that started the Bulimba Brewery in 1882. The business having failed, it went into liquidation, and the property was purchased by the newly-formed Queensland Brewing Co., who erected a new brewery on the site.

See also Queensland Brewing Co. Ltd.

Bulimba Ferry Brewery 1883–92
Vernon Terrace, Newstead

The Bulimba Ferry Brewery was started by West Ablin & Co. It was located in Vernon Street on the west bank of the Brisbane River, a bad position since the brewery was washed away by floods. The brewery was rebuilt in 1887, but the beer never regained its popularity. Following voluntary liquidation of the company in 1892, the brewery was eventually purchased by the Castlemaine Brewery, and closed to prevent a competitor from restarting the brewery.

Carlton & United Breweries Ltd 1961–93
The Valley

The Melbourne-based brewers, Carlton & United Breweries Ltd, purchased all interests of the Queensland Brewing Co. Ltd in 1961. The acquisition included all the hotels and the breweries in Brisbane and Toowoomba.

The brewery in Toowoomba, previously known as the Silverstream Brewery, continued to operate until its closure in 1976. The name of the brewery at Brisbane was changed to Carlton & United Breweries (Queensland) Ltd in November 1971, changing again in 1975 to Carlton & United Breweries Ltd. Following the purchase of Power Brewing Co. Ltd in 1993, the old Valley Brewery was closed, and all CUB and Power beers were then brewed at the Power plant at Yatala, 70 km south of Brisbane.

Carlton & United Breweries (Queensland) Ltd
See Carlton & United Breweries Ltd.

Castlemaine Brewery
See Castlemaine Perkins Ltd.

Castlemaine Brewery & Quinlan, Gray & Co. (Brisbane) Ltd
See Castlemaine Perkins Ltd.

Castlemaine Perkins Ltd 1878–
Milton Road, Milton

In 1871 M. Quinlan and N. Donnelly formed Quinlan, Donnelly & Co., and traded as general merchants and shipping agents. They started with modest capital, but business quickly expanded with the development of the rich pastoral, farming and mining districts of Queensland.

By the late 1870s the business had become quite

An early etching of the Castlemaine Brewery, Brisbane, c. 1880. At that time, it was owned by Fitzgerald, Quinlan & Co.

Gray. In 1888 the Milton Distillery, which had operated alongside the brewery for ten years, was closed.

In 1889 the Castlemaine Brewery became the first brewery in Queensland to produce lager beer, which retailed for sixpence per bottle.

In 1893 the Phoenix Brewing Co. Ltd in Chester Street and the liquidated Bulimba Ferry Brewery were purchased and closed.

On 3 December 1894 the well-known XXXX trade mark was applied for.

After surviving the financial crisis of the 1890s and the disastrous flood that followed, the company decided to off-load its general trading business in 1914 and to concentrate on brewing and the wine-and-spirit agencies it had acquired over the years.

During 1916 the continental method of storage was adopted. Instead of three weeks' storage, three months became standard, resulting in improvement in the quality of the beer. Castlemaine XXX Sparkling Ale had been in production since the company first started in 1878, and in 1916 an extra X was added and XXXX Sparkling Ale was put on the market. The famous Castlemaine XXXX Bitter Ale, with a yellow label, the name in red, and a picture of the brewery in the background, was first introduced in February 1924, and the label style has continued with little change since that time.

1 August 1928 marked the formation of Queensland's largest brewery, Castlemaine Perkins Ltd, with the takeover of Perkins & Co. City Brewery by the Castlemaine Brewery & Quinlan, Gray & Co. (Brisbane) Ltd.

The new company was listed on all eastern states stock exchanges, and the acquisition of Perkins & Co. included their two breweries, the City Brewery in Mary Street, Brisbane, and the Downs Brewery at Toowoomba. Included in the purchase agreement was the trade of nineteen freehold hotels and fifty leasehold hotels. The City Brewery was closed, but the Downs Brewery continued to operate at Toowoomba until 1958.

In November 1979 Castlemaine Perkins Ltd merged its operations with those of the Sydney-based brewer, Toohey's Ltd, to form Castlemaine Tooheys Ltd. Six years later, in August 1985, the new company was taken over by Bond Corporation Holdings Ltd, owner of the Swan Brewery in Perth, and the business then traded as Bond Brewing Queensland Ltd. The company then owned the Swan Brewery in Perth, Toohey's Brewery in Sydney, and Castlemaine Perkins Brewery in Brisbane. All of these breweries were taken over from Bond Corporation by the New Zealand brewer, Lion Nathan, in October 1990, and the three Australian breweries were then operated by National Brewing Holdings Ltd.

Today, Castlemaine XXXX Bitter Ale remains one of Australia's most popular beers, and the name and product are very much a part of Queensland's heritage.

substantial, and the partners considered opening a brewery in Brisbane. They began negotiations with the Fitzgerald brothers, Edward and Nicholas, of the well-known Castlemaine Brewery in Victoria, a wise choice for a partner since Castlemaine breweries were already successfully established in Castlemaine, and also in Melbourne, Sydney and Newcastle.

Meanwhile, there were changes to the Quinlan & Donnelly partnership. Donnelly had sold out to Quinlan, who died soon after, and his widow, Kate, took in George Gray as a partner. They traded as Quinlan & Gray, and went ahead with the brewery proposal. In 1877 Fitzgerald, Quinlan & Co. was formed. The partners were Edward and Nicholas Fitzgerald of Victoria, Robert Prendergast of Sydney, and Kate Quinlan and George Gray of Brisbane. The newly-formed company purchased the Milton Distillery (established in 1870) from Robert Forsyth in September 1877, and they built the Castlemaine Brewery on land adjoining the distillery.

The first batch of beer was ready for sale on 13 September 1878. It was called Castlemaine XXX Sparkling Ale, and was described by the *Brisbane Courier* as 'a delicious ale of the brightest amber, pleasant to the taste'. The company's advertisement read: 'Ale and Porter, equal in general quality to the famed Castlemaine Ale so popular for many years in the southern colonies'.

In 1880 the company was the first in Queensland to install a telephone line, which linked their brewery at the suburb of Milton to their city offices in Queen Street. The business, frequently referred to as the Milton Brewery in the early years, was highly successful, and on 5 August 1887 the Castlemaine Brewery & Quinlan, Gray & Co. (Brisbane) Ltd was incorporated, with shares being oversubscribed by 60 per cent. The new company, generally called the Castlemaine Brewery for simplicity, acquired the assets of two businesses: Fitzgerald, Quinlan & Co., which owned the brewery, and the well-established wine-and-spirit business of Quinlan &

On 1 August 1928 Perkins & Co. City Brewery was taken over by the Castlemaine Brewery to form Castlemaine Perkins Ltd.

Castlemaine Brewery (Fitzgerald, Quinlan & Co.)	1878–87
Castlemaine Brewery (Castlemaine Brewery & Quinlan, Gray & Co. (Brisbane) Ltd)	1887–1928
Phoenix Brewery and Bulimba Ferry Breweries purchased	1893, closed
Castlemaine Perkins Ltd Formed by the merger of Perkins & Co. City Brewery, and the Castlemaine Brewery	1928–79
Castlemaine Toohey's Ltd Formed by the merger of Castlemaine Perkins Ltd and Toohey's Ltd	1979–85
Bond Brewing Queensland Ltd Bond Corporation Holdings Ltd: now controlling Swan Brewery, Perth; Castlemaine Brewery, Brisbane; and Toohey's Brewery, Sydney	1985–90
National Brewing Holdings Ltd Now control Swan, Castlemaine and Toohey's breweries	1990–

City Brewery　　　　1864–1928
Mary Street

Patrick (Paddy) Perkins and his brother, Thomas, arrived in Victoria with their families in 1855. Paddy began his career as a barman at the Victorian township of Kyneton in 1856, and subsequently became involved in merchandising. For a brief period, he held a small interest in the Castlemaine Brewery in Victoria, and was also the owner of the Alpine Brewery at Wood's Point, Victoria, for two years.

The Perkins brothers moved to Queensland, and built the Downs Brewery at Toowoomba in 1868. The business prospered, and Paddy went to Brisbane several years later, becoming involved in real estate, hotels and politics. Eager to expand their brewing interests into the large Brisbane market, in 1872 the brothers purchased the brewery of Stanbridge & Harrison, founded in 1864; they traded as Perkins & Co. City Brewery.

With their successful Downs Brewery at Toowoomba, and an already-established brewery in Brisbane, the brothers held a virtual monopoly in the beer trade for the whole of Queensland. There were no other breweries in Brisbane at that time, and only two others in country Queensland, both at Gympie.

William Gooley was the manager of the City Brewery in 1876, and in the ensuing years he had much to do with the growth and success of the business. Included in their range of products was the popular Perkins XXX Bitter Ale.

Thomas Perkins died in 1879. Two years later the business was floated as Perkins & Co. Ltd. Paddy retained 25 per cent of the shareholding, and the breweries at Toowoomba and Brisbane were extensively upgraded. New brands of ale were released, and by 1885 the City Brewery was arguably the largest and most profitable in Queensland. However, the depression years of the 1890s seriously affected the business, causing the company to be wound up and reconstructed in 1894.

Gradually trade and profit improved, and by 1901 the company was operating depots at Cairns, Townsville, Bowen, Mackay, Rockhampton and Bundaberg along the east coast. Inland, depots were located at Winton, Barcaldine, Charleville and Cunnamulla. Business was booming for the City Brewery, and a record was achieved for the month of December 1905 when the output of bottled beer reached 276,000 bottles.

By the 1920s business began to decline again. Fierce competition from the popular Castlemaine XXXX Bitter Ale contributed to the fall-off in sales, and Perkins City Brewery tried to upstage their competitor by putting out a XXXXX beer.

On 1 August 1928 Perkins & Co. Ltd was taken over by the Castlemaine Brewery & Quinlan, Gray & Co. (Brisbane) Ltd. The acquisition included the Downs Brewery in Toowoomba, the City Brewery in Brisbane, and a large number of freehold and leasehold hotels. The new company continued to operate the Downs Brewery, but the City Brewery was closed and subsequently demolished. Later, the site became a garage for Telecom.

The partnership of Stanbridge & Harrison had started Queensland's second brewery in Mary Street, Brisbane, in 1864. Eight years later the Perkins brothers purchased the brewery, and traded as Perkins & Co. City Brewery.

Stanbridge & Harrison	1864–72
City Brewery	
Perkins & Co.	1872–81
Perkins & Co. Ltd	1881–1928
Taken over by Castlemaine Brewery & Quinlan, Gray & Co. (Brisbane) Ltd	1928

Eclipse Brewing Co.　　c. 1889–c. 1918
Wickham Street, Fortitude Valley/cnr Grey & Tribune Streets, South Brisbane

The brewery was first located in Fortitude Valley. After ten years the owner, Timothy Lane, shifted the operation to South Brisbane.

The business was taken over by Richard Early, who retired in 1917, and Frank Early then ran the brewery for another year.

Lion Brewery　　　　1889
Spring Hill

The partners in the business were Edmeades & Wright.

Milton Brewery
See Castlemaine Perkins Ltd.

Perkins & Co. Ltd
See City Brewery.

Phoenix Brewing Co. Ltd   1887–93
Cnr Chester & Leopold Streets, Fortitude Valley

First known as the Valley Brewery Co. in 1887, the name was changed to the Phoenix Brewing Co. Ltd a year later. Walter Lanfear, formerly the brewer at the Queensland Brewing Co. Ltd, was the proprietor in 1890, and J. F. Nicol was a partner for a short period.

In July 1892 the company adopted the system of artificial carbonation that many Australian breweries were using to make beer at that time.

The Castlemaine Brewery, Brisbane, bought the Phoenix in 1893, and closed it.

Queensland Brewery Co.
See Queensland Brewing Co. Ltd.

Queensland Brewing Co. Ltd   1882–1961
Brunswick Street, New Farm

The Bulimba Brewery, as it was first known, was built in 1882 on the east bank of the Brisbane River near the ferry. It had good wharfage facilities, and was part-owned and managed by R. Tooth, who went into liquidation in 1883. The newly-formed Queensland Brewery Co. acquired the property and equipment, and built a new brewery on the site, appointing Henry Bolton as managing director, and Walter Lanfear in charge of the brewing. The brewery officially opened on 24 November 1883, and the daily output of beer soon reached 50 hogsheads, a considerable quantity for Brisbane at the time. Because of its earlier name, the brewery continued to be referred to as the Bulimba Brewery until well into the twentieth century.

Early in 1885 the Queensland Brewery Co. was sold to the Queensland Brewing Co. Ltd for £55,490, and the shares, which were offered in Victoria, New South Wales and Queensland, were quickly secured. On 6 May 1887 the Queensland Brewing Co. Ltd was registered, twenty-eight years after the state of Queensland was granted self-government.

Substantial losses were incurred in 1890, and there was even talk of winding up the company. Three years later disastrous floods washed away a portion of the brewery, causing a financial crisis. Then there were more problems in 1896 when a price war between breweries took a heavy toll on the company's profits. During 1898 the company began to pasteurise its bottled beer, and the introduction of Gold Top Pale Ale that year saw a gradual return to profitability.

At that time the excise duty for bottled beer was 6d per dozen bottles. This increased progressively over the years to: 1s in 1915; 2s in 1918; 3s 6d in 1920; 5s 6d in 1940; 6s in 1941; 9s 2d in 1945; 14s 4d in 1952; and 19s 8d in 1956.

The company had purchased property in Brunswick Street, New Farm, previously used by Cameron & Co. as a tobacco factory. After much renovation and upgrading of the equipment, brewing operations

The Old Brewery — the original premises of the Queensland Brewing Co. Ltd. It was located on the east bank of the Brisbane River, near the ferry, and commanded a view of the Bulimba Reach. In the early years it was called the Bulimba Brewery.

were shifted to this large three-storey brick building. As it was close to Fortitude Valley, the locals and the media frequently referred to it as the Valley Brewery. The old brewery at Bulimba was sold in 1906 to Dalgety & Co. Ltd as valuable wharf-frontage property.

On 21 January 1908 the company suffered a severe loss when fire destroyed all of the stock and much of the equipment. The bottle department was completely gutted, and all the malt, hops and sugar were ruined by water. The refrigeration plant was destroyed, but fortunately much of the building structure remained intact. Rebuilding was slow and costly.

The Elizabeth Street offices, and the wine-and-spirit department, were moved to Queen Street in 1914. In 1923 the company purchased the Silverstream Brewery in Toowoomba, and built a new modern brewery on the site. A vital period in the company's history began in 1934 when the directors embarked on a policy of purchasing freehold hotels across the state of Queensland, ensuring outlets for the products of their Toowoomba and Brisbane breweries.

According to company records, the first rise in the price of beer for thirty years occurred in 1950, and it was another seven years before a further increase. A new bottling plant was installed with a capacity of 1200 dozen bottles per hour, and for the first time since 1942 in the state of Queensland bottled beer then became freely available, and not on quota.

In 1956 the company purchased the remaining properties adjoining their Brisbane premises, making it

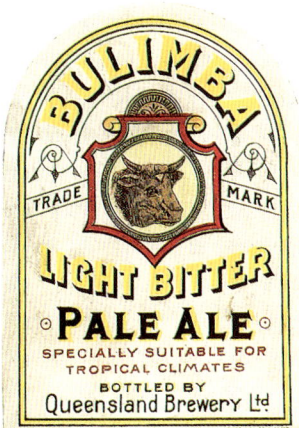

Label used by the Queensland Brewery Co. Ltd, shortly after its formation in 1885. It is interesting to note that, at that time, a Light Bitter was being produced.

Two views of the Queensland Brewing Co. Ltd.

Above: The original building in Brunswick Street, New Farm. The name Valley Brewery was commonly used at that time.

Left: The names Valley Brewery and Bulimba Brewery were used synonymously for the Queensland Brewing Co. Ltd. After extensions, the buildings now include an additional storey.

The Queensland Brewing Co. Ltd first introduced Gold Top Pale Ale in 1898.

Bulimba Brewery	1882–83
Queensland Brewery Co.	1883–85
Queensland Brewery Co. Ltd	1885–1961
(location changed to Brunswick Street, New Farm, 1906)	
Silverstream Brewery, Toowoomba, purchased	1923
Carlton & United Breweries Ltd	1961–71
Acquired the Queensland Brewery Co. Ltd breweries at Brisbane and Toowoomba	
Carlton & United Breweries (Queensland) Ltd (name change)	1971–75
Carlton & United Breweries Ltd	1975–93
Brewery at Toowoomba closed	1976
Brewery at New Farm, Brisbane, closed	1993
All brewing operations then transferred to Carlton & United Breweries Ltd brewery, Yatala	

the owner of the entire block bounded by Brunswick, Martin and Curphey Streets.

Carlton & United Breweries Ltd, Melbourne, acquired all the interests of the Queensland Brewery Co. Ltd in 1961, including all hotels and the breweries in Toowoomba and Brisbane. In November 1971 the name was changed to Carlton & United Breweries (Queensland) Ltd, and in 1975 the word 'Queensland' was deleted.

The brewery was closed in 1993 following the acquisition by CUB of the Power Brewing Co. Ltd, Yatala, 70 km south of Brisbane.

Stanbridge & Harrison
See City Brewery.

Terrier Brewing Co.   1883–98
North Quay

Robert Bond had worked at a number of breweries in Tasmania, and in 1883 he decided to start a brewery of his own in Brisbane.

In the meantime, John Hocker had been the proprietor of the Victoria Brewery at Kangaroo Point, Brisbane, and in 1884 he sold the brewery to August Thorsborne, cordial-maker of Beenleigh. Thorsborne may not have worked the brewery for very long, if at all. The next owner was Robert Bond, and in August 1896 he changed the name to the Terrier Brewing Co. The old name, Victoria Brewery, was misleading since the brewery was in Queensland.

The brewery closed in 1898, and the equipment was sold to the Licensed Victuallers' Brewery Co. Ltd in Gympie the following year. Three years later Robert Bond and his son, George, started another brewery at Gympie, also called the Terrier Brewing Co.

Valley Brewery
See Queensland Brewing Co. Ltd.

Valley Brewery Co.
See Phoenix Brewing Co. Ltd

Victoria Brewery
See Terrier Brewing Co.

West End Brewery Ltd   1886–1913
Montague Road, West End

A brewery was started by Albert Lanfear and George Nicol in 1886, and two years later the partners formed the West End Brewing & Malting Co. Ltd. Very soon the company was shipping 120 hogsheads of beer to northern ports each week, and their trade in Shamrock Stout was steadily increasing.

It was reported that two men were suffocated in a well at the West End Brewery on 3 December 1889. The well was 65 feet deep, and when the men climbed down to test the depth of water they were overcome by foul air. Doctors succeeded in saving the rescuers, who were also overcome by fumes, but the first two men were beyond recovery.

Above: *The West End Brewery, 1886.*
Below: *The brewery suffered from severe floods in 1889. After reconstruction in 1890 it was again badly damaged by a cyclone. Brewing ceased in 1913.*

> ## FATALITY AT A BRISBANE BREWERY
>
> Two men were suffocated in a well at the West-End Brewery, Brisbane, on the evening of the third inst., and one or two others had a narrow escape.
>
> The well had been sunk 60 feet and it contained about 14 feet of water; but operations were discontinued owing to the presence of foul air. The men were discharged during the afternoon but two of them, John Lennon and William Rees, remained on the premises and got into a dispute about the depth of the water. Lennon went down the well to investigate and Rees followed, but the latter only went as far as the staging, some distance above the water level.
>
> Cries for assistance were shortly afterwards heard and the cooper, Samuel Milman, descended into the well. He immediately became overpowered and fell into the water. John Hughes, a pupil at the brewery, then went to the men's assistance, but was unable to rescue them.
>
> McBride, the contractor, was let down the well, found Rees lying on the staging and brought him up insensible. McBride again went down and recovered Milman's body and, descending a third time, brought up Lennon's body. The doctors succeeded in bringing Rees around, but in the other two cases, life was extinct.
>
> *Australian Brewers' Journal*, December 1889

The brewery was rebuilt in 1890, having suffered from floods that washed away the rear section of the building and 500 hogsheads of beer. After reconstruction the West End Brewery Ltd was formed to take over the assets of the brewery and also the wine-and-spirit business, all of which had been the property of the partners Lanfear and Nicol.

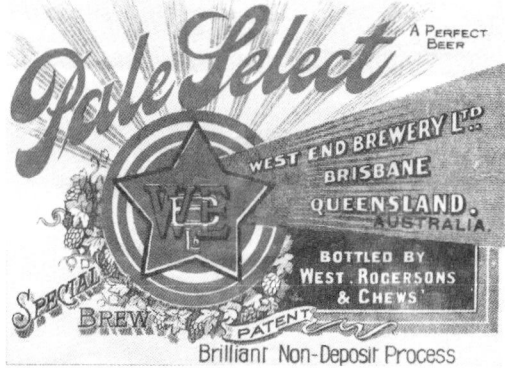

During 1906 the defunct North Queensland Brewing Co. Ltd at Mareeba was taken over with the idea of reopening it as another West End brewery, but the plan was abandoned.

Business and profit gradually declined, and in 1913 there was an unsuccessful attempt to take over the West End Brewery to form the proposed Co-operative Brewery of Queensland. A few months later the buildings were purchased by the Brisbane Bottle Exchange Co.

West End Brewing & Malting Co. Ltd
See West End Brewery Ltd.

Bundaberg

The growing of sugarcane is Bundaberg's principal industry. The first distillery was built in 1888, and Bundaberg has gained more recognition for its production of rum than the brewing of beer. The request for a 'Bundy and Coke' has been a familiar call for generations, and although brewing has long since ceased the town did produce a lot of beer.

Bundaberg Brewery Co. Ltd   1888–1932
Cnr Princess & Brewery Streets, East Bundaberg

Having sold his interest in the City Brewery, Bundaberg, to his partner Lionel Fleming, Gustav Steindl built another brewery and began business on his own in 1888, trading as the Bundaberg Brewery.

In 1893 the Bundabery Brewery was flooded, and larger premises were built on higher ground. They consisted of four main buildings, two of which were two storey. There was an underground cellar, and at the front of the brewery, in what is now Tomlin Street, there was a tall arched gateway with the words 'Bundaberg Brewery' in wrought iron at the top. The front fence had a top rail where farmers hitched their horses.

Pasteurised lager, bitter ale, light ale and stout were sold in bulk and also in 'recessed-bottom' green bottles. Labels were applied by hand. The company also bottled brandy and other products under the Seppelt label.

Gustav Steindl won four medals in a Commonwealth brewing competition conducted in 1894, and his ale and lager were considered to be among the best in the country.

After the death of Steindl in 1903, the Bundaberg Brewery continued under the management of the executors of his estate, J. Steindl, O. R. Steindl and G. A. Steindl.

The Bundaberg Brewery Co. Ltd was registered in 1923, with the ten shareholders all members of the Steindl family. As well as canefarming interests, the family owned five hotels, including the Metropolitan and the Gympie. Competition from the larger city breweries gradually took its toll, and brewing ceased in 1932. The company continued to run a liquor agency, and became involved in soft-drink production.

The Bundaberg Brewery, c. 1910.

Bundaberg Brewing & Ice Works
See City Brewery.

Central Brewing Co.   1895–97
Crofton Street

The cordial manufacturer, O. W. Short, built a small brewery in 1895, and employed W. J. Chardon as the brewer. The local press said the beer was 'found to be light and delicate, clear as sherry and entirely free from colonial twang'. Despite the favourable review, the following year there was a new brewer, John Fleming, and also a new owner, the Duffy Brothers.

City Brewery   1883–95
6 Princess Street

Gustav Steindl migrated from Austria with his wife and twelve children, and took up residence in Bundaberg in 1877. With Lionel Fleming as a partner, they formed the Bundaberg Brewing & Ice Works, and began brewing in 1883.

The partners sank a well and, with the aid of a steam pump at the bottom, they had ample water of excellent quality. With Steindl's brewing experience and family formulas, the partners brewed first-class beer, and were soon delivering to many country towns. The brewery prospered and became an important industry in Bundaberg, employing a large staff and supporting local coopers, cartage contractors, farmers and other suppliers.

Steindl & Fleming were awarded a Commemorative Diploma and Medal for their ale at the Indian and Colonial Exhibition held in London in 1886. Gustav Steindl became the mayor of Bundaberg. He was also the brother of Louis Steindl, who owned the Federal Brewery in Maryborough, Queensland. After the partnership was dissolved by mutual consent in 1888, Gustav Steindl started another brewery, the Bundaberg Brewery, and Fleming and his son continued at the City Brewery. Unfortunately, Fleming's business didn't prosper, and in 1895 his old partner, Gustav Steindl, took over the City Brewery and closed it.

Union Brewery   1897–99
The proprietor was George Klein.

Cairns

Cairns is situated on the west shore of Trinity Bay. It was established in 1875 on a swampy mangrove area, and, after clearing, it served as the outlet for the Hodgkinson goldmines and later for the Herbertson tinfields.

Burton Brewing Co. Ltd   1887–92

In 1887 the partnership of Cock & Horn started the Burton Brewing Co. Ltd. Shortly after, R. W. Cock leased the brewery to E. W. Cockrane, who arranged a formal opening of his newly-acquired brewery on 19 March 1890.

After two years the company went into voluntary liquidation, and E. W. Bushell & Co. purchased all the equipment and shifted it to the newly-formed Barron River Brewery Co. at Mareeba. The old Burton Brewery premises were sold in 1893 for £510.

Cairns Brewery
See Carlton & United Breweries (Queensland) Ltd.

Cairns Brewing Co. Ltd
See Carlton & United Breweries (Queensland) Ltd.

Carlton & United Breweries (N.Q.) Ltd
See Carlton & United Breweries (Queensland) Ltd.

Carlton & United Breweries (Queensland) Ltd   1925–92
113 Spence Street, Portsmouth

The company was formed in June 1924 as the Cairns Brewing Co. Ltd, and the first brew was tapped on 7 July 1925. At that time the consumption of beer in Cairns was greater than in Brisbane, even though the population of Cairns was only 9000! In fact, Cairns boasted the highest consumption of alcoholic beverages per head in Australia.

Beer was expected to be on the market by 15 July 1925 according to the *Northern Herald*; the editorial continued with the statement that 'Cairns water is thought to be one of the best waters in the world'.

J. L. Breheny was the chairman and head brewer, but lack of finance and technical skills forced the company to liquidate and reform on 3 September 1927 as Northern Australian Breweries Ltd. There was very little improvement in the business, and in 1930 R. F. C. Fogarty was appointed managing director.

In 1931 Carlton & United Breweries Ltd of Melbourne purchased the brewery, and the facilities were improved and expanded. Beer was made at Cairns, and stout was freighted up from Melbourne and bottled at Cairns under the Irish Terrier Treble Stout label. This was discontinued in 1940, but the brand name was reintroduced after World War II.

N.Q. Lager, which was brewed and bottled from about 1933, was discontinued a few years later, but brought back again in the early 1960s. Cairns Bitter Ale was marketed in 1952, and Gold Top Pale Ale from 1963 by arrangement with Queensland Breweries Ltd, Brisbane.

The name Northern Australian Breweries Ltd continued in use until 1972, and the business then operated as Carlton & United Breweries (N.Q.) Ltd, to be changed again on 1 July 1986 to Carlton & United Breweries (Queensland) Ltd.

When CUB's Darwin Brewery closed in February 1989, CUB's Cairns Brewery supplied the Darwin depot with Fosters Lager, N.T. Draught and the well-known king-size Darwin Stubby.

Throughout its history the brewery was mostly referred to as the Cairns Brewery. Brewing ceased in June 1992, and the company's regional beers such as North Queensland Lager, Cairns Draught and N.T. Draught, were brewed by CUB's Brisbane brewery, and transported to the Cairns Brewery, which continued to operate as a depot.

Northern Australian Breweries Ltd
See Carlton & United Breweries (Queensland) Ltd.

Cawarral

Cawarral Brewery   1889–1901
The brewery in the tiny town of Cawarral, 35 km north-east of Rockhampton, had two owners, Edward McAree from 1889 to 1900, and Powell & Sons in 1901.

Charleville

Charleville, the second-largest town in outback Queensland, was gazetted in 1868, and has been referred to as being in the heart of Queensland's 'Mulga Country'. The famous Cobb & Co. coaches, which served the outback before motor vehicles took over, were built in a factory in Charleville.

In 1922 Qantas began its first regular air service between Charleville and Cloncurry. Today, the town is an important air centre, and serves as a base for the Royal Flying Doctor Service.

Albert Park Brewery
See Charleville Brewery.

Charleville Brewery   1888–1905
Albert Park

There was only one brewery at Charleville. It was run by the owner of the Charleville Hotel, Albert Aeschimann, who was partnered by G. J. Fitzwalter for a few years. Locals tended to use the name Albert Park Brewery.

The brewery closed, and after negotiating a lease with Aeschimann, Charles Lanfear took his family to Charleville, and started brewing in May 1901. Part of the deal with Aeschimann related to a well on the premises. Aeschimann had said there was an inexhaustible supply of splendid water about 35 feet deep. After five months Lanfear found that the water was not 35 feet deep, that the supply was not inexhaustible — in fact, it was dry. He took Aeschimann to court, claiming that the brewery was worthless and that the claim about the water in the well was false. Aeschimann won the case when the decision was handed down two years later. Ironically, it was subsequently found that the sides of the well, at the bottom, had clogged up. When this was cleaned and some holes drilled into the sides, water flooded in.

Charles Lanfear had long since left the town when in 1903 the owner, Albert Aeschimann, renovated the place and changed the name to the Western Brewery Co. The following year, Thomas Holmes became a partner, in charge of the brewing.

Western Brewery Co.
See Charleville Brewery.

The Cairns Brewing Co. Ltd was formed in 1925. The name was changed to Northern Australian Breweries Ltd in 1927, and although CUB, Melbourne, took over the brewery in 1931, the business continued as Northern Australian Breweries Ltd until 1972. At that time the company operated as Carlton & United Breweries (N.T.) Ltd, to be changed again in 1986 to Carlton & United Breweries (Queensland) Ltd.

Charters Towers

Gold had been discovered in the Charters Towers district in 1872, and the township was named after W. E. Charters, the first mining warden. The 'Towers' was added to the name because of the similarity of the surrounding countryside to the Dartmoor Tors in England.

Anchor Brewery
See Northern Breweries (Queensland) Ltd.

Charters Towers Brewery Co. Ltd
See Northern Breweries (Queensland) Ltd.

Hargrave's Brewery　　　c. 1878
The only reference to Hargrave's Brewery is in an editorial that mentioned that the brewery had to be demolished in 1878 to prevent the spread of a fire.

Northern Breweries (Queensland) Ltd　　　1891–1936
Adelaide Hill

Ralph Clifton was a man of considerable determination. He had built the Anchor Brewery at Macrossan in 1884, where one problem had followed another. The local water became polluted, then floods washed away most of the brewery. After rebuilding, fire destroyed the tower and most of the buildings. That was enough for Ralph. He left Macrossan in 1890, moved 30 km south-west to Charters Towers, and was ready to start brewing again. He formed the Charters Towers Brewery Co. Ltd, built the brewery on the north side of Towers Hill, and the first batch of Towers beer that was ready in January 1891 was declared 'a good drop'. Clifton still used the name Anchor Brewery, although there were frequent references to the Towers Brewery. The building had a very high tower that was a prominent feature in the landscape of the town, and the huge cellar was 150 feet long and 50 feet wide. Clifton's method of cooling freshly brewed beer was unique. He had a large copper vessel, 20 feet square and about 2 feet deep, capable of holding the equivalent of 30 hogsheads of beer. This huge shallow tank was on the top floor, and rapidly revolving fans were placed over the top to cool the fresh beer.

Hector Perkins was a partner in the business for a brief period in 1893, and a Mr Lancia followed as a major shareholder. During 1899 Northern Breweries (Queensland) Ltd was formed to acquire the assets and businesses of three breweries — the Townsville Brewery and the Lion Brewery, both of Townsville, and the Towers Brewery, Charters Towers.

Ralph Clifton sold his interest in the Towers Brewery, and invested heavily in Queen's Cross (Qld) goldmining shares, a well-placed investment, since at the time of his departure to America in 1903 he was drawing £20,000 in yearly dividends.

The Anchor Brewery, Charters Towers, 1891. The founder of the brewery, Ralph Clifton, sold out in 1899, invested the proceeds in gold mining shares, and became one of the wealthiest men in the state.

Lancia had died in 1924, and his interest in the brewery was sold by his widow to the new proprietors, Samuel Allen & Sons, who ran a successful business until the brewery closed in 1936.

At the peak of its activities the brewery had twenty-eight men on the payroll, a large number considering the fact that the industry was not labour intensive and the brewery was of modest size. A popular product was Palo Draught Beer, which was sold in green champagne-type bottles with the corks wired in.

After the closure of the brewery the Allen family became the northern distributors for Carlton & United Breweries (CUB), and supplies of beer were sent from CUB's brewery at Cairns, known at that time as Northern Australian Breweries Ltd. Bottled beer was sold as Towers Brewery Bitter Ale, and stout was freighted up from Melbourne and bottled under the Irish Terrier Treble Stout label.

Towers Brewery
See Northern Breweries (Queensland) Ltd.

Towers Brewery Co.　　　1894–95
Brewery Road

When J. A. Benjamin started the Towers Brewery Co. in 1894, the only other brewery in the town at that time was the Charters Towers Brewery Co. Ltd. If there was any conflict over the choice of name, that was soon resolved, since Benjamin closed his brewery after one year.

Weimer's Brewery　　　1876
This brewery may have been the forerunner of Hargrave's Brewery.

West End Brewery　　　1896–97
Gill Street

The proprietor was L. O'Sullivan.

Cooktown

Cooktown was the site where in 1770 Captain James Cook and the crew of HMS *Endeavour* spent forty-eight days while repairing their ship. After the departure of Cook, the area remained untouched for more than a century until 1873 when gold was discovered in the nearby Palmer River. Cooktown suddenly became a prosperous seaport for the goldfield, becoming for a time the wealthiest town in Australia and Queensland's second-busiest seaport. From an uninhabited area, the population grew to over 30,000 including 18,000 Chinese.

In 1899 a cyclone hit the Cooktown area, resulting in the loss of 307 lives.

Cooktown Brewery
See Mount Cook Brewery Co.

Mount Cook Brewery Co. 1885–93

The Cooktown Brewery, as it was first known, started up in 1885. It was built by William Lakeland, a successful prospector on the Palmer River goldfield. The brewing expertise came from his partner, James Oddy, who had a special recipe for Tropical Beer, and the exotic brew soon became a favourite drink of the miners — admittedly, it was the only beer available at the settlement at that time!

In January 1889 Lakeland sold his interest in the brewery to the firm of Power, Thomas & Madden, who changed the name to the Mount Cook Brewery Co. Madden was the manager, and James Oddy continued making his Tropical Beer.

Some years later Oddy accidentally drowned in a tall vat of beer. Unable to climb out and with no one nearby to hear his cries for help, he perished through involuntary overconsumption of his own product. It was a tragedy also for the company, since no one knew the recipe for Oddy's famous Tropical Beer. Employees tried to make the same brew but without success, and the brewery went out of business late in 1890.

The original owner, William Lakeland, reopened the brewery in September 1891, and brewed for two more years.

Quick & Matchett 1889–c. 1890

The partnership of Quick & Matchett started a small brewery at the time when the Mount Cook Brewery was in difficulty. The partnership was soon dissolved, leaving W. Quick to continue on his own.

Croydon

City Brewery c. 1889–93

Croydon is a small township in the remote far north of Queensland. The population has always been small, even when Peter Martin and his son, Frederick, brewed there in the 1880s.

Cunnamulla

The name Cunnamulla is derived from an Aboriginal term meaning 'long stretch of water', and relates to the Warrego River, which passes through the town.

The small town of Eulo, about 40 km to the west of Cunnamulla, boasts the only memorial in the world erected to the memory of a cockroach. It commemorates the accidental death of a racing cockroach named Destructo, which died when an excited punter accidentally stood on it.

Next to the engraved monument is the Paroo Lizard Race Track, where the world lizard-racing championships have been held.

Burton Brewery 1886–1903

The proprietor of the Burton Brewery, Cunnamulla, was Henry Tatham who ran a satisfactory business for seventeen years. The fact that the township lies almost 1000 km west of Brisbane, in the vast semi-arid outback, gave Tatham a business free from competition — but not free from storm and tempest. During 1892 the brewery was almost blown away when a violent storm blew the roof off the brewery, and destroyed the adjacent cordial factory.

Eidsvold

The Eidsvold goldfield was extremely productive for the twelve years from 1888, and remains an attractive district for gem fossickers.

Humberstone & Pinniger 1889–90

The partnership of Humberstone & Pinniger chose Eidsvold as a likely township to start a brewery. Business could never have been very successful because of the small population of the region. When Pinniger left, the brewery closed.

Gympie

Gold was discovered in the Wide Bay district in 1867, and in common with all gold 'strikes' swarms of prospectors came flooding into the area. Overnight, shanties and tents appeared, and the township of Gympie had come into being.

A map of Gympie published in early 1869 shows over seventy pubs in Mary Street, from the foot of Carlton Hill to the top of Commissioner's Hill. There were even more pubs in the dusty side streets of the busy goldmining town. The map also shows the location of Gympie's first brewery, Farley's Brewery, which was just over the brow of Commissioner's Hill in Duke Street.

Ashton's Brewery

See Gympie Brewing & Ice Co. Ltd.

Brewery Tap Hotel & Brewery 1868–c. 1875

Reef Street

Within a year of the gold discovery a German migrant, Mr Finselbach, had set up a small hotel on the dirt track called Reef Street. The hotel was almost directly behind Farley's brewery and hotel. Finselbach's hotel was a very primitive building, and he made his own beer out the back and sold it across his hotel counter at the front.

W. J. Coghlan, nephew of the well-known brewer James Coghlan of Ballarat, Victoria, joined Finselbach for a few years. Later Carl Eisert took over, and kept brewing for the local market.

The Courage Brewery, Melbourne, released this label in 1970, commemorating the bicentenary of the landing of Captain Cook in Australia.

Farley's Brewery 1868–c. 1880
Duke Street

Farley's Brewery was a small conglomerate business, with the brewery operating in conjunction with the hotel. There were substantial livery stables, and for a short period the proprietors operated a coach service between Gympie and Maryborough.

Federal Brewery
See Gympie Brewing & Ice Co. Ltd.

Gympie Brewing & Ice Co. Ltd 1885–1907
Brewery Road, off Pine Street, near the Mary River

One of the most enterprising of Gympie's early citizens was Dr Benson. Apart from his medical practice, he set up a miners' hospital, dabbled in politics, agriculture and winemaking, and formed a company to start a brewery at the river end of Pine Street.

An imposing group of buildings was constructed, and the Gympie Brewing & Ice Co. Ltd was registered in 1885. Some of the brewery effluent drained into the river below the brewery, attracting fish, and the area became a popular spot for fishing and picnics.

Under the management of the head brewer, W. C. Lanfear, the brewery made excellent-quality beer that won first prize at the 1885 Brisbane Exhibition. A competitor, Brisbane's Bulimba Brewery, came second, and the Townsville Brewery, third.

When Dr Benson retired, the brewery's fortunes began to decline. J. S. Cullinane, the chairman of the company, had the unenviable task of arranging the voluntary liquidation of the company in December 1894, and the brewery then closed.

Walter Lanfear, previously the head brewer, together with Gilbert Garrick, the senior partner, started brewing again in 1898 as the Federal Brewery. The following year the name was again changed, this time to the Licensed Victuallers' Brewing Co. Ltd. When Thomas Ashton bought the business in August 1906, he simply used the name Ashton's Brewery, but brewing ceased soon after and the business became a trading company.

Gympie Brewing & Ice Co. Ltd	1885–94, closed
Federal Brewery Lanfear & Garrick	1898–99
Licensed Victuallers' Brewing Co. Ltd	1899–1906
Ashton's Brewery	1906–7

Licensed Victuallers' Brewing Co. Ltd
See Gympie Brewing & Ice Co. Ltd.

Terrier Brewing Co. 1902–6
Horse Shoe Bend

The last brewing venture in Gympie was started in 1902 by Robert Bond and his son, George. They had recently closed their Terrier Brewing Co. in Brisbane, and the site that they chose for their brewery at Gympie was just below the Wide Bay Dairy Co-operative Society's premises.

Robert Bond organised the setting-up of the brewery, and then left George to manage the business. The Terrier Brewing Co., Gympie, brewed XXXX brand draught ale and Terrier brand bottled ale and stout for a few years, and then George accepted the position of chief brewer at Toohey's Standard Brewery in Sydney.

Harrisville

Blantyre Brewery c. 1885–c. 1890

Herberton

Herberton Brewery 1886–92
Nigger Street

Patrick Dunne worked the brewery for four years, and sold in 1890 to J. James.

Hughenden

Hughenden Brewery c. 1890

Hughenden is a small township located beside the Flinders River, 1500 km north-west of Brisbane. In the late nineteenthth century, before motor-vehicle transport, it was a long, slow, 400 km trek to Townsville, the nearest township with a brewery.

Although Charters Towers was closer, there was no brewery operating there in 1890 at the time when M. Flynn thought that a brewery at Hughenden would be a good idea. It was the last outpost to the vast areas

The Federal Brewery, Gympie, 1898. Note the timber ventilation louvres at the top of the tower and also on the lower building in the foreground.

to the north and west; it would be free from competition and, with the hot dry climate, there would be a great demand for beer.

Unfortunately, Flynn overlooked the fact that very few people lived or travelled through those far-distant semi-desolate regions, and lack of customers forced Flynn to abandon the venture.

Ipswich

The city of Ipswich, on the Bremer River, is 40 km west of Brisbane. It is Queensland's most important industrial centre outside the Brisbane metropolitan area and is also the commercial centre for the surrounding farming and dairying districts.

The largest RAAF base in Australia, Amberley, is situated within the city's boundaries.

Booval Brewery Ltd
See West Moreton Brewery Co. Ltd.

Ipswich Brewery
See Standard Brewery.

Ipswich Brewing & Bottling Co. Ltd
The prospectus of the Ipswich Brewing & Bottling Co. Ltd was available in February 1887, and the objectives of the proposed company were to brew and sell first-class ale and stout in casks and bottles.

Henry Edmeades, the proposed manager, said that Ipswich, with a population of nearly 10,000, was the largest town he had seen without a brewery. The project fell through because of lack of investor support.

Standard Brewery   1887–97
Cnr Wharf & Bremer Streets

It was just after 10 p.m. on Tuesday, 30 December 1902. A large crowd had gathered, gazing at the spectacular fire engulfing the old Standard Brewery. The building, which was totally destroyed, had been a landmark in the town. Built in 1862, it was used as a wholesale and retail store until 1887, when John Johnston purchased the building and converted it to a brewery. Johnston soon had eight hands working at the brewery, and he obtained first prize for his beer at the Ipswich Show.

The business was first called the Ipswich Brewery, and with W. J. Chardon as his brewer, Johnston supplied most of the hotels in Ipswich and the surrounding districts of West Moreton. In 1893 the name was changed to the Standard Brewery.

John Johnston became the West Moreton agent for the Castlemaine Brewery in Brisbane, and, after closing his brewery in 1897, he concentrated on the sale of Castlemaine beer and spirits, using the Standard Brewery premises as a warehouse.

West Moreton Brewery Co. Ltd   1898–1903
The Booval Brewery was close to the Booval railway station, about 3 km on the Brisbane side of Ipswich. When the brewery was built in 1898, hardwood was used throughout. It had a 35-foot tower and three 400-gallon tanks were mounted on the third floor, one for hot water and the others for cooling. It was reported that everything about the brewery was scrupulously clean, and the facilities included a deep well, large cellars, and a bottling department complete with a syphon and corking machine.

The brewer was W. J. Chardon, late of the Standard Brewery in Ipswich, which had closed the year before. Chardon's beer was classed as a light mild beverage, particularly suited to the Queensland climate, and the first production was 'on tap' at nearly all Ipswich hotels in May 1898.

On 24 August 1900 the West Moreton Brewery Co. Ltd was registered, and it took over the assets of the Booval Brewery. The promoter, H. J. Atkinson, appointed Herbert Prewett as the brewer. After three years the brewery closed, and in 1906 Tom Meagher purchased the equipment and transferred it to Toowoomba, where he was in the process of setting up a new brewery.

Longreach

Of historical importance is the Qantas (Queensland and Northern Territory Aerial Service) hangar at Longreach airport, the first Qantas operational base, which was used from 1922 to 1934. Said to be the oldest airline in the English-speaking world, Qantas began its first regular airmail and passenger service in 1922. The first overseas flight was in 1934.

City Brewery   1888–1901
Wren Street

A few years after starting the brewery, the owner, W. J. Humphreys, took on W. W. Tucker as a partner, and they traded as the Western Brewing Co.

Late in 1897 Humphreys & Tucker transferred their interests in the brewery to the partnership of H. E. Tucker & R. E. Tucker. By 1900 the name had changed to the City Brewery, and the following year W. J. Humphreys came back into the business, this time leasing the brewery in partnership with his nephew, George F. Hunter Jnr. By the end of that year the brewery had closed.

Some residents recollect the story told by their parents that, when the brew was good, the brewery staff would ring a bell in town. If it was a failure, the brew was used to make vinegar.

Western Brewing Co.
See City Brewery.

Mackay

Within a decade of its settlement in 1862 Mackay became Queensland's largest sugar-producing region. The city gradually developed as a service centre for the sugar and rich pastoral industries, and a brewery was soon in business to meet the needs of the growing population.

City Brewery   1884–1922
Cemetery Road

In 1884 the Northern Australian Brewery Co. Ltd was formed by Benjamin McKay (unrelated to Captain John Mackay, the founder of the town). J. G. Lehman was a partner in 1888. Two years later McKay leased the brewery to Samuel Cooke & Co. for a term of five years. The name was later changed to the North End Brewery, although Mackay Brewery was used in advertisements.

George Johnston took over in 1893 but, shortly after, the lease was transferred to the partnership of Henry Bolton and Edward Terry. They renovated the place, and changed the name to the City Brewery. By 1895 Bolton was running the brewery on his own, producing an ale, 'bright and clear with no sediment'.

Henry Bolton died early in 1900, and Alfred Bredwell leased the brewery during the early 1900s, but continued in business until 1922 as H. Bolton & Co.

Northern Australian Brewery Co. Ltd
Benjamin McKay	1884–88
McKay & Lehman	1888–90
Samuel Cooke & Co.	1890–93

North End Brewery
George Johnston	1893

City Brewery
Bolton & Terry	1893–95
Henry Bolton	1895–1900
Alfred Bredwell (lessee)	1900–22

Lion Brewery   1900–4

Samuel Allen and Albert Lanfear were men of considerable brewing and business experience. They were the founding partners of the Lion Brewery in Townsville in 1894, and in 1899 they were the principal partners in Northern Breweries (Queensland) Ltd, owners of three breweries, including their Lion Brewery, Townsville.

Their Lion Brewery at Mackay was not as successful, and closed after four years.

Mackay Brewery
See City Brewery.

McKay, William   c. 1889
Romeo Street

William McKay, probably a relative of Benjamin McKay of the City Brewery, owned and operated a brewery in Romeo Street, near the railway station.

Mount Pleasant Brewery & Ice Works Co.   1898

This brewery may have been nothing more than a proposal. W. T. Kemp was to be the manager, and a Mr Harding, a previous employee at the local City Brewery, was to be the brewer. It was planned to convert a disused sugar-crushing mill into a brewery.

North End Brewery
See City Brewery.

Northern Australian Brewery Co. Ltd
See City Brewery.

Macrossan

Anchor Brewery   1884–90

The goldmining town of Charters Towers was first established on the bank of the Burdekin River at Macrossan, about 25 km east of where Charters Towers

---

BEER DRINKERS' STRIKE

There are over 600 men in the copper-mining districts of Hawdon and Mount Elliott in Northern Queensland and, for six weeks, they have not had a drink in any of the local hotels — at least all but two, and the latter were so dealt with by the others that they are not likely to patronise the hotels again.

The noble 600 are not temperance advocates. They are passive resisters to the tariff of one shilling a drink. They warned the six hotel keepers in the two towns named that unless the price for drinks was reduced, they would go on strike. The temperature was about 90 in the shade and the hotel keepers smiled. They are not smiling today.

On each pay-day, a special watch is kept in the hotels by the loyalists to see that none break away from the no-drink compact. One day, two backsliders were observed stealthily approaching. They went into one of the hotels and hot and thirsty vigilants were horrified to observe them quaffing the cooling ale.

A meeting of the vigilance committee was hastily summoned and the two men were arraigned. After very little discussion, it was decided to treat them as such traitors should be dealt with. They were thereupon taken out and ducked in the creek. When they emerged, they were put through the ordeal of tarring and feathering, with the substitution of treacle for tar.

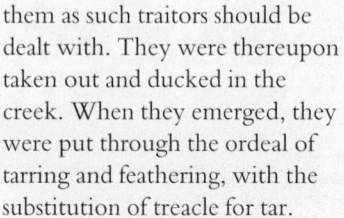

Australian Brewers' Journal,
October 1910

stands today. There was no reticulated water at Charters Towers until 1902, which was probably the reason Ralph Clifton set up his brewery beside the river at Macrossan.

When the brewery started in 1884, it was formed as the Burdekin Brewery Co. Ltd. In addition to brewing, the company stated as its objects

> to acquire saw-milling properties; to deal in malt and grain; to extract gold, silver, tin and any other metals from ore or quartz by crushing or any other method whatsoever.

Ralph Clifton kept to brewing. He had previously worked at the Anchor Brewery in Dublin, Ireland, which influenced his decision to change the name of his brewery at Macrossan to the Anchor Brewery. He had a well that was at a distance of only 80 feet from the edge of the river. It was sunk to a depth of 25 feet, and held a level of 6 feet of cool, clear water. River water was also used after being filtered three times. The first filtering was before the water was pumped up from the river to the top of the brewery tower. From there, the water gravitated down, passing through 6 feet of charcoal and coarse sand. Finally, the water passed through a Rawlin's Patent Filter, where it was thoroughly purified.

By 1890 Clifton had decided to leave Macrossan. There were several reasons for the move. The river water was becoming polluted from the outflow of waste from a crushing mill upstream. Then, one night, the river rose 60 feet and most of the brewery was washed away in the flood. Clifton rebuilt after the flood had subsided, but, to make matters worse, further damage was caused by a fire that destroyed the brewery tower. The Anchor Brewery at Macrossan was finished, and Ralph Clifton then moved to a safer location at Charters Towers, and started another Anchor Brewery there.

Burdekin Brewery Co. Ltd
See Anchor Brewery.

Mareeba

Mareeba is a small township on the Barron River, 60 km west of Cairns. At the turn of the century, the principal industry was timber, cedar being found in such abundance that it was used locally as a substitute for pine. Most of the buildings in the town were constructed of cedar.

There was a goldfield near the township, and it was the transient success of this field that induced some daring speculators to become involved in the town's only brewery.

Barron River Brewery Co.   1893–1902
The equipment of the bankrupt Burton Brewery, Cairns, was quite new, and E. W. Bushell purchased the lot, sent it to Mareeba, and started the Barron River Brewery Co. Bushell chose a good site, on the bank of the Barron River, above a popular swimming spot that became known as the Brewery Hole. On Sunday afternoons many of the town people would gather at the brewery, where free beer was available. A journalist, visiting the brewery one Sunday in 1894, said that he saw as many as eighty men lying about in groups on the bank of the river next to the brewery, drinking as much as they wanted of the complimentary beer, but, 'let the local publicans offer them the same beer during the week, to be paid for, the air would become heavy with strange oaths'.

Within a year of the brewery starting, it had new owners, Mr and Mrs Arthur Taylor. Perhaps Arthur died or left since in 1894, since Mrs Taylor then ran the business with the help of Charles Powell, who attended to the brewing.

Six years later the brewery closed, but was reopened late in 1900 as the North Queensland Brewing Co. Ltd. C. M. W. Chateau was the brewer manager, and the brewery was rebuilt and refitted.

The expected flood of population never came, and the few who remained coined nasty names for the beer and refused to drink it. One reporter said, 'I never tasted such stuff before or since. It was as thick as pea soup and the same colour — no words can convey the taste'. The only publican in town who tried to sell the beer was also the local carter. He had to take a certain quantity of the beer to offset his account for cartage of materials and the few hogsheads that he delivered for the brewery 'up the country'.

The North Queensland Brewery was a failure, even though it struggled on for a year or so. It closed in 1902, and some years later it was converted to a meatworks. In 1906 the West End Brewery Ltd from Brisbane purchased the equipment and property. It was intended to reopen the brewery as the West End Brewery, but the proposal was abandoned. They were still trying to resell the property in 1912.

Mareeba Brewery
See Barron River Brewery Co.

WANTED — A BREWER

We are frequently asked to engage brewers for our subscribers and have always pleasure in doing our utmost to select the most suitable applicant for the position.

But when we are asked, 'Are we sure he is a good brewer?' or, 'Will you guarantee that he'll produce good beer?' we find ourselves face to face with the fact that there is a lot of the element of chance in it.

Like marriage, 'it is a lottery,' and brewers who have been successful in some places, are failures in others.

Australian Brewers' Journal, February 1899

North Queensland Brewing Co. Ltd
See Barron River Brewery Co.

Maryborough

First settled in 1847, the town of Maryborough became a port for the Wide Bay, Hervey Bay and Burnett districts in which sugargrowing, dairying, grazing, coalmining, fishing, engineering and timber-milling are important industries. These products are now transported by road and rail. Today, Maryborough is one of Queensland's important industrial cities.

Bavarian Brewery
See Federal Brewery Ltd.

Federal Brewery Ltd 1878–1930
Bowen Street

Steindl & Son was one of very few Queensland country breweries where a family concern operated a successful brewing business for fifty years. Louis Steindl Snr, known as Lee by his friends, built his brewery at Granville in East Maryborough in 1878. He was his own architect and builder, and the spring water on the property was ideal for the production of beer. Although it was first named the Bavarian Brewery, it was frequently referred to as the Granville Brewery.

Considerable extensions and improvements were carried out in 1881, but four years later the brewery was almost destroyed by fire. It was rebuilt, and by 1901 the brewery was unable to cope with the demand. Later that year Steindl purchased the Maryborough Brewery, and all brewing was then carried on at that address.

Lee Steindl and his son, Louis Emanuel Steindl, changed the name from the Bavarian Brewery to the Federal Brewery, and traded as Steindl & Son. The old Bavarian Brewery was used for bottling only.

The Federal Brewery supplied beer to twenty-four hotels in Maryborough, and sent bulk beer far and wide. Once a week Lee Steindl would travel around Maryborough in his horse-drawn jinker, visiting the hotels and testing the beer. If the standard was not right, the cask of beer would be sent back to the brewery for a replacement. Steindl was described as 'a man of comparatively little ostentation and was keenly alive to anything that tended to the welfare of the town and its immediate surroundings'.

Lee Steindl died in 1913, and his son carried on the business until 1928. On 2 October of that year the brewery was sold to a group of Maryborough businessmen, who successfully floated the Federal Brewery Ltd. The brewer and manager was William Gooley, who was apparently never sober and kept drinking away the profits of the struggling company. He was sacked, but the company went out of business and the brewery closed in 1930.

Finselbach's Brewery 1875–78
Adelaide Street

The town of Maryborough nestles in a curve of the Mary River, and was first settled in 1847. The first brewer in the town was a Mr Finselbach who opened a small brewery at the back of his hotel.

Granville Brewery
See Federal Brewery Ltd.

Kerridge & Co. 1893–94
A. Kerridge was an old and respected resident of Maryborough. He was connected with the sugarcane industry, and started brewing in 1893, trading as Kerridge & Bond.

Maryborough Brewery 1881–1901
Bowen Street

The Maryborough Brewery, built by Charles Powell in 1881, had a large wooden tower and the whole structure was described as looking like a fortress. The business became the Maryborough Brewing & Mercantile Co. Ltd in 1884, but, with losses mounting year after year, the brewery was forced to close in 1890. Two years later Powell decided to try again, and ran the brewery until 1901.

Louis Steindl of the Bavarian Brewery in Granville, East Maryborough, took over Powell's Brewery and centralised his brewing operations at that address, continuing then as the Federal Brewery.

Maryborough Brewing & Mercantile Co. Ltd
See Maryborough Brewery.

Mungindi

Border Brewery 1896–1905
The township of Mungindi is located on both sides of the Queensland, New South Wales border, in a vast outback area of sparse grazing land. The Border Brewery was built on the Queensland side of the state border line by John Tabulo in 1896. His brother, Thomas, owned a successful brewery at St George at that time.

Within a year the partnership of Heiller & Capp Brothers had taken over Tabulo's Border Brewery.

Edward Thomas was involved during the years 1899 to 1901, but the brewery was never much of a success.

Millbong

Blantyre Brewery 1887–1903
The proprietor of the brewery was George Gordon Jnr.

Miriwinni

Tusa, Stephen   1934–37

Nerang

Eagle Brewery   1886–88

Owanville

Biddles, Charles & Thomas   c. 1874

Reid River

Reid River Brewery   1888–89
Reid River lies about 40 km south of Townsville, and was chosen as the place for a brewery by Frederick E. Russell back in 1888. He had been the founder of the Fitzroy Brewery in Rockhampton eight years earlier.

Rockhampton

In 1856 William Wiseman, a land commissioner, was sent by the Queensland government to find a suitable site on the Fitzroy River for a township. His ultimate choice of location was about 60 km from the mouth of the river; he named it Rockhampton, meaning 'town near the rocks in the river'.

Rockhampton is the principal city of central Queensland, and the outlet of a vast pastoral and mining area. The city is laid out with broad, tree-lined streets, and more than fifty buildings have been classified by the National Trust. Many of these are in Quay Street, adjacent to the river wharves, and were built between 1882 and 1903.

Abbotsford Brewery   1922–33
Quay Street

Boldeman's Brewery   c. 1860
The township of Rockhampton was quite small when William Boldeman, a soapmaker by trade, tried to make beer for a very brief period.

Carlton & United Breweries (Rockhampton) Pty Ltd
See Fitzroy Brewery.

Coorooman Creek Brewery
See Rockhampton Brewery Ltd.

ACHING TEETH

The Australian colonies are noted for their soft, tasteless water, deficient of carbonates, sulphates and all the other chemicals which combine to impart a pleasant, refreshing flavour to good drinking water. This is duly borne out by the well-known fact that the majority of Australians suffer from aching teeth, which is attributed to the lack of chemicals in the water, as it is insufficient to replenish the wear on the teeth by the mastication of the food.

Australian Brewers' Journal, February 1891

Fitzroy Brewery   1880–1976
Quay Street (later Richardson Street)

The Fitzroy Brewery was the longest-running brewery in country Queensland, spanning a period of ninety-six years, but Frederick E. Russell was not to know these statistics when he started the brewery in 1880. He was in partnership with A. L. Bourcicault, and the brewery was in Quay Street, about midway between Fitzroy and Denham Streets. It overlooked the Fitzroy River, and was said to be the most up to date of any brewery north of Brisbane.

The first brew was released at the official opening and inaugural banquet held in October 1880, and the beer was described as 'a nice light drink possessing a rich hop flavour with none of the hardness of other colonial beers on the market'. Fred Russell was no doubt proud of the review.

In February 1881, only four months after the brewery opened, the hopes for its future were shattered when it was put up for auction, either as a going concern or in lots. The two principal bidders were Thomas McLaughlin and William Higson. McLaughlin merely wanted to buy an engine that formed part of the plant, while Higson was a trader, buying anything that could be resold at a profit. Neither of the men had any intention, at that time, of getting into the brewing business, but having met at the auction, and after some lengthy discussion, they decided to have a go at running the brewery, and ended up buying it. The partners knew nothing about brewing, and employed Benjamin McKay as the brewer. McKay had a successful cordial and icemaking business, but little, if any, experience in brewing.

The McLaughlin and Higson partnership broke up after three months, and Higson sold his share in the brewery to his partner for £450. Although they remained friends, it was rumoured that the reason for the split was due to the unsatisfactory quality of the beer, and neither the owners nor the the brewer knew what the problem was, let alone how to fix it.

In 1884 Thomas McLaughlin moved the brewery to a new site further along Quay Street, and with more

The Kent Brewery, Rockhampton. The owner, John Headrick, died in 1895, and his two sons kept the business going until 1905. Many successful breweries were family affairs, with the business continuing for generations.

knowledge and improved techniques the Fitzroy Brewery's beer, known as Mac's, gradually became the popular beer on the market.

Thomas McLaughlin lost his life in tragic circumstances when he was washed overboard during a storm while on a voyage to New Zealand. The business was carried on by his two sons, Daniel and Thomas, and later by Thomas's sons, Terry, Robert and Laurie. The family company, Thomas McLaughlin & Co., was registered in 1893, and C. E. Lanfear was appointed head brewer in 1895. Mac's beer and stout were widely distributed inland and along the north and south coasts of Queensland, and the company prospered.

The Kent Brewery in nearby East Street was purchased in 1905, and closed.

In 1961 Carlton & United Breweries Ltd, Melbourne, bought the Fitzroy Brewery, and continued brewing the popular Mac's beer. A new brewery was built in Richardson Street in 1970, and the name was changed to Carlton & United Breweries (Rockhampton) Pty Ltd.

The brewery was closed in March 1976, almost a century after Fred Russell sat on the verandah of his old brewery, looking out over the Fitzroy River, quietly sampling a fresh batch of his 'nice light drink with a rich hop flavour'.

Russell & Bourcicault	1880–81
McLaughlin & Higson	1881
Thomas McLaughlin	1881–84
Thomas McLaughlin (new site)	1884–93
Thomas McLaughlin & Co.	1893–1961
Carlton & United Breweries Ltd	1961–70
Carlton & United Breweries (Rockhampton) Pty Ltd	1970–76

Kent Brewery 1889–1905
24 Bolsover Street

The Hon. Henry Bolton started the Kent Brewery in 1889, but the following year he was bankrupt, with liabilities of £33,000. John M. Headrick & Co., wine and spirit merchants, became the owners in 1894. They built a new brewery in East Street and brewed Bull's Head stout, and draught and bottled ale.

John Headrick died in 1895, and the two sons, J. M. and A. H. Headrick, kept the business going until 1905 when Thomas McLaughlin & Co. bought the brewery, and closed it.

Rockhampton Brewery Ltd 1892–1901

The founder of the Coorooman Brewery, as it was called in 1892, was Edwin Macree, a worthy citizen of North Rockhampton who was involved with educational projects and served as mayor for one term. He

The Rockhampton Brewery, c. 1895. It was located close to the Coorooman Creek, among the eucalypt trees, and was said to resemble either a church or a fort. The brewery lasted for only nine years.

was born in London, served in the British Navy, fought in the Crimean War, and arrived at Rockhampton in the 1860s. His career was varied and included such occupations as pawnbroker, ship salvager, carrier, auctioneer, land broker, and brewer.

Edwin Macree's family had some association with the famous Bass Brewery in Britain, and through them tests were taken of the Coorooman Creek water to determine its suitability for brewing. Although the water was satisfactory and the beer quite drinkable, the business failed, and the brewery was forced to close. It was claimed that there were not enough 'untied' hotels to purchase their beer.

The brewery, which was said to resemble either a church or a fort, was reopened in 1892 by a syndicate comprising W. J. Humphrey, F. E. Russell and others, and they formed the Rockhampton Brewery Ltd in 1893.

The following year the company announced their intention to bottle their own products at their own brewery, instead of having the bottling contracted out through an agency. Hotelkeepers were assured that 'the Coorooman brand ales and stout, now bottled at the brewery, may be relied on'.

The original owner, Edwin Macree, returned to the business in 1895, but the brewery closed two years later.

The last owners of the Rockhampton Brewery were C. R. Powell & Sons, who started the brewery going again in 1899.

Coorooman Brewery
Edwin Macree	1892, closed
Humphrey & Russell	1892–93

Rockhampton Brewery Ltd
Humphrey & Russell	1893–95
Edwin Macree	1895–97, closed
C. R. Powell & Sons	1899–1901

Roma

A vineyard was planted at Romaville in 1863, and the wine produced was the first to be sold in Queensland. The town was gazetted in 1867 and named after Diamantina Roma, wife of Sir George Bowen, the first Governor of Queensland.

Roma Brewery   1884

D. and J. Benjamin were owners of the local Royal Mail Hotel, and they built a brewery in Chinatown, Roma. A well on the premises maintained a constant supply of soft, clean water, even in the driest season. The brewery was a simple structure, and produced sufficient beer for the local trade and the outback western grazing districts, but, regrettably for the customers, only for about a year.

St George

St George Brewery   1888–1905
Barlee Street

The market for the brewery's beer was limited to the town residents, a few travellers and the inhabitants of the sparsely populated surrounding districts.

The owner of the St George Brewery, Thomas Tabulo, sold the business in 1904 to William Nieves who resold the following year to Hugh Robertson. Prospects for the brewery lasting much longer looked grim. The poor-quality water, the handful of customers and the stifling heat all remained. Earlier, Martin Harris had been listed as the owner, possibly a partner.

Stanthorpe

Stanthorpe Brewery   c. 1887–89

Thargomindah

Federal Brewery   c. 1890–1905

When H. J. Hine started his small brewery and cordial business around 1890, rainwater was the only source of supply of water for cleaning and the production of beer and other beverages. By 1893 the town's artesian bore became the source of energy for Australia's first municipally operated electric street lights. The power was supplied by a generator coupled to a water turbine, driven by the bore's natural water pressure, and the method continued in use until 1951.

During 1899 P. J. Leahy purchased the brewery from Hine, and worked it for a few more years. The population of the town at that time was only 400, and although its remoteness, over 1000 km west of Brisbane, ensured freedom from competition, there were not enough customers.

Tiaro

Biddles, Frank   c. 1874
Oakey Creek

Toowoomba

Originally called 'the Swamp', Toowoomba developed in a marshy area, in the 1850s, as a suburb of the neighbouring township of Drayton. Development of Toowoomba was rapid. An aerated-water and cordial factory, and a tannery, were opened in 1861, and a brewery was established in 1869. Pastoral and other industries soon followed.

Located 130 km west of Brisbane, Toowoomba is

> ## STANDARD BEER
>
> Beer shall not contain strychnine or cocculus indicus or picric acid or lead, and shall not contain more than one-hundred and fiftieth part of a grain of arsenic per gallon and not more than two grains per gallon of sulphurous acid calculated as sulphur dioxide.
>
> *Allowed addition (a)*
> Sulphurous acid or sulphites, calculated as sulphur dioxide, may be added to beer as preservative substance in such proportion that the total content of sulphur dioxide shall not exceed eight grains per gallon.
>
> *Allowed addition (b)*
> To beer containing not more than two per cent of proof spirit, saccharin may be added in a proportion not exceeding two grains per gallon.
> *Australian Brewers' Journal*, November 1906

now Queensland's largest inland city. It is the commercial, industrial and educational centre of a rich agricultural and pastoral region that produces much of Queensland's wool, prime beef, wheat and barley.

Breheny's Brewery Ltd
See Silverstream Brewery.

Carlton & United Breweries (Queensland) Ltd
See Queensland Brewery Ltd.

Castlemaine Perkins Ltd   1869–1958
Margaret Street

Patrick Perkins, or Paddy as he was mostly known, was born in Ireland in 1838. He arrived in Victoria in 1855 with his father, Thomas, and brothers, James and Thomas, and they travelled to the goldfields of Ballarat and Bendigo. Within a few years Paddy and brother Thomas had set up a successful general merchandising store in Castlemaine, Victoria.

For a brief period the brothers held an interest in the Castlemaine Brewery in Victoria, owned by the Fitzgerald brothers, but Paddy often clashed with Nicholas Fitzgerald over company policy.

In 1867 the Perkins brothers left Castlemaine to settle in Queensland's Darling Downs district. They purchased land at the bottom of Margaret Street, Toowoomba, late in 1868, built their substantial Downs Brewery, and commenced brewing on 13 December 1869. A malthouse was added two years later, and leased out to a private contractor.

Paddy Perkins bought the City Brewery in Brisbane in 1872. It was the only brewery in Brisbane at that time, and the acquisition gave Paddy a monopoly in the Brisbane and southern Queensland beer market. Both the Brisbane and Toowoomba breweries survived the many difficulties of the late nineteenth century, and the businesses prospered and expanded. By the 1920s profit began to decline, caused mostly by the fierce competition from the popular XXXX Bitter Ale put out by their competitor, the Castlemaine Brewery, Brisbane.

The Perkins & Co. Ltd Downs Brewery in Toowoomba and the City Brewery in Brisbane were sold on 1 August 1928 to the Castlemaine Brewery Ltd, Brisbane, and the business was then restructured as Castlemaine Perkins Ltd. The City Brewery was closed, and the Downs Brewery continued brewing until 1958, putting an end to a Queensland country brewery that had operated continuously for eighty-nine years. The Downs Brewery was demolished in 1960, and a shopping centre was built on the site.

Downs Brewery (Perkins & Co. Ltd)	1869–1928
City Brewery, Brisbane, purchased	1872
Castlemaine Perkins Ltd	1928–58
Both the Downs Brewery, Toowoomba, and the City Brewery, Brisbane, purchased	1928
City Brewery closed	1928
Downs Brewery closed	1958

Darling Downs Brewing Co. Ltd   1897–99
Black Gully

The prospectus for the Darling Downs Brewing Co. Ltd was issued in July 1897, and the company was successfully subscribed. George Nicol, late of the West End Brewery Ltd, Brisbane, was appointed manager, and brewing commenced on 11 November 1897. Competition and other problems caused the liquidation of the company late in 1899, and the property was purchased by Perkins & Co. Ltd.

Downs Brewery
See Castlemaine Perkins Ltd.

New Brewery   1894
Bell Street

The New Brewery was described as a very compact modern plant. The owner, D. T. Dillon, had considerable brewing experience, firstly at Maryborough, Queensland, then at Townsville, and finally, a long period of employment as head brewer at the Downs Brewery in Toowoomba. Trading as Dillon & Co., the brewery started in 1894, but must have closed soon after.

Queensland Brewery Ltd   1924–76
Having purchased the Silverstream Brewery in Toowoomba from the Breheny Brothers in 1923, the Brisbane-based Queensland Brewery Ltd set about building a substantial new brewery, which was officially opened on 3 December 1924. The only competition in Toowoomba then was from the Perkins Downs Brewery.

In 1961 CUB, Melbourne, acquired all assets of the Queensland Brewery Ltd. This included the breweries at Brisbane and Toowoomba. The Toowoomba Brewery, illustrated on this label, continued to operate until March 1976.

The Queensland Brewery operated a successful business in Toowoomba for thirty-seven years until 1961 when Carlton & United Breweries Ltd of Melbourne purchased all the assets of the Queensland Brewery Ltd, which included the breweries at both Brisbane and Toowoomba.

In 1971 the name was changed to Carlton & United Breweries (Queensland) Ltd, but March 1976 saw the closure of the brewery.

Silverstream Brewery   1881–1923

The Silverstream Brewery was built on a large block of land next to the Belle Vue Hotel. The water supply came from a well sunk 100 feet through solid granite, and was said to be the most suitable for brewing purposes that could be found anywhere in the Commonwealth.

The proprietor, Edmund Meagher, installed the most modern equipment available, and brewing was under way in 1881. Edmund Meagher's father, Tom, owned the Western Hotel in Toowoomba, and two other hotels in the town. In 1906 father and son built a new brewery on a site that provided an ample supply of good artesian water. Some of the equipment came from the Booval Brewery in Ipswich, which had been purchased and closed.

John and J. Leslie Breheny purchased the brewery in 1908, and traded as Breheny's Brewery Ltd until 1923. The brewery was then taken over by the Brisbane-based Queensland Brewery Ltd. They built a new modern brewery in Toowoomba, which opened in 1924 as the Queensland Brewery Ltd.

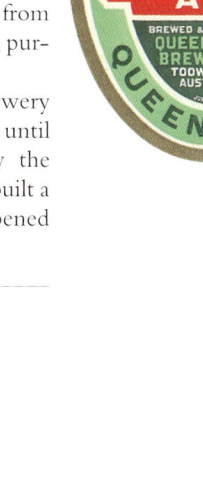

Silverstream Brewery	
Edmund Meagher	1881–1906
Edmund & Tom Meagher (new location)	1906–8
Breheny's Brewery	
John & J. Leslie Breheny	1908–23
Queensland Brewery Ltd (new brewery)	1923–61
Carlton & United Breweries Ltd	1961–71
Carlton & United Breweries (Queensland) Ltd	1971–76

Townsville

Townsville was named after Robert Towns, a sea captain and merchant who, in the early 1960s, acquired large pastoral holdings in the district.

Many of the city's beautiful old buildings are the product of Townsville's boom days when the gold-rushes at nearby Ravenswood and Charters Towers contributed to the city's growth and wealth.

Magnetic Island, 8 km across Cleveland Bay from the city, is a favourite tourist destination. There are spectacular views from the summit of Mt Cutheringa, commonly known as Castle Hill, which rises to 285 metres above sea-level, quite close to the city.

City Brewery   1885–92
Charters Towers Road

The premises of the Townsville Ice Co. were purchased in July 1885 by P. J. Martin & Sons, former owners of the Australian Brewery in Melbourne. They built their City Brewery alongside the iceworks, and produced their first beer in October 1885. The company also made and sold ice to the Townsville and other nearby communities, and the coastal and overseas shipping trade provided good custom for beer and ice.

In February 1886 the North Queensland Brewing Co. Ltd was formed for the purpose of acquiring the City Brewery and the Townsville Brewery of Ecklin & Dillon. The new company was not a success, and after a year or two the City Brewery was for sale. There were no buyers, and the brewery was closed. The brewery was leased to W. J. and A. Byrne in 1891, but the brewery closed again the following year.

Cleveland Brewery c. 1884
Frederick Russell was the proprietor. He had been involved in a number of breweries, and had started the Fitzroy Brewery in Rockhampton a few years earlier.

Lion Brewery 1894–1906
Flinders Street

The Lion Brewery was built and operated by Samuel Allen and Albert Lanfear. Allen, a successful general merchant, was one of the best-known and widely respected men in North Queensland. His partner, Albert Lanfear, had been a founding partner in the West End Brewery, Brisbane, and possibly for this reason the brewery was often referred to as the West End Brewery.

The brewery was described in 1895 as

> one of the most handsome structures in Townsville … none can compare with the Lion Brewery for picturesqueness of design, gracefulness of outline and completeness of detail. The 95 feet high tower is of a handsome and massive design, the roof being surmounted by a large railed-in flat, on the top of which is a crown of elaborate design.

The partners formed Northern Breweries (Queensland) Ltd in October 1899 with the purpose of taking over their own Lion Brewery, and also to acquire the Townsville Brewery, which had belonged to the North Queensland Brewing Co. Ltd before it was liquidated in 1891. The new company also purchased the Towers Brewery at Charters Towers. The Townsville Brewery was closed, and brewing continued at the Lion Brewery.

The directors of the new company included Christopher and Gerald Allen, and Albert Lanfear. Although Lanfear had had a long association with the Allen family, he filed a writ against Samuel Allen & Sons for £20,000 on 26 April 1902.

From 1906 the business continued as the Townsville Brewing Co. Ltd.

Lion Brewery
Allen & Lanfear 1894–99

Northern Breweries (Queensland) Ltd 1899–1906
(still trading as the Lion Brewery)

Townsville Brewing Co. Ltd 1906–39

North Queensland Brewing Co. Ltd 1886–91
The North Queensland Brewing Co. Ltd was formed in February 1886 and acquired the assets of two Townsville breweries, the City Brewery of P. J. Martin & Sons and the Townsville Brewery of Ecklin & Dillon.

The new company failed and was put into liquidation on 2 January 1891. The City Brewery, which had ceased operating, was leased for a year before closing in

Allen and Lanfear's Lion Brewery, Townsville, c 1895. Appearing around the parapet at the top of the second storey is the name 'Allen & Lanfear Limited established 1894'.

1892, but the Townsville Brewery stayed in business. It was taken over again in 1899, this time by Northern Breweries (Queensland) Ltd.

Northern Breweries (Queensland) Ltd
See Lion Brewery; North Queensland Brewing Co. Ltd.

Townsville Brewery
See Townsville Brewing Co. Ltd.

Townsville Brewing Co. Ltd   1884–1939
Flinders Street

The two-storey brick brewery was built in Flinders Street, opposite the railway station. The partners were Hugh Ecklin and D. T. Dillon, and the official opening of the brewery, on 11 January 1884, was a day-long affair. Publicans were invited, and some even arrived by express train from Charters Towers. There were many speeches and toasts to the success of the new brewery, and by late afternoon no one argued that the beer was the best they had ever tasted.

Sadly for some, the Townsville Brewery closed after less than two years, to be reopened by the newly-formed North Queensland Brewing Co. Ltd. The new company took over two Townsville breweries, the City Brewery and the Townsville Brewery, in February 1886.

On 2 January 1891 the North Queensland Brewing Co. Ltd went into liquidation. The City Brewery closed the following year, but the Townsville Brewery, after restructuring, continued under the management of F. Johnson, with S. G. Elliott in charge of the brewing.

Brewing ceased at the Townsville Brewery in 1899. During October of that year Samuel Allen and Albert Lanfear, of the Lion Brewery, Townsville, formed a new company, Northern Breweries (Queensland) Ltd, which took over their own Lion Brewery, and also the Townsville Brewery, which was closed. Later, about 1906, the Lion Brewery continued in business under the name of the Townsville Brewing Co. Ltd.

West End Brewery
See Lion Brewery.

Warwick

Warwick Brewery   1873–98
Victoria Street

The Warwick Brewery was close to the Condamine River, and the owner, John G. Wilson, began operating in August 1873. The brewery did quite well, supplying the local trade and the railway workers when the line was extended beyond Warwick.

Mark Brelsford, in his sketchbook, *Sandstone and Cedar*, describes the brewery as a four-roomed brick building, with verandahs louvred from floor to ceiling:

> A cellar under one room was reached through a trap door with steep steps below. Behind it was a timber building which was the manufacturing area. It had three rooms in a row with a loading platform in front and under one end of it was another cellar.

In 1885 an Act was passed to impose duty on beer manufactured in Queensland, and to provide for the registration of breweries. The brewer was required to pay an initial registration fee of £5, and a bond each year.

Safety precautions were almost non-existent in the nineteenth century, and few breweries had any form of guard rails around their large vats. A gruesome incident happened at the Warwick Brewery in 1896 when a workman fell into a vat of boiling liquid, and died almost instantly. Such fatalities were not uncommon at breweries, and yet little was done to regulate safety equipment and procedures.

The brewery owner, John Wilson, died in 1895, and his eldest daughter, Mary, together with her husband, James Thompson, continued to work the brewery for a few more years. The brewery closed in 1898, and the buildings, which had been added in later years and used as a residence, were demolished in 1960.

Yatala

Carlton & United Breweries Ltd   1993–
Cnr Pacific Highway & Mulles Road

In August 1992 Carlton & United Breweries Ltd (CUB) entered into a joint venture agreement with the Power Brewing Co. Ltd, a substantial modern brewery producing a range of widely marketed popular beers. It is located at Yatala, 70 km south of Brisbane.

Carlton & United Breweries Ltd closed their old brewery in the Valley, Brisbane, in February 1993, and all CUB beers that had been produced in the Valley were then brewed at Yatala. The brewery became totally owned by CUB on 28 October 1993, and CUB brand beers and some of the popular Power brands are now produced at Yatala.

Power Brewing Co. Ltd
See Carlton & United Breweries Ltd.

South Australia

During July 1836 a group of settlers landed at Nepean Bay on Kangaroo Island, a short distance off the coast of South Australia. A month later the party shifted to the mainland, and made a temporary settlement at Holdfast Bay (now the Adelaide suburb of Glenelg). This site was also unsuitable, and the settlers moved their tents and possessions to the Torrens River area, where a permanent settlement began late in 1836. Eight shiploads of immigrants and supplies had already been offloaded at Holdfast Bay before the arrival of Governor John Hindmarsh in December 1836.

By March 1837 the Surveyor-General, Colonel William Light, had completed a survey for the township of Adelaide, named in honour of Queen Adelaide, wife of King William IV of England. Colonel Light showed remarkable vision in the town plan, and Adelaide is now considered by many to be the most beautiful of the Australian cities.

Subsequent surveys of country land were hampered by inadequate staff and equipment, and the delays led to disastrous consequences for the settlers who were forced to wait for their allocation of land. More than 2000 people had arrived in South Australia, but only a few were able to settle and work their land. More settlers began to arrive, adding to the chaos. Food supplies ran short, and provisions had to be imported at great expense from the colonies of New South Wales and Van Diemen's Land. The cost of food became prohibitive, and some farmers, lacking the capital to see them through the unexpected delays, had to sell the very implements essential for them to earn their livelihood.

Compared with the hard-drinking early settlers of most other Australian colonies, the South Australian immigrants were sober, respectable and industrious middle-class people who were keen to work and build. Some had knowledge and experience in winegrowing, and others in the brewing industry. They were all free settlers, and the colony was unique in that there was no transportation of convicts.

The First Brewery

One of the more fortunate settlers was John Warren. Frustrated with the endless waiting for his land, he managed to gain permission from Governor Hindmarsh to start a brewery:

Warren first erected a brewery on the park lands by permission of Captain Hindmarsh, to whom encouragement was given that he should hold it for seven or ten years on consideration of supplying the inhabitants with good beer and yeast at a moderate price.

Just one year after the colony was established, Adelaide had its first locally produced beer. John Warren's brewery, known as the Torrens Brewery, was unfortunately built on the bank of the Torrens River, and on 4 September 1844 it was washed away by heavy floods. During the seven years of its operation ten other breweries had started in Adelaide, but most were relatively short-lived. There were three notable exceptions. The Union Brewery and the Adelaide Brewery had both commenced brewing in 1844, and, by coincidence, both continued in business until 1902, a span of fifty-eight years. Adelaide's longest operating brewery was the Walkerville, which also began in 1844. In spite of several insolvencies, many changes in name and various locations, it continued to brew popular beer for ninety-four years.

After the allocation of land, most of the population derived their livelihood directly or indirectly from wheatfarming. Later, mining industries brought wealth to the colony, following the discoveries of rich lodes of copper ore at Burra and Kapunda in the 1840s. More copper mines were opened at other locations, and townships began to mushroom with the outward spread of farming.

The South Australian Brewing Co. Ltd issued this label during the 1960s as a tribute to South Australia's first Surveyor-General and the founder of the city of Adelaide, Colonel William Light.

Country Breweries

South Australia's first regional brewery was opened at Oakbank, 30 km east of Adelaide, in 1843 by Scottish immigrants James and Andrew Johnston. The brewery became the longest-surviving country brewery in South Australia, continuing for seventy-one years until its closure in 1914.

For many years the picturesque town of Burra was the site of the world's richest copper mine. There were two substantial breweries in the town, the first of which opened in 1846.

As other pastoral and mining towns developed, the inhabitants needed provisions, churches, schools — and a regular supply of beer. Breweries were started at Gawler, Reynella and Noarlunga in 1847; Kapunda in 1848; and Clare, Littlehampton, McLarenvale and Macclesfield in 1850.

Although South Australia lacked the good fortune of many of her sister-colonies with their rich gold discoveries, the continuing output of copper and co-products added substantially to the colony's wealth. By 1880 nearly half the farmland in Australia was to be found in the colony, and by the turn of the century South Australia led the continent in agriculture. The fruit, wine, fishing and brewing industries also added to the economy.

During the 1870s there were no fewer than forty-five breweries in South Australia, and fifty in the 1880s.

Decline

Toward the end of the nineteenth century road conditions had improved, and there were rail links to most provincial towns. The larger Adelaide breweries were able to despatch their beer and other products quickly and economically to almost any destination, and the country breweries began to feel the effect of competition. Most of the mines had closed, leading to the inevitable departure of the miners and their families. Severe droughts had brought destitute farmers back to the city, and the brewing business in country districts declined rapidly.

Another contributing factor to the decline was the Commonwealth Act that came into force on 1 January 1902. Among many other conditions this stated, 'no person shall make beer unless licensed to do so'. Previously there had been few restraints, and the new regulations were so stringent and required so much paperwork that only the larger breweries could afford to comply with them.

The closure of breweries, in both city and country, had started in the late 1880s. The number of country breweries had dropped from twenty-three in 1888 to five in 1920. By 1930 there were only two; ten years later there were no country breweries. In Adelaide the peak was reached in 1888 when nineteen breweries were operating. In 1920 there were six, and now there are only

The West End Brewery, Hindley Street, Adelaide, 1880.

South Australia's most famous brewery is the South Australian Brewing Co. Ltd. Formed on 1 March 1893, it was originally incorporated as the South Australian Brewing, Malting & Wine & Spirit Co. Ltd in 1888 by the merger of the Kent Town Brewery, the West End Brewery and the wine-and-spirit business of Rounsevell & Simms.

The Kent Town Brewery had been built by Edwin Smith in 1876. The West End Brewery, Hindley Street, was established in 1859 by William Henry Clarke. Following the merger, it continued to be the major beer production unit for the South Australian Brewing Co. Ltd until 1983, when the buildings were demolished.

The Kent Town Brewery, Rundle Street, Adelaide, c. 1876.

two, both of which have a strong and flourishing marketing presence in the industry nationally.

The larger of these is the South Australian Brewing Co. Ltd, which was formed in 1888 by the merger of two of Adelaide's largest breweries, the West End Brewery (established in 1859) and the Kent Town Brewery (which started in 1876). The new company acquired many city and country breweries, which were closed either forthwith or soon after. Hotels were bought and, although the company has diversified, brewing remains the group's major activity.

The other South Australian brewery, Cooper & Sons Ltd, has a proud history dating back to 1862 when Thomas Cooper started brewing as a one-man business, supplying a few private customers with bottled beer. The family company has grown through good management and the excellence of its products, and is a highly efficient brewery of international repute.

High on Montefiore Hill overlooking Adelaide stands the statue of the founder of the city, Colonel William Light. From this scenic vantage point and with a little imagination, it may be possible to see the site on the Torrens River where pioneer settler John Warren first began brewing in 1837.

South Australia

#	Location	Grid
1	Adelaide	F6
2	Auburn	F5
3	Beltana	G1
4	Blinman	G2
5	Burra	F5
6	Clare	F5
7	Gawler	F6
8	Goolwa	F7
9	Gumeracha	G6
10	Jamestown	F4
11	Kadina	E6
12	Kapunda	F6
13	Langhorne Creek	G7
14	Laura	F4
15	Littlehampton	F6
16	Lobethal	G6
17	Macclesfield	F7
18	McLaren Vale	F7
19	Melrose	F4
20	Milang	F7
21	Moonta	E6
22	Morphett Vale	F7
23	Mt Barker	F7
24	Mt Gambier	H10
25	Murray Bridge	G7
26	Naracoorte	H9
27	Noarlunga	F7
28	Normanville	F7
29	Nuriootpa	G6
30	Oakbank	F6
31	Penola	H10
32	Pichi Richi	F3
33	Port Augusta	E3
34	Port MacDonnell	H10
35	Port Pirie	F4
36	Quorn	F3
37	Reynella	F7
38	Robe	H10
39	Second Valley	F7
40	Strathalbyn	F7
41	Yankalilla	F7

Adelaide

Adelaide Aerated Waters & Brewing Co. Ltd 1883–98
Angus Street

The company was registered on 28 March 1883, and F. W. Klauer was appointed managing director. The previous month, the company advertised in the *Licensed Victuallers' Gazette and Sporting Chronicle*: 'We are now prepared to supply Aerated Waters, Cordials, Blended Ales and Stout etc, at lowest current rates'.

In 1898, after fifteen years of operation, the company was wound up voluntarily in order to facilitate the amalgamation with the Adelaide Co-operative Aerated Waters Co. Ltd. The new company continued to produce a variety of non-alcoholic beverages.

Adelaide Brewery 1844–1902
Pirie Street

The Adelaide Brewery was owned and operated by James Walsh, who at one time had been the Captain of the Brighton Rifles, and was also one of the largest shareholders in the Kadina and Wallaroo Railway Co. He started brewing in 1844, but may not have been the first owner of the Pirie Street Brewery, as it was called at that time. Ed Moger, a brewer in Pirie Street, was there in 1844, but there are no other references to Moger operating in Adelaide, although he had a brewery at Gumeracha in the late 1860s.

Another brewer, George Moger, presumably a relative of Ed, operated during 1849 to 1850. An assessment notice for Town Acre 158 listed 'Brick and wood sheds used as a brewery, Moger's Lane'. Moger's Lane runs north from Pirie Street.

In 1851 James Walsh let his Pirie Street Brewery to the partnership of William K. Simms, Samuel W. Humble, James Chambers and John Hayter. They continued for three years, and then the brewery changed hands a number of times until 1858, when it was closed.

James Walsh was still the owner, and in November that year he advertised the Pirie Street Brewery 'to let with the right of purchase'. The brewery remained unoccupied until 1860.

Edward J. F. Crawford then became the proprietor, but only for a year, and once again the brewery closed. During the sixteen-year period since the brewery had started, no fewer than eight people had been financially involved, none with any degree of success.

In 1863 James T. Syme and Frederick S. Sison remodelled the Pirie Street Brewery, and commenced brewing in 1864 as the Adelaide Brewery. Prospects for success seemed better than in the past.

Fred Sison was a well-known Adelaide identity, and had been a traveller for the Hindmarsh Brewery, while Syme had been the brewer at the Union Brewery. This combination of talent and experience led to profitable growth for the Adelaide Brewery. James Walsh, who had retained ownership of the property, died in 1873, and Syme & Sison purchased the brewery.

The Adelaide Brewery sold XX Ale and Pale Ale. Galatea Ale was also brewed without sugar, and Porter and their popular Stout were delivered in bottles, as well as in bulk.

Syme & Sison sold their Adelaide Brewery on 1 June 1882, but retained their freehold hotels. The new owners of the brewery were Henry S. Anthony, William Wickstead and Andrew McIntyre, and they continued to trade as Syme & Sison until 1902, when the South Australian Brewing Co. Ltd purchased and closed the brewery.

Pirie Street Brewery

James Walsh	1844–51
Simms, Humble, Chambers & Hayter	1851–54
Simms, Humble & Hayter	1854–55
Simms & Humble	1855–57
R. Wilcox	1857–58
William Clark	1858, closed
Edward Crawford	1860–61, closed

Adelaide Brewery

Syme & Sison	1864–82
Anthony, Wickstead & McIntyre	1882–1902
Taken over by South Australian Brewery Co. Ltd	1902

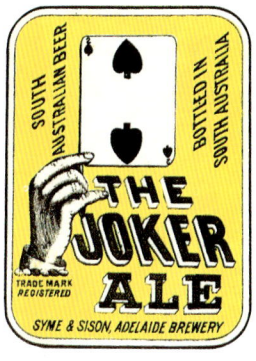

Originally the Pirie Street Brewery, the name was changed to the Adelaide Brewery by James Syme and Frederick Sison when they took over in 1864. The colours of the firm, yellow and black, were used for this Joker Ale label — even the drays and the brewery buildings were painted yellow and black.

Adelaide Brewery Co. Ltd 1933–38
Victoria Terrace (now Belair Road), Mitcham

In 1933 George Mallen sold his Waverley Brewery to the newly-formed Castlereagh Brewery Co. Ltd; the Waverley Brewery had been started by George's father, Charles Mallen, fifty-five years earlier, in 1878.

The new Castlereagh Brewery lasted a year, and then another new company was formed, this time the Adelaide Brewery Co. Ltd.

After four years the Adelaide Brewery Co. closed, and the premises were taken over by the Springfield Brewery Ltd.

Adelaide Hotel Brewery 1845
Hindley Street (north corner of Gray Street)

During the early years of the nineteenth century it was not uncommon for a hotel to set up a small brewery in the premises and brew beer for its own trade. A report in the *Adelaide Register* of 25 June 1845 describes a dinner held for the opening of the Adelaide Brewery in Hindley Street — the addition of a brewery to the Adelaide Hotel where John Auld had been the licensee since 1841.

John Auld and John Shand were the owners of the Torrens Brewery, and they had been using the Adelaide Hotel as an outlet for their Torrens Brewery beer before adding the brewery to the Adelaide Hotel.

Adelaide Malting & Brewing Co. Ltd 1894–1915
King William Street, Kent Town

The company started in business by purchasing the Macclesfield Brewing & Malting Co. from the owners, Messrs Wigg, Beevor and Clare. The old building was previously Logue's Brewery, which had its origin in 1856.

Beer was produced and sold still using the Macclesfield label. The company was put into liquidation in 1915. The premises were later used by Williams Breweries as a branch factory for the production of non-alcoholic beverages, including their popular 1 per cent alcohol Temperance Beer, oddly named Boshter Beer.

Alfa Brewing Co. 1908–28
17 Mary Street, Unley

During the early 1900s Alfred Schramm was one of three partners involved in the OK Brewery in the Adelaide suburb of Medindie. After four years the business went into voluntary liquidation, and Schramm moved to Broken Hill.

The Broken Hill venture was brief, and in 1908 Schramm returned to Adelaide and started the Alfa Brewing Co. Hop beer appears to have been the main product. During World War I Alfred Schramm changed his name to Alfred Seaton, and four years after his death in 1924 the factory was closed.

Anchor Brewery 1855–83
Morphett Street

The Anchor Brewery, which was started by John and Isaiah Reid, was located in Morphett Street near North Terrace, and was frequently called Reid's Brewery or the Morphett Street Brewery. According to the *South Australian Register* of February 1861, the brewery was the second-best in Adelaide. John Reid died in 1863. When the company became insolvent in 1866, the partners at that time were Isaiah Reid and John Harrison.

Frederick Fuller purchased the Anchor Brewery in 1868, and produced XX and XXX pale ale that was sold mostly in bottles. After three years Fuller also became insolvent.

In 1871 the brewery was taken over by Charles Chambers and his brother-in-law, Frederick Blades, who owned the Dragon Brewery. After operating the Anchor Brewery for a short period, they moved all the equipment to their Dragon Brewery in South Terrace.

Simms & Chapman of the West End Brewery used the Anchor Brewery premises as a bottling plant from 1871 to 1873, and the building was then left unoccupied.

Henry Edmeades reopened the brewery in 1877, and brewed there until 1883. He purchased the Kangaroo Brewery that year, and used the Anchor Brewery as a bottling depot until 1899.

J. & I. Reid	1855–63
I. Reid & J. Harrison	1863–66, closed
F. Fuller	1868–71
Chambers & Blades	1871
Simms & Chapman	1871–73, closed
(used as a bottling plant only)	
H. Edmeades	1877–83
(used as a bottling plant only)	1883–99

F. J. Anthony & Co. 1902–18
Payneham Road, East Adelaide

F. J. Anthony, son of H. S. Anthony of Adelaide Brewery fame, purchased a malting house in 1900, converted it to a brewery and started brewing beer in 1902.

Barleycorn Brewery 1841–44
Rundle Street

An advertisement in the *Adelaide Register* of September 1843 describes Thomas Moulden as a brewer at the Barleycorn Brewery in Rundle Street, near Stephen Street.

Thomas Moulden was the licensee of the Sir John Barleycorn Hotel during the period 1841 to 1844, and advertised 'Moulden's Porter — Barleycorn Brewery, Rundle Street. Splendid Draught and Bottled Porter made from South Australian Malt'. The bottled porter sold for 8s per dozen and the draught porter for 2s per gallon.

For a brief period in 1851 Moulden ran the Deepdell Brewery at Brownhill Creek, but on 13 July that year he was insolvent.

Big Gun Brewery
See Cannon Brewery.

Black Horse Brewery
See Walkerville Co-operative Brewing Co. Ltd.

Caledonian Brewery 1884–1902
Elizabeth Street, Eastwood/Edgeware Road
(now Opey Avenue), Hyde Park

The location of the Caledonian Brewery from 1884 to 1893 was Elizabeth Street, Eastwood. Charles Shand had leased the property from William Farrow, and 'he brewed in a tub holding 3 or 4 gallons and cooled in a hand basin'. The editorial was published in the *Licensed Victuallers' Gazette and Sporting Chronicle* of 10 July

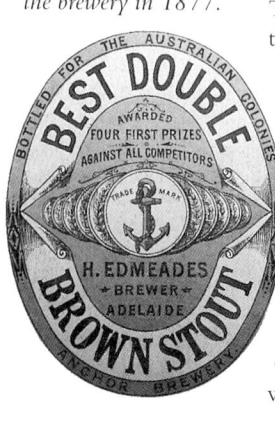

The Anchor Brewery, Adelaide, was started in 1855 by John Reid and his son, Isaiah. Several changes in ownership occurred before Henry Edmeades took over the brewery in 1877.

William Knapman's Cannon Brewery, Cannon Street, Port Adelaide.
Courtesy Brian Samuels collection

1886, and continued, 'No such abomination as glucose is admitted inside his brewery ... the beer was nectar'.

In 1885 Charles Shand advertised in the same gazette:

> Caledonian Brewery, Parkside, Chas. Shand Proprietor. The above brewery has now been established for 12 months and the brew has been pronounced by the public to be excellent ... good measure, low prices.

By 1886 Shand was 'turning out 30 or 40 hogsheads a week', but two years later he was insolvent.

John Schickel then leased the brewery from the owner, Elizabeth Farrow, for a period of five years, and when Richard Jaentsch became a partner in 1893 they bought the brewery from her. A few weeks earlier the partners had purchased the Hyde Park Brewery in Edgeware Road, Hyde Park. The brewery had been idle for three years, and Schickel & Jaentsch closed their Caledonian Brewery at Eastwood and shifted the equipment across to Hyde Park. The Hyde Park Brewery then became known as the Caledonian Brewery. At that time there were stables behind the main building, and the brewery was connected to the town by telephone.

Richard Jaentsch died three years later, and Schickel appointed Albert Dussenberg as manager in 1896. Retaining ownership of the brewery, Schickel then went to Kalgoorlie, Western Australia, to become the resident manager of the Kalgoorlie Brewing & Ice Co. Ltd. When John Schickel died in 1897 at the age of thirty-five, the Caledonian Brewery closed. Two years later it was reopened by William Bone, but even at that time it was still occasionally referred to as the Hyde Park Brewery. Bone lasted two years, and the brewery closed in 1902.

Caledonian Brewery (Elizabeth Street, Eastwood)

Charles Shand (lessee)	1884–88
John Schickel (lessee)	1888–93
Schickel & Jaentsch (owners)	1893

The Caledonian Brewery was closed, and the equipment was shifted to the premises of the old Hyde Park Brewery; trading continued as the Caledonian Brewery

Caledonian Brewery (Edgeware Road, Hyde Park)

Schickel & Jaentsch (owners)	1893–96
J. Schickel (owner)	1896–97, closed
A. Dussenberg (manager), W. Bone (owner)	1899–1902

Cannon Brewery   1865–1910
Cannon Street, Port Adelaide

William Knapman was twenty-four years of age when he migrated to Australia with his young bride. When he landed at Adelaide, he had only one shilling in his pocket, but he was soon able to find work as a carpenter. In 1860 he leased, with the right of purchase, the old White Horse Cellars Hotel at the corner of Commercial Road and Vincent Street, Port Adelaide. It had been built in 1851 as a masonic hall and theatre, and the Knapmans lived in the upstairs theatre area.

By 1865 William Knapman had converted the rear of the premises into a small brewery. It was known as the Steam Brewery, and 7 hogsheads of beer were brewed at a time. A carpenter by trade, Knapman built the Pioneer Hotel at Port Pirie in 1873, and shifted there three years later with his family. He continued to oversee the running of the brewery at Port Adelaide, and in 1883 he transferred the equipment to larger premises in Cannon Street and traded as the Cannon Brewery.

William Knapman and his son, William Henry Knapman, gradually acquired a number of hotels. They produced bottled ale that was sold under the brand name Big Gun, and the brewery was also referred to by that name. William Knapman Jnr died in 1900, and his father in 1908.

Sam Knapman and George Smith continued the business, but when brewing ceased in 1910 the property was sold to Walter & Morris, timber merchants. The buildings were subsequently demolished.

Castlereagh Brewery Co. Ltd
See Adelaide Brewery Co. Ltd.

Cooper & Crabb Ltd   1933–35
88 Durham Street, Glenelg

Cooper & Crabb Ltd was incorporated in 1933, and on 28 November 1935 the brewery closed. The address at Glenelg was near the site of the first mainland settlement of South Australia.

Cooper & Sons Ltd   1862–
9 Statenborough Street, Leabrook

Shortly after his arrival in 1852 in Adelaide, then a city with a population of about 33,000, Thomas Cooper went to work at his trade of shoemaking. Later he worked for a stonemason. By 1857 he had become a dairyman, and kept six cows on rented land opposite his home in George Street, Norwood, on Waterfall Creek Gully next to Gillard's vineyard.

When Thomas Cooper started brewing in 1862, he was a one-man enterprise and very inexperienced. He supplied only private customers. Whereas the large breweries produced mostly draught beer at that time, Thomas bottled his beer using any kind of bottles available. By 1867 he had more than 120 customers, but he didn't sell to hotels as it was against his principles. There were ten breweries in business in Adelaide at that time, and a further twenty-two in country areas.

During 1867 Thomas Cooper began to have serious problems with his brews. Time and again his batches were not up to standard, and he had to offload these wherever he could at lower prices. With the problems persisting, he was brewing less and selling less. Expenses exceeded income, debts mounted, and by 1869 his land and buildings were reclaimed. All his hard work and expectations, after almost eight years, were reduced to nothing. He had his wife and large family to keep, and he had to rent premises on the corner of Charles Street (now Phillips Street) and High Street, Kensington. He was not declared insolvent, and had the determination to continue brewing. With a small loan Thomas set up a very modest brewing plant in 1871 and tried to make ends meet. Then, in 1872, his wife died, leaving him with seven children to look after.

By 1878 business began to improve, and his son John, then twenty-one years old, started work at the brewery. In February 1881 Cooper purchased land in Statenborough Street, Upper Kensington, and a brewery was constructed using some of the equipment from the High Street premises. Son John began to introduce improved methods of production, and the quality and consistency of their beer improved greatly.

Cooper's continued as a small family concern, still bottling, and showing no interest in supplying hotels. The business expanded very little during the 1880s and the difficult years of the 1890s, and output represented only about 1 per cent of the state's consumption in 1900. Thomas Cooper had retired, and following his death in December 1897 the business then operated as a partnership with the four older sons — John, Christopher, Samuel and Stanley. Other sons, Frederic and Charles, worked at the brewery, and John's eldest son, Frank (grandson of Thomas), was made a partner in 1918.

John Cooper now headed the business. Hotels were being supplied, and this accounted for 40 per cent of sales in 1910, rising to 76 per cent by 1918. The Coopers had no interest in buying hotels, nor did they make draught beer, being content to sell their products in bottles.

In 1915 a referendum in South Australia resulted in 6 p.m. closing of hotels. Other Australian states soon followed, with Victoria, New South Wales and Tasmania in 1916, and Queensland soon after. The Act was not repealed until 1968, when hotel bars could then remain open until 10 p.m.

Cooper & Sons Ltd was formed in 1923, although the business still remained a Cooper family concern. When John Cooper died in 1935 at the age of seventy-eight, he had been head of the company for nearly forty years, and its guiding hand for even longer. Since then, successive members of the family have assumed control.

As well as producing lager beers, Cooper's has also used the top-fermentation method, a process that has varied little from that of the 1880s. Until recently Cooper's Sparkling Ale has been the only true ale produced by a major brewery in Australia, and its popularity has been acclaimed internationally.

Today the company's products are marketed throughout Australia, and exported to many countries. Cooper & Sons Ltd operate a brewery that is unique in Australia, being the only major brewery still privately controlled by the descendants of its founder.

Cooper's Brewery
See Cooper & Sons Ltd.

Deepdell Brewery
See Barleycorn Brewery.

Dragon Brewery   1871–1901
South Terrace

If the choice of name for a brewery meant anything, the Dragon Brewery could give rise to a number of both pragmatic and fanciful interpretations. There was even

Left: *Chambers & Blades Dragon Brewery, South Terrace, Adelaide, c. 1901.*
Courtesy Mortlock Library, South Australia

a sketch of a dragon on the bottle label, but whatever view was taken the brewery put out first-class beer.

Charles Chambers and his brother-in-law, Frederick Blades, purchased the Anchor Brewery in 1871, merely for the equipment, which they transferred to their newly-constructed Dragon Brewery in South Terrace. The three-storey building had extensive cellars, and was built using Glen Osmond stone, galvanised iron, and timber.

When Charles Chambers died in 1887, his brother William joined the firm, which continued to trade as Chambers & Blades. The brewery was put on the market in 1892 but there were no buyers. The following year Chambers & Blades were insolvent. However, the brewery kept going after a modest settlement with creditors.

Frederick Blades died in 1895. His son then joined the firm, which continued as Chambers & Blades Dragon Brewery. After six more years the company became insolvent, and the brewery was taken over by the Walkerville Co-operative Brewing Co. Ltd, and closed. During its life of thirty years the trade of the Dragon Brewery was principally local, and the company brewed 'a fine, pale, bitter beer of an English type'.

East Adelaide Brewery   1895–98
Seventh Avenue, St Peters

W. W. Warren started the East Adelaide Brewery, and was joined by Edward Clark, son of W. H. Clark, an experienced South Australian brewer. Warren had won a considerable sum of money as the result of successful turf speculations, and in 1891 he had become the licensee of the Napoleon Hotel. He built his brewery a few years later, and after working it for a year or two, he sold to his partner, who traded as E. Clark & Co.

The East Adelaide Brewery amalgamated with the Torrenside Brewery on 3 March 1898 to form Clark, Ware & Co. Brewing was then carried on at the Torrenside Brewery, and the East Adelaide Brewery was closed.

Enterprise Brewery   1885
Waymouth Street

Stephen & Co. were cordial manufacturers, and had been in business in Currie Street, Adelaide, since 1877. The company advertised in April 1885:

> Enterprise Brewery, Stephen & Co., Brewers and Bottlers of Superior Ales and Stout. Manufacturers and Importers of Wines, Liqueurs, Bitters, Cordials and Vinegar. Orders addressed to the Brewery, Waymouth Street, W. Adelaide, will receive immediate attention.

J. H. Foureur Ltd   1876
Jetty Road/Murray Street, Clapham

Joseph Foureur was originally a brewer and aerated-water manufacturer at Jetty Road, Glenelg, and it is doubtful if any alcoholic drinks were made after 1876. In later years the company, J. H. Foureur Ltd, formed in 1913, produced olive oil, a range of cordials, vinegar, cider, tonic ales and shandy. The factory was then at Murray Street in Clapham.

Glanville Brewery   1879–1907
Cnr Marion & Dislander Streets, Glanville

The Glanville Brewery was conveniently located between the Port River and St Vincent's Gulf, where the cool breezes from the sea reduced the temperature during the summer months. The founder of the brewery was William Goodier, who ran a successful business making ale, stout and tonic. He used a sailing ship as a trademark.

William Goodier's Granville Brewery, Adelaide, 1894. Goodier's five-roomed home, complete with a picket fence, is to the right.
Courtesy Port Adelaide Historical Society

> ## UNCHARITABLE COMPLAINT
>
> The brewers, as usual, gave Christmas beer to the gaols, lunatic asylums, and charitable institutions of Adelaide this year. This brought a protest, addressed to the Premier, from the Christian Endeavour Union, asking him to refuse the gift.
> I wonder if any other colony can beat this for narrow-minded Christianity? No public notice of the protest has been taken by anyone, much to the chagrin of the Endeavourers to provoke a discussion.
>
> *Australian Brewers' Journal*, January 1898

On 26 February 1906 William Goodier took on Mrs Martha Reid as a partner, and they formed the Goodier, Reid Brewing Co. Ltd, which went into liquidation the following year.

Goodier, Reid Brewing Co. Ltd
See Glanville Brewery.

Grenfell Street Brewery   1839–40
Grenfell Street

One of the colony's earliest breweries, the Grenfell Street Brewery, advertised in the *Southern Australian* of 6 November 1839:

> Brewery, Grenfell Street, opposite Fordham's Hotel, XX Ale, 2 shillings and 6 pence per gallon delivered in any part of Adelaide. Bottled Ale, 8 shillings per dozen bottles not included. Orders received at the brewery.

Another advertisement appeared in the 1840 *South Australian Almanac*, but beyond that nothing further is known of the brewery.

Hackney Brewery   1883–93
Junction of Walkerville Terrace & Park Terrace

The Phillipson brothers started the Hackney Brewery in 1883, and they won a gold medal for their ale and stout at the 1884 Calcutta Exhibition.

After the brewery closed, James Phillipson left the district and moved to Cue, Western Australia, where he started the Murchison Brewing Co.

Halifax Street Brewery   1843–63
Halifax Street

William Henry Clark owned and operated his Halifax Street Brewery from 1843 to 1857. During 1853 he built a steam flourmill, granary, malthouse and biscuit factory. These all adjoined the brewery, a towering five storeys high, described as one of the most imposing structures in the colony. From 1857 Clark leased the brewery to various operators.

Simms & Clark	1857
Simms & Noltenius	1857–58
W. K. Simms	1859–60
E. J. F. Crawford	1860
J. Smith	1861–63

The Halifax Street Brewery closed in 1863, and remained unoccupied for twelve years. It was reopened in 1875 by William Disher who chose the name Imperial Brewery. Of Scottish descent, Disher had been a wine-and-spirit merchant in Adelaide, and the proprietor of the Standard Brewery in Echuca, Victoria. Both ventures had been burdened with problems, both legal and financial, and in spite of his enthusiasm and perseverance at the old Halifax Street Brewery, now the Imperial Brewery, he was forced to close after one year.

Hindley Street Brewery   1843–47
Cnr Hindley & Morphett Streets

Andrew Birrell was one of the first Adelaide City councillors, and served from 1840 to 1843, and again in 1857. He was also one of Adelaide's early brewers, and advertised in the *Adelaide Examiner* of 11 February 1843: 'To Publicans and Families — on sale at the Hindley Street Brewery ... an excellent lot of ale ... 2 shillings per gallon. Andrew Birrell'.

By 1847 Andrew Birrell had left Hindley Street. The previous year he had leased the Burra Brewery, north of Adelaide, where there was much better profit potential in the rapidly-growing coppermining town. All the equipment from the Hindley Street Brewery was taken up to the Burra Brewery. He sold his business there in 1850, and started another brewery, the Enterprise Brewery, at Clare, 40 km south of Burra.

Hindmarsh Brewery
(Richard Street)   1859–1927
Richard Street, Hindmarsh

This Hindmarsh Brewery was started in 1859 by James Watson and Brocardius Bauer, on the western side of Richard Street. Watson & Bauer lasted less than a year, and the next lessee, J. Coultard, fared no better.

Then along came Edward Crawford to try his luck. He had done reasonably well when he was at the other Hindmarsh Brewery (in Robert Street), but not very well at all when he had rented the Halifax Street Brewery and then the Pirie Street Brewery, both of which had failed within a year. But luck favoured the brave, and Crawford continued at the Hindmarsh Brewery in Richard Street for about six years, until 1868.

The business and property were then taken over by Herman Henry Haussen and his brother-in-law, George Catchlove, and they traded as Haussen & Catchlove, Hindmarsh Brewery.

The brewery had extensive cellars known as the 'warren' which completely undermine the brewery building and extend for some

distance on either hand [sic]. There are seven passages in all, running out of the central cellar.

The company also had a central office and store at 63 Hindley Street.

Herman Haussen died in 1870, only two years after taking over the brewery. His widow, Rosa, then carried on the business with her brother, George Catchlove, until he retired in 1874.

Rosa Haussen's second husband was Frederick Bucknall, and with a third partner, Frank South Botting, they continued trading as Haussen & Co. The company also owned several hotels and a wine-and-spirit business.

After Fred Bucknall retired in 1881 Frank Botting ran the brewery by himself, and in 1893 he was joined by his father, Francis Joseph Botting. They introduced a double-B trademark, registered in December 1893, the letters referring to 'Botting and Botting'. Hindmarsh Brewery bottled ales and stout were pasteurised, and the bottling department was connected with the cellars by electric bells and a speaking tube.

Frank Botting died in 1894, and the father kept the business going until his death in 1906 at the age of eighty-seven. Haussen & Co. Ltd was incorporated in 1910, and the company continued brewing until 1927. Arrangements were then made with the Walkerville Brewery and the South Australian Brewery to supply beer to their various hotels. At the time the brewery closed it was one of Adelaide's longest operating breweries, spanning a period of sixty-eight years.

Watson & Bauer	1859–60
J. Coultard	1860
E. J. Crawford	1861–68
H. Haussen & Catchlove	1868–70
R. Haussen & Catchlove	1870–74
R. Haussen, Bucknall & Botting	1874–81
Frank Botting	1881–93
Frank & Francis Botting	1893–94
Francis Botting	1894–1906
Trustees	1906–10
Haussen & Co. Ltd	1910–27

Hindmarsh Brewery
(Robert Street) 1841–59
Cnr Robert Street (now Orsmond Street) & Manton Street, Hindmarsh

Irishman Daniel Cudmore was more of a speculator than a brewer. One of the very early settlers, he built a malting house in Melbourne Street, Adelaide, in 1837, and added a brewery in 1840. It was simply called the Melbourne Street Brewery, which he either leased or sold the following year.

In 1841 Cudmore built the Hindmarsh Brewery and malthouse, which he rented to Edward James Crawford in 1843. Two years later Crawford bought the brewery.

Still the brewing entrepreneur, Cudmore started the Allen Creek Brewery at Kapunda, where rich lodes of copper had been discovered. Ultimately, Cudmore returned to his pastoral and hotel interests.

Meanwhile, Edward Crawford was doing well at the Hindmarsh Brewery, and within a few years his brothers, James, Sydney, Thomas and Henry, were involved in the business. To prove the quality of his ales Crawford sent some casks on a return trip to Singapore, and the result, after the ale was tasted on return, was 'A colonial ale of choice brewing which sampled very well'.

Crawford began to speculate in land, and also invested in several hotels. By 1859 he was trying to rent his brewery. While this was going on, he took out a three-year lease on the Halifax Street Brewery. That venture failed within a year, but apparently obsessed with breweries he started out again by renting the Pirie Street Brewery. Once again, Crawford was out of luck, or out of good beer, or both, and within a year he was out of business.

The Hindmarsh Brewery had been idle since 1859, and three years later the malthouse section was taken over and used by W. K. Simms of the West End Brewery. Many years later, in 1876, the brewery premises were acquired by the newly-formed Kangaroo Brewery.

See also Kangaroo Brewery.

Holland Street Brewery
See Victoria Brewery.

Hyde Park Brewery 1883–90
Edgeware Road (now Opey Avenue), Hyde Park

When Robert Tilley and Henry Buckerfield were ready for business, they put an advertisement in the *Port Augusta Dispatch* of October 1883:

> Hyde Park Brewery, Adelaide. Tilley and Buckerfield proprietors. Sparkling Draught Ales, £3 per hogshead; 2½ per cent allowed for cash.

The price was very competitive for beer at that time.

Early in 1885 Guilford E. Gray purchased the brewery, and invited the trade to sample his brew, 'a genuine article' as he called it, and still priced at £3 per hogshead. Gray was an experienced brewer, having worked with his brother, Charles, at Melrose, and later at Strathalbyn, before becoming the head brewer at the Lion Brewery in Adelaide. He brewed at Hyde Park with considerable success, and exhibited his India Pale Ale at the Colonial and Indian Exhibition in London in 1886.

In December 1887 Gray leased the brewery to Theodore Bruce and George Aldridge. According to the *South Australian Sentinel* of 31 March 1888:

> Mr Guilford Gray of the Hyde Park Brewery has taken charge of a new brewery at Broken Hill … intends keeping the Hyde Park Brewery going and superintending the Broken Hill Brewery as well.

In 1889 Gray returned to Adelaide, and sold the Hyde Park Brewery to Charles Todd.

The brewery was vacant from 1890 to 1893, and was then purchased by the owners of the nearby Caledonian Brewery, John Schickel and Richard Jaentsh. They closed their Caledonian Brewery and shifted the equipment over to their newly-acquired Hyde Park Brewery in Edgeware Road, but continued in business as the Caledonian Brewery.

Imperial Brewery
See Halifax Street Brewery.

Kangaroo Brewery 1876–85
Manton Street, Hindmarsh

In 1876 R. Strutton and C. W. F. Trapman purchased the premises of the old Hindmarsh Brewery, which had been built in 1841 by Daniel Cudmore and had remained vacant since 1859. The partners used the name Kangaroo Brewery, and produced ale and porter with a kangaroo as their trademark.

In earlier years Strutton had been the sole bottler of ales and porter for Haussen & Co.'s Hindmarsh Brewery, and the partners continued to bottle some of their competitor's products at their Kangaroo Brewery well into the 1880s.

Trapman retired in 1882, and the following year Strutton sold the Kangaroo Brewery to Henry Edmeades. Edmeades had been the proprietor of the Anchor Brewery, but after two years, he closed the Kangaroo Brewery.

Kent Town Brewery 1876–88
Cnr Rundle Street & Dequetteville Terrace, Kent Town

Edwin Thomas Smith (later Sir Edwin) had considerable experience in the brewing industry. He had been operating his Logue's Brewery in King William Street for sixteen years, and having outgrown the brewery, he decided in 1876 to build a new and much larger brewery in Rundle Street. He also had nine workmen's cottages built at the rear of the brewery. Nothing was spared in the construction of the magnificent brewery, which was fitted out with the latest equipment and facilities available.

Edwin Smith was devoted to his trade, and became one of Adelaide's wealthiest businessmen. He was a member of the House of Assembly, representing East Torrens for twenty-one years, and in 1879 he was elected Mayor of Adelaide. He was knighted in 1888, and it was during that year that the Kent Town Brewery amalgamated with the West End Brewery to form the South Australian Brewing, Malting & Wine & Spirit Co. Ltd. Brewing continued at the West End Brewery, and the Kent Town Brewery was used for malting.

In 1896 the Kent Town Brewery premises were leased to the malting company of Barrett & Burston of Melbourne. Although there have been alterations since, the old Kent Town Brewery building has retained much of its original character.

Lion Brewery
See Lion Brewing & Malting Co. Ltd.

Lion Brewing & Malting Co. Ltd 1872–1914
Jerningham Street, North Adelaide

In March 1871 the partners William Bailey and Frederick Stanley called for tenders for the excavation of a large cellar and the construction of a brewery. Bailey had been in the hotel business, and Stanley was a wine-and-spirit merchant. The brewery took a year to complete, and in 1872 the partners started in business as the Lion Brewery.

Within a year William Bailey had become the sole proprietor, but shortly afterwards he sold the brewery to William Henry Beaglehole. James Johnston was a partner, and although there were two more partners, W. J. James and J. McD. Gasquoine, the company traded as Beaglehole & Johnston, Lion Brewery.

William Beaglehole had been a successful gold prospector in Victoria, and after returning to South Australia he started business as a building contractor. He built the Kapunda railway station, and several buildings in Rundle and Hindley Streets in Adelaide, before becoming a member of parliament.

The Lion Brewing & Malting Co. Ltd was formed

on 12 April 1888 for the purpose of acquiring the Lion Brewery property and ongoing business, its twenty-three freehold hotels, several parcels of vacant land, and its interest in sixteen leasehold hotels. At that time the Lion Brewery was producing only draught beer and stout. Bottling started in 1892, and beer sold for 4s per dozen bottles.

In 1914 arrangements were made for the Walkerville Co-operative Brewery to supply some of the Lion hotels with beer, and the brewing section of the Lion Brewery was closed, although the company continued to produce aerated waters and cordials.

Much of the original structure of the old brewery and malting premises remain. The buildings and the Lion Hotel were sold in 1970, and subsequently converted to a modern boutique-style brewery, which has retained the original name, Lion Brewery.

Lion Brewery

W. Bailey & F. Stanley	1872–73
W. Bailey	1873
Beaglehole & Johnston	1873–88
Lion Brewery & Malting Co. Ltd	**1888–1914**

Logue's Brewery 1857–76
King William Street, Kent Town

In 1857 Edward Logue built his brewery on the site of Dr Kent's flourmill in King William Street. Edwin Smith became a partner in 1860, but Logue died later that year and Smith took over the business, still retaining the name Logue's Brewery.

The energetic and industrious Smith (later Sir Edwin Smith) quickly went about extending the premises and updating the equipment. He also kept a large piggery that added to his income. With beer sales rapidly expanding, Logue's Brewery became too small, and in 1876 Smith built a grand new brewery in Rundle Street. He called it the Kent Town Brewery.

Logue's Brewery was vacated and the buildings were used, in turn, by several other firms: the Co-operative Mineral Water Co.; Macclesfield Brewery; Adelaide Malting & Brewing Co. Ltd and Williams Breweries Ltd.

Macclesfield Brewing & Malting Co. Ltd 1888–94
King William Street, Kent Town

On 1 August 1888 the partnership of Wolton Wigg, Miles Beevor and William Clare opened the Macclesfield Brewery (originally Logue's Brewery, which had closed in 1876). The partners had also purchased the Macclesfield Brewery, Macclesfield, in the hill country 50 km south-east of Adelaide, in 1888. After a few years the country brewery was closed, and the equipment was transferred to their brewery in Adelaide.

In 1894 the Macclesfield Brewery in Kent Town was sold to the Adelaide Malting & Brewing Co. Ltd. Brewing continued, and the beer was still sold under the Macclesfield label.

Melbourne Street Brewery 1840–c. 1858
Lot 983, Melbourne Street, North Adelaide

The man who started the brewery in 1840, Daniel Cudmore, moved on after a year, and started the Hindmarsh Brewery, in the Adelaide suburb of Hindmarsh.

The Melbourne Street Brewery may have been idle for some years. Others came and went, all attempting to earn a living at the brewery: James Hearn, 1849–55; then B. Higgins, 1856–58; and finally Sam Higgins in 1858.

Morphett Street Brewery
See Anchor Brewery.

Nathan Brewery
See South Australian Brewing Co. Ltd.

OK Brewery 1903–7
41 Main North Road, Medindie

Alfred Schramm ran the OK Brewery with the support of two partners, Messrs Newing and Alderman. They started in August 1903, and went into voluntary liquidation in October 1907.

Pirie Street Brewery
See Adelaide Brewery, Pirie Street.

Primrose Brewery
See Union Brewing & Malting Co. Ltd.

Prince Albert Hotel & Brewery
See Tasmanian Hotel & Brewery.

Reedbeds Brewery 1850
The *Adelaide Register* of 30 October 1850 stated:

> A correspondent has been pleased to express in terms of ecstasy the satisfaction he lately experienced in imbibing a glass of Mr Fisher's ale. The gentleman, we are told, has recently commenced brewing at Reedbeds and the beverage produced is not only superior to the ordinary run of colonial swanky, but a near approach to the genuine imported Burton.

George Fisher was the brewer referred to, and with such a grand editorial it is surprising that more is not known of Fisher and his 'near approach to the genuine imported Burton' beer.

Reid's Brewery
See Anchor Brewery.

Salisbury Brewery 1855–84
In January 1860, five years after starting the brewery, the owners, Patrick Wauchope and John Parker, sold the brewery to Amos Sargent for £365.

Sargent worked the brewery until 1863, and then sold to Dennis Nash for £507. With his father, Owen Nash, they stayed at the brewery for the next twenty years.

In 1884 Dennis Nash left the district, and purchased the Solomontown Brewery at Port Pirie.

South Australian Brewing Co. Ltd   1888–
107 Port Road, Thebarton

The South Australian Brewing Co. Ltd has a remarkable history of acquisitions and growth, and has dominated the South Australian beer market since its inception. The company was formed by a three-way merger of the West End Brewery, established by William Clark in 1859, the Kent Town Brewery built in 1876 by Edwin Smith, and the wine-and-spirit business of Rounsevell & Simms. The new company was incorporated on 15 March 1888 as the South Australian Brewing, Malting & Wine & Spirit Co. Ltd. Robert Stock, brother-in-law of Edwin Smith, remained as managing director until his death in 1904.

The prospectus of the new company offered a guaranteed dividend of 10 per cent for the first three years and securities were represented by the three merged companies, forty-four freehold hotels, sixty-five leasehold hotels, extensive freehold stores and other properties. The capital of the company was £400,000.

The Kent Town Brewery was used as a malthouse, and all brewing operations were carried out at the West End Brewery in Hindley Street.

In 1891 the company disposed of the wine-and-spirit section to A. E. & F. Tolley and Milne & Co. The name of the company was changed to the South Australian Brewing Co. Ltd on 1 March 1893.

The Broken Hill Brewery was purchased in 1889, and the company continued to expand with the takeover in 1893 of South Australian country breweries at Laura and Port Augusta. The Laura Brewery was closed the following year, and brewing continued at the Port Augusta Brewery until 1898. It was during that year that the company commenced bottling with the well-known 'Pick Axe' emblem embossed on the bottles.

By the turn of the century lager beer was becoming the most popular beer in the eastern states, and in 1902 the South Australian Brewery set up a new department specially designed for the production of lager beer.

The Adelaide Brewery of Syme & Sison was taken over in 1902, and the Walkerville Co-operative Brewing Co., one of the main competitors, acquired in 1938. Walkerville had previously purchased the Torrenside Brewery in 1898, and had relocated to that site in Winwood Street, Southwark. At the time of takeover the Winwood Street premises were renamed the Nathan Brewery, to be changed again in 1949 to the Southwark Brewery. When the West End Brewery premises in Hindley Street were demolished in 1983, all brewing operations were then carried out at Winwood Street.

The closure and demolition of the West End Brewery was a sad occasion. It meant the loss of a historic landmark, and the end of 124 years of brewing from the time William Clark had started the brewery in 1859.

From the early twentieth century the South Australian Brewery entered into agreements with many breweries that were then either taken over and closed, or, having ceased beer production, still required a reliable source of beer for their hotel interests. These business strategies effectively shut out competition, and

The South Australian Brewing Co. Ltd, Hindley Street brewery, shortly after the company was formed in 1893. It was still referred to as the West End Brewery, a major beer producer for the South Australian Brewery until 1983.

La Trobe Library, State Library of Victoria

An early label of the South Australian Brewing, Malting & Wine & Spirit Co. Ltd. Formed in 1888, the company continued under that name until 1893, when it became the South Australian Brewing Co. Ltd.

paved the way for both Adelaide and country districts to be supplied with beer from the company's own breweries in Adelaide.

Breweries whose hotels were supplied by the company include:

Supplied from the Southwark Brewery
Dragon Brewery	1901–
Adelaide Brewery	1902
Lion Brewery	1914
Oakbank Brewery	1914
Hindmarsh Brewery	1927

Supplied from the West End Brewery
Cannon Brewery, Port Adelaide	1905
Gawler Brewery, Gawler	1909
Victoria Brewery, Kapunda	1909
Standard Brewery, Mt Gambier	1923
Waverley Brewery, Mitcham	1933
Dorset Brewery, Oakbank	1938

The company continued to invest in the brewing industry by acquiring a 25 per cent interest in Cooper & Sons Ltd in 1962, and two years later a licence was obtained to brew the world-renowned Guinness Stout. Over time, about 160 hotels were acquired, and the company diversified with strategic shareholdings in other companies. Although investments and property ownership have grown in importance, brewing has remained the group's major activity.

In the earlier years the South Australian market accounted for most of the company's sales. Aggressive marketing, attractive packaging and, most importantly, consistently high-quality products, have resulted in strong growth in sales throughout Australia and overseas. With a brewing history of more than 100 years, the South Australian Brewing Co. Ltd has well earned its reputation as one of Australia's most respected and successful companies.

On 1 August 1993 the company became part of the New Zealand-based Lion Nathan group, but the popular range of West End beers and other products continue to be brewed.

South Australian Brewing, Malting
& Wine & Spirit Co. Ltd   1888–91
Formed by the merger of West End Brewery (established 1859), Kent Town Brewery (established 1876) and Rounsevell & Simms, wine & spirit merchants
Brewing continued at the West End Brewery, Hindley Street

South Australian Brewing Co. Ltd   1891–
Acquisitions:
Broken Hill Brewery Co.	1889–1925
Laura Brewery	1893–94
Port Augusta Brewery	1893–98
Adelaide Brewery, Pirie St.	1902, closed
Walkerville Co-operative Brewing Co.	1938
Renamed Nathan Brewery	1938
Renamed Southwark Brewery	1949
West End Brewery, Hindley Street	1983, closed

Brewing continued at the Winwood Street brewery

National Brewing Holdings Ltd
  (Lion Nathan Group)   1993–

South Australian Brewing, Malting & Wine & Spirit Co. Ltd
See South Australian Brewing Co. Ltd.

Southwark Brewery
See South Australian Brewing Co. Ltd.

Springfield Brewery Ltd   1938–48
Cnr Princes & Belair Roads, Mitcham

When the Springfield Brewery Ltd was formed in 1938, the premises of the old Adelaide Brewing Co. were purchased. It was previously the Castlereagh Brewery and, before that, the Waverley Brewery built by Charles Mallen in 1878.

William Joseph Jacka (previously the owner of the Melrose Brewery, at Melrose in the Flinders Ranges) was involved in the Springfield Brewery.

From about 1950 the premises were used as a

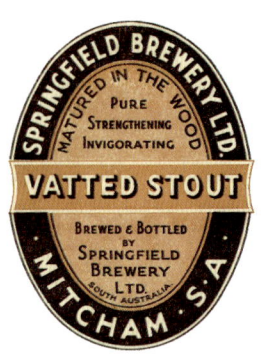

butter-and-cheese factory, but later they were demolished to make way for the Mitcham shopping centre.

Waverley Brewery
Haimes, Mallen & Co./Mallen & Co. 1878–1933
Castlereagh Brewery Co. Ltd 1933–34
Adelaide Brewery Ltd 1934–38
Springfield Brewery Ltd 1938–48
(only the premises of the Adelaide Brewery Ltd were taken over, not the business)

Steam Brewery
See Cannon Brewery.

Tasmanian Hotel & Brewery 1839–47
Cnr Hindley & Morphett Streets

The Tasmanian Hotel & Brewery was advertising consistently from 1839 to 1845. One advertisement in the *South Australian Almanac* of 1844 stated:

> Tasmanian Brewery, Hindley Street, near the corner of Morphett Street. Brewery at the back of the Tasmanian Hotel. Six pence per quart.

John Wheland was the licensee.

From 1846 to 1847 William Williams was the owner, and he changed the name to the Prince Albert Hotel & Brewery. Council assessment notices for the two years show John Chanter as the occupier of the 'Prince Albert Hotel and Brewery, brick house and out-buildings on town acre 72'.

Thwaites Brewery 1896–97
Cator Street, Hindmarsh

Thomas Thwaites's efforts at brewing lasted less than a year.

Torrens Brewery 1837–43
Park Land, River Torrens

John Warren was South Australia's first brewer. He started one year after the colony was founded, and his tiny premises were on the bank of the River Torrens, at the rear of the present North Terrace railway station.

Captain Sturt, writing to His Excellency, Governor Grey, on 14 October 1841, commented:

> I believe that an individual by the name of Warren first erected a brewery on the Park Lands by permission of Captain Hindmarsh, to whom encouragement was given that he should hold it for seven or ten years on consideration of supplying the inhabitants with good beer and yeast at a moderate price.

John Warren had arrived in the colony to take up farming land, but with the protracted delays in land allocation he started brewing in 1837 as a means of livelihood. He soon had competition when a Mr Lillyman set up a brewery, also adjacent to the River Torrens. These early breweries were quite small, and the ale was brewed using wheat, since no barley was available in the colony at that time.

Warren didn't stay in the brewing business for the suggested seven or ten years, and in 1841 he sold the brewery to the partnership of John Auld and John Shand. In December of that year they advertised their

> Best Ale, £5 per hogshead Light Ale, 7 shillings per dozen bottles and Good Porter at equally low prices. On sale, wholesale and retail at the Adelaide Brewery, Hindley Street.

John Auld happened to be the licensee of the Adelaide Hotel, which was used as an outlet for the beer the partners brewed at their brewery, now named the Torrens.

Brewing ceased at the Torrens Brewery in 1843 when Auld and Shand were declared bankrupt. Shand was later imprisoned as an insolvent debtor, but Auld was able to stay on as the licensee of the Adelaide Hotel.

On 5 September 1844 heavy floods destroyed the Torrens Brewery. As recorded in the *South Australian Register* of 25 September 1844,

> between one and two o'clock, the destruction of Shand's brewery … was not too fearfully evident. By four in the afternoon, the brewery was completely undermined and came down with a tremendous crash.

This was a tragic end to South Australia's first brewery. Some of the equipment was salvaged and taken over by John Primrose of the Union Brewery. By this time there were at least eight other breweries operating in Adelaide.

Torrenside Brewery 1886–98
Winwood Street, Southwark

The Torrenside Brewery, built on the southern bank of the River Torrens, was very much a family affair, and was managed by Alexander W. Ware and his brother, Thomas L. Ware. Brewing commenced in 1886, and two other brothers, George J. Ware and Charles Boxer Ware, joined the company in 1893.

NEW CURE FOR INFLUENZA

'ALCOHOL ONLY ANTIDOTE', SAYS NOTED LONDON DOCTOR
London, Monday, 3rd Feb., 1919

Sir James Cantlie, the noted Surgeon and Authority on Tropical Medicine, states that alcohol is the only valuable antidote for the new Influenza.

Many physicians are prescribing alcohol, the scarcity of which is considered a disgrace to the controlling authorities.

Australian Brewers' Journal, February 1919

The senior partner, Tom Ware, had learnt the trade at the South Australian country town of Kapunda, and also at the Castlemaine Brewery in Melbourne. He became one of the best-known and most popular men in Adelaide, and earned distinction as a brewer when he took the silver medal against the brewers of the world at the Paris Exhibition of 1889.

According to the *South Australian Sentinel* of 18 May 1889, the company was producing Jubilee Lager Beer, and it guaranteed that any of its bottled ales would keep for at least two years. 30,000 dozen bottles of the Jubilee Lager were kept in stock, as well as large quantities of Bitter Beer and Stout.

Tom Ware died in December 1896 at the young age of thirty-two, and the brothers continued to run and build the business into a highly successful enterprise. The year 1898 saw the amalgamation of the Torrenside Brewery with Edward Clark's East Adelaide Brewery to form Clark, Ware & Co. Brewing continued at the Torrenside, and the East Adelaide Brewery was shut down.

In the same year, 1898, the newly-formed business of Clark, Ware & Co. sold all their brewing interests to the Walkerville Co-operative Brewing Co. Ltd, who closed their own Walkerville premises and shifted all the equipment over to the Torrenside Brewery at Winwood Street, Southwark. In 1938 all assets of the Walkerville Brewery were taken over by the South Australian Brewing, Malting & Wine & Spirit Co. Ltd, which later became the South Australian Brewing Co. Ltd. At the time of acquisition, the name Walkerville Brewery was changed to Nathan Brewery, and later changed again to the Southwark Brewery, in 1949.

Union Brewing & Malting Co. Ltd 1844–1902
Union Lane, off Rundle Street

John Primrose arrived in Adelaide in 1839, and started a distillery in Rundle Street. This was at the Union Brewery site, which had been listed for sale in the *Port Lincoln Herald and South Australian Commercial Advertiser* of 6 April 1839:

> Desirable Investment. Union Brewery, to be disposed of by private contract; the lease of the premises, together with the plant, utensils and stock in trade of the well known Union Brewery recently completed at great cost, with capacious cellaring, malt house, kiln and every material for immediately carrying on an extensive business.

The advertisement offered 'the low rent of £24 per annum' and suggested that only a very small capital would be required. The property was finally sold by auction on 8 May 1839.

John Primrose and John Richmond began distilling, and in 1844 they commenced brewing at the same site. By December of that year the partnership had been dissolved by mutual consent, leaving Primrose to continue on his own. In the early 1860s the Primrose Brewery was described as the largest in Adelaide (there were ten at the time), and Primrose Pale Ale and XXX Ale were distributed widely throughout the colony.

Following the death of John Primrose in 1876, W. R. Sawers managed the brewery and estate, and continued to uphold Primrose's good name and reputation in the hotel trade in South Australia.

In 1883 W. R. Sawers and Thomas D'Arcy Burke purchased the business.

Five years later the Union Brewing & Malting Co. Ltd was formed. Burke left to start the Union Barrier Brewery at Silverton in New South Wales, and Sawers ran the Union Brewery until his retirement in 1892.

The brewery cellars, which had a capacity to hold 1000 hogsheads of beer, extended out under Rundle Street, and beneath the site of the Academy of Music. In November 1890 the *Australian Brewers' Journal* reported a fatal accident at the brewery when an employee slipped and fell into a large vat of boiling liquor, twelve feet deep: 'he scrambled out and screamed for help. He was rubbed down with oil and yeast but died the next day'.

The well-known brewer, Guilford E. Gray, was the manager of the Union Brewery in 1892, and he continued brewing draught beer under the Primrose name. There were no facilities for bottling. In 1902 brewing was discontinued, and the following year saw the amalgamation of the Union Brewery with the Walkerville Co-operative Brewery Co. Ltd.

The mayor of Thebarton, Adelaide, Mr C. B. Ware.

Charles Boxer Ware came from a brewing family, and entered the business as soon as he left school; his father had opened a brewery in Kooringa in 1867, and by 1886 had started the Torrenside Brewery in Adelaide.

Boxer Ware soon became a vital member of the family business. With his brother, Thomas, they opened the Lion Brewery in Coolgardie, one of the best known on the Western Australian goldfields.

With Boxer Ware in charge of the brewing, the Torrenside Brewery gained a silver medal at the Paris Exhibition in 1891; two years before that, a diploma in the Brewers' Exhibition in London; and at the Adelaide Exhibitions no fewer than eight orders of merit in ales and stout. Boxer Ware's specialty was a 1 per cent alcohol temperance drink that he named Ware's Jubilee Lager Beer.

La Trobe Library, State Library of Victoria

Union Brewery	c. 1839
Primrose & Richmond	1844
John Primrose	1844–76
W. R. Sawers	1876–83
Sawers & Burke	1883–88

Union Brewing & Malting Co. Ltd	
W. R. Sawers	1888–92
Guilford E. Gray	1892–1902

Victoria Brewery 1889–1919
Holland Street (off King William Street)/103 Sturt Street

The brewery, frequently called the Holland Street Brewery, was started by Edward Clark in 1889.

Later that year he sold the brewery to Louis Werthheimer, who brewed for a year or so, and resold to his brewer in April 1891. The brewery then traded as Dussenberg & Co.

More changes followed: Schalinger & Co. in 1892, then Grenville & Co. in 1895; the brewery's name was then changed to Victoria Brewery. The brewery closed in 1899.

Five years later the equipment was shifted to 103 Sturt Street, only a few streets away, and Grenville & Co. continued as the Victoria Brewery until 1919.

Walkerville Brewery

See Walkerville Co-operative Brewing Co. Ltd.

Walkerville Co-operative Brewing Co. Ltd 1844–1938
Cnr Richman Street (later Walkerville Terrace) & Fuller Street, Walkerville

During the long life of the Walkerville Brewery there were many changes in ownership, several changes in name and location, and many acquisitions. The brewery was finally taken over by the South Australian Brewing Co. Ltd in 1938.

The *Adelaide Register* of 2 March 1844 reported that W. H. Colyer had established a brewery in Richman Street, Walkerville. A later report, in December 1846, stated that a malthouse, store and other buildings had been completed.

White & Phillips had put out some 'very creditable Walkerville beer and stout' before becoming insolvent, and after 1858 the brewery was idle for six years.

George Ball and George Huntley, two of the old employees, started brewing in premises adjoining the old Walkerville Brewery in 1864, and the brewing equipment was transferred to the new location. They changed the name to the Black Horse Brewery when production commenced, and advertised under that name in commercial trade directories.

George Ball, the leading partner, died in 1882, and that left Huntley to continue alone. He brewed for the next seven years, and his principal sales were to local families.

A major change took place in 1889 when the Walkerville Co-operative Brewing Co. was formed by a syndicate of four hotelkeepers. They had purchased the Black Horse Brewery, and extended the premises; with new equipment, capacity was trebled. In 1895 sixteen other hotelkeepers were invited to join the group.

The Walkerville Co-operative Brewing Co. Ltd was incorporated on 7 May 1898, and, shortly after, the Torrenside Brewery of Clark, Ware & Co. was purchased. The new company then closed their brewery at Walkerville, and continued to brew at the Torrenside Brewery in Winwood Street, Southwark.

At the formal opening of the Walkerville Co-operative Brewing Co. Ltd on 4 November 1899 the Hon. E. Ward, MLC, had a few appropriate words to say:

The Walkerville Brewery, Adelaide, c. 1918. Founded in 1844, it was taken over by the South Australian Brewing Co. Ltd in 1938.

Look at the national importance of this great industry, not merely in providing so well for the pleasant quenching of their thirsts, but in the liberal employment of labour, in the beneficial circulation of cash and in its very material contribution to the revenue of the state.

The Walkerville Brewery premises were sold to their head brewer, Charles Williams, in 1901, and during that year the Dragon Brewery was purchased and closed. The Gawler Brewery and its hotel trade were also acquired the same year, and brewing continued there for the next five years. In 1903 the company amalgamated with the Union Brewing & Malting Co. Ltd. The Union was closed, and the Walkerville Co-operative continued at Southwark.

Accidents and tragedies at breweries were by no means uncommon. A tragic incident occurred in December 1897 when a driver for the company committed suicide by hanging himself in a shed at the brewery. There was also a fatal accident early in 1903 when the head cellarman went to test a vat of fermenting stout on the second floor of the brewery. His body was later found floating in the vat — he had been overcome by the carbonic acid fumes, had overbalanced, and fallen in. A verdict of accidental death was recorded, the contents of the vat were poured to waste, and the vat was destroyed. Cold comfort indeed for the family of the victim, where in those times there was no compensation.

The Williams Breweries Ltd was taken over in 1906, primarily for the purpose of acquiring the equipment and premises needed for expansion. At that time there were five breweries in Adelaide, the Walkerville

was one of the largest, and the company continued to grow and prosper.

In 1938 the business and properties of the Walkerville Brewery were acquired by the South Australian Brewing Co. Ltd. They continued brewing at the Walkerville Brewery in Winwood Street, Southwark, but used the name Nathan Brewery. By 1949 the South Australian Brewing Co. Ltd chose to use the name of Southwark Brewery.

The company's central brewing complex address is now 107 Port Road, Thebarton — the district of Southwark was renamed Thebarton in 1969. Products are still marketed under West End and Southwark labels.

Waverley Brewery   1878–1933
Cnr Princes Road & Victoria Terrace (now Belair Road), Mitcham

After leaving the West End Brewery in Adelaide, where he had been the brewer and manager, Charles Mallen built his own brewery at West Terrace. He called it the Waverley Brewery, and was ready for business in December 1875. The following year William Simms bought the brewery, with the proviso that Mallen would not open another brewery within 50 miles of Adelaide for a period of ten years, subsequently reduced to two years. This first Waverley Brewery lasted for a very brief period, and became the Waverley Vinegar Works.

In 1878 Mallen built his second Waverley Brewery at Mitcham, and formed a partnership with John Haimes, Marie Mallen (a daughter) and Arthur Bean. The firm was called Haimes, Mallen & Co., and traded as the 'Waverly [sic] Brewery', according to some media references. The company specialised in Sparkling Waverly Ale. Bean retired in 1879, and after the death of Haimes, the name was simplified to Mallen & Co.

In time Charles Mallen gained the reputation of being the largest owner of freehold property in Adelaide, and was still involved at the brewery in 1909 at the age of eighty-nine. He was quoted as saying that he was 'determined not to rust but to wear out'.

In 1933 the Waverley Brewery stopped brewing, and arrangements were made for the South Australian Brewing Co. to supply Mallen's hotels with beer. Charles Mallen, the benefactor, for more than thirty years had supplied a half-barrel of beer free of charge, each week, to the Home for Incurables.

George Mallen, son of the founder, sold the Waverley Brewery to the newly-formed Castlereagh Brewery Co. Ltd in 1933, but the new company ran into difficulties.

Another company, the Adelaide Brewery Co. Ltd, was formed. It took over the brewery in 1934, and operated for four years.

The Springfield Brewery purchased the property in 1938, and continued brewing there for the next ten years.

West Adelaide Brewery   1838
Torrens River

One of the early Adelaide settlers was a Mr Lillyman, a general trader and part-time brewer, who apparently built and sold his brewery in the same year.

W. H. Colyer	1844–47
William Williams	1847–51
	(insolvent)
James Thompson	1851–54
White & Phillips	1855–57
	(insolvent)
James Thompson & Claude Shuttleworth	1858 (insolvent)
Black Horse Brewery	
Ball & Huntley	1864–82
George Huntley	1882–89
Walkerville Co-operative Brewing Co.	
Syndicate	1889–98
Walkerville Co-operative Brewing Co. Ltd	
Torrenside Brewery acquired	1898–1938
Brewery closed at Walkerville; now at Winward Street, Southwark	
Amalgamation with Union Brewery (Union Brewery closed)	1903
South Australian Brewing Co. Ltd	
Nathan Brewery	1938–49
Southwark Brewery	1949–

An auction notice in the *South Australian Gazette* on 29 September 1838 refers to 'Mr Lillyman's Brewery' and lists various items of brewing equipment for sale, including 18 gallons of vinegar, 50 prime Westphalia hams, and half a chest of fine green tea. The vinegar was no doubt the end-result of undrinkable ale.

West End Brewery 1859–88
Hindley Street

The West End Brewery was built in 1859 by William Henry Clark, a brewing entrepreneur who had started several other breweries that had failed to prosper. Once again, his attempt at Hindley Street was a disaster, and within a year he was declared bankrupt. He had no way of knowing at that time that his failed brewery would ultimately grow and flourish over the next 124 years.

The brewery was taken over by William K. Simms, a man of substance and brewing experience, who later became a member of the Adelaide City Council. In 1866 a partnership was formed between William Simms and Edgar Chapman. They produced three types of beer — XX, XXX and Pale Ale — most of which was sold in bottles. A less-than-favourable report in the *South Australian Register* of June 1868 said that the quality of the beer lacked uniformity. This was a common complaint of most of the beer put out by the breweries of the day.

Simms & Chapman West End Brewery, Adelaide, c. 1880.

From 1862 Simms & Chapman used some of the buildings of the disused Hindmarsh Brewery, and from 1871 to 1873 those of the Anchor Brewery premises as a bottling plant. They employed sixteen men and two boys, and the West End Brewery was a profitable and well-run business. Edgar Chapman died in 1886.

Two years later it was decided to sell the brewery. Alfred Simms took over his father's interest in the business, and in 1888 both the West End Brewery and the Kent Town Brewery were acquired by the South Australian Brewing, Malting & Wine & Spirit Co. Ltd.

The West End Brewery was a major beer-producer for the South Australian Brewery until 1983, when the buildings were demolished.

Williams Breweries Ltd 1901–6
Walkerville

Williams Walkerville Brewing Co. Ltd was formed by Charles Williams in 1901, and in December of that year the name was changed to Williams Breweries Ltd. Williams had purchased the old Walkerville Co-operative Brewery, which had been vacated a few years earlier — he had actually been the head brewer there for many years. Now that the brewery was his, he made a range of cordials, non-alcoholic beverages and also beer.

Williams Breweries Ltd was liquidated in June 1906, and the assets were taken over by the Walkerville Co-operative Brewery. Later, Williams Breweries returned to business, and produced many popular brands of aerated waters, cordials and brewed soft drinks. Among these were Boshter Beer and Boshter Shandy, both temperance beers, but actually containing 1 per cent alcohol. In those years the word 'Boshter' was a slang expression meaning 'very good'.

Williams Walkerville Brewing Co. Ltd
See Williams Breweries Ltd.

Auburn

Auburn Brewery
See Enterprise Brewery.

Enterprise Brewery 1865–88

Thomas Robinson owned and operated the Auburn Brewery for three years, and then sold to Edward Clark, who brewed with reasonable success from 1868 to 1878.

When Fanny Filgate and John Christison of the Enterprise Brewery of Clare took over, they changed the name to the Enterprise Brewery, and ran the business from 1878 to 1887.

Thomas Davies worked the brewery for about a year, and finally, in 1888, Morris Trimming.

Jacka, William, Jnr 1871–76

In 1866 William Jacka Jnr left the family business in Adelaide, and moved to Auburn, where he commenced work as a baker and soft-drink manufacturer.

In 1871 he started brewing with the assistance of his two sons, William John Jacka and Joseph Henry Jacka. They may have taken over the Phoenix Brewery, which had started the year before.

William Jacka and his sons stayed at Auburn for five years, and then moved on to Melrose, and started the Melrose Brewery.

Phoenix Brewery 1870
King Street

The only known reference to the brewery is an advertisement that appeared in the *Northern Argus,* Clare, on 9 December 1870:

> Phoenix Brewery, King Street, Auburn. Superior XXX Ale and Porter; also lemonade, soda water, sarsaparilla, ginger beer and cordials made at the above brewery, All orders promptly attended to.

Beltana

The old railway township of Beltana is now a historical reserve, and many of the old buildings are gradually being restored. Beltana was one of the major camel-breeding stations in the early years; it was also the base for the pastoralists, Thomas Elder and Robert Barr-Smith, co-founders of Elder Smith & Co.

Beltana Brewery 1876–78

Charles Henry Gray sold his brewery at Blinman in 1876, and started another brewery at Beltana, 70 km north-west in the Flinders Ranges district. After two years he closed the brewery, and moved to Pichi Richi, near Quorn, to become the brewer for the Pichi Richi Brewery.

Blinman

Blinman was a bustling coppermining town from the 1860s to 1890. It was 'Pegleg' Robert Blinman, a shepherd with a wooden leg, who first discovered traces of copper in the area in 1859, and the township was named after him.

Blinman Brewery 1869–1901

The Blinman Brewery was started by Charles Henry Gray in 1869. He moved to Beltana in 1876 after selling the Blinman Brewery to Guilford E. Gray. Other owners followed.

Charles Henry Gray	1869–76
Guilford E. Gray	1876–83
D. Hart	1883–84
W. Hocking	1885–86
George Armstrong	1886–1901

Burra

Burra is one of Australia's oldest mining settlements. Copper had been discovered in the district in the early 1840s, and soon there was a collection of small mining townships, none of them called Burra, but all fathered by the Burra Burra mine. Locally, these townships were known as Kooringa, Redruth, Aberdeen, Hampton, Llwychr and Copperhouse. Collectively, they became known as Burra.

For years Burra was the world's richest coppermining town. It became Australia's seventh-largest town, and the largest inland centre before the discovery of gold in eastern Australia. Today the district supports some pastoral activity, and the beautiful old town is a popular tourist attraction.

Burra Brewery 1846–74

A new hotel named the Burra Burra was licensed in 1846, and a small brewery was erected alongside by Edward J. Crawford. In 1846 he leased the brewery to Andrew Birrell, who brought up all the equipment from his Hindley Street Brewery in Adelaide. By 1850 the owner–operator was Andrew Paxton.

Competition forced the brewery to close when the new modern Unicorn Brewery, complete with the latest equipment and facilities, was built at Burra.

Andrew Birrell	1846–50
Andrew Paxton	1850–55
Charles Ware	1855–63
Edgar Chapman	1863–64
W. H. Williams	1864–74
F. T. Jones	1874

Unicorn Brewery 1873–1902
Paxton Terrace

William Henry Banks was twenty-four years of age when he arrived at Burra. Newly married, he bought the Miners Arms Hotel in Kooringa, one of the early districts of Burra, and in 1873 he built the Unicorn Brewery. The cellars could hold 500 hogsheads of beer, compared to a mere 50 hogsheads at the Burra Brewery, which closed the following year.

Banks died suddenly in 1878 at the age of thirty-three. His widow, Catherine, unable to carry on, sold the brewery to George Catchlove, late of the Hindmarsh Brewery in Adelaide.

The new company, George Catchlove & Co., was a family affair. The managing director was a nephew, Edward Catchlove Lockyer, and his brother, Henry Lockyer, was the head brewer. William Jacka was involved in the business in 1892, the year that George Catchlove died. The following year the registered name of the company was E. C. Lockyer & Co.

Toward the end of 1902 the brewery was taken over by the Walkerville Co-operative Brewing Co. Ltd, and closed.

In April 1905 the brewery and its fifteen hotels were put up for sale, but no offers were received. Seven months later the brewery was put up for auction. Again, not a single bid. Gradually, some of the equipment was sold — old vats for use as horsefeeders, and wood and iron from outbuildings were sold at 'very fair prices'. But the brewery stood unwanted. Part of the property was bought by the South Australian Education Department, and in 1913 the massive tower was dismantled and the dressed stone used for the construction of cottages.

At the time the brewery closed it was supplying beer to most of the hotels in the northern railway towns, and the seven hotels in Burra that they owned. There were three types of ale — pale, dark, XXX — and also porter.

An artist's impression of the Unicorn Brewery, Burra.

Clare

This small town of Clare was named after County Clare in Ireland, and the district is now famed for its wine production, dairy produce and wool.

Clare Brewery
See Enterprise Brewery.

Clare Co-operative Brewing Co. Ltd
See Enterprise Brewery.

Enterprise Brewery   1850–1916
Main Street

Andrew Birrell had been the lessee of the Burra Brewery in Burra and, having moved out of there in 1850, he built his own brewery in Clare. Within two months of the opening of his Enterprise Brewery in Clare, in February 1850 Birrell was offering the brewery to anyone who would lease it. But no one was interested.

Birrell then ran the brewery himself. He had to wait four years before he found a lessee. In 1854 W. McKenzie, owner of the local Travellers Rest Hotel, leased the brewery at a cost of £120 per year. After five years McKenzie decided not to renew the lease. The lessee from 1859 to 1865 was Jonathon Filgate.

Meanwhile, in 1858 William Kerr had a brewery and malthouse on his farm at Emu Flat near Clare. He had supplied some of the local market with beer until his death in 1859, and his widow then leased the property to Alex Paterson. Another brewery had been built in Main Street by the late William Kerr, who had intended to shift his brewing business from Emu Flat to the larger premises in Main Street. After his death this new unused brewery was taken over by Charles Fenton.

In 1865 Jonathon Filgate moved out of the brewery in Union Street that he had been leasing, and negotiated the purchase of Fenton's newer and larger complex in Main Street. Sadly, Filgate died the following year, and his widow, Fanny, persevered with the brewery with the assistance of Walter Davies.

In 1878 Fanny Filgate took her future son-in-law, William Richardson, into partnership, and formed the firm of Filgate & Richardson. They built a larger brewery at the northern end of Clare township, and became the owners of several local hotels. They supplied their own hotels and others in the district with Clare Sparkling Ales, which were delivered in wagons drawn by mules.

Richardson left the firm in 1880, and John Christison became Mrs Filgate's new partner in 1881. Filgate and Christison ran the brewery for the next twenty-four years until 1905. Christison then became sole owner, and he changed the name from the Enterprise to the Clare Brewery.

John Christison died in 1911, and the brewery was auctioned the following year. Bidding reached £27,750, but was below the reserve. Much of the value was in the fifteen hotels that had been acquired over the years, including three at Clare.

In June 1912 the brewery was taken over by the newly-formed Clare Co-operative Brewing Co. Ltd, and shares were offered to the public and to the lessees of the brewery-owned hotels. The new company then set about upgrading the brewery on a grand scale. The buildings were extended, new equipment installed, the roof was lifted to provide an extra storage floor, the tower was reconstructed and an elevator was fitted. A refrigeration plant was installed, automatic bottling machines put in place, and the company introduced the first motor trucks for the delivery of beer.

Despite this massive upgrading and expenditure, brewing had stopped by 1916. Frank Bulfield, the company secretary, continued the aerated-water and cordial section of the business.

In earlier years the Enterprise Brewery had been described as 'the prettiest brewery in Australia'.

Enterprise Brewery (Union Street)	
Andrew Birrell	1850–54
W. McKenzie (lessee)	1854–59
J. Filgate (lessee)	1859–65
Meanwhile:	
W. Kerr (Emu Flat)	1858–59
A. Paterson (lessee)	1859–65
C. Fenton (Main Street)	
Jonathon Filgate moved out of his brewery in Union Street, and shifted into the brewery in Main Street (purchased from Charles Fenton)	
J. Filgate	1865–66
F. Filgate	1866–78
Filgate & Richardson	1878–80
(new location at the northern end of the town)	
Filgate & Christison	1881–1905

Clare Brewery	
J. Christison	1905–12

Clare Co-operative Brewing Co. Ltd 1912–16

Gawler

Gawler Brewery 1847–1906
Murray Street

Gawler is South Australia's oldest country town, its official birthday being 31 January 1839. The area soon began to develop, and in 1847 John Auld and his brother, Thomas, started a brewery in the township. Later that year they sold their brewery to James Fotheringham. James was joined by his brother, Robert, in 1855, and by his other brother, Thomas, the following year.

The brothers purchased the Kapunda Brewery in 1858, and Thomas Fotheringham then left Gawler to become the manager at Kapunda. Robert and James stayed at Gawler. Robert was said to have been a very genial and popular man, and when he left Gawler in 1868 he was presented with a clock, and a silver cup containing 117 sovereigns, a substantial gift for that time.

Various members of the Fotheringham family continued to operate the Gawler Brewery. James had died in 1866 and, following the death of Robert in 1885, Thomas Fotheringham's sons, Sydney and Thomas Jnr, were in charge of the business.

The Walkerville Co-operative Brewing Co. Ltd bought the brewery in 1901, and continued brewing there until it was closed in 1906.

Goolwa

The river-port township of Goolwa was founded in the 1850s, and shipbuilding, timber milling and brewing were early industries. One of the first railway lines to operate in Australia was opened between Goolwa and Port Elliot in 1854.

Dutton's Brewery
See River Murray Brewery.

River Murray Brewery 1865–95
Richard Street

Edward Dutton's brewery was about 200 metres from the Murray River. He had previously brewed at Noarlunga and Yankalilla for brief periods before settling in Goolwa in 1865. He brewed good beer, which was sent to the townships along the Murray, Darling and Murrumbidgee Rivers by paddle-steamer. Dutton's Ale was also delivered as far as Wilcannia in New South Wales, and to the townships in between.

Several other brewers became involved at different times, either leasing the brewery or as owners. Edward Clark ran the brewery from 1880 to 1885. He advertised in the *Licensed Victuallers' Gazette* of 5 May 1883:

> River Murray Brewery; Prize Ales, Porters etc. Edward Clark, having taken the above extensive

Dutton's Brewery, Goolwa, c. 1890. Goolwa, today, is an attractive tourist township, and the old brewery building still stands near the wharf.

> ### LEAD IN BREWERY PLANT
>
> Brewers have often been warned against using lead in connection with brewery plant, but many continue to use it as if there were no fear of contamination at all, instead of which the danger from the solution of the metal is very great.
>
> The new lead, in constant contact with a moist atmosphere, undergoes surface change; a grey powder appearing, which presumably represents a suboxide of the metal, while this, in contact with moist air, continues to absorb oxygen with avidity, undergoing gradual conversion into lead oxide, which is slightly soluble in water. Our opinion is that brewers will do well to have as little lead about their brewing plant as possible.
>
> *Australian Brewers' Journal,*
> March 1891

and old established brewery, is prepared to supply ales and porters, in casks or bottled.

Other brewers were John Boult, 1885–90; and John Spencer, 1888–95.

Gumeracha

Moger, Ed   1866–69

Jamestown

Emu Brewery   1879–80

Edmund Humphris was the owner of the Emu Brewery, and the brewer was James Bryan. Bryan had a reputation for brewing good XX and XXX ales when he was a brewer at Macclesfield and Strathalbyn. At Jamestown all went well until July 1880 when Bryan died, only one year after the brewery had started. Humphris, who knew nothing about how to make beer, was unable to run the brewery, and it was converted to a skating rink the following year.

Kadina

Kadina Brewery   1860–74

Copper was discovered at Kadina, on the Yorke Peninsula, in 1859, and many Cornish and Welsh miners migrated and settled in the area. Copper was also found at Wallaroo, a few kilometres to the west, and the population of the district quickly grew.

In 1860 H. Nankervis began brewing at Kadina. After a few years he sold his brewery to Edward Hughes. Hughes worked the brewery from 1864 to 1874, and then sold to James Thompson later that year.

Kapunda

Allen Creek Brewery
See Victoria Brewery.

Teagle's Brewery   1893–1919
Christchurch Street

George Teagle had been the head brewer for the Fotheringham brothers' Victoria Brewery in Kapunda for many years, and decided to start up on his own in 1893. His son, Albert, was in charge from 1912.

Victoria Brewery   1848–1909
Allendale, 4 km from Kapunda

An outcrop of green copper ore was discovered in 1842 in the area later known as Kapunda, and Australia's first significant copper mine was opened in 1844. Four years later Daniel Cudmore was listed as a brewer on Section 1520 at Allen Creek, near Kapunda, and when he started brewing he used the name Allen Creek Brewery. Cudmore was one of South Australia's early brewers, having brewed as early as 1838 at North Adelaide. He also built and operated the Hindmarsh Brewery in Adelaide.

At Kapunda Daniel Cudmore worked the brewery for four years, and after selling to Richard Haimes he went on to become one of Australia's leading pastoralists. Haimes ran the brewery with the help of two partners, J. D. Cossins and J. Brewster, but only for three years, since Haimes became insolvent in 1857.

In 1858 the Fotheringham brothers, brewers of Gawler, purchased the Allen Creek Brewery, and promptly changed the name to the Victoria Brewery, with Thomas Fotheringham in charge. Later his nephews, George and Robert Fotheringham, ran the business. Thomas died in 1894, and Andrew Thompson, an employee at the brewery since 1888, purchased the brewery and continued trading as Thompson & Fotheringham.

Langhorne Creek

Langhorne Creek Brewery   1892–96

Charles Henry Gray was an itinerant brewer, moving from place to place, apparently unable to settle for any length of time. He had started brewing at Melrose in 1859, then moved to Blinman, followed by Beltana, Pichi Richi, Mt Barker, Littlehampton, and then Langhorne Creek. Four years there was sufficient for Charles.

Laura

Nestled into the eastern slopes of the lower Flinders Ranges lies the pretty town of Laura, which developed as the result of the expanding agriculture and dairy industries of the surrounding districts.

Laura Brewery Co. 1874–94
West Terrace

John Gleeson and Thomas Sabine were operating a timber yard at Laura in 1873 and, as a sideline, they held a wine licence. They accepted orders for beer from the Enterprise Brewery at Clare, which was run by Gleeson's sister, Fanny Filgate.

The rapidly-expanding beer market, both local and to the north, encouraged the partners to start a brewery in 1874. They called it the Laura Brewery. John Gleeson's share of the brewery was taken over by Fanny Filgate in 1876.

Four years later there was a new group of partners: F. Filgate, T. F. Sabine, A. E. Glibbon and J. Spicer. They operated as brewers, and aerated-water, gingerbeer, cordial and ice manufacturers.

The partnership was dissolved in 1882, and the business was then conducted by Thomas Sabine and Edward Martin. Thomas Sabine, one of the original partners, was the owner in 1886 when the Laura Brewery Co. was formed.

The next year the company accounts showed a massive deficit, and Henry Hodgson was placed in charge of affairs. The brewery continued to operate, and A. J. Whittle became the owner in 1888.

From 1891 Henry Hodgson, Charles William and W. C. Shand were involved at the brewery, and in 1893 it was purchased by the South Australian Brewing Co. Ltd and closed in 1894.

Littlehampton

Littlehampton Brewery 1850–1906

Benjamin Gray migrated from Littlehampton, Sussex, England. In 1849 he built an inn and brewery, having already laid out the township that he named Littlehampton after his home town.

Robert Hunt joined Gray when the brewery was opened in 1850, but Hunt withdrew after two years. Gray continued on his own for the next twenty-six years.

The Johnston brothers of the Oakbank Brewery in Oakbank took over in 1878, and ten years later Gray again became involved in the business.

The proprietor from 1887 to 1902 was E. F. Miels, and Guilford E. Gray, son of the founder, ran the business for the last few years.

Lobethal

Lobethal Brewery 1864–74

F. W. Kleinschmidt was a sugar boiler by trade, and was also involved in contract building work and farming. He moved to Lobethal, and in 1851 he built the Lutheran Church by himself.

In 1864 he built the Lobethal Brewery, which he sold to the Johnston brothers of the Oakbank Brewery in Oakbank in 1873.

Macclesfield

The abundance of marble, slate and walling stones in the Macclesfield district is evident in the many examples of beautiful buildings in the town, located 40 km south-east of Adelaide.

Macclesfield Brewery 1850–93
Bank of the Angas River (off Venables Street)

An incredible number of owners and operators came and went during the life of the Macclesfield Brewery. The first was Henry Lewis, who purchased several lots of land at Macclesfield in 1850, and built his brewery on the river bank.

Henry Lewis leased the brewery to Miller & Bouquett, but William Miller died after falling into a vat of boiling liquid. Other lessees and owners followed.

Henry Lewis (lessee)	1850–51
Miller & Bouquett (lessee)	1851–53
Sam Coleman (lessee)	1853–63
John Coleman (lessee)	1864–67
Henry Lewis	1867
John & George Davenport (lessee)	1868
John Fox (lessee)	1868–71
Lewis Deane (lessee)	1871–73
Henry Lewis	1873–77

Albert Landseer and William Dunk bought the brewery in 1877. They employed James Bryan, formerly of the Strathalbyn Brewery, as their brewer, and he put out a good brew of XX and XXX Emu Beer, but not for long.

One year later the Conigrave brothers, Benjamin and Henry, advertised in the *Southern Argus* of 12 April 1879 that they had erected 'a substantial and elegant building in contrast to the old one and greatly improving the outlook of the main road'. The Conigrave brothers were awarded First Prize for their bottled beer at the Adelaide Exhibition. Before that they had also won First Prize and a Gold Medal for bottled beer at a London Exhibition. More operators followed.

Landseer & Dunk	1877
Conigrave brothers	1877–83
Alexander Crooks	1883–84
James Mott	1884–86
Mott & Wade	1886–87
William & Gustav Danker	1887–88
Wigg, Beevor & Clare	1888–90
B. G. Edwards (lessee or manager)	1890–93

Wolton Wigg, Miles Beevor and William Clare had started another Macclesfield Brewery in King William Street, Adelaide, and they worked both breweries for a short period. When they closed the brewery at the Macclesfield country town in 1893, they transferred the equipment to their brewery in Adelaide.

McLaren Vale

The McLaren Vale district, south of Adelaide, is an important wine-producing area, but at one time brewing was also a local industry, producing beer for the small population of the town and surrounding districts.

McLaren Vale Brewery c. 1850–63
Brewery Hill

After arriving in Adelaide from Middlesex, England, James Pavey settled in McLaren Vale. He built a brewery at the foot of a hill that attracted the name of Brewery Hill. Pavey chose the area as the colony's finest barley was grown in the district.

The location of the brewery, however, was not well chosen. The site was a former swamp, and the black soil often resulted in the well-water being tainted. Each time this occurred a new well had to be excavated for fresh water.

In January 1867 the brewery, cottage, malthouse, together with all the fittings and utensils were advertised for sale. Apparently the brewery had been idle, since an earlier directory had reported that J. Pavey had worked the McLaren Vale Brewery until 1863.

Melrose

Melrose is the oldest of the towns in the South Flinders Ranges district, and dates from the early 1850s when copper was discovered in the area.

Gray's Brewery 1859–68
Brewery Street

In 1859 Charles Henry Gray ran a brewery on Section 38A of the small township. In June the following year he was charged with supplying Aboriginals with liquor, but the case was dismissed when it was found that the beer had been stolen.

In 1893 Jacka's Melrose Brewery was shifted to this old flourmill. Brewing continued until 1934.

Charles Gray's brother, Guilford E. Gray, joined the business, and during the last year that the brewery operated Thomas Robinson was the occupier. Both Charles and Guilford Gray were sons of Benjamin Gray, who had started the Littlehampton Brewery in Littlehampton in 1850.

Jacka's Brewery
See Melrose Brewery.

Melrose Brewery   1877–1934
Lambert Street

The Jacka brothers, William and Joseph, commenced brewing at Melrose on 3 January 1877. Although properly known as the Melrose Brewery, it was frequently called Jacka's Brewery.

William Jacka sold his share in the business to his brother Joseph in 1885, and moved to Sydney where he worked as the brewer at the Pyrmont Brewery. By 1892 he was at the Unicorn Brewery in Burra, and then in 1894 he settled in Adelaide and opened a coffee palace on North Terrace.

The brewing operations at Melrose were shifted to an old flourmill in 1893, and cellars were excavated under what was originally the corn store. In the 1890s there were only two hotels in Melrose, and the brewery had to find markets in other, larger towns. This required the maintenance of a large stable of horses for transport, eight horses being needed to haul one dray loaded with 20 hogsheads of beer. A farm adjacent to the brewery provided fodder.

Melrose beer was remarkably popular over a wide area of the countryside, and even hotelkeepers tied to opposition breweries said that Jacka's beer was first class.

When Joseph Jacka died in 1901, the business passed to his son, William Joseph Jacka. In 1905 his uncle, William John Jacka, sold his coffee palace in Adelaide and returned to Melrose to assist his young nephew.

Sales reached their peak in the early 1900s, but by 1917, after the retirement of the uncle, business began to decline. In 1924 the main building was badly damaged by fire, and the final blow to the business was caused by the economic depression of the 1930s. This, coupled with local droughts and shrinking population in the northern districts, forced the brewery to close in 1934.

William Joseph Jacka later became associated with the Springfield Brewery in Adelaide.

North Star Hotel & Brewery   1854–58
William St George was the licensee of the North Star Hotel, and brewed sufficient beer for his hotel trade only.

Milang

Pavey's Brewery   1856
Henry and Phillip Pavey were sons of James Pavey, who had owned and operated the McLaren Vale Brewery. The sons completed the construction of a

Moonta

Moody's Brewery c. 1880

The township of Moonta, to the north of the Yorke Peninsula, was another of South Australia's early coppermining towns.

About 1880 John Moody was working his brewery at Moonta, and advertised: 'Prize Ale. Prize Porter, Prize Cooper, Draught or Bottled. Orders from all parts of Yorke Peninsula and the areas promptly attended to'; there was no mention of what 'Prize' referred to.

Morphett Vale

Morphett Vale Brewery 1851–67

Having sold his Emu Inn at Morphett Vale, Peter Anderson took up farming. He built a house on the opposite side of the road to his farm, planted a garden and vineyard, and built a flourmill and a brick brewery.

Various brewers were involved at the brewery: J. Edwards, 1851; C. Catchlove, 1859; J. Hosking, 1860; and W. A. Gerloff, 1866–67.

Mt Barker

Mount Barker Brewery 1887–88

Charles Gray, a member of a family of brewers, had first brewed at Melrose at Gray's Brewery in 1859. He brewed at Mt Barker for a year, and then moved on to brew at Littlehampton Brewery, and, after that, at the Langhorne Creek Brewery.

Mt Gambier

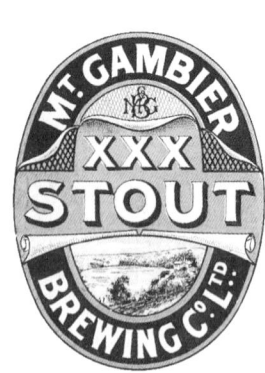

Mt Gambier, built on the lower slopes of an extinct volcano, has two famous attractions. The Blue Lake in the main crater changes colour from winter-grey to an intense blue in November each year. The other interesting feature, in the centre of the city, is an open cave, with attractive gardens set out in the depression at the entrance to the cave. In earlier years this had been the source of the town's water supply.

Molony's Brewing Co.

See Standard Brewery.

Mount Gambier Brewing Co. Ltd 1898–1911

In 1885 Charles Engelbrecht started a whisky-distilling business. It failed in 1898, and the premises were converted to a cordial factory. Shortly after, a brewery was added by the enterprising partners, W. Jaeger and T. Tormay. They named their brewery the Swallow, but after three years the brewery closed.

The Mount Gambier Brewing Co. Ltd was formed on 22 November 1902 as a private company. The shareholders were the Anderson family, owners of the local Standard Brewery, and the Gebhardt family, owners of the South Australian Brewery, also in Mt Gambier. The new company took over Jaeger & Tormay's Swallow Brewery, which was vacant, but after a year the families decided to discontinue the joint venture in order to concentrate on running their individual breweries.

Charles Reineke and Eugene Marie took over the Mount Gambier Brewery in 1903, but the partnership was dissolved the following year, and the brewery was again closed.

It was offered for sale at auction, and in 1904 the brewery was purchased by J. Anderson, a nephew of Walter Anderson of the local Standard Brewery. After seven years the business was wound up voluntarily.

In 1912 John Molony, the owner of the local Standard Brewery, purchased some of the machinery for use at his own brewery.

Swallow Brewery
Jaeger & Tormay	1898–1901, closed

Mount Gambier Brewing Co. Ltd
Anderson & Gebhardt families	1902–3
Reineke & Marie	1903–4, closed
J. Anderson	1904–11

South Australian Brewery 1867–1920
Commercial Street

In 1867 William Gebhardt built a single-storey brewery in Commercial Street, east of the Park Hotel. He called it the South Australian Brewery — no connection with the more famous South Australian Brewing Co. Ltd of Hindley Street, Adelaide, which did not come into being by that name until 1891.

William Gebhardt was also a partner in the Penola Brewery, 50 km north. He worked the South Australian Brewery at Mt Gambier for twenty-four years before passing the business to his sons, Charles and Ernst, in 1891. They continued for a further twenty-nine years.

Standard Brewery 1868–1923
Commercial Street, west

After leaving the West End Brewery in Mt Gambier, which they had been leasing, Robert Anderson and George Sharp built a brewery of their own further down Commercial Street. They called it the Standard Brewery. Five years later, in 1873, Robert Anderson was on his own, and he continued at the brewery until his death in 1881. He had been a prominent citizen in Mt Gambier, and became Mayor in 1879.

Robert's brother, Walter L. Anderson, took control of the brewery, and on 7 May 1898 John Tothill joined the firm. Three years went by, and Walter became sole proprietor. He used an image of the Commonwealth flag as his trademark.

When John Molony purchased the Standard Brewery in November 1911, he traded as Molony's Brewing Co. John Molony died in 1915, leaving a wife and eight children. The eldest son, Edward A. Molony, then in his early twentiess, assumed responsibility for the business, which expanded and prospered under his direction.

When brewing was discontinued in 1923, the company continued to expand its aerated-water and cordial business, and acquired a number of hotels in Mt Gambier and other country districts.

Standard Brewery
Anderson & Sharp	1868–73
Robert Anderson	1873–81
Walter Anderson	1881–98
Tothill & Anderson	1898–1901
Walter Anderson	1901–11

Molony's Brewing Co.
John Molony	1911–15
Edward Molony	1915–23

Swallow Brewery
See Mount Gambier Brewing Co. Ltd.

West End Brewery   1856–c. 1871
Commercial Street, west

Robert Cock was one of Mt Gambier's early pioneers, and he opened his brewery and distillery in Commercial Street in 1856. Robert, the brewer and distiller, had two sons, both staunch members of the temperance movement.

In 1865 the Anderson family set up the Pioneer Distillery. Later that year Robert Cock decided to lease his West End Brewery to Robert Anderson and George Sharp. They left after three years, and started up in competition by building their own Standard Brewery further down the street.

Robert Cock's West End Brewery was then leased to the partnership of Maud & Draper. It is uncertain when the brewery closed. Maud & Draper had taken over in 1868, and the owner, Robert Cock, died in 1871.

Murray Bridge

Drovers had to swim their cattle across the Murray River before bridges were built, but at the township of Murray Bridge, or Edwards Crossing as it was known in 1865, crossing was easier. Empty beer kegs were used to buoy up the wagons so that they could be hauled across the river more quickly and with safety.

Murray Bridge Brewery   1887–1905
The bridge was opened at Murray Bridge in 1879, the railway arrived in 1886, and the brewery started in

The South Australian Brewery at Mt Gambier had no connection with the South Australian Brewing Co. Ltd of Adelaide. The brewery at Mt Gambier was a family concern that remained in business for fifty-three years.

1887. W. A. Gerloff was the owner, at least for a year or so, and then the brewery closed.

In 1901 James Opie reopened and upgraded the brewery. He stayed in business for about five years.

Naracoorte

The history of Naracoorte can be traced back to the 1840s when the first hotel and store were built. A commercial centre developed, and the town was proclaimed in 1870; the name Naracoorte was derived from the Aboriginal word meaning 'running water'. The town is now world renowned for its limestone caves.

Naracoorte Brewery   c. 1870–90

During the 1870s the brewery, 'a stable-like structure', was established by A. S. Malcolm in the town centre. By 1880 John Lobban was running the brewery. William Goedecke operated the Naracoorte Brewery from 1883 to 1886, and J. A. Smith was the owner for the last few years.

Noarlunga

Noarlunga Brewery   1847–67
Bank of the Onkaparinga River

During 1847 William Edmonds built a brewery at Horseshoe, then a flourishing township 30 km south of Adelaide. Some of the historic buildings in the district date back to 1840, and the Noarlunga market square was in use in 1841.

Edmonds's substantial brewery was erected on the bank of the river. He was an old English brewer, and made very good beer that found a ready sale in the few hotels in the area. A malthouse was added in 1851, but six years later Edmonds was insolvent.

Edward Dutton and Henry Aldersley took over, but their partnership was dissolved in 1863, leaving Aldersley to carry on alone, as Dutton had moved on to Yankalilla.

Normanville

Normanville Brewery   1860–69

Benjamin Pascoe brewed at Normanville for nine years, and then took over the brewery at Yankalilla, 3 km east. The reason for the move is unknown, but both townships were quite small and relatively remote.

Nuriootpa

Angus Park, later known as Nuriootpa, in the Barossa Valley, is a well-established winegrowing district. In earlier years brewing was also an important industry, and for half a century local beer was supplied to the town and surrounding districts.

Angus Park Brewery   1858–1912

John Williams started brewing at Angus Park in 1858. Within ten years his property had developed to include the brewery — a compact two-storey stone building with an iron roof, a five-roomed cottage for the foreman, deep underground cellars, stables and pigsties, and tanks of water scattered about for washing and cleaning. The private residence of John and Elizabeth Williams was in front of the brewery, facing the main road, and was surrounded by a well-laid-out flower and fruit garden.

The XX and XXX ales were well liked throughout the district, and the high reputation continued after the death of John Williams in 1876. The son, Charles Williams, leased the brewery from his mother from 1877 to 1880. The brewing licence was then transferred to William White, followed by Sarah Kevern in 1881.

August Friederich Kruger took possession of the brewery and property in 1883. Before that he had a small brandy distillery on his property at nearby Keyneton, where he also made and sold beer. Having shifted to Nuriootpa, Kruger ran a prosperous brewing business until his death in 1903. His two sons, Heinrich and Friederich, then continued the business.

By 1906 William H. R. Appelt owned the brewery. He built a new factory opposite the railway station in 1912, and stopped brewing alcoholic beverages at that time. However, the company engaged in the bottling of ale and stout, which they obtained in bulk from the Macclesfield Brewery in Adelaide. Brewing of non-intoxicating beverages continued at Nuriootpa, under the brand names of Barossa Bitter Beer, Barossa Lager Beer and Barossa Hop Beer.

Oakbank

Dorset Brewery   1886–1938

When the Dorset Brewery started at Oakbank, there was already a sizable brewery in the village. In fact, it had been brewing there since 1843, but that didn't discourage the owners of the new brewery, which traded as Pike, Son & Beasley.

Henry Pike was a carpenter by trade, and while doing carpentry work at a brewery, he carefully observed how beer was made and decided to try brewing himself, it seemed so easy. He started brewing at his home, using a small and very primitive plant consisting of a copper and a few tubs. He managed to brew one hogshead of beer at a time, and put out a fairly drinkable beer that he sold to neighbours. He kept brewing this way for three years, then added more tanks and tubs, and employed his two sons, W. H. and E. F. Pike, and his son-in-law, E. A. Beasley.

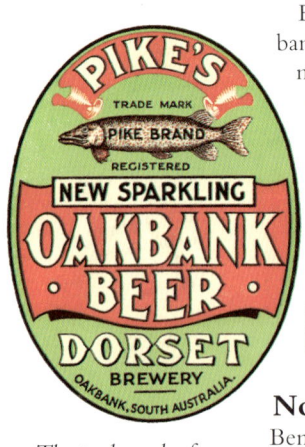

The trademark of a pike fish (using the surname of the owner of the Dorset Brewery, Henry Pike) was registered in March 1906, and used on the labels of most of the brewery's products.

The business grew rapidly and the firm's products were in strong demand. They also ran a dairy, and in the slack season, if there ever was one, they raised pigs and cured bacon. The name of the business was changed from Pike, Son & Beasley to H. Pike & Co. Ltd in 1910. The father, Henry Pike, had died in 1904.

After fifty-two years brewing stopped in 1938, and supplies of beer and stout were obtained from the South Australian Brewing Co. Ltd. The Dorset Brewery continued to make soft drinks until the premises were closed on 30 August 1975.

Oakbank Brewery Ltd   1843–1914

James and Andrew Johnston migrated from Scotland with their parents, and settled in the Onkaparinga district of South Australia, 30 km east of Adelaide. They subdivided land, and established the township of Oakbank, named after a village near their home in Scotland.

In 1843 the brothers set up a brewery and malthouse on the bank of the Onkaparinga River, trading as J. & A. G. Johnston. This was South Australia's first, and also longest operating, country brewery, continuing for seventy-one years until its closure in 1914.

In 1873 the brothers purchased the Lobethal Brewery, 10 km north, and five years later they took over the Littlehampton Brewery, a few kilometres south. The expansion of their business through acquisitions continued. In 1874 the Johnston brothers, together with W. H. Beaglehole and J. McD. Gasquoine, acquired an interest in the Lion Brewery of Adelaide. They also started the Waverley Brewery at Broken Hill in 1890, in conjunction with Simpson and Beaglehole.

At Oakbank James Johnston's son, John Disher Johnston, joined the firm in 1886. Following the death of Andrew Johnston that year, and James in 1891, the respective sons, Andrew and William, took charge of the business, and it became a 'Limited' company in 1901. At that time there were two breweries in the town, but no hotels.

It was reported by the company in 1905 that one of their employees, C. Smith, had been in continuous employment in the firm for fifty-eight years — he had started at the age of fifteen and was now seventy-three and 'still going strong'. At the time this was thought to be a record in South Australia for long service with one company.

About twenty hotels had been gradually acquired, but brewing ceased in 1914. Production of various soft drinks continued, and beer for the company's hotels was supplied by the South Australian Brewing Co. Ltd.

One of the reasons why the company stopped brewing was the problem of wild yeasts. Before 1 January 1902, the date when brewers were required by Act of Parliament to take out a licence to brew, the alcoholic content of their beer was very high; 17 per cent alcohol by weight was not uncommon. After this date brewers were forced to make a much milder brew with a lower alcohol content. As a consequence, wild yeast attacked the lower-alcohol beer more readily. The Johnstons experienced this problem, which spread throughout the brewery, and continued to affect batches of beer up to the time that brewing was stopped.

> ### BREWERY AS A GAOL
>
> It is not often that a brewery serves the purpose of a gaol, but during the progress of the great picnic race meeting at Oakbank, S.A., on Easter Monday, the brewery of Messrs. T. & A. G. Johnson was requisitioned for this purpose.
>
> The police had under their notice a suspicious character from one of the other states, and thought it better to get him confined than allow him to exercise a doubtful calling among the public. He was temporarily placed in a room at the brewery, but rather smartly managed the removal of the screws from the hinges of the door and escaped.
>
> *Australian Brewers' Journal*, April 1907

Penola

Penola Brewery   1867–1902

The oldest town in the south-east region of South Australia is Penola, located close to the Victorian border and a short distance south of the renowned wine-producing district of Coonawarra.

When the Penola Brewery opened on 16 September 1867, the owners were William Gebhardt and Ernst Seeliger. They had two employees, and their output was a modest 8 hogsheads of beer per week.

Gebhardt had recently started the South Australian

Brewery in Mt Gambier, and in 1873 he decided to sell his interest in the Penola Brewery to his partner.

Pichi Richi

The Pichi Richi Pass is a long gorge, north-east of Port Augusta. It was used by the pioneer settlers as a transport route, and the original narrow-gauge Central Australian railway, completed in 1879, went through the pass.

Willow Brewery   1879–c. 1881

The brewery, which opened on 3 July 1879, employed 'a brewer of experience', Charles Henry Gray. Gray had been brewing at Melrose twenty years earlier, then at Blinman. Before moving to Pichi Richi he had been the owner of the Beltana Brewery for two years.

The brewery was described as a first-class stone building that could be easily extended to cope with expanding business. It was also said that the well had an inexhaustible supply of fresh water, supposedly equal to the best in the world. Although the quality of the water was apparently not a problem, the brewery closed not long after it started. The railway department refused to erect a siding at Pichi Richi stating that 'the grade was too steep'.

W. Taylor & Co. owned the brewery during its final year. Two years later the buildings were destroyed by fire.

Port Augusta

The town of Port Augusta, appropriately known as the 'Gateway to the Outback', was founded in 1854, and developed into one of the major South Australian ports for the shipment of wool, wheat and minerals until 1973.

Glenrowan Brewing & Aerated Water Co.   1916

The proprietors, H. Jones and S. Young, dissolved their partnership on 16 May 1916.

Port Augusta Brewery   1876–98
12 Jervois Street

Isaiah Reid and his brother, John, had been the owners of the Anchor Brewery in Adelaide. When John died, Isaiah moved to Port Augusta, and started the Stone Brewery in 1876. He died the following year, and his widow, Jane, continued with it for two years.

In January 1879 she sold the brewery to Henry Hilton and William Perrers who changed the name from the Stone Brewery to the Port Augusta Brewery.

Henry Hilton sold his share in the business to H. V. & T. Moyle in June 1879. After that the other partner, William Perrers, had a succession of partners: Perrers & Barker, January 1880; Perrers, Briggs, Aldridge & Co., February 1880, and Perrers, Aldridge & Co., December 1880.

It had been a hectic year for Perrers, and from April 1881 he was trading as Perrers & Co. He was then on his own for twelve years, before becoming insolvent in 1893.

The South Australian Brewing Co. Ltd bought the brewery in 1893, and continued making beer at Port Augusta until 1898. They then used the premises as a depot.

Stone Brewery	
Isaiah Reid	1876–77
Jane Reid	1877–79
Port Augusta Brewery	
Perrers & Hilton	1879
Perrers & Moyle	1879–80
Perrers & Barker	1880
Perrers, Briggs, Aldridge & Co.	1880
Perrers & Aldridge & Co.	1880–81
William Perrers	1881–93
South Australian Brewing Co. Ltd	
(Port Augusta Brewery)	1893–98

Stone Brewery
See Port Augusta Brewery.

Port MacDonnell

Port MacDonnell, situated on the South Australian coast close to the Victorian border, was surveyed in 1860 and named after the then-Governor, Sir Richard MacDonnell. Between 1860 and the 1880s the town was second only to Adelaide as a port for South Australian produce.

Port MacDonnell Brewery   1863–74

By the early 1860s the town was growing rapidly, and the opportunity was there for someone to provide the population with locally made beer. The nearest brewery was at Mt Gambier, 40 km north.

Robert Anderson formed a partnership with his wife's brother-in-law, George Clark, and they set up a brewery at Port MacDonnell in 1863. The following year the business was carried on by George Clark and James Thompson, but the partnership was dissolved on 1 February 1866, leaving Thompson to carry on alone.

Port Pirie

Port Pirie Brewery   1876–1929
Solomontown, Port Pirie

The *Port Pirie Gazette and Area News* of 12 May 1876 displayed an advertisement: 'Port Pirie Brewery. New brew now ready, T. Garlick, proprietor'.

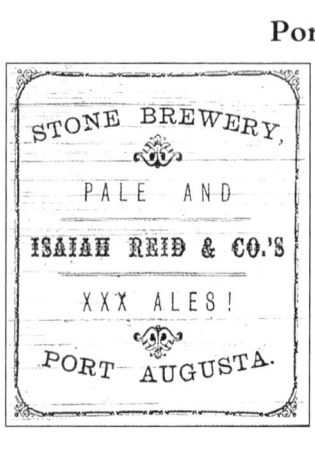

Dennis Nash, who had been working for his father at the Salisbury Brewery in Adelaide, purchased the Port Pirie Brewery in 1884.

Meanwhile, at that time Barrington Knight was operating a general store in Port Pirie, in partnership with his father-in-law, John Barton. They sold ales and porter, which they bottled at their store from bulk shipments that they obtained from Syme & Sison's Adelaide Brewery. They also sold wines and spirits.

The Port Pirie Brewery, frequently referred to as the Solomontown Brewery, was taken over by Knight in 1896. Trading as B. J. Knight & Sons, they extended the building, and brewed with considerable success, winning First Prize for stout at the Adelaide Wine Shows of 1896 and 1897.

Other brewers who were involved in the business were E. H. Martin, James Burgess and Richard Mackay.

Solomontown Brewery
See Port Pirie Brewery.

Quorn

The small township of Quorn was the original starting point for the famous Ghan train that travelled north to Oodnadatta. More recently the district has been noted for the making of such films as *The Shirralee*, *Gallipoli* and *Sunday Too Far Away*.

Quorn Brewery   1896–1901
Before moving to Quorn in 1896 Charles Medlin had been making and selling soft drinks at Port Augusta. At Quorn he continued making soft drinks and, to expand his business, he also brewed beer.

Reynella

Reynella Brewery   1847
A small brewery began operating near Reynella about 1847, but its trade with the local farmers was insufficient to keep the brewery going. The township is named after John Reynell, who made the first wine in South Australia in 1840.

Robe

Situated on the south-east coast of South Australia, Robe was an important port for wool shipment during the latter half of the nineteenth century.

Robe Town Brewery   1869
George Lord Snr owned the Robe Town Brewery, and apparently brewed for one year only.

Second Valley

Second Valley Brewery   c. 1855
During the middle years of the 1850s a Mr Fox began brewing at Second Valley, but there was not enough trade in the neighbourhood for the brewery to continue.

Strathalbyn

Strathalbyn Brewery   1867–71
Eastern corner of Murray Street & South Terrace
James Bryan built the Strathalbyn Brewery at the south-eastern end of the township, a short distance from the Angus River. The large cellar, hewn out of solid rock, was cool and dry, but shortage of water was a problem from the beginning. Bryan's solution was to build a large underground tank, which was filled with the overflow water from Murray Street. There was an open drain that carried the floodwaters straight from the dirty road into the tank, and that was the water used for brewing and everything else.

James Bryan left after two years, and Guilford E. Gray then worked the brewery for another two years. The building was later used by C. Stowe, coach painter.

Yankalilla

Yankalilla Brewery   1864–92
Although the Yankalilla Brewery was in business, off and on, over a period of twenty-eight years, it was never very substantial, due in part to its location in a sparsely populated area.

Edward Dutton had been a partner in the brewery at Noarlunga, about 40 km north, and in 1864 he moved south and started brewing at Yankalilla. One year later he left the district, and started another brewery in the more prosperous township of Goolwa.

The brewery at Yankalilla remained closed for five years, and was reopened in 1869 by H. J. Edmonds. One year was enough for Edmonds. After that Benjamin Pascoe took over, and ran the brewery for the next thirteen years. He had been the owner of the Normanville Brewery, a mere 3 km to the west. Pascoe stopped brewing at Yankalilla in 1883 and, once again, the brewery was idle.

The last brewer was Edgar Martin, who struggled on from 1889 to 1892.

Western Australia

The brewing industry in Western Australia was never as extensive as most of the other Australian states. In total, less than 100 breweries have operated in Australia's largest state since its colonisation in 1829, the main reason being the relatively small population. After twenty years of settlement, the population of the colony was only 5000. Twenty years later the number was a mere 23,000; and by 1869, sixty years after the first settlement, there were still less than 43,000 inhabitants in the colony.

A New Colony

When the British government founded the colony of New South Wales in 1788, it claimed only the eastern half of Australia. The land to the west was known at that time as New Holland. The first attempted settlement of New Holland took place on Christmas Day, 1826, when a small party of convicts and soldiers arrived at what is now Albany on the southern coast. The penal settlement was not successful, and the garrison was withdrawn in 1831.

Early in 1827 a naval officer, Captain James Stirling, explored the Swan River region, and his enthusiastic report of the area led to permanent settlement. On 2 May 1829 Captain Charles Fremantle arrived at the mouth of the Swan River, and took possession of all the remaining unclaimed land of Australia, to the west, for the British Crown.

Captain Stirling was in command of the new colony, and there were no plans for the transportation of convicts to the settlement. Emigrants were offered incentives to settle, and on 1 June 1829 the first party arrived at the Swan River. On 18 June the colony was proclaimed.

Pioneers

The site of the capital, Perth, named on 12 August 1829 after the Scottish town of that name, offered ample fresh water, timber and clay for brickmaking. Fremantle, situated at the mouth of the Swan River, about 20 km south-west of Perth, was established as a port shortly after. The land for both townships was surveyed but allotment was slow, leading to disastrous consequences for the inhabitants. Some settlers had to wait a year for their land, while others less patient left the colony to settle in Sydney on the east coast.

More than 2000 immigrants came to the colony during the first twelve months, but very few knew anything about farming, and, even so, their land had not yet been allotted. These early pioneers suffered severe deprivation and hardship, and the flow of settlers came to a standstill. With long delays in the arrival of an occasional ship, the colony had to be totally dependent on its own resources by 1830.

Fertile land was discovered in the Avon Valley, and this was opened up for farming in 1831. However, overland transport was difficult and tedious, and hostile natives caused further distress. Crops that were planted tended to be used for private consumption and not for commercial trade.

As the years passed the conditions of the settlers began to improve. There were formed dirt roads, and the Swan River ferries that connected Perth to the port of Fremantle became the main source of transport between settlements further upstream. By the early 1840s there were modest exports of timber and wool, supplemented by whaling, but progress was still slow. Capital and labour were in short supply, and in 1850, contrary to earlier intentions, the first shipload of convicts arrived. They were of considerable help to the emerging colony, and were deployed in public works programmes such as the construction of roads, bridges and public buildings.

The Breweries

The first breweries in Western Australia were located in Perth. Toward the end of 1830, with the population a little over 2000, there were a few wayside inns between Perth and Fremantle. Beer was at a premium, if available at all, since there were long periods of waiting until the next ship arrived. Even then, supplies of liquor that did arrive were mainly rum and other spirits. Lieutenant R. N. Bull, having taken up a land grant near the Canning Ford, put up a small building, and in 1830 he began brewing beer, which he sold for the exorbitant price of 3s per gallon. Technically, Lieutenant Bull was Western Australia's first brewer.

In 1835 William Devenish advertised that, because of the pureness of the water in the well behind his East Guildford Tavern, he was producing 'the best beer in the colony'. His was the only brewery in the colony at that time.

The first commercial brewery in Perth was the Albion, which was started by James Stokes in 1837. His beer sold for 9d per gallon, and, although much of it was more often than not barely drinkable, people kept buying it. By 1840 Stokes had to extend the brewery. The *Perth Gazette* praised the beer: 'a wholesome beverage produced in the colony is far better than the trashy stuff generally imported'. The locals held a different opinion, and called Stokes's beer 'Colonial Twang', which, after a sip or two, would cause the drinker to experience an involuntary shudder and a jerk of the head. The 'Twang' put out by Stokes was heavy, black and bitter, 'to be consumed only as a last resort'. The Albion Brewery later became the Stanley, then the Emu Brewery, and finally the Swan Brewery.

Other small breweries opened in Perth around 1840. Sergeant Edward Barron was brewing at Wattle Grove in 1838, and two years later beer was produced at

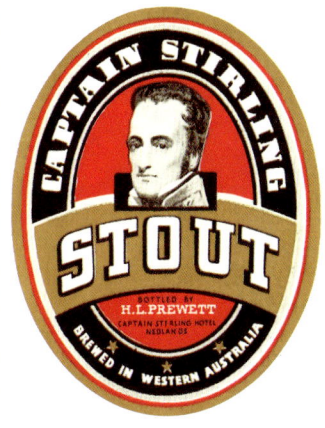

Captain James Stirling was the commander of the Swan River Colony when it was first settled and proclaimed in 1829. This label was used during the 1950s.

> ### BEER DECLARED BLACK
>
> Following an announcement by the goldfields (WA) publicans to increase the price of beer to; imperial pots 9 pence, public meetings were held and all beer was declared 'black'.
>
> *Australian Brewers' Journal,*
> *February 1920*

Western Australia's first commercial brewery was started by James Stokes in 1837. It was called the Albion Brewery, later becoming the Stanley, then the Emu Brewery, and finally the Swan Brewery.

the Western Australian Brewery and also at the Rose and Crown Hotel and Brewery, now claimed to be the oldest hotel in the west.

Regional

Breweries started up in two provincial towns in 1843. James Childs, a whaler by trade, ran a brewery at Bunbury, 180 km south of Perth, while at Fremantle Anthony Curtis added a brewery to his Stag's Head Inn. In the course of time, breweries were established in thirty-five country towns, many of which had more than one brewery: Albany had seven breweries; Kalgoorlie also had seven; Bunbury, Coolgardie and Fremantle, four each; and the townships of Geraldton and Kanowna each had three breweries.

Gold

Traditionally, Western Australia had been a primary-producing colony, with wool, wheat and sandalwood being the main contributors to the economy. Whaling and pearling also provided export income, but much more was to follow. In the late 1880s gold was discovered in many of the dry outback regions to the east, and the flood of fortune hunters that followed led to the emergence of a scattering of townships. During the 1890s, and at the turn of the century, most of these small mining towns had one or more breweries,

towns such as Broad Arrow, Menzies, Kookynie, Leonora, Laverton, and many others. The average life of a brewery in these towns was only six years. Many of these places in the desolate regions of the far outback are now little more than ghost towns.

The greatest of all goldrushes occurred at Coolgardie in 1892, and at Kalgoorlie in 1893. Thousands of immigrants poured into the areas, and the population of the colony rose from 43,000 in 1889 to 100,000 in 1895. Nine years later the number had grown to 240,000. Four breweries were working at maximum capacity at Coolgardie, two more at nearby Boulder, and by the turn of the century seven breweries were in business in Kalgoorlie.

Beer Duty

Government beer duty had to be assessed, and it was the task of an excise officer to carry out brewery inspections, travelling incredibly long distances into remote areas, either by Cobb & Co. coach, or camel or horseback. A typical travel routine for an officer would involve travelling from Perth down to Albany (400 km), then east across to Esperance (530 km), up north to Wiluna via Kalgoorlie (950 km), west to Geraldton (730 km) and then south, back to Perth, another 500 km.

Only One

In the early 1880s there were eleven breweries operating in the colony. A decade later, as the result of the goldrushes, the number had soared to forty-eight. The peak was reached in 1905 when there were fifty-six breweries spread out across the state. By the 1920s there were only twelve, and the decline continued. Three breweries were left by the early 1950s: the Swan, Emu and the Kalgoorlie, all owned by the Swan Brewery. In due course the Emu and Kalgoorlie breweries were closed, and Western Australia then had only one brewery, the Swan Brewery Co. Ltd.

For the first hundred years of its history Western Australia remained relatively isolated from the rest of Australia. To a large extent its development was a continuance of the determination and courage of the pioneers, where self-reliance was the essence of their livelihood. The brewers of the day were typical of this spirit of individual effort, where their experiments and failures and achievements added in no small way to the growth of the colony.

Western Australia

#	Location	Grid	#	Location	Grid
1	Albany	D10	16	Lawlers	E7
2	Boulder	E8	17	Leonora	E8
3	Broad Arrow	E8	18	Menzies	E8
4	Bulong	F8	19	Merredin	D9
5	Bunbury	C10	20	Mt Magnet	D7
6	Coolgardie	E8	21	Mt Malcolm	E8
7	Cue	D7	22	Mt Margaret	F8
8	Esperance	F10	23	Mt Morgans	F8
9	Fremantle	C9	24	Mullewa	C8
10	Geraldton	C8	25	Narrogin	D10
11	Greenbushes	C10	26	Norseman	F9
12	Kalgoorlie	E8	27	Northam	D9
13	Kanowna	E8	28	Perth	C9
14	Kookynie	E8	29	Port Hedland	D4
15	Laverton	F7	30	Ravensthorpe	E10
			31	Sandstone	D7
			32	Wagin	D10
			33	Wiluna	E7
			34	Yalgoo	C7
			35	York	D9

Albany

The southern coastal town of Albany was the site of the first attempt at European settlement in Western Australia in 1825. Named after the Duke of York and Albany (second son of George III of England), it was to have been a penal settlement, but it was abandoned after three years.

Development of the town was slow, and thirty-seven years passed before locally-brewed beer was available. The population was never large, and it is surprising that so many breweries operated in Albany. There were no nearby townships to provide a larger market, and the beer produced was only for local consumption and the passing shipping trade.

Albany Brewing Co. Ltd   1906–34
Middleton Road

The best-known brewer at Albany was James Myers. While he was working at the Southern Brewery in Albany, he learnt a lot about brewing from the proprietor, Gustavus Heinzmann, and by 1890 he was ready to start his own brewery. He called it the Lion, and as time progressed, his five sons joined the business: James Jnr, John, Arthur, Charles, and the youngest son, Walter.

During 1906 the Albany Brewing Co. Ltd was formed for the purpose of acquiring the assets of the Lion Brewery, and a new brewery was built in Middleton Road just below the present Albany Senior High School. The site was chosen for the excellent supply of clear water that came from a spring running out of the rugged slopes of Mt Clarence. By December 1906 the brewery was advertising bulk and bottled beers, aerated waters, cordials and ice. No deposits were required on bottled beer.

In 1910 the brewery was leased to Holland, Long & Co. Archibald Holland did the brewing, Long looked after the administration. They continued brewing under the old name of the Lion Brewery until May 1918.

The brewery was then taken over by Michael Brady, a former cartage contractor and produce merchant. Jim Clancy, a retired farmer, was a partner. The new owners relied on two of the Myers boys coming back to the brewery, Jimmy (who had become bankrupt after running the Excelsior Brewery for a year) and Walter: Jimmy was to do the brewing, and Walter was to look after the machinery.

While all this was going on, Mick Brady's brother, Bill, bought Jim Clancy's share, which meant that the brewery then functioned with the two Myers brothers and the two Brady brothers. The brewery closed on 30 June 1934, and the equipment was sold as junk. Walter Myers helped to cut up and load the copper vats and other items to be taken away. No trace of the brewery remains.

Cambridge Brewery   1883–1907
Short Street, west

George Pettit had started the brewery in January 1883, but after a few months he sold to Fred Ward. Ward died five years later, and the brewery closed. It was reopened in 1897 by Timothy Cullinane, previously the owner of the local Oriental Brewery.

Two years went by, and the next owner of the Cambridge Brewery was John Ward, presumably a relative of Fred Ward, one of the earlier owners. By 1907 the brewery had gone out of business.

City Brewery
See Oriental Brewery.

Crown Brewery   c. 1880–90
The brewery was in business for about ten years. In 1890 it amalgamated with the Southern Brewery to form the Southern Brewery Co. Ltd.

Excelsior Brewery
See Southern Brewery Co. Ltd.

Great Southern Brewery
See Southern Brewery Co. Ltd.

Lion Brewing, Aerated Water & Cordial Manufacturing Co.   1890–1906
Perth Road (now Albany Highway)

James Myers, a German migrant, built his Lion Brewery on 5 acres of land along the Perth Road. He had gained his brewing experience with Gustavus Heinzmann at the Southern Brewery in Albany, and left there in 1890 to start out on his own. Within a few years he was advertising as a brewer and aerated-water and cordial manufacturer, and traded as Jas Meyers & Son. Actually, there were five sons in the business — James Jnr (Jimmy), who was the brewer, John, Arthur, Charles and, later, the youngest son, Walter.

In March 1906 a prospectus was issued for the Lion Brewing, Aerated Water & Cordial Manufacturing Co. The capital of the new company was £30,000 with James Myers Snr retaining 50 per cent of the shares. Later that year the company was acquired by the newly-formed Albany Brewing Co. Ltd. The Lion Brewery was closed, and the equipment was transferred to a new brewery in Middleton Road.

See also Albany Brewing Co. Ltd.

The Lion Brewery, Albany, was founded by James Myers in 1890. In 1906 it was taken over and reformed as the Albany Brewing Co. Ltd. Four years later, the brewery was leased to Holland, Long & Co. who continued to trade under the old name of the Lion Brewery.

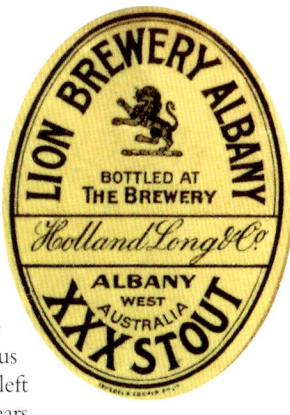

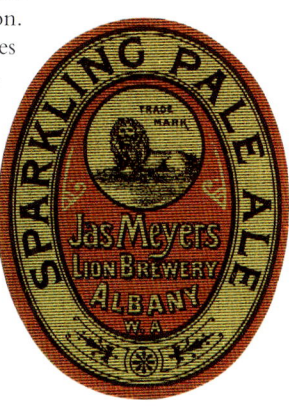

Lion Brewery		
James Myers		1890–1906
Lion Brewing, Aerated Water & Cordial Mfg. Co.		1906
Albany Brewing Co. Ltd		
James Myers		1906–10
Holland, Long & Co. (lessees)		1910–18
Michael Brady & Jim Clancy (owners)		1918
Brady Bros. & Myers Bros.		1918–34

Oriental Brewery 1880–97
Cnr Gordon & York Streets

Bartholomew Arienti had changed his name to Argent when he started the Oriental Brewery in 1880. He was in partnership with George Pettit, who left the following year. Several years later the brewery was conducted by Argent & Galle.

During 1888 the brewery was put up for sale, but it took two years to find a buyer. Timothy Cullinane became the new owner. He changed the name from the Oriental Brewery to the City Brewery in 1896. The City Brewery lasted a year.

Cullinane had reopened the Cambridge Brewery that had been idle for several years. Having closed his City Brewery, he shifted all the kegs, vats and utensils over to the Cambridge Brewery and continued brewing there.

See also Cambridge Brewery.

Southern Brewery Co. Ltd 1869–1907
Top of York Street

William Mumme had been an apprentice brewer in Hamburg, Germany. He arrived at Mt Gambier, South Australia, and for the next twelve years he improved his knowledge of colonial brewing in the company of South Australia's largest German community.

In 1869 Mumme joined his friend, Gustavus Heinzmann, at Albany, and they started a brewery. After some difficulties, Mumme left, and became the brewer and joint lessee at the Swan Brewery, Perth. Heinzmann remained in Albany.

As well as running his brewery, he became a pastoralist and real-estate agent. At the brewery he had two good men working for him: young James Myers, who quickly learnt the art of brewing, and Nathaniel McKail, who became the manager and secretary when the Southern Brewery Co. Ltd was formed in October 1890. The nearby Crown Brewery was taken over at this time. It was during that year that James Myers left to start his own Lion Brewery at Albany.

Nat McKail became a director of the Southern Brewery in 1894, and by the early 1900s he was the owner. The company also owned the Weld Arms Hotel. At times the brewery was called the Great Southern Brewery. Gus Heinzmann had continued as the manager of the brewery, working for Nat McKail, but Heinzmann died early in 1906. Later that year the company was in liquidation.

James Edward Myers (James Jnr) put an advertisement in the *Albany Advertiser* of 20 October 1906:

> having purchased the plant and all interests of the Southern Brewery Company, begs to intimate that it is his intention to carry on the business under the name of the Excelsior Brewery. The brewery will henceforth be conducted by him personally and those mindful of his capacity as a brewer at the Lion Brewery for 14 years are notified that they have still only to ask for Meyers' Beer … Excelsior Brewery (late Southern) James Myers Jnr, Owner and Brewer, top of York Street. October 12, 1906.

One week after this advertisement, James Myers Jnr lost his wife as the result of fatal burns when the family home was destroyed by fire. Jimmy, as he was known, kept going at the brewery, and advertised early in 1907:

> Now Albanians, just listen while I read to
>   you this tale
> About a new discovery — a good and well-
>   brewed ale
> They call it the XLCR which signifies it's good
> And I'm sure you'll not get better from the bottle
>   or the wood.

This was the first of four verses extolling the superior qualities of Jimmy's beer and telling the reader to 'Impress upon your memories the name Excelsior'.

It was a sad situation in many ways when, on 4 July 1907, after only nine months of trying to establish a good business for himself, Jimmy put the Excelsior Brewery up for sale — he had been declared bankrupt. He explained that, after purchasing the Southern Brewery, he had very little capital left and that was quickly used up for stock. He had previously worked for his father since he was thirteen years old and 'his father would not entertain his reasonable claim for more wages'. His father had sold out (the Lion Brewery, which had become the Albany Brewing Co. Ltd earlier that year). Working on his own, Jimmy said that 'he could not understand a succession of bad brews, since he had been brewing for 14 years'.

That was the end of the Excelsior, formerly the Southern Brewery, which had put out its first beer in 1869. As for Jimmy, he later became the brewer and a partner in the Albany Brewing Co. Ltd.

Mumme & Heinzmann	1869–72
G. Heinzmann	1872–90
Southern Brewery Co. Ltd	**1890–1900**
Crown Brewery taken over, and closed	
Nathaniel McKail (owner)	1900–6
Excelsior Brewery	
James Myers Jnr	1906–7

Ward's Brewery 1863
Near Short, Earl & Spencer Streets

In 1860 John Ward applied for permission to establish a brewery, and requested a licence to brew in 1863. The location of the brewery was at the old flourmill site in the vicinity of Short, Earl and Spencer Streets, and the beer was called 'Tanglehead'.

Shortly afterwards, the brewery closed, and Ward returned to Scotland.

Boulder

The town of Boulder was built to accommodate the miners and their families who came to the area in the early 1890s following the discovery of gold. It adjoins

Kalgoorlie, and derives its name from an early mine, the Great Boulder.

At the turn of the century it was a dirty, dusty place with crushing mills, mining plants and hot furnaces. The place was crowded and unhygienic, with no flowing water and very little sanitation. In spite of these handicaps, some brewers managed to produce beer that was acceptable to the thirsty miners.

The old city is now considered to be one of the most significant historical areas in the state.

Boulder Brewery 1898–99
Boulder Block

Tom and Bill Elliott came to Western Australia in 1893, and moved immediately to the goldfields where they began business as cartage contractors. After two years Tom built a cordial factory near the railway; he also built the Federal Brewery in Kalgoorlie for F. W. Whitfield. In 1898 he built a brewery for himself at the Boulder Block. The tiny brewery was unique; it had a frontage of only 12 feet and the depth was 75 feet. It was wedged in between a group of six hotels, almost in the centre of the Boulder Block area, frequently referred to as the 'dirty acre', and later known as Finiston.

Within a few years of the goldmining town being established, Boulder had thirty-six hotels, plus the six on the Block. All were open twenty-four hours a day, and most were only small frontages with small bars at the back, catering to the ever-optimistic peggers of blocks and those who worked various shifts at the mines. They all earned a drink or two, but it rarely stopped at that, and drunkenness was a common sight in the small community.

The total output of the Boulder Brewery was delivered to hotels close by. No transport was needed since the kegs of beer were simply rolled out of the brewery and down the street to the pubs.

Boulder City Brewery Co. Ltd 1898–1924
Cnr Wittenoom & Ivanhoe Streets

When the Toorak Brewery in Coolgardie closed in 1897, the Coolgardie Brewing & Ice Co. Ltd bought the equipment, dismantled everything and transported it to Boulder, about 25 km north-east, where they set up the Lion Brewery. Brewing commenced on 2 February 1898.

During 1900 the brewery was put up for sale, and it was ultimately taken over by a local syndicate for £4000, 'a rattling good bargain and a few thousand pounds less than its original cost'. The name was changed to the Boulder City Brewery, and the company was incorporated in 1903.

In spite of the lack of an ample supply of fresh clean water, the Boulder City Brewery was doing quite well. The plant was modernised, and the buildings, which were extended, ultimately covered four town blocks. The company's Boulder Stout gained a wide reputation, and was sold as far afield as Lawlers and Norseman. In a good month output could reach 48,000 bottles of stout.

In 1924 the Boulder City Brewery was taken over and closed by the Kalgoorlie Brewing & Ice Co. Ltd. A few years later the equipment was once again dismantled and reassembled, this time at Merredin, 340 km west, for the newly-formed Kalgoorlie Brewing & Ice Co. Ltd.

The Boulder City Brewery, December 1913. A record Christmas order loaded ready for delivery to the Lake View Hotel, Boulder City. It consisted of 500 dozen bottles of Boulder Stout, weighing 12 tons.
La Trobe Library, State Library of Victoria.

Lion Brewery
See Boulder City Brewery Co. Ltd.

Broad Arrow

Broad Arrow, Bardoc & Black Flag Brewing, Aerated Water & Ice Co. Ltd 1896–1911

The brewery name was derived from the districts with the rather unusual names of Broad Arrow, Bardoc and Black Flag. Before 1896 the township of Broad Arrow was known as Kurawa.

Jim Elliott and his brother, Tom, were the founders of the brewery that was incorporated in 1896 as the Broad Arrow, Bardoc & Black Flag Brewing, Aerated Water & Ice Co. Ltd. (Another company, Broad Arrow Brewers Ltd, was formed at the same time, but liquidated the following year.)

The official opening of the brewery, commonly called the Broad Arrow Brewery, took place during the afternoon of 10 February 1897, and more festive celebrations followed, with a gala ball being held in the evening.

The Elliott brothers changed the name to the Shamrock Brewery in 1901, but with several members of the family involved in the business, it was more commonly referred to as Elliott's Brewery. Richard Elliott was the manager at the time the brewery closed.

Broad Arrow Brewery
See Broad Arrow Bardoc & Black Flag Brewing, Aerated Waters & Ice Co. Ltd.

Carlton Brewery 1898–1905
H. M. Smalpage started trading as the Credo Brewery in 1898, but five years later the name was changed to the Carlton Brewery by the new owners, Fagan & Hegarty.

The brewery closed a year or so later, and the equipment of the Carlton Brewery was sold at auction in November 1905.

Credo Brewery
See Carlton Brewery.

Elliott's Brewery
See Broad Arrow, Bardoc & Black Flag Brewing, Aerated Water & Ice Co. Ltd.

Shamrock Brewery
See Broad Arrow, Bardoc & Black Flag Brewing, Aerated Water & Ice Co. Ltd.

Bulong

Bulong Brewery 1898–1910
Near Bulong

When a syndicate opened the Bulong Brewery in 1898, it was the only brewery in Western Australia east of Kalgoorlie. It was built on the side of a hill about 2 km from Bulong, and James McIntyre was the manager.

Timothy Keogh was a syndicate member from 1905

Mr and Mrs James Elliott, Elliott's Brewery, Broad Arrow, WA.

Born at Deniliquin, NSW, 'Jim' Elliott came from a family of well-known brewers. His father, Albert Elliott, had been the brewer at Hodges Brothers Brewery, Geelong, Victoria, and his brothers Syd and Tom, were also well known in the brewing industry.

Jim Elliott was educated at the Church of England Grammar School, Geelong, Vic., and was then trained as a brewer by his father. After fourteen years, 'young Elliott became an expert in the art of turning out the bright and sparkling', and received tempting offers to go to Tasmania and Western Australia.

After a brief period at the Lion Brewery, Coolgardie, he purchased the brewery at Broad Arrow, in partnership with brother Tom, and they were soon 'doing one of the largest goldfields outputs'.

Jim Elliott was devoted to his trotting horse, kennel of hounds, a collection of game fowls, canaries and finches, and he called his tame emu 'Carbine'. He was a member of the local council and, with his interest and participation in cricket and football, he became president of the District Athletic Association.

La Trobe Library, State Library of Victoria.

The Bulong Brewery operated from 1898 to 1910. It was built on the slope of a hill; note the primitive construction and the mound of soil built up against the side of the building as protection against the hot summer winds.

to 1907. Turnover was small, and the brewery sold ale to the few small settlements in the vast outback areas bordering the Nullarbor Plain.

Bunbury

The second-largest city in Western Australia, Bunbury is the principal port for wheat and timber shipments. The nearby township of Worsley processes bauxite, and the alumina is transported by rail to the port of Bunbury for export.

In earlier years American whalers sheltered on the shores where the modern city stands.

Beigel's Brewery Co. Ltd 1903–16
On the bank of the Leschenault Estuary

Before starting his own brewery, Herman Beigel had been bottling beer that he purchased in bulk from the Bunbury Brewery Co. Ltd. Then, in 1902, fire completely destroyed his bottling factory. At that stage he planned to make his own beer, so he went ahead and built a brewery.

In 1903 Beigel advertised his beer as 'not merely the best but the champion', and went on to win first prize at the National Show in 1905.

About four years later he set up a branch brewery at Wagin, 180 km to the east, and at Bunbury he started selling wine and spirits. Herman Beigel was for many years a member of the Bunbury Municipal Council, and became associated with the Bunbury Harbour Board as its chairman.

In 1912 Beigel's local competitor, the Bunbury Brewery Co., then in liquidation, was purchased by Beigel, and closed. Competition from the powerful Perth breweries gradually took its toll. After running at a loss for several years, the Beigel breweries at Bunbury and Wagin were sold. Brewing was never started again in either town.

Bogue's Brewery
See Federal Brewery.

Bunbury Brewery Co. Ltd 1897–1912
Victoria Street

Although the Bunbury Brewery Co. Ltd was formed in 1896, the first beer was not produced until November 1897. Artesian-bore water was used, and bottling was subcontracted to Herman Beigel in Bunbury, and to H. Sherwood & Co. in Perth. Later, the company decided to do the bottling themselves for southern district sales.

The Bunbury Brewery advertised its famous Terrier Brand Pale Ale and Stout, which sold so fast that the brewer, Archibald Holland, had to put in more plant late in 1898. Beer was selling for 6d per bottle, and the Bunbury's thriving trade expanded to nearby towns and timber mills.

After ten good years the brewery began to suffer the same fate as most other country breweries and yearly losses finally forced the company into liquidation. Herman Beigel of Beigel's Brewery Co. Ltd, the other brewer in town, purchased and closed the Bunbury Brewery in 1912.

Burton Brewery Co.
A prospectus for the proposed brewery was issued in January 1905, but the venture failed to proceed.

Childs, James 1843–45
Victoria Street

One of the earliest whalers to operate from Port Leschenault, Bunbury, was James Kay Childs. He was suffering from tuberculosis when he arrived from England at the age of twenty-two, and it was thought that the warmer climate would cure him. His whaling endeavours, however, were minimal and he opened a store in Victoria Street. In those days Victoria Street was little more than a lane — muddy and boggy in winter, and black with dust in summer. At one section of the street, logs were placed along the road to provide a foundation for horsedrawn vehicles.

Childs's beer was a relatively light sugar-beer, and it was reported that 'he makes it very well'. Unfortunately his health did not improve, and after only five years in the colony he died at the age of twenty-seven.

Federal Brewery 1897–1905
Picton Road, South Bunbury

When Frederick Bogue first began advertising in February 1897, he used the name Bogue's Brewery, but changed it the following year to the Shamrock Brewery: 'Drink Bogue's Ale and Stout, a splendid tonic, absolutely pure. Bogue's Shamrock Brewery and Bottling Works', that was the advertisement in the *Bunbury Herald* of 12 January 1899.

At the same time, in the same newspaper and for the same products of ale and stout, Bogue's competitor, the Bunbury Brewery, chose to use the descriptive terms of 'Bright, Sparkling and Delicious' for their beer. A few weeks later the Shamrock countered with 'A good thing for this district is [that] the delegates attending the Municipal Conference have agreed that Bogue's Bunbury Beer and Stout are superior to all other brands'.

In 1902 the name was changed to the Federal Brewery, and, superior or not, no more beer was produced after 1905.

Shamrock Brewery
See Federal Brewery.

Coolgardie

Gold was first discovered in Coolgardie in 1892 when the district was nothing more than a wasteland. Four years later there were 10,000 inhabitants, and more

Beigel's Brewery, Bunbury, c. 1910. The owner, Herman Beigel, used a picture of a beagle dog on most of his beer labels.

BEER DRINKER LYNCHED

An extraordinary affair is reported from Woolgangi [approx. 80 km west of Coolgardie, WA]. A few weeks ago, a gang of men stationed there had a tarpaulin muster and 10 shillings was collected. The subscribers deputed [*sic*] one James Mead to proceed to Woolgangi and return with the value of the money in beer.

In the course of time, the messenger came back but without the liquor. His mates there-upon held a court martial over the erring one and sentenced him to be hanged. Mead was immediately strung up and was left for some time suspended.

When taken down, he was found to be in an insensible condition and almost dead. Considerable difficulty was experienced in taking the rope off the unfortunate man's neck and hours elapsed before he was brought round.

Australian Brewers' Journal, May 1898

prospectors kept arriving to fossick for gold. The town was then the third-largest in Western Australia; only Perth and Fremantle were larger.

By 1900 the township had a population of 15,000, two stock exchanges, sixty stores, twenty-three hotels, five newspapers, many churches and two breweries. During the previous eight years two other breweries had started and closed, the main problem being the lack of an ample supply of fresh water.

Coolgardie is now Western Australia's best preserved historical goldmining town, and has a busy tourist trade.

Coolgardie Brewing & Ice Co. Ltd 1895–1906

The Coolgardie Brewery was set up by a syndicate in 1895, and John Cocks was appointed brewer and manager. The brewery was a small galvanised-iron building, with underground cellars alongside, dug into the side of a hill. Within months the business was registered as the Coolgardie Brewing & Ice Co. Ltd.

At the Criminal Court, Perth, on 10 July 1897 John

Cocks, brewer, of Coolgardie, was charged with attempting to set fire to his house with intent to defraud an insurance company. He was acquitted, but left Coolgardie to form a brewery syndicate in Guildford, Perth.

The *Coolgardie Miner* of 25 May 1898 described the Coolgardie Brewery as 'about the most extensive structure on the goldfields'. The editorial continued:

> the beer, which is acknowledged to be about the best made in Western Australia, is sent to Menzies, Niagara, Mt. Leonora, Mt. Malcolm and many other parts and has the largest sale of any beer in Coolgardie.

Earlier that year a branch brewery was started at the nearby township of Boulder, using the equipment from the Toorak Brewery in Coolgardie, which had closed the previous year. By 1906 the Coolgardie Brewing & Ice Co. Ltd had been taken over by the W.A. Lion Brewery & Ice Co. Ltd, and closed.

Goldfields Brewing Co. Ltd   1895–97
Bayley Street

The brewery was operating profitably in 1896 under the direction of J. H. Wiechert, but the company was wound up the following year. When asked for an explanation, the chairman said, 'The brewery had five brews which turned out failures causing a loss of £450 and much of the outstanding debts would not be realized'.

Lion Brewery
See W.A. Lion Brewery & Ice Co. Ltd.

Toorak Brewery   1894–97
Hunt Street

The Toorak Brewery was owned and operated by Robert Cross for a brief three-year period, after which the equipment was purchased by the Coolgardie Brewing & Ice Co. Ltd. They dismantled it, and took it 25 km north-east to Boulder, where it was reassembled for their Lion Brewery.

W.A. Lion Brewery & Ice Co. Ltd   1896–1917
Cnr Renou & Lindsay Streets

Tom Ware of the Torrenside Brewery, Adelaide, had been involved in a brewery at Norseman in 1895. Anticipating better opportunities further north, he started a brewery in the goldmining town of Coolgardie, in conjunction with C. Vincent and J. Lipman, owners of the adjacent Lion Hotel and four other hotels in the town.

The formal opening of the brewery took place on 7 February 1896. A flag was unfurled at the top of the 60-foot tower, and the guests celebrated the occasion by sampling the beer in the spacious cellars.

The basis for good beer production has always been clean, fresh water, and that was a constant problem for brewers working in the hot, dry, inland regions where there were no rivers, lakes or streams. Sometimes water was the most expensive component in the production of beer — in 1896 brewers in Coolgardie were paying 8d a gallon for condensed water. James (Jim) Elliott, the brewer and manager of the W.A. Lion Brewery, seemed to be able to overcome the water problem, and put out beers 'noted for their soundness and regularity and have stood the test of long and hot journeys of several hundred miles by camel without injury'.

Beer in Coolgardie was 1s a pint for a long time, then the Globe Hotel dropped the price to 9d. When the other hotels followed suit, the Globe reduced the price again to 6d. To stay in business the other hotels had little option but to meet the competition. There was considerable rivalry between the hotels tied to the Lion Brewery and those tied to the Toorak Brewery. One hotel had a sign: 'Why go to rack and ruin when you can get good Lion beer here straight off the ice?'; the sign also had a picture of a block of ice and a pot of beer. The opposition countered with 'Why suffer from cramp when you can get good Toorak beer here?' — they had a picture of a barrel of beer with an enticing counter-lunch on top.

During 1898 the brewery was on the market, and had been for sale for some time. The vendors, Vincent & Lipman, finally concluded a sale, reportedly for £70,000. It was said to be a bargain, since 'some of the best hotels on the fields were included'. The new owners of the Lion Brewery bought the Coolgardie Brewing & Ice Co. Ltd in April 1906, and closed it, effectively reducing the competition; for the same reasons the Lion Brewery itself was taken over by the Kalgoorlie Brewing & Ice Co. Ltd in 1912.

The Lion continued to operate, but an order for the winding up of the company was made in December 1916. Beer production ceased on 31 December 1917.

Cue

The township of Cue, 640 km north-east of Perth, was tagged the 'Queen of the Murchison' during its heyday, and was named after Tom Cue, the first man to discover gold in the district.

Cue Brewery
See Murchison Brewing Co. Ltd.

Excelsior Brewery   1899–1908
Dowling Street

The owner of the brewery was Thomas Marshall, although Reg Smith was involved, either as a partner or brewer.

In 1902 Chris Hansen was the manager, and Reg Smith the following year.

Murchison Brewing Co. Ltd   1894–1910

When James W. Phillipson began brewing at Cue in 1894, there was no other brewery for 500 km in any direction. The local water was said to be 'admirably

suited', and the brewery cellars were dug out of the soft kaolin rock, providing cool storage.

The Murchison Brewing Co. Ltd was formed in 1896. The prospectus advised that annual turnover was expected to be £27,000, with more than 50 per cent profit, and a guarantee of 10 per cent return for two years. Phillipson, previously the owner of the Hackney Brewery, Adelaide, held most of the shares, and the balance was taken up by shareholders from Adelaide. George Bone was the brewer and manager.

The gold ran out, and the brewery failed when the customers left the district.

Esperance

Coleman's Brewery　　　　　　　　1895
John Coleman, proprietor.

Esperance Brewing & Aerated
Water Co. Ltd　　　　　　　　1897–1906

The company was incorporated in Perth in 1896, and in September of that year the *Australian Brewers' Journal* noted: 'a gigantic new brewery is being erected at Esperance'. The company was probably a continuation of Coleman's Brewery, since in March 1898 the *Australian Brewers' Journal* reported that John Coleman had resigned as manager, and John Allt had taken his place. Louis Weisse was the brewer when the company started in 1897.

The brewery was not as gigantic as had been forecast. It was a corrugated-iron structure with a tower at the north end, and an external beam with a tackle at the end, enabling bags of grain to be hoisted to the upper floors of the tower. Output was quite small, and the excise duty paid for the year 1899 was a mere £44.

John Desterbeque, nicknamed Dustyback, joined Louis in 1902, and they brewed until 1906. The equipment was then shifted 200 km west to the larger township of Ravensthorpe, and the name was changed to the Phillips River Brewing & Aerated Water Co. Ltd.

Situated on the southern coast of Western Australia, the Esperance district has a natural vegetation cover of low shrub in semi-desert country. Its remoteness gave the Esperance Brewery some degree of protection from competition, since the nearest breweries were at Coolgardie, 370 km to the north, and Albany, 490 km west. But the brewery was never really a viable proposition from the start; there were simply not enough customers in the small community.

Fremantle

Fremantle, the major port of Western Australia, is at the mouth of the Swan River, 20 km from Perth, and is now part of the Perth metropolitan area. The city was named after Captain Charles Fremantle, who, on 2 May 1829, raised the Union Jack flag and took formal possession, in the name of H.M. King George IV of England, of 'all that part of New Holland which is not included within the territory of New South Wales'. Effectively, England then owned all of Australia.

Castlemaine Brewing Co.　　　1897–1929
Canning Road/Riverside Road

The *Australian Brewers' Journal* of May 1897 reported that

> J. H. Gracie, formerly of Hobart, and H. N. Sleigh, purchased and dismantled the old brewery at Koondrook, Victoria and had the equipment freighted over to Fremantle where they were to start the Fremantle Brewing Co. Ltd.

Nicholas Fitzgerald of the Castlemaine Brewery in Castlemaine, Victoria, played an important role in the establishment of the brewery in 1891. In conjunction with Harry Sleigh, he built the first brewery in Canning Road.

Shortly after, Sleigh & Co. became the proprietors. By 1902 the partnership of John H. Gracie and W. F. Walkley were the owners. They built a new brewery in Riverside Road, and used the old brewery as a bottling department where Penguin brand ale and stout was bottled.

The Castlemaine Brewery, Fremantle, c. 1905. It was built on the bank of the Swan River, and the local council threatened legal action if the brewery continued to allow its waste water, stale beer and rubbish to be dumped into the river.

The Castlemaine Brewery seemed to regard the Swan River as a convenient dumping place for its refuse, upsetting the nearby Swan Yacht Club. The council wrote the brewery and threatened legal action if the brewery continued to tip its rubbish into the river.

The business was known as the Castlemaine Brewery, and for most of the time it traded as Sleigh & Co. The brewery was taken over by the Swan Brewery Co. Ltd in 1927, and production of the popular Castlemaine Perkins Stout continued for two more years.

Gracie & Sleigh (Canning Road)	1897–98
Sleigh & Co.	1898–1902
Gracie & Walkley (Riverside Road)	1902–27
Taken over by Swan Brewery	1927–29

Fremantle Brewing & Ice Co. Ltd
See Phoenix Brewery.

Phoenix Brewery   1898–1904
Riverside Road

The company was started in February 1898 as the Fremantle Brewing & Ice Co. Ltd by Albert Walmsley. He had a 60-foot suspension bridge built across the river from his house to the brewery, but after less than three years he went into voluntary liquidation.

The name was changed to the Phoenix Brewery in 1902, but the brewery closed on 30 April 1904. The premises were later purchased by the nearby Castlemaine Brewery.

Port Brewery Co. Ltd   1893–1908
Beach Street

The old Port Brewery, owned by Ernest Birch, used to operate not far from the wharves and sheds of Victoria Quay. It commanded an excellent view of the Swan River, and was the second brewery to operate in Fremantle, forty years after the Stag's Head Inn & Brewery had stopped brewing. The Port Brewery Co. Ltd was incorporated in 1895.

The beer, which was pasteurised, was 'of excellent quality with good 'body' suitable for the varied tastes of all consumers'. Bulk ale and stout were sold mainly to local hotels and private families, and were sent to the goldfields in bottles bearing the Ship brand label.

The company was proud of its refrigeration plant

> which renders the process of cooling a much shorter operation than the old system of flat shallow coolers taking twelve to twenty-four hours, now only two to three hours.

The brewery closed on 30 October 1908, but was reopened later as Clayton's Brewery, which made non-alcoholic beer using the name Golden Ale.

Left: *The Port Brewery, 1893–1908, from across the Swan River.*

Right: *The same building, now the Clayton's Brewery, which started in 1908.*

This display of the Phoenix Brewery, Fremantle, obtained First Prize in the Trade and Firms Display competition, 1902. The brewery operated from 1898 to 1904.

La Trobe Library, State Library of Victoria.

Stag's Head Inn & Brewery   1843–53
Cnr High & Pakenham Streets

On 1 January 1834 Anthony Curtis opened the Stag's Head Inn; later he owned several other inns, including the Black Swan Inn. Many years after, in 1843, Curtis began brewing at his Stag's Head Inn, and the *Perth Gazette* of 11 November 1843 reported:

> We are informed that Mr Curtis of Fremantle has prepared an extensive brewery establishment on a scale equal to the demands of the colonists. Our informant has tasted the beverage produced at this brewery and reports most favourably of its quality ... we hope this venture will prove successful and banish from our shores the execrable trash which is foisted upon us in the shape of beer ... heads of families, the publicans, indeed all who have any consideration for their health and cannot live without beer, would do well to resort to this establishment.

The Stag's Head Inn and Brewery became a hostelry of some importance, and, following the death of Curtis in 1852, it was described at the time of the sale of the property as

> a first rate house and premises with every convenience, having a number of bed and sitting rooms, a billiard room, a shop, kitchen, sculleries, pantries, a capital piggery, a large store, a brewery and all the conveniences for carrying on a large baking and butchering business.

Geraldton

Geraldton, now the second-largest port in Western Australia, is an important distribution centre for agricultural products, wool and minerals. Brewing also became an important industry from the 1880s until 1949.

Referred to as the Sun City, Geraldton was proclaimed a city during the visit of Her Majesty, Queen Elizabeth II, in April 1988.

Castlemaine Brewery
See Geraldton Brewery Co. Ltd.

Geraldton Brewery Co. Ltd   1882–1905
Durlacher Street

The partners Harwood and Meloy owned the Lion Brewery in Perth. After upgrading it with new equipment, they packed up the leftover brewing equipment and utensils, and sent it all up to Geraldton for their new brewery, which they had named the Victoria.

Harwood & Meloy advertised in the *Victoria Express* on 1 January 1883 that their new brewery was in full production, and that their 'Victoria Ale is pronounced by the public and the press to be superior to the Perth and Albany brews'. The Victoria Ale sold for 17s 6d in 10-gallon lots, a good average price for the time.

The business became the Geraldton Brewery Co. Ltd in 1885, and traded as F. Maley & Son (Harwood had left, and later started another brewery in Perth). The Maley combination of father and son produced excellent beer. Hops were purchased from Adelaide, and malt, corks and other requirements came from Melbourne, but unfortunately, deliveries were irregular, causing delays in beer production. Customers went elsewhere and business gradually declined. The cash position deteriorated, and some creditors had to be paid in promissory notes three months to a year in advance.

The Geraldton Brewery was put up for auction. Frederick Maley's son, J. S. Maley, negotiated the purchase of the brewery. He renovated and repaired where necessary, but had to close the brewery in 1893.

Some attempts were made to lease the brewery. Finally, in January 1900, the property was sold to John Enright for £2200. Enright started another brewery, the Star Brewery, at Chapman River, Geraldton, and leased the old Geraldton Brewery in Durlacher Street to J. S. Maley, who decided on a new name, the Castlemaine Brewery. It closed in 1905.

Victoria Brewery

| Harwood & Meloy | 1882–85 |

Geraldton Brewery Co. Ltd

F. Maley & Son (owner)	1885–c. 1890
J. S. Maley (owner)	c. 1890–93, closed
J. Enright (owner)	1900

Castlemaine Brewery

| J. S. Maley (lessee) | 1900–5 |

Globe Brewery Ltd   1908–49
16 Evans Street (now Cunningham Street)

The brewery was built in 1907 by Quain Brothers. of Perth for the proprietors, Charles Speed and Walter Hetherington. The best equipment available was installed, and when construction was completed the brewery was an impressive landmark. It was the largest building in the town, and had a 65-foot-high square tower. Brewing commenced late in 1908.

Toward the end of 1915 the brewery was offered for sale. Early the following year the owners sold their interests to the newly-formed company, the Globe Brewery Ltd. The directors of the company were O. S. Green (Railway Hotel), F. H. Hansen (Freemasons Hotel) and M. Quain (Commonwealth Hotel), all from Geraldton.

Within a few years the Globe was sending beer north to Broome and Port Hedland. It enjoyed good business, despite tough competition from larger Perth breweries. The well-paid brewer and manager, Jim Elliott, was a popular personality; and in 1923 he paid £705 for an imported six-cylinder Studebaker car to motor from Geraldton to Perth, a two-day trip.

During the 1920s the business began to deteriorate. In 1925 the manager complained that, despite the firm's excellent output, hotels throughout the Murchison district were beginning to favour imported German beer and beer from the eastern states of Australia. Many of the locals had stopped buying Globe beer because they said it tasted strongly of salt water. Export to Singapore and elsewhere was considered, but ships had suddenly stopped calling at Geraldton and only sailed from the port of Fremantle, 450 km south.

Another problem that contributed to the company's declining profits was the government's imposition of excise duty. In 1902 the rate had been 2d per gallon; by March 1920 it had risen to 1s 3d and by 1943 it was 4s 7d.

The company was heavily in debt, and in May 1949 it was announced that the brewery would close down as the equipment was no longer adequate and replacement would require enormous capital. Even so, it would not be a viable proposition because of the comparatively small market and the considerable competition. The Swan Brewery was approached as a possible purchaser, but they declined, and the brewery closed. However, the Swan did eventually buy the brewery property in 1962, together with the six hotels at Geraldton and one at Carnarvon that the Globe had acquired over the years. The old brewery premises were later used as a refrigerated storehouse for fruit and fish.

Lion Brewery   1908–10

Archibald Holland had been the head brewer at the Swan Brewery in Perth, and later at the Bunbury Brewery. In December 1907 he formed a syndicate, and at a cost of £10,000 he constructed a new modern brewery that he called the Lion.

The Lion Brewery traded as Holland, Long & Co. in 1910, but the brewery closed shortly after. Eager to continue in the business of brewing, the partners moved south and leased the Albany Brewery.

Star Brewery   1895–1905
Chapman Street

Shortly after the Star Brewery was built, it was purchased by John Enright. He also purchased the Geraldton Brewery in 1900 and leased it to the former owner, J. S. Maley.

Star beer was a popular drink, and was shipped 'all the way from Geraldton to Peak Hill'. John Enright changed the name from the Star Brewery to the Victoria Brewery in 1904, but the brewery closed on 31 May the following year.

Victoria Brewery (Chapman Street)
See Star Brewery.

Victoria Brewery (Durlacher Street)
See Geraldton Brewery Co. Ltd.

Greenbushes

The area around the tiny township of Greenbushes was a rich tinfield. By 1900 the population of the newly-settled township was 1500–2000 miners.

South Western Brewery & Cordial Co. Ltd   1900–1

While the South Western Brewery was under construction early in 1900, John Allt was given the job of brewer and manager, but he resigned before the brewery was completed. However, the directors were able to find a replacement in K. Lewin.

To get the brewery going, one of the partners in the Castlemaine Brewery in Fremantle assisted by supervising the erection of the brewery and attending to the first six brews.

K. Lewin, well-known in the trade in the west, then continued to brew and manage the business. However, all this organising and construction and expense had been for a business that lasted for only one year.

Kalgoorlie

Together with the adjoining town of Boulder, Kalgoorlie owes its existence to one of the world's richest gold-bearing reefs. Gold was first discovered in the Kalgoorlie area by Patrick (Paddy) Hannan in June 1893, and the flamboyant days of prosperity and extravagance continued well into the twentieth century.

Tourists today can gain an insight into the way things were in the boisterous days of the past by visiting various museums, tours of the area, and a chance to go underground into a real goldmine in safety.

Eastern Goldfields Brewery   1910
Egan Street

Elliott's Brewery   1909–18
109 Forest Street

Alfred Langford had been the brewer at Hannan's Brewery in Kalgoorlie from 1900, and with his know-

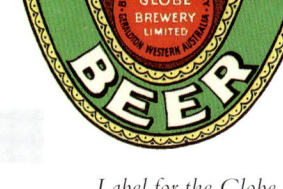

Label for the Globe Brewery.

Left: *Langford's Brewery, c. 1910.*

Right: *The same brewery after it was taken over by James Elliott in 1912. It was then called Elliott's Brewery. For the previous fifteen years Elliott had been at the Broad Arrow Brewery, 40 km north.*

ledge and experience he ventured into business on his own in 1909. He traded as Langford & Co., but the business was liquidated in 1912.

Another experienced brewer, James (Jim) Elliott, bought the brewery. He had previously been the brewer and managing director of the Lion Brewery in Coolgardie. At his own brewery, Jim ran into trouble in 1913 when he was charged with having committed a breach of the Excise Act — it was alleged that he had removed seven bottles of beer without paying the duty. In spite of his plausible explanations, he was fined £2 10s with 2s costs, a ridiculous penalty and humiliation, considering he owned the brewery and the whole thing was over a paltry seven bottles of his own beer.

In its quest to curtail competition, the Kalgoorlie Brewing & Ice Co. Ltd bought Elliott's Brewery in 1918, and closed it.

Federal Brewery
See Union Brewery.

Hannan's Brewery Co. Ltd 1895–1916
Parkeston

Kalgoorlie, which has the Aboriginal meaning of 'dog chases kangaroo', was founded in 1894. The following year a brewery started about 3 km from Kalgoorlie, near the richest gold-bearing belt in the world at that time. The brewery and the homes of the employees formed most of the small area of Parkeston.

The major shareholders in Hannan's Brewery Co. Ltd were Messrs Ibister, George Gray, Charles de Rose and Pat Whelan. The brewery was named after Kalgoorlie's most famous personality, Paddy Hannan, considered to be the first man to discover gold in the area.

Hannan's Brewery opened in August 1895, with Alfred Langford in charge of the brewing. He was only seventeen years old, and during his employment at the brewery it was said that 'he never once had a bad brew'. In 1909 Langford left to start a brewery of his own. Hannan's Brewery started another brewery at Mt Margaret in 1897, not a wise decision since it lasted less than two years.

At Kalgoorlie the company had been in financial difficulty soon after it started. Credit was restricted, and there was no money for wages. The chairman, Pat (Paddy) Whelan (later the proprietor of the Union Brewery) advanced £500 of his own money to allow the company to pay wages and obtain supplies. This provided temporary relief, but by 1899 the company had gone into voluntary liquidation.

Before 1903 all water used in the district had to be condensed, and plumbers did a roaring trade constructing and installing condensing equipment. Hannan's Brewery first obtained water from the government bore, but later they installed a 50 h.p. engine, and pumped salty water from a nearby mine to an elevated 20,000-gallon tank. From there, the water flowed into twenty-eight condensing boilers. Stokers worked three shifts, feeding wood into the furnaces to keep up the supply of condensed water. Water used for the cleaning of barrels was used twice. After washing the barrels and other utensils, the waste was condensed again. The company had no refrigeration or icemaking facilities, since the owners thought that 'the cool nights made this device unnecessary'.

John and Adam Wilkie, formerly at the local Federal Brewery, acquired a controlling interest in Hannan's Brewery in 1904, and Gerald McKenna, an experienced brewer from Victoria, was appointed general manager and chief brewer. After four years the brewery was extensively upgraded, and it was then ranked as one of the best in the Commonwealth. It had about thirty employees in all, including a blacksmith, a wheelwright and two coopers. Bottled beer output alone had reached 10,000 dozen per month during the hot season.

The brewery was highly profitable, paying out £70,000 to its shareholders over the five-year period from 1904 to 1909; the subscribed capital was only £3500.

But by the end of 1911 the company was again in liquidation. In March 1912 the brewery was auctioned,

General view of Hannan's Brewery, Kalgoorlie, c. 1910. It was the largest brewery on the goldfields.

La Trobe Library, State Library of Victoria.

and the successful purchasers were the syndicate members John, Adam and Leonard Wilkie, J. O'Connell and Walter Ruse. They paid £17,000, and traded as Hannan's Co-operative Brewery Ltd.

Business did not improve. Then, on 1 October 1915, fire destroyed the main building and seriously damaged others. Perhaps it was a coincidence that, four weeks earlier, the company had again decided in favour of voluntary liquidation. The insurance cover was £20,000 and the claim was for £13,500 — a later enquiry found that the fire was caused intentionally by a person or persons unknown.

Attempts were made to get some of the plant working, and the brewery struggled on, but the reduced scale of operation was not profitable and the brewery was forced to close in 1916.

Hannan's Co-operative Brewery Ltd
See Hannan's Brewery Co. Ltd.

Kalgoorlie Brewing Co. Pty Ltd
See Kalgoorlie Brewing & Ice Co. Ltd.

Kalgoorlie Brewing & Ice Co. Ltd   1896–1983
Porter Street

The Kalgoorlie Brewing & Ice Co. Ltd was incorporated on 24 February 1896, and brewing commenced in September of that year. J. H. Schickel, owner of the Caledonian Brewery in Adelaide, was the brewer and manager, and was full of praise for the district, commenting, 'This place is going to be the Ballarat of Western Australia, in fact, everyone here thinks that Kalgoorlie will eclipse Johannesburg in the near future'.

Output was 50 hogsheads of beer per month at the start, and by 1908 this had risen to an incredible 1100 hogsheads, with much of the credit due to the chief brewer, Syd Elliott, who built an enviable reputation for 'the stuff he put out'.

The company installed a cask 'pitching' machine, which lined the inside of the barrels with pitch, rolling the surface until it looked like polished glass, effectively preventing any trace of wood flavour in the beer. Another innovation was a wiring machine, the first and only one of its kind in the west. It could wire corks into bottles at the rate of 600 bottles per hour, 'very methodical, neat and with perfectly tied knots'.

Depots were opened in the more important towns of the outback, and during the long life of the brewery many other breweries were taken over.

1912	Lion Brewery, Coolgardie; closed a few years later.
1918	Elliott's Brewery, Kalgoorlie; closed.
1919	Union Brewery, Kalgoorlie; became the company's headquarters.
1924	Boulder City Brewery, Boulder; closed. The equipment was sent to the town of Merredin, where the company established another brewery.

By this time all of the local opposition had been taken over, and there were no other breweries operating in Kalgoorlie or the nearby towns of Boulder and Coolgardie. But soon opposition of another kind began to have a profound impact on the brewery's trade. Tastes in beer were changing: lager was becoming the popular beer, and the company's Big K brand was losing favour. Richmond Tiger Lager, Swan Lager and South Australian Nathan Lager were taking over the bottle trade.

In 1936 a new brewery was built, specially designed and equipped to produce Hannan's Lager Beer. After the launch of the new product, the company began to regain some of its lost trade. The driving force behind the brewery's expansion was James Cummins, a former mayor of Kalgoorlie and hotel-owner. He had large investments in the mining industry, owned a number of farming properties, and took an interest in political affairs.

After Cummins's death in 1936 his daughter, Alice, became managing director, and ruled the business with

In 1936 the Kalgoorlie Brewing & Ice Co. Ltd built a new brewery specially designed for the production of its new product, Hannan's Lager. The popular brand continued in production until the brewery closed in 1983. The brewery had been taken over by the Swan Brewery, Perth, in 1945, and the name had then been changed to the Kalgoorlie Brewing Co. Pty Ltd.

A FAST TRIP

Mr. Arthur Simpson, head brewer for the Union Brewery, Kalgoorlie, WA, recently had the unique experience of motoring from Perth to Kalgoorlie, a distance of about 400 miles.

Mr. Simpson drove a 20-h.p. Hupp car — a very fine model — and the machine behaved splendidly during the trip. The roads in some places were mere bush tracks; in others, sandy desert. The trip took 4 1/2 days to accomplish.

Australian Brewers' Journal, July 1912

equal flair, determined to prevent the Swan Brewery in Perth from taking over her Merredin and Kalgoorlie breweries. She was not to know that that would ultimately happen since, in 1943, she died of a heart attack.

In its attempt to take advantage of the large and growing beer market in Kalgoorlie and surrounding districts, the Swan Brewery Co. Ltd, Perth, had started bottling at their brewery in Kalgoorlie during the late 1890s. But it was almost fifty years later before Swan actually brewed in the area. In fact, Swan was the only brewer in Kalgoorlie when it acquired all the interests in the Kalgoorlie Brewing & Ice Co. Ltd in February 1945. The acquisition included both the Kalgoorlie and Merredin breweries, and the name was changed to the Kalgoorlie Brewing Co. Pty Ltd.

The Merredin Brewery was closed in 1949, and the brewery at Kalgoorlie continued until 1983.

Langford's Brewery
See Elliott's Brewery.

Workers at the Shamrock Brewery, c.1900, line up neatly for the photographer — nobody thought of cleaning up the mess in the foreground. Originally the Federal Brewery, the name was changed to the Shamrock Brewery in 1899 and changed again to the Union Brewery in 1903.
Courtesy Eastern Goldfields Historical Society (Inc.)

Shamrock Brewery Co.
See Union Brewery.

Swan Brewery & Bottling Co. 1898
Hannan Street

The Swan Brewery Co. Ltd of Perth installed a bottling plant at Kalgoorlie in the late 1890s. Bulk beer was transported across from Perth to Kalgoorlie where it was bottled. It was almost fifty years later before Swan was actually brewing in the town. It took over the Kalgoorlie Brewing & Ice Co. Ltd in 1945, and continued brewing there for the next thirty-eight years.

Union Brewery Co. 1897–1919
86 Brookman Street

During the life of the brewery it was known by four different names: the Federal Brewery, the Shamrock Brewery Co., the Union Brewery Co., and the Kalgoorlie Brewing & Ice Co. Ltd.

The Federal Brewery was built by Tom Elliott and taken over on completion in 1897 by Frank Whitfield. The difficulties of producing a palatable beer, particularly in the hot dry regions of the eastern goldfields, proved far greater than Whitfield had anticipated, and after many anxious months both his health and the brewery failed.

A. H. Newsham was involved for a brief period, and then the business changed hands to John and Adam Wilkie. The Wilkie brothers were railway contractors; their attempt at brewing also failed.

On 26 June 1899 the mortgagee sold the brewery to three young and enthusiastic partners: A. H. Paton, H. M. Mair and F. Scott. They changed the name to the Shamrock Brewery, and employed John Cocks as their brewer. He was soon replaced by Phil Hardwick. The task ahead was not easy, since the brewery's reputation had suffered badly through the terrible quality of the beer put out by the previous brewers.

The Shamrock Brewery, as such, lasted just over four years, but in that short period the three partners built up quite a reasonable business. An advertisement to promote their new beer had a touch of poetry and rhyme:

> Then here's to a drink that's always the same
> Glistening and sparkling and bounding to fame
> Fearless of rivals and chemical skill
> Secure in its merits, unvarnished with frill
> Brewed by experience, guided by brains
> Perfection and progress go with its name
> Drink to its triumph, swear to it here
> The drink of the goldfields, Shamrock Beer.

Perhaps the beer was not 'always the same, glistening and sparkling', since ownership changed, first with the retirement of Mair in 1901, and then by late 1903 to Frank Scott as the sole proprietor. He changed the name to the Union Brewery. A year later Scott was joined by Pat (Paddy) Whelan, who gave the business the expertise and direction it needed.

Paddy Whelan had been a director and substantial shareholder in Hannan's Brewery. He was one of the early settlers at the goldfields, and had a long association with the hotel and brewing trade. He was also something of an extrovert and amateur actor, and when he joined Scott he had a lot of new ideas.

Unfortunately, within a few months of forming the partnership, Frank Scott died. Paddy took over, and with his experience and enormous energy the brewery soon grew to be the busiest at the goldfields. The proprietors were now Mrs Mary Scott, Paddy Whelan and Arthur George Simpson, who was also the head brewer (Arthur was the son of George Simpson, owner of the Waverley Brewery in Broken Hill). Arthur's skill and experience ensured the continuing success of the Union Brewery. Buildings were extended, new equipment put in place, and the brewery was an impressive landmark in the centre of town, with its high tower visible for miles.

In 1906 Whelan purchased a large bottling plant, formerly the Federation Bottling Co. The factory was in McDonald Street, and employed thirty men. The bottle-washing machine was loaded with bottles, each containing a small quantity of lead shot, and the carriage was then agitated with a force of water squirting into the bottles. The lead certainly cleaned the bottles, but nobody knew or bothered about any possible contamination.

Harwood's Brewery in Perth was acquired in 1913, and upgraded, giving the Union Brewery an operating base in the much larger Perth market. In 1915 the Union Brewery sponsored the first locally-built aeroplane to fly in Western Australia. It was appropriately named 'Kalgoorlie', and had 'Union Beer' painted under the lower wing.

The Kalgoorlie Brewing & Ice Co. Ltd found the competition from the Union Brewery more than just a nuisance, so they bought out the Union in 1919 and made it their headquarters.

Federal Brewery
F. J. Whitfield	1897–98
A. H. Newsham	1898
J. & A. Wilkie	1898–99

Shamrock Brewery Co.
Paton, Mair & Scott	1899–1901
Paton & Scott	1901–3

Union Brewery Co.
F. Scott	1903–4
Whelan & Scott	1904
M. Scott, Whelan & Simpson	1904–19

Kalgoorlie Brewing & Ice Co. Ltd   1919–83

Victoria Brewing & Bottling Co. Ltd

The promoter of the company was Thomas Aitken, formerly of the Victoria Parade Brewery in Melbourne. Details of the prospectus were advertised in the *Coolgardie Miner* of 15 February 1896. It was proposed to 'purchase a suitable piece of land and establish a brewery in the rising township of Kalgoorlie'. However, there was insufficient application for shares, and the venture did not proceed.

West End Brewery   1902
Hannan Street

There was very little chance of the West End Brewery succeeding when W. Herdsmann and E. Bushell began brewing ale in January 1902. Selling it was one of the problems, and after a few months, the brewery closed. The owners said that there was too much competition

The Union Brewery, Kalgoorlie, c. 1909. It was previously the Shamrock Brewery, and before that the Federal. The Union Brewery sponsored the first locally-built aeroplane to fly in Western Australia. It was named Kalgoorlie and had 'Union Beer' painted under the lower wing.

La Trobe Library, State Library of Victoria.

from the other large local breweries that controlled the market with their tied houses.

Paton & Scott of the Shamrock Brewery leased the premises as a bottling store.

Kanowna

Kanowna Brewery Co. Ltd — 1896
A prospectus was issued for the Kanowna Brewery Co. Ltd, which was incorporated in 1896, but apparently the company never started in business.

Standard Brewery — 1905–9
The Standard Brewery closed soon after it opened, and was reopened late in 1906 by M. A. McCabe who had been in the drapery and grocery business. He had also been the mayor of the borough. The brewery closed again in 1909, and the equipment was advertised for sale the following year.

White Feather Castle Brewery Co. Ltd — 1897–1913
Isabella Street

The White Feather Castle Brewery was started in 1897 by R. C. Barnes. It was incorporated in 1901. One newspaper reporter, who commented in July 1898 on the Western Australian outback breweries, had this to say:

> the beer being much liked locally, in fact all the beer turned out seems to me uniformly good. Whether this is due to the fact that the salty nature of the dust makes me unusually thirsty I cannot say.

The company set up a bottling plant at Kalgoorlie in 1903, the manager at that time being R. W. Cock.

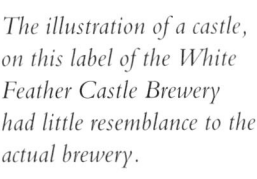

Label for the Kookynie Brewing & Bottling Co. Ltd.

The illustration of a castle, on this label of the White Feather Castle Brewery had little resemblance to the actual brewery.

James Elliott ran the brewery from 1905 to 1906 and the following year it was up for sale.

There were two more owners of the brewery before it closed: the partnership of McCaughey & Jelly in 1909, and James McIntyre in 1910.

James McIntyre wrote to the editor of the *Australian Brewers' Journal*:

> Owing to my being unfortunate enough to start this brewery in a declining township, I am compelled to close down.
>
> *James McIntyre,* January 1, 1914.

The buildings were demolished in 1918.

There was little success for any of the brewers at the hot, dry, outback township of Kanowna. This may have been due to its close proximity to Kalgoorlie, where there were several large well-established breweries with better beer and better prices.

R. C. Barnes	1897–1903
R. W. Cock	1903–5
J. Elliott	1905–6
McCaughey & Jelly	1909–10
J. McIntyre	1910–13

Kookynie

Kookynie Brewing & Bottling Co. Ltd — 1903–12
Tom Elliott formed a syndicate of hotelkeepers, and they purchased the City Brewing & Bottling Co. at Menzies, about 60 km south-west of Kookynie. The proprietor at Menzies was Syd Elliott, and all of his brewing equipment was packed up and shifted to Kookynie. This was in 1903 when the thriving town had a population of about 1000 and seven hotels.

The brewery did quite well for almost ten years, but had to close down in 1912 when the local mining operation was shut down. During its ten years the brewery sold 356,000 gallons of beer, and was one of at least thirty breweries operating in the various towns scattered across the goldfields. Today the old town is a recommended stop on ghost-town tours.

Laverton

Arbitration Brewery
See Laverton Brewery.

Belfast Brewery — 1902–6
Of all the breweries that have operated in Western Australia, none would have been in a location more remote than Laverton. Situated 950 km north-east of Perth, the tiny township is close to the edge of the vast, desolate Great Victoria Desert. Gold had been discovered in the area in 1896, and prospectors quickly

arrived. Within a few years there were two breweries in the town, trying to make good beer in the sweltering heat and dust.

The Belfast Brewery, sometimes called the City Brewery, was started in 1902 by A. Burrowes. The owner of the building was J. O. McArdell, previously the owner of the Mount Malcolm Brewery. After Burrowes left, the brewery was leased, in May 1904, to F. W. Smalpage.

City Brewery
See Belfast Brewery.

Laverton Brewing Co. Ltd   1900–4
The owner of the Laverton Brewery, John Sprunt, put out Star brand bottled beer, and sold Sprunt's Tipple for the outrageous price of £8 per hogshead.

John Cocks and B. E. Haddy leased the brewery from Sprunt in 1904, and they changed the name to the Arbitration Brewery. Cocks had been the brewer at the other brewery in Laverton, the Belfast Brewery.

Lawlers

Crown Brewery   1906
The Crown Brewery was operated by the partnership of West & O'Toole, who may have taken over the Lawlers Brewery, and changed the name.

East Murchison Brewery
See Lawlers Brewery Co.

Lawlers Brewery Co.   1899–1906
Lawlers was once a small goldmining town in the eastern goldfields, about 130 km north of its nearest neighbour, Leonora. Today, Lawlers no longer appears on any maps of Western Australia, since the township was destroyed by open-cut mining.

The brewery was known as the East Murchison Brewery when George Coote started in 1899. Several years later Fred Maley took over, and the business then became Lawlers Brewery Co. Fifteen years earlier Maley had been involved in the Geraldton Brewery.

Leonora

Leonora Brewery   1898
The following article appeared in the *Australian Brewers' Journal* of August 1898:

> W. J. Suiter, late of the Menzies Brewery and owner of the Eighteen Mile Hotel, has completed arrangements for starting a new brewery at Leonora, one of the most advanced and promising points of the gold-producing area.

Nothing further is known of the Leonora Brewery. Perhaps it never existed.

Menzies

Menzies is named after L. R. Menzies, one of the men who first discovered gold in the area in 1894. The following year, when the municipality was proclaimed, there was an estimated population of 10,000, but similar to many other goldmining towns, its prosperity was shortlived. In recent years there have been some discoveries of emeralds in the area.

Burton Brewery Co. Ltd   1888–89
J. F. Hunter started the Burton Brewery during the middle of 1888; he closed it early the following year. Early failure of a brewery was not an uncommon occurrence, and the history of the industry in Australia is studded with breweries, similar to the Burton Brewery at Menzies, which failed as quickly as they started. This happened throughout all the Australian colonies, and, although there would be a complexity of reasons for the failures, the common factor was the inability of the brewers to produce batch after batch of consistently top-quality beer.

City Brewing & Bottling Co.
See Menzies Brewery Co. Ltd.

Menzies Brewery Co. Ltd   1895–1903
Brown Street

During the late 1890s the eastern goldfields breweries, which were scattered over vast dry areas, suffered a general downturn in business. Mines were closing, the population was moving on, and many brewers were out of work. Desperate for income, some would start a small brewery in another town, mostly with disastrous results. In some towns, when a brewer was needed, it was common practice for a notice to be put up in the window of the public bar of a hotel. One such notice, 'Wanted, a First Class Brewer, Apply within', attracted thirteen responses for the only brewery in the town of Menzies.

The Menzies Brewery was started by W. J. Suiter in

The Menzies Brewery, Menzies. Some of the workmen can be seen standing on top of a water tank. Note the five barrels, on top of one another, displaying the range of sizes available. The brewery commenced in 1895 and lasted eight years.
Courtesy Eastern Goldfields Historical Society (Inc.)

October 1895. He had the backing of six local hotel proprietors and, according to an early report, the company was fortunate in selecting a site where a 60-foot water shaft gave a good supply of fresh water. In districts where there was no fresh water, all underground water used had to be condensed because of the high salt content. Breweries on the goldfields had to buy their water at a cost of between 15s and 30s per 100 gallons. The water had to be used not only for the beer but also for washing the utensils, vats and barrels, and for personal use. All this meant an extremely high price for beer, which the Menzies Brewery sold for just under £10 per hogshead.

Shortly after the brewery started at Menzies, there was some alarming news. It was found that the water supply was insufficient for brewing, and that some additional construction materials and brewing equipment had somehow gone astray. On the site of the brewery there was not enough clean water to give the workmen a drink.

Two companies were incorporated in 1896: the Menzies & Niagara Brewing Co. Ltd, which was liquidated the following year, and the Menzies Brewery Co. Ltd, which went into voluntary liquidation in 1899.

The Menzies Brewery was taken over by Sydney George Elliott in March 1901, and the next year he shifted the brewing operations into the town — before this the brewery had been located 5 km away. Elliott used a new name, the City Brewing & Bottling Co., and his bulk ale, bottled beer and stout were said to be 'very superior'.

In 1903 a syndicate of hotelkeepers, headed by Tom Elliott, purchased the equipment, and transported it to the township of Kookynie, 60 km north-east, where it was used for their new Kookynie Brewery.

Merredin

Kalgoorlie Brewing & Ice Co. Ltd 1929–49

In 1892, after gold had been discovered at Coolgardie, a stream of prospectors took the 600 km journey from Perth to the goldfields, and a steady procession of men and wagons moved eastward from one waterhole to the next. One of these waterholes, about halfway from Perth to Coolgardie, was Merredin Peak. The present town lies about 3 km from the Peak.

The Kalgoorlie Brewing & Ice Co. Ltd was well established at Kalgoorlie, and had been brewing there since 1896. In 1924 the company purchased the Boulder City Brewery in Boulder, and four years later the equipment was dismantled and sent to Merredin. At the same time a number of houses were transferred from Boulder to Merredin, and re-erected in the general neighbourhood of the brewery.

The first brew of stout was ready in 1929, and gradually the company, frequently called the Merredin

Brewery, produced a wide range of products, including Merredin Bitter, Oatmeal Stout and King Lager.

The brewery was taken over by the Swan Brewery in 1945, and closed in October 1949.

Merredin Brewery
See Kalgoorlie Brewing & Ice Co. Ltd.

Mt Magnet

Mt Magnet, 350 km east of Geraldton, was discovered in 1854 by surveyor Robert Austin, who named the area Mt Magnet after a prominent nearby hill that contained magnetic rocks. Development, however, did not take place until the 1890s when gold was found in the area. By the end of the twentieth century gold was still being mined at the famous Hill 50 goldmine, and amateur gemstone hunters now frequent the area.

Mount Magnet Brewery & Cordial Co.   1897–1912
The *Australian Brewers' Journal* of 1896 noted that Attwood & Moore intended to start a brewery at Mt Magnet. Perhaps they did, but in 1897 John Perryman was working his Mount Magnet Brewery and cordial factory, which was formed into a company two years later. The capital was subscribed by residents of Mt Morgans and the township of Cue, 80 km due north. F. W. Brown was the manager, and H. Parsons the brewer.

In 1903 Mr Flanagan, previously the brewer at the Cue Brewery, bought the Mount Magnet Brewery for £1000. According to a 1909 issue of *Victoria and Murchison Districts, Illustrated*, the company made

> a light sparkling beer much resembling lager beer, it only needs to be tried to be appreciated ... those who drink Magnet Beer know that they are drinking a perfectly pure, refreshing beverage.

The stout was claimed to be equal to any imported from England, 'more healthy and wholly free from obnoxious gases'.

Mt Malcolm

Great Northern Brewery   1899–1908
According to J. O. McArdell, who started the Mount Malcolm Brewery, very little capital was required, and during construction he even provided space for future expansion. The brewery was near the North Star goldmine, and since the town was relatively isolated, many drays and teams of horses were needed to cart the beer across dry sandy country to areas extending over a radius of 40 km.

The brewery closed after two years, and was reopened in 1903 by Syd Elliott, who changed the name to the Great Northern Brewery, an odd choice since the brewery was located close to the centre of Western Australia.

The brewery suffered some fire damage in 1905, but the partnership of Chambers & Box managed to get the brewery going again.

Mount Malcolm Brewery
See Great Northern Brewery.

Mt Margaret

Mount Margaret Brewing Co. Ltd   1897–98
The Mount Margaret Brewing Co. Ltd was formed as a subsidiary of Hannan's Brewery Co. Ltd of Kalgoorlie in 1897. J. H. Coad held the position of manager, and Joseph Freeman was in charge of the brewing. The town, which was little more than the mine itself, plus a few outbuildings, was located at the northern end of Lake Carey, a dry saltpan with surrounding saltbush and desert.

By the end of 1898 the district was almost deserted, and the company went into liquidation. Some of the plant was taken over by the Mount Malcolm Brewery.

Mt Morgans

The district, 300 km north-east of Kalgoorlie, was commonly called the Morgans.

Mount Morgans Brewing & Malting Co. Ltd   1900–4
The brewery was incorporated in 1900, and went into voluntary liquidation late the following year as the result of the death of the owner, Alex Forrest.

Otto Hansen reopened the brewery in 1902, but after two years he left to take up a position at the Belfast Brewery in Laverton.

For the year 1902 the brewery produced 13,000 gallons of beer, sold in small wooden casks.

TRY MUSTARD SEED

Aromatic Bodies in Reference to Beer Flavour
The fact has been brought before us that mustard seed is likely to prove an aromatic body of service to the brewer, in reference to the palate flavour and body of beer, There is so far as we can see, no objection to be urged to the employment of a seed so entirely innocent in its influences and we see no reason not to try an ounce to the quarter of malt in the mashing operation.

Australian Brewers' Journal, June 1884

Mullewa

Mullewa Brewery   1905–6

The small township of Mullewa lies 100 km east of the coastal town of Geraldton, and is the centre of a wheat-farming district.

After leaving the Castlemaine Brewery at Geraldton, Fred Maley decided to move east to Mullewa and start another brewery there — a poor move since he brewed at Mullewa for less than a year.

Narrogin

Narrogin Brewing Co. Ltd   1903–13
Smith Street

Nicholas Bushalla was born at Mt Lebanon in Syria. He migrated to Melbourne in 1887, and left the following year to seek his fortune in the booming colony of Western Australia. Ten years later he settled in Narrogin, married there, and built a hotel with a mineral-water factory alongside.

Bushalla started his brewery company in August 1903, and he built a solid wood-and-iron structure with a tall cooling tower. His brother-in-law, Sam Dowsett, was the manager. The *Narrogin Advocate* of 21 December 1904 said that Charles E. Lanfear was then the brewer, and went on to describe the brewery operations in detail. At first, Bushalla carted the water, and then he ran it down to the brewery by pipes from a spring on his farm, a kilometre north-west of the town. The water was always thoroughly boiled the day before brewing in order to kill germs and to precipitate minerals.

Lanfear left in May 1905, after only one year of employment. Nick Bushalla knew very little about brewing, and apparently his beer was far from the best — cynical locals called Bushalla's brew 'mallet bark juice' (mallet bark was used for tanning, and the water used in the process turned to a dirty, dark, muddy colour).

W. J. Brennan managed the brewery from 1910, and after the brewery closed in 1913 Bushalla continued to make aerated waters. The brewery building was subsequently destroyed by fire.

Label for the Avon Brewing & Ice Co. Ltd.

Norseman

The statue of the horse, Norseman, can be seen in the main street of the town. The horse allegedly pawed at the ground and unearthed the nugget of gold that started the Norseman gold-rush. The town is the first major town on the western side of the Nullarbor Plain.

Norseman Brewery Co. Ltd   1896–1911
Lake Cowan

A prospectus for the Norseman Brewery Co. Ltd was issued in October 1895, and the brewery was built that year under the direction of an Adelaide syndicate headed by the well-known brewing entrepreneur, Tom Ware of the Torrenside Brewery, Adelaide. The first beer was ready in June 1896, and at the official opening the following October about 100 of the prominent men in Norseman were present.

The brewery was built on the shore of Lake Cowan, 3 km south of the town, and the water was produced by a large condenser. During 1903 the business was restructured as the Norseman Co-operative Brewing Co. Ltd.

An Aboriginal Christmas spree was investigated at the Norseman Police Court on 11 January 1910, and three Aboriginal police trackers were sentenced to three months' imprisonment each for looting the Norseman Brewery and stealing 120 bottles of beer. When the robbery was reported, one of the trackers was put on to follow the trail, but conveniently reported that the ground was too dusty. A week later the police, on searching the native camp, discovered a pile of bottles that the trackers had indeed stolen and taken to their camp for Christmas celebrations.

Norseman Co-operative Brewing Co. Ltd
See Norseman Brewery Co. Ltd.

Northam

Northam was linked with Perth by rail in 1886, and it became the gateway to Kalgoorlie and the eastern goldfields for the steady movement of prospectors, miners and tradesmen. The picturesque Avon River flows through Northam, which was named by Governor Stirling after Northam in Devonshire, England.

Avon Brewing & Ice Co. Ltd   1896–c. 1935
Fitzgerald Street

Gustavus Luber was a Jewish grocer and draper who came to Northam in 1894. Two years later he built the Eclipse Brewery in Fitzgerald Street, and engaged Henry Edmeades, a man with twenty years' brewing experience, as the brewer and manager.

In April 1897, after only five months, Luber sold the brewery to a syndicate. Edmeades stayed on as the brewer, and ended up buying the brewery in July 1901. After a year or two Paul Solomon became a partner, and handled the business side of the brewery.

The Avon Brewing & Ice Co. Ltd was formed in January 1907 for the purpose of acquiring the business and property of the Eclipse Brewery.

Barleycorn Brewery
See Northam Brewery & Refrigerating Co. Ltd.

Eclipse Brewery
See Avon Brewing & Ice Co. Ltd.

Northam Brewery & Refrigerating Co. Ltd 1907–34
York Street

The official opening of the Northam Brewery & Refrigerating Co. Ltd took place on 11 December 1907 at the new brewery that had been built in York Street. The company brewed John Barleycorn ale and stout, and Star Bitter; wagonloads of these were carted long distances, as far as Leonora and Wiluna in the north-west and to Denmark on the southern coast. For most of the time locals used the name Barleycorn Brewery.

The company was wound up in 1917, and reformed in 1922. However, competition from Perth breweries forced the company into liquidation in 1932. Attempts were made to revive the business, but these failed and the plant was sold in a realisation sale in November 1933.

The buyers resumed operations without success, and the brewery was finally closed in 1934.

The last physical evidence of the brewery disappeared when it was demolished in 1938. The closure of the brewery was a severe loss to the economy of Northam as the retrenchments affected about eighty-three people, and many supporting industries suffered loss of trade.

Perth

Aitken Brewing & Bottling Co. Ltd
See Cottesloe Brewery.

Albion Brewery 1837–48
Spring Street

One of the early commercial brewers in Western Australia was James Stokes. He migrated from Bristol, England, in 1834, and three years later, only eight years after the founding of the Swan River colony (Perth), he was brewing and selling beer.

The brewery site had been carefully chosen — on the bank of the Swan River, at the foot of what is now Spring Street, where a sufficient supply of clear, fresh water came from the escarpment above. The long brewery building was constructed of rough limestone that was plastered with cement, and the timber used was Swan River mahogany (otherwise known as jarrah). Although the brewery was sometimes referred to as Stokes' Brewery, James Stokes chose the name Albion Brewery, an ancient name for Britain.

Brewing began in 1837, with a gallon of Stokes's poor-quality beer selling for 9d. Stokes also traded as a general merchant, and advertised building materials, cartage and storage. He was also in partnership with Dubois Aggett as land agents and auctioneers. The population of Perth was then only 590.

The brewery was extended in 1840, and the *Perth Gazette* of that year gave some praise: 'a wholesome beverage produced in the colony is far better than the trashy stuff generally imported'. The locals held a different opinion, preferring British ale when they could get it, and calling Stokes's beer by such disrespectful names as 'tanglefoot' and 'she-oak', to be consumed only as a last resort.

In the hot summer months Stokes had great difficulty producing anything at all palatable. The brew was heavy, black and bitter, and had a 'colonial twang' that could cause a drinker to experience an involuntary shudder. James Stokes also had other problems. He lost heavily in his attempts to establish a distillery because of the government's failure to make adequate compensation for his expenses when an Act was passed rendering the distillation of spirits illegal. To make matters worse, his trading partner, Aggett, blew off an arm while attempting suicide.

To boost business, Stokes imported large quantities of spirits, even bottled ale and stout. He also imported the raw materials for his own beer production, since there was nothing available locally in those early years.

On 3 November 1848, with some fanfare, Stokes opened his new Stanley Brewery and began brewing 'a nutritious body ale, superior to any imported variety'. It sold for £4 a hogshead, in bulk. He also supplied a light ale 'suitable for invalids and nursing mothers', for about the same price.

The Stanley Brewery continued in business for sixty years and continued after that as the Emu Brewery for another twenty years. It was then taken over by the Swan Brewery Co. Ltd. James Stokes would have been proud if he had known the destiny of his Albion Brewery when he was brewing his 'colonial twang' in 1837.

See also Stanley Brewery Co. Ltd.

Barron, Sergeant Edward 1838–39
During 1838 and 1839 Sergeant Barron was advertising his brewery at Wattle Grove. Before that he had worked at the Wheat Sheaf Tavern.

Bond Brewing W.A. Ltd
See Swan Brewery Co. Ltd.

Bond Corporation Holdings Ltd
See Swan Brewery Co. Ltd.

Bull, Lieutenant (R.N.) 1830–31
Toward the end of 1830 the population of the Swan River colony was only a sprinkling of struggling pioneers. Between Perth and Fremantle there were a few wayside inns, and unless the owners made their own beer there would be long periods of waiting until the next ship arrived with a further supply — Fremantle was the port, and Perth was 20 km upstream.

The earliest reference to a brewery in Western Australia is to that of Lieutenant Bull, who took up a land grant near Canning Ford in 1830, and began making beer and selling it for 3s a gallon. Bull Creek, which joins the Canning River, was named after him.

Label for the Northern Brewery & Refrigerating Co. Ltd.

The Swan Brewery Co. Ltd took control of the Emu Brewery in the summer of 1928. This new brewery was built and began operating in March 1938. Although the brewery was then a division of the Swan Brewery, the Emu Brewery continued to use the Emu name and logo on its packaging until 1980.

Commonwealth Brewing Co.   1901–2
Ocean Street, Cottesloe.

Cottesloe Brewery   1897–1901
Main Road, Cottesloe Beach

The brewery first went under the name of Aitken Brewing & Bottling Co. Ltd, and the owner was Thomas Aitken, possibly a relative of Thomas Aitken (a pioneer of the brewing industry in Melbourne who had died in 1884).

The Cottesloe Brewery started up in 1897, went into liquidation the following year, and the property was then sold by auction, and closed.

In September 1899 it was reopened by the partnership of Langford & Nilsen, still as the Cottesloe Brewery.

Elliott's Brewery   1922–29
Riversdale Road, Belmont Park

Sydney George Elliott had been involved in breweries all his adult life, either as a brewer, a partner or as sole owner. He had been well known as a competent and reliable brewer when he was in charge of brewing at the Kalgoorlie Brewing & Ice Co. Ltd at the turn of the century.

Emu Brewery Ltd   1909–80
Mounts Bay Road

The Emu Brewery was formerly the Stanley Brewery, and before that, the Albion Brewery, which had been started by James Stokes in 1837.

During 1905 the business of the Stanley Brewery

was divided so that the Stanley Brewing Co. Ltd operated all the company's hotels and freehold properties and the Stanley Co-operative Brewing Co. Ltd handled the brewing side of the business. The two names became confusing, and led to a further change in 1908 to the Emu Co-operative Brewery Co. Ltd. This was simplified to the Emu Brewery Ltd in June 1909.

The brewer, Ernest Terry, had been trained by his brother-in-law, Colonel John Ballenger at the Carlton Brewery in Melbourne, and it was due to Terry's efforts that the company's sales and profits showed remarkable improvement, even though the output of the competitor, the Swan Brewery, was four times that of the Emu. There was bitter rivalry between the two breweries.

During October 1923 Emu launched 'Emu Bitter' beer, ordering two million bottle labels in three colours, priced at 1s 8d per 1000. Although the new brew was popular, company sales slumped to 10 per cent of the Western Australian market by 1927; Swan held 65 per cent.

In January 1928 the Swan Brewery, took control of the Emu Brewery and Colonel Ballenger, ex-CUB, Melbourne, was appointed head brewer. He created his own version of Emu Bitter Ale, which held its popularity for the life of the brewery. Swan rebuilt the Emu Brewery as the most modern brewery in the west. It was completed in March 1938, and during the period of construction beer was supplied by the parent Swan Brewery Co.

The Emu Brewery worked independently of the Swan, and continued to use the Emu name and logo until brewing ceased in 1980.

Emu Co-operative Brewery Co. Ltd
See Emu Brewery Ltd.

Guildford Brewery   1835–68
James Street, Guildford

In 1835 William Devenish advertised that, because of the pureness of the water in the well behind his East Guildford Hotel, he was producing 'the best beer in the colony'. He had arrived with his family five years earlier, and he and his wife, an excellent cook, turned their humble home into Devenish's Hotel.

In 1841 the hotel was extended to cater for dinners such as those held by the Agricultural Society. Public auctions were held at the inn, which served as a meeting place for the Guildford Town Trust. It was also a popular place for newlyweds to honeymoon. Beer production at the Devenish was not large, merely sufficient to satisfy local customers, travellers and nearby farmers.

The economy of the 1830s was generally unfavourable for business activity. Shortages, and the first trough of depression, were felt in the colony in 1832. The cost of essential food items soared, and some settlers literally faced starvation. Nevertheless, the consumption of beer and spirits saw very little decline, and the producers and sellers of liquor in any form still made a very comfortable living.

William Devenish died in 1854, and his only surviving son, Henry, left his bakery business in Perth and returned to Guildford to take over the running of the family business. He advertised in the *Perth Inquirer* of 26 October 1859:

> Guildford Brewery. Henry T. Devenish begs most respectfully to acquaint the public [that] he has on sale large quantities of excellent beer. To the trade, £3 3 shillings per hogshead; in smaller quantities, 1 shilling 3 pence per gallon; bottled beer, 5 shillings per dozen.

The Devenish family moved to Terrace Road, Guildford, in 1868, where Henry set up a bakery and a store. During that year the inn in James Street was advertised under the name of the Liverpool Arms, licensed to P. D. Connolly, and apparently brewing had been discontinued.

Guildford Brewing Co. Ltd   1897–98
This was another one of the hundreds of breweries throughout Australia that lasted in business for very brief periods, some of them for only a month or two.

John Cocks had been the brewer and manager of the Coolgardie Brewing & Ice Co. Ltd for the first two years of its operation. In 1897 he was charged with attempting to set fire to his house. When he was acquitted he moved to Perth, where he organised a syndicate, formed the Guildford Brewing Co. Ltd, built a brewery, and went broke the following year.

Harwood's Brewery Ltd   1907–10
59 Palmerston Street

David Harwood had been a joint lessee of the Stanley Brewery in Perth as early as 1850. Much later, in the early 1880s, he had been a partner in the Victoria Brewery in Durlacher Street in Geraldton, and also a joint proprietor of the Lion Brewery in Perth until 1888.

No longer a young man, Harwood started his brewery in 1907, and employed his brother, Samuel, as the engineer. In the summer of 1910 Sam fell into a vat of boiling wort while checking some overhead piping; he died two weeks later.

The Swallow Brewery Co. Ltd had been taken over by Harwood in 1908, but after Sam's death both Harwood's Brewery and the Swallow Brewery were closed. The Union Brewery of Kalgoorlie purchased Harwood's Brewery premises in January 1913, installed new equipment, and started in business in Perth as the Union Brewery.

Hawkeswood, Alfred   c. 1895–96
Randell Street

Hay Street Brewery   1870–71
Hay Street

William Meloy was an experienced brewer, and when he started his own Hay Street Brewery in 1870 he let

Label for the Emu Brewery Ltd.

the public know in no uncertain terms. He advertised 'Meloy's Unrivalled Ale, Porter. Ginger Wine and Ginger Beer', and reminded readers of his 'uninterrupted connection of nearly 32 years with the Stanley [Stokes] Brewery'. Meloy had actually been the brewer at Western Australia's first commercial brewery, the Albion, which had started in 1837.

Meloy sold his beer and porter, both at £4 per hogshead, but he was better at brewing than conducting a business, and the brewery closed after a year or so.

Horonda Brewing Co. 1905–27
498 Hay Street, Subiaco

The owner of the Horonda Brewery was Arthur Gardner. After two years he was trading as Gardner & Chapman, and the company specialised in brewed soft drinks. Although the company name included the word brewing, it may not have produced any alcoholic beverages.

Lion Brewery 1876–91

When David Harwood sold his interest in the Stanley Brewery, he started a brewery of his own in 1876 and called it the Lion Brewery. With John Smith as a partner, in 1882 William Meloy took over from Smith, and the Lion Brewery then traded as Harwood & Meloy. They put in new equipment, and all the old vats, boilers and other leftover utensils were sent up to Geraldton where they had started the Victoria Brewery.

The Lion Brewery was taken over by the Swan Brewery in May 1888, and David Harwood stayed on as the brewer.

National Brewing Holdings Ltd
See Swan Brewery Co. Ltd.

Perth Brewery Co. Ltd 1898–1907
Brown Street, East Perth

The proprietor was W. E. Cross.

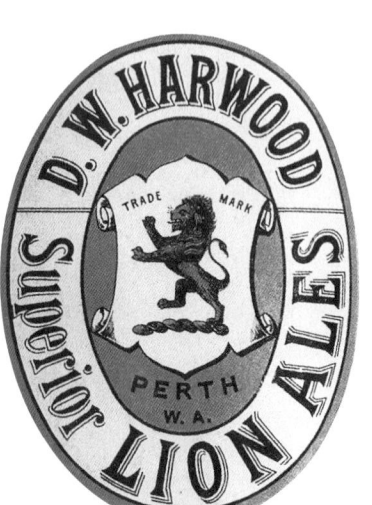

As an enticement to customers who preferred English beverages to colonial, the Horonda Brewing Co., Perth, identified the label of their product as English Ale by the British flag flying above.

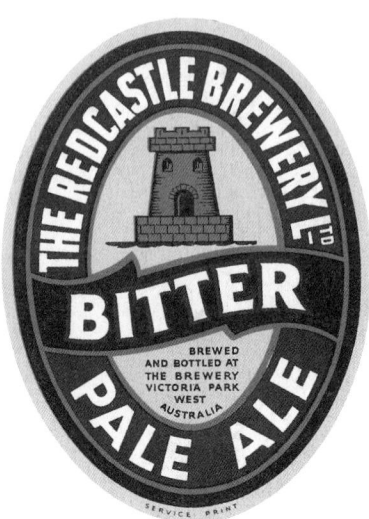

Redcastle Brewery Co. Ltd 1912–53
Ascot Road, Victoria Park

The Redcastle Brewery opened in January 1912, and the owners, Syd Elliott and George Hughes, sold their beer for 8d a bottle.

After two years Don Curtis, owner of the Perth Glass Works, acquired a one-third share, and by 1918 he was the sole owner. The business was incorporated in July 1924.

A 'Pale Ale' plant, probably for lager beer production, was installed in 1927, together with new refrigeration and bottling equipment. Syd Elliott was then the manager. The company had no 'tied houses' and did not advertise, but it enjoyed a sound and profitable business because of the popularity of Redcastle Ale and Stout.

The Swan Brewery took over the Redcastle Brewery in 1951, changed the name to the Stirling Brewery Ltd, and continued to brew under the Stirling name until the brewery was shut down in 1953.

Rose & Crown Hotel & Brewery c. 1841
Swan Street, Guildford

The historic Rose & Crown Hotel was built with adobe bricks, and was opened by Thomas Jecks in July 1841. There was a cellar below the building, and also a well that provided ample water for brewing and hotel use.

Brewing was apparently a lesser consideration, and its prime purpose was as a wayside inn for travellers and as a social meeting place for drinkers. Today, the property remains the oldest hotel in Western Australia, having been meticulously restored from the details shown in early photographs.

Stanley Brewing Co. Ltd 1848–1908

The Stanley Brewery was originally the Albion Brewery, which was started by James Stokes in 1837. He changed the name to the Stanley Brewery in 1848. Stokes continued to run the business, leasing the property from the wealthy landowner, Edward Hamersley (the now-famous Hamersley Range was named after him by F. T. Gregory, the first European to explore the area in 1861; Hamersley was a generous supporter of the explorations).

Stokes had a good brewer, William Meloy, while Hamersley looked after the management of the business.

In 1850 the Stanley Brewery was leased to the partnership of Harwood & Jones. During that year the company advertised its Harvest Ale and Brown Stout as being

> brewed for the purpose of giving increased vigour and strength to the sinews of the working men and also to their employers. In good sound quarter casks at one shilling and six pence per gallon.

Another advertisement in the *Enquirer* in 1853 advised 'they had brewed specially for the ploughing season some "Stunning and Never-Give-Up" ale and porter'.

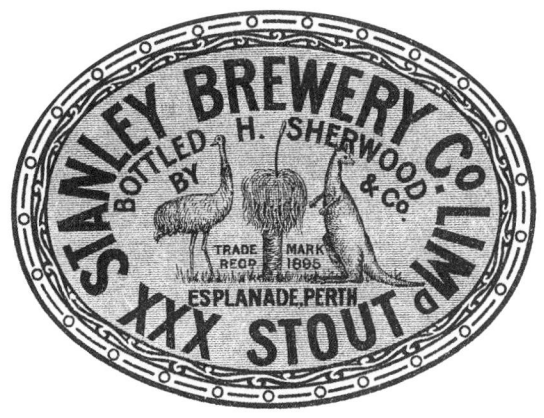

When James Stokes died in 1861, his friend, the highly-respected merchant and storekeeper, Henry Saw, renewed the lease and ran the business, looking after the interests of Stokes's daughter, Julia; he received one-eighth of the brewery profits. Unfortunately Saw died in 1870, and the brewery was advertised to let.

The handsome seafarer, Captain John Ferguson, leased the brewery in 1872, and the following year the jovial German migrant, William Mumme, became a partner. Ferguson was away most of the time, and as an experienced brewer William Mumme ran the business. He became dissatisfied with the quality of his beer, complaining that organic matter, the curse of the brewer, had crept into the Stanley water supply.

It so happened that the Swan Brewery was available for lease at that time, and Ferguson & Mumme shifted out of the Stanley Brewery premises, and opened for business at the Swan Brewery on 1 January 1875. The vacated Stanley Brewery was back in the hands of one of the early lessees, David Harwood, who sold the brewery to Jones & Hall in 1882.

In November 1887 the Stanley Brewery Co. Ltd was formed. There were eight local directors, including Henry Sherwood and a former owner, John Jones, who stayed on as the brewer. The name was changed in January 1891 to the Stanley Brewing Co. Ltd, the word 'Brewery' being changed to 'Brewing'. The business was showing steady profits, in sharp contrast to the plight of the breweries in the eastern states, where the devastating depression was forcing many to close. In the west the great Coolgardie–Kalgoorlie goldrush had begun, bringing prosperity to the state, and within ten years the population of Western Australia had increased from 45,000 to 180,000.

A new Stanley Brewery was built early in 1893. During construction, part of the building collapsed, killing one of the workmen, who was buried under the rubble.

In November 1905 the company sold the brewing side of the business to the Stanley Co-operative Brewing Co. Ltd, leaving the Stanley Brewing Co. Ltd to carry on as the owner and operator of the company's hotels and other freehold properties. The two names were confusing, and led to the change of name in May 1908 to the Emu Co-operative Brewery Co. Ltd, being simplified in June 1909 to the Emu Brewery Ltd.

For a summary, see Swan Brewery Co. Ltd.

See also Emu Brewery.

Stanley Co-operative Brewery Co. Ltd
See Stanley Brewing Co. Ltd.

Stirling Brewery Ltd
See Redcastle Brewery Co. Ltd.

Stokes' Brewery
See Albion Brewery.

Subiaco Brewery   1886–98
Broome Road

Captain John Ferguson and William Mumme had been two very prominent men in the brewing industry since the days when they had been partners in the Stanley Brewery and, after that, the Swan Brewery.

Ferguson had severed his connection with the Swan in 1886, and started the Subiaco Brewery as sole proprietor. His old associate, William Mumme, joined the firm around 1895, and was on his own until he was declared bankrupt a few years later, a very sad end for the man who had done so much for the industry over twenty-five years.

Swallow Brewery Co. Ltd   1906–10
Cnr Brown & Jewell Streets, East Perth

Two years after the Swallow Brewery started, it was taken over by Harwood's Brewery Ltd. The date was August 1908, and the brewery kept going for another two years until the death of David Harwood's brother, Samuel.

Swan Brewery Co. Ltd   1857–
Canningvale

Although the Swan Brewery commenced in 1857, the acquisition of the Emu Brewery in 1928 gave the company a lineage that dated back to 1837 when it had been founded by James Stokes as the Albion Brewery. It changed to the Stanley Brewery in 1848, and to the Emu Brewery in 1909.

When Frank Sherwood and his family arrived from England in 1842, they settled near Bunbury, where, as sponsored migrants, Sherwood had agreed to survey land in the area. A year later they moved to Fremantle and then to Perth in 1844. Sherwood took on various work, and opened a school of classics and languages that he conducted at the family home. It was a tragic time for Frank Sherwood in 1855 when his wife was killed in a carriage accident, leaving him with the daunting task of bringing up six young children.

By mid-1857 Sherwood had closed his school, and had started building his Swan Brewery. The site was in the vicinity of a hillside spring that ran down to the Swan River. When Captain Stirling was making his first probing trip up the river, the area was a favourite camping spot for local Aboriginal people.

With his brewery well under way, Sherwood began to advertise on the front page of the local newspaper:

> Superior Pale Ale, £1 10 shillings per hogshead exclusive of cask, also 2 shillings per gallon and in bottles for 3 shillings per gallon including the bottles which will be allowed for when returned.

Within a year Sherwood was advertising the Swan Brewery as the only malt brewery in the colony, and with disregard to the prices of beer elsewhere he was offering a hogshead of Swan Pale Ale for 10s more than the Stanley Ale of his competitor, James Stokes of the Stanley Brewery. Neither Sherwood nor Stokes could know that, over the next hundred years, more than ninety breweries would come and go in Western Australia, and the only ones to survive would be their breweries, the Swan and the Stanley, and ultimately only one, the Swan.

Sherwood's sons travelled to country districts selling Swan beer and farm produce, at the same time purchasing carefully selected barley to bring back to the brewery for malting. They had little interest in the brewing business, and when their father died in 1874 the brewery was leased.

Two years earlier John Ferguson and William Mumme had leased the other brewery, the Stanley, but the experienced German brewer Mumme was never satisfied with the quality of his beer, blaming this on impurities in the water supply. When the Swan Brewery came on the market, they took up the lease, left the Stanley, and on 1 January 1875 they were open for business as the Swan Brewery. Four years later the partners purchased land at the foot of Mt Eliza (now King's Park), and also a larger tract of land in Mounts Bay Road, and built a malthouse, icehouse and a new brewery on the site.

Mumme's beer, made this time from clear, pure water, became a favourite in the town and country, but after twelve years of successful brewing the partners decided to separate in 1886. John Ferguson then started his own Subiaco Brewery.

On 7 September 1887 the Swan Brewery Co. Ltd was floated on the Melbourne stock exchange. The new company now owned the brewery and several cottages, all on 5 acres of land facing the Swan River. It also owned hotels and other freeholds, and had absolute rights to supply its ale to twenty-four hotels. Under the dynamic leadership of the general manager, Thomas Hardwick, and the wise counsel of the Melbourne-based chairman, Montague Cohen, the Swan Brewery became the largest and most profitable brewery in the west.

There was very little competition from outside the state, and what there was came mainly from England and Germany. The imported beer sold for 1s to 1s 3d a bottle, compared with 7d for Swan.

The brewery was extended, and improvements were carried out in 1890. In the following year William Mumme resigned as the head brewer, and took on the position of manager at the rival Stanley Brewery. In 1895 he joined his old partner, John Ferguson, at the Subiaco Brewery. He was the sole owner for a year, but was declared bankrupt in 1896, a sad end to the brewing career of one of Perth's most colourful personalities; William Mumme had also been the founder of the yachting fraternity that was to become the Royal Perth Yacht Club.

Swan Brewery workers enjoyed their regular supervised daily intake of beer — two glasses before starting work at 7.30 a.m., two at the ten o'clock smoko, two at lunch, two at about three o'clock and another two before leaving the brewery. Night-shift workers drank the same amount. Bosses thought that such a system encouraged punctuality. Some workers managed to confuse whoever was looking after the keg to sneak an extra glass or two.

During 1903 the company installed Australia's first automatic bottle-wiring machine which assembled wire-tie corks in place. Imported from Ireland, the machine had a capacity to assemble 800 bottles per hour.

Much of the company's expansion was due to acquisitions. The Lion Brewery was taken over on 25 May 1888, the Castlemaine Brewery, Fremantle, in 1927, and the Emu in 1928. The Kalgoorlie Brewing & Ice Co. Ltd was acquired in February 1945, giving Swan a strategic base to the east. By the end of 1932 Swan owned fifty-two hotels; and by the late 1960s the company owned more than 120 hotels spread throughout the state.

Following the acquisition of the Redcastle Brewery in 1951, Swan changed the name of that brewery to the Stirling Brewery Ltd, and began marketing Stirling Lager, while retaining Redcastle Stout.

From almost sixty breweries that had been operating half a century earlier, only the Swan and its three subsidiary breweries now remained in business in Western Australia — the Stirling, Emu and Kalgoorlie.

One of the few unprofitable Swan ventures was the

FROTH

'This is beautiful beer,' said the brewer,

As the cask he did carefully skewer

With a gimlet and held out a ewer

To catch the malt liquid so pu-er;

But, alas for his boast, it was truer

Acid water than beer to be su-er,

And humble and sad was that brewer,

As he emptied the cask in the sewer.

Australian Brewers' Journal, May 1889

Swan Brewery label, 1873, used when the brewery was taken over by the partnership of Ferguson & Mumme.

From the 1860s the Black Swan has been a trademark of the Swan Brewery, and it continues to be used by the company for its advertising and packaging.

Swan Brewery, Perth	1857–87
Frank Sherwood	1857–74
Ferguson & Mumme	1875–86
William Mumme	1886–87
Swan Brewery Co. Ltd	1887–1966
Emu Brewery taken over	1928
Swan Brewery closed	1966
All production then at the Emu Brewery	1966–78
Built at Canningvale	1978
Emu Brewery closed	1980
Bond Corporation Holdings Ltd	1982–87
Bond Brewing, W.A. Ltd	1987–90
National Brewing Holdings Ltd (still called the Swan Brewery)	1990–

ACQUISITIONS AND EXPANSION:

Lion Brewery, Perth	
Harwood & Smith	1876–82
Harwood & Meloy	1882–88
Taken over by Swan Brewery	1888–91
Castlemaine Brewing Co., Fremantle	
Gracie & Sleigh (Canning Road)	1897–98
Sleigh & Co.	1898–1902
Gracie & Walkley (Riverside Road)	1902–27
Taken over by Swan Brewery	1927–29
Albion Brewery, Perth	
James Stokes	1837–48
Stanley Brewery (name change only)	
James Stokes (lessee)	1848–50
Harwood & Jones	1850–61
Henry Saw	1861–70
John Ferguson (lessee)	1872–73
Ferguson & Mumme (lessees) (shifted from the Stanley Brewery to the Swan Brewery in 1875)	1873–75
David Harwood	1875–82
Jones & Hall	1882–87
Stanley Brewery Co. Ltd	1887–91
Stanley Brewing Co. Ltd	1891–1905
Stanley Co-operative Brewing Co. Ltd	1905–8
Emu Co-operative Brewery Co. Ltd	1908–9
Emu Brewery Ltd	1909–28
Taken over by Swan Brewery	1928–80
Kalgoorlie Brewing & Ice Co. Ltd, Kalgoorlie	1896–1945
Acquisitions:	
Lion Brewery (Coolgardie)	1912–17
Elliott's Brewery (Kalgoorlie)	1909–18
Union Brewery (Kalgoorlie)	1897–1919
Boulder City Brewery (Boulder)	1898–1924
Taken over by Swan Brewery	1945–83
Kalgoorlie Brewing & Ice Co. Ltd, Merredin	
Branch Brewery	1929–45
Taken over by Swan Brewery	1945–49
Redcastle Brewery, Perth	
Elliott & Hughes	1912–14
Elliott, Hughes & Curtis	1914–18
Don Curtis	1918–24
Redcastle Brewery Co. Ltd	1924–51
Taken over by Swan Brewery; name changed to Stirling Brewery Ltd	
Stirling Brewery Ltd	1951–53
Stuart Brewery Ltd, Darwin	
Started by Swan Brewery	1958–73
Joint venture with CUB Ltd then wholly owned by CUB Ltd	1973–82

building of the Stuart Brewery Ltd in Darwin in 1958. Later, this brewery was acquired by Carlton & United Breweries, Melbourne.

In August 1966 brewing ceased at the Swan Brewery premises in Perth, and all brewing operations were then based at the Emu Brewery in Spring Street, the Swan Brewery premises being used for fermentation and storage.

About five years earlier there had been local criticism of the old brewery being an eyesore and a hazard to passing traffic. The brewery may have looked untidy during the day, but at night it presented a unique and spectacular sight. In 1962, with the Commonwealth Games being held in Perth, the brewery was illuminated at night with 1792 light globes placed around the contours of the buildings to form a 200-metre-long static facsimile of a sailing ship, representing the arrival of the Swan River colonists. In June 1981 the old brewery buildings were sold, and in September 1985 the property was purchased by the state government.

On 18 March 1978 the first bottles of beer rolled off the line at Swan's newly completed brewery and packaging plant at the Perth suburb of Canningvale. The Emu Brewery continued to operate until 1980. On 1 April 1982 the Swan Brewery became a subsidiary of Bond Corporation Holdings Ltd, changing to Bond Brewing W.A. Ltd in June 1987. In October 1990 the New Zealand-based Lion Nathan group acquired the interests of all the Bond breweries: Swan in Perth, the Castlemaine Brewery in Brisbane, and Toohey's in Sydney, through the new company, National Brewing Holdings Limited.

Union Brewery 1913–24
59 Palmerston Street

There was also a Union Brewery in Kalgoorlie, the proprietors being M. Scott, P. Whelan and A. G. Simpson. In January 1913 they bought Harwood's Brewery premises in Perth, put in new equipment, and started another Union Brewery. The Perth operation was managed by J. C. Innes.

In 1922 the company introduced a non-alcoholic drink called Spot Light Lager, similar in colour to lager beer and with a slightly bitter taste.

W.A. Burton Brewery Co. Ltd 1899
Barrack Street

West Australian Brewery Co. Ltd 1896–1905
Barndon Hill

The company built a new brewery, and the first brew was sampled in June 1896. James Liddington was the manager for a while, followed by G. H. Palmer, and then Ernest Bushell from 1900.

Western Australian Brewery c. 1840–41

The Perth Hotel, founded in 1830, survived for many years under a number of owners and licensees, and became, in turn, an inn, a store, and a brewery. Henry Hall was the owner of the Perth Hotel in 1837, and he added a brewery some years later. In 1841 he advertised: 'To Let or For Sale, the Western Australian Brewery and unexpired licence, formerly known as the Perth Hotel ... apply Henry Hastings Hall'.

Woodville Brewing & Bottling Co. Ltd 1898–1900
Wanneroo Road

William Cooper was the owner and operator of the brewery, which was incorporated in January 1898. By 1901 it had been struck off the register.

Port Hedland

Pioneer pastoralists had first settled in the Port Hedland region in the 1860s, and when pearls were found off the coast in the 1870s the port became the base for a host of luggers and other pearling vessels. In Port Hedland's early days the small village frequently ran out of beer because of the long wait for the arrival of ships. There was no regular land transport at that time.

Today Port Hedland is the largest port, by tonnage, in Australia, shipping enormous quantities of iron ore mined from the Pilbara, a region in Western Australia that holds the largest iron-ore deposits in the world.

North West Brewing, Refrigerating & Ice Co. Ltd 1907

In 1906 a group of residents decided to build a brewery in the town, a decision that was later regretted. In October that year a meeting of shareholders was called, and directors were provisionally appointed. By February the following year the brewing equipment was nearly ready, and the icemaking plant installed.

A meeting at the Esplanade Hotel in June 1907 resolved to increase the capital, but the following month action was taken to wind up the company. It was said that the promoter, F. H. West, previously the brewer at the Swallow Brewery in Perth, still had confidence in the venture. One of the reasons for the failure was that no one had made certain that there was an adequate supply of suitable water.

Ravensthorpe

Phillips River Brewing & Aerated Water Co. Ltd 1907–10

The Esperance Brewery at Esperance had operated from 1897 to 1906, and it was decided at that time to pack up all the equipment and relocate to Ravensthorpe, 200 km west, as there was greater sales potential at Ravensthorpe. The town was the centre of a district renowned for its rich tin and other mineral deposits, and had a much larger population. In spite of these better prospects the brewery closed on 30 June 1910.

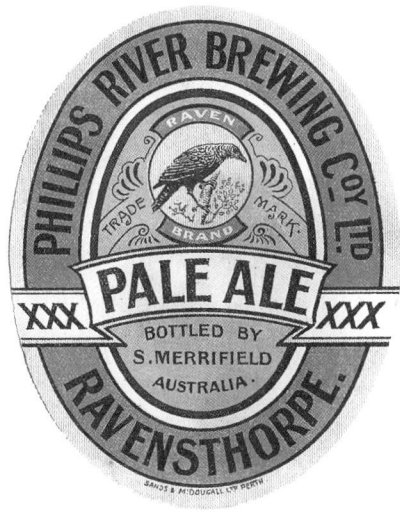

Sandstone

Black Range Brewery 1907–11

Gold was discovered in the region in 1902, and when the brewery started five years later the township of Sandstone boasted four hotels, many cafes, four butchers, and several large stores.

The Black Range Brewery was owned by Percy Wacher, who worked in the blistering heat until January 1911.

Wagin

Beigel's Brewery Co. Ltd 1909–16

Herman Beigel owned a brewery of the same name at Bunbury on the south-west coast, and started another at Wagin, 180 km east of Bunbury, in 1909. His aerated-water and cordial business was sold in 1914, and two years later the breweries at Bunbury and Wagin closed.

Wiluna

Lake Way Brewery

See Phoenix Brewery.

Phoenix Brewery 1901–4

Very shortly after the Lake Way Brewery started, the name was changed to the Phoenix Brewery. Located in harsh arid country, lack of sufficient clean, salt-free water was probably the reason the brewery closed.

Yalgoo

Yalgoo Brewery 1898

The tiny township of Yalgoo, 216 km east of Geraldton, was a thriving goldfield in the late 1890s. Traces of gold and gemstones are still found in the area.

The owner of the Yalgoo Brewery was Fred Richardson.

York

York Brewery 1882–1901

From as early as 1830 York had been established as a small farming community, and it had its own post office by 1840.

Half a century later York became an important commercial centre for the flow of prospectors as they passed through the town to the eastern goldfields — pausing in the town for a glass or two of beer from the York Brewery.

Today York is Western Australia's most historic inland town.

Tasmania

In 1803 Governor Philip Gidley King selected a small party to leave Sydney, with instructions to form a settlement at the Derwent River area of Van Diemen's Land. As well as convicts and troops, the small group included some free settlers who had been attracted by offers of land grants. In September 1803 the party of forty-nine people, led by Lieutenant John Bowen, settled at Risdon Cove on the eastern bank of the Derwent River, 8 km upstream from the present site of the city of Hobart.

An Island Colony

Meanwhile, a larger settlement party headed by Captain David Collins (later Lieutenant-Governor of Van Diemen's Land) had left Port Phillip Bay, having considered that area near the entrance (now known as Sorrento) as being unsatisfactory for settlement. Collins continued south, across Bass Strait, to the Derwent River region of Van Diemen's Land, unaware of Bowen's group, and within five days of his arrival in February 1804 Collins had selected a site at Sullivan's Cove on the western bank of the Derwent River (now the port of Hobart).

Three months later John Bowen's small group joined Captain Collins's larger settlement, which was then named Hobart Town. The name remained in official use until 1881, when it was shortened to Hobart. Hobart is Australia's second-oldest city, founded in 1804, sixteen years after Sydney, and named in honour of Lord Hobart, British Secretary of State for the Colonies. Van Diemen's Land functioned as part of New South Wales until 1825, when it was proclaimed a separate colony. The colony itself became known as Tasmania after 1855.

The Governor of New South Wales, Lachlan Macquarie, visited the settlement in 1811, and drew up a plan for the township. The suburb of Battery Point was Hobart's first residential area, and the waterfront, particularly Salamanca Place, recalls the days when Hobart was a great whaling port, a shipbuilding town, and a shelter for sailing vessels from all corners of the world.

In the years following settlement Tasmania had its convicts, bushrangers, mining booms, world-famous apples, tigers and devils, and a procession of breweries.

The First Brewer

Richard Clark can be given credit for being the first brewer in Van Diemen's Land. He started brewing about 1818 and the location of his 'home brewery' was at Pattersons Plains, now the Launceston suburb of St Leonards. Clark's output was minimal, sufficient only for his family and friends. Surprisingly, commercial production of beer did not commence in Van Diemen's Land until sixteen years after settlement.

Hobart

Commercial brewing commenced in Van Diemen's Land during 1820 when the Scotsman James Whyte set up his Tasman Brewery in Liverpool Street, Hobart. He was licensed 'to brew beer, ale and porter from grain, the product of Van Diemen's Land only'. Imported grains were in short supply, and needed for more essential food products. The Tasman Brewery was noted for its Tasman's Stingo — said to be better than imported ale. Whyte grew his own barley and hops, and these fresh ingredients may have accounted for the excellence of his beer. The brewery continued to operate for fifty-seven years, under various names and ownerships.

With the success of the Tasman Brewery, other breweries quickly followed in Hobart. The Newtown Brewery advertised in the *Hobart Town Gazette* of 11 August 1821: 'porter at 4 shillings per gallon and table beer at 1 shilling and 6 pence per gallon'. Four more breweries started in 1822: John Blanchard's Phoenix Brewery, located at the wharf; Presnell's Brewery in Argyle Street; the Hobart Town Brewery in Davey Street; and another brewery owned by Joseph Bonney. By the mid-1830s seventeen breweries had started, of which nine were still operating. All these breweries were located in Hobart.

Launceston

The history of Launceston, Australia's third-oldest city, dates back to 1798 when the seamen-explorers, George Bass and Matthew Flinders, named the river estuary Port Dalrymple. It was here, at the entrance to the Tamar Estuary, that Colonel William Paterson, with seventy-five convicts, established another outpost in 1804. Two years later the settlement was relocated to the present site of Launceston.

Twenty years went by before Launceston had its first commercial brewery. It was appropriately named the Port Dalrymple Brewery by William Barnes when he began brewing in 1824. The location was at the north end of Margaret Street on the bank of the Tamar River. Barnes grew his own barley and wheat, and brewed a heavy malt liquor, a pewter pot of which was said to be as good as a square meal. Within five years there were five more breweries in Launceston.

The Country

Exploration of the island of Tasmania was rapid, and small townships soon spread across the colony. Apart from the rugged wilderness areas to the south-west, only minor tasks of exploration remained to be done after the 1830s.

The first regional brewery was at Austin's Ferry, 15 km north of Hobart. James Austin had started the first ferry service across the Derwent River about 1818; he also owned a hotel on the west bank of the river, and by 1820 he had added a brewery. To keep his customers drinking his beer at the hotel, Austin would contrive reasons why the ferry was delayed. A similar complex of hotel, brewery and ferry service was also operating in 1820. It was owned by John Cawthorn, and was located at New Norfolk, 20 km upstream from James Austin.

During the 1820s there were breweries at Kempton, New Norfolk, Perth and Sorrel. For such a small Australian colony, with a slow rate of growth in the population, it is quite remarkable that, at one time or another, there were breweries in no fewer than thirty-eight country towns, many of which supported more than one brewery. Over the years several townships had three breweries — some were attached to hotels, and others were quite small and existed for very brief periods. Bothwell, Burnie and New Norfolk each had four breweries, while at Kempton and Oaklands five breweries had been in business in each of these towns during the first fifty years of settlement.

Haughton Forrest's painting of the Cascade Brewery, Hobart, c. 1886. It is Australia's oldest operating brewery, having continued in business since its foundation in 1832. The founder, Peter Degraves, built the brewery on the lower slopes of Mt Wellington where there was a series of small waterfalls nearby, hence the name Cascade Brewery.
Courtesy Carlton & United Breweries Ltd

The First Foster's

There have been two Foster's breweries in Australia. The most famous was started by the Foster brothers in Melbourne in 1888, later amalgamating with five other Melbourne breweries to form Carlton & United Breweries Pty Ltd. Tasmania, however, can lay claim to having Australia's first Foster's Brewery, which was brewing well before Melbourne was founded.

Thomas Foster started his brewery in 1832 at Glenorchy, now a northern suburb of Hobart. Sadly, by December that year the sheriff had arranged to auction most of Thomas Foster's brewing utensils, his bullocks, cart and plough, and a quantity of his household furniture. His situation deteriorated further, and in 1835

> that old established brewery known as Fosters, together with dwelling house and farm of 100 acres ... an extensive malthouse, brewery, granary, servants dwellings and every requisite for brewing on a grand scale.

All of Thomas Foster's worldly possessions were auctioned, and that was the end of Australia's first Foster's Brewery.

Growth and Decline

The colony of Van Diemen's Land began to grow and prosper. Whale and seal oil and sealskins were the main exports of the 1830s, to be replaced in the following decades by wool, wheat, hops and timber. During the 1870s and 1880s a mining boom added to economic growth following the discovery of tin, lead and silver. The brewing industry kept pace with the gradual growth in population, and the number of breweries reached their peak in the 1850s. At that time close to seventy breweries were operating in Tasmania, most of them in country towns. Two decades later the number had dropped to less than thirty, and the decline continued. By the turn of the century only nine breweries remained, and by 1932 only two, one in Hobart and the other in Launceston.

Heritage

The Cascade Brewery, known today as Tasmanian Breweries, is Australia's oldest operating brewery, having continued in business since its foundation in 1832. The founder, Peter Degraves, was a pioneering industrialist, a man of energy and vision, who became one of the most civic-minded personalities in early Tasmanian history. His brewery, located on the lower slopes of Mt Wellington, Hobart, grew to become the largest in Tasmania.

The Launceston-based Esk Brewery of J. Boag & Sons was taken over by Cascade in 1922, and both the Esk and Cascade breweries continue to produce their individual brands of beer.

The Cascade Brewery buildings in Hobart stand today on the original site chosen by Peter Degraves, an attractive landmark, popular tourist attraction and a brewing enterprise of considerable economic and historic importance to Tasmania.

Tasmania

#	Location	Grid	#	Location	Grid	#	Location	Grid	#	Location	Grid
1	Austin's Ferry	F8	11	Deloraine	E4	22	Jerusalem	D5	33	Scottsdale	G3
2	Avoca	G5	12	Devonport	D3	23	Kempton	F7	34	Sorell	G8
3	Bagdad	F7	13	Don	D3	24	Latrobe	D3	35	Spreyton	D3
4	Bothwell	F7	14	Dundas	B5	25	Launceston	F4	36	Stanley	B2
5	Brighton	F7	15	Evandale	F4	26	Longford	F4	37	Strahan	B6
6	Burnie	C3	16	Fingal	H4	27	Lymington	F9	38	Swansea	H6
7	Campania	F7	17	Franklin	F9	28	Mangalore	F7	39	Waratah	B4
8	Campbell Town	G5	18	George Town	E3	29	New Norfolk	F8	40	Westbury	E4
9	Carrick	F4	19	Hadspen	F4	30	Oatlands	F6	41	Wynyard	C3
10	Cygnet	F9	20	Hamilton	E7	31	Perth	F4	42	Zeehan	B5
			21	Hobart	F8	32	Richmond	G8			

Austin's Ferry

Austin, James   1820–24

One of Tasmania's early brewers was James Austin, who began brewing on a small scale some time before December 1820. He had arrived in Van Diemen's Land in 1804, and later set up his brewery and a hotel at Roseneath, on the bank of the Derwent River, 15 km north of Hobart.

James Austin also owned a ferry, and another hotel at Old Beach on the opposite bank of the river. The ferry crossed the river, landing and departing from where his hotels were located. A shrewd and crafty businessman, he would contrive reasons why the ferry was delayed, so that customers could fill in time drinking his beer at his hotels while waiting for the ferry.

The brewery section of the business was shortlived and was for sale after a few years. Austin died in 1831.

Avoca

Gray's Arms Inn & Brewery   c. 1841–44

The brewery was attached to the Gray's Arms Inn, and both were owned by Charles Peters. During 1844 he tried to sell the inn and brewery, and subsequently moved to Fingal where he started another brewery, the Fingal Brewery.

Bagdad

Bagdad Brewery   c. 1835–49

William Mawle had worked as a brewer in Hobart, and in the mid-1830s he began brewing at his hotel in Bagdad. Jacob Wing was the proprietor in 1844, followed by Robert Stodart who adopted the name Bagdad Brewery.

Bothwell

Most settlers in the district came from Scotland and the town was named after the Scottish town of Bothwell.

Bothwell is one of several classified historic towns of Tasmania where most of the old buildings were built by convict labour. Situated on the Clyde River, this beautiful township dates back to 1824, when its fine wide streets were laid out by the early Scottish settlers. They brought with them their own native sport — golf — and established Australia's first golf course.

Bothwell Brewery   1839–1902

William Dyke started a brewery in Bothwell early in 1839, but sold out later that year to George Larkins. Larkins had closed his Clyde Brewery, also in Bothwell, in February that year. He advertised for a competent, sober and industrious man to manage his newly acquired brewery: 'None need apply whose character will not bear the strictest investigation'. Larkin also offered to lease the brewery.

In the meantime Robert Whitway, proprietor of the White Hart Inn, which was licensed for the sale of wine, spirits and beer only, decided to move into the brewing business. He bought the Bothwell Brewery and also William Horne's brewery in nearby Alexander Street, both during 1859; he then closed the Alexander Street brewery.

In 1864 the Bothwell Brewery was purchased by Isaac Blake, who conducted a successful business for twenty years. William Blake, who had been a partner for five years, became the proprietor in 1884. He supplied local inns with beer that was described as 'mild, clear, sparkling and free from acid'.

William Dyke	1839
George Larkins	1839–59
Robert Whitway	1859–64
Isaac Blake	1864–84
William Blake	1884–1902

Clyde Brewery   1836–39

George Larkins was Bothwell's first brewer. He built the Clyde Brewery in 1836, but three years later he closed it, having bought the larger Bothwell Brewery from William Dyke.

Horne, William   1854–59
Alexander Street

When William Horne started brewing, he was faced with competition from the Bothwell Brewery, which had been in business for fifteen years. After running his brewery for five years, Horne sold to Robert Whitway, one of the local hotelkeepers, and the brewery was closed.

McWaide, John   1856–67

Although the brewery was started by John McWaide in 1856, Esther McWaide was advertising the property for sale in 1863. This included the brewery and tannery on 18 acres of land along the bank of the River Clyde. The property was finally sold to John Easton in 1865, and he resold shortly after to Benjamin Jackman.

Brighton

The town was named Brighton by Governor Lachlan Macquarie in 1821 for reasons unknown. It would seem unlikely that it was named after the English seaside town of Brighton, since the Tasmanian town is close to the Derwent River, and inland from the sea.

Brighton Brewery   1835–50

The owner of the Brighton Brewery, James Evans, would have been pleased with the editorial in the *Colonial Times* of 28 July 1835:

We have seen and tasted some of the beer lately brewed by Mr Evans. It is extremely bright and beautifully clear ... what a burning shame it is that we import beer so largely when we can make most excellent beer of our own.

James Evans sold the Brighton Brewery to Edward Rand in 1842, but three years later Rand was declared insolvent.

J. Davis ran the brewery from 1845 to 1850, and the property was then offered for lease but nobody was interested. Although brewing had ceased, the property remained in the Davis family for many years.

Burnie

The town was named after William Burnie, a director of the Van Diemen's Land Company, which opened land to tenants in 1842. After the discovery of tin at Mt Bischoff in 1871, Burnie became the port for the mines. The city's principal secondary industry is the milling of pulp and paper.

Bridley, Francis   1877–81
E. Medwin was the owner of the cottage and small brewery, but the occupier and brewer was Francis Bridley.

Burnie Inn Brewery   1856–57
The first hotel in Burnie (or Emu Bay as the settlement was known at that time) was built in 1847 and was called the Burnie Inn. The hotel licence was held by Joseph Law. When Thomas Wiseman bought the inn during 1856, he added a small brewery to boost the family hotel business. Very soon, he found that it was easier to sell beer than to make it.

TOO MUCH SCIENCE

We are getting too scientific nowadays. The tendency to overlay plain matters of fact with technical and chemical jargon is on the increase, especially amongst the younger school of brewers who consider that it sounds well to talk metaphysically; *i.e.*, about something they don't clearly understand themselves, neither do those whom they address. Young men who wish to be thought clever, talk of chemical terms and formulae in a glib manner which excites mingled feelings of derision and pity. Chemical science has rendered the art of brewing great service, but there is a danger that chemistry will smother brewing. We admit the great advantage of a scientific training to a young brewer, but for a 'high falutin' science, which is mainly composed of a knowledge of words, we have a mild contempt.

Australian Brewers' Journal, April 1891

Star Brewery   1855–70
West Beach

Joseph Law was a substantial landowner, holding properties that now form much of the central and western business districts of Burnie. One of his occupations was brewing, and he continued at his Star Brewery for fifteen years, after which the brewery closed, later becoming a boarding house, and then one of Burnie's first schools.

Tasmanian Brewery Co. Ltd   1903–7
The land for the brewery was leased, oddly enough, from Burnie's pioneer methodist minister, the Rev. W. H. Walton, who lived in what later became the Wivenhoe schoolhouse. Construction of the brewery began early in 1902, and by November that year the brewery had been completed at a cost of £500, plus an extra £600 for the equipment. The formal opening of the brewery, at Wivenhoe (now an eastern suburb of Burnie) took place on 26 January 1903. Howard N. Sleigh and George Leighton were the owners — Sleigh was previously the proprietor of the Castlemaine Brewery in Fremantle, Western Australia.

The company soon ran into difficulties, and went into liquidation later that year. One letter, written in March 1904, said that the affairs of the company 'were in a delightful muddle'.

Wiseman & Co. operated the brewery from 1905, but they also folded up after two years.

From time to time the brewery was referred to as the Wivenhoe Brewery because of its location.

Late in 1912 the brewery was reopened by Mr Southerwood.

Wivenhoe Brewery
See Tasmanian Brewery Co. Ltd.

Campania

Ticehurst Brewery   1845
The brewery was on the Ticehurst farm, which was beside the Coal River, near Campania, 35 km north of Hobart. The owner was Dr George Desailly.

Campbell Town

Campbell Town is of considerable historic interest, with many fine old buildings, such as Powell's Hotel built in 1834, and the red brick bridge built by convicts in 1836. The town was named by Governor Lachlan Macquarie, after his wife's maiden name, during his visit in 1821.

Campbell Town Brewery   1832–70
High Street

The Campbell Town Brewery was started in 1832 by James Hume. He had arrived in Van Diemen's Land nine years earlier, and had previous experience as a brewer, distiller and malt-extract manufacturer. In spite of this background, Hume brewed in Campbell Town for only two months, and never went back to brewing again. His son, Richard, continued for about a year.

In 1833 David Murray purchased the brewery. Later that year Murray was trying to resell the brewery.

James Lord became the owner in 1843, and he put the brewery on the market as a going concern, to let only and not for sale.

Meanwhile, Hubert Kean was 'building a brewery, a handsome edifice, in High Street on the bank of the Elizabeth River'. The year was 1846, and the construction may have been on the site of Hume's old brewery. Kean ran the brewery until about 1855, and then ran into financial difficulty. This resulted in a new owner, Eleanor Morrison. She leased the brewery to Francis Turnbull and, one after another, other lessees followed for the next four years. Eleanor Morrison also owned the Evandale Brewery.

There was a new owner of the Campbell Town Brewery in 1860, Mary McNeal, and she leased the brewery to Thomas Bonney, followed by James Bonney in 1862. On 25 August 1864 the brewery and other properties were put up for auction by order of the Supreme Court of Tasmania. Two years later Hubert Kean's son, Richard, was offering to let the re-equipped brewery.

Four more years passed, and in 1870 Esther and Robert Spencer took over. Brewing ceased later that year.

The premises were converted to a cannery in 1882, and later the building was used as a Masonic Hall and a Methodist Sunday School.

First Brewery

James Hume	1832
Richard Hume	1832–33
David Murray	1833–43
James Lord	1843

Second Brewery

Hubert Kean	1846–55
Eleanor Morrison	1855
Francis Turnbull (lessees)	1855–57
Adam Turnbull (lessee)	1857
Edwin Whitchurch (lessees)	1857–58
Turnbull & Henslowe (lessees)	1858–59
F. B. Henslowe (lessee)	1859
Mary McNeal	1860
Thomas Bonney (lessee)	1860–62
James Bonney (lessee)	1862–64
Richard Kean	1866
E. & R. Spencer	1870

Carrick

Carrick Brewery 1854–63

Frederick Rudge had been declared insolvent in 1846 when he was living in the nearby township of Deloraine. Eight years later he moved to Carrick and started a brewery, complete with a steam-mill and malthouse. As well as selling beer, Rudge sold 'superior colonial malt, crushed or whole'. This was in 1859 when the town population was only 400.

During 1861 the brewery failed to sell at auction. Two years later the entire property was sold, and Fred Rudge moved back to Deloraine and took over the lease of the Deloraine Brewery in December 1863.

Cygnet

The township was first named Port de Cygnes because of the large numbers of black swans in the estuary. A convict settlement operated at Port de Cygnes during the 1840s, and the name was officially changed to Cygnet in 1915.

Port Cygnet Brewery 1855–60

Francis Burslem received his brewer's licence in 1855. The property where he brewed was mortgaged from William Lindsay and consisted of a steam flourmill, sawmill, cottages, public house, malthouse and brewery, all on 500 acres of land. The brewery section had been the subject of a dispute between Francis Burslem and James Lee, who happened to be the brewer when the whole property was auctioned in January 1861.

Deloraine

The Deloraine area was first settled in 1825, and named after the town of Deloraine in Scotland. Many of the town's buildings and homesteads date from the 1830s, and are now used as galleries, craft centres and museums.

Beefeater Street Brewery 1869

The brewery operated for a short time under an unusual arrangement. Samuel Henry owned the property; he engaged Adolphus Rooke to manage the brewery and brew the beer. There must surely have been some conflict of interest since Rooke was the owner of the Retreat Brewery, also located in Deloraine.

Deloraine Brewery 1856–69
Church Street

James Morse owned the brewery. He leased it to John Nunn, who became bankrupt after working the brewery for five years. The lease was then taken over by George Whiley.

Frederick Rudge had been a resident of Deloraine before leaving to start a brewery at the nearby township of Carrick. After ten years he moved back to Deloraine, and in December 1863 took over the lease of the Deloraine Brewery. When the lease ran out, the owner, James Morse, continued to operate the brewery himself.

Retreat Brewery 1850–79

Although the Deloraine district was first opened up for agriculture in the 1820s, almost thirty years went by before brewing commenced in the town. In 1850 Adolph Frederick Rooke was advertising for a malster, to work at his new brewery on his farm several kilometres east of Deloraine. An article in the *Examiner* of 18 June 1851 stated that, after a certain meeting, 'bread and cheese, with Rooke's X Ale will be provided for committee men'.

In 1869 Rook was also the manager and brewer of the Beefeater Street Brewery, also in Deloraine.

Adolph Rooke stopped brewing in 1879 and the premises were used as a cordial factory. The brewery building was destroyed by fire in 1885, and eleven years later the malthouse met with the same fate.

Devonport

The city and port of Devonport in Northern Tasmania is situated at the mouth of the Mersey River. First called Port Frederick, and subsequently Mersey River, the present town was known as Devonport in the 1890s. The port is now the terminal for vehicular-passenger ferries from the mainland.

Mersey Brewery 1857–59

Bartholomew Thomas built his Mersey Brewery at Appledore (the earlier name for Devonport) in 1856, and a brewer's licence was granted on 1 January 1857. His attempt at brewing was not very successful, and in July 1858 the goodwill and plant were advertised for sale 'with the use of premises and a malthouse and the lease of a first class site for business on a creek of fresh water'. The brewery closed in 1859.

Don

North West Coast Brewery 1889–91

This was another shortlived brewery; it had three owners in as many years, and very little production of beer. John Pierce had converted a stable into a brewery, but ran into trouble almost immediately for breaches of the Beer Duty Act, and the brewery closed.

G. S. Gardiner bought the brewery. He then resold to J. A. Campbell & Co. in December 1890. Three months later the new owners were trying to sell the brewery, which fortuitously burned to the ground in October 1891.

Dundas

West Coast Brewery Co.
See Zeehan & Dundas Brewery Co. Ltd.

Zeehan & Dundas Brewery Co. Ltd
1892–96

The *Zeehan and Dundas Herald* of 10 September 1892 reported that the Zeehan & Dundas Brewery was to begin operating the following week. And it did, turning out Dundas beer 'fit to take the place of any imported draught article'.

The founder and promoter of the brewery was Henry Simpson who worked in conjunction with a brewery consultant, J. Tizard Welsh. The previous year the promoters had been inviting capital for the West Coast Brewery Co., the name subsequently being changed to the Zeehan & Dundas Brewery Co. Ltd.

The brewery closed in 1893 after voluntary liquidation. One of the difficulties was the poor quality of the water, which mineralised to the extent that fish could not live in it. The brewer, T. F. Usher, also complained about the loneliness of the place.

Edward Burgess and his brother, William, decided to reopen the brewery as the West Coast Brewery Co. in 1896, but by the end of that year the company was wound up.

Evandale

Evandale Brewery
See Tasmanian Brewery.

Patriot King William the Fourth Inn & Brewery
1849–53

Many hotel breweries operated throughout Australia during the nineteenth century, brewing relatively small quantities of beer for sale to their hotel customers. One such enterprise was the Patriot King William the Fourth Inn & Brewery, owned and operated by John Williatt. Most of these hotel breweries found that brewing was not such an easy or profitable endeavour, and after a few years they returned to buying their beer from reputable breweries.

Tasmanian Brewery
1855–66

Many women took over the running of a brewery after their husbands had died, but one enterprising lady started up on her own. Eleanor Morrison started the Evandale Brewery and after three years, she sold to Henry Gee, then moved to Campbell Town and became the owner of the Campbell Town Brewery, which she leased.

At Evandale Henry Gee brewed for one year, and then sold to William Perkins. He resold the same year to William East. He changed the name to the Tasmanian Brewery, and continued in business for the next seven years. Brewing ceased at Evandale in 1866, and William East moved to Perth, Tasmania, where he purchased and operated the Esk Brewery.

Fingal

Fingal Brewery
1851–73

Talbot Street

The first payable gold was found in Tasmania at the Nook, near Fingal, in 1852. The previous year Charles Peters (previously the brewer at Gray's Arms Inn & Brewery in Avoca) had started a brewery at the local Talbot Arms Inn. He had gained his hotel and brewing experience at nearby Avoca during the 1840s, and the gold discovery at Fingal boosted business at his brewery.

In 1854 the brewery was leased to William Duncan Jnr. After Duncan's retirement from the trade in 1861, the lease was taken over by Edward Watson. He became insolvent later that year.

Charles Peters still owned the brewery, and in 1866 John Gatty ran the business for three years.

The brewery was purchased by William East in 1869, and he used the name Fingal Brewery. At that time he was also the owner of the Perth Brewery in Perth, Tasmania, and had previously owned the Tasmanian Brewery in Evandale.

The last reference to the Fingal Brewery shows Cecil Frederick Greene as the brewer from 1872 to 1873.

Pestell's Brewery
1854–79

Daniel Pestell had been brewing at his Tasmanian Hotel in Fingal since 1854. Needing more capacity, he built a new brewery at the Tasmanian Hotel in 1862.

Five years later the brewery was taken over by Robert Viney. In 1879 William Viney (probably the son), advertised: 'To let, cheap, the brewery and plant at Fingal — or a thoroughly competent man taken in as a partner'.

That appears to be the end of the brewery, although in 1887 the partnership of Thomas Spencer & Hamlet Fletcher received a brewer's licence for a period of one year.

Franklin

Franklin Brewery
1855–72

Thomas Spooner received his brewer's licence on 6 January 1855. Rave reviews followed about the excellence of his Huon Ale, but after four years Spooner was insolvent. As a consequence, he lost his house and contents, dairy, malthouse, kiln, and his spacious brewery. Such were the risks that were taken by brewers. Spooner also lost all his poultry and pigs, and two fine boats.

Elijah Brown took over the brewery in 1861, but didn't do much better. He tried to let the business later that year, and finally sold the brewery to John Tabor in

1863. Three years later Tabor was in trouble and was trying to sell or rent the brewery; he was out of business altogether by 1872. Fortunately, he was able to sell the property to James Griggs, who was not licensed as a brewer.

George Town

The history of the George Town district dates back to 1804, when Lieutenant-Colonel Patterson raised the Union Jack on Monument Point, and took possession in the name of King George III of England. The town was named after the King in 1811.

Public signs in the town attest to the fact that George Town is the oldest 'town' in Australia (Hobart and Sydney, although settled earlier, were by then 'cities').

George Town Brewery — 1855–58
Anne Street

Elizabeth Davies, the local postmistress, was granted a brewer's licence on 6 January 1855. She was the brewer for Benjamin Hyrons, who owned the Freemason's Hotel, which included the brewhouse. The hotel and brewery were offered for sale in 1858 and brewing ceased.

Hadspen

Hadspen Brewery — 1871–72

Cecil Frederick Greene was the owner and operator of the brewery for about two years. He left the Hadspen district and settled in Fingal, bought the Fingal Brewery, but fared no better there than at Hadspen.

Hamilton

Hamilton Inn & Brewery — 1855–59

Richard Baldwin began brewing at the Hamilton Inn in 1855, then sold both the inn and brewery to Oliver Lang in 1858.

Hit or Miss Brewery — c. 1850–81
Cnr George & Rider Streets

It is difficult to understand why the founder of the brewery, James Middleton, would call his business the Hit or Miss Brewery, a name unlikely to attract public confidence in anything to do with the brewery, including the quality of the beer.

James Middleton must have been working the brewery before 1851, since the *Hobart Town Courier* of 8 January 1851 carried an advertisement: 'To be let: The public house and stables called the Hit or Miss Brewery … late in the occupation of James Middleton, deceased'. Middleton had come to a tragic end when he dropped a loaded musket on the floor, and shot himself in the foot; he died the next morning.

Jacob Trott, a blacksmith and wheelwright by trade, decided to get into the brewing business, and bought the Hit or Miss Brewery in 1856. Knowing nothing about brewing, Trott soon had the brewery up for sale or rent and, when nobody was interested, he employed Robert Spencer as a brewer for £150 per year. Spencer continued for three years, then left after a legal dispute with Trott. It is uncertain what happened to the brewery after that, but in 1868 E. G. Hooke was running the business.

James Bryant Snr was the owner in 1875, and his son, James Jnr, ran the brewery until it closed in 1881.

Jackson's Brewery — 1844–64

James Jackson was Hamilton's first brewer, and he stayed in business for twenty years, a remarkable achievement for one man during those early years. He also owned a malthouse in Grace Street, which he rented to Jacob Trott of the Hit or Miss Brewery, the other brewery in the town.

Rotherwood Brewery — 1845

George Pogson began brewing in December 1845. His 'backyard' brewery was on his property, about 18 km out from the township of Hamilton.

The brewer, Alexander Smith, was fined £100 for operating an illicit still in his private home. He was jailed in default, and Pogson's Rotherwood Brewery closed.

Hobart

Adams Tasmanian Brewery 1902–5
Cnr Elizabeth & Warwick Streets

George Adams became one of the wealthiest and most influential businessmen in Hobart. After holding a variety of jobs during his first twenty years in Australia, he purchased a Sydney city hotel with a Tattersall's gaming club, based on the rules of the famous Tattersall's Club of London. His reputation for fair dealing and honesty ensured the growing popularity and success of his Tattersall's Sweeps, and in the early 1890s he was invited by the Tasmanian government to rescue the failing Bank of Van Diemen's Land by disposing of its property assets. He achieved this by organising a lottery of 100,000 tickets at £1 each. Adams then took up residence in Hobart, and Tattersall's became the official Tasmanian lottery in 1895.

In 1902 George Adams purchased the old Tasmanian Brewery premises in Elizabeth Street, and immediately began extensions and improvements on a grand scale. Much of the equipment was purchased from the Zeehan & Dundas Brewery in Dundas, which had closed seven years earlier. Adams's ambitions for the brewery profits were also on a grand scale. He planned to capture most of the Tasmanian market and to develop a large export business to the Australian mainland, and would spare no expense in order to achieve these objectives.

Adams's ale was reasonably popular, but the grand plans ended suddenly when George Adams died in Hobart in 1904. The building was leased by the Cascade Brewery Co. Ltd, and was used for malt storage.

In 1911 the premises were used by an upholstery and spring-mattress company. Later still, in 1927, the newly-formed Co-operative Breweries of Tasmania Ltd acquired the property, and brewing commenced once again.

Albion Brewery 1823–46
4 Argyle Street

The Albion Brewery was first known as the Eagle Tavern Brewery, with both a tavern and a brewery housed in the one building. Brewing commenced in 1823; the proprietor was G. W. Robinson. The *Hobart Town Gazette* of 8 November 1823 displayed an advertisement of G. W. Robinson of the Eagle Tavern, Argyle Street, informing the public that he could supply 'genuine home brewed beer at 2 shillings per gallon, minimum order five gallons'.

John L. Roberts leased the brewery in 1829, but died three years later. His eldest son, John V. Roberts, continued, but hard times followed. In 1835 he was the subject of court actions by his creditors, but he managed to survive for a few more years.

George Adams of Tattersall's fame operated his own brewery at Hobart for three years until his death in 1904.
Courtesy Cascade Brewery Co. Ltd

The wine-and-spirit merchant, John Clarke, bought the business in 1839 and kept on brewing under the name of the Albion Brewery. 'Families would do well in trying his [Clarke's] beer which is an excellent beverage at the price, only 6 shillings per dozen [bottles], so said the *Hobart Town Advertiser* of 12 July 1839.

The following year the same newspaper advised:

> The public are respectfully informed that the undersigned has for sale, ale and beer of a description and quality which cannot fail to give satisfaction to those who may favour him with their orders. A. F. Angus.

A year had barely passed and the new owner, A. F. Angus, was attempting to sell the brewery.

W. J. Disher became the proprietor in 1843, but after three years he started the Artillery Brewery in Gore Street, Hobart, and that was the end of the Albion.

Anchor Brewery (Liverpool Street) 1820–77
Liverpool Street

During the life of the brewery there were at least twelve operators and four different names. Scotsman James Whyte started the Tasman Brewery in 1820, making it the earliest commercial brewery in Tasmania. Whyte was licensed to brew beer, ale and porter from grain, the product of Van Diemen's Land only. In the early years imported grains were in short supply, and needed for more essential food products.

The Tasman Brewery was noted for its Tasman's Stingo, which was said to be superior to the famous Yorkshire Stingo — and, for that matter, better than any other beer according to one journalist of the day.

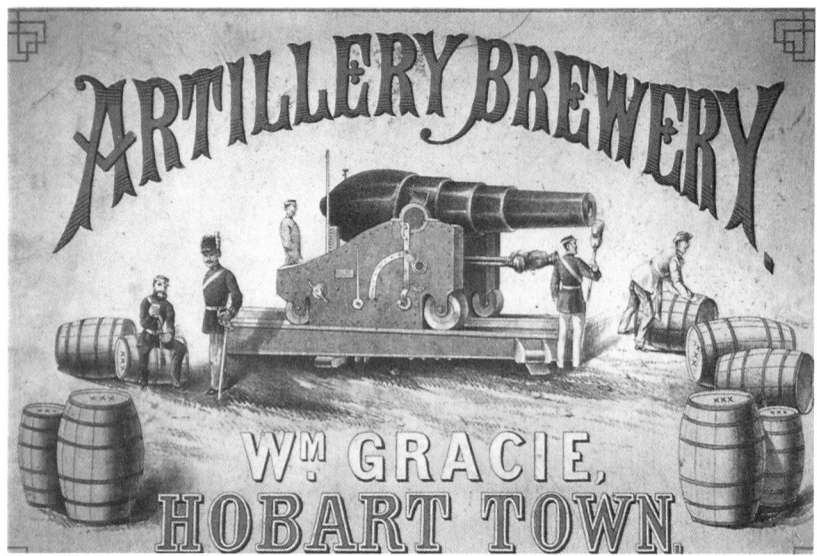

Whyte grew his own barley and hops and 'turned out a first class article [beer]'.

James Whyte met with an accident in November 1823, necessitating the amputation of his leg. He died forty-eight hours later, and his wife, Sarah, then endeavoured to run the business.

When John Macdougall purchased the brewery in 1825, he changed the name to the Tasmanian Brewery, worked it for two years, and then leased it to William Stallard and Stephen Coombs. John Mills worked at the brewery at this time. In 1830 when Coombs was running the business, the name was changed again, this time to the Britannia Brewery.

Coombs was on his own from 1830 to 1834.

For the next eight years Macdougall, the owner, was involved in the operation of the brewery from time to time, with leases being granted in between. John Stracey joined Macdougall for a few years, and later leases were held by Peter Miller, followed by Stracey & Burn.

Frederick Patterson purchased the brewery in 1842. He sent several shipments of ale to California in the 1850s, hopeful of establishing an export market in that area where a goldrush had begun.

After working the brewery for twenty-three years, Patterson was ready to sell. Finally, in 1865 the partnership of Wood & Spencer negotiated the purchase, and decided to trade as the Anchor Brewery.

The brewery was close to the Hobart Town Rivulet and frequently suffered flood damage. The various owners and operators obviously put up with the problem, since the brewery was not relocated. There were two more owners before the brewery closed in 1877.

Anchor Brewery (Macquarie Street) c. 1855–56
3 Macquarie Street

There were two breweries in Hobart using the name Anchor Brewery. This one, near the Bridge Inn in lower Macquarie Street, had been operating for some time when it was purchased by a veterinary surgeon, John Coulson. His advertisements told everyone how good his ale was, and with colonial pride, he finished with 'Advance Tasmania'. His greater claim to fame though, was as a veterinary surgeon. He regularly advertised his practice: 'No cure, no pay, in any disease'.

The brewing effort lasted a year, and Coulson moved to the St Patrick's Inn, which he renamed the Lame Horse, not a particularly appropriate name for the premises of a practising veterinarian.

Artillery Brewery 1846–83
Macquarie Street (now Gore Street)

The *Hobart Town Gazette* of 20 January 1820 featured an article that described the laying of the foundation stone of a brewery by the owner, R. W. Loane. The location is at the end of Loane's premises in Macquarie Street, and part of the old building still stands.

Although the building, when completed, was intended as a brewery, it was used as a warehouse for the first two or three years. By the end of 1823 it was used for the production of spirits, and was named the Derwent Distillery. Loane tried to dispose of the property on numerous occasions, either by sale or lease, even by auction in 1825. It was still on offer in 1842.

The premises were finally used for brewing by W. J. Disher (former owner of the Albion Brewery) in 1846, and he chose the name Artillery Brewery. After three years Disher sold the brewery to Thomas Pascoe, who supplied Ales and XX and XXX Porter in bottles.

The Benson family owned the brewery in the late 1860s, but brewing ceased about that time and the brewery remained idle for many years.

After additions and alterations the Artillery Brewery was reopened in 1873 by William Gracie, an experienced brewer who had worked at the Cascade Brewery for sixteen years. After ten years Gracie was persuaded

Tasman Brewery
James Whyte	1820–23
Sarah Whyte	1823–25

Tasmanian Brewery
John Macdougall	1825–27
Stallard & Coombs	1827–30

Britannia Brewery
Stephen Coombs	1830–34
Macdougall & Stracey	1834–36
John Macdougall	1836–38
Peter Miller	1838–39
Stracey & Burn (lessees)	1839
Frederick Patterson	1842–65

Anchor Brewery
Wood & Spencer	1865–74
R. R. Wood	1874–75
R. A. McLean	1875–77

to sell to the Cascade Brewery Co. Ltd, and the Artillery was closed in 1883.

Bevley Bank Brewery 1830–39
Newtown Road

Henry Condell was one of the few businessmen who made a success at brewing in Van Diemen's Land in the early years. He was born in Madiera, and at an early age he went to Scotland to learn the art of brewing and distilling from his grandfather.

In 1822 Condell sailed from England to Van Diemen's Land. By 1830 he had built a substantial home and brewery. He sold ale and porter for 1s per quart, and even exported porter to Sydney. Local barley was used to make malt, and the hops were imported from England. Although the brewery was named the Bevley, the name Condell's Brewery was also commonly used.

In 1839 Condell migrated with his family to the infant settlement of Melbourne. Before his departure, all his properties were offered for sale, but six years went by before the brewery and most of his Hobart estate were sold. In Melbourne Condell set up another large and highly successful brewery.

Black Swan Brewery 1839
Argyle Street

William Cutts brewed for a very brief period. His main business was as a merchant, selling wine and spirits. He also sold his own beer, but soon found that it was easier to buy from reputable brewers than to brew his own.

Blue Bells of Scotland Hotel & Brewery 1855
Murray Street

The brewery formed part of the Blue Bells of Scotland Hotel, and the owner was George Wickins.

Bonney, Joseph 1822

A small advertisement in the *Hobart Town Gazette* of 23 November 1822 said that Joseph Bonney was offering his brewery for sale or to let. (Thomas and James Bonney, possibly his sons, were both involved in the Campbell Town Brewery in Campbell Town in the early 1860s.)

Britannia Brewery
See Anchor Brewery (Liverpool Street).

Bruford, Alexander 1843
Collins Street

Alexander Bruford was a miller, and for several years he operated the Old Mill at the upper end of Collins Street. He became insolvent in 1836, and some years later he decided to try brewing as a means of livelihood. He advertised for an experienced brewer and malster, and took out a brewer's licence — that is all that seems to be known of Bruford and his attempt at brewing.

Cascade Brewery Co. Ltd 1832–

The Cascade Brewery is Australia's oldest operating brewery, having continued in business since its foundation in 1832. Throughout its long history it has been of considerable economic importance to the state, and is a classic example of Australia's industrial heritage.

Accompanied by his brother-in-law, Major Hugh McIntosh, Peter Degraves, his wife and eight children arrived at Hobart Town from England on 10 April 1824. Degraves was a pioneering industrialist, and a man of energy and vision, who became one of the most colourful and civic-minded personalities of early Tasmanian history. His many business ventures included sawmilling, flourmilling, brewing, shipbuilding, and the ownership of a fleet of ships used for the local and mainland coastal trade.

Soon after his arrival Peter Degraves received a grant of 2000 acres of heavily timbered land on the lower slopes of Mt Wellington. The well-chosen site was at the junction of the Hobart Town and Guy Fawkes Rivulets, where a series of small waterfalls gave rise to the name Cascades.

In partnership with Hugh McIntosh, Degraves started business as a sawmiller. The water-powered equipment had accompanied them on their voyage, and business was soon under way.

Misfortune followed when some English creditors obtained a judgement against Degraves, and he spent the next five years in the Hobart gaol. While in prison, he designed a new gaol and offered the plans free of cost to the authorities.

After his release from gaol, Degraves immediately started work on the construction of the Cascade Brewery. The year was 1832, and although there were already eight breweries operating in Hobart Town at that time Degraves had the advantage of an unlimited supply of fresh, clear water, free from the contamination that was common in the town. The population was approaching 10,000, and the town's water supply came from the Hobart Town Rivulet, which collected sewerage outfall and all sorts of litter. In summer months the water was particularly filthy and putrid when the flow was reduced to a trickle. Later, Degraves arranged for river water, which passed through his land holdings, to be supplied to the town.

The first beer was produced by the Cascade Brewery early in 1832, and was quickly considered superior to other beers, even those shipped down from the mainland. As an indication of the popularity of the beer, the story is told of the notorious Tasmanian bushranger, Nugget Brown, who, in 1849, held up a coach on the road to Milton Mowbray. He ignored the mailbags and passengers' valuables, preferring to ride off with a 5-gallon keg of Cascade beer.

Peter Degraves designed and built the Hobart Theatre Royal, which was officially opened on 6 March 1837, and continues in use, as a theatre, to this day. It is an enduring reminder of the man who gave so much to the industrial, economic and cultural development of Tasmania.

The Cascade Brewery, Hobart, 1899. At that time, the brewery was one of the largest in Australia and exported its beer to the mainland. It is Australia's oldest operating brewery, having continued in business since its foundation in 1832.
La Trobe Library, State Library of Victoria

It was a sad time when Peter Degraves died at his home at the Cascades on 31 December 1852. His two capable sons, Charles and John, continued to run the various business enterprises, and their brother-in-law, James Wilson, managed the brewery. Charles died, and two years after the death of his brother, John, James Wilson, husband of one of the Degraves daughters, arranged the sale of the brewery and hotels to a Melbourne-based syndicate headed by John Syme. The acquisition was on 8 December 1881.

During 1883 the syndicate purchased the Artillery Brewery from William Gracie, the Tasmanian Brewery (Elizabeth Street) from Henry James, and the brewery interests of Mrs Emma Walker at Walker's Brewery, and formed the Cascade Brewery Co. Ltd on 26 May 1883. The three breweries were closed, leaving Cascade and two other breweries, the Jolly Hatters and the Globe, the only breweries operating in Hobart. The company had a Melbourne office and depot in Hoddle Street, Clifton Hill, from 1886 to 1904, and a large aerated-water department was added in 1886.

An important event occurred on 1 March 1922 when the brewing interests of J. Boag & Son (1911) Ltd of the Esk Brewery in Launceston were acquired. A wholly-owned subsidiary of Cascade, Tasmanian Breweries Pty Ltd, was formed to control the affairs of the Cascade and J. Boag & Son Esk River breweries, both continuing to produce their individual brands of beer and under their own brewery names.

The Derwent Brewery was taken over in 1922, and closed.

Disaster struck on 7 February 1967 when raging bushfires swept down Mt Wellington and reduced a large part of the Cascade Brewery to ashes. Arrangements were urgently made for supplies of beer, firstly from the Esk Brewery in Launceston, and then from their friendly competitor, Carlton & United Breweries Ltd in Melbourne. Twelve weeks later the Cascade Brewery was back in production.

The Cascade Brewery came under foreign ownership in 1984, following the acquisition by Industrial Equity Ltd of New Zealand. Ownership changed again in 1988 to the New Zealand-based company, Wilson, Neill Australia Ltd. The name was changed to the Cascade Group Ltd, which became a wholly-owned subsidiary of Wilson, Neill Ltd, New Zealand, in 1990.

The Cascade Group Ltd and Carlton & United Breweries Ltd formed a joint-venture company in January 1993 to acquire the Cascade Brewery, Hobart. The joint venture, called the Cascade Brewery Co. Pty Ltd, was now controlled and operated by CUB. Boag's Brewery in Launceston continued under the ownership of the Cascade Group Ltd.

Regardless of ownership, the Cascade Brewery has a rich and proud history. In Melbourne William Degraves's name is remembered by Degraves Street, which runs into Flinders Street near Swanston Street. The Cascade Brewery buildings today stand majestically on the original site chosen by Peter Degraves in 1824, an attractive landmark in Hobart and a popular tourist attraction.

Cascade Brewery

Peter Degraves	1832–52
C. & J. Degraves	1852–81
Melbourne-based syndicate	1881–83

Cascade Brewery Co. Ltd   1883–1922
Acquisitions:

Artillery Brewery	1883, closed
Tasmanian Brewery	1883, closed
Walker's Brewery	1883, closed
Derwent Brewery	1922, closed
Esk Brewery, Launceston	1922–

Tasmanian Breweries Pty Ltd   1922–

Formed to control both the Cascade Brewery, Hobart and the Esk Brewery, Launceston; both breweries continue to operate under their own names

Ownership changes:

Industrial Equity Ltd	1984
Wilson, Neill Australia Ltd	1988
Name changed to Cascade Group Ltd	1990

Joint venture: Cascade Group Ltd and Carlton & United Breweries Ltd form Cascade Brewery Co. Pty Ltd   1993

Breweries now trade as:
Cascade Brewery Co. Pty Ltd (Hobart brewery), CUB controlled
J. Boag & Son Esk River Brewery (Launceston brewery)

City of Norwich Inn & Brewery
1853–55

Cnr Argyle & High Streets

William Champion sold his Jolly Hatters Brewery in Melville Street in 1853, and bought the City of Norwich Inn, where he brewed for two years.

Coates, Edward   1858–66
Cascade Road

Although the property was owned by Robert Warrior, the brewery was operated by Edward Coates.

In 1865 Coates was charged with operating an illicit still, but the case was dismissed.

Commercial Brewery   1851–58
The Old Wharf

In addition to running his Commercial Brewery, William Green was also managing his Commercial Steam Mills, both with considerable success. He also owned a malthouse in Adelaide Street.

When Green retired in 1858, all his business properties were sold to William Searle, who decided not to continue brewing in order to concentrate on the milling business.

Condell's Brewery
See Bevley Bank Brewery.

Co-operative Breweries of Tasmania Ltd   1927–31
245 Elizabeth Street (cnr Warwick Street)

Following the death of George Adams of Tattersalls fame, his Adams Tasmanian Brewery closed in 1904 Twenty-three years later the premises were used by the newly-formed Co-operative Breweries of Tasmania Ltd, who brewed a variety of lager beers for a brief four years.

> ## SELF PRAISE
>
> What power is beer. It cements friendships, loosens tongues, clinches dullness, defeats diplomacy, opens difficult doors, unlocks hearts, wins confidence, renews hope, sharpens wits and appetite, creates and inspires courage, softens sorrow, gives pleasure, dulls pain and prepares the way for peace.
>
> Brewers themselves stressed to each other and everyone else, the nutritional value of their beer, its relatively low alcohol level compared with spirits, and its digestive properties. They compared the composition of beer with milk, arguing that beer was adapted to the adult in much the same way as milk to the child.
>
> The brewers had more to say,
>
> Beer assists intellectual activities, diminishes feelings of hunger and helps to overcome physical and psychological weakness. Sound beer does not cause corpulence but gives energy and health.' Finally, they reminded each other that beer made women 'wonderfully warm-hearted and winsome.'
>
> *Australian Brewing and Wine Journal*, August 1936

The person responsible for raising the share capital was Thomas Breheny, formerly the head brewer at Tooth & Co. in Sydney. The best equipment was installed, and Breheny was the brewer. Despite the 'tied houses' of their competitor, the Cascade Brewery, demand for the new brewery's beer was excellent, and a lucrative trade was developed in the north-western districts. Some sales were obtained in New South Wales.

The brewery closed in 1931, and it was rumoured that sabotage was one of the reasons for the collapse of the business — it was claimed that pieces of soap had been thrown into the large brewing vats. Thomas Breheny and the shareholders lost all their investment.

A very good stout had been brewed, so much so that, at the end, the Cascade Brewery purchased the last brew, together with the recipe and yeast, and advertised the stout as their special Christmas brew. At the time of closure, townspeople had a quaint saying: 'Why did the Co-op. fail? — because the Cascade Bit-'er'. The equipment was purchased by Carlton & United Breweries in Melbourne, and sent to Cairns in Queensland, where it was installed in their recently-acquired Northern Australian Brewery.

Davey Street Brewery 1822–64
Davey Street

For the first nine years the brewery was called the Hobart Town Brewery — no connection with the Hobart Town Brewery in Campbell Street, which started in 1832. Shortly after starting his brewery in Davey Street, the proprietor, William Wood, had problems with the quality of his beer. Nothing unusual about that; there was hardly a brewery in Australia that didn't have problems at one time or another. Wood's customers said the beer was barely drinkable. Wood thought his beer was good, the drinkers were the problem — they were too fussy and couldn't tell good beer from bad. Disillusioned, Wood reduced his price of draught beer to 9d a quart and bottled beer down to 12s a dozen. The next year he dropped the price again, draught down to 6d a quart, and the best bottled ale for 9s a dozen.

William Wood took on John Petchey as a partner in 1823, and then left the business three years later.

Petchey stayed on until 1831, and then sold to William Wilson, who wisely changed the name to the Davey Street Brewery — there were too many lingering memories of the Hobart Town Brewery's poor-quality beer.

William Wilson was a prominent Hobart Town merchant, and during 1836 he built a new three-storey brewery on the site, reputed to be the finest and most complete brewery in the colony. Wilson died ten years later, and his wife, Anne, carried on until 1853; then she accepted an offer of £10,000 for the brewery.

The new owner, William J. Clark, leased the brewery to John Stewart, who had a bad experience at the brewery the following year. One of his employees, when washing out the vessels, became suffocated from gases and fell into a vat. When he was pulled out, he was found to be 'quite dead'.

John Stewart continued to work the brewery until 1863, and then W. B. Watchorn took over. The brewery closed a year later.

Derwent Brewery (Collins Street) 1823–50
Collins Street

On 6 September 1823 James Ogilvie advertised in the *Hobart Town Gazette* that he 'has now on sale, for ready money, porter at £5 and ale at £5 5s, per hogshead'. He added that yeast and grains were also available at the brewery.

During 1825 Ogilvie attempted to sell the brewery, and finally concluded a sale on 2 January 1826. The new owners, Peter Dudgeon and Frederick Bell, traded as Dudgeon & Bell, but Bell dropped out the following year. Dudgeon was also a merchant, and in his advertisements he offered the very best wines, spirits and home-brewed ale, even malt and hops, in exchange for barley. Bartering was commonplace at the time.

After brewing for eight years, Dudgeon was forced to sell the brewery because of his financial problems. At the auction in 1835 the successful bidder was William Brodribb Snr, who leased the brewery to a number of brewers over the next five years.

David Lord was the owner in 1839, and he leased

the brewery to L. J. Prentice & Son, followed by Blackburn & Bilton. John Walker & Son bought the brewery in 1850, and converted it to a malthouse.

James Ogilvie	1823–26
Dudgeon & Bell	1826–27
Peter Dudgeon	1827–35
William Brodribb Snr	1835–39
George Lukin (lessee)	
John Brown (lessee)	
Luckman & Stallard (lessee)	
T. Knight (lessee)	
Reeves, Boreham & Co. (lessee)	
David Lord	1839–50
L. J. Prentice & Son (lessee)	
Blackburn & Bilton (lessee)	

Derwent Brewery (Melville Street)
See Jolly Hatters Brewery.

Derwent Distillery
See Artillery Brewery.

Dusty Miller Brewery   1833
Liverpool Street

Luke Milward set up a small brewery at his licensed house, the Dusty Miller, having learnt something of the brewing business when he worked at the Newtown Brewery in Hobart.

Milward brewed sufficient to meet the needs of a small number of private families, and was better known as a cooper than a brewer.

Eagle Tavern Brewery
See Albion Brewery.

Ellis's Brewery   1842–45
Campbell Street

R. A. Roberts started the brewery in 1842, and sold it as a going concern to Henry Ellis in 1844. The brewery was destroyed by fire in 1845.

Fergusson's Brewery   1829
Fergusson's Brewery was highly respected at the time, but there is no indication as to why the brewery failed.

Foster's Brewery   1832–35
Glenorchy

There have been two Foster's breweries in Australia. The most famous was started in Melbourne in 1888; after amalgamation in 1907 to form Carlton & United Breweries Pty Ltd the name has continued to this day as an internationally famous beverage, Foster's Lager. Tasmania, however, can lay claim to having Australia's first Foster's Brewery, which was in business well before Melbourne was founded.

Thomas Foster's brewery was at Glenorchy (originally Glenarchy), now a north-western suburb of Hobart. Foster was in financial difficulty very early in his brewing career. The Sheriff's Office issued a notice on 29 November 1832:

> In the Supreme Court: Hewitt, Smith, Gellibrand and Walker, versus Foster. On Monday next, December 3, at 1 o'clock, the Sheriff will positively cause to be put up for sale by public auction, on the premises of the defendant, situate at Glenorchy; 2 working bullocks, 1 cart, 1 plow [sic], 1 harrow, some brewing utensils and a quantity of household furniture, unless these executions be previously satisfied.

The land and buildings were not being auctioned, so presumably Foster remained on the property and continued to farm and to brew.

But the end came in 1835 as a result of the following advertisement:

> That old established brewery known as 'Fosters', together with dwelling house and farm of 100 acres of land adjoining, situated at Glenorchy about 8 miles from town. The premises consist of an extensive malt house, brewery, granary, servants' dwellings and every requisite for brewing on a large scale, conveniently arranged by the side of a never-failing rivulet. The residence comprises 10 rooms surrounded by an excellent garden commanding delightful views of the Derwent. The whole is admirably adapted for the purpose, being close to the main road and water carriage.

So ended Australia's first Foster's Brewery. Thomas Foster certainly didn't make any Foster's Lager, as lager beer was unknown in Australia at that time.

Globe Brewery
See Hobart Brewery.

Golden Cross Hotel & Brewery   c. 1845
Murray Street

This was another example of a hotel attempting to make its own beer, with very little success. Most hotel proprietors who made their own beer stopped brewing when they found that it was cheaper and easier to buy ale and porter from established breweries. The owner of the Golden Cross Hotel & Brewery was H. Wilks.

Green, Richard   1853
Arthur Street, Battery Point

The brewer, Richard Green, rented the brewery building from the estate of D. Kelly. The annual rent was £37, but Green only needed to make one payment as he stopped brewing within a year.

Hobart Brewery   1882–1920
Cnr Antil & Davey Streets

The first reference to the brewery was in 1882 when George Nicholls received a licence to brew at his

Globe Inn. He knew how to make good beer, and went on to win two first prizes (gold medals) for his malt ales at the Melbourne International Centennial Exhibition of 1888. Three years earlier he had appointed William Sander as his Melbourne agent at 144 Little Collins Street West.

The business was highly successful, and James Boag & Sons of the Esk Brewery, Launceston, eager to enter the Hobart market, made an attractive offer, which was accepted in 1889. The name was then changed to the Hobart Brewery. An earlier name used by the company was the Tasmania Dandelion Ale Co. Ltd.

Hobart Town Brewery (Campbell Street) 1832–34
Campbell Street

William Cowley and John Mills started in business making malt, and then tried their hand at brewing.

Mills left in 1833, and Cowley brewed by himself for about a year before renting the premises to Andrew Wright.

Hobart Town Brewery (Davey Street)
See Davey Street Brewery.

Hodgson's Inn & Brewery 1857
Argyle Street

Thomas Hodgson was the owner of the inn and brewery.

Jolly Hatters Brewery 1845–1922
43 Melville Street

William Champion purchased a building in Melville Street, fitted it out as a brewery, and started making and selling beer in 1845. Before that he had made some money in the beaver-hat industry (the hats were not actually made from beaver fur, but from the fur of silver-grey rabbits that had been released on Betsy Island in Storm Bay). As a reminder of his hatmaking days, he called his brewery the Jolly Hatters.

William Champion enjoyed considerable success as a brewer, and arranged for his elderly father to travel from England. Then one catastrophe followed another. Soon after his arrival, the father died at the age of eighty-seven. A year later Champion's son died (aged twenty-six), leaving a widow and one child. This was sad enough, but then William's wife died in 1855, and his daughter lost her husband. After all this, Will Champion, described as a hardworking and generous man, returned to England to see his remaining relatives.

The Jolly Hatters Brewery was purchased by John Armstrong and James Robertson in 1853, the year that transportation of convicts to the colony ended. Armstrong left three years later, and, after working the brewery on his own for twelve years, Robertson sold the brewery to William Cowburn.

The Cowburn family had connections at various times with a number of hotels in Hobart, Glenorchy and New Norfolk, and they also maintained their family hotel at the Jolly Hatters Brewery. In addition to beer, they made a range of cordials, aerated waters and ginger beer.

A number of changes in brewery ownership followed, firstly to Esther Johnson and then to Maria Johnson, both residing in Victoria. In 1881 the *Hobart Town Herald* reported that ownership had passed from Mrs Johnson to George Amott, a Hobart butcher.

In 1882 the Blake family took control of the brewery: first Henry Blake, then Isaac Blake in 1885. Isaac's son, Edwin Blake, who was to run the brewery for the next twenty years, was joined by Henry James in 1911. There was a public announcement at that time that James had become a partner and 'the business, previously known as the Jolly Hatters Brewery, will now be called the Derwent Brewery'. They traded as James & Blake until 1921 and the business was then reformed as Boag & James Pty Ltd.

The premises were purchased by the Cascade Brewery in 1922. Brewing had ceased, and the property was later resold to a machinery merchant.

Jolly Hatters Brewery

William Champion	1845–53
Armstrong & Robertson	1853–56
James Robertson	1856–68
William Cowburn	1868–80
Esther Johnson	1880–81
Maria Johnson	1881–81
George Amott	1881–82
Henry Blake	1882–85
Isaac Blake	1885–91
Edwin Blake	1891–1911

Derwent Brewery

James & Blake	1911–21
Boag & James Pty Ltd	1921–22

Newtown Brewery 1821–48

An advertisement in the *Hobart Town Gazette* of 11 August 1821 said that

> a constant supply of porter and beer is available from Mr Gatehouse's Brewery; porter at 4 shillings per gallon and table beer at 1 shilling per gallon.

George Gatehouse was one of Hobart's early brewers. His brewery and malthouse, both quite considerable, were built on his farm at Newtown, now an inner suburb of Hobart.

Original letters selected by Mrs A. Prinsep, London, in 1833 state that

> the brewer [Gatehouse] is a favourable instance of the rise of a convict to respectability. He is now, by his good conduct and industry, not only rich but his family are grown up and settling respectably.

The first recorded death at a Tasmanian brewery occurred during April 1830 when a wall at the Newtown Brewery collapsed on an employee, and crashed

First known as the Jolly Hatters Brewery in 1845, the name was changed to the Derwent Brewery by Henry James and Edwin Blake in 1911. The brewery closed in 1922.

through the floor to the cellar: 'the poor man's right leg was crushed in a most dreadful manner … a surgeon amputated his leg but he died half an hour later'.

George Gatehouse died in 1838, and the brewery was taken over by Captain Robert Jacomb, late of the Royal Navy. Jacomb seemed predisposed toward taking people to court. The brewery was on the lower reaches of the Newtown Rivulet and was frequently polluted by 'filth and other nauseous matter' caused by effluent from industries operating higher upstream. One example was reported in the *Colonial Times* of 1842: 'Mr Regan, tanner, was charged with defiling the water and thereby spoiling Mr Jacomb's beer'. Jacomb won the case, and Regan was fined £10, plus costs. After operating the Newtown Brewery for ten years, Captain Jacomb sold the business in 1848 to Jonathon Watson, but the brewery closed later that year.

Old Bell Inn & Brewery 1834–48
Elizabeth Street

Having left the Hobart Town Brewery in Campbell Street in 1833, John Mills started brewing again at the Old Bell Inn in Elizabeth Street. The small brewhouse supplied a limited clientele with XX ale, which was sold in bottles and also small casks.

Mills left early in 1837, and established the Melbourne Brewery & Distillery in Melbourne.

Pack Horse Inn & Brewery 1856
Melville Street

The proprietor was James A. Thompson.

Phoenix Brewery 1822–25
The Wharf

One of Hobart Town's very early breweries was the Phoenix. It was owned by John Blanchard, and a condition of his brewer's licence stated that he could brew beer only from grain produced in the colony — all brewer's licences at this time were qualified by this condition.

Blanchard left the brewery after three years, and went to Parramatta, NSW, where, for reasons unknown, he 'blew his brains out with a pistol'.

Presnell's Brewery 1822–26
Argyle Street

A number of breweries operated in Argyle Street, Hobart, at various times, and one of these was Presnell's Brewery, owned by Thomas and William Presnell. Most of these breweries were in business for very short periods.

Punshon, William 1838–c. 1843
Cnr Argyle & Patrick Streets

William Punshon started malting and brewing in 1838. In 1841 he advertised that his 'home-brewed' ale was recommended by the medical fraternity as a cure-all for patients recovering from sickness.

Poor William Punshon ended his days at the New Norfolk Lunatic Asylum.

> **ALCOHOLIC PATENT MEDICINES**
>
> Those who make their living by the sale of intoxicating beverages, must always be permitted a feeling of unholy glee upon consideration of the large consumption of patent medicines and of the many who 'never touched a drop of liquor in their lives,' yet resort to these 'patent' preparations for every pain or ache.
>
> Were the attention of these people directed to the fact that many of the patent medicines on the market at present, contain from 10 to 60 per cent of alcohol, they would probably scout the idea and say they never heard of the suggestion before, in spite of the fact that the newspapers and magazines are full of references to this great evil.
>
> *Australian Brewers' Journal*, December 1903

Tasman Brewery
See Anchor Brewery (Liverpool Street).

Tasmania Dandelion Ale Co. Ltd
See Hobart Brewery.

Tasmanian Breweries Pty Ltd
See Cascade Brewery Co. Ltd.

Tasmanian Brewery (Elizabeth Street)
See Tasmanian Pale Ale Brewery.

Tasmanian Brewery (Liverpool Street)
See Anchor Brewery.

Tasmanian Pale Ale Brewery 1862–83
Elizabeth Street

When George James started the Tasmanian Brewery at the upper end of Elizabeth Street in 1862, he was the sole proprietor, but within the first year of operation he took on Henry James as a partner. A year later John Clarke entered the business, which then traded as Clarke, James & Co.

For some unknown reason, Clarke left after a few months and Henry James assumed control, using the name Tasmanian Pale Ale Brewery.

Henry James advertised James's Six Guinea Ale, and was awarded first prizes for his Tasmanian Pale Ale and Porter at the Sydney International Exhibition of 1880.

The business was doing extremely well, and the Cascade Brewery made an attractive offer to James, which he accepted in 1883. Under the terms of the agreement James continued to own the brewery property, and accepted an important position at the Cascade Brewery. The Tasmanian Pale Ale Brewery was closed.

The wealthy entrepreneur, George Adams of Tattersall's fame, purchased the property almost twenty years later, in 1902, and after much rebuilding and the installation of new plant, he started another brewery on the site.

Walker, Robert 1844–50
5 Davey Street

Robert Walker had been in partnership with his father, John, and after a year or two he decided to start his own brewery in Davey Street. He began brewing Hobart Ale, and installed a substantial bottling plant. By 1850, instead of competing with his father, he closed his brewery and rejoined his father's business at Walker's Brewery.

Walker's Brewery c. 1843–83
Cnr Barrack & Macquarie Streets

During 1843, possibly earlier, John Walker and his son Robert were making beer, and traded as J. & R. Walker.

In 1844 Robert started a brewery of his own in Davey Street and made Hobart Ale. He returned to his father's brewery in 1850, and the business then traded as John Walker & Son.

A new brewery was built on the site in 1845, and the complex of buildings and stables covered almost a town block.

The business passed into the hands of Robert. When he died in 1877, his wife, Emma, ran the business. Her friends advised her to close the brewery and retire. 'No', she said.

> The name of Walker has been before the public so many years that I would not like to see it die out. If the brewery is closed, a number of men who have worked all their lives here will be thrown out of work.

A proud and courageous woman, Mrs Walker. She continued to manage the brewery and the business until 1883, when the Cascade Brewery bought the business, and closed the brewery.

White Horse Inn & Brewery 1841
Wellington Bridge

Jerusalem

Jerusalem Brewery 1855–57

John McConnon was granted a brewer's licence on 6 January 1855, and immediately set up his brewery at Mt Jerusalem, slightly north-east of Cradle Mountain. There would have been very few customers in the region at that time.

Kempton

Exchange Inn & Brewery 1869–79

Daniel Brown Snr had been the owner of the Triumph Brewery at Kempton, and he transferred the business to his son, also Daniel, in 1871. Two years earlier the father had taken over the ownership of the Exchange Inn & Brewery, which he leased to William Mullings in 1878, and George Hurd in 1879.

Gorringe's Brewery 1823–29

The township of Kempton had been known as Green Ponds, and also Cross Marsh, during the early years of settlement. When Dr Thomas Francis Gorringe started brewing in 1823, his address was Green Ponds. Common with all Tasmanian brewers' licences of the time, it was a condition of the licence that only locally-produced grain could be used — the imported grain that was available was required for more essential uses.

Some of the local population held a poor opinion of the doctor, as one journalist noted in 1826:

> Doctor Gorringe, once a dispenser of drugs, but of late converted them into beer, he farms miserably, rents land which he does not think of paying for, takes sheep on the thirds of which he gives no account and notwithstanding all his shifts as doctor, farmer and brewer, is nearly insolvent.

William Whitchurch arrived at Green Ponds at the same time as Gorringe, and worked for him at the brewery during 1826.

Royal Oak Hotel & Brewery 1856–66

The brewery section of the Royal Oak Hotel lasted for much longer than most hotel breweries, ten years in all; the owner was John Picken.

Triumph Brewery 1856–71

Daniel Brown Snr started the Triumph Brewery in 1856. Nine years later he was charged with receiving stolen wool. The incident attracted considerable local curiosity, and at the hearing the court was packed. Brown was acquitted.

In 1871 the Triumph Brewery was passed on to the son, Daniel Brown Jnr.

Victoria Hotel & Brewery 1850–63

James Brown rented the Victoria Hotel and the detached brewery from Francis Flexmore, a neighbour of the Dr Gorringe who, twenty-seven years earlier, had tried his hand at brewing at Gorringe's Brewery.

In 1863 Joseph Graves, the lessee and brewer at the time, sold his stock-in-trade, furniture and all his brewing utensils, and beer was no longer brewed at the hotel.

Latrobe

Latrobe Brewery 1858–77
On the bank of the River Mersey

The first brewer at Latrobe appears to be W. Mitchell. He was a baker by trade, and brewed very briefly in 1857.

Adam B. Turnbull, formerly of the Campbell Town Brewery, opened the Latrobe Brewery in 1858, but because of ill health he had to sell the brewery the following year.

Edward Allen became the new owner in 1859. He had built many buildings in the area, including the Town Hall, but his success as a brewer was less notable. He became bankrupt in 1872, but, with dogged determination, he was back in business the next year, and continued brewing until his death four years later.

The brewery was later converted to a Salvation Army barracks.

Rudge's Brewery — 1877–84
Regent Street

Frederick Rudge had been a brewer at the Carrick and Deloraine Breweries. With his son, George, he operated a brewery and flourmill in Regent Street, Latrobe. A few years later brewing ceased, and George became a shipping agent.

William Metcalf started the brewery again in 1883, brewed for a year, and then moved on to Spreyton.

Launceston

Aaron, Abraham — c. 1827

The *Colonial Times* of 18 May 1827 displayed this advertisement:

> Mr A. Aarons informs the public that he continues to brew beer from barley and the best colonial hops, at £5 per hogshead. Families may be supplied by the 9 gallons. Apply at the Commercial Tavern, Launceston.

Abbott, William H.

See Cornwall Brewery; Phoenix Brewery.

Black Swan Brewery — 1840–45
Cnr Charles & Brisbane Streets

It was common practice for a new owner of a brewery to advertise the fact: Thomas Dudley did so in the *Launceston Advertiser* on 23 April 1840, and told the readers that he was able to deliver 'a pure unadulterated article suitable for private families'. Wine and spirits were also available.

Many of the advertisements of Australian breweries of the 1820s to the 1860s made claims that their beer was particularly suitable for private families, any families for that matter. This seemed to infer that the whole family were beer drinkers — the wife, and sons and daughters of any age, as well as the father — for the whole family to sit down and drink beer while father kept tapping the barrel, refilling the mugs and tankards for mother and the children. This conclusion, however, would seem most unlikely. A more reasonable interpretation would be that the casks or barrels or bottles of beer were better taken home to be consumed there, an infinitely better option than having the husband out drinking at taverns and elsewhere until all hours.

> ### MAN BOILED IN A VAT OF BEER
>
> A shocking fatality occurred on August 9th [1900] at Messrs. James Boag and Sons' Esk Brewery, Launceston, Tasmania. James Kirby, aged 26 years, the assistant brewer, was sent to take the temperature of 1500 gallons of wort in a tank nine feet deep, with a railing round it three feet high along the top.
>
> Mr. J. B. Webb, the brewer, saw him at work and warned him not to lean over the rail, but to kneel down. The proper way to take the temperature of the liquor entering the copper was to kneel and take hold of the railing with one hand. Instead of doing this however, it was a habit of Kirby's, Mr. Webb informed the coroner's jury at the inquest, to ascertain the heat by standing, to accomplish which meant leaning over the railing.
>
> Mr. Webb had repeatedly cautioned him as to the risks of the practice, but the assumption is — for no one saw the accident — that he neglected the precaution once too often and fell headlong into the boiling cauldron.
>
> Mr. Webb had left Kirby and about a quarter of an hour later, missed him and on searching, found his cap floating in the vat. The liquor was immediately run off into a gutter and the body of Kirby was found lying at the bottom in a frightful state, being literally boiled.
>
> An inquest was held, when the evidence showed that deceased must have fallen into the vat head first and that death was instantaneous.
> *Australian Brewers' Journal*, August 1900

In 1842 Thomas Dudley was a little more adventurous in his advertising and included prices:

BEER BEER BEER
Now selling by the undersigned [Thomas Dudley]
Five gallons XX ale for 8 shillings, cash. Also bottled ale from 4 shillings and 6 pence per dozen, bottles to be returned. He can also malt barley at a price.

It is a saddening fact that many brewers had their dreams shattered after building a business that they hoped would be their livelihood, a means of supporting a wife and family. Dudley was just another statistic when, by order of the Sheriff, his house, brewery and all his belongings were auctioned in 1843.

Thomas Lecky became the new owner of the Black Swan Brewery, and more advertisements followed: 'begging to inform', etc., 'superior ale and porter', 'best in the colony', 'suitable for families', and finishing by hoping to merit a share of patronage. Lecky lasted a year.

In 1844 George Burgess became the next owner, and immediately offered the brewery to let.

The following year the property was again up for sale, this time by auction, but brewing at the Black Swan Brewery was by now a thing of the past.

An Esk Brewery poster from the late nineteenth century.
Courtesy Cascade Brewery Co. Ltd.

The Esk Brewery of James Boag & Son, at the turn of the century.

J. Boag & Son Esk River Brewery 1881–
Cnr William Street & The Esplanade

Charles Stammers Button had a long history of brewing. He had managed the Launceston Brewery for six years, and then joined Edward Ditcham in a twenty-year partnership — Ditcham, Button & Co. Not content to retire, he set about building the Esk Brewery, unaware that the brewery would ultimately form part of the largest brewing company in Tasmania.

On 1 February 1882 Charles Button sold his Esk Brewery to the newly-formed partnership of James Boag and his son, James Boag Jnr. Boag Snr had been the brewer and subsequent manager of the Cornwall Brewery for close to thirty years, and the son had recently left the Cataract Brewery.

When the Boags took over the Esk Brewery, it was said to be the most complete in Tasmania. The name Esk Brewery was retained, although Boag's Brewery became a frequent reference, and in later years came to be known officially as the J. Boag & Son Esk River Brewery. The brewery had frontages onto William Street and The Esplanade, and was close to wharves, the railway station and the Esk River.

In their advertisements J. Boag & Son claimed that their celebrated ales and stout were 'recommended by the leading medical facility as an excellent tonic', a claim that was apparently not misplaced since Boag's beer soon gained an excellent reputation. Boag, the father, retired in 1887, and before his death in 1891 he transferred his brewery interest to his son. Boag's Brewery prospered and expanded, and the succeeding years saw many extensions, new equipment and acquisitions. The brewery itself and the block of buildings formed an ornamental feature of the city.

In 1889 the adjacent Cornwall Brewery was taken over, and the brewing operations were subsequently merged with the Esk. In the same year the company bought the Globe Brewery in Hobart, and its name was changed to the Hobart Brewery.

A new company, J. Boag & Son (1911) Ltd, was formed in 1911 to consolidate the company's business interests, and during that year the Union Brewery was purchased from the Tasmanian Co-operative Brewery Co. Ltd.

More acquisitions followed: the Tamar Brewery was bought and closed in 1917; and in 1922 the company purchased and closed the Derwent Brewery, Hobart (formerly the Jolly Hatters Brewery).

James Boag III was born in 1881, and he joined the J. Boag & Son Brewery in 1919, the year of his father's death.

On 1 March 1922 the brewing interests of Boag's Brewery were taken over by the Cascade Brewery Co. Ltd. J. Boag & Son (1911) Ltd retained ownership of its brewery property and Launceston hotels until 1957. The new company, now Tasmanian Breweries Pty Ltd, a wholly-owned subsidiary of the Cascade Brewery Co. Ltd in Hobart, controlled both the Boag's and Cascade breweries. Boag's Brewery retained the Boag and Esk breweries' package names on all products produced in Launceston.

Tasmanian Breweries Pty Ltd was taken over in 1984 by Industrial Equity Ltd of New Zealand.

Ownership changed again in 1988 to the New Zealand-based company, Wilson Neill Australia Ltd, and in 1990 the name was changed to the Cascade Group Ltd. In 1992 the Cascade Group was aquired by Cadenza International Ltd. A joint venture was formed in January 1993 between Carlton & United Breweries Ltd, Melbourne, and the Cascade Group Ltd. The Cascade Brewery was sold to CUB. J. Boag & Son retained the distribution rights for Cascade brands in Tasmania for twenty years, and was relisted on the Australian Stock Exchange in November 1994. Since listing, J. Boag & Son was appointed as agent by Scottish & Newcastle, the Boston Beer Co. and Carlsberg to represent their brands throughout Australia.

In 1998 the company's flagship brand, James Boag's Premium Lager, was awarded the title of Grand Champion over 425 beers representing 100 breweries entered into the Australian International Beer Awards, the first time an Australian beer had won this prestigious title. In the same competition the brewery itself was also awarded the title of 'Best Brewery in Australasia' Such awards have firmly established the company's credentials throughout the world as 'Australia's Premium Brewer'.

Esk Brewery

C. S. Button	1879–82
James Boag & Son	1882–87
James Boag (Jnr)	1887–1911
Acquisitions:	
Cornwall Brewery	1889, closed
Globe Brewery (Hobart)	1889–1920,
(name changed to Hobart Brewery)	closed

J. Boag & Son (1911) Ltd 1911–22

Acquisitions:	
Union Brewery	1911–31, closed
Tamar Brewery	1917, closed
Derwent Brewery (Hobart)	1922, closed

Cascade Brewery Co. Ltd (Hobart) 1922–90
Tasmanian Breweries Pty Ltd formed, to control the interests of the Cascade and J. Boag & Son Esk River breweries

Bridge Brewery 1844–60
Westcombe Street (near the Tamar Bridge)

After starting the Bridge Brewery, George Westcombe transferred the business to his sons, but retained ownership of the property. During the 1850s one of the sons, Daniel, advertised with some pride 'Superior Colonial Brewed Pale India Ale and Best Stout'.

George, the father, died in 1858, and the other son, George Jnr, ran the business until 1860. The brewery buildings and considerable land holdings were auctioned.

Burton Brewery
See Wharf Brewery.

Caledonian Brewery 1829–40
Another early brewer in Australia's third-oldest city was Newman Williatt, an ex-postmaster who brewed a table ale said to be superior to London porter.

After a year or so Williatt sold his Caledonian Brewery to Robert Towers, a distiller of some note, but he lasted as a brewer for about a year.

David McGowan then purchased the brewery. His Entire was 'confidently recommended' in editorials, but the property and 2000 acres of best grazing land were sold at auction in 1840.

Cape's Brewery 1873
John Cape's attempt at brewing was a failure. His brewery consisted of nothing more than a shed at the wharf, which he rented from the Trustees Savings Bank.

Cascade Group Ltd
See Cascade Brewery Co. Ltd, Hobart; Esk Brewery.

Cataract Brewery 1835–91
79 Patterson Street

James Kirk built a brewery in 1834 with the sole purpose of gaining rental income. The scenic location was at the head of the Tamar, fronting the river and close to Cataract Gorge. Kirk tried to rent the brewery but, because there was no interest, in 1835 he decided to start brewing himself. He was a farmer, not a brewer, and after a few months he was fortunate in finding a lessee, James Gerrard. The name of the brewery was the Cataract, although Gerrard's Brewery was commonly used.

By 1838 Gerrard was trying to sublet the brewery. He had a pawnbroking business, and ran into trouble from time to time, having to pay fines for various reasons. In 1843 he decided to leave the pawnbroking business and concentrate on brewing. Still in financial difficulty, James Gerrard was chased by creditors, and there were several court actions.

The Cataract Brewery was bought at auction in 1845 by William Sackville Turner for £725. Turner also owned the Cornwall Brewery that he was leasing to James Fawns. The Cornwall happened to back onto the Cataract Brewery, and Turner, an investor rather than a brewer, set about finding a lessee for the Cataract Brewery. Although he was asking for only a modest rental, Turner had no response. Heavily in debt, he was declared bankrupt in 1848, and both the Cornwall and Cataract breweries were put up for auction.

Some time later Edward French became the owner of the Cataract Brewery. He had purchased the premises of the old Tasmanian Brewery that John Williams had started and closed in 1832, and these premises were apparently used in conjunction with the operation of the Cataract. French died in 1864 at the age of thirty-six, and again the brewery was put up for auction without attracting a single bid.

The following year George Glenwright, previously the licensee of the Prince Albert Hotel, bought the brewery and ran it for the next twelve years. A fatal accident occurred in May 1866 when a workman

Labels for two of the brands from J. Boag & Son Esk River Brewery.

James Kirk	1835
James Gerrard (lessee)	1835–45
William Turner	1845
Edward French	1855–64
George Glenwright	1865–77
John Glenwright	1877–80
Glenwright & Boag	1880–82
John Glenwright	1882–84
Glenwright & Rockliff	1884
John Glenwright	1884–91
William Abbott	1891

Label from John Fawns's Cornwall Brewery, Launceston, c. 1882. It was started in 1827 by John Fawns Snr, who ran the brewery until his death in 1881. The son, also John, took over at that time, but eight years later he sold the brewery to the Esk Brewery, Launceston.

The Australian coat of arms, or a stylised version, was a popular label motif used by many breweries of the nineteenth century.

slipped into a vat of boiling wort. He was dragged out and stripped, tearing away skin with the clothing, and his body was rubbed with linseed oil and flour. He died in hospital fourteen hours later, leaving a wife and five small children.

By 1877 the brewery was owned by George Glenwright's estate, and the son, John, was running the business. James Boag Jnr was a partner from 1880 to 1882, and Roger Rockliff during 1884, otherwise John Glenwright operated the brewery by himself.

The brewery was taken over in 1891 by William Abbott, presumably for the equipment, since he had built a new and larger Phoenix Brewery on a site, still in Patterson Street, at the rear of the Phoenix cordial works.

Clark, Richard c. 1818

Richard Clark can be given the credit of being the first person to brew beer in Van Diemen's Land. The location of his 'home brewery' was at Patterson's Plains (now the Launceston suburb of St Leonards). Clark brewed sufficient only for himself and his friends.

Cornwall Brewery 1827–89
Margaret & Patterson Streets

When John Fawns started brewing in 1827, he worked in a small shed on the Esplanade. In his opinion, the water from the North Esk River was unsuitable for brewing, so he arranged for fresh water to be brought down-river in shallow-bottomed barges from Cataract Gorge, about a mile upstream. In 1845 the investor, William Turner, bought the brewery and leased it back to Fawns.

About this time Turner purchased the Cataract Brewery, which backed onto the Cornwall Brewery. Within a year or so Turner was desperately trying to resell both breweries, but became bankrupt in 1848.

> ### TAP FROM THE TOP
>
> Cause of Sour Beer: By actual experiment, it has been found that beer taken from the centre of a cask of beer is sound and good; but when taken from the bottom, where the liquor was in immediate contact with the wood, it was sour.
>
> There was only one inference possible and that was that the pores of the wood of which the cask was made were full of acidity and foul ferments and that the beer immediately in contact with the sides went sour at once, while that in the centre of the cask, for a time remained sound.
>
> Bottlers may have had trouble from the same source and wondered what was the matter with their beer when several boxes [casks] were good and the remainder sour. This can only be overcome by thorough enamelling of the casks and the bottler should call the attention of his brewer to this fact when once discovered.
>
> *Australian Brewers' Journal*, April 1893

The Cataract and Cornwall breweries were passed in at auction, but the Cataract was ultimately sold and continued in business. The Cornwall was leased to the partners, Britton Jones and Richard Wallis, but Jones left after a few months. Wallis stayed on, as his lease was for ten years. Following his death, the unexpired lease period of four years was auctioned, together with a large quantity of brewing equipment and stock.

John George Fawns became the lessee again in 1854. Two years later he purchased the Cornwall Brewery and employed James Boag (later of Esk Brewery fame) as the brewer, and ultimately the manager. Boag stayed with the company for close to thirty years.

John Fawns Snr died in 1881, and his son, John J. S. Fawns, took control. He formed a partnership with William Abbott in 1886, and they traded as Fawns & Abbott, Cornwall Brewery, until 1889, when the brewery was purchased by the Esk Brewery and closed shortly after.

John Fawns	1827–45
John Fawns (lessee)	1845–48
Jones & Wallis (lessee)	1848–48
Richard Wallis (lessee)	1848–54
John Fawns (lessee)	1854–56
John Fawns (owner)	1856–81
John J. S. Fawns	1881–86
Fawns & Abbott	1886–89
Purchased by the Esk Brewery	1889

Ditcham, Button & Co. 1858–78
St John & York Streets

Edward Ditcham was an experienced brewer, and he joined Charles Stammers Button in a partnership that was to last twenty years. Button had just left the Launceston Brewery, and together they built a new brewery and traded as Ditcham, Button & Co.

The company also traded as general merchants, with a timber yard and a well-equipped joinery, leasing the premises from John Cameron Trustees. The brewery made a range of products, including strong and bitter ales, a double-brown stout, Red Label ale, and a non-intoxicating Blue Label East India pale ale.

A fire completely destroyed the brewery in May 1866, and the flames could be seen as far away as Westbury and Longford. After rebuilding on the same site, the partners were back in business, but decided to stop brewing in 1878.

Esk Brewery
See J. Boag & Son Esk River Brewery

Fawkner, John Pascoe c. 1828

Although largely self-educated, John Pascoe Fawkner became a leading citizen of Launceston. In his time he was a hotelkeeper (the Cornwall Hotel), unofficial lawyer, newspaper proprietor, librarian, money lender, and part-owner of a brewery that was part of the hotel.

John Pascoe Fawkner is generally credited with being the founder of Melbourne. Although John Batman had arrived at Port Phillip Bay from Van Diemen's Land some months earlier, Fawkner's settlement in 1835 was the more permanent.

Fawns Brewery
See Cornwall Brewery.

Gerrard's Brewery
See Cataract Brewery.

Houghton, James 1828–29
Brisbane Street

James Houghton was the proprietor of the Globe Tavern. He advertised his wares in the *Hobart Town Courier* of 2 February 1828, thanking his patrons for their support and advising of his latest shipment. He could now offer

> choice Cape Madeira and Catalonia wine, by the pipe or the gallon, full-proof Jamaica rum and cognac brandy. Also home brewed beer by the cask or gallon. Saddle horses and neat chaise for hire at any hour and good entertainment for man and horse.

There was no mention as to what was the entertainment for the horse!

The following year, the whole business was on the market, including a 'Needham's Patent Brewing Machine and all appurtenances'. He begged to state that his sole reason for selling was his wish to retire with his family.

Launceston Brewery 1824–58
Margaret Street North (on the Tamar River)

Shortly after arriving at Hobart Town from England in 1824 William Barnes moved to Launceston. He received a substantial land grant that year, and began brewing not long after, using the name Port Dalrymple Brewery. He produced a heavy malt liquor made from Tasmanian barley and wheat, and it was said that a pewter pot of his brew was as good as a square meal.

William Barnes wrote many letters back to England to his brother-in-law, William Manifold, the first of which, relating to the brewery, was dated 15 March 1824. He wrote:

> I am building a small brewery which will cost about £200. There is in this town a population of about 1,100 souls and no brewery in the place.

He added that beer was shipped down from Sydney, and some came up from Hobart, and that the selling price was around £9 per hogshead. He figured that he could produce beer for £2, and by selling it even at £6 there was a tidy profit to be made.

Further letters from Barnes, late in 1824, informed his brother-in-law that 'I am doing so well that I am afraid to tell you for fear you would not believe me'. Barnes, however, was short of capital, and paid his assistant, William Robertson, a share of the profits instead of a salary.

The business expanded rapidly, and Barnes decided to lease the brewery to Williams & Waddell in 1835, followed by William Button and Jonathon Waddell in 1839. The name was changed to the Launceston Brewery.

Charles Stammers Button, son of William, operated the brewery from 1853 to 1858, and then left to start another brewery in York Street with his friend, Edward Ditcham (Ditcham, Button & Co.).

The Launceston Brewery was then vacant, and the owner, William Barnes, must have sold the property shortly after. It was operating as a shipyard in 1865.

McDiarmid, John 1829–30

John McDiarmid arrived from Scotland in 1824, and took over the Cornwall Hotel from John Pascoe Fawkner in 1828. There was a small brewery at the hotel.

In 1830 he was fined £10 for selling ginger beer without a licence. Actually, he was a licensed victualler and was openly selling ginger beer, probably alcoholic, around the town. Someone had reported him for delivering short measure, and the matter ended up in court.

Phoenix Brewery 1891–1900
79 Patterson Street

William Abbott purchased the Cataract Brewery from John Glenwright in 1891 and built a new brewery on the site, which was at the rear of the Phoenix cordial factory. The new brewery, called the Phoenix, was an impressive six storeys high, and was fitted out with the latest equipment, including an aerating plant, the first of its kind in the colony.

The Phoenix Brewery opened for business on 1 October 1891, and quickly gained a high reputation for its ales and stout. At the Tasmanian Exhibition of 1891–92 William Abbott won First Award for his Bottled Ale, Second Award for Light Running Beer on Draught, and First Award for Ale on Draught. He also brewed a non-alcoholic Dandelion Ale that was 'Good for the liver and kidneys, purifies the blood and assists digestion'.

The Phoenix Brewery was the first brewery in Tasmania to adopt the eight hours' system of employment, and a Saturday half-holiday.

At the turn of the century it was decided to discontinue brewing and to concentrate on the production of soft drinks.

Port Dalrymple Brewery
See Launceston Brewery.

Rayner, James 1832
Charles Street

James Rayner was selling his 'Superior Ale' for between 1s 6d and 2s per gallon. He also had a cooperage that may have kept him in business, since nothing further is known about his brewing activity.

Right: *Tasmanian Co-operative Brewery Co. Ltd, Union Brewery, York Street, Launceston, c. 1910.*

Royal Brewery 1852–54
Wellington Street

Ale — Ale —Ale. Good Wholesome XXX to be had at the Royal Hotel for 6 pence a quart, out of doors for persons bringing their own vessels. I am not in the habit of puffing, but I mean to say my ale is the best in Launceston.

In those days 'puffing' meant boasting, and the advertisement was put in the *Examiner* of 18 September 1852 by the owner of the Royal Hotel & Brewery, Benjamin Hyrons. He was also the owner of the Freemason's Hotel in Georgetown.

Because of ill health, Hyrons advertised his hotel and brewery for lease at £6 per week. Edward Knight rented the brewery during 1853 and 1854, and James Clydesdale followed later in 1854.

Sydney Place Brewery 1847–58

A compact little malthouse and brewery belonging to James Smith was offered to let in 1847. Smith had been making 'colonial bottled ale', but had decided to return to England.

A. O. Gordon continued at the Sydney Place Brewery for some time, and then John Raven bought the brewery. He also owned the store next door to the brewery, and sold both in 1858.

Tamar Brewery 1855–1917
Charles Street (fronting the Tamar River)

John Scott served in both houses of parliament during his political career in Tasmania. He was born in Hobart, and was left an orphan at the age of ten. As a young man he went to Launceston, where he worked at John Fawns's Cornwall Brewery, and later at the Wharf Brewery.

In 1855 John Scott joined his future father-in-law, John Griffiths, and the partnership traded as John Scott & Co., Tamar Brewery.

Griffiths had interests in milling, whaling and shipbuilding. In 1864 he built the ship called the *Bitter Beer*, but, sadly, the ship and two of his sons were lost at sea.

John Scott was the first to produce bottled beer in Launceston, and his corks were branded Scott & Co.'s Tasmanian Ale. Bitter ale and stout were also supplied in casks, as well as in bottles.

By 1872 the Tamar Brewery was quite impressive, with substantial buildings and facilities covering a large area. Thomas Griffiths became a partner in 1873; the business then traded as Scott & Griffiths.

Years later the brewery was running below capacity. The cause was said to be 'a combination of general poverty, excessive competition and lack of promotion'. After brewing for sixty-two years the Tamar Brewery was purchased by the Esk Brewery in 1917, and closed.

Tasmanian Breweries Pty Ltd
See Cascade Brewery Co. Ltd, Hobart.

Tasmanian Brewery 1832
John F. Williams began brewing in 1832, but left for Sydney five months later and told his creditors to send their bills to his accountant. Some years later the premises were used by the Cataract Brewery.

Tasmanian Co-operative Brewery Co. Ltd 1908–31
214 York Street

Subscribers to the newly-formed company were mostly hotelkeepers from Launceston and other Tasmanian towns. Although the company was registered as the Tasmanian Co-operative Brewery Co. Ltd, it was also known as the Union Brewery.

In 1911 J. Boag & Son Ltd took over, and continued to operate as the Union Brewery. By the middle of 1912 the company was in liquidation, but managed to reconstruct and continued to brew for another nineteen years.

Towers Brewery c. 1838–c. 1850
Lyttleton Street

Before starting their brewery the Towers brothers, Robert and James, had been distilling whisky that they sold for 8s a gallon. Robert had gained some brewing experience when he worked at the Caledonian Brewery in 1830, and now, at their own brewery, the brothers did reasonably well for twelve years or so.

Union Brewery (Lyttleton Street) 1835–c. 1840
Lyttleton Street

During 1835, perhaps earlier, John Adams started his brewery. He tried to sell it privately the following year. The best he could do was to lease it to James Hearn, who was joined by Walter Cousens for a brief period. It is quite possible that the brewery was taken over by the Towers brothers.

Label for the Tasmanian Co-operative Brewery Co. Ltd.

Union Brewery (York Street)
See Tasmanian Co-operative Brewery Co. Ltd.

Wharf Brewery 1841–59
St John Street

When brewing commenced, the partners were William Colyer and George Lukin, but after two years Lukin was running the Wharf Brewery on his own. He had been the lessee of the Derwent Brewery in the mid-1830s. When George Lukin died in 1849, his widow, Mary Ann, ran the business with the assistance of her brewer and manager, John Scott, of later Tamar Brewery fame.

Thomas Saunders leased the brewery in 1856 and changed the name to the Burton Brewery. Three months later, on 14 May, he left, and the lease was taken over by William Evans. The Burton Brewery never traded under that name, and the new lessee continued to operate as the Wharf Brewery. Evans had been a prominent baker and general merchant in Launceston, certainly not a brewer, and after another three months he also left.

The brewery property was still owned by Mary Ann Lukin, and another lease was granted to William Brown and his son, William Jnr. The son was running the brewery at the time it closed in 1859. The premises were later sold to Archibald & Jackson, and then to a teetotaller, a Mr Shield, who converted the brewery into a coffee palace.

Colyer & Lukin	1841–43
George Lukin	1843–49
Mary Lukin	1849–56
Thomas Saunders (lessee)	1856
William Evans (lessee)	1856
W. Brown & Son (lessee)	1856–59
William Brown Jnr (lessee)	1859

Wilson, Thomas 1831–34

Thomas Wilson stepped off the *Greenock* in Hobart on 3 January 1828. He was twenty-three years of age, and had brought with him £150 worth of implements and £900 in cash, a small fortune in those days. By 1831 he had started brewing at 'an old established brewery', possibly that of A. Aarons or J. Houghton or J. McDiarmid. All of those breweries had closed a year or two earlier.

Thomas Wilson had a somewhat cynical way of advertising his 'most superior article'. He was 'convinced that a good article is always cheap while the smallest coin is too much for the trash often sold as beer'.

The *Launceston Advertiser* of 29 May 1834 reported:

> A melancholy event took place early on Sunday morning last. A Mr Wilson, brewer, in a fit of insanity, attempted to put an end to his existence by cutting his throat with a razor. Medical assistance was speedily called and some hopes are entertained for his recovery.

Longford

First known as Norfolk Plains, Longford was officially named by Governor George Arthur in 1830.

Longford Brewery 1839–85
Wellington Street

Forty-six years was a long time for any country brewery to stay in business and to be owned by the one family. The brewery owner was Isaac Noake, and for much of the time it was referred to as Noake's Brewery. Isaac died in 1860, and his widow, Elizabeth, kept the business going. She was an enterprising lady, but she needed assistance for the day-to-day running of the brewery, and frequently advertised for experienced staff.

A distressing accident occurred at the brewery in September 1864, when a workman named Forster fell into a vat of boiling liquid. He was a steady, hardworking man with a wife and four small children, and there was no hope of his recovery. Later, the police arrived to witness the throwing away of the vat of ale in which Forster had been scalded, a necessary procedure to reassure customers that the ale would not be resold.

Elizabeth Noake had problems of a different kind in 1872 when the South Esk River flooded, and rose 12 feet. All hands worked through the night and the next day to remove goods to higher ground, and, after the flood had subsided, to clear up the mess, and to start brewing again.

It was a proud time for Mrs Noake when, in 1879, she won a prize for her bottled ale at the Sandhurst Exhibition in Bendigo, Victoria, but by then she was thinking of retiring. She rented the brewery to Frederick Webb in 1879, and by 1882 she was advertising the whole property for sale, including the brewery.

Mrs Mary Davis purchased the property in 1885, but brewing had ceased. Four years later the brewery was completely destroyed by fire.

Noake's Brewery
See Longford Brewery.

Lymington

Ayton, George 1863

George Ayton had worked at the Longford Brewery, and decided to move south to the small township of Lymington on the Port Cygnet Estuary. His attempt at running his own brewery lasted a year.

Mangalore

The small township of Mangalore, originally known as Black Brush, lies about 30 km north of Hobart, on the north side of the Derwent River.

Perriman's Brewery c. 1850–63

G. L. Perriman settled at Mangalore about 1850, and developed a substantial estate with servants' quarters, two stables and a large orchard. Many of the larger estates during Australia's pioneering days were self-sufficient — everything was grown and raised on the property — and Perriman's spread was a typical example. He had all the farm animals, vegetables and fruit, a carpenter's shop, blacksmith's shop, granary and a brewhouse.

Perriman's Brewery supplied the needs of his family, friends, relatives, staff and neighbours — where supplies of beer from the breweries of distant towns were infrequent and costly. The brewing of beer at pastoral and cattle stations, particularly those in remote areas, was relatively common, and frequently no brewing licences were applied for, and therefore there were no official listings in public records.

New Norfolk

New Norfolk is in the Derwent Valley, 35 km northwest of Hobart. When the Norfolk Island colony, off the coast of New South Wales, was closed in 1813, many of the inhabitants shifted to the Derwent Valley district, hence the name New Norfolk.

Cawthorn's Brewery c. 1820

John Henry Cawthorn arrived in Van Diemen's Land in 1818, and was soon working an inn, a brewery and a ferry service, in much the same manner as James Austin, who had a similar set-up beside the Derwent River, 20 km downstream at Austin's Ferry. Brewing became too much trouble for Cawthorn, and was soon discontinued.

Derwent Brewery

See New Norfolk Brewery.

Mann's Brewery 1855–60
Humphrey Street

After working his brewery for five years, Anthony Mann was declared insolvent.

Martin, John 1831–35

John Martin owned stables, a blacksmith's shop, butcher's shop, offices and a brewhouse, all of which were for sale. He bought the Star & Garter Hotel and Brewery, but he put it up for auction in 1835. He then moved on to become the licensee of the Ordnance Arms Hotel and, later, the British Hotel.

New Norfolk Brewery 1823–40

The brewery, which was started by Major Henry Oakes in 1823, was located at the 'Falls' of the Derwent River.

In 1834 Oakes sold the brewery to G. Cope, who advertised in the *Hobart Trumpeter* that he was ready to supply ale and beer 'far superior to any to be got in the colony … the water used is taken from the Derwent … free from impregnations of mineral substances'.

Cope died six years later, and at that time the brewery name was changed from the New Norfolk to the Derwent Brewery, but apparently brewing ceased very soon after.

Oatlands

The classified historic town of Oatlands has the greatest number of sandstone buildings in a village situation in Australia, and is said to have the largest collection of pre-1837 buildings in Australia.

Horehound grew profusely around the Oatlands area, and was used as an essential ingredient for the beer brewed in the district.

Albion Brewery 1844

The brewer, E. Barwick, was a member of the Barwick family who owned a number of hotels in the district.

Boreham, J. E. 1840

John Boreham had worked at the Derwent Brewery for about a year, and then shifted to Oatlands where he began brewing again at Carrington Mill, north of the town.

Kentish Brewery 1854–59

William and Joseph Barwick brewed at the family-owned Kentish Hotel for five years.

Much later, William Barwick took out a lease on the local Oatlands Brewery from the owner, Samuel Page, for a period of eight years.

Oatlands Brewery 1835–81
High Street

The first brewer in the town of Oatlands was Joseph McEwan, who brewed at the Inverary Castle Inn owned by Samuel Page. McEwan tried unsuccessfully to sublet the brewery in 1838, and therefore had to continue paying rent to the owner.

Samuel Page also owned the Oatlands Hotel, and when brewing operations were shifted to that location a succession of lessees followed:

Henry Coop	1854–56
John Bailey	1856–63
Robert & Esther Spencer	1866–67
Edwin Currie	1869
William Barwick	1871–79
John Bailey	1879–81
George Bagley	1881

At the Oatlands Hotel and Brewery, when a new brew was 'on', a keg of the beer would be placed outside the door and a mug was fixed to the keg for potential customers to sample the brew.

Following the death of the owner, Samuel Page, the hotel and brewery were put up for auction by his widow in 1880; the lessee at the time was John Bailey.

Just before the brewery closed, George Bagley made a final attempt to keep it going.

Royal Hotel Brewery 1855

Edward Knight was brewing at the Royal Hotel, left a pile of debts, and disappeared. Ten years earlier he had been imprisoned for twelve months for stealing a spade.

Perth

Esk Brewery

See Perth Brewery.

Perth Brewery 1856–80

Edward Sherwood started the brewery in 1856, and was joined by George Ingram a few years later.

Many changes in ownership followed. When William East, owner of the Fingal Brewery in Fingal and former owner of the Tasmanian Brewery in Evandale, was running the Perth Brewery, he won prizes for his bottled ale and porter at the Sandhurst Exhibition in Bendigo, Victoria. Unfortunately, East was declared bankrupt in 1880.

During the life of the Perth Brewery it was frequently called the Esk Brewery.

Edward Sherwood	1856–58
Sherwood & Ingram	1858–59
George Ingram	1859–66
William East & John Sidebottom (lessees)	1866–78
William East	1878–80

Whitchurch, William 1826–57
Charles Street

William Whitchurch was an auctioneer and butcher, and then a brewer at a property known as Belle Vue near the South Esk River. In 1830 he advertised, for sale at his residence in Charles Street, 'Colonial Beer by the hogshead or in quantities not less than five gallons'. He was declared insolvent in 1849, but was back brewing again in 1855 at Clifton, near Perth, for two more years.

Richmond

The settlement of Richmond, named in 1824, is arguably the best-known of Tasmania's historic villages. The many beautiful sandstone buildings that survive were built by convict labour. The Richmond Bridge, also built by convicts, is the oldest bridge in Australia still in use, and is a popular tourist attraction.

Bridge Hotel & Brewery 1855–57

The brewery was at the back of the Bridge Hotel, and the owner, Daniel Murphy, brewed for only two years. He then bought his beer from other brewers.

Richmond Brewery 1845–53

This was another of the many hotels that brewed beer, to be sold to customers across the counter of their hotels. Most soon found that it was not such a good proposition, and went back to buying their beer from established breweries.

The Richmond Brewery lasted longer than most. It was attached to the Lennox Arms Inn and, according to the *Colonial Times* of March 1845, the owner, Thomas Ockerby, produced 'Excellent beer, a clean, wholesome, palatable beverage, a hundred to one better than the miserable slop called tea'.

Woodburn Brewery 1830–34

The Woodburn estate, which bordered the tiny township of Woodburn, also had a broad frontage to the Coal River. The many buildings on the property included a brewery that was operated by Gilbert Robertson about 1830. A few years later William Stallard was doing the brewing, but by 1834 brewing had stopped and the brewery building was offered for sale.

Scottsdale

Scottsdale Brewery 1883–95
Ringarooma Road (near Tucker's Corner)

For Charles Stammers Button, making beer and running a brewery was his business, and he was very good at both. Early in his career he had been the owner-operator of the Launceston Brewery. This was followed by a twenty-year partnership with Edward Ditcham in a brewery they had built in York Street, Launceston.

In 1879 Button built the Esk Brewery, unaware that it would become part of the largest brewing company in Tasmania.

Charles Button sold his Esk Brewery to James Boag and his son in 1882. The following year he moved to Scottsdale, and built another brewery and also a cordial factory in Ringarooma Road. He sent word to the township of Devonport for his son and daughter to join him. The distance from Devonport to Scottsdale is 170 km, and the condition of the mountain tracks in those days led to the journey taking the greater part of three and a half days.

During the late 1870s Charles Button built a cordial factory in Spreyton, a few kilometres south of Devonport. When brewing started there in 1881, his son, Edmund, was left in charge. Two years later, when he was asked to join his father at Scottsdale, the Spreyton Brewery was leased.

Edmund Button worked long hours for his father at the Scottsdale Brewery. He started at four in the morning, winter and summer, and delivered beer as far as Weldborough and Alberton, along treacherous muddy tracks in high mountain country. The father and son brewed bottled ale, strong XXX and light body, and held a virtual monopoly on the beer trade in those areas, since there were no other breweries anywhere near the districts.

Sorell

Downard, Richard   1826–44
Richard Downard was a farmer and flourmiller at Pitt Water, and in between these activities he found time to brew small quantities of beer until his retirement in 1844.

Reardon's Brewery   1824–79
On the Forcett River, Greenhills, Pitt Water District

During the life of the brewery, ownership remained with members of the Reardon family. The brewery was started by Bartholomew Reardon in 1824 and was offered for sale in 1832. Since there were no buyers Mrs Elizabeth Reardon continued as the owner, and her son, Edward, as the manager.

For a few months in 1847 Samuel Iles and Charles Cue leased the brewery, but after they left the brewery was idle for some years.

Edward Reardon started up again, and in 1858 Sam Parsons leased the brewery. He married Elizabeth Reardon in 1864, and ultimately Edward became the owner of the brewery.

For the last two years George Hayton was the lessee.

Sorell Brewery   1846–48
The small brewery was attached to the Gordon Highlander Inn, and the owner, Mrs Elizabeth Willis, leased the brewery section to Jonathon Watson.

Spreyton

Devon Brewery   1881–95
When Charles Stammers Button, of Launceston brewing fame, moved to Spreyton in 1879, he started in business as a manufacturer of cordials and aerated waters, using the name Devon Steam Factory. Brewing commenced in 1881, and his son, Edmund, was put in charge. They called it the Spreyton Brewery.

Edmund Button left in 1883 to help his father, who had set up a brewery at Scottsdale. The Spreyton Brewery and cordial factory was then leased for the next five years to several lessees, the last being William Devine and his wife, Mary, who changed the name to the Devon Brewery in 1888.

The following year Richard Jamieson advised the public that he was the sole proprietor of the business and that all monies had to be paid to him.

There were a number of changes in ownership in 1889 and 1890, the second-last being Charles Forrester, who purchased 'the old established Devon Brewery and will shortly be able to supply ale, beer and stout in bulk and in bottles'. Unfortunately, Forrester had little opportunity to supply very much of his ales and beer, since he died early the following year.

The last person to run the brewery was Frederick Barnes. The brewery was close to the Mersey River, and it was often referred to as the Mersey Brewery.

Spreyton Brewery
Charles Button	1881–84
William Metcalf (lessee)	1884–85
Edwin Cleaver (lessee)	1885–88

Devon Brewery
W. E. & M. Devine (lessee)	1888–89
Richard Jamieson	1889
Allen & Kellam	1889
Crick & Kellam	1889–90
Albert Kellam	1890
Charles Forrester	1890–91
Frederick Barnes	1891–95

Mersey Brewery
See Devon Brewery.

Spreyton Brewery
See Devon Brewery.

Stanley

Stanley Brewery   1855–74
Rougemont Street

Robert Nunn started brewing at the coastal town of Stanley in 1855. His son, Allen, became a partner, and by 1860 they were trading as R. & A. Nunn. The father wanted to retire about 1861, but kept working for nine more years after the property failed to sell.

Allen Nunn ran the brewery by himself for the last four years.

Strahan

Cascade Brewery Co. Ltd   1899
The Hobart-based Cascade Brewery Co. Ltd built a cordial factory at Strahan. It was intended to be a brewery, and if beer was brewed at Strahan it would have been for a very brief period. W. J. Gee was the manager.

Swansea

This is the sad story of a brewery that had been well planned but, through tragic circumstances, never started.

This Devon Brewery label, Spreyton, was used during the brief Crick & Kellam partnership, 1889–90. Note the central motif of a platypus.

Thomas Large had been the licensee of the Royal Oak Hotel in Hobart. He moved to Swansea in 1850, and purchased the old Swansea Inn, intending to convert into a brewery.

The *Hobart Town Courier* of 11 November 1850 reported:

> WRECKS: We regret to announce a melancholy occurrence which took place last Monday week at Oyster Bay, near Swansea. The wind was blowing high at the time and the cutter, 'Resolution', hence for Swan Port, with Mr and Mrs Large and six children varying in age from 2 to 12 years, and a cargo comprising articles for establishing a brewery at Swan Port, on board, was totally wrecked, the whole of the goods and the lives of the six children falling a sacrifice to the ruthless elements. We hear that so sudden was the catastrophe, the poor father, who was formerly a publican in Hobart Town and has now lost his all, had barely time to escape himself and that he was insensible for several hours after being thrown on shore by the surf. How Mrs Large escaped has not correctly transpired …

A convict servant gained his freedom for attempting to rescue one of the children. Mr and Mrs Large returned to Hobart, and subsequently raised seven more children.

Hurst, James 1861
James Hurst built the Pier Hotel at Swansea in the mid-1850s at a cost of £3500. He brewed there for a short period, and advertised 'English and Good Cape Barley'.

Waratah

There was a brewery under construction at Waratah in 1876, but no further details are known. Tin had been discovered in the district, but the population at the time was only 300.

Westbury

Lyall's Brewery 1864–87
King Street

The brewery had been started by Robert Lyall in 1864, but for the next twenty-three years it was closed for much of the time.

William Webb leased the brewery in 1880, and then Alexander Duncan in 1887.

Westbury Brewery 1854–64
William Street

Moore Simmons, the owner of the Westbury Brewery, tried to lease it soon after it was built. He finally sold the brewery to Jessie Pullen, who in turn leased it to Alfred Edmeades in 1856. Alfred was joined by his brother, Henry Edmeades, but the brewery closed not long after.

Wynyard

Wynyard Brewery 1864–81
The Esplanade

The Wynyard Brewery was started by John Quinn in 1864. He sold out the following year to Joseph Alexander who brewed from 1865 to 1872, with J. Garner assisting in 1868. John Durant was the occupier in 1872, Honoria Jones in 1877, and finally Andrew Rubock for the last four years.

Zeehan

Cowburn, Thomas c. 1890–c. 1895
Thomas Cowburn had worked with his father, William, at the Jolly Hatters Brewery in Hobart. With his wife and six children, Thomas moved to Zeehan and began brewing there about 1890. Within two years the brewery was one of the biggest assets of the mining district, supplying most of the sixteen hotels in the town at that time.

The miners at Zeehan were a thirsty lot, and the *Zeehan and Dundas Herald* of 4 November 1896 gave this account:

> On the Dundas line last night, driver Baillie and guard Smith averted what would have been a most sensational rail-road disaster. When approaching the brewing junction, the keen eyes of the guardians of the train were struck by an inanimate form peacefully reposing in the middle of the track. The engines were promptly reversed to avert running over the obstruction. It was found that the obstacle was a human being entitled William Hawkes. The danger of his position was intimated to the recumbent form. The only answer was, 'Fill 'em up again', so the careful railway officials rolled him to one side and the train resumed its journey.

Northern Territory

Nobody seemed to be interested in the Northern Territory. It had been annexed to South Australia in 1863, and before that it was part of New South Wales. From 1911 it was administered by the federal government. Finally, in 1978, the Northern Territory was given self-government.

Many names had been suggested for the Territory, such as Alexandra Land and Prince Albert Land. During World War II there was a proposal to name it Churchill Land, and in 1954, when Queen Elizabeth II visited Australia, there were advocates for the name Elizabeth. In spite of all the suggestions and proposals, the name Northern Territory has prevailed.

Settlement

The first British settlements in the Northern Territory were made at Melville Island in 1824 and Port Essington in 1838; but both were abandoned. Port Darwin was discovered in 1839 by John Stokes who named the harbour after his good friend and famous naturalist, Charles Darwin.

The area remained unexplored until 1869 when Surveyor-General George Goyder selected a site on the Port Darwin shore, and sent his men to find water, cut timber, plant vegetables and carry out preliminary surveys. Within three months the new infant township, called Palmerston, was ready for settlers, but few came. After Goyder and his team left, only forty-three inhabitants remained.

Streets in the settlement had been named by George Goyder after the surveyors in his party. Bennett Street was named after an unfortunate draughtsman, who was speared to death by Aboriginals three months after his arrival. Smith Street, now part of the Mall, was named after the surveyor in charge of the many survey parties sent out from Palmerston. Gradually, the township became known as Darwin, and officially so in 1911.

The overland telegraph from Darwin to Adelaide, a distance of 3200 km, was completed in 1872.

Although development of the Darwin township was slow, private and commercial buildings began to emerge, and government offices were built along the Esplanade. By the end of 1874 the population had grown to about 1700 Europeans, of which only fifty were women.

Disasters

Darwin has suffered three major disasters. The first occurred in 1897 when a cyclone swept the area, leaving very few buildings undamaged and completely destroying the trees for a considerable distance.

The next disaster was in 1942 when Darwin became the first Australian city to be attacked by an outside enemy force. The Japanese bombing raids, which continued for ten months, resulted in considerable loss of life and the destruction of much of the city. Rebuilding was slow, but by the 1970s the city was well established and expanding rapidly. Then, within the time span of a single day, that progress was tragically halted.

On Christmas Day 1974 the fury of Cyclone Tracy destroyed 90 per cent of Darwin's buildings, and killed 50 people. Within three days, after the largest evacuation in Australia's history, only 11,000 of the city's 47,000 population remained to clean up the mess and begin the task of rebuilding.

The First Brewery

The population of Darwin had been too small during the nineteenth and early twentieth centuries for a brewery to be a viable proposition. There were only 3300 European inhabitants in the whole territory in 1911, including less than 1000 in Darwin.

The first brewery in the Northern Territory was at Alice Springs, a tiny settlement at that time, located 1500 km south of Darwin, and with practically no habitation in between. It was called the Alice Springs Brewery, and the owner was Thomas Gunter.

The township of Alice Springs was not expanding, the population was a mere handful, and Gunter's brewery closed after a few years.

Darwin Breweries

Apart from Thomas Gunter's brief brewing endeavour in Alice Springs, there have been no other breweries anywhere in the Northern Territory, except for the capital city, Darwin.

The Territory's second commercial brewery was started by Harry Ellis-Kells at Darwin in 1950. Apparently very little beer was produced,

Although Darwin's first commercial brewery, the Ellis Kells Brewery, operated for only a year or so from 1950, some of the bottle labels that remain are among the most attractive in capturing the spirit of Aboriginal Australia.

The Darwin Stubby, the largest bottle of beer in Australia — and perhaps the world — was first introduced in Darwin in 1958. It then contained 80 fluid ounces of beer, later becoming 2.25 litres and later again 2 litres. People of the Northern Territory have been renowned as the thirstiest drinkers in the world — said to consume 230 litres of beer per head in a thirsty year. The record for drinking a Darwin Stubby was set in 1979 at 1 min. 2 secs.

and the brewery closed. The property, stock and all the equipment were auctioned in March 1952.

The Melbourne-based Carlton & United Breweries Ltd (CUB) began brewing in the Darwin suburb of Winnellie in 1957, one year before the Perth-based Swan Brewery, who started their Stuart Brewery at Parap, another Darwin suburb, in 1958. By 1973 there was only one brewery, following the merger of the Stuart Brewery with CUB's Darwin Brewery. Brewing ceased altogether in 1989, and the CUB premises at Winnellie have since been used as the company's depot. CUB commenced brewing again, in the suburb of Berrimah, in 1996.

The economy of the Northern Territory has been based mainly on the cattle industry, although more recently mining has increased in importance, following the discovery of uranium ore in 1948. Tourism has grown considerably with the opening of the Kakadu National Park, and also the building of tourist facilities at the world's largest rock, the legendary Uluru (formerly known as Ayers Rock), in the Uluru National Park. Brewing, however, has never been a major industry in the state.

The population of the Territory is now quite substantial, and with the rapidly-growing tourist industry there is an ever-increasing demand for beer. Shiploads, trainloads and truckloads of all manner of beers now pour into the Territory from all the other states of Australia.

Alice Springs

Alice Springs was originally gazetted under the name of Stuart, and was changed to Alice Springs in 1933. For most Australians, Alice Springs is the symbol of the centre of Australia, an oasis of civilisation in the vast arid expanses of central Australia.

Alice Springs Brewery   c. 1897–1900

Thomas Gunter, the owner of the Alice Springs Brewery, sent a letter to the editor of the *Australian Brewers' Journal*, which was published on 20 December 1897:

> This last winter, I started to brew on my own efforts having been disappointed so many times with brewers who drank too freely and neglected to carry out their work.

When the brewery was operating, the township consisted of three stores and Gunter's Hotel. Business was mainly dependent on travellers moving to and from the goldfields, 110 km away. David Hart was the proprietor of the Alice Springs Brewery when it closed in 1900.

Stanlake, Charles

Charles Stanlake of Scotts Hotel, Melbourne, submitted applications in 1945 for a brewer's licence and also for the construction of a brewery at Alice Springs. He was advised in January 1946 that it was not practicable to issue a permit for the building because of the post-war shortage of building materials.

Undaunted, Stanlake tried again early in 1947, this time to operate at Coomalie Creek, 100 km south of Darwin. The application was approved, and a prospectus issued, but the project did not proceed.

Darwin

Carlton & United Breweries Ltd
(Darwin Brewery)   1957–73; 1996–
Winnellie Road, Winnellie/Lilwall Road, Trade Development Zone East Arm, Berrimah

Carlton & United Breweries Ltd, Melbourne (CUB), had been well aware of the Perth-based Swan Brewery's interest in the Darwin market. By 1956 Swan had purchased five Darwin hotels, and owned a non-operating company called the Darwin Brewery Ltd.

According to Reg Fogarty, the general manager of CUB, Melbourne, at that time, 'if anyone is to start a brewery in Darwin, CUB will be the first'. The prediction came true with the formal establishment of the CUB's Darwin plant on 21 November 1957, one year ahead of Swan's Stuart Brewery Ltd. Although CUB was not the first company to be granted a brewer's licence in the Territory, nor the first actually to brew

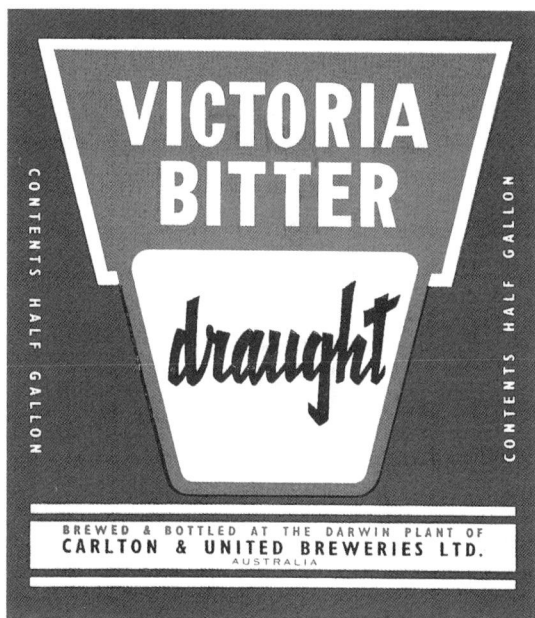

The first label used on the Darwin Stubby. The bottle held half a gallon (2.25 litres) of Victoria Bitter.

beer, it was the first commercial brewery to operate successfully in Darwin.

CUB had bought some secondhand brewing equipment for their proposed brewery in Fiji. Instead, it was sent up to Darwin to their small brewery at Winnellie. In the rush to be first, CUB discovered, at the opening ceremony of their modest Darwin Brewery, that the beer they had produced was completely flat — no sparkle at all. The embarrassed manager quickly had to order a crate of Scotch whisky to carry on the party.

The beer, however, was soon considered to be excellent by anyone's standard, and was quaffed in great quantities by ever-thirsty Territorians. In the course of time Darwin drinkers gained the reputation of consuming more beer per head than any other town or city in Australia — some said the world.

The famous Darwin Stubby was released in April 1958, and was an immediate success. It was the largest beer bottle in Australia, and believed to be the largest in the world. The giant-sized bottle contained 80 fluid ounces (2.25 litres), changing to 2 litres in 1983.

Meanwhile, the Swan Brewery of Perth had started their Stuart Brewery Ltd, Darwin, in 1958. The venture was never successful, in spite of the fact that the company owned almost all the hotels in Darwin. There wasn't enough business to support two breweries in Darwin, and on 1 April 1973 the Swan Brewery merged its Northern Territory interests with those of CUB, Darwin, to form N.T. Brewery Pty Ltd. Swan held a 49 per cent interest, and CUB 51 per cent. The new company acquired both breweries, five hotels owned by the Swan group, and one hotel owned by CUB.

The new company was to produce a new product called NT Lager, and also sell both Swan and Carlton beers, but the agreement meant the end of Swan in the Northern Territory. CUB took 95 per cent of the

Northern Territory

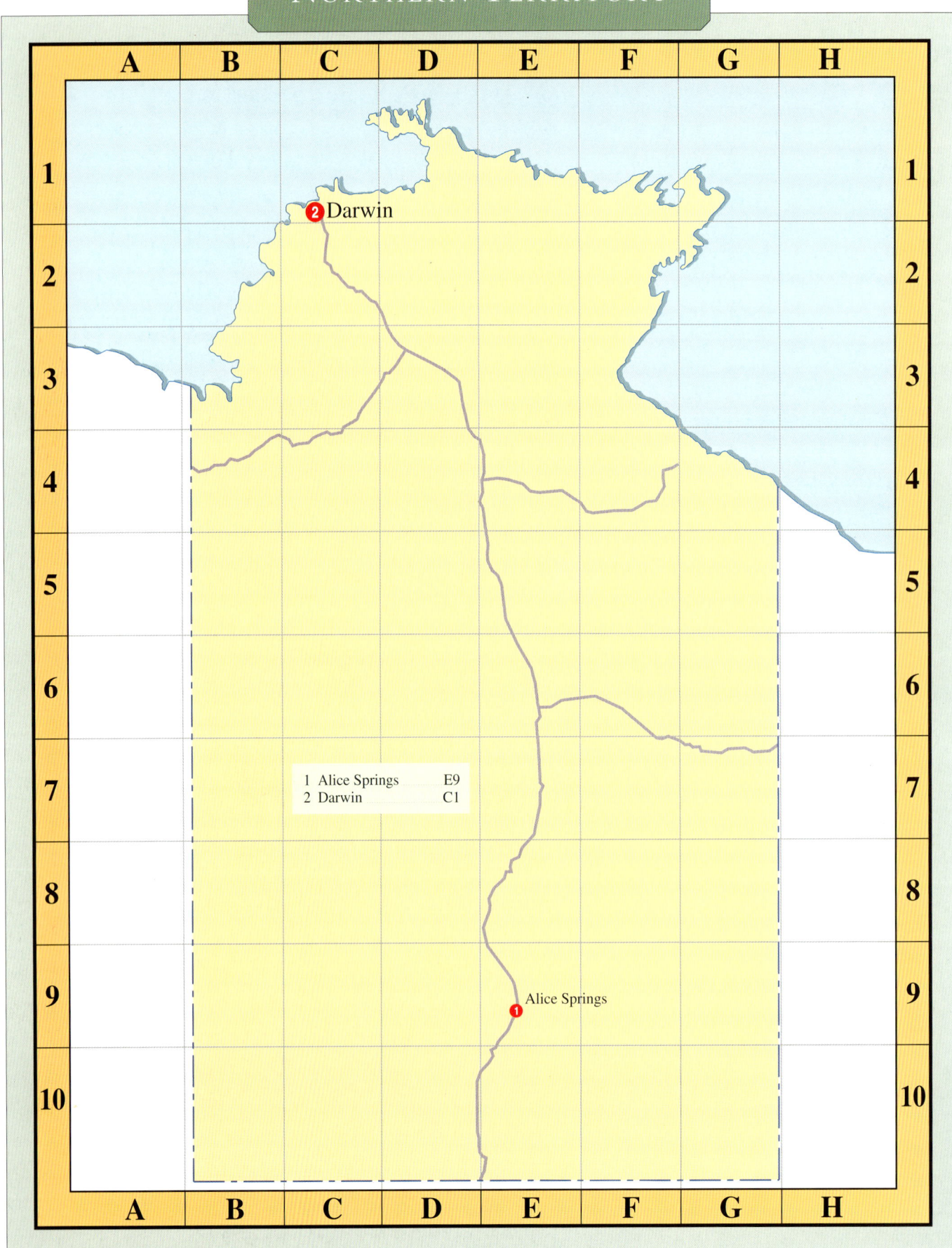

1 Alice Springs E9
2 Darwin C1

Many commemorative and other special labels have been used on Darwin Stubby bottles.

market, brewed its draught beer in the larger Stuart Brewery at Parap, and converted its Winnellie Brewery to a warehouse. By July 1982 N.T. Brewery Pty Ltd had become a wholly-owned subsidiary of CUB.

The company continued to brew its popular NT Draught until February 1989 when the Parap plant (the old Stuart Brewery) was closed, leaving the Winnellie warehouse and offices as the company's Darwin depot.

The Darwin Stubby and NT Draught were then brewed and bottled at CUB's Cairns Brewery (Qld) and shipped to Darwin. When the Cairns Brewery closed in 1989, supplies were then shipped from CUB breweries in Brisbane and Melbourne.

In 1994 a consortium, led by Pars Ram Brothers (Australia) Pty Ltd, a Brisbane-based importing and exporting company, formed Goldchill Australia (Darwin) Pty Ltd. Modern brewing equipment had been purchased from the Eumundi Brewery in Queensland, and this was installed in premises at Darwin's Trade Development Zone in Berrimah. The company was to trade as the Goldchill Brewery, but the brewery at Darwin was never completed. A year or so later it was acquired by the Melbourne-based company, Visy Board Pty Ltd.

Carlton & United Breweries Ltd
(Winnellie Road, Winnellie) 1957–73

N.T. Brewery Pty Ltd
(Bishop Street, Parap) 1973–82
Merger with Stuart Brewery Ltd;
Winnellie plant converted to a warehouse, brewing continued at Parap
Wholly owned subsidiary of CUB 1982–89, closed

Carlton & United Breweries Ltd 1996–
New brewery started at the Darwin suburb of Berrimah

The brewery, still not completed, was taken over by Carlton & United Breweries Ltd on 31 October 1996. It was quickly put into working order, and the official opening was on 18 December 1996. The company's initial plans were to produce only one beer, Victoria Bitter, for the local market and for export.

Ellis-Kells Brewery (Darwin) Ltd   1950–52
Brewery Road

Darwin's first commercial brewery was planned by Harry Ellis-Kells in Brewery Road, off the Stuart Highway, to provide the local population with a regular supply of several different styles, of beer and at a price free from the high freight costs from other states. At the time there was no brewery in Darwin, and supplies of beer had to be shipped thousands of kilometres from Brisbane, Sydney, Adelaide or Melbourne.

The brewery started in 1950, but closed early in 1952. The beer produced was apparently quite good, but insufficient capital forced the closure. On Saturday, 1 March 1952, the property, plant, equipment and stock of malt, hops, syrups and cordials were put up for auction.

The brewery has left a legacy of some interesting bottle labels, with very attractive Australian Aboriginal designs, today highly desirable collectors' items.

Northern Territory Brewery Ltd
When the Northern Territory Brewery Ltd was incorporated, there was much publicity surrounding the venture, but the brewery was never built and the

project was abandoned. The *Centralian Advocate* of 26 May 1947 said:

> Approval has been granted for the erection of the first brewery in the Northern Territory. It will be built at Coomalie Creek about 60 miles south of Darwin. When functioning, the brewery will supply the whole of the Northern Territory with beer and will probably eliminate the need to ship supplies from the southern states at high freight costs. The floating of a public company with a capital of £1,000 has been sanctioned by the Commonwealth Treasurer.

An update on the venture was reported in the *Northern Standard* on 15 August 1947:

> Northern Territory Brewery Ltd has now been incorporated under the Companies Act and has issued a prospectus which shows an authorized capital of £100,000. The brewery is to be built on the roadside at Coomalie Creek, 55 miles south of Darwin. Directors are Charles Stanlake, MD (late of Scotts Hotel, Melbourne), Harry Phillips and Albert Moir.

The article continued with details of the issue of the brewer's licence, and that the Coomalie Creek Hotel licence would be taken over:

> The cost of erection of the brewery is estimated at £38,700 and a bottling, casks and delivery plant at £18,825. The water at Coomalie Creek has been analysed by industrial chemists who report that it is of high standard. Good supplies of silica and sand are available in Darwin for a glass blowing furnace.

During World War II there was a RAAF airstrip in the area. It was the base for the No. 1 Photographic Reconnaissance Unit, and an important intelligence-gathering centre for the North-West Area Headquarters, located 6 km south of Coomalie Creek. Today there is nothing more than the sign 'Coomalie Creek' at the Stuart Highway bridge over a small creek that looks more like a stagnant waterhole than the main water source for a brewery.

N.T. Brewery Pty Ltd
See Carlton & United Breweries Ltd.

Stuart Brewery Ltd   1958–73
Bishop Street, Parap

Years ago it was said that, given the chance, Darwinians could consume more than 50 gallons of beer per head annually, leaving the rest of Australia far behind. Before the establishment of a brewery in Darwin, the Swan Brewery, Perth, and Carlton & United Breweries, Melbourne, fed the incredible thirst by transporting their beer north in anything that moved. Ships, aircraft and trucks laden with beer headed north to Australia's Top End, still barely able to satisfy Darwin's population of 16,000.

By 1954 Swan had started a profitable agency agree-

ment in Darwin, and had begun to think seriously about setting up a brewery there. It so happened that in January 1956 a gentleman by the name of Paul Cullen had registered a Darwin-based brewery company on the Sydney Stock Exchange. Cullen approached three of the largest breweries in Australia — Tooth's, Toohey's and CUB — offering the non-operating registered company for sale, but all three refused. He then approached Swan, which bought the company that was re-registered in Darwin as the Darwin Brewery Ltd. The company never operated.

Swan began to buy or lease Darwin hotels, and in 1957 the foundation stone was laid for the company's brewery at Darwin, Stuart Brewery Ltd, named after a prominent early Territory explorer. The modern German-designed brewery began operations in 1958, one year after CUB had started their plant in the Darwin suburb of Winnellie.

The Stuart Brewery began brewing Swan Export Bitter and Swan Draught, and sold Swan Lager for 4s a bottle, compared with 5s 2d for CUB's Victoria Bitter. The Stuart Brewery used a number of company names on their bottle labels; some were identified with Stuart Brewery Pty Ltd or Stuart Brewery Ltd, others used Swan Brewery Co. (N.T.) Pty Ltd or Swan Brewery Co. Ltd, Darwin.

Although the company owned five hotels in Darwin, plus the local newspaper and a part-interest in Darwin's first radio station, the Stuart Brewery was not a successful venture. Two breweries in Darwin was one too many, and finally Swan merged its Northern Territory interests with those of CUB, Darwin, forming the N.T. Brewery Pty Ltd on 1 April 1973. Swan contributed their Darwin-owned hotels and the Stuart Brewery, to retain a 49 per cent interest in the new company; CUB had 51 per cent.

By July 1982 the N.T. Brewery Pty Ltd had become a wholly-owned subsidiary of Carlton & United Breweries Ltd, marking the end of Swan's brewing endeavour in the Northern Territory.

Swan Brewery Co. Ltd (Darwin)
See Stuart Brewery Ltd.

Norfolk Island

 Norfolk Island, the oldest of the Australian external territories is situated about 1600 km east-north-east of Sydney. It was discovered by Captain Cook in 1774, and named in honour of the 9th Duchess of Norfolk.

The first settlement of Norfolk Island began on 6 March 1788 when Lieutenant Philip King (later governor of New South Wales), under orders from Governor Arthur Phillip, arrived with a party that included nine male and six female convicts. Subsequently, additional parties of convicts, guards and marines arrived on the island. This first period of settlement, which had begun only forty days after the arrival of the First Fleet in Australia, operated as a branch of the penal settlement of New South Wales. Early in 1814 the inhabitants were evacuated to Van Diemen's Land and the island was left unoccupied.

The island was again settled as a penal colony in 1825 with the arrival of Major R. Turton with a party of soldiers and convicts. They set about cultivating the land and building many of the now historic buildings, most of which are located in the Kingston area of the island. So harsh was this second period of settlement that the women and children were returned to Van Diemen's Land. The island became a 'place of extreme punishment short of death'; mercifully, it closed as a penal colony in 1854.

The third and current settlement of Norfolk Island was by the descendants of the mutineers of HMS *Bounty*, who had been living on Pitcairn Island since 1790. After a long and arduous sea voyage they arrived with all their belongings, and established a free settlement on Norfolk Island on 8 June 1856.

By an Order-in-Council of 1856 Norfolk Island was separated from Tasmania, and was created a distinct settlement of the British Crown under the administration of the Governor of New South Wales. By the *Norfolk Island Act 1913* Norfolk Island was accepted by the Australian parliament as a territory of Australia; in July 1914 the island became an external territory under the authority of the Australian government.

Under the *Norfolk Island Act 1979* Norfolk Island has a degree of responsible legislative and executive government, and now conducts its own affairs to a significant extent. The Australian government remains responsible for the island as a territory under its authority.

Most of the island's coastline has precipitous cliffs and several sandy beaches. The picturesque landscape is dominated by endemic Norfolk Island pines, *Araucaria heterophylla*. Only 8 km by 5 km, Norfolk Island has a mild and subtropical climate. The historic buildings of the early convict days and the scenic beauty of the island attract an increasing number of tourists.

Norfolk Island Brewing Co. 1995–

Douglas Drive (opposite the airport terminal)

The permanent population of Norfolk Island is in the vicinity of 1800, about a third of whom are descendants of the Pitcairn Islanders of the mutiny on the *Bounty* fame. Although imported beers, mostly from Australia, are to be found in the few resort hotels and stores on the island, in 1995 the owners of the Norfolk Island Brewing Company courageously started a local brewery.

Influencing their decision was the growing number of tourists visiting the island — 30,000 in 1997. The English-designed and built micro-brewery sells its products to customers in the front saloon bar. Behind the counter, beer can be tapped from any of the three large wooden kegs while customers watch, a novel and attractive way to serve the beer.

Beers produced include Beesting, which is brewed with some local unrefined honey; also Mutineer, made from a blend of pale ale, crystal and chocolate malts. Bligh's Revenge, 6.5% alc./vol., is a traditional top-fermented English porter.

'We are proud to be producing 100% malt beers', says Richard Woodward, the owner–brewer and Pitcairn Island descendant. And he can be justly proud of the growing popularity of his beers and the success of the brewery.

Thompson, William 1804

Dr David Hughes, in his article, 'The Brewing Industry in Early Australia', refers to a brewer, named William Thompson, who had established himself on Norfolk Island, where he had succeeded beyond his 'most sanguine expectations'.

At first glance Thompson's success on this small penal settlement island would seem an exaggerated claim, given the small population of guards, marines and administrators. Convicts could not have been customers. However, considering the harsh conditions of the time, and the isolation and boredom, a ready supply of beer would have provided considerable relief to the small community.

This attractive label of the Norfolk Island Brewing Co. shows some of the many historic penal settlement buildings in the Kingston area, with Norfolk Island pines in the background.

The Boutique Breweries of Australia

Toward the end of the nineteenth century the number of breweries in Australia steadily declined. A peak had been reached during the late 1880s, when there were more than 300 breweries operating throughout the colonies. Thirty years later the number had dropped to less than half, and by 1940 only twenty-nine breweries remained.

During the period 1940 to 1980 there were very few attempts to establish new, independent breweries in Australia. The large and powerful breweries in the capital cities held a virtual monopoly in their respective states. They had the economy of large-scale production, marketing strength through hotel ownerships, and their beers were popular and consistent in quality. Moreover, there was little, if any, competition between the breweries of any of the Australian states. Under these conditions, it was little wonder that there were very few who had the courage to challenge the supremacy of the giant breweries by starting up in competition.

A few small breweries started after 1950 — one at Darwin, another in Sydney and one at Mildura — but all had no significant effect on the trade of the major city breweries. There was, however, one major challenge to Australia's well-established breweries in Melbourne and Sydney, and this occurred in 1968 when Courage Breweries Ltd, partly-owned by the British brewer, Courage, erected a substantial brewing plant in Melbourne. After enormous capital expenditure and extensive promotion and the marketing of a range of new beers, their attempt to compete was eventually unsuccessful, and the brewery closed in 1982.

Tradition

Apart from the introduction of low-alcohol beers in the late 1970s, Australian breweries had kept to their proven recipes and brand names, many of which had continued for half a century or more. There was no need for product change or innovation. Historically, Australian beer-drinkers were parochial in their drinking habits, and tended to stay with their favourite local brand of beer for years on end. Without provocation, they would pass unfavourable comments about other beers, particularly from other states, whether they had tasted the beers or not. This old-fashioned culture was to change dramatically in the 1980s when a new era emerged in the history of Australian brewing, and in the preferences and tastes of the consumers.

A Welcome Change

After almost half a century, with the same beers being produced by the same few breweries, a new breed of brewing entrepreneurs began to set up small breweries that offered the drinking public an amazing variety of new styles of beers. These were the boutique breweries, small-scale independent breweries, many of which were set up in conjunction with an up-market, renovated hotel. The hotels and diningrooms were quite often the main retail outlet for their products, and sales were generally only for a local or regional market.

These new pub breweries have generally been referred to as 'boutique' breweries, although because of their small output other names such as 'mini' brewery or 'micro' brewery are occasionally used. With the exception of one or two of these boutique breweries, none had any intention of competing with the long-standing mainstream breweries. With considerable entrepreneurial flair, they set about brewing new beers, some of which had not been produced in Australia for almost eighty years. Brewing on a small scale allowed for more experimentation, which resulted in handcrafted beers of different and distinctive character, new flavours, and in an incredible variety. They offered the consumer an interesting, if not exciting, alternative to the traditional mass-produced commercial beers.

The Beginning

The first of the boutique breweries was started in 1984 by Brewtech Pty Ltd, who purchased and restored the historic Freemasons Hotel in Fremantle, Western Australia. A small state-of-the-art brewery was installed, and the hotel was renamed the Sail & Anchor Pub Brewery. Later that year the Old Ballarat Brewery in Ballarat, Victoria, became the first of the boutique breweries to operate in eastern Australia.

The immediate success of these breweries was an invitation for others to follow. By 1992 no fewer than fifty boutique breweries had been set up across Australia, brewing hundreds of different types of highly-priced, fashionable beers. Many of the breweries were linked to a hotel, and took pride in featuring their brewing equipment by installing glass walls so that customers could view the highly-polished brewing utensils and the production layout.

The growth of the boutique breweries in Australia in the 1980s was similar in many ways to the expansion of the brewing industry during the boom period of the 1880s. Although a hundred years apart, both periods supported the notion that investment in a brewery was a sure and safe way to success.

The Anchor Brewing Co. was Australia's first boutique brewery. The company began in business by purchasing and restoring the historic Freemasons Hotel in Fremantle, Western Australia. A small brewery was installed and the hotel was renamed the Sail & Anchor Pub Brewery. Brewing commenced in July 1984 and, at the outset, only barrelled beer was produced. Shortly after, another larger brewery was established at the Perth suburb of Nedlands and a new company, the Matilda Bay Brewing Co. Pty Ltd, was formed. Carlton & United Breweries Ltd, Melbourne, acquired total control of the company in 1990.

Consolidation

The closing years of the nineteenth century and the early years of the twentieth century marked a period of closures, amalgamation and takeovers, through which the large brewing companies of today were formed.

To a much lesser extent, the economic downturn of the late 1980s, coupled with the passing wave of consumer enthusiasm, led to the closure or resale of many of the boutique breweries. Some ventures were shortlived when customers returned to their earlier beer preferences, while others continued to trade with difficulty as sales declined because of competition and the high prices of their products. With the surge of beer imports from overseas, and more and more local varieties becoming available, there were too many brands seeking markets that were not expanding.

Two of the larger boutique breweries were absorbed by national brewers, while others throughout Australia, after careful consideration of their product range and market niche, continue to operate efficiently, serving a well-established demand for variety.

There is no doubt that the introduction of new products such as wheat beer, old English-style ales, and many other varieties of beer and stout, has had a profound influence on the drinking preferences and habits of the Australian drinking public. The boutique breweries across Australia can claim credit for this change, and their existence is a healthy and important part of the Australian brewing industry.

New South Wales/ACT

Ballina

York Breweries Pty Ltd 1988–
36 Bonview St, East Ballina

The York family had started in business as engineers on the northern New South Wales coast as early as 1907. They became involved in the shipbuilding and mining industries, and in the late 1980s they set up a small brewery as a model so that potential customers could order a similar brewery to be built at a location of their choice. An arrangement was made with Coopers Brewery in Adelaide to supply concentrate for the proprietors of the new breweries. The Grogfathers Brewery in Lismore was one such project.

Canberra (ACT)

Australian Pizza Kitchen Brewery 1991–
London Circuit, Canberra City

Trading leaflets referred to the business as the A.P.K. Brewery, using the initials of the Australian Pizza Kitchen. The brewery formed part of a restaurant and bar in the basement of premises at a shopping centre in Civic, Canberra. Only draught beer is produced for sale at the restaurant and bar.

Gang Gang Brewery 1990–91

The brewery formed part of a licensed restaurant that was in the Glebe Park Eatery of the shopping complex in suburban Canberra. Under the unlikely name of the Gang Gang Brewery, brewing commenced at the back of the restaurant late in 1990, and continued for about a year. Two styles of draught beer were produced: a lager and an English-style ale.

Wig & Pen Restaurant & Brewery 1995–
Alinga Street

The licensees are L. & J. McOmish, and brewing is carried out by Richard Pass. The small brewery section produces different lagers, and all in bulk.

Goulburn

Old Goulburn Brewery 1991–
Bungonia Road

The original Goulburn Brewery, maltings, mill and mews complex was established in Goulburn by the Bradley family and, although the mill bears the date of 1836, brewing commenced in 1838. When Tooth & Co. Ltd took over in 1920, the premises were then used as a warehouse and depot until 1956.

The Goulburn Brewery is of considerable historical importance, being the oldest intact brewery and flour-mill in New South Wales. Restorations began in 1982 under the direction of Father Michael O'Halloran, and the grand old buildings became licensed premises, open to the public for various functions.

In 1991 a small brewery facility was installed, and several beers were produced for local consumption. Late in 1996 three different beers were released in huge 3-litre flagons: a full-bodied fine sparkling ale, a traditional stout, and a light ale.

Griffith

William Bull Brewery 1998–
Bilbul, on the eastern outskirts of Griffith

In June 1997 the De Bortoli family, of winemaking fame, purchased the brewing equipment from the Horizon Brewery in Tatura, Victoria. The Horizon had gone into liquidation two years earlier. At Bilbul the equipment was put into storage for a year or so. After it was finally installed and operating, the first beer was tapped on 1 December 1998. It was called William Bull Premium, available in draught form only, to be sold, at first, to hotels and clubs in the immediate area.

Lismore

Grogfathers Brewery 1994–
73 Keen Street/107 Dawson Street

With a somewhat peculiar name, the Grogfathers Brewery formed part of the Gollan Hotel, and put out excellent-quality lager, ale, a darker beer, and also Capone's Bullet Draught. Early in 1997 the owner, Chris Hayward, shifted the brewery to form part of the Little Brewery Steak House in Dawson Street. Draught beer is sold locally.

Maitland

Valley Brewery 1988–93
Ken Tubman Drive, West Maitland

The Valley Brewery operated at the back of Alfie's Bar & Grill. Draught beer only was produced and sold through the tavern. Brewing ceased in 1993. Five years later the brewing equipment was still on the premises.

Mudgee

Mount Vincent Meadery 1971–
Common Road

The meadery, owned by Mrs Jane Nevell, began operating in 1971, and produced a mead with a strength of

12 per cent alc./vol. Production of Skal Mead Ale commenced in 1990, and, according to the label, was inspired by an authentic Viking recipe. It is 5 per cent alc./vol., naturally fermented from honey and hops, with no preservatives.

Newcastle

Newcastle Brewing Co. Ltd
Munibung Road, Cardiff

Early in 1990 a consortium of investors, led by Kim Butler, planned to establish a brewery in the Newcastle suburb of Cardiff. Equipment was ordered, and it was intended to float a public company to raise the necessary $14 million capital, build the brewery, produce a beer to be called Butler's Premium Bitter, and develop a broad distribution network. Unfortunately, the project failed to proceed, although some bottle labels remain as a reminder of the proposal.

Queens Wharf Hotel Brewery   1988–
150 Wharf Road

Situated on Newcastle's harbour foreshore, the Queens Wharf Brewery brews a range of beers from concentrated wort supplied by Cooper's Brewery, Adelaide. The equipment for the mini-brewery also came from Cooper's. The beers produced include Nobby's Pale, Waterfront Bitter, Newcastle Old, and Boltons Ginger Beer, claimed to be the first commercially-produced, alcoholic ginger beer in Australia. The brewery forms an attractive part of a large tourist attraction complex, which includes a nightclub, restaurant and the hotel.

Picton

Scharer's Little Brewery   1987–
Old Hume Highway

In the late 1970s Geoffrey Scharer, the son of a Sydney publican, applied for a brewing licence at a time when new small-scale breweries were unheard of in Australia. Although the licence was granted in 1980, it was seven years before Scharer commenced brewing.

Geoff Scharer set up his small brewery in the historic George IV Inn at Picton, 80 km south-west of Sydney. Scharer's first brew, Scharer's Lager, was released in mid-1987, and was so well accepted that it was soon the only beer available at his hotel.

A year later a heavier beer, Burragorang Bock, was put on the market. Both beers were brewed in a traditional fire-kettle, lagered for a minimum of thirteen weeks, and neither filtered nor pasteurised.

The George IV Inn is believed to have been built in 1819, and was first licensed in 1839. In earlier years the cellars were used to house road gangs and convicts in transit on their way to the Berrima and Goulburn gaols.

Sutton

Eagle Hawk Hill Brewing
Co. Pty Ltd   1987–93
Federal Highway

In late 1987 a large tourist resort opened on the Federal Highway at Sutton, about 500 metres into New South Wales from the Australian Capital Territory border. One of the features of the resort was the Eagle Hawk Hill Brewery, which produced draught beer for the resort customers, and also bottled beer that was distributed as far as Sydney and Melbourne.

The brewery had a very strong English connection: the plant was from the Inn Brewery of the United Kingdom; the brewer, Simon Brook-Taylor, came from Bass Breweries in Sheffield; and the beers were top-fermented English-style ales.

The brewery produced a number of special and private bottlings, such as Speaker's Ale and President's Lager, for sale through Parliament House, Canberra.

Sydney

Balmain Brewery Ltd   1987–90
18 Hornsey Street, Rozelle

The Balmain Brewery, the inspiration of Sydneysider Ian Pike, was located in the inner Sydney suburb of Rozelle, but took its name from the nearby and more affluent suburb of Balmain.

In the spring of 1987 the first beer was released. It was called Balmain Bock, a relatively strong beer at 6.8 per cent alc./vol., 'not a beer to be consumed before driving', and claimed to be made to a 400-year-old recipe.

The brewery was sold late in 1988. The new owners reduced the strength of the Bock, and introduced a lager at 3.1 per cent alcohol/volume. Despite these efforts, the business did not succeed, and by late 1990 the brewery had closed. The last batch of beer was brewed for the company by the Sovereign Brewery in Ballarat, Victoria.

Craig's Brewery, Bar & Grill   1988–92
Festival Market Place, Darling Harbour

The renovation and development of Sydney's Darling Harbour area converted an ugly industrial dockland into one of Australia's largest tourist attractions. Within the complex are numerous restaurants and bistros, and one of these was Craig's Brewery, Bar & Grill. From

the middle of 1988 it brewed its own beer from concentrated wort, producing two beers — a Strong Ale and a Premium Lager — most of which was sold by the glass at the bar. Early in 1990 both beers were bottled and labelled by hand for the tourist trade, but by July 1992 the brewery had closed.

Hahn Brewing Co. Pty Ltd 1988–98
101 Pyrmont Bridge Road, Camperdown

Dr Charles Hahn and three other partners, together with Kimberley Securities, the major shareholder, formed the Hahn Brewing Co. Pty Ltd. By March 1988 beer had begun to flow at their new brewery in the inner Sydney suburb of Camperdown. Chuck Hahn had gained considerable brewing experience with Coors Brewery in the USA, Tooth's Brewery in Sydney, and the New Zealand Breweries in New Zealand.

The three large copper kettles, a showpiece of the Hahn Brewery, originally came from Germany in 1952, and were purchased in New Zealand after the Standard Brewery had closed. When brewing commenced, there was only one beer, Hahn Premium Lager, an all-malt, unpasteurised lager that was intended for the restaurant and prestige hotel trade. The beer was an immediate success, and its popularity rapidly spread. Draught and bottled beer were distributed throughout eastern Australia, and other products were introduced to a receptive market.

In March 1989 Kimberley Securities sold their equity in the company to an investment company of Stephen Woods with extensive experience in liquor marketing and distribution. A new product, Sydney Bitter, was introduced in 1991, and different brewing techniques were employed to reduce the brewing and cellaring time, and production costs.

Several factors contributed to the company's difficulties in the early 1990s, and in January 1993 the Hahn Brewery was taken over by the Sydney brewer, Toohey's Ltd. The brewery at Camperdown continued to brew a range of beers, including many of the popular Hahn brands.

Toohey's, however, ceased brewing their own beers at Hahn's Brewery in 1998, following an agreement with the founder of the brewery, Dr Charles Hahn. The premises at Camperdown were renamed the Malt Shovel Brewery Pty Ltd, and, as brewmaster, Dr Hahn then continued to brew and market his own specialty beers.

Harbour Beer Co. 1998–
90 Sydenham Road, Marrickville

In April 1998 Bob Wessler and his partners opened their brewery in the inner Sydney suburb of Marrickville. Wessler had gained his brewing experience at the Steam & Anchor Brewery in San Francisco, USA. A great deal of effort went into developing a beer of very high quality. Early production was bottled and labelled by hand, and sold to a small number of restaurants in the area. The first beer was Full Sail Amber Ale, and another went under the unusual name of Raspberry Wheat Beer.

Lord Nelson Brewery Hotel 1987–
Cnr Argyle & Kent Streets, The Rocks

The Lord Nelson Hotel is the oldest in Sydney, dating back to 1831 when it was known as the Shipwright Arms; it became the Lord Nelson in 1841. Situated in the historic Rocks area of Sydney, the three-storey sandstone building was carefully restored in recent times, and became Sydney's first brewery hotel.

Production of beer commenced in 1987, and the names for the beers reflected some association with Lord Nelson: Trafalgar Pale Ale, Victory Bitter, Nelson's Blood, and Old Admiral, a very strong ale that is said to come served with the local taxi phone number.

Similar to a number of other pub breweries, the Lord Nelson has a glass wall that allows customers to view the brewery equipment and its operation.

In recent times the company won a competition in Japan for its Old Admiral beer.

Malt Shovel Brewery Pty Ltd 1998–
99 Pyrmont Bridge Road, Camperdown

The Hahn Brewing Co. Pty Ltd was started by Dr Charles Hahn in 1988. Toohey's Brewery took over five years later, and continued to brew a range of the popular Hahn beers. In 1998 an arrangement was made between Dr Hahn, the founder of the brewery, and the Lion Nathan Group, owners of Toohey's Brewery — Toohey's was no longer brewing at the brewery at Camperdown.

The premises at Camperdown were renamed the Malt Shovel Brewery Pty Ltd, and Charles (Chuck) Hahn then continued to brew and market his own specialty beers. The first, released in December 1998, was Amber Ale, with the labels commemorating James Squire, Australia's first brewer.

Pumphouse Brewery
See Tankstream Brewing Co.

Tankstream Brewing Co. 1989–96
17 Little Pier Street, Darling Harbour

In the late 1800s, before the use of electricity became widespread, hydraulic power was an important source of energy. Water, under pressure, was fed through cast-iron pipes to operate lifts, cranes, wool presses and other mechanical equipment. The building, now known as the Pumphouse, at Sydney's Darling Harbour, was commissioned in 1891 to supply the demand for this form of energy, and did so until its closure in 1975.

During the 1980s the New South Wales govern-

Craig's Brewery, Darling Harbour.

The Hahn Brewing Co.'s first beer, Hahn Premium Lager, was released in January 1988.

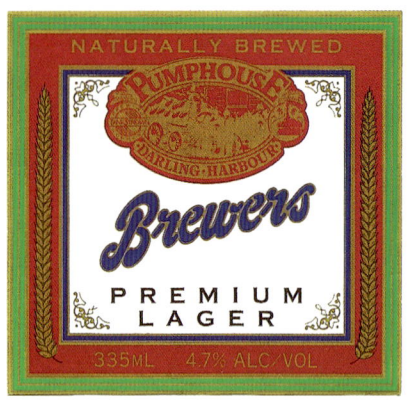

ment undertook a major redevelopment of the whole Darling Harbour area, and a thirty-year lease was granted to Centrepac, an owner of inner-city hotels, to renovate and use the Pumphouse. The old building was transformed into a tavern, restaurant and small brewery, to be operated by Centrepac's Tankstream Brewing Co.

The Darling Harbour complex opened before the brewery was ready and the beer was initially supplied by Britten's Brewery in Tamworth, which was also owned by the company. Operating as the Pumphouse Brewery, its own beer became available in March 1989, and was supplied on tap at the bar and in the restaurant. Some bottled beer was produced for the tourist trade.

The brewery closed in November 1996, and the equipment was taken over by Sharer's Brewery, Picton.

Tamworth

Britten's Brewery   1988–94
New England Highway

Britten's Brewery was next to the Lonyard Tavern, both of which formed part of a tourist complex on the outskirts of Tamworth in north-eastern New South Wales. The parent company, Tankstream Brewing Co. in Sydney, also operated the Pumphouse Pub Brewery at Darling Harbour.

Only draught beer was produced at Tamworth, and products included Golden Wheat Beer, Best Bitter, Federation Ale and Thunderbolter Strong Ale.

After the brewery closed in 1994, the equipment went to New Guinea.

Victoria

Ballarat

Old Ballarat Brewery   1984–87
Elsworth Street

The Old Ballarat Brewery was the second of the modern-day boutique breweries in Australia, and the first to become established in Victoria. The Anchor Brewery in Fremantle, WA, began in July 1984, and the Old Ballarat Brewery followed later that year.

John Gilbert built a large motel and convention centre on 16 hectares of land opposite Ballarat's renowned Pioneer Village. The complex had its own tennis courts, restaurant and pottery factory on the hill at the back. Gilbert had seen the success of mini-breweries in England, and, with considerable vision and even more courage, he ventured into a new era of

The Old Ballarat Brewery produced only one style of beer, most of which was packaged in small bottles and supplied to hotels, restaurants, clubs and corporations, with the bottle label carrying the name, emblem or logo, as required by the customer. More than 120 different labels were produced.

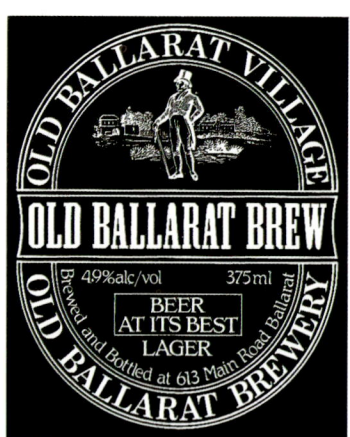

Australian brewing by building a brewery on the slope of land just above the convention centre.

The Old Ballarat Brewery produced just the one style of beer, a full malt lager with a fine flavour and texture. Most of the production was packaged in small bottles, many of which were supplied to convention customers, hotels, clubs and corporations, with the bottle label carrying the name, emblem and any other distinctive feature required by the customer. A small printing factory operated at the site; it designed and printed more than 120 different labels during the life of the brewery, where a minimum order of 20 dozen bottles of Old Ballarat Brew would be processed and specially labelled.

The market was expanded to Melbourne, and several shipments went to Sydney, but penetration of the market was difficult. Early in 1987 the brewery was sold to Sovereign Brewery Pty Ltd, a wholly-owned subsidiary of Pacific Maltings Pty Ltd, and brewing continued under the Sovereign name.

Sovereign Brewery Pty Ltd   1987–90
Elsworth Street

Pacific Maltings Pty Ltd was formed in 1986 and the company began to supply the brewing companies of South-east Asia with malted barley. Early the following year, the Old Ballarat Brewery was taken over and the name was changed to the Sovereign Brewery. At the outset the new company continued to brew the same style of beer and to use the same style of label, modified only by name, as its predecessor. The new company also continued to supply bottled beer with special labels for restaurants, companies and clubs.

A stout was released, followed by a new lager, Ballarat Gold, and in 1988 the capacity of the brewery was increased to one million litres per year.

Financial difficulties led to the appointment of a receiver and manager in August 1990. The brewing equipment was subsequently purchased by the newly-formed Lederberger Brewery in Tatura, Victoria.

Bendigo

Rifle Brigade Pub Brewery   1988–
137 View Street

The Rifle Brigade Pub Brewery is a tastefully renovated country hotel with its own mini-brewery, a restaurant, and a unique walk-down wine cellar where diners can select their own wine.

The beers are brewed from concentrated wort, and are given colourful topical names, such as Quartz Dry, Bendigo Best, Rifle Lager, Cannon Lager, Rimshot and Corporal Punishment. In addition to these, there are never less than ten different beers on tap, and up to eighty Australian and international brands are available in bottles.

Boorhaman

Buffalo Brewery   1996–
Boorhaman Road

The small township of Boorhaman lies 20 km north of Wangaratta, the larger town that had a Buffalo Brewery during the first half of the twentieth century.

Len David, the owner of the Buffalo Brewery at Boorhaman, claims it is the smallest brewery in Australia. Even so, the tiny brewery won a silver award for its beer at an Australian and international competition in 1998.

Production of lager and a porter-style draught ale began in April 1996, and the limited quantities produced are mainly for the local market.

Dixons Creek

Yarra Flats Brewery   1998–
Melba Highway

Brian and Denise Lovey set up their Yarra Flats Brewery as an addition to their Lovey's winery and restaurant and reception centre, 8 km north of Yarra Glen. The brewery, finally completed in August 1998, had earlier been launched at the Yarra Valley Grape & Wine Festival in March that year.

Before the brewery was completed, beer had been obtained from the Traditional Brewery Co. in Hawthorn, Melbourne.

The Yarra Flats Brewery beers were sold in bottles, with attractive shrink-wrapped labels. Included in the range were Golden Goose Wheat Ale and Golden Goose Porter.

Geelong

Geelong Brewing Co. Pty Ltd   1988–
80 Point Henry Road, Moolap

The Geelong Brewery Co. Pty Ltd was started by Henry Peeters, a former brewer at Carlton & United Breweries, and with the assistance of several colleagues, he commenced production at the well-equipped brewery on 4 January 1988.

At first three beers were introduced to the mainstream beer market — Geelong Draught, Geelong Bitter and Geelong Lager — followed a year later by Geelong Light. The competitively-priced beers are not unlike Carlton & United Breweries' beers in taste, and are distributed throughout Melbourne. The company also conducts a considerable business in specialty labelling for commercial houses, restaurants and hotels.

Scottish Chief's Tavern Brewery   1990
Cnr Corio & O'Connell Streets

Despite its modern appearance, part of the Scottish Chief's Tavern Brewery has a history dating back to 1839. In that year the owner John Cummings began brewing his own beer. In 1857 the Volum Brewing Co. took over, and continued brewing on the site until 1953. The next owner was the Ballarat Brewery, but when Carlton & United Breweries, Melbourne, took over the Ballarat Brewery in 1958, brewing ceased at Geelong and the premises were used as a depot.

The former Scottish Chief's Hotel and the old Volum Brewery bluestone malthouse were converted

The Geelong Brewery's beer production includes an extensive range of special labels for restaurants, companies and special events.

The bottling and labelling for the Scottish Chief's Tavern Brewery, Geelong, was carried out by the Geelong Brewery.

into a modern tavern and mini-brewery by a developer, David Trew, and bulk beer became available early in 1990. Only one batch was brewed, and the brewery section of the tavern was closed.

Steam Packet Brewing Co. 1996–
Cnr Corio & O'Connell Streets

The brewery section of the Scottish Chief's Tavern was leased by Gavin Gamble, and brewing started again in September 1996. The beers produced are sold mainly through the tavern.

Melbourne

Bell's Hotel & Brewery 1988–
157 Moray Street, South Melbourne

In 1988 Bill Bell installed a small brewing facility in his century-old hotel in South Melbourne. It was intended that this would be one of a number of pub breweries to be set up throughout Australia with the assistance and expertise of the Matilda Bay Brewing Co. in Perth.

Although the expansion plan did not proceed, Bill Bell continued to brew draught beer in the English style, putting out a porter, two ales, a Best Bitter and a ginger beer.

Geebung Polo Club Hotel & Brewery
See Traditional Brewing Co. Pty Ltd.

Kiewa Brewing Co. Pty Ltd 1988–93
20 Gatwick Road, Bayswater

The year 1987 was a busy time for Peter Thompson and Brian Griffin as they experimented with various recipes in their endeavour to perfect an all-malt, unpasteurised lager beer. The name chosen for the brewery, Kiewa, is taken from the Aboriginal name for 'sweet water'.

Having decided on their recipe and the sources of supply for the ingredients, the partners built their brewery in the outer Melbourne suburb of Bayswater. For purity, water was trucked from Victoria's Kiewa Valley in order to avoid the chlorine, fluoride and other undesirable characteristics of town-supply water.

The first beer, Wattle Lager, was released in January 1988, and continued to be the main product widely available in Melbourne. Some shipments went interstate, and in 1992 quantities of Wattle Lager were shipped to Japan.

A special brew, Kiewa Gold, was made with the addition of banksia honey, and released early in 1989. Other special beers were made for local hotels and liquor merchants, but by January 1993 the brewery had closed.

Loaded Dog Pub Brewery 1986–90
St Georges Road, North Fitzroy

In 1985 Geoff Chamberlain left his position as manager of the Sail & Anchor Pub Brewery in Fremantle, WA, and returned to Melbourne. With other associates, he formed the Traditional Brewing Co. Pty Ltd, and purchased the old Aberdeen Hotel in North Fitzroy from Carlton & United Breweries Ltd. The exterior of the hotel, with its balconies and iron lace, was restored to its former Victorian-period splendour, the interior was extensively remodelled, and a small-scale brewery was installed behind a glass wall, allowing the passing public to view the brewery. This was the first of the new

Although the Loaded Dog Pub Brewery produced only draught beer, some bottling and labelling was done by the Geelong Brewery.

breed of pub breweries to operate in Melbourne. It was named the Loaded Dog, a name taken from a story by Australia's famed poet and story writer, Henry Lawson.

Top-fermented English-style ales were produced, including Corbunga Bitter, Razorback Stout, Thunder Ale, and a Ruby Bitter, which, when poured into a glass, looked very much like a glass of red wine. At the bar about twenty different beers were on tap, plus up to eighty local and imported bottled beers

The venture was highly successful, and in May 1987 the owners acquired the Auburn Hotel in Hawthorn, which they also upgraded, and installed a mini-brewery.

The Loaded Dog Pub Brewery was sold, and the new owners carried on for some time but with little success, and by the middle of 1990 the brewery had closed.

Metropolitan Brewing Co. 1989
16 French Street, Coburg

Although the opal-mining township of Lightning Ridge is more than 1000 km north of Melbourne, Lightning Ridge was the name given to the lager that the Metropolitan Brewing Co. brewed at Coburg. Using equipment from the former Botanic Hotel Brewery in Adelaide, the Metropolitan opened in January 1989.

It produced only one beer, Lightning Ridge Lager,

This attractive label, featuring a spray of wattle, Australia's floral emblem, was released when the Kiewa Brewery, Bayswater, Melbourne, opened in 1988.

which was available in bottles and draught. By June that year the brewery had closed.

Port Melbourne Brewing Co. 1988–90
75 Flemington Road, North Melbourne

It is rather odd that the name Port Melbourne was chosen for the brewery, since its location, at North Melbourne is 5 km from that seaside suburb.

The Royal Hotel at North Melbourne was purchased by the Port Melbourne Brewing Co. in a joint venture with the Matilda Bay Brewing Co. Ltd of Fremantle, WA. The old hotel was renovated, a brewery was installed, and a two-storey glass partition allows customers to view the highly-polished copper kettles and to see the layout of a modern boutique brewery.

Brewing began in the second half of 1988. The Matilda Bay Brewery later took control of the entire project. For a while, the business traded as the Tiger's Head Brewery, and then as the Redback Brewery.

Following the acquisition in 1990 by Carlton & United Breweries, Melbourne, of all the Matilda Bay Brewery operations, the Port Melbourne Brewery continued to brew Matilda Bay specialty beers.

The Port Melbourne Brewing Co. produced only draught beer. All bottled beer was produced by the parent company, Matilda Bay Brewing Co., Fremantle, Western Australia.

Redback Brewery
See Port Melbourne Brewing Co.

Station Tavern & Brewery   1987–90
96 Greville Street, Prahran

The Station Tavern and Brewery, situated close to the Prahran railway station, began brewing late in 1987, and produced a range of six beers. The hotel had been renovated, and, as a touch of eccentricity, the front end of a Victorian Railways locomotive was fitted to the front of the building, giving the appearance that it had crashed through the wall.

The brewery section of the business was apparently never very successful. Brewing was spasmodic, and brewers and owners came and went until a receiver took control of the business in August 1990. Some of the beers had most unusual names, such as Ballbiter Stout, Boofhead Strong Ale and Brown-nosed Dark Ale.

Tiger's Head Brewery
See Port Melbourne Brewing Co.

Traditional Brewing Co. Pty Ltd   1989–
85 Auburn Road, Hawthorn

Geoff Chamberlain and his associates started Melbourne's first pub brewery in 1986 at the Aberdeen Hotel at North Fitzroy. Although the company was registered as the Traditional Brewing Co. Pty Ltd, it traded as the Loaded Dog Pub Brewery. Several years later the brewery was sold, and in May 1987 Chamberlain and associates bought the Auburn Hotel, Auburn.

The stately old Auburn Hotel was extensively upgraded, and a small brewery was installed in a separate building behind the hotel. The name of the hotel was changed to the Geebung Polo Club Hotel, and traded as the Traditional Brewing Co. Pty Ltd.

Draught beer was ready early in 1989, and some deliveries were sent as far as Sydney and Canberra. Bottled beer became available early in 1993.

This label was used by the Station Tavern and Brewery, Melbourne. The bottling and labelling of their beer was carried out by the Sovereign Brewery, Ballarat.

The Traditional Brewing Co. Pty Ltd, Hawthorn, also traded as the Geebung Polo Club Hotel and Brewery.

Mirboo North

Grand Ridge Brewing Co. Ltd   1988–
Baromi Road/Main Street

In December 1988 the Grand Ridge Brewing Co. Pty Ltd assumed control of the failed Strezlecki Brewery, located in an old butter factory in the pretty but lonely township of Mirboo North in Victoria's Gippsland district.

The new company began brewing Gippsland Gold, Brewers Pilsener, Moonlight, and an extra strong Moonshine, one of Australia's strongest beers at 8.5 per cent alc./vol. Some years later another, stronger beer was put

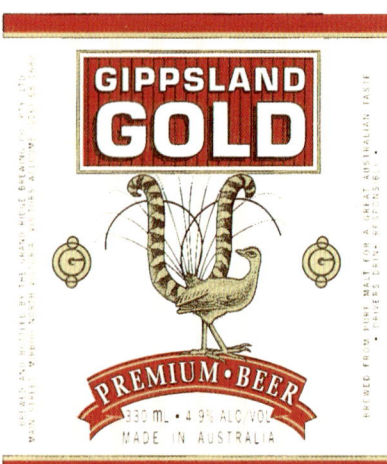

One of the attractive labels of the Grand Ridge Brewing Co., Mirboo North, Victoria.

on the market; named Thunder Ale, it has a powerful 11 per cent alc./vol. All are full-malt beers with no chemicals or additives. As well as the local trade, the company's award-winning range of beers is sold to many clubs, pubs and bottleshops in Melbourne.

The brewery is also a tourist attraction, where visitors are welcome to see the brewing operations, sample the beers in the bar and dine in the fashionable restaurant.

Strezlecki Brewing Co. Pty Ltd 1988–89
Baromi Road

Tucked away in the mountains of Victoria's Gippsland district is the tiny town of Mirboo North. The butter factory there had been empty for some time, and it was taken over late in 1987 by the Strezlecki Brewing Co. The name Strezlecki was taken from that of the Polish explorer who passed through the area in the 1850s.

Over the next twelve months, the building was remodelled, and new brewing equipment was installed. In September 1988 the first beers were released. These included the English-style Country Bitter, Powerhouse Stout and Pure Malt Beer. There was also a very heavy Scotch-type ale called '1080' with an alcoholic content, by volume, of 8.5 per cent. The 1080 was the specific gravity of the beer, an old measure of alcoholic strength — '1080' also happened to be a brand of a popular rabbit poison at the time!

By June 1989 a receiver had been appointed, and in March 1990 the newly-formed Grand Ridge Brewing Co. Pty Ltd took over, and started brewing again.

Tatura

Goulburn Valley Brewery 1992–93
See Horizon Brewery Co. Pty Ltd.

Horizon Brewery Co. Pty Ltd 1993–95
Cnr Hogan & Thompson Streets

Lederberger's Brewery started brewing at the small northern Victorian town of Tatura, the centre of a productive irrigation area where dairying, fruit growing and tomato growing are the major rural activities.

The equipment for the brewery was originally used by the Old Ballarat Brewery (which later became the Sovereign Brewery). When the Sovereign closed in 1990, Lederberger bought the equipment from the receiver, and transferred it to Tatura.

The first of a range of beers was ready in March 1992, but five months later a receiver was appointed.

The receiver appointed in August 1992 allowed the manager to run the brewery while he searched for a buyer for the brewery. This was an almost impossible task, given the failure of the brewery, the remote location and very limited market.

The manager took over in his own right but, trading as the Goulburn Valley Brewery, he produced only two batches of beer.

The Melbourne-based Horizon Fund Ltd took over late in 1993, used the name Horizon Brewery, and appointed Nick Cleave as the brewer.

Production of Horizon Bitter began in December 1993, and sales were through distributors and to clubs.

The company went into liquidation in 1995.

Lederberger's Brewing Co. 1992
See Horizon Brewery Co. Pty Ltd.

Wodonga

Palatinat Brewery 1998–
Lincoln Causeway

The name Palatinat derives from Palatina, the area in Germany where the owners of the brewery, Fritz and Ingrid Walter and family, had lived before migrating to Australia in 1996.

In setting up the Palatinat Brewery, and the large convention centre and restaurant, the owners said they wanted to create something new — 'something different from the usual restaurants and hotels, a place for the family, where there would be no poker machines or gambling'.

The brewery was opened by Jeff Kennett, the Premier of Victoria, in May 1998. At that time four beers were released, including Palatinat Dark and Golden Lager, with the bottling and labelling carried out, at that stage, by hand.

The attractive, well-designed buildings of the restaurant, bar and brewery complex, is considered one of the largest of any recently established.

Queensland

Brisbane

Brisbane Brewery Pty Ltd 1987
Off Lytton Road, Morningside

Many of Australia's boutique breweries that started in the 1980s had very short lives, but none shorter than the Brisbane Brewery. In fact, the brewery was never built and consequently no beer was ever produced. The company's parent was the Lifestyle Beverage Corporation, which had its origin in British Colombia, Canada, in 1981. By April 1987 it had become a distributor of beverages in the USA, including wines from Victoria. In conjunction with Australian Beverage Corporation Ltd, a privately-held Australian company, it was intended to build a brewery and produce 1.7 million cases of beer annually, mostly for export to the USA.

This label was for beer that was never produced. The Brisbane Brewery Pty Ltd was formed in 1987 with the intention of producing and selling large quantities of Australian Premium Lager to the USA. Unfortunately for the investors, the brewery was never built.

It was planned that, while their own brewery was being built, beer would be obtained from the South Australian Brewery in Adelaide. The labels that were printed are all that remain of the concept of the Brisbane Brewery.

Colonial Brewing Co.   1987–89
4 Commercial Road, Fortitude Valley

Brewhouse Operations Australia Ltd was a company set up by Graham Howard, who intended to design and build small breweries for anyone who was interested in starting up a boutique brewery. The idea had merit, since in the mid-1980s entrepreneurs were clamouring to get into the apparently highly-profitable, specialty-brewing business.

The Colonial Brewing Co. was formed, and Graham Howard set up a working example of his proposed breweries at the Waterloo Hotel in Fortitude Valley at a cost of $500,000. The brewery and tavern complex, with glass viewing-windows and highly-polished copper kettles and vats, was largely aimed at the tourist market. The variety of beers produced included Valley Gold Pilsener, Colonial Real Ale and Settlers Extra Stout. Most of the beer was sold in draught through the Waterloo Hotel and to other Brisbane hotels.

The brewing side of the business was not a profitable venture, and by September 1989 brewing had been discontinued.

Kelly's Brewery   1988–c. 1997
521 Stanley Street, South Brisbane

Kelly's Brewery is in the former Castle Hotel, South Brisbane, and has something of an international background, even though the name Kelly may immediately be associated with Ned Kelly, the infamous Irish-Australian bushranger who rode and robbed throughout north-eastern Victoria.

The equipment, which had come from Bavaria fifty years earlier, had also been used in a brewery in Zimbabwe. It was found in an old shed in Brisbane, and after restoration it was installed at Kelly's Brewery.

The brewer, of German descent, was trained in Bavaria and had lived in Papua New Guinea for a number of years. The hops came from Tasmania and Czechoslovakia, and the bottles from Mexico. Where the yeast came from was Tim Kelly's secret.

Kelly released his first beer, Kelly's Premium Beer, at the end of 1988. This was followed later by Kelly's Premium Dark and Kelly's Special Lager. Corporate customers were supplied with Premium Beer in small bottles with individually designed labels.

In June 1992 the brewery was sold, but continued to brew the same range of beers. However, brewing ceased after a few years.

Eumundi

Eumundi Brewing Co. Ltd   1988–92
Memorial Drive

The attractive small township of Eumundi nestles in the hinterland rainforests of Queensland's Sunshine Coast, 110 km north of Brisbane, perhaps an unlikely location for a brewery. During 1987 John Lynch, a brewing engineer and developer, had invited a number of Queensland businesspeople and hotelowners to invest in a brewery at Eumundi, which could 'grow with demand'.

On behalf of the group, Lynch purchased the beautiful old Imperial Hotel at Eumundi, and began construction of an adjacent brewery. In February 1988 Eumundi Lager was on the market, and the beer sold as fast as it could be brewed — from the keg at the Imperial, and in long-necked bottles throughout southeast Queensland. The beers — Eumundi Lager, Gulf Beer and Laguna Bay Lager — quickly attracted cult followings. The bottle labels of all of the company's beers are particularly attractive, and the beers themselves gained widespread popularity.

Several Australian boutique breweries have used an image of Captain Cook on their bottle labels, including this label that was used by the Colonial Brewing Co., Brisbane.

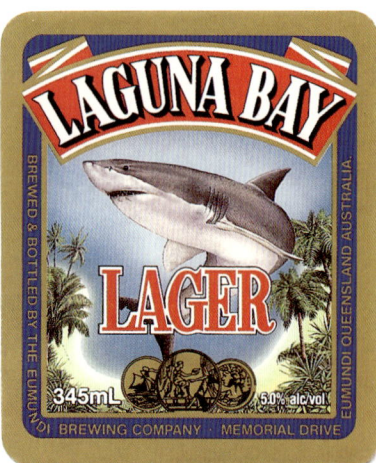

Labels of the Eumundi Brewing Co., Queensland, featured colourful illustrations of Australia's unique fauna.

A prospectus was issued in 1989, and the share issue was oversubscribed. Shortly after, however, the new company, Eumundi Brewing Co. Ltd, was faced with a number of problems. Eumundi was always meant to be a premium beer but at a premium price, and gradually it became a luxury few drinkers could afford or were prepared to pay. Local residents took exception to the smells coming from the brewery, and, to make matters worse, there were huge cost over-runs at the brewery.

By early 1991 mounting losses required the infusion of further capital, but the problems persisted. In December 1991 an agreement was reached with the Power Brewing Co. of Yatala to produce and distribute Eumundi's beer.

In February 1992 the Eumundi Brewery closed. Brewing ceased, but Eumundi beers continue to be brewed for the company by other major brewing companies.

Hope Island

Gold Coast Brewery Pty Ltd   1988–
Casey Road, Hope Island

Queensland's luxury Sanctuary Cove Resort was built on Hope Island, a short distance north of the Gold Coast. It was officially opened in January 1988. A few months later the Sanctuary Cove Brewing Co., at the adjacent marine-village tourist complex, commenced production of Island Lager.

The brewing equipment was imported from Germany, and had a capacity to produce one million litres of beer annually. Both draught and bottled beers were brewed in the European lager-style, unpasteurised to retain the full flavour.

An extensive Queensland market was developed for bottled beer, with custom-designed labels for restaurants, companies, clubs and special events. Regular products became available in most of the capital cities in the eastern states, and the brewery began exporting beer to Japan.

The resort, including the brewery, was taken over by Japanese investors. In July 1992 it was decided to close the brewery, which was then leased to a soft-drink manufacturer.

Brewing started again in October 1992, this time as the Luka Brewery, and continued until April 1995. The holding company of the Luka Brewery was Almond Tower Pty Ltd, and during 1994 ownership changed to Sabina Pacific Ltd.

Carlton & United Breweries Ltd took over the brewery late in 1995, and reopened it as the Gold Coast Brewery Pty Ltd.

Luka Brewery
See Gold Coast Brewery Pty Ltd.

Sanctuary Cove Brewing Co.
See Gold Coast Brewery Pty Ltd.

Maroochydore

Sunshine Coast Brewery   1998–
The brewery opened on 26 January 1998 at Kunda Park, an industrial estate just west of Maroochydore on the Sunshine Coast. It has a bar area at the front of the brewery. Draught beer, including Sunshine Coast Extra Bitter, Sunshine Coast Premium and other specialty beers are supplied to a number of clubs in the area.

Yatala

Power Brewing Co. Ltd   1988–93
Cnr Pacific Highway & Mulles Road

One of the largest of the boutique breweries to commence in Australia in the 1980s was the Power Brewing Co. Ltd — in fact, it was well above the boutique brewery class. It was a large major brewery, which set out to compete on the domestic market with the two long-established Queensland breweries, Castlemaine with their well-entrenched XXXX Bitter Ale, and Carlton & United Breweries Ltd (CUB) with their Foster's Lager. Power also planned to export draught, bottled and canned beer to the southern states of Australia.

The driving force behind the venture was Bernard Power, the owner of a number of hotels in Queens-

Some of the many special labels which the Sanctuary Cove Brewery has supplied to clubs, restaurants, companies and other customers.

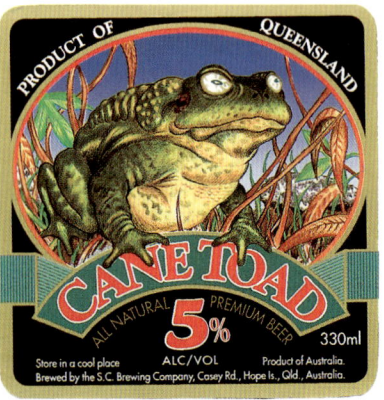
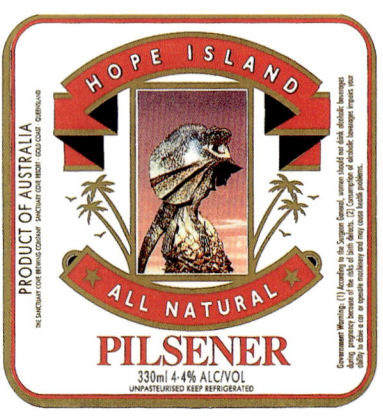

The Power Brewing Co.'s Power's Bitter was first released in September 1988 and rapidly gained in popularity throughout Australia's eastern states. The Power Brewing Co. became totally owned by Carlton & United Breweries in September 1993, and a number of new beers were progressively put on the market.

land. In 1985 he set about developing a huge 30 ha brewing complex at Yatala, 70 km south of Brisbane. When completed, after enormous capital expenditure, the brewery was claimed to be one of the most modern and efficient in the world.

Power's Bitter was launched in September 1988, and Power's Light a year later. Such was the popularity of the beers that, after two years of operation, the brewery had expanded to a capacity of 140 million litres of beer a year. Bulk and packaged beer gained widespread acceptance throughout Queensland, and also in Sydney and Melbourne, where Power's beer could be purchased from almost every hotel and liquor store. Bernie Power's brewery was an undoubted success.

In August 1992 a joint venture between Power Brewing Co. Ltd and CUB resulted in the formation of Queensland Breweries Pty Ltd. The new company would brew for both companies at Yatala, with distribution carried out independently by both Power and CUB.

On 28 October 1993 the brewery became totally owned by CUB. They closed their old brewery in Fortitude Valley in Brisbane in February 1993, and all CUB beers that had been produced at the Valley were then brewed at Yatala. Some of the popular Power brands continue to be produced at Yatala.

South Australia

Adelaide

Botanic Hotel Brewery 1986–87
309 North Terrace

The Botanic Hotel is a gracious three-storey Victorian building situated on Adelaide's elegant North Terrace.

A small brewing plant was installed, and a beer called Old Botanic Brew became available in November 1986. It was an all-malt, lager-style beer, which was sold in bottles and also draught.

Despite the best efforts of the brewer and hotelkeeper to build up a profitable business, the brewery closed in December 1987. The equipment was later purchased by the Metropolitan Brewery in Melbourne.

Clarendon Brewing Co. 1986
Chandlers Hill

In February 1986 at Chandlers Hill, a southern suburb of Adelaide, the Clarendon Brewing Co. produced the first of only two batches of beer. The owners also operated Norman's Winery where the beer was made.

After three months the production of beer was discontinued. The first batch had been bottled and sold, but apparently the second batch was never released.

Cooper's Ale House 1987–94
Cnr Carrington & Pulteney Streets

The Schmidt Corporation owned a chain of hotels in Adelaide, and over time, they had developed a close working relationship with Cooper's Brewery in Adelaide. In a joint venture the Earl of Aberdeen Hotel was renovated into a stylish hotel, complete with its own fermentation plant, where wort, prepared by Cooper's Brewery, was transformed into the final product.

Brewing commenced at the Earl of Aberdeen Hotel in March 1987, and three beers were produced: Carrington Pale Ale, Aberdeen Scotch Ale and Earl's Best Light.

Jerningham Street Brewery 1996–
8 Peekarra Street, Regency Park

The Lion Brewing & Malting Co. Pty Ltd started in Jerningham Street, North Adelaide, in 1986, had closed, and was taken over by the Lion Brewing Pty Ltd in 1992.

After several more closures the equipment was purchased by the Jerningham Street Brewery, and relocated to Regency Park. Their first production, Red Ant Lager, was apparently the first red-coloured lager to be

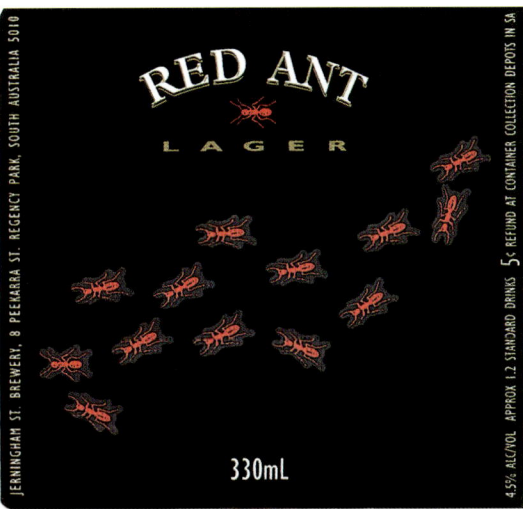

The Jerningham Street Brewery purchased the equipment of the defunct Lion Brewery, Adelaide, and installed it at a new brewery at Regency Park. The new company's first beer was named Red Ant Lager.

made in Australia. Although now located some distance from the old Jerningham Street site, the company has continued to trade as the Jerningham Street Brewery.

Kent Town Brewery 1990–95
2 Rundle Street

The original Kent Town Brewery had been started by Sir Edwin Smith in 1876, and later amalgamated with the West End Brewery to form the South Australian Brewing Co. Ltd. At the time of amalgamation, in 1888, brewing was discontinued at the Kent Town Brewery. For the next hundred or so years, the premises were mainly used for the preparation of malt.

In recent times malting has been carried out by a Scotsman, Gordon Welsh, who decided in late 1990, to set up a brewery, and produce what he called Kent Town Real Ale. At the outset the Real Ale was supplied in casks to about thirty Adelaide hotels, and later it was available in bottles. The yeasty, cask-conditioned ale was made with the technical assistance of the South Australian Brewing Co. Ltd, but brewing was discontinued late in 1995.

Lion Brewing & Malting Co. Pty Ltd
See Lion Brewing Pty Ltd.

Lion Brewing Pty Ltd 1986–95
31–39 Jerningham Street, North Adelaide

The original Lion Brewery started in business in 1850, and continued to brew beer until 1914. Aerated-waters and cordials were made after that. The old brewery and malting buildings, together with the Lion Hotel, were sold in 1970, and converted into one of Adelaide's fashionable hotel entertainment venues.

In 1986 the Lion Brewing & Malting Co. Pty Ltd was formed, and a joint venture was entered into with the Perth-based Matilda Bay Brewing Co. Ltd (Brewtech Pty Ltd, as it was then known). A modern brewery was installed, and the first draught beer was produced in November 1986. Bottling was subcontracted, and the labels featured a lion in stylised form — crown on the top of the head, and holding a foaming mug of beer. The two popular beers were Dark Lager and Pilsener.

The partnership with Matilda Bay was terminated in September 1989, and the Lion Brewery then became fully independent.

March 1990 saw the introduction of a wheat beer named Copperhead, but the company began to experience financial difficulty, and in June 1991 the State Bank assumed control of the company. At the auction in October 1991 the brewery was passed in, but six months later it was purchased by a new company, Lion Brewing Pty Ltd, which began producing Sparkling Bitter Ale and Adelaide Porter.

The brewery closed in October 1992, then reopened early in 1995, and closed again later that year. Shortly after, the equipment was purchased and relocated to Regency Park by the newly-formed Jerningham Street Brewery.

Port Dock Brewery Hotel 1986–
10 Todd Street, Port Adelaide

The lovely old Port Dock Hotel building dates back to 1883. It survived the decline of the port area, but closed following the temperance campaign that saw a third of Port Adelaide's hotels closed in 1909.

On 5 December 1986 the South Australian Premier officiated at the reopening of the beautifully restored hotel. The intervening seventy-seven years had seen it used as a brothel, a boarding house and a stevedore's office. The renovation included a small brewery and restaurant, and Cooper's Brewery supplied the concentrated wort for the production of the beer. The Port Dock Brewery produced Old Preacher Ale, Collectors Pale Ale, Lighthouse Ale and Black Diamond Best Bitter.

The hotel and brewery then had a number of changes in ownership, and brewing was intermittent until it stopped altogether late in 1989. Brewing commenced again in 1990, and the bulk beers produced were primarily for use by the hotel.

Label used by the Lion Brewing & Malting Co., Adelaide, when production commenced in November 1986.

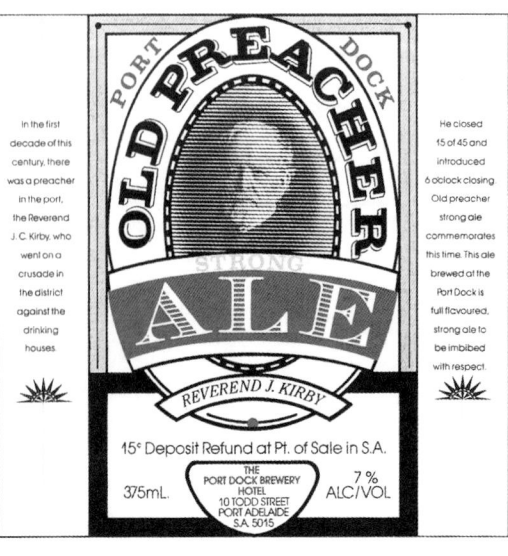

With a touch of irony, the Port Dock Brewery Hotel named its strongest beer, Old Preacher Ale. The bottle label was complete with a picture of the late Reverend John Kirby of the Temperance Society, the man who led the campaign that saw the hotel close in 1909.

Western Australia

Armadale

Darling Range Brewery 1992–
Canns Road

The Elizabethan Village is in Armadale, 30 km south of Perth, and with its magnificent Tudor-style buildings it hosts a wide variety of first-class tourist facilities. There are full-sized replicas of both William Shakespeare's birthplace and Anne Hathaway's cottage (near Stratford-upon-Avon in England). A later addition by the owner, Walter Lenz, was the Elizabethan Village Pub & Brewery, housed in a replica of the famous White Swan Inn at Stratford.

Brewing commenced late in 1992, the beer being of the true pilsener-style lager, with a big bouquet, a gentle bitterness and a creamy head.

Six types of beer, including a wheat beer, are served across the counter of the Brewhouse Inn, and also sold in kegs.

Toward the end of 1996 the name was changed to the Darling Range Brewery.

Elizabethan Village Pub & Brewery
See Darling Range Brewery.

Broome

Broome Brewery 1997–
60 Hamersley Street

Matso's Gallery & Coffee House includes a restaurant, as well as the Broome Brewery, which was opened on 10 May 1997. All are contained in two of Broome's most historic buildings: the Union Bank of Australia, built in 1900, and the home of master-pearler, Captain Ancell Gregory, erected in 1917. The old bank building had been moved twice, and Captain Gregory's home once. The present site faces Roebuck Bay.

The total operation is operated by Royal Harmony Pty Ltd. Mick Gayfer is the chairman, and Perth historian and businessman, Anthony Ellis is managing director.

Beers produced include such topical names as Lugger, Pearl, Cyclone and Governor Broome.

Fremantle

Anchor Brewing Co. Pty Ltd
See Matilda Bay Brewing Co. Ltd.

Brewtech Ltd
See Matilda Bay Brewing Co. Ltd.

Fremantle Brewing Co. Pty Ltd 1993–97
7 Blamey Place, Fremantle

In 1992 Irishman Brian Deighan set up the Fremantle Brewing Co. Pty Ltd. Brewing commenced early in 1993, and within a year or two the company claimed to have established about 300 outlets throughout Western Australia. Popular beers were Mariner Bitter and Mariner Light Bitter.

The brewery was taken over by the Swan Brewery in Perth in 1996. Brewing continued with the release of new products such as 1857 Pilsener, Swan Stout

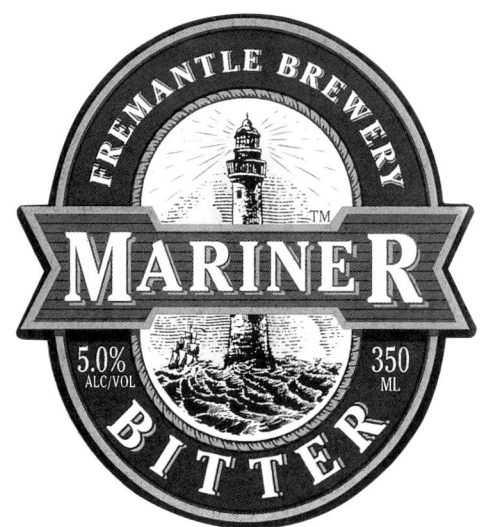

The historic township of Broome, on the far north-east coast of Western Australia, began as a pearling station. Today, the cultured pearl industry and tourism account for much of the town's economy. The label illustrated was used during the 1930s by H. E. Mau. He purchased bulk beer from breweries in Perth, and then bottled it for resale in Broome and nearby areas.

and O'Flanagan's Cream Stout, all under the Fremantle Brewery name. The brewery closed in November 1997.

His Lordship's Larder — 1986–89
2 Mouat Street, West Fremantle

His Lordship's Larder is an old hotel located in the west end of Fremantle. After the installation of a small brewery, several beers were ready in August 1986, including Murphy's Mild, Old Fremantle Stout and Tobruk Lager.

Early in 1989 it was decided to close the brewery section of the hotel.

Matilda Bay Brewing Co. Ltd — 1984–90
130 Stirling Highway, North Fremantle

The Matilda Bay Brewery was the first of the modern-day boutique pub-breweries to operate in Australia. Completely independent of the long-established and powerful breweries, including the Swan Brewery in Perth, the new company was the pioneer in introducing a new range of specialty beers and old-style English ales.

The promoter of this profoundly courageous venture was Philip Sexton, a young man who had worked for years at the Swan Brewery, and had been involved in developing the highly successful Swan Special Light. In 1983 he left Swan and completed a master's degree in biochemistry in Britain, specialising in the fermentation of beer.

Returning to Fremantle, Sexton began to shape his vision of an up-market hotel brewery into reality. A company was formed in October 1983 as Dallenton Pty Ltd, changing to Brewtech Pty Ltd, and then Brewtech Ltd in December 1987.

The company began in business by purchasing and restoring the historic Freemasons Hotel in Fremantle. A small brewery was installed, and the hotel was renamed the Sail & Anchor Pub Brewery. Business was conducted as the Anchor Brewing Co. Pty Ltd at 64 South Terrace, Fremantle, and when brewing commenced in July 1984 Australia's first pub-brewery this century was born. A new era in the history of brewing in Australia had begun, and the foundation was laid for the boutique breweries that were to follow throughout all states of Australia.

A range of new-style beers was introduced to an eager public, who were able to sample Real Ale, Porter, Lager and Steam Beer. Many other brands followed, including the popular Redback, said to be the first wheat beer to be commercially brewed in Australia this century.

Shortly after the establishment of the Sail & Anchor Pub Brewery, another, larger brewery was built at the inner Perth suburb of Nedlands, and the Matilda Bay Brewing Co. Pty Ltd was formed. It became a 'Limited' company on 23 May 1988.

Other hotels were purchased, and with increasing demand for the company's ales, lagers and stout, a major new brewery was fitted out by converting the old Ford assembly factory in North Fremantle into a brewing complex. Production of beer began in May 1989, with the official opening the following August.

Markets were expanded by the acquisition of hotels in the eastern states, and the company rapidly became a national specialist brewer and hotelier. During 1988 in a joint venture, the Port Melbourne Brewing Co., later called the Redback Brewery, was formed, and a small modern brewery was installed in the Royal Hotel, North Melbourne. Also during 1988 a distribution agreement was executed with Elders IXL Wine & Spirits Co., a division of Carlton & United Breweries Ltd (CUB), for the national distribution of all Matilda Bay beers.

On 20 October 1988 the company was listed on the Australian Stock Exchange, and CUB acquired a share-

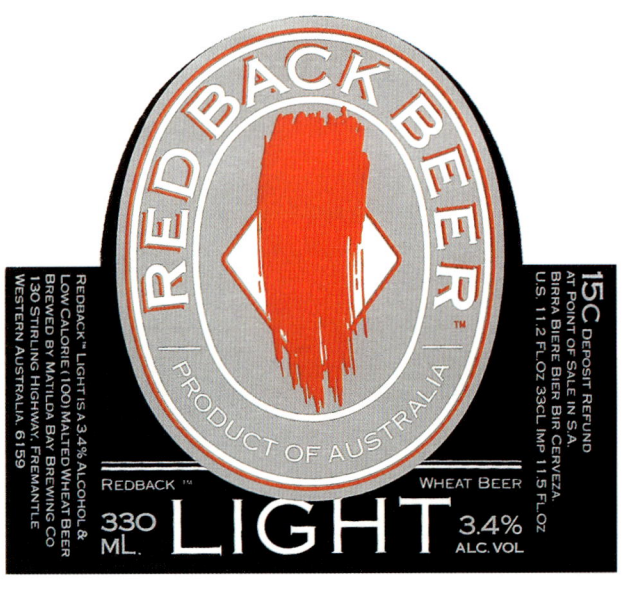

holding. This ultimately led to the takeover and total control of the Matilda Bay Brewing Co. Ltd and its operations by CUB in April 1990.

Sail & Anchor Pub Brewery
See Matilda Bay Brewing Co. Ltd.

Margaret River

Bootleg Brewery 1994–
Pusey Road, Willyabrup, Margaret River

For some, the name Bootleg Brewery may invoke thoughts of an illicit whisky still in some remote region far from the scrutiny of the law. However, when the brewery was started by Tom and Sue Reynolds, it certainly had a licence to brew, and was located in the well-known winegrowing district of Margaret River. The equipment came from the Glencoe Brewery at Yallingup, which had closed. Oddly

enough, the Glencoe had also been known as the Moonshine Brewery, another name for 'liquor illicitly distilled'.

Using Moonshine Brewery equipment, the Bootleg Brewery opened on 23 November 1994, and twelve or more beers were progressively put on the market, all with the same style of green-coloured bottle labels, the only difference being the names. They included Special Beer, Bush Beer, Christmas Ale, Wills Pils, Raging Bull and Black Magic. More recently other colours have been introduced to the labels.

Perth

Inchant Brewery Co. 1998–
Rose & Crown Hotel, 105 Swan Street, Guildford

The historic Rose & Crown Hotel at Guildford, was built by Thomas Jecks, and was opened in July 1841.

Brewing became part of the hotel's business. Although there have been improvements to the property over the many years, and recent restoration to the buildings, the property remains the oldest operating hotel in Western Australia.

Ian Jeffrey and his partner, Steve Milosz, added a brewery to the property in 1998. According to Ian Jeffrey, it had taken two years of experiments to perfect his recipes. At the launch in October 1998, guests were able to sample three beers — Bull Ant Bitter, Thomas Jecks Commonwealth Ale and Guildford Porter.

Rare Amber Brewing Co. 1998–
13A/18 Milford Street, East Victoria Park

The Rare Amber Brewery Co. was established by the owners, John Green and Meg Pitcher, in mid-1998, and the first beer was ready in November that year. Located on a small industrial estate, it is a stand-alone brewery with no hotel or restaurant attached.

The beers produced include a wheat beer, bitter ale, a brown ale and a stout. Initially, these will be available through the restaurant trade, and will also be delivered direct to customers. This a similar marketing practice used by many early breweries such as the Richmond Brewery, Melbourne and Coopers in Adelaide. The delivery vehicle, for the Rare Amber, is a fully restored 1948 Austin truck.

Witchcliffe

Leahdale Brewery 1996–
Lot 1, Sebbes Road, Witchcliffe

The Leahdale Brewery is located 10 km south of Margaret River, in the heart of a well-renowned winegrowing district. It operates on weekends only, and the owner, Andy Scothern, produces four different beers. Named after the Scothern children, Leah and Dale, the brewery is said to rank as one of the smallest in Australia.

Yallingup

Glencoe Brewing Co. 1990–94
Wild Wood Road

The township of Yallingup, about 200 km south of Perth, is close to the Margaret River winegrowing district. The Kiepo Vineyards, one of many in the area, were established in the late 1980s by Bill and Pam McKay. They added a brewery, and production of beer commenced in 1990.

Two of the beers, Moonshine Bitter and Moonshine Pale, were made from barley malt, with a small quantity of wheat malt added to give a distinct flavour and creamy character to the beer. Most of the output was consumed locally.

The brewery, frequently referred to as the Moonshine Brewery, closed in 1994, and the equipment was purchased by the Bootleg Brewery.

Tasmania

Cygnet

Cygnet Brewery 1979–85
Bafles Hill

The Cygnet Brewery was licensed as part of the Chateau Lorraine Winery at Bafles Hill, 3 km south of the small township of Cygnet and 60 km south of Hobart. The beer, first produced in 1979, was bottled in clear bottles and, according to some unkind Melbourne critics, very much resembled a bottle of muddy Yarra River water.

Beer production was spasmodic, and both the brewery and winery closed in 1985.

Glenorchy

Taverners Products 1989–
1 Nichols Street

Taverners Products began as a partnership between Stephen Nichols and David Thomas, at the original address of Ranelagh Road, Ranelagh. Later, the business moved to Glenorchy, and was incorporated.

Officially, the business was a winery and not a brewery. The proprietors preferred the term 'Meadery' as being more descriptive of the products, which included a champagne-style Sparkling Mead and a Good Ale Mead. The former was self-carbonated by a second fermentation in the bottle, which allowed the mead to mature with age. The Good Ale Mead was made from honey and hops, with an alcohol/volume content of 8 per cent.

Golconda

Lone Star Brewery 1989–

The tiny Lone Star Brewery was set in a picturesque valley surrounded by state forest, in the north-eastern region of Tasmania. It was one of the more unusual breweries to open during the late 1980s where, instead of the traditional ingredients of malt, hops and sugar, the Lone Star's Horehound Ale Mead was made from the bitter aromatic horehound herb and local bush honey.

Brewing began in September 1989 by the Rooke family, who also operated a small organic farm where the horehound was grown. The small quantities of Ale Mead produced were available mostly at the premises.

Hobart

Battery Point Brewery
See St Ives Brewery.

St Ives Brewery 1986–
86 Sandy Bay Road, Battery Point

First known as the Battery Point Brewery, it operated from the St Ives Hotel at Battery Point, a short distance from the central business district of Hobart. The original owner was the Port Melbourne Brewing Co., Melbourne, and brewing commenced in 1986 under the guidance of George McMasters.

The Matilda Bay Brewing Co. Ltd of Fremantle, WA, took over in 1988, but by July 1989 Romi Nominees were in control. Twelve months later brewing had ceased; only draught ale had been produced, under the brand names Classic Blue Water and Battery Ram.

In 1992 James Bleasel became the new owner of both the hotel and brewery. The brewery was relocated to another part of the hotel and beer went on sale again in 1992. The brewery was then referred to as the St Ives Brewery, with the master brewer, Ken Holmes, in charge. Beers produced include Gothic Gold, Old Bastard, Vicar's Bitter and St Ives Draught.

Wineglass Bay Brewing Co. 1996–
86 Sandy Bay Road, Battery Point

The business was first operated by Matthew Robinson and Claudio Radenti. They had the unusual arrangement to use the facilities of the St Ives Brewery at the St Ives Hotel to produce their own beer. One of the products is Hazards Ale, sold at the St Ives Hotel and several other hotels in Tasmania.

In August 1997 the business was conducted by Ken Holmes and Claudio Radenti.

Rosevears

**Rosevears Waterfront
Brewery Pty Ltd** 1989–90
Rosevears Drive

The old Rosevears Hotel was first licensed on 24 September 1831, and has held a licence as a hotel since that date. Although the hotel was rebuilt many years ago, some of the original brickwork can still be seen. The site of the hotel, on the west bank of the Tamar River, 20 km north of Launceston, provided a delightful view across the broad upper reaches of the river.

During 1989 the proprietor and licensee of the hotel, Peter Tonkin, commenced brewing at the hotel, and produced Batman's Best Bitter, Brady's Mild Ale and Tamar Porter.

Toward the end of 1990 the hotel was auctioned, and the new owner, Bruce Appleby, sold the brewing equipment and continued to run the hotel.

Northern Territory

Darwin

Frontier Brewery 1988–96
Cnr Daly & Mitchell Streets

The Northern Territory's first pub-brewery, aptly named the Frontier Brewery, formed part of the Top End Frontier Hotel & Motel complex, owned and operated by an amalgamation of two family companies.

Brewing commenced in June 1988 with production of a range of appropriately-named beers, including Old Buffalo, Kakadu Lager, Top End Premium Pilsener and Frontier Gold.

When Carlton & United Breweries Ltd closed its Darwin Brewery early in 1989, the Frontier became the only brewery in the Northern Territory. The nearest breweries were in Cairns in Queensland and Adelaide, South Australia.

Lager Beer

Many Australian settlers held a poor opinion of colonial beer and, more often than not, their criticism was justified. During the nineteenth century, while some colonial brewers managed to put out reasonably good beer, most were unable to brew anything of consistent quality. Breweries struggled through continual changes in ownerships, bankruptcies, failures and closures.

Better-quality imported beers were preferred by those who could afford the higher price, although, with long and rough sea voyages, these were sometimes not much better. Some of the beers that came from Germany were new to the colonies. They were lager beers.

The Ale of the Future

By the 1850s and 1860s in the USA, Germany, and some other European countries, a change in drinking preferences began to emerge. People began to favour a new style of beer called lager; it was lighter, less intoxicating, more gaseous and better-conditioned than the old-style ales and porters. This was a beer more suited to Australian conditions where, in the hotter climates, men often wanted a long drink rather than a strong one. The *Australian Brewers' Journal* of November 1882 reported that

> the lager beer of Germany is the type of ale to the manufacture of which we would like to see some of the Australian brewers turning their attention. It is gradually obtaining a footing in England where several large breweries have been quite lately built for its manufacture, and is practically the only kind of ale drunk in the United States of America …

The article continued, with rather odd comparisons,

> People are beginning to find out that drinking hot tea three times a day, as is often done in this country, is nothing less than poisonous, medical men affirming that its present excessive use affects the digestion, heart, &c., and generally upsets the whole nervous system. They recommend the use of light clarets. We ask, why not light ales, in which there would be more nourishment. A gentleman who had just returned from Europe said he was astonished to see the enormous quantities of lager beer the Germans drank without becoming intoxicated …

Year after year the journal continued its crusade, urging Australian brewers to start making lager beer. This again, in January 1886:

As we have said over and over again, a beer of the lager type is the beer of the future … the public in this hot country will demand their ale cold, full of gas and a long drink for their money. To insure all this, the beer must be packed in ice and the temperature kept down from the time the fermentation starts till it is handed to the thirsty customer.

The Beginning of Change

One of the pioneer brewers of lager beer in Australia was Sam Marks, joint-owner of the Sydney Brewery in George Street, Sydney. The *Australian Brewers' Journal* of August 1883 reported on Sam and his lager beer:

> Our representative, Mr. Setzer, during a late visit to New South Wales, was surprised to find that Lager Beer was being successfully manufactured by Messrs Marks and Murphy of Sydney. The beer was of the American type, with a very fine flavour, in good condition, brilliant and without sediment, and as it had been pasteurised, it should keep well. Mr. Marks has had 15 years' experience of lager beer brewing in the United States of America, where hardly anything else is drank.

Very little lager beer was brewed and sold by the Sydney Brewery. There were four changes in ownership, a change of address, and three different brewery names over a lifespan of eight years.

For German migrants Leopold Rennie and Rudolph Friederich 1885 was going to be a great year. They

> secured a splendid site on the Yarra River at Collingwood, [Melbourne] … the fermenting cellar is 36 feet underground and has some 10 feet of solid earth on top, and buildings again on this.

The partners installed the latest equipment specially designed for lager beer production, and registered the Gambrinus Lager Beer Brewery Co. Ltd on 25 September 1885. All the employees were German, and Rennie knew how to make lager beer, but soon after the company was formed it was wound up. The brewery was taken over, but the new owner closed it permanently the following year.

Cohn Brothers' Victoria Brewery in Bendigo, Victoria, can be credited with being Australia's first successful commercial brewer of lager beer. In 1880, at the age of eighteen, Julius Cohn, the elder son of Moritz Cohn, was sent to the brewing college in Worms, Germany. This was the premier brewing college in the world at that time, and specialised in teaching the art of brewing lager beer. Julius returned in 1882 with his 'degree', and persuaded the partners to erect the first lager beer brewery in the Australian colonies. Cohn Brothers called their new product Excelsior Lager.

A letter of protest and indignation was sent by Cohn Brothers to the editor of the *Australian Brewers' Journal*. Dated 26 June 1885, the letter was published in the July 1885 issue of the journal:

The Victoria Brewery of Cohn Brothers, Bendigo, Victoria, was the first to commercially produce lager beer in Australia. The label for their Excelsior Lager Beer did not show the name of the brewery and gave the appearance of an imported German Lager. Later, the company overprinted the labels with the letters C and B, centrally placed to the sides of the Eagle emblem, the CB standing for Cohn Brothers.

This beautiful label was produced for the ill-fated Gambrinus Lager Beer Brewery, Melbourne. The company was registered in September 1885 but was wound up shortly after. At the time, lager beer production was very experimental and did not have public acceptance.

Dear Sir,

We notice an article in your last journal headed 'A New Lager Beer Brewery, Melbourne' [this was the defunct Gambrinus Brewery], in which you state 'that it is the first time you are aware that a brewery specially fitted out for the production of lager beer has been started in Australia.' … such is not the case, as not only have we a brewery specially fitted up for the production of lager beer, but we have also imported a large amount of machinery from Germany, together with a large ice machine, the latter being absolutely necessary for a lager beer plant, as it is impossible to manufacture the beverage without it. We have had our plant erected for three years, during which time we have turned out a large quantity of lager beer, which has been pronounced by critics as being quite equal to the imported article.

Yours truly,
Cohn Bros.,
Sandhurst, Victoria.

By 1885 there had been very little public acceptance of this new lager beer, but some Australian brewers had faith in the future of the product and began brewing and selling lager under their own brand names. Montgomerie's Brewery in Jeffcott Street, West Melbourne, advertised lager beer from about 1886. Another Melbourne brewery, Ernest Miller's Royal Artillery Brewery in Elsternwick, put out a Lager Bier in the mid-1880s.

Thomas Ware of the Torrenside Brewery in Adelaide was brewing lager in 1888. The company guaranteed that any of their bottled ales would keep for at least two years, and said that they kept 30,000 dozen bottles of Jubilee Lager in stock. The Castlemaine Brewery in Brisbane became the first in Queensland to produce lager, which sold for 6d per bottle. The *Brisbane Courier* said, in October 1889, that

> Its quality has been found to be excellent, the Pasteur system of destroying yeast germs — immersion of the beer after being bottled in hot water — preventing it from losing its bright condition.

Through the 1880s lager beer production in Australia had been mostly experimental. The technique was new and difficult, and the public was sceptical. The industry was making little headway in mastering the brewing processes, and the quality of the lager, particularly without refrigeration, was no better than the old-style ales. Under such conditions it was almost impossible to educate and influence a public resistant to change. But change was on the way, and that tide of transition was to be Foster's Lager.

A New Era

William Foster and his brother, Ralph, arrived in Melbourne from New York in 1887, bringing with them a German-American who had studied lager brewing in Cologne, Germany. The brothers built an ultra-modern lager-beer brewery in the inner Melbourne suburb of Collingwood, and installed special lager-brewing equipment and an icemaking plant, all brought from the USA.

Brewing commenced in November 1888, and the public received its first taste of Foster's Lager on 1 February 1889. The product was an instant success: the public liked it, and the quality was consistently good, no doubt due to the services of the experienced chemist, August de Bavay.

From the beginning hotels taking the new lager received free ice to keep the beer cool, and chilled casks were delivered during the hot summer months. Later, small 5-gallon kegs of lager were supplied to leading cafes. Foster's Lager was developing an ever-increasing market, not only in Melbourne but in country Victoria and in other states. This success and influence on public taste motivated other breweries to start making lager.

Slowly but surely, more and more breweries began to follow the trend. In 1894 the Bundaberg Brewery in Queensland was brewing pasteurised lager, and the following year the Victoria Brewery in East Melbourne extended its floor space to accommodate a new 50,000 barrel capacity lager-beer plant. Similar installations took place in Sydney. The New South

AUSTRALIAN BEER IN ENGLAND

The advent of a few barrels of Australian-brewed beer has apparently created some little sensation in England, judging by the fact that the London *Daily Telegraph* of the 24th of October 1891 contained the following:-

> misfortunes are falling thick upon the beer trade. In addition to home difficulties and 'lager' rivals [lager beer had recently been introduced in Melbourne and had become extremely popular], it has now come to count upon colonial [Australian] competition.
>
> The first consignment of Australian beer ever exported to this country by our Antipodean offspring has arrived in the Thames by a Peninsular and Oriental steamer. Should it prove palatable to English consumers, the trade, it is said, will be rapidly pushed ahead. What with beer, wine, mutton, kangaroos' tails, oranges, apples and other articles too numerous to mention, Australia will soon be able to supply us with the complete equipment of a substantial dinner. It may be added that the judgment of those who have sampled the new importation is distinctly favourable to the Antipodean brew.
>
> The Melbourne *Evening Standard*, a few days ago, seized upon the above and made it the text for a somewhat gushing leading article, wherein the British brewer was advised to beware, inasmuch as the 'glory of the pale ale of old England was waning above the rising might of the Australian article.'
>
> The beer of Australia, which is described as light, mild and wholesome, is supposed to be fighting its way merrily in the London markets, where heavy beer is said to 'giving place to this light and sparkling beverage from across the sea.'

Australian Brewers' Journal, December 1891

The Foster brothers, William and Ralph, were the pioneers of the successful commercial production of lager beer in Australia. Although not the first to brew lager in Australia, they laid the foundation of change where lager is now the beer of the nation. The label illustrated is one of the first to be used by the company in 1889, the letter F being the forerunner symbol for all the Foster beers that have followed.

Wales Lager Bier Brewing Co. Ltd was formed in 1896, and a magnificent brewery was built, fully equipped to produce lager beer. Other breweries followed. Marshall's Paddington Brewery in Sydney put out their first lager beer under the label Imperial Lager in December 1900, and the South Australian Brewing Co. created a new lager beer department in 1902. Others started much later, such as Tooths in Sydney and the Queensland Brewery in Brisbane, both in 1918.

The Pretenders

As a supplement to their regular brewing business, some Australian brewers imported bulk lager beer from the Continent, generally from Germany, and bottled it, using their own name on the label. Frequently the customer had no idea where the lager came from, and didn't really care. But lager beer was being sold in Australia as early as the late 1860s.

As an example, Jabez Wheeler was operating his brewery at 19 La Trobe Street, Melbourne, though the 1860s. The label illustrated shows Lager Bier, and could give a first impression that Wheeler was brewing his own lager beer. This would have been fifteen or more years earlier than any other Australian brewery. The label has the German words '*Gebraut — einzig und allein fur Jabez Wheeler*'. Few Australians spoke German at that time, and would easily assume that Wheeler had made the lager. Even today there could be that assumption. However, the translation is 'Brewed specifically and only for Jabez Wheeler'; it was brewed *for* Wheeler, not *by* him, and was obviously imported lager.

Since the 1930s virtually all beer produced in Australia has been lager beer and the prophesy of the *Australian Brewers' Journal* of August 1890 in many ways has been fulfilled:

> The system of brewing introduced into Australia from England has proved an utter failure and the old methods and systems will disappear like chaff before the wind. We have over and over again asserted that really good and satisfactory beer cannot be continuously produced in Australia on the old system, obsolete so far as this country is concerned. A change is near and the establishment of a considerable lager beer brewing concern will be a real boon to the inhabitants of our hot and dusty cities.

During the late nineteenth century casks of lager beer were imported from Germany, then bottled and sold, frequently under an Australian brewery name.

How Many Xs?

For centuries the letter X has been used by brewers as a means of identifying the strength of their beer, for their own purposes as well as for the benefit of the public. The origin of its use, or rather one interpretation, is found in an old English book on brewing:

> At a certain period, in distinguishing between small beer and strong, all beer sold at or above 10 shillings per barrel was reckoned to be strong and was therefore subjected to a higher duty. The cask which contained this strong beer was then first marked with an X, signifying ten. Hence the present quack-like denominations of XX (double X) and XXX (treble X) which appear unnecessarily on the casks and in the accounts of the strong ale brewers.

Commenting on the question, the *Australian Brewers' Journal* of July 1889 had this story to tell:

> A certain country brewer in a small way of business, one day received an order for eighteen gallons of 'strong' ale. He took the ale from the cellar and then, with a stencil, proceeded to mark four Xs on the cask, whereupon a friend, who happened to be present, asked ironically, 'Why don't you paint another X on it?' and received the reply: 'Because the cask ain't big enough!'

Most breweries of the nineteenth and early twentieth centuries used the letter X as part of their product description. XXX was the most commonly used.

Only one solitary X was originally marked on the kegs, but over time the use was extended to include XX (double X) and XXX (treble X), but nobody knew exactly how much each additional X made to the strength of the beer. By inference, more Xs had to make the beer stronger, presumably higher in alcoholic content, and presumably 'better' whatever 'better' meant.

In the earlier years of Australia's brewing history it was fashionable to use Xs. There was a certain degree of prestige and status in having Xs on a barrel. If a brewery had a lot of Xs on its kegs and barrels, it gave the impression of being 'up with the times' and a 'better' brewery than one that didn't use an X. There also appeared to be some influence over public preference, that XXX ale had to be 'better' than just plain ale.

Australian brewers have been using Xs since 1835 when John Tooth of the Kent Brewery in Sydney advertised his X, XXX, and XXXX ales. Prices increased according to the number of Xs. The XXXX ale was more than twice the price of the X ale.

When the Castlemaine Brewery in Brisbane first started brewing in 1878, it put out an XXX Sparkling Ale that was described by the *Brisbane Courier* as 'a delicious ale of the brightest amber, pleasant to the taste'. The innovative company went one further, and applied for their well-known XXXX trademark in 1894, but didn't use it until 1916. During that year they sold XXXX Sparkling Ale. The more famous Castlemaine XXXX Bitter Ale followed in 1924, and became so popular that the other brewery in town, the City Brewery, tried to upstage the Castlemaine Brewery by producing a 5X beer.

The letter X seemed to be the wrong symbol for beer right from the start. There were too many negative connotations: whereas a tick means yes or approval, an X means no or disapproval; X is used to indicate something that is wrong or incorrect, and in mathematics it is the symbol for an unknown quantity or a variable. X, either used in the singular or in multiples, has been used for generations on bottles of poison. Why label beer with an X?

If X has to be used, why not use 6X? The more Xs the better! If X is any criteria, 6X should sell better than the rest. Taken further, make it 8X. But there has to be a limit — XXXXXXXXXX beer would be going too far!

Today the use of X is no longer necessary other than to identify a product, such as the popular XXXX Bitter Ale. By law, breweries are required to

Left: *The Castlemaine Brewery, Brisbane, used this label when they introduced their XXXX Bitter Ale in 1924.*
Right: *In an endeavour to compete, Castlemaine's competitor, Perkins City Brewery, added an X and produced XXXXX Prize Pale Ale.*

clearly identify the amount of alcohol in their products, and the old X beer has gone for ever.

At another time, long ago, it would have been a unique and interesting experience to sample and evaluate all the different X beers, starting from X and then working up the scale to whatever number of Xs were available — but not 6X, as Australian breweries never made any.

The Temperance Movement

It was not easy to make a living as a brewer. On a social level, brewing was about the bottom of the list. A terrible smell always lingered around the brewery premises, and the unpleasant odours wafted away to other properties. People complained, not only about the smell but about the beer that was barely drinkable at times. Given the vagaries of the brewing business, bankers were sceptical about lending, and bankruptcies, frequent changes in ownership and closures were commonplace.

It was difficult enough having to put up with all these problems without the interference of the members of the temperance movement. They wanted to ban the production and sale of every form of liquor. It was as simple as that. The loud calls of 'Down with the demon drink' and 'Close the breweries' echoed across the country as the temperance movement planted its heavy foot on the brewers and their 'despicable trade'.

In some ways the brewers themselves contributed to the problem by putting out beer of substandard quality. They could 'doctor' their beer with all sorts of undesirable ingredients to offset bad smell or taste — anything to avoid waste. Nobody knew how much alcohol was in the beer, least of all the brewers, and much of the beer served could quickly put the drinker into a stupor.

Governments of the day did little to ease the problem of excessive drinking, other than fining or jailing the offenders. Governments actually supported the brewing industry, which provided a steady source of excise revenue. More beer was a good thing — for the treasury. Governments also saw the industry as a provider of employment, and there was a chain of service industries, from the farmer and bottlemaker to the barmaid in the hotel.

Disillusioned with government apathy, and the urgent need for reform, concerned and sober members of communities banded together to form well-organised temperance groups. The moral and economic decay caused through drunkenness had to be stopped, and the presence and influence of the temperance crusaders was sorely needed. For generation after generation the anti-liquor activists engaged in meetings and rallies, planning and lobbying for their cause.

Although it is doubtful if any breweries ever closed as the direct result of temperance movement action, the moral and social disruption associated with excessive drinking attracted much-needed publicity. Many members of parliament became staunch supporters of the cause, and, in time, a number of hotels were converted to what became known as 'Coffee Palaces', where liquor was prohibited. By the late 1880s there were fifty coffee palaces in Melbourne alone.

Temperance Societies

Problems associated with drunkenness started as soon as the Australian colonies were settled. With breweries spreading out across the country, temperance societies were quick to follow. The Port Phillip Temperance Society was founded as early as 1837, just two years after Melbourne was settled, while the Diemen's Land Temperance Society began in Hobart in 1832, with the aim of 'preventing the formation of habits and intemperate drinking'. Six years later the Tasmanian Teetotal Society was founded in Launceston.

In Western Australia the Swan River Auxiliary Temperance Society held its first meeting in January 1838 with the members promising, as an example to others, to abstain from drinking any form of alcoholic beverage. One journalist of the time reported:

> The sounds of revelry echoed through the silent bush and the terrible sin of drunkenness deluged the young colony [Perth]. Settlers lurched from wretched shanties to harass women and terrify children or to slump senseless in the dirt.

The description was no idle exaggeration. According to a member of the government, 90 per cent of deaths in the colony were caused by alcohol.

By 1857 there were three breweries in Perth, the population had grown to 14,000, and the drunkenness persisted.

> Each week, the courthouse collected crowds of drunks, both men and women. Binge drinkers with pay cheques could disappear into public houses for a week at a time and farmers would lure workers out to the bush with promises of drink.

The temperance advocates had much work to do.

Society in Need

The Victorian government took some action in 1854, and set up a Select Committee to 'Inquire into Intemperance'. Dr J. Singleton, President of the Victorian Liquor Law

---

THE BARMAID — MUST SHE GO?

Quite a lot of excitement is being created of late in Sydney circles by the action of a small coterie of feminine busybodies of the gimlet brigade, who are crying aloud to Heaven and the State Parliament for the abolition of the barmaid and pointing out that the average girl who serves behind a bar cannot possibly be a nice, respectable girl.

She would be a much more reputable citizen if engaged in scrubbing pots in a sixpenny restaurant, or wheeling somebody's twins out in the family go-cart around the domain. Recently a deputation of 50 ladies waited on the New South Wales Treasurer to urge that in the new Licensing Bill, a clause be inserted prohibiting the employment of barmaids. One of the deputationists suggested that a law be enacted debarring any female under the age of 21 from doing bar work.

Another Christian soul gave, as her opinion, that the age should be raised to 31; a suggestion which, carried into effect, would be doing away with our fair bar tenders altogether, as no bar-lady would ever own up to 31.

Australian Brewers' Journal,
June 1902

League, found that 'the committals for drunkenness during the past year [1853] have been enormous in Melbourne, 7,329, or one in ten of the population'. Melbourne's one in ten compared to London's one in 230. The brewers, full of self-righteousness, declared they were not responsible for the excessive drinking habits of the minority, and continued brewing at full capacity.

Dr Alleyn Best comments in his book, *The Liquor Trades Union in Victoria*, that, 'the medical profession freely prescribed alcohol for fevers, consumption, chills and to help recovery from operations'. The indignant temperance societies highlighted the amazing dispensing records of the Melbourne Hospital in the 1870s and 1880s:

> Outpatients looked upon the dispensary as a free grog shop. In 1882, 350 gallons of wine and spirits and about 3,000 gallons of porter were dispensed. Mr. Fitzgerald, the surgeon who owned the famous painting of Chloe, had 61 patients for the month of January 1884 and he prescribed 271 ounces of brandy, 74 ounces of wine, 2 bottles of champagne and 29 bottles of ale and porter.

Debate

Temperance advocates were usually well-intentioned, although at times their accusations bordered on the hysterical. An emotive article in their journal, the *Alliance News*, in 1892, said:

> It is well known that the rate of mortality amongst the brewers' assistants is very great and this is largely due to the drink with which their veins are habitually loaded. Slight accidents — sometimes a mere scratch, inflaming and mortifying — easily prove fatal to them and numbers of them are cut off by disease long before their time. The brewery educates them into the evil habit and, as we see, special effort is made in this direction by some of them, in celebration of the birth-time of our Lord and Saviour.

The reference was to the free beer handed out to brewery staff at Christmas time.

Arguing against the temperance 'fanatics', the breweries were no less modest in their rhetoric, and boasted that 'beer was the best barometer of a country's prosperity and healthful vigour'. They admitted that the pleasures of beer-drinking could be abused, but emphasised that 'the English language suffered much greater abuse when uttered by lying,

DRUNK ON BREAD

'You could get drunk on fresh bread if you could eat enough of it at once,' said a chemist to a woman with a white ribbon in her button-hole.

'I don't believe it.' the woman answered.

'And yet it is a fact,' the chemist continued. 'It used to be thought that the alcohol, which bread, in its fermentation generated, all passed out in the baking; but Thomas Bolas, a distinguished scientist, has proved that bread, after it is ready for eating, still contains alcohol. The other day, twelve loaves of fresh bread were examined and found to contain, on average, alcohol in the proportion of 0.314 per cent. When, therefore, you have eaten 100 lbs. of bread, you have consumed five ounces of alcohol. That is quite as much alcohol as you would get in a pint of whisky.'

Australian Brewers' Journal, June 1907

venomous and slanderous teetotallers'. They warned that 'British doctors had noted a remarkable increase there in the number of deaths from nervous complaints largely due to tea shops and coffee palaces'.

Continuing Action

Temperance groups met in workshops, houses or church halls, and enrolled large numbers of adults and children who signed the pledge of teetotalism. Typical of the movement was the Corio Total Abstinence Society in Geelong, Victoria, which frequently used the local fire brigade station for meetings and concerts. William Stitt Jenkins was the leader of the choruses, and a hard worker for the cause. One of the choruses offered this advice:

> Leave your port and leave your sherry
> Both are very bad indeed;
> Haste young men and maidens merry
> Sign the pledge with Charlie Read.

Charles Read, a former member of the Legislative Assembly, was the chairman at the concerts. The government had granted a site for a Temperance Hall, and the ceremony of laying the foundation stone was performed by Charlie

Temperance movement advocates were a constant force of condemnation and pressure against the breweries and their wretched trade. To show some measure of appeasement, most of the larger breweries produced non-intoxicating beverages.

Read. A vase, placed beneath the foundation stone, contained newspapers, a pledge card, reports, rules, and a statement, of which the following is an extract:

> The Geelong Total Abstinence Society erects this building for the purpose of advocating total abstinence from all intoxicating drinks and to train up the children of the land so that they may abhor these dreadful beverages which have for generations spread want and woe, death and eternal misery, broadcast over the earth …

During the second decade of the twentieth century there were five breweries in Perth. All were working to capacity, and the temperance groups were just as active in fighting the evils of alcohol. At that time the Band of Hope and other temperance organisations were busy with their rallies, and took particular interest in teaching young children in Sunday Schools. Small children were told of the evils of alcoholic drinks, and were invited to sign the pledge, promising never to touch the terrible beverages. The initials of the five breweries gave the Sunday School teacher the opportunity to round off a well-prepared talk by writing on the blackboard a summing up:

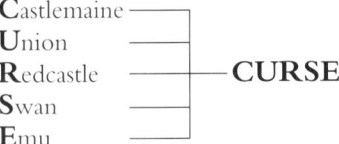

As a gesture of goodwill, many breweries made and sold a few brands of soft drink, but this meagre concession was looked on with scorn by the temperance zealots — after all, the breweries were still making beer. The 'movement' was also having trouble with so-called 'temperance' drinks, and time and again, the makers of hop beer, dandelion ale and other brands of 'soft drink' were brought before the courts, charged with selling beverages containing alcohol. Some of the 'soft drinks' had up to 11 per cent alcohol.

Brewers would look for any excuse to ridicule their temperance adversaries, and jokes and tall stories were common. The following advertisement was published in the *Australian Brewers' Journal* of January 1890:

> Lost — A small satchel, containing the manuscript of a temperance lecture, a number of unreceipted bills and a flask. If the finder will return the flask, with its contents, he may keep the lecture and bills.

Another story was published in May 1897:

> It was at a teetotal meeting and there had been the usual speeches and songs, full of the usual self-glorification of teetotallers and the usual vituperation of moderate drinkers. The chairman asked if there was anyone present who would come forward and bear his testimony on the important question of drink. After repeated appeals, a working man was seen making his way up the room from the back of the hall. Loud cheers followed until he reached the platform. The chairman shook his hand and introduced him as 'our worthy friend who has kindly come to assist the good cause.' The newcomer was a sturdy, healthy looking man and when the cheers subsided, he began. After saying that he was no orator, he proceeded — 'We have been invited here to bear our testimony on the important question of drink — (*Cheers*) — and I stand here to bear mine. (*Loud cheers*) Twenty years ago, ladies and gentlemen, there were two young men living next door to each other. They were both healthy young men as anyone could wish to see. (*Cheers*) They were the same age and followed the same trade and their circumstances were exactly alike. (*Cheers*) There was, however, one point on which they differed. (*Cheers*) That was the all important question of drink. (*Loud cheers*) One of those two young men took a pint of beer every day. (*Groans*) The other took a pint of water every day. (*Great cheering*) One of those two young men has for some time been in his grave. (*Sensation*) The other young man now stands before you. (*Immense cheering and waving of hats*) 'Ladies and gentlemen', he added, lapsing into his common vernacular, 'It was him as is dead what took the water.' (*Great uproar, during which the man was roughly hustled off the platform*).

There is no doubt that the temperance movement played an important and necessary and effective role in improving the morale, and, to some extent, the economic conditions of the Australian community. At times it may have appeared to some to be a lost cause, but it did maintain a presence and exerted much influence in improving the wellbeing of family life. It helped to restrain the excesses of irresponsible indulgence during those times when the nation was in need of this discipline.

The Number of Breweries

The table below lists the known number of breweries that have operated in Australia since colonisation. The numbers shown, however, are not entirely accurate for a number of reasons.

In the early years many publicans brewed their own beer, and continued to do so for some time without any registration, licence or record. As an example, Mr W. J. Wooldridge bought land in St Vincent Street, Port Adelaide, in 1850, and built the Carpenters Arms Hotel. The beer that he brewed in the adjoining premises was for sale at his hotel only. The hotel burnt down, the brewery portion was abandoned. and a new hotel, the Globe, built on the site in 1856. No official records show W. J. Wooldridge as a brewer, nor is the Carpenters Arms Hotel listed as a brewer. There were quite a number of small hotels throughout the colonies where their in-house brewing was limited, and no records were ever kept.

Shanty towns appeared overnight where gold was discovered, and during the second half of the nineteenth century almost all colonies had their share of goldrushes. The demand for any sort of strong drink was enormous, and opportunists quickly took advantage. They set up illicit stills, made all sorts of spirits and also beer, and operated illegally in tents, tin sheds or anywhere else that would suit their purpose.

People brewed beer at home, in the cellar, in a shed out the back, or in the kitchen for that matter. And in difficult times they sold their homemade beer to make ends meet. The authorities didn't know, and of course, there are no records, even though these 'home brewers' were in business, making and selling beer.

Frequently the information about a brewery that had changes of name are given under only one name of the brewery: for example, the Federation Brewery Co., Melbourne. In total there was a continuance of the brewery with various changes of address and brewery name. It started in Richmond and became known as the Richmond Brewery. Later, the business was shifted to La Trobe Street, Melbourne, and the name was changed to the Metropolitan Brewery Co. Later still, the brewery was moved further up La Trobe Street, and became the Metropolitan Brewery Co. Ltd., and, finally, the Federation Brewery Co. This listing of only the one brewery in the text, where there were many different names for the brewery, occurred frequently. If each of the brewery names were included, the number of breweries listed would be substantially increased.

Early records are not always accurate, and information in directories, gazettes and other government documents sometimes differ, one to the other. With research involving many information sources and spanning a period of 200 years, some errors and omissions will inevitably occur.

Number of breweries that have operated in Australia since colonisation

State	No. towns	No. breweries			Total
		Country	City		
New South Wales	99	168	Sydney	73	241
Victoria	94	211	Melbourne	91	302
Queensland	37	66	Brisbane	12	78
South Australia	41	51	Adelaide	47	98
Western Australia	35	68	Perth	26	94
Tasmania	42	96	Hobart	38	134
Northern Territory	2	1	Darwin	3	4
Additional boutique breweries, Australia wide					72
TOTAL	350	661		290	1,023

Glossary

Alcohol by volume (alc./vol.) This indicates the strength of a beer by the percentage of alcohol it contains, by volume. In Australia this is the standard way of describing strength, and is required by law to be shown on the bottle or can.

Ale Beer made by the top-fermentation process, and generally with less hops than other beers. Ale was the traditional Australian beer of the nineteenth century. Today, almost all beer produced in Australia is lager.

Barrel A wooden vessel of slightly ovoid cylindrical shape, made of staves bound together with hoops. A barrel may be a specific size such as a firkin, 9 gallons (41 litres); barrel, 36 gallons (164 litres); and hogshead, 54 gallons (245 litres). Almost all beer barrels are now made from stainless steel, and are typically referred to as kegs.

Beer A fermented liquor brewed from malt or from a mixture of malt and malt substitutes and flavoured with hops or other bitters. In Australia the word 'beer' is used in a very general sense to include ale, lager, pilsener, bitter, draught, stout and others. See also *Wheat beer*.

Bitter A term used to describe a beer that has been well hopped to give it a bitter flavour.

Bottom fermentation The method of fermentation used to produce lager-style beer. During fermentation the used yeast sinks to the bottom of the fermentation vessel.

Cask A general term for a wooden barrel made of staves of varying size.

Cooper A person who makes or repairs wooden vessels made from staves and metal hoops, such as casks, barrels and tubs.

Draught A term describing beer that may be served directly from a barrel. This beer is generally drawn from a barrel, under pressure, through pipes to a dispensing tap at a bar. Until the 1960s and 1970s draught beer was only available in barrels. Today, draught beer has become a style of beer where most breweries market draught beer in cans and bottles.

Fermentation The action of yeast on sugar, causing a conversion to alcohol and carbon dioxide.

Hogshead A large wooden barrel, made of staves; 52½ gallons capacity, but 54 gallons for beer or cider.

Hop (*Humulus lupulus*) A perennial climbing plant, preferring a cooler climate. The 'cones' or flowers are referred to as hops. Most beers are brewed using hops as a flavouring agent to give the beer a bitter flavour.

Keg A small wooden cask, usually of 5–10 gallons capacity. The term is also frequently used for the stainless-steel beer barrels used by the breweries.

Lager The literal meaning is 'storage'. Lager is beer made by the bottom-fermentation process, and stored for conditioning at cold temperatures.

Light beer Beer with a reduced alcohol content; in Australia this is generally between 0.9 and 3.3 per cent alc./vol.

Malt Grain, generally barley, is softened with water until it begins to germinate; this produces sugars and enzymes. The grain is then heated in a kiln, which stops the process, and then ground. Rice and other grains were sometimes used; and more recently some boutique brewers have used wheat in place of barley.

Pilsener Named after the Czech town of Pilsen, where a light-coloured, bottom-fermented, lager-style beer was first brewed.

Porter A heavy, dark-brown beer, originally a mixture of ale and stout. In earlier times in England it was named 'porter' because of its popularity with the hardworking market porters.

Stout A dark beer, sometimes top fermented, and made with highly roasted malt. Possibly because of the very dark colour (almost black), stout may give the impression of being a very strong beer, but generally stout is much the same strength as regular beers.

Top fermentation A traditional method of fermentation where the yeast rises to the top of the beer during the process.

Wheat beer Made from malt that contains a percentage of wheat, although rarely all wheat. Wheat beer has a characteristic flavour, noticeably different to beers brewed from barley malt.

Yeast A single-celled micro-organism that brings about fermentation, producing alcohol, carbon dioxide and flavour components.

Conversion Table

Before Australia converted to the metric system in 1966, brewers used the old imperial systems of currency and measurement. Original terminology has been retained to preserve the character of the times.

Where pre-metric currency is mentioned, no sensible metric equivalent can be given.

1d (penny)
1s (shilling: 12 pence)
£1 (pound: 20 shillings)

1 inch	2.54 cm
1 foot (12 inches)	30.5 cm
1 yard (3 feet)	91.5 cm
1 mile	1.61 km
1 acre	0.405 ha
1 lb	0.454 kg
1 ton	1.02 tonnes
1 pint	0.568 litres
1 quart (2 pints)	1.137 litres
1 gallon (4 quarts)	4.546 litres
1 barrel (36 gallons)	164 litres
1 hogshead (54 gallons)	245 litres

Bibliography

Books, Journals and Manuscripts

Andrews, Dr A. *The History of Albury 1824–1895*. History Pamphlets, vol. 13, Albury, NSW, 1912.

Arnold, K. *A History in Bottles and Stoneware, 1852–1930*. K. Arnold, Bendigo, [1978].

Arnold, K. *A Victorian Thirst*. Crown Castle Publishers, Bendigo, 1990.

Arnold, K. *Australian Antique Bottle Collector*. Quarterly journal, Crown Castle Publishers, Bendigo, Vic..

Auld, I. *In Cellar Cool*. Burra, SA, 1974.

Australian Brewers' Journal. 1882–1921.

Australian Brewing and Wine Journal, Spirit and Cordial Review. 1921–59.

Australian Encyclopaedia. Australian Geographic Society, 1988.

Australian Wine, Brewing and Spirit Review. 1958–.

Barrett, B. *The Inner Suburbs: The Evolution of an Industrial Area*. Melbourne University Press, Carlton, Vic., 1971.

Bassett, J. *Benalla Sketched*. Neptune Press, Newtown, Vic., 1984.

Bayley, W. A. *Blue Haven: History of Kiama Municipality, New South Wales*. Kiama Municipal Council, 1976.

Best, A. *The History of the Liquor Trades Union in Victoria*. Federated Liquor and Allied Industries Employees Union of Australia, Victorian Branch, North Melbourne, 1990.

Bingham, M. *Cascade: A Taste of History*. Cascade Brewery, Hobart, 1992.

Black Swan (magazine of the Swan Brewery Co. Ltd), Perth.

Blume, M. Castlemaine Breweries. Unpublished research notes, Castlemaine, Vic.

Bradfield, R. A. *Campbells Creek: Some Early History*. R. A. Bradfield, Vaughan, Vic., [1978].

Brelsford, M. *Sandstone and Cedar*. Aline, Toowoomba, Qld, 1983.

Brooke, B. & Finch, A. *A History of Horsham: A Municipal Centenary*. City of Horsham, 1982.

Brownhill, W. *History of Geelong and Corio Bay*. Wilks & Co., Melbourne, 1955.

Burton, B. K. *Flow Gently Past*. Corowa Shire Council, Corowa, NSW, 1973.

Cammilleri, C. *Anthony Curtis, Merchant and Trader, 1830–1853*. [np, nd].

Cannon, M. *Old Melbourne Town Before the Gold Rush*. Loch Haven Books, Main Ridge, Vic., 1991.

Carr, C. The Brothers Resch in New South Wales. Unpublished notes, Canberra, ACT.

Charlton, R. *History of Kapunda*. Hawthorn Press, Melbourne, 1971.

Clunes, F. *Saga of Sydney*. Halstead Press, Sydney, 1961.

Cohn, A. A., Cohn, J. M. & Cohn, L. J. *Tablets of Memory: The Bendigo Cohns and their Descendants, 1853–1989*. Antelope Press, Melbourne, 1990.

Cohn, J. M. *115 Years of Service: Cohn Bros. Limited, 1856–1971*. J. M. Cohn, Bendigo, Vic., 1971.

Commonwealth of Australia. *Year Books*.

Concise Encyclopaedia of Australia. David Bateman Pty Ltd, Qld, 1984.

Craig, G. F. *Looking Back: The Early Days of Stanley*. Ovens & Murray Advertiser, Beechworth, Vic., 1958.

Cyclopaedia of South Australia. 1909.

Cyclopaedia of Tasmania. 1900.

Cyclopaedia of Victoria. 1905.

Drew, G. H. *Discovering Historic Burra*. [Adelaide], 1988.

Driscoll, W. P. *The Great Aussie Beer Book*. Ellsyd, Sydney, 1984.

Dunstan, K. *The Amber Nectar*. Viking O'Neill, Melbourne, 1987.

Dunstan, K. *Wowsers*. Castle Australia, Melbourne, 1968.

Finch, P. & Auld, I. *Burra in Colour*. Rigby, [Adelaide], 1973.

Firkins, P. *A History of Commerce and Industry in Western Australia*. University of Western Australia Press, Nedlands, WA, 1979.

Garden, D. *Albany: A Panorama of the Sound from 1827*. Thomas Nelson (Australia), West Melbourne, 1977.

Garden, D. *Hamilton: A Western District History*. City of Hamilton, North Melbourne, 1984.

'Garryowen'. *The Chronicles of Early Melbourne 1835–1852*. Heritage Publications, Melbourne, 1976.

Guritson, J. *Tibooburra: Corner Country*. Tibooburra Press, [1981].

Hardy, J. *Norwesters of the Pilbara Breed*. Shire of Port Hedland, Port Hedland, 1981.

Harvey, R. *Background to Beechworth from 1852*. Beechworth Progress Association, 1981.

Historical Records of Melbourne, vol. 3, 1984.

Historical Records of Victoria, vol. 4, 1985.

Hoch, I. *Barcaldine 1846–1986*. Barcaldine Shire Council, 1986.

Hodge, H. *The Hill End Story*, Book 1: *Toorak*. Hill End Publications, Melbourne, 1986.

Howard, S. A History of Brewing in New South Wales 1788–1935. Unpublished manuscript, 1935.

Hughes, Dr D. 'Australia's First Brewer'. *Journal of the Royal Australian Historical Society*, vol. 82, part 2, December 1996.

Hughes, Dr D. *The Brewing Industry in Early Australia: The Dynamics of the International Brewing Industry Since 1800*, edited by R. G. Wilson & T. R. Gourvish. Routledge, 1998.

Hull, H. M. *Guide to Tasmania*. Hobart Town, 1870.

Hunt, G. *When Narrabri Was Young*. Narrabri Municipal Council, 1980.

Huntington, H. W. H. *History of the Beer and Cordial Industry in Australia*. Huntington, Newcastle, NSW, 1888.

James, W. S. *History of Shepparton 1838–1938*. Shepparton Centenary Celebrations Committee, 1938.

Jones, D. *Trinity Phoenix: A History of Cairns*. Cairns and District Centenary Committee, 1976.

Kearns, R. H. B. *Silverton: A Brief History*. Broken Hill Historical Society, 1976.

Kennedy, Brian & Barbara. *Australian Place Names*. Hodder & Stoughton (Australia), Rydalmere, NSW, 1989.

Kimberley, W. B. *Ballarat and Vicinity*. F. W. Niven, Ballarat, Vic., 1894.

Kimberley, W. B. *Bendigo and Vicinity*. F. W. Niven, Ballarat, Vic., 1895.

Lawson, W. R. *West Australian Breweries Since Federation, 1901–1958*. Customs Museum, Fremantle, WA.

McDonald, L. *Rockhampton: A History of City and District*. University of Queensland Press, St Lucia, Qld, 1981.

Manifold, W. G. *The Wished-for-Land*. Neptune Press, Newtown, Vic., 1984.

Moore, A. *Breweries of South Australia 1836–1936*. Working Paper 10, University of Adelaide, 1981.

Morris, S. *The Brewing Industry in Wagga*. [np], 1987.

Morrison, W. F. *The Aldine Centennial History of New South Wales*. Aldine Publishing Co., Sydney, 1888.

New Ways in an Ancient Land. Bay Books, Sydney, [1986].

Newbold, R. J. The Economic Development of the Brewing Industry in Queensland 1870–1901. Thesis, University of Queensland, 1989.

O'Hara, M. History of Carlton & United Breweries Ltd. Unpublished manuscript, 1958.

Osborn, B. & Dubourg, T. *Maryborough: A Social History, 1854–1904*. Maryborough City Council, 1985.

Osbourne, R. *History of Warrnambool 1887*. H. Worland, Warrnambool, Vic., [1970].

Painter, A. *The History of Cooper's Brewery, 1862–1987*. Cooper's, Adelaide, 1987.

Palmer, Y. S. *Track of the Years: The Story of St Arnaud*. Melbourne University Press, Carlton, Vic., 1955.

Roper-Power, M. The History of Brewing in Tasmania. Unpublished manuscript, 1987.

Shueard, H. & Tuckwell, D. *Brewers and Aerated Water Manufacturers in South Australia 1836–1936*. Stepney, SA, 1993.

Steele, J. *Early Days of Windsor*. Tyrell's, Sydney, 1916.

Stubbs, B. J. The Brewing Industry in Country New South Wales, 1946–1961. Thesis, University of New England, Armidale, NSW, 1991.

Stubbs, B. J. The Liquor Control Legislation of New South Wales and the Evolution of the Licensed Public House, 1788–1837. Unpublished manuscript.

Tuckfield, T. *Early Colonial Taverns and Inns*, vol. 7. Royal Western Australian Historical Society, 1971.

Victoria and its Metropolis: Past and Present. [np], Melbourne, 1888.

Ward, M. H. *Brief Records of Brewing in South Australia, Adelaide*. Pioneers' Association of South Australia, 1950.

Weeding, J. *History of Bothwell*. Telegraph Printery, Launceston, Tas., [1958].
Welborn, S. *Swan: The History of a Brewery*. University of Western Australia Press, Nedlands, WA, 1987.
What's Brewing (magazine of Carlton & United Breweries Ltd).

Wiedemann, E. *World of Its Own: Official History of Inverell, 1827–1920*. Devill Publicity, Inverell, NSW, 1981.
Withers, W. B. *The History of Ballarat*. F. W. Niven, Ballarat, Vic., 1870; revised edn, 1887.

Directories and Gazettes

Adelaide Directories
Ballarat District Directories
Bathurst and Western District Directories
Bendigo Directories
Birtchnell's Ballarat, Creswick, Buninyong, Clunes, Smythesdale and Browns Directories
Butler & Brooke Ovens District Directories
Castlemaine District Directories
Cox & Co.'s Sydney Post Office Directories
Geelong and Western Districts Directories
Geelong, Ballarat & Creswick's Creek Commercial Directories
Geelong Commercial Directory and Almanac
Kerr's Melbourne Almanac & Port Phillip Directory
Kyneton, Malmsbury, Taradale Directories
Melbourne Commercial, Professional & Legal Directories
Melbourne Directories
New South Wales & Port Phillip General Post Office Directories
New South Wales Government Gazettes
Official New South Wales Directories
Ovens District Directories
Port Phillip and Victorian Government Gazettes
Port Phillip Directories
Port Phillip Patriot Almanac & Directory
Port Phillip Separation & Melbourne Directory
Queensland Almanac & Brisbane Directories
Queensland Government Gazettes
Queensland Post Office Directories
Sampson New South Wales National Directory
Sandhurst and District Directories
Sands & Kenny Melbourne Directories
Sands & Kenny Sydney Directories
Sands & McDougalls Melbourne Directories
Sands & McDougalls Melbourne, Suburban & Country Directories
Sands Sydney Directories
South Australian Almanacs
South Australian Directories
South Australian Government Gazettes
South Australian Post Office Directories
Stephens and Bartholomew's District Directories
Sydney Gazettes
Tasmanian Directories
Tasmanian Post Office Directories
Victorian Government Gazettes
Walch's Tasmanian Almanacs
Western Australian Government Gazettes
Western Australian Post Office Directories
Wises New South Wales Directories
Wises Tasmania Post Office Directories
Wood's Point and Gippsland General Directories

Newspapers

Adelaide Examiner
Adelaide Observer
Advocate (Burnie, Tas.)
Albany Advertiser
Albany Mail
Albury Banner
Albury Border Post
Alpine Observer (Bright, Vic.)
Ararat and Pleasant Creek Advertiser
Argus (Melbourne)
Australian
Australian Advertiser
Avoca Mail

Bairnsdale Courier
Ballarat Miner and Weekly Star

Banner of Belfast (Port Fairy, Vic.)
Barrier Miner (Broken Hill, NSW)
Bathurst Times
Belfast Gazette (Port Fairy, Vic.)
Benalla Standard
Bendigo Advertiser
Bendigo Independent
Braidwood Dispatch
Brisbane Courier
Britannia (Hobart)
Broad Arrow Standard
Bunbury Herald

Camperdown Chronicle
Castlemaine Mail
Centralian Advocate (Darwin)

Charleville Times
Chronicle Despatch (Wangaratta, Vic.)
Clunes Guardian and Gazette
Colonial Times (Hobart)
Colonial Times (Launceston, Tas.)
Coolgardie Miner
Cootamundra Herald
Cornwall Chronicle (Tas.)

Darling Downs Gazette
Daylesford Mercury
Deloraine–Westbury Advocate
Devon Herald (Tas.)

Evening Echo (Warrnambool, Vic.)
Every Week (Gippsland, Vic.)
Examiner (Launceston, Tas.)

Federal Standard (Chiltern, Vic.)
Forbes and Parkes Gazette
Free Press and Mining Journal (Bathurst, NSW)

Geelong Advertiser
Geraldton Guardian
Gippsland Daily News
Gippsland Mercury
Gippsland Times
Glen Innes Examiner
Goulburn Evening Penny Post
Goulburn Herald

Hampden Guardian (Camperdown, Vic.)
Herald (Melbourne)
Hill End and Tambaroora Times
Hobart Town Advertiser
Hobart Town Courier

Hobart Town Gazette
Horsham Times
Hunter River Gazette

Illustrated News (Sydney)
Independent (Tas.)

Jamieson and Wood's Point Chronicle

Kalgoorlie Miner
Kilmore Advertiser

Launceston Advertiser
Launceston Examiner
Licensed Victuallers' Gazette and Sporting Chronicle (Adelaide)
Lithgow Mercury

Mackay Standard
Mail (Adelaide)
Maitland Mercury
Mansfield Guardian
Maryborough Chronicle (Vic.)

Maryborough and Dunolly Advertiser (Vic.)
Melbourne Advertiser
Mercury (Hobart)
Miner and Weekly Star (Ballarat, Vic.)
Mining Record (Grenfell, NSW)
Moreton Bay Courier (Brisbane)
Morning Advertiser (Hobart)
Morning Bulletin (Rockhampton, Qld)
Morning Star (Hobart)
Mount Alexander Mail (Castlemaine, Vic.)
Mount Ararat Advertiser
Mudgee Guardian
Mudgee Newspaper and Mining Advocate

Narrabri Herald
Narrogin Advocate
Narrogin Observer
National Advocate (Bathurst, NSW)
New South Wales Magazine
Newcastle Chronicle
Newcastle Morning Herald
Newcastle Morning Star
Norseman Pioneer
North Coast Standard (Tas.)
North Eastern Ensign (Benalla, Beechworth, Vic.)
North Queensland Herald
North West Post (Tas.)
North Western Advocate (Tas.)
North Western Chronicle (Ballarat District, Vic.)
Northam Advertiser
Northern Argus (Clare, SA)
Northern Herald (Cairns, Qld)
Northern Miner Register (Charters Towers, Qld)
Northern Standard (Darwin)

Ovens and Murray Advertiser (Benalla, Vic.)

Pastoral Times (Deniliquin, NSW)
Pastoral Times and Echuca and Moama Chronicle
Perth Enquirer
Perth Gazette
Perth Herald (Tas.)
Picton Journal (Bunbury, WA)
Pilbara Goldfields News
Pleasant Creek News (Stawell, Vic.)
Port Augusta Dispatch
Port Lincoln Herald
Port Phillip Gazette (Melbourne)
Port Pirie Gazette and Area News
Portland Gazette and Belfast Advertiser
Portland Guardian
Portland Mirror

Queensland Times

Riverine Herald (Deniliquin, NSW)
Riverine Herald (Echuca, Vic.)
Rutherglen Sun

St Arnaud Mercury
Saturday Evening Mercury (Tas.)

Silver Age (Broken Hill, NSW)
South Australian Gazeteer
South Australian Register
South Australian Sentinel
Southern Australian (Adelaide)
Southern Star (Tas.)
Standard (Warrnambool, Vic.)
Stanley Times and Mining Journal (Vic.)
Sunday Times (WA)
Sydney Gazette
Sydney Gazette and New South Wales Advertiser
Sydney Monitor
Sydney Morning Herald

Talbot and North Western Chronicle
Talbot Leader and North Western Chronicle
Tarrengower Times (Maldon, Vic.)
Tasmanian Mail
Tasmanian News
Tasmanian and Port Dalrymple Advertiser
Tasmanian Weekly Dispatch
Toowoomba Chronicle
Towers Herald (Charters Towers, Qld))

Townsville Herald
Trumpeter (Hobart)
Victoria and Murchison Districts, Illustrated (WA)
Victoria Express (Geraldton, WA)

Wagga Wagga Express
Wangaratta Chronicle
Waranga Chronicle and Goulburn Advertiser (Rushworth, Vic.)
Waranga Echo (Rushworth, Vic.)
Warrnambool Examiner
Warwick Examiner
Weekly Mercury and Bendigo Mining Journal
Western Argus (WA)
Western Champion (Barcaldine, Qld)
Western Herald (Bourke, NSW)
Western Post (Mudgee, NSW)
Wilcannia Times
Wood's Point Times

Young Chronicle

Zeehan and Dundas Herald

Historical Societies

Albury & District Historical Society
Alexandra Historical Society
Ararat Genealogical Society
Australian Stockman's Hall of Fame
Avoca & District Historical Society

Bacchus Marsh & District Historical Society
Bathurst District Historical Society
Bathurst Family History Group
Beaufort Historical Society
Beenleigh & District Historical Society
Bega Valley Historical Society
Benalla & District Historical Society
Berrima District Historical & Family History Society
Boorowa Historical Society
Bourke Historical Society
Braidwood & District Historical Society
Bright & District Historical Society
Broken Hill Family History Group
Broken Hill Historical Society
Bunbury Historical Society
Bundaberg & District Historical & Museum Society

Cairns Historical Society
Camperdown & District Historical Society
Charleville & District Historical Society
Charters Towers & Dalrymple Family History Association
Chiltern Athenaeum Trust
Clunes Museum
Cobar Historical Society
Cooma–Monaro Historical Society
Coonamble Family History Society
Cootamundra Local History Society

Deniliquin Historical Society
Donald History & Natural History Group
Dubbo Museum & Historical Society

East Gippsland Historical Society
Eastern Goldfields Historical Society
Echuca Historical Society
Eldorado Museum Trust
Esperance Bay Historical Society

Geelong Historical Society
Geraldton Historical Society
Glen Innes & District Historical Society
Goldfields Historical & Arts Society
Goulburn & District Historical Society
Grenfell Historical Society
Gundagai & District Historical Society
Gunnedah & District Historical Society
Gwydir Family History Society
Gympie & District Historical Society

Hamilton & Western District Historical Society
Hay Historical Society
Healesville & District Historical Society
Hill End Family History Group
Horsham & District Historical Society

Inverell District Family History Group
Ipswich Historical Society

Jerilderie & District Historical Society

Kapunda Historical Society
Kiama & District Historical Society
Kilmore Historical Society

Lilydale & District Historical Society
Lithgow District Historical Society
Mackay Historical Society & Museum
Maitland & District Historical Society
Maldon Historical Group
Mansfield Historical Society
Midlands Historical Society
Molong Historical Society
Mudgee Historical Society

Narrabri & District Historical Society
Narrandera & Sturt Historical Society
Narrogin & District Historical Society
Newcastle & Hunter District Historical Society
Nyngan Museum & Historical Society

Orange & District Historical Society

Parkes & District Historical Society
Picton & District Historical & Family History Society
Port Fairy Historical Society
Portland Family History Group

Richmond River Historical Society
Rockhampton & District Historical Society
Royal Historical Society of Victoria
Rutherglen Historical Society

St Arnaud & District Historical Society
Sale & District Historical Society
Seymour & District Historical Society
Shepparton Historical Society & Family History Group
Singleton Family History Society
Stanthorpe & District Historical Society
Stawell Historical Society
Stroud & District Historical Society

Talbot Arts & Historical Museum
Tamworth Historical Society
Temora Historical Society
Toowoomba Historical Society
Tumut & District Historical Society

Wagga Wagga & District Historical Society
Wangaratta Historical Society
Warracknabeal & District Historical Society
Warrnambool & District Historical Society
Warwick & District Historical Society
Wellington Historical Society
Williamstown Historical Society
Woady Yaloak Historical Society

Yass & District Historical Society
Young Historical Society

Index

Aaron, Abraham 295
Abbott, William H. 295, 296, 297
Abbotsford Brewery (Melbourne) 128, 135, 148
Abbotsford Brewery (Rockhampton) 199
Abbott, George (Corowa) 35
Abbott, George (Lancefield) 124
Abbott, William 297
Abrahams, George 108
Adams, George (Adams Tasmanian Brewery) 285, 289
Adams, George (Red Lion Brewery) 34
Adams, Henry J. 49, 50
Adams, John 300
Adams, Oliver 87, 117–18
Adams Tasmanian Brewery 285
Adelaide Aerated Waters & Brewing Co. Ltd 211
Adelaide Brewery (Adelaide) 211
Adelaide Brewery (Bendigo) 101–2, 106
Adelaide Brewery (Sydney) 58, 74, 75, 76
Adelaide Brewery Co. Ltd 211, 220, 221, 225
Adelaide Hotel Brewery 211–12
Adelaide Malting & Brewing Co. Ltd 212, 219
Advance Brewery 110
Aeschimann, Albert 191
Aggett, Dubois 265
Ainley, Edward 97
Aitken, Anthony 167
Aitken, Archibald 133, 154–5
Aitken, Thomas 58, 118, 133, 135, 153, 154, 259, 266
Aitken Brewing & Bottling Co. Ltd 265
Albany Brewing Co. Ltd 245
Albert Park Brewery 191
Alberton Brewery 92
Albion Brewery (Ballarat) 94
Albion Brewery (Bathurst) 25
Albion Brewery (Bendigo) 102, 103, 128, 164
Albion Brewery (Hobart) 285
Albion Brewery (Inglewood) 113, 122, 160

Albion Brewery (Newbridge) 122, 160
Albion Brewery (Oatlands) 302
Albion Brewery (Perth) 265
Albion Brewery (St Arnaud) 163–4
Albion Brewery (Sydney) 58–9, 71, 165
Albion Brewery (Wagga Wagga) 80
Albury Brewery 21, 22, 23, 99
Albury Brewing & Malting Co. Ltd 21–2, 23, 99
Alderman, Mr 219
Aldersley, Henry 236
Alex Cowan & Sons 147
Alexander, Joseph 305
Alexander, T. B. 141
Alfa Brewing Co. 212
Alice Springs Brewery 307, 310
Allan/Allen, Eli 42, 52
Allen, Mr 109
Allen, Christopher 204
Allen Creek Brewery 230
Allen, Edward 295
Allen family 192
Allen, Frederick 100, 169
Allen, Gerald 204
Allen & McKay 150
Allen, Samuel 196, 204, 205
Allen, William (Cambridge Brewery) 131
Allen, William (Mountain Brewery) 25, 27, 40
Allt, Howard 123
Allt, John 252, 255
Allt's Brewery & Wine & Spirit Co. Ltd 59, 70, 74, 75, 76
Alpine Brewery (Jamieson) 122–3
Alpine Brewery (Stratford) 169
Alpine Brewery (Tumbarumba) 78–9
Alpine Brewery (Walhalla) 165, 171
Alpine Brewery (Woods Point) 175, 176, 185
Alpine Brewery & Cordial Co. (Bendigo) 102
Alton, W.H. 29
American & German Lager Beer Brewing Co. Ltd 59, 144
Amour & Hatton 110
ANA Brewery 128

Anchor Brewery (Adelaide) 212, 215
Anchor Brewery (Bendigo) 102, 103, 104
Anchor Brewery (Charters Towers) 192
Anchor Brewery (Hobart) 285–6
Anchor Brewery (Macrossan) 196–7
Anchor Brewery (Sydney) 59
Anchor Brewery (Walhalla) 171
Anchor Brewing Co. Pty Ltd (WA) 135, 331
Anderson, John 111, 112, 153, 234
Anderson, Peter 234
Anderson, Robert 234, 235, 238
Anderson, Thomas 79
Anderson, Walter 234, 235
Anderson's Brewery (Castlemaine) 110
Anderson's Brewery (Tumut) 79
Andrews, William 110
Andrews Brewery 110
Anglo-Australian Brewery (Sydney) 59, 145
Anglo-Australian Brewery Co. Ltd (Beechworth) 22, 99, 100, 101, 169
Anglo-Australian Brewery Co. Ltd (Yarrawonga) 177
Anglo-Bavarian Brewery Co. 128
Angus, A. F. 285
Angus Park Brewery 236
Annandale Brewery 60
Anthoness, George 152
Anthony, F. J. 212
Anthony, Henry S. 211, 212
Appelt, William H. R. 236
Appleton, Frederick 117
Araluen Brewery 24
Ararat Brewery 92–3
Arbitration Brewery 260
Archibald, Glen 109
Argyle Brewery 40
Arienti, Bartholomew 246
Armidale Brewery 24–5, 39
Armstrong, Alfred 128
Armstrong, George 227
Armstrong, James 104, 106
Armstrong, John (Great Northern Brewery) 54

Armstrong, John (Jolly Hatters Brewery) 292
Arnold, Augustus 27
Arnold, F. P. 159
Arnold, Henry 64
Arnott, George 292
Artillery Brewery (Hobart) 286–7
Artillery Brewery (Melbourne) 128, 136, 156, 157
Ashton, Sir James 33
Ashton, Thomas 194
Ashton's Brewery 193
Atkinson, Anne 79
Atkinson, H. J. 195
Atkinson, James 27
Atkinson, John 27, 33–4, 36, 82
Auburn Brewery 226
Auld, Georgina and Thomas 24, 38, 53
Auld, John 212, 222, 229
Auld, Thomas 229
Austin, Henry 145
Austin, James 171, 276, 279
Austral Brewing Co. 128
Australasian Breweries Ltd 60
Australia Inn & Brewery 58
Australian Brewery (Bourke Street, Sydney) 60, 62
Australian Brewery (Cobar) 32
Australian Brewery (George Street, Sydney) 59, 60
Australian Brewery (Melbourne) 26, 128
Australian Brewery & Aerated Water Co. 115
Australian Brewery & Malthouse 128
Australian Brewery & Wine & Spirit Co. Ltd 60, 62
Australian Brewing Co. 32
Australian Natives Association Brewing Co. 128–9
Australian Pizza Kitchen Brewery 319
Avon Brewing & Ice Co. Ltd 264
Ayton, George 301

Bacon, Matthew 76
Bagdad Brewery 279
Bagley, John 302, 303

Bailey, John 302
Bailey, William 218
Bain, Elliott & Jackson 102, 103
Bairnsdale Brewery 93
Bairnsdale Brewing & Distilling Co. Ltd 93–4
Baker, Henry 145
Baker brothers 38, 39
Baldwin, Richard 284
Ball, George 131, 224
Ball, William E. 171
Ballarat Brewing Co. Ltd 94–5, 119, 120, 134
Ballenger Brewery Co. Pty Ltd 129, 134, 158
Ballenger, John 129, 136, 158, 267
Balmain Brewery Ltd 320
Balranald Brewery 25
Balsillie, Andrew 160
Banks, Catherine 227
Banks, William Henry 227
Barcaldine Brewing Co. Ltd 182
Barker, George 130
Barker's Creek Brewery 110
Barleycorn Brewery (Adelaide) 212
Barleycorn Brewery (Northam) 264
Barley Sheaf Brewery (Ballarat) 94, 95–6
Barley Sheaf Brewery (Hill End) 44
Barnes, Annie 170
Barnes, Frederick 304
Barnes, J. & E. 34
Barnes, Joseph 113, 170
Barnes, R. C. 260
Barnes, William 275, 299
Baron, Edmond 166
Barrett, Charles 139
Barrett, Thomas 102, 103
Barringun Brewery 25
Barron, Sergeant Edward 241, 265
Barron River Brewery Co. 197
Barr-Smith, Robert 226
Bartlett, William 41
Bartlett's Brewery 40
Bartley, A. E. T. 113
Bartley, Benjamin 34, 113, 127
Bartley, Alfred 34
Bartley, Edmund 34
Bartley, Nehemiah 73
Bartley & Co. 78
Bartley's Brewery (Chiltern) 113
Bartley's Brewery (Maryborough) 113
Barton, Edmund 141
Barton, John 239
Barwick, E. 302
Barwick, Joseph 302
Barwick, William 302
Barwon Brewery 87
Bathhurst Co-operative Brewing Society Ltd 25, 26
Bathurst Street Brewery 60
Battery Point Brewery 334
Bauer, Brocardius 216
Bauer, R. 122
Bavarian Brewery 198
Baxter, Robert 33
Baynes, Arthur 173, 174, 175
Baynes & Hearn 172, 173
BB Brewery 102, 103
Beach, John Stewart 181–2
Beaglehole, William Henry 29, 218, 237
Beale, Johnnie 21, 79
Bean, Arthur 225
Beasley, E. A. 236
Beatie, James 80

Beatty, John 26, 27
Beauvais, C. E. 43
Beckworth Brewery 159
Bedding, Thomas 68
Beechworth Brewery Co. Ltd 99
Beefeater Street Brewery 281
Beenleigh Brewery 182
Beet, George 37
Beevor, Miles 212, 219, 231
Bega Brewing Co. Ltd 27
Beigel, Herman 273
Beigel's Brewery Co. Ltd (Bunbury) 249
Beigel's Brewery Co. Ltd (Wagin) 273
Belfast Brewery (Laverton) 260–1
Belfast Brewery (Port Fairy) 161
Bell, Frederick 290
Bell, R. 142
Bell & Holmes 110
Bell Brewery 82
Bellair, James 78, 80, 85
Bellett, Christopher 65
Bellman, John 133, 135, 150
Bell's Hotel & Brewery 324
Belltopper Brewery 170
Bellvue Brewery 110
Belperound, Alex 92, 108, 160
Beltana Brewery 226
Benalla Brewing & Malting Co. 99, 101
Benallack's Brewery 110
Bendigo Brewery 102, 103
Bendigo & Nothern District Co-operative Brewing Co. Ltd 102, 103, 104, 134
Bendigo United Breweries Pty Ltd 103, 134
Bendigo & United Co-operative Breweries Ltd 103, 134
Benjamin, D. & J. 201
Benjamin, J. A. 192
Bennett, George H. 142
Bennett's Brewery 60
Benson, Dr 194
Benson family 286
Berliner, Louis 30, 129
Berliner Brewery (Broken Hill) 29
Berliner Brewing Co. (Melbourne) 129
Berrie, Alexander 49
Berry, J. B. 108
Berwick, Samuel 176
Bet Bet Brewery 125
Bevley Bank Brewery (Hobart) 139, 287
Biddles, Charles & Thomas 199
Biddles, Frank 201
Biegel, Herman 249
Big Gun Brewery 212
Billson, Alfred Arthur 99, 100, 101
Billson, George Henry 21–3, 57, 99, 100, 129
Billson, George (Jnr) 99
Billson, Walter Joseph 23, 24, 25, 101
Billson's Brewery (Albury) 22–3
Billson's Brewery (Beechworth) 99–100
Bilton, Thomas 164
Birch, Ernest 253
Birrell, Andrew 216, 227, 228
Birtles, Jack 51, 52
Bisby, John 77
Black Horse Brewery (Adelaide) 212, 224
Black Horse Brewery (Ballarat) 96

Black Horse Brewery (Echuca) 115
Black Horse Brewery (Hay) 34, 43
Black Horse Brewery (Lillicur) 125
Black Horse Brewery Co. Ltd (Wilcannia) 34, 83
Black Range Brewery 273
Black Swan Brewery (Hobart) 287
Black Swan Brewery (Launceston) 295
Blackford, R. 47
Blackshaw, John 40
Blackwell, William 71
Blackwood Brewery 107–8
Bladen, N. 70
Bladen & Borrows 76
Blades, Frederick 212, 215
Blain, James 92
Blake, Edwin 292
Blake, Isaac 270
Blake, William 279
Blanchard, John 275, 293
Blantyre Brewery (Harrisville) 194
Blantyre Brewery (Millbong) 198
Blaxland, E. J. & A. 63
Blaxland, Gregory 82
Blaxland, John 82
Blayney Brewing & Cordial Mfg Co. Ltd 27–8
Bleasel, James 334
Blencowe, Benjamin 24, 25
Blinman Brewery 227
Block, Joseph 92, 93
Blue Bells of Scotland Hotel & Brewery 287
Blue Mountains Brewery (Lithgow) Ltd 47, 48
Boag, James (Jnr) 296, 298
Boag, James (Snr) 135, 277, 292, 296, 297, 298, 300, 303
Boag, James (III) 296
Boag's Brewery 296; see also J. Boag & Son (1911) Ltd; J. Boag & Son Esk River Brewery; James Boag & Son Ltd
Bogie, William 60
Bogue, Frederick 249
Bogue's Brewery 249
Boldeman, William 199
Boldeman's Brewery 199
Bollington Brewery 129–30
Bollington, George 129–30
Bollington Hop Beer Co. 118, 130
Bollington's Temperance Brewery 130
Bolton, Henry 101, 121, 166, 196, 200
Bond, Berry & Underwood 48
Bond, George 188
Bond, Robert 48, 188, 194
Bond Brewing Queensland Ltd 183, 185
Bond Brewing W.A. Ltd 265
Bond Corporation 55, 72, 73, 184, 265, 271, 272
Bone, George 252
Bone, William 213
Bones, Henry 166
Bonham, Samuel 46
Bonney, James 281
Bonney, Joseph 275, 287
Bonney, Thomas 281
Bootleg Brewery 333
Booval Brewery Ltd 195
Border Brewery 198
Border United Co-operative Breweries Ltd 22, 23, 99, 100
Boreham, J. E. 302

Borsa, Antonio 114
Borsa, Battista 114
Boston, John 16, 60–1, 70
Botanic Hotel Brewery 329
Bothwell Brewery 273
Bothwell, James 57
Botting, Frank South 217
Boulder Brewery 247, 257
Boulder City Brewery Co. Ltd 247
Boult, John 230
Bourcicault, A. L. 199
Bourne, Henry 98
Boxall & Connolly 36
Boxall, Henry W. 55
Boyd, Charles J. K. 152
Boyd & Head 133, 141, 152
Boyd, Henry 141, 152
Boyle, Henry 110
Boyle, R. J. 34
Boynton, Thomas 25
Bradbury, Alfred 57
Bradbury's Brewery 57
Bradley, Thomas 40
Bradley, William 40, 41
Bradley's Brewery 40
Brady, John 123
Brady, Michael 245
Brady, Thomas William 35
Brain & Humphreys 121
Bray, William 38
Bredwell, Alfred 196
Breheny Brothers 98, 103, 104, 202
Breheny, Edward 164
Breheny, J. L. 191, 203
Breheny, James 148
Breheny, John 128, 203
Breheny, Michael B. 164
Breheny, Peter 148
Breheny, Thomas 148, 290
Breheny's Brewery Ltd 202
Brelsford, Mark 205
Brennan, W. J. 264
Brett, William 130
Brewery Tap Hotel & Brewery 193
Brewster, J. 230
Brewtech Ltd 317, 331
Brickfield Hill Brewery 61, 69
Bridge Brewery 297
Bridge Hotel & Brewery 303
Bridgewater Brewery 106, 108
Bridley, Francis 280
Bright Brewery & Alpine Aerated Water Works & Cordial Co. 108, 160
Brighton Brewery (Brighton, Tas.) 279–80
Brighton Brewery (Brighton, Vic.) 130
Brinkley family 93
Brisbane Brewery 182–3
Brisbane Brewery Pty Ltd 326–7
Britannia Brewery (Braidwood) 28
Britannia Brewery (Hobart) 286, 287
Britannia Brewery (Melbourne) 40, 86, 130
British Breweries Pty Ltd 61, 66
British Tobacco Co. (Australia) Ltd 140
Brittania Brewery (Prahran) 130
Britten's Brewery 322
Broad Arrow, Bardoc & Black Flag Brewing, Aerated Water & Ice Co. Ltd 248
Broad Arrow Brewery 248
Brodribb, William 290
Broken Hill Brewing Co. 29, 30, 220, 221

Brombee Brewery 51
Bromilow, Charles W. 55, 56
Brooker, Charles 161
Brookvale Brewing Co. Pty Ltd 61
Broome Brewery 331
Broughton, Frank 39
Brown, Daniel 294
Brown, Elijah 283
Brown, F. W. 623
Brown, Gilbert 170
Brown, James 294
Brown, Patrick 161, 162
Brown, Thomas 106
Brown, William 301
Brown's Brewery 170
Bruce & Barrett 102
Bruce, Robert 84
Bruce, Theodore 29
Bruce, William 102, 103, 105, 106
Bruford, Alexander 287
Brunswick Brewery Ltd. 130
Bryan, James 230, 231, 239
Bryant, Charles 112, 126, 166, 168, 171
Bryant, Garnet 171
Bryant, James 284
Bryant & May 142
Bryant, Walter 171
Bryant, William John 126
Bucknall, Frederick 217
Buffalo Brewery (Boorhaman) 323
Buffalo Brewery (Wangaratta) 171
Bulimba Brewery 134, 183, 186, 188
Bulimba Ferry Brewery 183, 184
Bull, Lieutenant (R.N.) 265
Bullock, Thomas 21, 22
Bulong Brewery 248
Bunbury Brewery Co. Ltd 249
Bundaberg Brewery Co. Ltd 190
Bundaberg Brewing & Ice Works 190
Buninyong Crystal Temperance Malt Ale Co. 109
Burbury, W. T. 129
Burdekin Brewery Co. Ltd 197
Burgess, George 295
Burgess, James 239
Burke, Thomas D'Arcy 31, 48, 58, 80, 143, 223
Burnie Inn Brewery 280
Burnley Brewery 130, 137
Burnley Brewery Co. 130
Burns, James and William 62
Burnt Creek Brewery 115
Burra Brewery 227
Burrows, A. 261
Burrows & Gleeson 75–6
Burrows, H. 70
Burrows, Oscar 68, 70
Burrundulla Brewery 32
Burslem, Francis 281
Burton Brewery (Alexandra) 92
Burton Brewery (Bathurst) 25, 26, 27
Burton Brewery (Bendigo) 102, 103
Burton Brewery (Cootamundra) 34, 35
Burton Brewery (Cunnamulla) 193
Burton Brewery (Launceston)) 296
Burton Brewery (Lithgow) 47
Burton Brewery (Maitland) 49
Burton Brewery (Orange) 55
Burton Brewery (Sydney) 62
Burton Brewery (West Melbourne) 29, 131, 137
Burton Brewery & Aerated Water Co. Ltd (Broken Hill) 29, 116
Burton Brewing Co. Ltd (Bunbury) 249

Burton Brewing Co. Ltd (Cairns) 190
Burton Brewing Co. Ltd (Melbourne) 131
Burton Brewing Co. Ltd (Menzies) 261
Bush, W. D. 175
Bushalla, Nicholas 264
Bushell, E. W. 190, 197, 259
Button, Charles Stammers 296, 297, 298, 303, 304
Button, Edmund 304
Button, William 299
Bux Brewing Co. 96, 131, 152
Bymes, Stephen 33
Byrne, A. 204
Byrne, James 131
Byrne, W. J. 204
Byrne's Brewery 62
Byrnes, Thomas 44

Cadell, George 52
Cadell, Thomas 77, 84
Cadenza International Ltd 296
Cairns Brewery 190
Cairns Brewing Co. Ltd 134, 190
Calder, Frank 38
Caledonian Brewery (Adelaide) 212–13
Caledonian Brewery (Launceston) 206, 297
Caledonian Brewery (Sydney) 62, 73
Callaghan, Mathew 82
Calvert, Florence 93
Calvert, James 92, 93
Cambridge Brewery (Melbourne) 131, 139
Cambridge Brewery (Albany) 245
Campbell, D. 45
Campbell, J. A. 282
Campbell, Robert 77
Campbell Town Brewery 280–1
Cannon Brewery 213–14, 221
Cape, John 297
Capel, Mrs 40, 86–7, 130
Capel, Thomas 40, 86, 130
Capel's Brewery 40
Cape's Brewery 297
Carcoar Brewery 32
Carden, Robert 160
Cardwell, William 108–9
Carisbrook Brewery 110
Carlington O'Keefe Ltd 135
Carlisle Brewery 28
Carlton Brewery Ltd 130, 133, 135–7, 155, 158, 166
Carlton Brewery (Broad Arrow) 248
Carlton Brewery (Fiji) Ltd 133
Carlton & United Breweries Ltd (CUB) 37, 46, 74, 89, 95, 103, 107, 111, 112, 119, 128, 129, 131–5, 137, 138, 140, 144, 147, 149, 150, 151, 152, 155, 158, 179, 183, 188, 191, 192, 200, 205, 277, 291, 296, 308, 310–11, 328, 335
Carlton & United Breweries (Darwin) Ltd 133
Carlton & United Breweries (N.Q.) Ltd 134, 191
Carlton & United Breweries (Queensland) Ltd 134, 183, 188, 191, 202, 203
Carlton & United Breweries (Rockhampton) Pty Ltd 134, 199
Carlton & United Breweries Ltd, Darwin Brewery 134
Carlton & West End Breweries 128, 133, 135, 136, 156, 157

Carmichael, Samuel 34
Carrick Brewery 281
Carrington Brewery 59, 62, 144
Cascade Brewery (Hobart) 73, 135, 277, 290
Cascade Brewery (Melbourne) 133, 137, 139
Cascade Brewery Co. Pty Ltd 135, 287–9, 296, 297, 304
Cascade Group Ltd 135, 289, 296, 297
Castlemaine Brewery (Brisbane) 111, 180, 183, 185
Castlemaine Brewery (Castlemaine) 62, 110, 112, 113, 160
Castlemaine Brewery (Geraldton) 254
Castlemaine Brewery (Newcastle) 54, 111
Castlemaine Brewery (Walgett) 82
Castlemaine Brewery & Quinlan, Gray & Co. (Brisbane) Ltd 183, 184, 185
Castlemaine Brewery & Wood Brothers & Co., Newcastle, New South Wales Ltd 54, 73
Castlemaine Brewing & Malting Co. 62
Castlemaine Brewing Co. (Fremantle) 111, 252–3
Castlemaine Brewing Co., Melbourne, Ltd 111, 132, 133, 137–8, 158
Castlemaine Brewing Co., Sydney 60, 62
Castlemaine Brewing, Malting & Wine & Spirits Co. Ltd 62
Castlemaine Perkins Ltd 54, 72, 73, 180, 183–5, 202
Castlemaine Toohey's Ltd 54–5, 72
Castlereagh Brewery Co. Ltd 211, 214, 222
Cataract Brewery 296, 297–8
Catchlove, C. 234
Catchlove, George 216, 217, 227
Cawarral Brewery 191
Cawthorn, John Henry 276, 302
Cawthorn's Brewery 302
Centennial Brewery 62–3, 66
Central Brewing Co. 190
Chamberlain, Charles 101
Chamberlain, Geoff 324, 325
Chambers, Allan 112
Chambers, Charles 212, 215
Chambers, James 211
Chambers, William 215
Champion, William 289, 292
Chanter, John 222
Chapman, Edgar 75, 227
Chapman, John 79
Chard, Henry 40
Chardon, W. J. 190, 195
Charleville Brewery 191
Charters Towers Brewery Co. Ltd 192
Chateau, C. H. 92, 93
Chateau, C. M. W. 197
Chateau Brewery 92, 93
Chester, Elizabeth 46
Childs, James 242, 249
Christison, John 226, 228
Churchman, James 145
Chynoweth, John 55
Chynoweth, Richard 24
Chynoweth & Co. 46
Cima, Charles 94
City Brewery (Albany) 245
City Brewery (Armidale) 24, 25

City Brewery (Bundaberg) 190
City Brewery (Brisbane) 180, 185, 202
City Brewery (Croydon) 193
City Brewery (Laverton) 261
City Brewery (Longreach) 195
City Brewery (Mackay) 196
City Brewery (Melbourne) 138, 147
City Brewery (Sydney) 63
City Brewery (Townsville) 63, 203–4
City Brewery Co. (Bendigo) 103–4, 106
City Brewing & Bottling Co. 261
City of Norwich Inn & Brewery 289
Clanchy, Michael 118
Clancy, Daniel 154
Clancy, Jim 245
Clare Brewery 228
Clare Co-operative Brewing Co. Ltd 228
Clare, William 212, 219
Clarence River Brewery Co. 35, 46
Clarence Street Brewery 63
Clarendon Brewing Co. 329
Clarion Brewery 29, 116
Clark, Edward 215, 223, 224, 226, 229
Clark, Francis 173
Clark, George 238
Clark, John 99
Clark, Maria 161, 162
Clark, Richard 275, 298
Clark, Thomas 161, 162
Clark, William Henry 211, 216, 220, 226
Clark, William J. 290
Clark, Ware & Co. 223, 224
Clarke, A. E. 172, 173
Clarke, Alfred 96, 131
Clarke, Alice 96
Clarke, E. 21, 22
Clarke, John (Albion Brewery) 285
Clarke, John (Malmsbury) 127
Clarke, John (Taradale) 170
Clarke, John (Tasmanian Pale Ale Brewery) 293
Clarke, Richard 101
Clarke, William 231
Clark's Brewery 161
Clarkson, Catherine 63
Clarkson, Thomas 63
Clarkson's Brewery 63, 64
Clayton, Edward 35
Clayton's Barrier Brewery 29
Clayton's Brewery Pty Ltd 138
Cleave, Nick 326
Clements, Henry 100
Cleveland Brewery 204
Clifton, David 35
Clifton, Ralph 192, 197
Clifton, Robert 50
Clifton Hill Brewery 138–9
Clifton's Brewery 35
Climas, Daniel 102
Clingin, James 167
Clyde Brewery 279
Coad, J. H. 263
Coates, Edward 289
Coates, George 102, 103
Cobb & Co. 70
Cock, Robert 101, 124, 235
Cock, R. W. 190
Cock, Thomas 108
Cockrane, E. W. 125, 190
Cocks, John 57, 250–1, 261, 267
Coffey, Michael 165
Coghlan & Crabbe 96

Index — 365

Coghlan, James 94, 95, 96, 97, 98, 157
Coghlan & Tulloch's Ballarat Brewing Co. Pty Ltd 94, 95, 96, 97, 98, 118, 127, 134
Coghlan, W. J. 96, 193
Cohen, Montague 270
Cohen, Nathan 77
Cohn Brothers 59, 106–7, 108, 133, 143, 145, 172
Cohn Brothers Brewery 104
Cohn, Jacob 106–7
Cohn, Julius Isaac 106–7, 139
Cohn, Moritz 106–7, 139, 169
Colac Brewery 109, 114
Cole, Charles 119
Coleman, John 231, 252
Coleman, Mark 57
Coleman, Maurice 165
Coleman, Sam 231
Coleman's Brewery 252
Colette, Horace 113
Collicott, Thomas 63
Collier, John 115
Collier, Sibley 115
Collingwood Brewery 139, 152–3
Collins, Albert 51
Collins, Charles 50, 51, 53, 82
Collins, Cornelius 167
Collins, Captain John 46
Collins Street Brewery 120, 121
Colonial Brewery 63
Colonial Brewing Co. 327
Colonial Porter Brewery 23
Colyer, William H. 224, 301
Comans, Daniel 33
Combes, E. 39
Comerford, Tom 36
Commercial Brewery 289
Commonwealth Brewing Co. 266
Condell, Henry 139–40, 146, 287
Condell's Brewery 139–40, 146
Condell's Brewery (Hobart) 289
Condoblin Brewery 33
Conigrave, Benjamin 231
Conigrave, Henry 231
Conlon, J. W. 43
Connell, W. M. 55
Connolly, John 36
Connolly, P. D. 267
Connolly's Brewery 35
Constitution Brewery 63
Continental Brewery 63
Cooke, Samuel 196
Cooktown Brewery 192
Coolgardie Brewing & Ice Co. Ltd 250–1
Cooma Brewery 33
Coomber, Herbert 28
Coombs, Stephen 286
Coonamble Brewing & Cordial Mfg Co. Ltd 33, 34
Coop, Henry 302
Cooper, Daniel 16, 59, 60, 70
Cooper, John 214
Cooper, Thomas 214
Cooper, William 272
Cooper & Crabb Ltd 214
Cooper & Sons Ltd 209, 214, 221
Cooper's Ale House 329
Cooper's Brewery 214
Co-operative Breweries of Tasmania Ltd 289–90
Coorooman Creek Brewery 199
Cootamundra Brewery 34
Coppin, George 140
Coppin's Brewery 140
Corbett, H. W. 141

Corbett, Henry P. 47, 48
Corio Brewery (Geelong) 118, 142, 168
Corio Brewery (Warrnambool) 174
Cornwall Brewery 296, 297, 298
Cornwell, John 60
Cornwell, Samuel 60
Corowa Brewery 35
Corowa & Wahgunyah Brewing & Malting Co. Ltd 35, 170
Cossins, J. D. 230
Cottesloe Brewery 266
Coulson, Hay & Co. 150
Coulson, John 286
Coultard, J. 216
Counsell, James 83
Courage Breweries Ltd 73, 74, 89, 134, 135, 140
Cousens, Walter 300
Cowan, Alex 147
Cowburn, Thomas 305
Cowburn, William 292
Cowley, Austin 79
Cowley, William 292
Cowlishaw & John Armstrong 54
Cowman, Richard 123, 168
Coyle, Holman & Inch 26, 27, 44
Coyle, Patrick 151, 159
Crabbe, Mr 96
Craig's Brewery, Bar & Grill 320–1
Crampton, Richard 65
Crane, Peter 55
Crawford, Edward J. F. 211, 216, 217, 227
Crawford, James 140, 141, 167, 174, 175
Crawford, Jane 167
Crawford, S. M. 104
Crawford, Thomas 160
Credo Brewery 248
Crellin, William 156
Cremorne Brewery 140–1
Creswick Brewery Co. Ltd 114
Crisp, John 170, 177
Crisp family 177
Crispe, Edward 131, 139, 153
Crooks, Alexander 231
Cross, Joseph 102
Cross, Robert 251
Cross, W. E. 268
Crossing, John 58
Crossing, Richard 51, 58
Crossing's Brewery 51
Crown Brewery (Albany) 245
Crown Brewery (Bathurst) 25–6, 27
Crown Brewery (Collingwood) 141
Crown Brewery (Fitzroy) 141, 152, 166
Crown Brewery (Lawlers) 261
Crown Brewery Co. Ltd (Castlemaine) 110, 141
Crown & Junction Brewery 141, 166
Crystal Fountain Brewery 53
Crystal Malt Ale Brewery (Melbourne) 139, 141
Crystal Malt Brewery (Buninyong) 109
Crystal Spring Brewery (Yackandandah) 176
Crystal Spring Brewery (Young) 85
Cudden, James 37
Cudmore, Daniel 217, 218, 219, 230
Cue Brewery 251
Cue, Charles 304
Cue, Tom 251
Cullen, Paul 312
Cullinane, J. S. 194

Cullinane, Timothy 245, 246
Cumming(s), John 118, 147, 323
Cummins, Alice 257–8
Cummins, James 257
Cunningham, Robert 154, 157
Currawang Brewery 36
Curry, William 144
Curtis, Anthony 241, 254
Curtis, Don 268, 271
Cutt, James 174
Cutt's Brewery 174
Cutts, William 287
Cygnet Brewery 334

Dale, Richard 123
Daley, James 27
Dalton, Albert 26
Daly, E. W. 51, 52
Daly, James 138
Daly, Michael 100
Dandelion Ale Brewery 141
Dandelion Ale & Weiss Brewery 141
Danker, William and Gustav 231
Darling Brewery 63, 70, 71
Darling Downs Brewing Co. Ltd 202
Darling Range Brewery 331
Dart, William 141, 142
Darwin Brewery 135
Davey Street Brewery 290
David, Len 323
Davies, Elizabeth 284
Davies, Thomas 226
Davies, Walter 228
Davis, J. 280
Davis, Mary 301
Davison, Robert 21, 22
Davoren, William 80
Day, Joseph 93
Day, Robert 122, 160
Daylesford Brewery 112, 114
de Bavay, August 144
De Bortoli family 319
de Grout, John 101
de Rose, Charles 256
Deane, Lewis 231
Dee, Charles 58
Deepdell Brewery 214
Defiance Brewery 26, 27
Degraves, Peter 277, 287–8, 289
Delaney, T. 105
Deloraine Brewery 281
Derwent Brewery (Collins Street, Hobart) 290–1
Derwent Brewery (Melville Street, Hobart) 291, 292, 296, 297
Derwent Brewery (New Norfolk) 302
Derwent Distillery 291
Derwin, John 59
Derwin family 32
Desterbeque, John 252
Deumer, E. L. 129
Devenish, William 241, 267
Devon Brewery 304
Dewar, George 51
Dickens, Daniel 84
Dickinson, James 111, 113
Dickson, John (Albury Brewing & Malting Co. Ltd) 21, 22
Dickson, John (Steam Engine Brewery) 70
Dieghan, Brian 331
Dillon, D. T. 204, 205
Dillon, George 202
Dilnot, George 121
Disher, William James (Adelaide and Echuca) 116–17, 128, 159, 216

Disher, William James (Hobart) 285, 286
Ditcham, Button & Co. 296, 298
Ditcham, Edward 296, 298
Dockendorff, R. E. 172, 173
Dodds, John 130
Dodimeade, Mr 47, 48
Dodsworth, John 171, 172, 173
Dodsworth & Moloney 172
Dodsworth Brewery 171–2
Dolphin, James 114
Dommichetti, Jonis 79
Donnelly, N. 183, 184
Dooen Brewery 115
Dorset Brewery 221, 236–7
Dougall, Thomas William 150
Dowling, Thomas 33
Downard, Richard 304
Downs Brewery 185, 202
Dowsett, Sam 264
Dragon Brewery 214–15, 221, 225
Drake Brewery 37
Dressler's Brewery 51, 52
Drew, Francis 96
Dubbo Brewery 37
Dubbo Co-operative Brewery 37
Dublin Brewery (Bendigo) 104
Dublin Brewery (Melbourne) 141–2, 151
Dudgeon, Peter 290, 291
Dudley, Thomas 295
Duffy brothers 190
Dunbar, James 128
Duncan, William 283
Dunk, William 231
Dunn, Alexander 167
Dunn, E. H. 100
Dunn, John 83
Dunne, Patrick 194
Durham, James 99
Durham, Patrick 99
Durham's Brewery 99, 100
Dussenberg, A. 213
Dussenberg & Co. 224
Dusty Miller Brewery 291
Dutton, Edward 229, 236, 239
Dutton's Brewery 229
Dyer, William 99
Dyke, William 279
Dyring, Charles 167

E. Resch & Co. 58
E. & R. Resch & Co. 35
Eagle Brewery (Glen Creek) 120
Eagle Brewery (Melbourne) 142
Eagle Brewery (Nerang) 199
Eagle Brewery (Sydney) 59, 63–4
Eagle Hawk Hill Brewing Co. Pty Ltd 320
Eagle Tavern Brewery 291
Eaglehawke Brewery 102, 104
Early, Frank 185
Early, Richard 185
East Adelaide Brewery 215
East End Brewery 142, 153
East Murchison Brewery 261
East, William 283, 303
Eastern Goldfields Brewery 255
Easton, John 279
Eaton & Tewksbury 81, 82
Eaton, William Henry 81, 82, 85, 156
Eaton, William Seymour 21, 23, 78, 79, 81, 82
Ecclestone, Robert 78
Echuca Brewing & Malting Co. Ltd 116
Ecklin, Hugh 205

Ecklin & Dillon 204
Eclipse Brewery (Northam) 264
Eclipse Brewing Co. (Brisbane) 185
Eden Brewery 38
Edhouse, Benjamin 112, 120, 126
Edhouse, Henry 123, 126, 151, 168
Edinburgh Brewery (Bendigo) 103, 104
Edinburgh Brewery (Sydney) 64
Edmeades, Alfred 305
Edmeades, Henry 45, 68, 195, 212, 218, 264, 305
Edmonds, H. J. 239
Edmonds, William 236
Edmunds, Thomas 45
Edwards, B. G. 231
Edwards, David 34, 51, 52
Edwards, Henry 45, 100
Edwards, J. (Morphett Vale Bewery) 234
Edwards, John (Billson's Brewery) 23
Edwards, John (Maitland Brewing Co. Ltd) 49, 50
Edwards, Joseph 167
Eisert, Carl 193
Elam, Benjamin 139, 153
Elder, Thomas 226
Elder Smith & Co. 226
Elders IXL 135
Elizabeth Village Pub & Brewery 331
Elliott, Albert 43, 44, 114, 116, 120, 121
Elliott, Bill 247
Elliott, George 36, 103, 104, 105, 106, 108, 113, 115, 122, 128, 160, 262, 266
Elliott, James 93, 248, 251, 255, 256, 260
Elliott, S. G. 116, 205
Elliott, Syd 260, 263, 268
Elliott, Tom 247, 248, 258, 262
Elliott's Brewery (Broad Arrow) 248
Elliott's Brewery (Kalgoorlie) 255, 257
Elliott's Brewery (Perth) 266
Ellis, C. H. 102
Ellis, James 60, 61
Ellis-Kells, Harry 307, 311
Ellis-Kells Brewery (Darwin) Ltd 307, 311
Ellis's Brewery 291
Elmes Brewery 142
Elmes, George 141
Elmes, Henry 118, 119, 142
Elwin, William 56
Emanuel, Alfred H. 68
Emmett, Edward 106
Emms, Jonathan 45
Emu Brewery (Jamestown) 230
Emu Brewery (Sydney) 64, 68
Emu Brewery Ltd (Perth) 265, 266–7, 269, 271
Emu Co-operative Brewery Co. Ltd 267
Engelbrecht, Charles 234
English Ale Brewery 64
Enright, John T. 125, 254, 255
Enterprise Brewery (Adelaide) 215
Enterprise Brewery (Auburn) 226
Enterprise Brewery (Clare) 228
Ernstsen, Ernst 36
Ernstsen's Brewery 36
Escott, Richard 114
Esk Brewery (Launceston) 277, 296–7, 298
Esk Brewery (Perth, Tas.) 303

Eskbank Brewery 47
Esperance Brewing & Aerated Water Co. Ltd 252
Eumundi Brewing Co. Ltd 327–8
Eureka Aerated Waters & Brewing Co. 96, 131
Evandale Brewery 283
Evans, Edward 51
Evans, F. J. (Jessie) 96, 131
Evans, James (Brighton Brewery) 279
Evans, James (Burnley Brewery) 130
Evans, John 175
Evans, William 301
Everett, Henry 49, 50
Evestaff, William 64
Evisson, William 63
Excelsior Brewery (Albany) 245, 246
Excelsior Brewery (Cootamundra) 34
Excelsior Brewery (Cue) 251
Excelsior Brewery (Hay) 43, 44
Excelsior Brewery (Melbourne) 142
Excelsior Brewery (Stawell) 168
Exchange Inn & Brewery 294

Fagan, Edward 76
Fair Hill Brewery 32
Falcon Brewery 57
Farley's Brewery 194
Farmer, J. G. 143
Farrell, John 41, 57
Farnell, Thomas Charles 70
Faulkner, Archie 110, 164, 168
Faulkner, Septimus 51
Fawkner, John Pascoe 298–9
Fawns Brewery 299
Fawns, Helen 103, 105
Fawns, James 103, 105, 106, 297
Fawns, John (Jnr) 298
Fawns, John (Snr) 298
Federal Brewery (Bathurst) 26
Federal Brewery (Bunbury) 249
Federal Brewery (Gympie) 194
Federal Brewery (Horsham) 122, 174
Federal Brewery (Kalgoorlie) 256
Federal Brewery (Sydney) 64
Federal Brewery (Thargomindah) 201
Federal Brewery (Wahgunyah) 170
Federal Brewery (Wagga Wagga) 73, 80
Federal Brewery (Warracknabeal) 173–4
Federal Brewery Ltd (Maryborough) 198
Federal Brewery Ltd (Mudgee) 51–2
Federal Dandelion Ale Brewery 142–3
Federation Brewery Co. 143
Felmingham, W. H. 68
Ferguson, John 269, 270
Fergusson's Brewery 291
Ferndale Brewery, Wine & Spirit Co. Ltd 54, 55
Ferrier, John 51, 52, 53
Filgate, Fanny 226, 228, 231
Filgate, Jonathon 228
Finch, Frederick 115
Findlay, Thomas 152, 157
Findlay, William 152, 157
Fingal Brewery 283
Fink, Benjamin 147
Finn, Daniel 122
Finn, John 161
Finn & Meagher 161
Finselbach, Mr 96, 193, 198
Finselbach's Brewery 198

Fisher, George 219
Fisher, Thomas 42
Fitzgerald, Edward 110, 111, 137, 138, 160, 184
Fitzgerald, Nicholas 54, 62, 111, 114, 138, 160, 184, 202, 252
Fitzgerald Brothers 134
Fitzgerald's Brewing & Malting Co., Castlemaine, Ltd 110, 111–12, 113, 133
Fitzpatrick, Daniel 25, 26
Fitzpatrick, Vincent 26
Fitzroy Brewery (Melbourne) 46
Fitzroy Brewery (Rockhampton) 134, 199–200
Fitzwalker, G. J. 191
Flanagan, Mr 263
Flanagan, Edgar 170
Flattelly, William 161
Flagstaff Brewery 143
Fleming, John 190
Fleming, Lionel 190
Fletcher, Ernest 34
Fletcher, John 34
Flowers, John 48
Floyd, Henry 39
Flynn, J. 44
Flynn, M. 194–5
Flynn, Mrs 50
Flynn & Unmack 176
Fogarty, R. F. C. 191
Fogarty, Reg 310
Forbes, Dr 38, 39
Forbes, Charles 139, 153
Foresters Brewery 162
Foristal, Robert 101
Forrester, Charles 304
Forsyth, Robert 184
Foster, A. W. 100
Foster, Ralph R. 59, 143–4
Foster, Thomas 143, 277, 291
Foster, William M. 143–4
Foster Brewing Co. Pty Ltd 59, 89, 132, 135, 143–4, 155
Foster's Brewery 143, 277, 291
Fosters Brewing Group Ltd 135, 144
Fotherington family 229, 230
Foston Brewery 40
Fountain Head Brewery 92, 93
Foureur, Joseph H. 215
Fox, John 231, 239
Francis, Robert 162, 163
Franklin Brewery 283–4
Fraser, David 167
Frayne, Peter 115
Frayne, William 168
Frazer, James 42
Freeman, Edward 33
Fremantle Brewing Co. Pty Ltd 331–2
Fremantle Brewing & Ice Co. Ltd 253
French, Edward 297
Frew, A. 23
Friederich, Rudolph 144
Frontier Brewery 335
Fuller, Alfred 145
Fuller, Frederick 212
Funnell, O. N. 43
Fynn, John 121, 123, 166

Gambrinus, Johann 145
Gambrinus Lager Beer Brewery Co. Ltd 144–5
Gamble, Gavin 324
Gang Gang Brewery 319
Gant, Richard 62
Gard, William 46

Garlick, T. 238
Gardiner, G. S. 282
Gardner, Arthur 268
Garrick, Gilbert 194
Gaslight Brewery 64
Gasquoine, J. McD. 218, 237
Gasse, Frederick 42
Gatehouse, George 292–3
Gatty, John 283
Gaulston, J. P. 160
Gavin Ralston & Co. 59
Gawler Brewery 221, 229
Gebhardt, William 234, 237
Gee, Henry 283
Gee, W. J. 304
Geebung Polo Club Hotel & Brewery 324
Geelong Brewery 118, 119, 134, 147
Geelong Brewing Co. Pty Ltd 323
George B. Kerferd & Co. 99
George Elmes & Co. 141
George Town Brewery 284
Geraldton Brewery Co. Ltd 254
Gerloff, W. A. 234, 236
German Brewery 23
Germantown Brewery 119
Gerrard, James 297
Gerrard's Brewery 297
Gibbons, Henry 162
Gibbs, John 161, 162
Gibson, James 177
Gideon & McKaige 145
Gideon & Wheeler 145
Gilbert, John 322
Gilchrist, W. J. 96
Gilchrist's Brewery 96
Gillett, A. 58
Gillies, Thomas C. 39
Gippsland Brewery Pty Ltd 164–5
Gisborne Brewery 120
Glanmire Brewery 39
Glanville Brewery 215–16
Gleeson, Hampton 75
Gleeson, John 231
Gleich, Frederich 23, 85
Glen Innes Brewery 39
Glencoe Brewing Co. 333–4
Glenrowan Brewing & Aerated Water Co. 238
Glenwright, George 297–8
Glenwright, John 297, 299
Glibbon, A. E. 231
Globe Brewery (Hobart) 291, 297
Globe Brewery Ltd (Geraldton) 254–5
Glynn & Co. 156
Gobur Brewery 120
Goddard, Charles 43, 48
Godhead, Chris 81
Goedecke, William 236
Goerin's Brewery 64
Gold Coast Brewery Pty Ltd 328
Goldchill Australia (Darwin) Pty Ltd 311
Golden Ale Pty Ltd 138
Golden Cross Hotel & Brewery 291
Goldfields Brewing Co. Ltd 251
Gooch, Henry 49, 73
Goodeare, Alfred 47, 48
Goodier, William 215–16
Goodier, Reid Brewing Co. Ltd 216
Goold, Michael 94
Goold's Brewery 94, 165
Gooley, William 185, 198
Gordon, A. O. 300
Gordon, George 198
Gorringe, Thomas Francis 294

Index — 367

Gorringe's Brewery 294
Goulburn Brewery (Goulburn) 40, 73
Goulburn Brewery (Jamieson) 123
Goulburn River Brewery Co. 166
Goulburn Valley Brewery 326
Goulburn Valley Brewery Co. Ltd 151, 159
Government Brewery 64
Gowers, W. H. 93
Gracie, John H. 25, 252
Gracie, William 286, 288
Gracie & Sleigh 123, 253, 271
Grafton Brewing Co. Ltd 41, 72
Graham, Charles 55
Graham, Duncan 104
Graham, James 77
Graham, Thomas 152
Graham's Brewery 133, 145, 152
Grand Ridge Brewing Co. Ltd 325–6
Grange Brewery 120
Granville Brewery 198
Graves, Joseph 294
Gray, Benjamin 231
Gray, Charles Henry 217, 226, 227, 230, 232, 238
Gray, George 184, 256
Gray, Guilford E. 217–18, 223, 227, 231, 232, 239
Gray's Arms Inn & Brewery 279
Gray's Brewery 232–3
Great Northern Brewery 263
Great Northern Brewery & Malting & Wine & Spirit & Aerated Waters Co. Ltd 54
Great Southern Brewery 245
Great Western Brewery Co. Ltd 26–7, 56
Greaves, J. C. 113
Green, John 333
Green, O. S. 255
Green, Patrick 101
Green, Richard 291
Green, William 289
Greene, Cecil Frederick 283, 284
Gregory, F. T. 268
Gregson, W. 39
Grenfell Street Brewery 216
Griffin, Brian 324
Griffin, Joseph 119
Griffiths, John 300
Griggs, James 284
Grogfathers Brewery 319
Groom, Henry 162, 163
Grose, J. H. 62
Gruenert, Oscar 131
Guilford Brewery 267
Guilford Brewing Co. Ltd 267
Guinn, Alfred 161
Guinn, Frederick 161
Guinn, George 36, 116
Guinn, Harry 116
Gulong Brewery 42
Gulson, R. A. 41
Gulson, Tom 41
Gunter, Thomas 310
Gwydir Brewery 50–1, 82
Gympie Brewing & Ice Co. Ltd 194

Hacker, Walter 130
Hackney Brewery 216
Haddy, B. E. 261
Hadspen Brewery 284
Haferkorn, Charles 120
Hahn, Charles 321
Hahn Brewing Co. Ltd (Sydney) 73, 321

Haimes, John 225
Haimes, Richard 230
Haimes, Mallen & Co. 225
Halifax Street Brewery 216
Halford, William 112, 113
Halfpenny, Tom 145
Hall, Alexander 162, 163
Hall, Henry 272
Hallahan, Dennis 35, 170, 175
Hallahan, John 170
Hallahan, Patrick 163, 170
Halligan, William 172, 173
Hamersley, Edward 268
Hamilton Brewery 120, 121
Hamilton Inn & Brewery 284
Hamilton, James 74
Hannan, Paddy 256
Hannan's Brewery Co. Ltd 256–7
Hannan's Co-operative Brewery Ltd 257
Hannay, A. W. 143, 163
Hannay brothers 128
Hansen, Chris 251
Hansen, F. H. 255
Hansen, Otto 263
Harbour Beer Co. 321
Harding, Mr 196
Hardwick, Philip 28, 258
Hardwick, Thomas 28, 55, 270
Hargen, Henry 27
Hargrave's Brewery 192
Harper, Robert 102
Harris, Albert 170
Harris, Herbert 55
Harris, J. 73
Harris, Martin 201
Harris, Thomas 114
Harrison, William 62
Hart, D. 227
Harwood, David 254, 267, 268, 269, 271
Harwood's Brewery Ltd 266, 269
Hattersley, John 177
Haussen, Herman Henry 216, 217
Haussen, Rosa 217, 218
Haustorfer, Heinrich 122
Haviland, Francis 57
Hawkesbury Brewery 84
Hawkeswood, Alfred 266
Hay, Peter Grant 89, 150–1
Hay, R. 153
Hay Street Brewery 267–8
Hayes, Pat 68
Hayter, John 211
Hayton, George 304
Hayward, Chris 319
Head, Francis 141, 152
Headrick, John M. 200
Headley, Henry S. 22, 23, 80, 81, 82
Healy, Matt 17, 41
Heap, Edward 56, 85
Hearn, James 219, 300
Hearn, William 172, 173
Hearty, Thomas 142
Heath, Richard 53, 81
Heathcote Brewery 121, 123, 166
Heathorn, Henry 26, 27, 46
Hedley brothers 106, 108, 113
Heinz, John 59
John Heinz & Co. 59
Heinze, Ferdinand 121
Heinzmann, Gustavus 245, 246
Heley, Edward 52
Heley, Frank 158
Heley, Walter 158
Henden, Henry 145
Henden's Brewery 145
Henderson, W. 149

Henfrey, William 66
Hennelly, James 131, 139, 143
Hennelly's Brewery 145
Henry, Samuel 281
Herald, A. T. 66
Herberton Brewery 194
Herdsmann, W. 259
Herman, Frank 120
Hetherington, Walter 254
Hibernian Brewery 122, 123
Hickson, John 48
Higgins, Sam 219
High Street Brewery 104
Higson, William 199
Hill, A. C. 77–8
Hillier, Steven 24, 25
Hills, William 85
Hilton, Henry 238
Hindley Street Brewery 216
Hindmarsh Brewery (Bendigo) 104
Hindmarsh Brewery (Richard Street, Adelaide) 216–17, 221
Hindmarsh Brewery (Robert Street, Adelaide) 217
Hine, H. J. 201
Hine, Henry 25
Hinyard, George 94
Hirons, Clifton & Hughes 50
His Lordship's Larder 332
Hit or Miss Brewery 284
Hobart Brewery 291–2, 297
Hobart Town Brewery (Campbell Street) 292
Hobart Town Brewery (Davey Street) 275, 292
Hobbs, Henry 161
Hobson's Bay Brewery 145
Hocker, John 188
Hocking, W. 227
Hodgens, D. 175
Hodges, Isaac 119
Hodges Brothers Brewery 118, 119, 133, 134
Hodgson, Henry 231
Hodgson's Inn & Brewery 292
Hoe, J. 79
Hoffmeyer, C. 106
Hogan, John 80
Holdsworth, T. 123
Holland, Archibald 245, 248, 255
Holland, Long & Co. 245, 255
Holland Street Brewery 217
Holler, Phillip 36, 108, 113
Holman, W. 26, 27
Holmes, Charles 159
Holmes, John 103, 104
Holmes, Ken 334
Holmes, Thomas 191
Holt, H. T. 79
Hooke, E. G. 284
Hood, Martin 128
Hooper, Ellen 108
Hooper, William 108
Hope & Anchor Brewery 169
Hopkins, George 53
Horizon Brewery Co. Pty Ltd 326
Hornby, William 128
Horne, J. L. 128–9
Horne, William 279
Horonda Brewery Co. (Perth) 268
Horonda Brewery Ltd 145
Horsham Brewing, Ice & Cordial Co. 122
Hose, Frederick 35
Hosking, J. 234
Hotchin, Thomas 146
Houghton, James 299
Hoverden, F. A. 45

Howard, Graham 327
Howe, Arthur 67
Howe, Rogers & Co. 106
Howison, James 35, 38, 39, 55, 57, 78
Howlong Brewery 45
Hughenden Brewery 194–5
Hughes, Mr 78
Hughes, Edward 163, 230
Hughes, George 268
Hughes, John Terry 59
Hughes, Thomas 71
Humberstone & Pinniger 193
Humble, Samuel W. 211
Hume, James 280
Hume, Richard 281
Hume Brewery (Wilson Street) 23
Hume Brewery (Wodonga Place) 21, 22, 23
Humphrey, W. J. 201
Humphrey, William 101
Humphreys, E. H. 163, 181
Humphreys, J. 195
Humphreys, W. J. 181
Humphris, Edmund 230
Hunt, George 46
Hunt, James 46
Hunt, Robert 231
Hunt, Thomas 123
Hunt Brothers 46
Hunter Brewery 54, 72
Hunter Brothers 104
Hunter, Elizabeth 104
Hunter, George Frederick 103, 104, 106, 195
Hunter, J. F. 261
Hunter, Thomas O. 104
Hunter River Brewery 49
Hunter Valley Brewing Co. Pty Ltd 29
Huntley, George 224
Hurd, George 294
Hurst, Edward 100, 172, 173
Hurst, James 305
Hustwick, C. F. 46
Hutchinson, William 60
Hutton, E. 174
Hyde Park Brewery 217–18
Hyrons, Benjamin 284, 300

Iles, Samuel 304
Illawarra Brewery 46
Illingworth, John 104
Imperial Brewery (Adelaide) 159, 218
Imperial Brewery (Castlemaine) 112
Imperial Brewery (Sydney) 63, 64–5
Imperial Inn & Brewery (Melbourne) 145
Inch, Charles 44
Inch, Edward 44
Inch, D. J. 28
Inch, Richard 44, 47
Inchant Brewery Co. 333
Industrial Equity Ltd 296
Ingham, Alfred 123
Innes, J. C. 272
Inverell Brewery 45
Ipswich Brewery 195
Ipswich Brewing & Bottling Co. Ltd 195
Isaacs, Wolf 150

J. Boag & Son (1911) Ltd 297
J. Boag & Son Esk River Brewery 296–7
J. T. & J. Toohey 71
Jacka, Joseph 233

Jacka, William 221, 226, 227, 233
Jacka's Brewery 233
Jackman, Benjamin 279
Jackson, James (Gulgong Brewey) 42
Jackson, James (Leura Brewery) 109, 114
Jackson, James (Jackson's Brewery) 284
Jackson, Jones & Nash 102
Jackson's Brewery 284
Jacobson, George 169
Jacomb, Robert 292
Jaeger, W. 234
Jaentsch, Richard 213, 218
Jager, Peter 83
James, Mr 149
James Boag & Son Ltd 135, 277, 298, 300
James, George 293
James, Henry 288, 292
James, W. J. 218
James, Walter 131, 141
Jamieson, G. H. 131, 158
Jamieson, Keith 140
Jamieson, Richard 164, 165, 304
Jecks, Thomas 268
Jefferson, M. J. 121
Jeffree, Albert 44
Jeffries, Joseph 141, 142
Jeffrey, Ian 333
Jenkins, Charles 24, 25
Jenkins, Richard 24, 25
Jerilderie Brewery 45, 73
Jerningham Street Brewery 329–30
Jerusalem Brewery 294
John C. Fletcher & Co. 64
John M. Headrick & Co. 200
John McKenna & Son 170
Johns, William 88, 126, 162
Johnson, C. F. 65
Johnson, Esther 292
Johnson, F. 205
Johnson, Maria 292
Johnson, Matthew 124
Johnson & McClelland 51
Johnson & Sands Brewery 65
Johnston, Andrew 237
Johnston, George 196
Johnston, James 218, 237
Johnston, John 195
Johnston, John Disher 237
Johnston, Samuel 78
Johnston, William 104
Johnston Street Brewery 145
Jolly Hatters Brewery 292
Jones, Mr 116
Jones, Britton 298
Jones, David 96
Jones, F. T. 227
Jones, Frederick 145
Jones, H. 238
Jones, J. Nelson 101
Jones, John 269
Jones, John Alexander Stammers 47, 48
Jones, Lincoln & Co. 43, 44, 45, 53, 78, 79
Jones, Thomas 45
Jones, William 34, 44, 45, 53, 59, 79
Jon's Brewery Ltd 65
Joseph, Benjamin 51
Joseph, Henry 51, 53, 82
Joseph Young & Co. 112
Jowett, William 124
Junction Brewery 171
Junee Brewery 45

Kable, George 84

Kable, Henry 84
Kable's Brewery 84
Kadina Brewery 230
Kalgoorlie Brewing Co. Pty Ltd 257
Kalgoorlie Brewing & Ice Co. Ltd (Kalgoorlie) 213, 247, 257–8
Kalgoorlie Brewing & Ice Co. Ltd (Merredin) 262–3
Kangaroo Brewery 212, 217, 218
Kanowna Brewery Co. Ltd 260
Kaleski, John 21, 22
Kanter, Gustave 122
Kean, Hubert 281
Kean, Michael 123
Kean, Richard 281
Kejam Pty Ltd 140
Kelloshiel Brewery 26, 27
Kelly, Hugh 83
Kelly, James 108
Kelly's Brewery (Bright) 108–9
Kelly's Brewery (Brisbane) 327
Kemp, W. T. 196
Kempnich, J. G. 48
Kenna, William 98, 118
Kennedy, Edward 40
Kennedy, Joseph 40
Kenny, Dennis 21, 42
Kenny's Brewery 42
Kent Brewery (Bendigo) 103, 104
Kent Brewery (Forbes) 38, 39
Kent Brewery (Melbourne) 145
Kent Brewery (Rockhampton) 200
Kent Brewery (Sydney) 65, 71, 73, 74, 80, 134, 135
Kent Brewery Co. (Melbourne) 145
Kent Town Brewery 209, 218, 220, 330
Kentish Arms Inn & Brewery 27
Kentish Brewery 302
Keogh, Timothy 248
Kerferd, George B. 99
Kerferd's Brewery 99, 100, 173
Kerr, William 228
Kerridge, A. 198
Kerridge & Co. 198
Kerry, J. 26, 27
Kett, Henry 172, 173
Kevern, Sarah 236
Kew Brewery 145
Kiewa Brewing Co. Pty Ltd 324
Kildare Brewery 118
Kilmore Brewery 121, 123
King, Louis 62
Kinkead, James 112
Kinsela, Enoch 63
Kirby, William 161, 162
Kirchner, C. F. W. 82, 83
Kirk, James 297
Kissing Point Brewery 65
Kite, Charles 39, 57
Klaeby, Gustavus 25
Klauer, F. W. 211
Kleinschmidt, F. W. 231
Knapman, Sam 214
Knapman, William 213, 214
Knight, B. J. 239
Knight, Edward 303
Knight, George 107–8, 127
Knight, Henry 92
Knight, J. 170
Kobbel, John 126
Kobbel, Louisa 126
Kobbell's Brewery 126
Kofoed, John (Jens) 92, 93
Kookynie Brewing & Bottling Co. Ltd 260
Kooyong Brewery 146
Kops Brewery Ltd 65

Kruger, August Friederich 236
Kyneton Brewing & Malting Co. Ltd 124
Kyneton & Trentham Breweries Ltd 124, 170
Kyngdon, F. B. 70

Lachlan Brewery Co. 38–9, 78
Laitz, William 162
Lake Way Brewery 273
Lakeland, William 193
Lakeman, Allan 43
Lancaster, Edward 176
Lancefield Brewery 124
Lancia, Mr 192
Landmann, August 175
Landseer, Albert 231
Lane, Thomas 56
Lane, Timothy 142, 185
Lane, W. 120
Lanfear, Albert 188, 196, 204, 205
Lanfear, Allen 204
Lanfear, Charles E. 200, 264
Lanfear, Frederick 37, 47, 48
Lanfear, W. C. 194
Lanfear, Walter 186
Lang, John 40
Lang & Parker 85
Langford, Alfred 255–6
Langford's Brewery 258
Langhammer, Mr 22, 23
Langhorne Creek Brewery 230
Large, Thomas 305
Largey, Thomas 42
Larkin, Patrick 65
Larkin, William 35, 38, 39
Larkin's Colonial Brewery 65
Larkins, George 279
Laski, Thomas 110, 126, 127, 169
Laski's Brewery 169
Latham, Edward 133, 136, 137, 152, 157
Latrobe Brewery 294–5
Launceston Brewery 296, 298, 299
Laura Brewery Co. 220, 221, 231
Laurance, Henry 55
Laverton Brewing Co. Ltd 261
Law, Joseph 280
Lawlers Brewery Co. 261
Lawrence, Nathaniel 62, 66
Lawther, John 115, 120, 126
Lawther's Brewery 126
Lawton, Alfred 176
Leahdale Brewery 333
Leahy, P. J. 201
Lederberger's Brewing Co. 326
Lee, George 96
Lee, James 281
Lee, John and Richard 129, 130
Lee & Hine 25
Lee & Hull 96
Lee's Barrier Brewery 29
Leggo, Charles 95
Leggo, Henry 94, 95
Lehman, J. G. 196
Leichhardt Brewery 62, 63, 65
Leon, Henry W. 32
Leonora Brewery 261
Leura Brewery 109, 114
Levi, A. 131
Lewin, K. 255
Lewis, Henry 231
Lewis, Hopkin 33
Liardet, Mr 60
Licensed Victuallers Brewery Co. Ltd (Gympie) 188, 194
Licensed Victuallers Brewery Co. Ltd (Melbourne) 146

Liddington, James 28, 44, 272
Liddle, James 21, 22, 23, 103, 104, 106, 117
Liddle's Brewery 23
Lillyman, Mr 222, 225–6
Lincoln Brewery (Hay) 43
Lincoln Brewery (Melbourne) 143, 146
Lincoln & Co. Ltd 44, 45, 53
Lincoln, Harry 53
Lincoln, Susannah 45, 53
Lincoln, Thomas F. 34, 44, 45, 53, 79
Lincolnshire Brewery 146
Linden, Clarence 55
Lindsay, C. 51
Lindsay, George 51, 123, 124
Lindsay, Henry L. 28, 32, 43, 44, 55, 78, 92, 113, 143
Lindsay, Rev T. 61
Lindsay, William 281
Lindsay Brewery Co. Ltd 28, 43, 44, 55
Lindsay's Brewery (Orange) 55
Lindsay's Brewery (Hay) 28, 43, 44
Lion Brewery (Adelaide) 218, 220
Lion Brewery (Alexandra) 92
Lion Brewery (Boulder) 248
Lion Brewery (Brisbane) 185
Lion Brewery (Coolgardie) 251, 257
Lion Brewery (Cootamundra) 34–5, 74, 84
Lion Brewery (Geraldton) 255
Lion Brewery (Mackay) 196
Lion Brewery (Perth) 268
Lion Brewery (Silverton) 57–8, 74
Lion Brewery (Sydney) 65
Lion Brewery (Temora) 35, 78
Lion Brewery (Townsville) 204
Lion Brewery (Wilcannia) 74, 83–4
Lion Brewing Pty Ltd 330
Lion Brewing, Aerated Water & Cordial Manufacturing Co. (Albany) 245
Lion Brewing & Malting Co. Ltd. (Adelaide) 31, 218–19, 330
Lion Nathan 184, 221
Lipman, J. 251
Lister, Charles 141
Lister, John 21, 22
Lithgow Brewery Ltd 47, 48
Lithgow Burton Brewing Co. Ltd 47
Littlehampton Brewery 231
Liverpool Brewery 102, 104
Loaded Dog Pub Brewery 324
Loan, Elizabeth and Lewis 171
Loane, R. W. 286
Lobban, John 236
Lobethal Brewery 231
Locke, James 109
Lockyer, Edward Catchlove 227
Lockyer, Henry 227
Logue, Edward 219
Logue's Brewery 219
London Brewery (A'Beckett Street, Melbourne) 139, 146
London Brewery (Bendigo) 43, 105, 103, 106
London Brewery (Clifton Hill, Melbourne) 146
Lone Star Brewery 334
Loddon Brewery (Bridgewater) 108
Loddon Brewery (Castlemaine) 112
Long, Charles 28, 44
Longford Brewery 301
Lonsdale Street Brewery 146
Lord, David 290

Lord, George 239
Lord, James 281
Lord Nelson Brewery Hotel 321
Lord's Place Brewery 55
Loughlin, Thomas 80
Louis King & Co. 62
Lovey, Brian and Denise 323
Lowden & Nash 116
Lowe, Francis 62
Luber, Gustavus 264
Lucan Street Brewery 105–6, 153
Luddenham Brewery 82
Ludlow, John 113
Lugton, P. 78
Luka Brewery 135, 328
Lukin, George 301
Lukin, Mary Ann 301
Lyall, Robert 305
Lyall's Brewery 305
Lyon, George 100

McArdell, J. O. 261, 263
McArthur, Neil 117
McAuley, J. & D. 48
McAuley, Neil 48
McBride, John 112, 113
McBride, Joseph 131
McBride's Brewery 112
McCabe, M. A. 260
McCarthy, J. H. 51, 52
Macclesfield Brewing & Malting Co. Ltd (Adelaide) 212, 219
Macclesfield Brewing & Malting Co. Ltd (Macclesfield) 231
McClelland, J. 106
McConnon, John 294
McCormack, Patrick 34
McCracken, Collier 147
McCracken, Peter 146–7
McCracken, Robert 146–7
McCracken & Robertson 133, 146–7
McCracken's City Brewery Co. Ltd 93, 132, 133, 146–7, 149, 158
McCullam, Archibald 37
McCullam, John 37
McDiarmid, John 299
McDonald & Co. 64
MacDonald, G. J. 24
McDonnell, Hugh 80
Macdougall, John 286
McDowell, John 116
McEwan, Joseph 302
McGee, Alex 23, 174
McGee, Francis 121, 143
McGee, John 143
McGee, James 174
McGee, W. T. 36
McGee, William 174
McGill, A. 118
McGowan, David 297
McGrath, James 125
McGrath, Patrick J. 26, 27, 39, 43
McGrath's Brewery 43
McGuigan, Patrick 60
McGuiness, John 160
Machin, Mr 141
McIndoe, Peter 29, 131
McIntosh, David 117
McIntosh, Hugh 287
McIntyre, Andrew 211
McIntyre, James 248, 260
McIntyre, Lincoln & Co. 34, 43, 44, 45, 53, 78, 85
McIver, John 165
McIver's Brewery 165
McKail, Nathaniel 246
McKay, Benjamin 196, 199
McKay, Bill 333
Mackay, David 112
McKay Brewery 196
McKay & Co. 150
McKay, Pam 333
Mackay, Richard 239
McKay, William 196
McKenna, Gerald 256
McKenna, John 170
McKenna, Martin 124
McKenny, F. 25, 26
McKenzie, W. 228
Mackie, David 162
Mackie, John 70
MacKinlay, Alexander 161
McKinley, J.F. 24, 25
McLaren, Thomas 97
McLaren Vale Brewery 232
McLaughlin, J. 145
McLaughlin, Thomas 134, 199, 200
McLean, Charles 164
McLean, William 108
McLennon, Kenneth 21, 22
McMasters, George 334
McMillan, A. 116
McMillan, Angus 169
McNamara, Michael 103, 106
McNeil, Mary 281
McOmish, L. & J. 319
Macpherson, Malcolm 131
Macquarie Brewery 37
Macree, Edwin 201
McRoberts, Gavinus 163
McSweeney, Eugene 170
McTherney, Michael 34
McWaide, Esther and John 279
Macedon River Brewery Co. Ltd 162
Magill, Alex 97, 161
Magill, William 94, 101, 109, 163
Magney, J. B. 54
Mahon, Patrick J. 80
Mair, M. 258, 259
Maitland Brewing Co. Ltd 49–50, 73
Malcomb, A. S. 236
Maldon Brewery Co. Pty Ltd 126, 168
Maley, Frederick 254, 261, 264
Maley, J. S. 254, 255
Mallen, Mr 47, 48
Mallen, Charles 75, 211, 225
Mallen, George 211, 225
Mallen, Maurie 225
Malt Shovel Brewery Pty Ltd 321
Malmsbury Brewery 127
Manchester Brewery 106
Manning, Robert 23
Mann's Brewery 302
Mapleback, George 116, 124, 163
Marceba Brewery 197–8
Marie, Eugene 234
Marine Stockade Brewery 128, 147
Marks, R. 126
Marks, S. 169
Marks, Sam (Mayton's Brewery) 92
Marks, Samuel 59, 67
Marr, H. F. 66
Marrin, Arthur 39
Marrin, Vincent & Co. 39
Marshall, James 66
Marshall, Joseph 65–6
Marshall, Thomas 251
Marshall, William 161, 162, 169
Marshall's Brewery (Portland) 162
Marshall's Brewery (Stawell) 168
Marshall's Co-operative Brewery Ltd 62, 63, 65, 66, 73
Marshall's Paddington Brewery Ltd 32, 65–6, 130, 340
Martin, Alfred 57
Martin, Edgar 239
Martin, Edward 231
Martin, Henry 50
Martin, John 55, 302
Martin, Peter J. 26, 116, 128, 131, 193, 203, 204
Martin, W. 174, 175
Maryborough Brewery 95, 127, 198
Maryborough Brewing & Mercantile Co. Ltd 198
Mason, Samuel 59, 121
Massey, James 143
Matilda Bay Brewing Co. Ltd 135, 332–3
Matthewman, John 64
Maude, A. J. 56
Maunsell & Co. 141
Mawle, William 279
Mayton's Brewery 92
Mead, Richard 33
Meadowbank Brewery 122
Meagher, Edmund 203
Meagher, Tom 195
Medlin, Charles 239
Medwin, E. 280
Melbourne Brewery Co. 131, 148
Melbourne Brewery & Distillery 86, 130, 133, 139, 147–8
Melbourne Brewery & Distillery Co. Ltd 133, 148, 155
Melbourne Brewing & Malting Co. 128, 133, 136, 148, 156, 157
Melbourne Co-operative Brewery Co. Ltd 89, 133, 148
Melbourne Street Brewery 219
Meldrum, James 173
Meldrum's Brewery 172
Meloy, William 267–8, 271
Melrose Brewery 233
Melville & Milne 41
Menindee Brewery 50
Mennon, John 43, 44
Menzies Brewery Co. Ltd 261–2
Menzies & Niagara Brewing Co. Ltd 262
Merredin Brewery 263
Merrin, Bruce 51
Mersey Brewery (Devonport) 282
Mersey Brewery (Spreyton) 304
Metcalf, William 295
Metropolitan Brewery (Sydney) 66
Metropolitan Brewing Co. (Melbourne) 324–5
Metropolitan Brewery Co. Ltd (Melbourne) 139, 143, 149, 153
Middleton, James 284
Middleton, T. W. 66
Miels, E. F. 231
Mildura Brewery Ltd 158
Millar, George 112
Miller & Brownscombe 142
Miller, Ernest 141, 142, 151
Miller, George 59, 121
Miller, James 119
Miller, Louis 141, 142, 151
Miller, Peter 286
Miller, Robert William 61, 66
Miller Lager Beer Brewing Co. 149, 151
Miller's Brewery Pty Ltd 61, 66, 72
Mills, John 86, 87, 130, 146, 147–8, 286, 292, 293
Millstream Brewery 49, 50
Milne, George D. 28, 41, 49, 50, 87, 136
Milne, John 77
Milne & Co 220
Milne & Woodman 85
Milosz, Steve 333
Milton Brewery 185
Milward, Luke 291
Mitchell, Francis 167
Mitchell, Henry 23
Mitchell, James 73
Mitchell, John 141
Mitchell, W. (Latrobe Brewery) 294
Mitchell, William (Cremorne Brewery) 141
Mitchell's Brewery 141, 149
Moger, Ed 211, 230
Moger, George 211
Moloney, Michael 172, 173
Molony, Edward A. 235
Molony, John 234, 235
Molony, John F. 31
Molony's Brewing Co. 234, 235
Montgomerie, Robert 147, 149
Montgomerie's Brewery 149
Moody, Joan 83
Moody, John 234
Moody's Brewery 234
Moonambel Brewery 159
Mooney, Richard 80
Mooney Valley Aerated Water & Cordial Co. 145
Mooroopna Brewery Co. 159
Moras, Henry 35
Moreland, J. W. 149
Morpeth Brewery 51
Morphett Street Brewery 219
Morphett Vale Brewery 234
Morrison, Eleanor 281, 283
Morrow, T. 49, 50
Morse, James 281
Morton, H. 48
Morton, William 167
Morton & Jackson 34
Moss, Henry 77
Moss, John 87, 147, 149
Moss's Brewery 130, 149
Mott, James 231
Moulden, E. T. 151, 159
Moulden, Thomas 212
Mount Alexander Brewery 113
Mount Baker Brewery 234
Mount Cook Brewery 193
Mount Gambier Brewing Co. Ltd 234
Mount Hope Brewery 51
Mount Macedon Brewery 159
Mount Magnet Brewery & Cordial Co. 263
Mount Malcolm Brewery 263
Mount Margaret Brewing Co. Ltd 263
Mount Morgans Brewing & Malting Co. Ltd 263
Mount Pleasant Brewery & Ice Works Co. 196
Mount Vincent Meadery 319–20
Mountain Brewery (Woods Point) 175
Mountain Brewery Co. Ltd (Blackheath) 27
Mountain Brewing Co. Ltd (Sydney) 66
Mountford, Charles 117, 175
Mountford, William 117
Moyes, Robert 109, 123
Mudgee Co-operative Brewing Co. 32, 51, 52
Mueller, A. 153
Mulgoa Brewery 82

Mullan, Isaac 55
Mullard, Isaac 39, 51
Muller, Narcisse 37
Mullewa Brewery 264
Mullings, William 294
Mullins, Charles 26, 27
Mullins, Edward 26, 27
Mumme, William 246, 269, 270, 271
Munro, David 149
Murchison Brewing Co. Ltd 251–2
Murcutt, Robert 152, 154, 157
Murcutt's Brewery 133, 149, 152
Murphy, Daniel 303
Murphy, James 106, 157
Murphy, John Robert 157
Murphy, Patrick 28
Murphy brothers 86
Murphy's Brewery (Bendigo) 106
Murphy's Brewery (Melbourne) 149, 157
Murray, David 112
Murray Breweries Pty Ltd 22, 99, 100
Murray Bridge Brewery 235–6
Murrumbidgee Brewery 80–1
Must, Thomas 162
Muswellbrook Brewery 52
Muter, James 167
Myers, James 245, 246
Myers, Walter 245
Myring, Annie 113
Myring, Joseph 112, 113

N.T. Brewery Pty Ltd 134, 311, 312
Nankervis, H. 230
Napier Brewery 96–7, 152
Narrabri Brewery 52–3, 82
Narracoorte Brewery 236
Narrandera Brewery 53, 73
Narrogin Brewing Co. Ltd 264
Nash, Dennis 239
Nash, Owen 220
Nathan Brewery 219, 223, 225
Nathan, Leopold 150
Nation, Alfred 133, 155, 170
Nation, James 133, 155, 170
Nation, Thomas 171
Nation, Walter 171
National Brewing Holdings Ltd 73, 184, 221, 268
Natty's Brewery 62, 66
Neal, John 25
Neave, James 92
Nectar Brewery 58
Nelson, Stephen 123
Nelson, Thomas 42
Nelson Brewery 66–7
Nepean Brewery 82
Nerrigundah Brewery 53
Nevell, Jane 319
New Brewery (Echuca) 116
New Brewery (Toowoomba) 202
New Brewery (Warrnambool) 174
New Brewery Ltd (Melbourne) 149
New Norfolk Brewery 302
New South Wales Lager Bier Brewing Co. Ltd 67, 74, 75, 339
New York Brewery 67
Newbridge Brewery Co. 112, 160
Newcastle Brewing Co. Ltd 320
Newdick, P. 47, 48
Newell, Michael 39
Newing, Mr 219
Newman, James 111
Newnham, Charles 46, 73
Newnham & Tooth 71, 134
Newsham, A. H. 258

Newton & Martin 92
Newtown Brewery (Geelong) 118
Newtown Brewery (Hobart) 292–3
Newtown Brewery (Wagga Wagga) 81
Nhill Brewery 160
Nicol, George 202
Nicol, J. F. 186, 188
Nicholas, Priscilla 96
Nicholls, George 67, 291
Nicholls, James 168
Nicholls Tasmanian Dandelion Ale Co. 67
Nichols, Stephen 334
Nieves, William 201
Noake, Elizabeth 301
Noake, Isaac 301
Noake's Brewery 301
Noarlunga Brewery 236
Noblett, George 115
Nolan, Michael 78
Norfolk Brewery 102, 103, 104, 106
Norfolk Island Brewing Co. 315
Norman, Charles 84
Normanville Brewery 236
Norseman Brewing Co. Ltd 264
Norseman Co-operative Brewing Co. Ltd 264
North Carlton Brewery 149
North End Brewery 196
North Eastern Brewery 101
North Hamilton Brewery 120
North Melbourne Brewery 132, 133, 135, 149–50
North Queensland Brewing Co. Ltd (Mareeba) 189, 198
North Queensland Brewing Co. Ltd (Townsville) 204–5
North Star Hotel & Brewery 233
North West Brewing, Refrigerating & Ice Co. Ltd 272–3
North West Coast Brewery 282
Northam Brewery & Refrigerating Co. Ltd 265
Northern Australian Breweries Ltd 191
Northern Australian Brewery Co. Ltd 196
Northern Breweries (Queensland) Ltd 192, 205
Northern Brewery (Lismore) 46, 74, 135
Northern Brewing Co. Pty Ltd (Mildura) 158–9
Northern Territory Brewery Ltd 311–12
Nunn, Allen 304
Nunn, John 281
Nunn, Robert 304
Nymagee Brewery 55
Nyngan Brewery 55

Oakbank Brewery (Narrandera) 53
Oakbank Brewery (Oakbank) 31, 220, 237
Oatlands Brewery 302–3
O'Brien, Thomas 33
Ockerby, Thomas 303
O'Connell, J. 257
O'Connor, G. H. 51, 52
O'Connor, Nicholas 127
O'Connor's Brewery 127
Oddy, James 110
Oddy, Joseph 41
O'Driscoll, Dennis 174, 175
O'Farrell, Edmund 66
Ogilvie, Harry 35
Ogilvie, James 290, 291

Ogilvie, Thomas 35, 170
O'Hara, P. 118
OK Brewery 219
O'Keeffe, Richard 21, 22, 23
Old Ballarat Brewery 317, 322, 326
Old Bell Inn & Brewery 293
Old Goulburn Brewery 319
Old Mill House Brewery 28
O'Meara, Patrick 121
O'Neill, Henry 56
Opie, James 236
Orange Brewery 55
Orient Brewery 67, 75, 76
Oriental Brewery 246
Orme, Frederick 150
Orme's Brewery 146, 150
Osborne, James 37
O'Sullivan, L. 192
Ovenden, William 81
Ovens Brewery 99, 100
Ower, William 109

Pack Horse Inn & Brewery 293
Paddington Brewery 67
Page, Samuel 302, 303
Palling, Mary 175
Palmer, Thomas Fyshe 61
Park, William 166
Park Brewery (Forbes) 38, 39
Park Brewery (Newcastle) 55
Parker, Eugene 25
Parker, James 32, 84
Parker, John 32, 219
Parker, T. L. 155, 156
Parker Brothers Brewery 150
Parkes Brewery 57
Parramatta Brewery (George & O'Connell Street, Sydney) 67–8
Parramatta Brewery (Macquarie Street, Sydney) 68
Pars Ram Brothers (Australia) Pty Ltd 311
Parsons, H. 263
Parsons, Henry 34
Parsons, Sam 304
Pascoe, Benjamin 239
Pascoe, Thomas 286
Pass, Richard 319
Passmore, Mr 47
Paterson, Alex 228
Paton, A. H. 258, 259
Patriot King William the Fourth Inn & Brewery 283
Patterson, Frederick 286
Patterson, John 116
Pavey's Brewery 233–4
Pavey, Henry 233
Pavey, James 232, 233
Pavey, Phillip 233
Paxton, Andrew 227
Payne, John 76
Pearson, George 141
Pearson & Gray 154
Pedley, Arthur 85
Penny, John 130
Penola Brewery 237
Penrose, John 57–8
Perkins City Brewery 111, 180, 185
Perkins & Co. 175, 176, 180, 185, 186
Perkins, Hector 192
Perkins, James 175
Perkins, Patrick (Paddy) 111, 171, 175, 180, 185, 202
Perkins, Thomas (Jnr) 111, 171, 175, 180, 185, 202
Perkins, Thomas (Snr) 175

Perkins, William 283
Perrers, William 238
Perriman, G. L. 302
Perriman's Brewery 302
Perrin, James 111, 114, 138
Perry, H. W. 125
Perryman, John 263
Perseverance Brewery (Gunnedah) 43
Perseverance Brewery (Wangaratta) 172
Petchey, John 290
Peters, Charles 279, 283
Perth Brewery (Tasmania) 303
Perth Brewery Co. Ltd 268
Pestell, Daniel 283
Pestell's Brewery 283
Pettit, George 245, 246
Pettit, James 94, 164, 165, 171
Peyroux, Augustus 109
Phillips, E. 58
Phillips, John 98
Phillips River Brewing & Aerated Water Co. Ltd 273
Phillipson, James W. 216, 251–2
Phimister, William 130
Phoenix Brewery (Auburn) 226
Phoenix Brewery (Ballarat) 94–5, 96, 97, 98, 134
Phoenix Brewery (Bendigo) 106
Phoenix Brewery (Castlemaine) 112, 113
Phoenix Brewery (Cowra) 36
Phoenix Brewery (Fremantle) 253
Phoenix Brewery (Hobart) 253, 275, 293
Phoenix Brewery (Launceston) 298
Phoenix Brewery (Melbourne) 133, 149, 150
Phoenix Brewery (Rushworth) 162, 163
Phoenix Brewery (Wiluna) 273
Phoenix Brewery Co. (Melbourne) 150
Phoenix Brewing Co. Ltd (Brisbane) 184, 186
Plunket, Sam 33
Picnic Point Brewery 93, 94
Pierce, John 282
Pike, Henry 236–7
Pike, Ian 320
Pirie Street Brewery 219
Pitcher, Meg 333
Pivot Brewery 118
Pogson, George 284
Pond, Alfred 64, 68
Pond's Brewery 64, 68
Port Albert Brewery 160–1
Port Augusta Brewery 220, 221, 238
Port Brewery Co. Ltd 253
Port Cygnet Brewery 281
Port Dock Brewery Hotel 330
Port Dalrymple Brewery 275, 299
Port MacDonnell Brewery 238
Port Melbourne Brewing Co. 325
Port Pirie Brewery 238–9
Portland 161, 162
Powell, Charles 197, 198, 201
Powell, Thomas 118, 119, 168
Powell's Brewery 119
Power & Blain 92
Power Brewing Co. Ltd 135, 180, 183, 205, 328–9
Power, Thomas & Madden 103
Power, William 123
Prendergast, Nicholas 127

Index — 371

Prendergast, Robert 54, 62, 111, 160, 184
Prentice, L. J. 291
Presnell, Thomas 293
Presnell, William 293
Presnell's Brewery 275, 293
Prewett, Herbert 195
Price, David 59
Price, Edward (Ted) 174
Price, Thomas 174
Primrose Brewery 219
Primrose, John 58, 223
Prince Albert Hotel & Brewery 219
Pritchard & Chamberlain 101, 106
Pritchard, Thomas 101
Puctalko, August 156
Pullen, Jessie 305
Pumphouse Brewery 321
Pushion, William 293
Pursy, Peter 102
Pyrmont Brewery Co. Ltd 68

Quain, M. 255
Quain Brothers 254
Quantong Brewery 162
Queen's Brewery 150
Queen's Wharf Hotel Brewery 320
Queensland Brewing Co. Ltd (Brisbane) 134, 179, 183, 186–8, 340
Queensland Brewing Co. Ltd (Toowoomba) 134, 202–3
Quick, W. 193
Quinlan, Kate 184
Quinlan, M. 183, 184
Quinn, John 305
Quinn, Thomas 114
Quorn Brewery 239

R. E. & F. Tooth 73
Radenti, Claudio 334
Ralston, Arthur 165, 171
Ralston, Gavin 59, 165, 171
Ralston, George 81, 82
Ralston & Wishart 165
Rampling, James 24, 25
Rampling & Scholes 24, 25
Rand, Edward 280
Rankin, E. 79
Rankin, George 26, 27
Rankin, J. D. 45
Rankin, Thomas 34
Rare Amber Brewing Co. 333
Rasp, Charles 30
Rayert, Nicholas 160
Raymond, James 41
Raymond, Robert (Goulburn Brewery) 41
Raymond, Robert S. (Carcoar Brewery) 32
Rayner, James 299
Reardon, Edward and Elizabeth 304
Reardon's Brewery 304
Red Heart Brewery 59, 68
Red Lion Brewery (Amherst) 92
Red Lion Brewery (Bourke) 28
Red Lion Brewery (Coonamble) 33–4
Red Lion Brewery (Cobar) 32, 33
Red Lion Brewery (Hay) 43–4
Red Lion Brewery (Orange) 55–6
Redback Brewery 325
Redcastle Brewing Co. Ltd 268
Reedbeds Brewery 219
Refreshment Tent & Brewery 106
Regentville Brewery 82
Reichelt, Frederick W. 141, 153

Reid, Isaiah 212, 238
Reid, John 212, 238
Reid, Jane 238
Reid, Martha 216
Reid River Brewery 199
Reid's Brewery 219
Renateau, John 28
Renne, Leopold 144, 145
Renou, Percival 166
Rentier, Francis 120
Resch, Edmund 34, 35, 57, 67, 74, 75, 76, 83, 84
Resch, Emil 57, 58, 74, 84, 133, 155
Resch, Richard 34, 35, 74, 84
Resch's Ltd 75; see also E. Resch & Co.; E & R Resch & Co.
Resch's Brewery 68, 75
Restall, John 83
Restall & Dymond 82
Retreat Brewery 282
Retreat Inn & Brewery 119
Reynell, John 239
Reynella Brewery 239
Reynolds, Sue 333
Reynolds, Thomas 100
Reynolds, Tom 333
Rice, James 171
Richards, John 41
Richardson, Fred 273
Richardson, William 228
Richmond, John 223
Richmond Brewery (Church Street, Melbourne) 141, 142, 150, 151
Richmond Brewery (Lincoln Street, Melbourne) 89, 139, 143, 150
Richmond Brewery (Perth) 303
Richmond N.S. Brewing Co. Pty Ltd 134, 150–1
Richmond River Brewery 46
Rickettson, Henry 125
Rieneke, Charles 234
Rifle Brigade Pub Brewery 323
Riley, Jonathon 81
Rippendale, Isabella 57
Ritchie, William 114
River Murray Brewery 229–30
Riverine Brewery (Echuca) 116
Riverine Brewery, Aerated Waters & Milling Co. Ltd (Deniliquin) 36–7
Riversdale Brewery 41
Robe Town Brewery 239
Robert Bruce & Co. 84
Roberts, John L. 285
Roberts, Lawrence 160
Roberts, R. A. 291
Roberts, Thomas 123
Roberts, William 130
Robertson, Gilbert 303
Robertson, James (McCracken's City Brewery) 112, 146–7
Robertson, James (Jolly Hatters Brewery) 292
Robertson, William 80
Robinson, G. W. 285
Robinson, J. 170
Robinson, John 123
Robinson, Thomas G. W. J. 146, 148, 226, 233
Robinson, Matthew 334
Robinson, William 161
Rock Brewery 123
Rockhampton Brewery Ltd 200–1
Rockliff, Roger 297, 298
Rocky Mouth Brewing Co. 48
Rodwell, George 62
Rogers, George 53
Rogers, Richard 27
Roma Brewery 201

Rooke, Adolphus 281, 282
Rose & Crown Hotel & Brewery 268
Rose Hill Brewery 68
Rosenberg, Theodore 132, 133, 149
Rosevears Waterfront Brewery Pty Ltd 335
Ross, John 100
Ross brothers 77
Rotherwood Brewery 284–5
Rottger, Johann 121
Rounsevell & Simms 220
Rowland, Henry 142–3
Rowley, John 174
Rowley, Thomas 63
Roxburgh Brewery (Melbourne) 151
Roxburgh Brewery (Sale) 165
Royal Artiller Brewery 151
Royal Brewery (Geelong) 119, 134
Royal Brewery (Hobart) 300
Royal Hotel Brewery 303
Royal Mint Brewery 151
Royal Oak Hotel & Brewery 294
Royal Standard Brewery (Ballarat) 94, 95, 97–8, 134
Royal Standard Brewery (Tamworth) 77
Rudge, Frederick 281, 295
Rudge's Brewery 295
Rudkin, Jonathon 145
Rule, R.E. 33, 34
Ruse, Walter 257
Rushton, Charles 69
Rushton, Thomas 63, 67, 68–9
Rushton's Brewery 68–9
Rushworth Brewery Co. Ltd 162–3
Russell, Frederick E. 199, 201, 204
Russell & Taylor 117
Ryan & Iveson 109
Ryan, Thomas 123
Ryan, William 111, 113, 122

Sabine, Thomas 231
Sackville, William 296
Sail & Anchor Pub Brewery 333
St Arnaud Brewery 164
St George Brewery 201
St George, William 233
St Ives Brewery 334
Sale Brewery 165
Salisbury Brewery 219–20, 239
Sanctuary Cove Brewing Co. 135, 328
Sander, William 292
Sanderson, Donald 55
Sandhurst Brewing & Malting Co. Ltd 105, 106
Sargent, Amos 219
Saunders, T. H. 53
Saunders, Thomas 301
Saunders, William 109
Savage, R. 170
Savage & Clifford 149
Saw, Henry 271
Sawers, W. R. 223
Sayer, Charles 103, 106
Sayer, James 103, 106
Sayers & Co. 128
Scarr, Thomas 55
Scarr's Brewery 55
Scharer, Geoffrey 320
Scharer's Little Brewery 320
Schickel, John 213, 218, 257
Schramm, Alfred 212, 219
Scott, David 78
Scott, Edward 127
Scott, Frank 258, 259

Scott, John 300
Scott, Mary 259, 272
Scottish Chief's Tavern Brewery 323
Scottsdale Brewery 303–4
Scrase Brothers Brewery 151–2
Scrase, Edwin 96, 97, 125
Scrase, George 121
Scrase, Samuel 125
Seage, John 37
Seager, Francis 46
Seager, John 46
Searle, William 289
Seaton, Alfred 212
Second Valley Brewery 239
Seeliger, Ernst 122, 237
Service, James 160
Sexton, Philip 332
Seymour Brewery 121, 166
Shamrock Brewery (Broad Arrow) 248
Shamrock Brewery (Broken Hill) 29, 31
Shamrock Brewery (Bunbury) 249
Shamrock Brewery Co. (Kalgoorlie) 258
Shamrock Brewing & Malting Co. Ltd 132, 133, 149, 152
Shand, Charles 212–13
Shand, John 212, 222
Shand, W. C. 231
Sharp, George 234, 235
Sharp, Peter 27, 82
Sheffield's Brewery 177
Sheil, William 126, 166, 171
Sheldrick & Co. 120, 121
Sheldrick, Walter 174
Sheldrick's Brewery 174
Shelley, John 29, 115
Shelley, William 40, 41
Shelley & Co. 29
Sheppard, Frank 114
Sheppard, Henry 113
Shepparton Brewery 166
Sheridan, John 117
Sherwood, Edward 303
Sherwood, Frank 269–70, 271
Sherwood, H. 248
Shone, E. R. 33, 34
Short, O. W. 190
Sibbald, Frederick 85
Siddall, Elias 110
Siddall, Paul 111, 141, 143, 166
Sieber, Mr 143
Silberg & Sidney 121
Silver City Mineral Water Co. 29
Silverstream Brewery 134, 188, 203
Silverstream Mfg Co. Pty Ltd 130, 152
Simmond, Henry 85
Simmons, Henry 25, 172
Simmons, Moore 305
Simms, William K. 75, 211, 217, 225, 226
Simpson, Arthur George 259, 272
Simpson, Beaglehole & Co. 29
Simpson, George 31, 39
Simpson, John 43, 130
Simpson, Johnston & Co. 31
Simpson, Peter (Armidale Brewery) 24, 25, 39, 44, 52–3
Simpson, Peter (Mountain Brewery) 175
Simpson, Thomas 43, 44, 82, 83
Simpson's Road Brewery 133, 152
Singleton Brewery 58
Sison, Frederick S. 211
Skerret, J. 119
Skinner, Archibald 82

Skinner, David 99, 100
Skinner, James 36
Slattery, John 106
Slattery's Brewery 104, 106
Sleigh, Harry 252
Sloan family 120
Sloan, James 29, 31, 55, 120
Sloan's Brewery 120, 121
Sloane, Thomas 162
Small, William 51
Smalpage, Frederick W. 29, 116, 261
Smalpage, H. M. 248
Smee, W. F. 131
Smith, Alexander 285
Smith, C. 237
Smith, David 46
Smith, Edward 28
Smith, (Sir) Edwin Thomas 218, 219, 220, 330
Smith, Elizabeth 69
Smith, George 214
Smith, Henry 51
Smith & Horwood 145
Smith, J. A. (Naracoorte Brewery) 236
Smith, James (Portland Brewery) 161
Smith, James (Sydney Place Brewery) 300
Smith, John 98, 121, 174
Smith, Joseph 77
Smith, Reg 251
Smith, Thomas (Albion Brewery) 160
Smith, Thomas (Grange Brewery) 120
Smith, Walter 110, 112
Smith and Laski's Brewery 127
Smithers, John B. 63, 64
Smith's Brewery 121
Smythesdale Brewery 166–7
Sneath, John 131
Solomon, A. M. 24, 25
Solomon, Cleveland 77
Solomon, Paul 264
Solomontown Brewery 239
Sommers, John 119
Sorell Brewery 304
South Australian Brewery 234, 237
South Australian Brewing Co. Ltd (Adelaide) 29, 209, 220–1, 231, 237, 238, 340
South Australian Brewing Co. Ltd (Broken Hill) 29, 30, 31, 92
South Australian Brewing, Malting & Wine & Spirit Co.Ltd 221
South Broken Hill Brewery 30, 129
South Western Brewery & Cordial Co. Ltd 255
Southern Brewery (Richmond, Melbourne) 136, 152, 157
Southern Brewery Co. Ltd (Albany) 246
Southwark Brewery 221
Sovereign Brewery Pty Ltd 322
Spargo, B. B. 93
Specimen Hill Brewery 96, 97, 98
Speed, Charles 254
Spencer, Esther 281
Spencer, John 230
Spencer, Robert 281, 284
Spicer, J. 231
Spier, J. A. 39
Spooner, Thomas 283
Spreyton Brewery 305
Spring Creek Brewery (Beechworth) 99, 100
Spring Creek Brewery (Maldon) 127

Spring Creek Brewery (Tallangatta) 169
Springfield Brewery Ltd 221–2
Springett, Colman R. 64
Springett, Robert 26, 27
Springs Brewery 127
Springvale Brewery 116
Sprunt, John 39
Sprunt, Thomas 38, 39
Spry, R. 161
Squire, James (Jnr) 69–70
Squire, James (Snr) 16, 60, 61, 69–70
Stabler, William 70
Stacey Brewing Co. 131, 152
Stacey, Thomas 139, 152
Stag's Head Inn & Brewery 253, 254
Stahl, Louis 47
Stallard, William 286, 303
Stanbridge & Harrison 185, 188
Standard Brewery (Ipswich) 195
Standard Brewery (Kanowna) 260
Standard Brewery (Mt Gambier) 31, 221, 234
Standard Brewery (Orange) 27, 56, 72
Standard Brewery (Sydney) 59, 70, 71, 72
Standard Brewery Co. Ltd (Castlemaine) 112–13
Standard Brewery Co. Ltd (Echuca) 116, 159
Stander, F. C. 117
Stanhope Brewery 201
Stanlake, Charles 310
Stanley, Frederick 218
Stanley Brewery 304
Stanley Brewing Co. Ltd 268–9
Stanley Co-operative Brewery Co. Ltd 269
Star Brewery (Burnie) 280
Star Brewery (Castlemaine) 113
Star Brewery (Geraldton) 255
Star Brewery (Hillston) 44–5
Star Brewery (Melbourne) 139, 152–3
Star Brewery (Walhalla) 171
Star Brewery (Yass) 85
Station Tavern & Brewery 325
Stawell Brewery 168
Stawell New Brewery 169
Steam Brewery 213, 222
Steam Engine Brewery 70
Steam Packet Brewing Co. 324
Steindl, Gustav 190
Steindl, J. 190
Steindl, Lee 198
Steindl, Louis 190, 198
Steindl, O. R. 190
Steindl & Son 198
Stephen & Co. 215
Stephenson, William 154
Stevens, Augustus 122
Stevens, James 37
Stevens, Peter 122, 173–4
Stevenson, John 64
Steward, James George 102, 128, 164
Steward & Hunter Pty Ltd 104
Stewart, Hugh 33
Stewart, James 25, 26
Stewart, John 290
Stirling Brewery Ltd 269
Stirton, T. A. 51
Stock, Robert 220
Stodart, Robert 279
Stokes, James 241, 265, 266, 268, 269, 271
Stokes, Samuel 141, 142

Stokes' Brewery 269
Stone Brewery 238
Strachan & Minter 154
Strathalbyn Brewery 239
Strathloddon Brewery 113
Stratton, Lang & Co. 34
Strezlecki Brewing Co. Pty Ltd 326
Strickland, Mr 81
Strickland, Robert 104
Strickland, Roy 39
Strickland, William (Crown Brewery) 26
Strickland, William (High Street Brewery) 104
Strickland, William (Leura Brewery) 109, 114
Strong Beer Brewery 63, 70
Strutton, R. 218
Stuart, James 49, 50
Stuart Brewery Ltd 308, 312
Studd, Samuel 59
Subiaco Brewery 269
Sudholtz brothers 170
Suiter, W. J. 261
Sunshine Coast Brewery 328
Surrey & Myers 57
Surrey Brewery 70, 75, 76
Sutherland, Hugh 33
Swallow Brewery (Mt Gambier) 234, 235
Swallow Brewery Co. Ltd (Perth) 269
Swan, J. G. H. 68
Swan Brewery (Molong) 50
Swan Brewery & Bottling Co. (Kalgoorlie) 258
Swan Brewery Co. Ltd (Darwin) 312
Swan Brewery Co. Ltd (Perth) 73, 243, 269–72, 308
Sydney Brewery (Burrundulla) 32
Sydney Brewery (Harris Street, Sydney) 59, 70
Sydney Brewery (Parramatta Road, Sydney) 70–1
Sydney Co-operative Brewery Co. Ltd 62, 66, 71
Sydney Place Brewery 300
Syme, James T. 211
Syme, John 288
Syme & Sison 220
Symington, William 93
Symington's Brewery 93

Tabulo, John 198
Tabulo, Thomas 198, 201
Taegtow, Frederick 145
Tait, Charles 166
Talbot Brewery 107, 169
Tamar Brewery 296, 297, 300
Tamworth Brewery 77–8
Tanjil Brewery 170
Tanksteam Brewing Co. 321–2
Tasman Brewery 275, 285, 286, 293
Tasmania Dandelion Ale Co. Ltd 292, 293
Tasmanian Breweries Pty Ltd 277, 293, 296, 297, 300
Tasmanian Brewery (Evandale) 283
Tasmanian Brewery (Hobart) 286, 293
Tasmanian Brewery (Launceston) 297, 300
Tasmanian Brewery (Melbourne) 131, 153
Tasmanian Brewery Co. Ltd (Burnie) 280

Tasmanian Co-operative Brewery Co. Ltd 296, 300
Tasmanian Hotel & Brewery 222
Tasmanian Pale Ale Brewery 293–4
Tatham, Henry 193
Taverners Products 334
Taylor, Arthur 197
Taylor, W. 238
Teagle, George 230
Teagle's Brewery 230
Temora Brewery 73, 78
Temperance Brewery 141, 153
Terrier Brewing Co. (Brisbane) 188
Terrier Brewing Co. (Gympie) 194
Terry, Albert 128, 136, 153, 154, 156, 157
Terry, Alfred 120, 136
Terry, C. N. Wingate 47, 48
Terry, Edward 130, 196
Terry, Ernest 267
Terry, Samuel 58–9, 60, 71
Terry's Brewery Ltd 47–8
Terry's West End Breweries Ltd 153, 157
Tewksbury, Alphonso R. 78, 81, 85
Thistlewaite, George 162
Thomas, Mr 51
Thomas, Bartholomew 282
Thomas, David (Nymagee Brewery) 55
Thomas, David (Taverners Products) 334
Thomas, Edward 93, 169, 198
Thomas, James 37
Thomas, John 45
Thomas, Joseph 37
Thomas McLaughlin & Co. (Qld) 134, 200
Thompson, Andrew 84–5, 230
Thompson & Bishop 64
Thompson, James 205, 230, 238
Thompson, Peter 324
Thompson, R. 63
Thompson, Robert 23
Thompson, Luke 113
Thompson, Welwood 64
Thompson, William 315
Thorne, Daniel 41
Thorne, George 41
Thorne, William 112, 127, 170
Thorne Brothers Brewery 41
Thorsborne, August 181
Thunder, Alfred 106, 153
Thunder & Co. 153
Thurston, Thomas 142
Thwaites Brewery 222
Thwaites, Thomas 222
Ticehurst Brewery 280
Tierney, James 121, 123, 166
Tiger Brewery 77, 78
Tiger's Head Brewery 325
Tighe & Co. 59
Tindale, William 36
Tinson, William 49, 52, 58
Tinson & Wharton 53
Tippins, Henry 36
Todd, A. W. 44
Tolley, A. E. & F. 220
Tonkin, Peter 335
Toogood, William 117
Toohey, James 59, 62, 66, 70, 71, 72, 73
Toohey, John 59, 62, 66, 70, 71, 72, 73
Toohey, Matthew 71
Toohey's Ltd 41, 54–5, 56, 66, 71–3
Toorak Brewery 247, 251
Tooth, Edwin 73

Tooth, Frederick 73
Tooth, John 71, 73, 134
Tooth, R. (Bulimba Brewery) 183, 186
Tooth, Robert 73
Tooth, Robert Lucas 73
Tooth Brewery 74, 79
Tooth & Co. Ltd 41, 45, 46, 49, 50, 53, 54, 60, 63, 66, 71, 73–4, 78, 80, 134, 135, 140, 290, 340
Topman's Brewery 58
Topp, Charles 109
Torrens Brewery 222
Torrenside Brewery 222–3
Tothill, John 235
Tovey, Harry 85
Towers, James 300
Towers, Robert 297, 300
Towers Brewery (Charters Towers) 192
Towers Brewery (Launceston) 300
Towers Brewery Co. 192
Townsville Brewery 205
Townsville Brewing Co. Ltd 205
Trade Union Co-operative Brewery Co. Ltd 153
Traditional Brewing Co. Pty Ltd 325
Trait, J. J. 96
Trapman, C. W. F. 218
Treacey, Elizabeth 80
Treacey, Martin 37, 80, 119
Treacy & Smith 122
Trent Brewery Co. 124–5, 170
Trentham Brewery 170
Trew, David 324
Trew, Digby 28
Tripp, J. P. 84
Triumph Brewery 294
Trott, Jacob 284
Tuck, John 24, 25
Tucker family 195
Tucket, P. S. 125
Tuena Brewery 78
Tulloch, W. H. 76
Tulloch, William 94, 95, 97
Tumbarumba Brewery 79
Tumut Brewery 73, 79
Turnbull, Adam B. 294
Turnbull, Francis 281
Turner, William 297, 298
Turrell, Samuel 62
Tusa, Stephen 199
Twedall, W. 39
Twigg, W. 174
Two Brewers Hotel & Brewery 127–8
Tyler, James E. 64
Tyrell, William 43

Ulladulla Brewery 79
Underwood, Frank 48
Underwood, Thomas 49
Unicorn Brewery (Burra) 227
Unicorn Brewery (Silverton) 58
Union Barrier Brewery 31, 58
Union Beer Co. 74
Union Brewery (Adelaide) 58
Union Brewery (Bendigo) 106
Union Brewery (Bundaberg) 190
Union Brewery (Grenfell) 42
Union Brewery (Launceston) 296, 297, 300–1
Union Brewery (Little Lonsdale Street, Melbourne) 153
Union Brewery (Perth) 272
Union Brewery (Richmond, Melbourne) 153–4

Union Brewery (Sydney) 74
Union Brewery Co. (Kalgoorlie) 257, 258–9
Union Brewing & Malting Co. 223
United Distillers Ltd 98
Unmack, Lawrence 176
Urana Brewery 79
Usher, T. F. 283
Usher, Thomas 52

Vallack, James 68
Valley Brewery (Brisbane) 188
Valley Brewery (Maitland) 319
Valley Brewery Co. 186, 188
Vaughan, Charles (Red Lion Brewery) 34
Vaughan, Charles: (Cambridge Brewery) 131, (Collingwood Brewery) 139, 153, (Star Brewery) 152
Vectis Brewery 170
Vezey, Henry 152
Victoria Brewery (Adelaide) 224
Victoria Brewery (Brisbane) 181, 188
Victoria Brewery (Castlemaine) 113
Victoria Brewery (Geraldton) 255
Victoria Brewery (Horsham) 122
Victoria Brewery (Kapunda) 221, 230
Victoria Brewery (Kilmore) 123
Victoria Brewery (Koondrook) 123
Victoria Brewery (Prahran) 154, 157
Victoria Brewery (Port Fairy) 161
Victoria Brewery (Portland) 161, 162
Victoria Brewery (Sale) 165
Victoria Brewery Co. Ltd (Bendigo) 59, 106–7, 133, 139, 143, 145
Victoria Brewery Co. Ltd (Wangaratta) 172–3
Victoria Brewery Pty Ltd (East Melbourne) 89, 132, 133, 135, 144, 154–6
Victoria Brewery & Malting Co. Ltd 154, 156
Victoria Brewing & Bottling Co. Ltd (Kalgoorlie) 259
Victoria Brewing, Malting & Distilling Co. Ltd 133, 155, 156
Victoria Flour Mill & Brewery 45
Victoria Hotel & Brewery 294
Victoria Parade Brewery 58, 118, 133, 156
Victoria Temperance Brewery 156
Victorian Hop Beer Co. 129, 156
Vienna Lager Beer Brewery 156
Vincent, C. 251
Vincent, George 64
Vincent, Thomas 64
Vine Street Brewery 107
Viney, Robert 283
Viney, William 283
Volum, Andrew 118, 119
Volum Brewery 95, 118, 119, 134, 323
Volum, James 118, 119

W.A. Burton Brewery Co. Ltd 272
W.A. Lion Brewery & Ice Co.Ltd 251
Wacher, Percy 273
Waddell, Johathon 299
Wade, Alfred C. 51, 52
Wagga Wagga Brewery 23, 80, 81–2
Walder, Thomas 113
Walder's Brewery 113
Walford, S. R. 41, 68

Walker, Emma 288
Walker, James 26, 27, 56, 62, 72
Walker, John 291, 294
Walker, Robert 291, 294
Walker's Brewery 294
Walkerville Brewery 224
Walkerville Co-operative Brewing Co. Ltd 215, 220, 221, 223, 224–5, 227, 229
Walkley, W. F. 252
Wall, Arthur 49, 50
Wallace, John Alston 167
Wallen, Robert 173
Wallis, Richard 298
Walmsley, Albert 253
Walsh, Edward 170
Walsh, James 211
Walter, Fritz 236
Walter, Ingrid 236
Walters, J. M. 172, 173
Walton, John 41
Wangaratta Brewery 173
Wangaratta Brewery Pty Ltd 171, 173
Wangaratta Brewing & Malting Co. 171, 172, 173
Waratah Brewery 82
Warburton, Joseph 144
Ward, Charles 171
Ward, Fred 245
Ward, George 170
Ward, John 245, 246
Ward, Louis McDermott 173
Ward's Brewery 246
Wardley & Potts 177
Ware, Alexander W. 222
Ware, Charles Boxer 222, 227
Ware, George J. 222
Ware, Thomas L. 222, 223, 251, 264
Warnock brothers 126, 127
Warnock, Samuel 126, 127
Warren, John 222
Warren, W. W. 215
Warrenheip Brewery 98
Warrior, Robert 289
Warrnambool Brewing & Malting Co. 139, 174–5
Warrnambool New Brewery Co. 175
Warwick Brewery 205
Watchorn, W.B. 290
Waterfield, William 121
Watson, James 216
Watson, James A. 112, 113
Watson, Jonathon 304
Watson & Young 23
Watt, William 62, 73
Watts, Jesse 101
Wauchope, Patrick 219
Waverley Brewery (Adelaide) 221, 222, 225
Waverley Brewery (Broken Hill) 29, 30–1
Waverley Brewery (Redfern) 67, 70, 73, 74–5
Waverley Brewery (Waverley) 35, 67, 73, 75–6
Waygood, William 162
Webb, William 305
Webster, Joseph 160
Wehlow, Edward 68
Weimer's Brewery 192
Weisse, Louis 252
Welch, F. (Welsh, J.) Tizard 128, 283
Well Park Brewery (Dubbo) 37
Well Park Brewery (Leigh Creek) 125
Wellington Brewery 76

Welsh, Gordon 330
Wentworth Brewery 83
Wessler, Bob 231
West, Absolem 7
West, F. H. 272
West Albin & Co. 183
West Adelaide Brewery 225–6
West Australian Brewery Co. Ltd 272
West Coast Brewery 283
West End Breweries Ltd (Melbourne) 128, 136, 153, 156–7
West End Brewery (Adelaide) 209, 221, 226
West End Brewery (Broken Hill) 30, 31
West End Brewery (Charters Towers) 192
West End Brewery (Geelong) 119
West End Brewery (Kalgoorlie) 259–60
West End Brewery (Mt Gambier) 235
West End Brewery (Townsville) 205
West End Brewery Ltd (Brisbane) 188–9
West End Brewing & Malting Co. Ltd 189
West Moreton Brewery Co. Ltd 195
Westbrook, Edward 76
Westbury Brewery 305
Westcombe, Daniel 297
Westcombe, George (Jnr) 297
Westcombe, George (Snr) 297
Western Australian Brewery 272
Western Brewery 174, 175
Western Brewery Co. 191
Western Brewing Co. 195
Western City Brewing Co. Ltd 121, 164
Western Creek Brewery 110, 168
Westley, A. C. 46
Wetherhill, Robert 76
Wetherhill's Brewery 76
Wharf Brewery (Melbourne) 87, 97, 130, 139, 154, 157
Wharf Brewery (Launceston) 301
Wharton, John 107
Wheeler, Ann 163
Wheeler, Edmund 112, 113, 174, 175
Wheeler, Jabez 157
Wheeler, James A. 112, 113
Wheeler, William E. 110, 164
Wheeler Brothers 112
Wheeler's Brewery 157
Whelan, Andrew 80
Whelan, John 80|
Whelan, Pat 256, 258–9, 272
Whickstead, William 211
Whiley, George 281
Whitchurch, Edwin 281
Whitchurch, William 294, 303
White, Edward 142, 143
White, Elliott 142
White Feather Castle Brewery Co. Ltd 260
White Hills Brewery 106
White Horse Brewery 162
White Horse Inn & Brewery 294
White & Phillips 224
White, William 236
Whitfield, Frank W. 247, 258, 259
Whitson, James 43–4
Whitway, Robert 279
Whyte, James 275, 285–6
Whyte, Sarah 286
Whyte, Thomas 83

Wickins, George 287
Wiechert, J. H. 251
Wig & Pen Restaurant & Brewery 319
Wigg, Wolton H. 162, 163, 212, 219, 231
Wilcannia Brewery 84
Wilcox, George 139, 154, 165
Wilcox, Henry 151
Wild, Edward 131, 139, 152, 153
Wildman, George 53, 81, 82
Wildman, W. 175
Wilkie, Adam 256, 257, 258, 259
Wilkie, John 256, 257, 258, 259
Wilkie, Leonard 257
Wilkins, Frederick 27, 43
William Bruce & Sons 102, 103, 106
William Bull Brewery 319
William, Charles 231
William Jones & Co. 59
William Mitchell & Co. 141
Williams Breweries Ltd (Adelaide) 212, 226
Williams Brewery (Beechworth) 100
Williams, Charles 100, 226, 236
Williams & Cohen 49, 50
Williams, Elizabeth 236
Williams, G. 33
Williams, James 170
Williams, John (Angus Park Brewery) 236
Williams, John (Australia Inn & Brewery) 58
Williams, John (Tasmania Brewery) 296, 300
Williams, Richard 160–1
Williams, Samuel 33, 36, 55, 58, 78
Williams Walkerville Brewing Co. Ltd 226
Williams, William 139, 222, 227
Williamstown Brewery 128, 157
Williatt, Newman 297
Willis, Elizabeth 304
Willis, Thomas 82
Willis, William 82
Willow Brewery 238
Wills, Horatio 92
Wilshire, James 68
Wilson, Hector 162
Wilson, James 288
Wilson, John G. 205
Wilson, Mary 205
Wilson, Neill Australia Ltd 288, 296
Wilson, T. 64
Wilson, Thomas 301
Wimmera Brewery 122
Windsor Brewery (Dunolly) 115
Windsor Brewery (Windsor) 84–5
Windsor Brewery (Sydney) 77, 85
Wineglass Bay Brewing Co. 334
Wing, Jacob 279
Winn, John C. 141
Wiseman, Thomas 280
Wiseman, William 199
Wittabrinna Brewery 78
Wittaker, William 28
Wivenhoe Brewery 280
Wodonga Brewery 175
Wodonga Place Brewery 23
Wolfensohn, Mr 47, 48
Wollondale Brewery 41
Wood Brothers & Co. 54
Wood, Charles 158
Wood, James 140, 141, 158
Wood, John 134, 158
Wood, Samuel R. 33
Wood & Ware 158
Wood, William 290
Woodburn Brewery 303
Woodbury, Richard 84
Woods, John 62
Wood's Point Brewery Co, Ltd 176
Woodstock Mill & Brewery 46
Woodville Brewing & Bottling Co. Ltd 272
Woodward, Richard 315
Woolpack Brewery 77
Wright, James 60
Wright, John 83
Wright, Uriah 28
Wyalong Brewery 85
Wyld, Alfred Norman 47, 48
Wyndham, Wadham 31
Wynyard Brewery 305

XXX Brewery 96, 98

Yackandandah Brewery 177
Yalgoo Brewery 273
Yankalilla Brewery 239
Yarra Flats Brewery 323
Yarrawonga Brewery 177
Yass Brewery 85
Ye Olde Tymes Brewerie 137, 152, 157–8
York Breweries Pty Ltd (Ballina) 319
York Brewery (York) 273
York family 319
Yorkshire Brewery (Sydney) 77
Yorkshire Brewery Co. Ltd (Collingwood) 89, 129, 131, 158, 134
Young Brewery 85
Young, Edmund 125
Young, George 51, 52, 53, 85
Young, Joseph 112
Young, S. 238
Young, Samuel 119
Young, William 27
Younger, Robert 120

Zeehan & Dundas Brewery Co. Ltd 283
Zig Zag Brewery 47, 48
Zwar, Albert 100